Administration of Programs for Young Children

Young Children

6th Edition

PHYLLIS M. CLICK

THOMSON

DELMAR LEARNING

Australia   Canada   Mexico   Singapore   Spain   United Kingdom   United States

THOMSON

DELMAR LEARNING

Administration of Programs for Young Children, Sixth Edition
Phyllis M. Click

Vice President, Career Education SBU:
Dawn Gerrain

Director of Editorial:
Sherry Gomoll

Acquisitions Editor:
Erin O'Connor

Developmental Editor:
Alexis Breen Ferraro

Editorial Assistant:
Ivy Ip

Director of Production:
Wendy A. Troeger

Production Editor:
J.P. Henkel

Technology Project Manager:
Joseph Saba

Director of Marketing:
Donna J. Lewis

Channel Manager:
Nigar Hale

Cover Design:
TDB

Composition:
Carlisle Publishers Services

Library of Congress Cataloging-in-Publication Data

Click, Phyllis.
    Administration of programs for young children / Phyllis M. Click.— 6th ed.
        p. cm.
    Rev. ed. of: Administration of schools for young children. 5th ed. ©2000. Includes bibliographical references and
        index.
        ISBN 1-4018-2644-X
1. Nursery schools—United States—Administration. 2. Day care centers—United States—Administration. 3. Early childhood education—United States. I. Click, Phyllis. Administration   of schools for young children. II. Title.
LB2822.7.C55 2003
            372.21'6'0973—dc21   2003053146

NOTICE TO THE READER

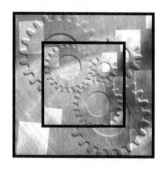

Contents

PART I Administration

Part V Beyond the School Itself

Preface

RATIONALE

Administration of Schools for Young Children was first published in 1976 when interest in the education of very young children was just beginning. Today, the importance of those early years is well established, and it is universally recognized that quality programs must have well-trained and knowledgeable teachers. This new edition, retitled *Administration of Programs for Young Children,* responds to the need for equally well-trained leaders. The job of an administrator is so multifaceted that it is important for courses and training materials to be available. This book can serve that purpose.

ORGANIZATION

The organization of this sixth edition has been changed in response to suggestions from reviewers who have used the text. Part I, Administration, includes the general responsibilities of a director and discusses the different kinds of settings. Chapter 1 emphasizes the importance of creating a democratic or collegial environment for staff members. Chapter 2 discusses the different kinds of programs and how each affects the job of the administrator.

In Part II, Planning: Program and Environment, Chapter 3 discusses how to plan a curriculum by setting goals and developing objectives. The reader is taken through the steps that lead to the development of a set of goals, then shown how to use these to develop objectives. Chapters 4 to 6 document planning for three age levels: infants and toddlers, preschool children, and school-age children. Each highlights developmental milestones, then discusses how to plan a developmentally appropriate program and arrange the environment. While the previous edition covered planning the program and planning the environment in separate sections, this edition combines the two into one chapter. In each chapter there are specific guidelines and suggestions for activities and areas to include in the environment. This enables the reader to get a complete picture of how to plan for each age level.

Part III covers hiring staff and developing personnel policies that encourage staff retention. Chapter 7, Staff Selection/Personnel Policies, takes the director through the process of determining staff qualifications, recruiting, and selecting. There are also sections on developing personnel policies and keeping employment records. Chapter 8, Staff Supervision and Training, suggests effective methods of supervising and evaluating staff as well as planning for staff development and training activities. Chapter 9 recommends strategies for developing and maintaining a core of student teachers and volunteers. The reader is shown how to have a dedicated group of volunteers and the most effective ways to work with student teachers.

Part IV, Management, details the process of putting together a budget, maintaining a safe environment, ensuring the health of children, and operating a food and nutrition program. Chapter 13, Beginnings: A New Program/A New Year, has been moved from the first section to this one since reviewers felt the information would provide students with a way to consolidate learning from previous chapters.

Part V, Beyond the School Itself, takes the student outside the facility to consider external influences. Chapter 14, Including Families and the Community, considers the role of families in early childhood education and how the surrounding community can impact the program. The final chapter, Maintaining the Quality of Child Care, addresses the issues of how to determine quality, how to measure it, and how to maintain it. This chapter also contains a discussion of the laws that pertain to personnel and families.

Appendix A still contains information about computer software programs that are useful to the administrative process, but it has been updated. Every vendor was contacted and asked to highlight additions or changes to its product. Appendix B lists professional organizations and sources of information for students and directors. Appendix C contains a list of publishers and suppliers of early childhood materials, equipment, supplies, and books.

Each time this text has been reviewed, the author has tried to be responsive to the concerns and suggestions of each reviewer. However, the changes may not always meet the needs of each group of students or individual instructors. The order of chapters can be changed as each situation warrants.

 ## FEATURES

The reader will still find the vignettes "A Day in the Life of . . ." in this edition, but new ones have been added. These snapshots of a director's activities give the student an opportunity to glimpse what it is like to be a leader of a program. They also sometimes provide a bit of humor to spark interest in the content and are not meant to be examples of appropriate practices.

Each chapter begins with a list of Key Terms that pinpoint important concepts. There are two additions at the end of chapters: a Case Study and Helpful Web Sites. The case study poses questions that foster critical thinking, and the Web sites provide access to additional information if the student chooses to pursue it.

INTERNET DISCLAIMER

The author and Delmar Learning affirm that the Web site URLs referenced herein were accurate at the time of printing. However, due to the fluid nature of the Internet, we cannot guarantee their accuracy for the life of the edition.

 NEW TO THIS EDITION

This edition reflects some of the changes that are taking place in early childhood education. There is a new discussion of ethical practices, including the National Association for the Education of Young Children (NAEYC) Code of Ethical Conduct. The need for well-trained directors led to the development of the Illinois Director Credential. Chapter 1 presents an overview of the credential. A growing need for child care in different settings has caused the proliferation of centers for mildly ill children. Military child care has incurred a great deal of interest because of its model programs. Both of these are discussed in Chapter 2.

Other new topics include developing a philosophy that embraces an understanding of the importance of cultural diversity and a culturally sensitive environment. Most children today will grow up in an environment in which they come in contact with others from many different cultures. It is essential that they develop attitudes that promote a positive image of themselves and others. Parents are an important part of creating cultural diversity so their input is stressed.

Recently, there has been a great deal of discussion about standardized testing of children at all levels of education. The text relates the NAEYC Position Paper on Standardized Testing. Information on professionalism has been expanded to include a discussion of ethical practices as they apply to both teachers and administrators.

Increasingly, programs have had to justify their existence by being fiscally sound. In order to do this, administrators need to know about good business practices, including marketing and public relations. They also need to have access to information regarding legal issues that affect not only their staff members, but the families they service.

 ONLINE RESOURCE™

An exciting new feature, Online Resource™, accompanies this sixth edition of *Administration of Programs for Young Children*. It is designed for use by the reader and is a link to early childhood education on the Internet. The Online Resource can be accessed at http://www.EarlyChildEd.delmar.com.

 Downloadable Forms

Throughout the book there are forms that have the Online Resources icon. These will be found on the Web site so they can be downloaded and printed out.

Case Studies

Additional case studies give students an opportunity to consider real-life situations. They will be challenged to consider how they might react or what would be some alternative reactions.

Discussion Forum

This segment presents information about issues that are relevant to each section of the text. Students are asked to respond to questions that can be discussed in a classroom setting or via e-mail to other students.

Internet Activities

Students are referred to a Web site that has information related to each chapter. Several questions ask them to assess the information, answer questions, or decide how a director might use the information.

The Online Resources can be found at http://www.EarlyChildEd.delmar.com. Review questions and activities at the end of each chapter also make it applicable to a self-study plan by individual readers.

HOW TO USE THIS TEXT

The revised sequence of chapters provides the student with a logical progression of topics that have been field-tested by many instructors using the text. The order can be adopted as is or changed to suit the needs of a particular setting. Review questions and activities at the end of each chapter also make it applicable to a self-study plan by individual readers.

A significant and timely addition to this edition is the list of Web sites at the end of each chapter. Many students have computers and are comfortable with searching out information on the Internet. The instructor can assign topics or pose questions to be answered by logging on to one of the sites. In addition, the Online Resource section to be found on the Delmar site provides the instructor with ways to enhance students' learning. Downloadable forms can be used as worksheets for in-class discussions or reproduced as transparencies to accompany lectures. The Case Studies are a rich source for augmenting learning. Students can read and discuss the studies on-line or in groups during class time. The author has posed questions at the end of each, but the instructor may want to phrase other questions.

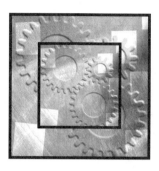

About the Author

Phyllis Click obtained her bachelor and master's degrees from the University of California at Berkeley in psychology and child development. Throughout a long career, she worked in a variety of settings with both children and adults. She taught in preschools, worked in summer camps, and developed and taught in a program for autistic children. She began working with adults, teaching college students, administering grant programs, and designing a curriculum for a private college for prospective teachers.

Now retired, she has been a consultant, helping others start or administer programs, and has published widely. Her publications include another textbook, articles in professional journals, and ancillary materials for other authors' texts. She belongs to the National Association for the Education of Young Children, the California School-Age Consortium, and the Association for Childhood Education International.

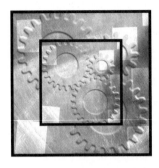

Acknowledgments

My thanks to those who generously gave of their time to make this edition of *Administration of Programs for Young Children* an effective tool for both beginning and experienced administrators. My special thanks to Erin O'Connor, Acquisitions Editor, and Alexis Breen Ferraro, Developmental Editor. I want to express my appreciation for the other Delmar Learning staff members who carry the project from one step to another until the final pages are put together.

A special thanks to the reviewers who took the time to read the previous edition and offered excellent suggestions for changes and additions to this edition:

Nancy Baptiste, Ed.D.
New Mexico State University
Las Cruces, NM

Elaine Camerin, Ed.D.
Daytona Beach Community College
Daytona Beach, FL

Meryl Glass
San Francisco Community College
San Francisco, CA

Berta Harris
San Diego City College
San Diego, CA

Linda Rivers
Signal Centers
Chattanooga, TN

Marie Saracino
Stephen F. Austin State University
Nacogdoches, TX

Jill Uhlenberg, Ph.D.
The University of Northern Iowa
Cedar Falls, IA

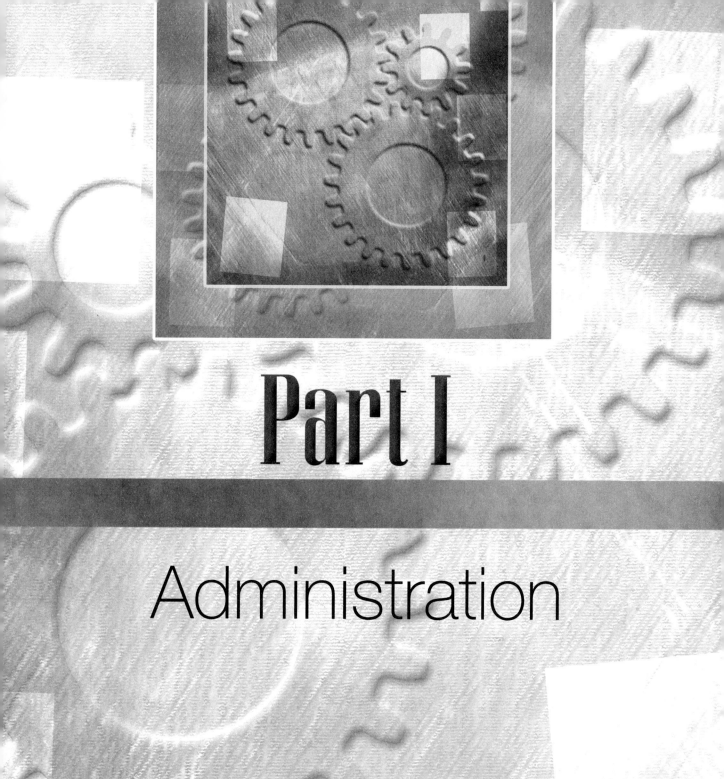

Part I

Administration

1

The Director:
A Broad View

KEY TERMS

authoritarian manager
authoritative director
collegiality
democratic manager
ethics
management skill
morality
nonverbal messages
permissive manager
values

OBJECTIVES

After reading this chapter, you should be able to:

- State the responsibilities of a director.
- Describe management style and methods.
- Identify ways the director organizes school resources.
- Discuss the role of director as communicator.
- Devise and use a self-evaluation tool.
- Discuss the relationship of a director to a board of trustees.

A Day In The Life Of …
A Director of a For-Profit Center

6:30 A.M. Arrive to open center. One parent waiting, teacher is late. Take child with me to vacuum hallway since cleaning crew did not show up last night. Phone ringing, a sick teacher. Child and I go to classroom to set out a few materials. Finally a teacher arrives.

6:45 A.M. Go to my office, notes from my assistant are on my desk. They concern a request from Michelle (an assistant teacher) to leave early, an upset mother, two scheduled tours with prospective families, and a need to order paper towels and tissues. The parents are arriving and the phone is ringing; further changes in attendance. I get out my daily schedule to make the changes, then call a sub from our list. She will come, but cannot get there for an hour and a half. No sub so Michelle can leave early. Maybe I'll be able to figure it out later.

7:00 A.M.   Jordan's mom comes into the office and closes the door. She wants to talk to me. Yesterday her son had dirt all over his face and his clothes were dirty when she picked him up at the end of the day. She did not like the teacher's attitude when she asked her about it. I assured her I would talk to the teacher and not let it happen again.

7:30 A.M.   I am in the toddler room covering until the substitute can arrive. I spend 45 minutes in the room helping the children separate from their parents. The phone is continuing to ring. I answer from the classroom. Three more children have called in sick. The cook enters the room to tell me there is no pancake mix for the morning snack. She stays in the room while I go get petty cash so she can go to the store for more. Snack will be about 20 minutes late.

8:20 A.M.   The substitute has arrived. I walk through the classrooms to see if everything is OK. I count to be sure the teacher/child ratio is correct. A parent comes in and hands me her tuition check.

8:40 A.M.   I finally get to my desk with my first cup of coffee. A staff member comes in to request a day off the following week. I talk to a prospective parent for 10 minutes and schedule a tour for this afternoon at 2:00.

9:00 A.M.   My assistant director arrives. We talk briefly about the day and yesterday afternoon. She tours the center again to do the ratio count. There is now an extra teacher in one room.

I begin the daily bank deposit and work on the payroll report, cash flow report, and payment status log. This usually takes 1 hour if there are no interruptions. I'm almost finished, but my tour arrives 10 minutes early. We tour the building, then sit in the office.

10:30 A.M.   The tour leaves and I get back to my paperwork. Two staff interruptions, but I finish at 11:00.

11:00 A.M.   My interview begins. The phone rings with another inquiry from a prospective parent. I take her phone number and say I will call her back.

12:00 P.M.   I leave the building to make the bank deposit and to purchase supplies needed for tomorrow. I return to the center just in time for some leftovers from lunch and once again pick up the daily schedule to see if I can let Michelle leave early. I decide to shift the extra teacher to Michelle's room. She's very happy.

I begin tomorrow's schedule and look at my list for things I need to accomplish today. I write a parent a note, write 10 reminders to pay tuition, and call back the prospective parent who wants to tour the school. I begin work on a grant application that is due next week.

2:00 P.M.   My tour arrives and we spend about 20 minutes together. I give my assistant a list of the three things I did not get done today. I make a new list for tomorrow. We talk for a few minutes until I realize I am going to be late picking up my six-year-old from school. I run out of the building and tell my assistant to call me at home. I hope she has time after she completes her own list of curriculum items.

Karen, Director of Kiddie Academy

Directors of child care centers sometimes laughingly describe their job as being like the "master of ceremonies in a three-ring circus" or the "head of a large and disparate family." Their description has some validity since the task is certainly complex and multifaceted requiring a wide variety of skills. A director must see that all aspects of the program and the people involved work together effectively. It is a challenge that sometimes can be frustrating and at others extremely rewarding. Let us look at some of the daily occurrences that require a director's attention. He or she may do the following:

In the morning

- Greet parents and children as they arrive.
- Help some children separate from their parents.
- Find a substitute for a teacher who is ill.
- Talk to teachers about their schedules because it is raining.
- Call the roofers to repair a leak.
- Write an agenda for the next staff meeting.
- Answer several telephone calls from parents interested in the school.
- Show a parent and child around the school.
- Discuss next week's lunch menu with the cook.

At noon

- Attend a luncheon meeting of a local organization to discuss a fund-raising activity.

In the afternoon

- Meet with a licensing worker to review the latest inspection report.
- Have a conference with a parent who is concerned about her child's behavior at home.
- Begin a report for the next board of trustees meeting.
- Discuss with another director plans for a future activity of a local advocacy group.

In the evening

- Meet over dinner with two teachers who are having problems working together.

There are additional demands on directors as well. Many directors are pressured to learn efficient business methods in order to control costs. This may mean they must take business or computer courses. In schools that are part of a large child care corporation, the director must schedule time to meet with a designated executive. If the early childhood center is part of a school system and located on a school campus, the director must work with central office personnel and cooperate with staff members at the school site. Directors of nonprofit schools may have to plan and coordinate fund-raising activities. For a more detailed list of a director's duties and responsibilities, see Figure 1-1.

The director has general responsibilities:

Determines requirements that must be met regarding licensing, health, and safety regulations from the state and local regulatory agencies. Works with agencies to meet requirements.

Serves as an ex officio member of the board of directors and attends committee meetings as necessary.

Provides leadership for setting overall goals for the school—to be used as a basis for curriculum objectives.

Plans reports on school as required by board or corporation.

Evaluates own work as a director and plans for continuing professional growth.

The director has enrollment duties:

Enrolls children and keeps an accurate waiting list.

Interviews prospective parents, giving information about the school.

Plans orientation for new parents.

Knows the changing needs of the community in order to maintain full enrollment.

Prepares a parent handbook and keeps it current.

The director supervises curriculum:

Provides direction to staff in setting curriculum objectives appropriate to the school goals.

Works with staff to implement and maintain goals and objectives.

Provides leadership in evaluating curriculum.

Provides up-to-date information on curriculum issues.

The director is responsible for the physical plant and equipment:

Plans, allocates, and uses space effectively.

Maintains the physical plant by providing custodial care and repair services.

Plans for the future needs of the school for space and equipment.

Keeps records such as inventories, repair schedules, and purchase information.

Manages supplies, reordering as needed.

Monitors the health and safety aspects of the environment.

The director is in charge of finances:

Sets up a budget.

Controls budget expenditures.

Collects fees and tuition.

Manages disbursements for payroll, equipment, and supplies.

Keeps adequate records of income and expenditures.

Handles petty cash disbursements.

Prepares monthly reports on expenditures to date.

FIGURE 1-1 ■ Responsibilities of a director *(continues)*.

Prepares a year-end analysis of budget and expenditures.

Reports to board or corporation.

The director is concerned with staff relationships:

Recruits and hires staff.

Plans and conducts staff orientation.

Prepares job descriptions for each position.

Formulates and implements personnel policies.

Assists staff in implementing school goals.

Provides a continuing assessment of staff development needs.

Plans with staff for in-service training.

Encourages staff involvement in community activities.

Meets with staff members to resolve problems.

Prepares a staff handbook and keeps it current.

Keeps personnel records.

The director provides leadership in parent involvement and education:

Communicates goals of the school to parents.

Plans and implements parent education activities.

Confers with parents regarding their child's progress.

Encourages a variety of ways for parents to be involved in school activities.

Keeps adequate records of parent involvement and education activities.

The director must plan for health and safety:

Maintains an adequate health program for the school.

Keeps health records on all children enrolled.

Keeps staff informed concerning the health status of each child.

Confers with parents as needed about child's health and nutritional status.

Refers families to community agencies for special help when necessary.

Continues to be informed regarding legal responsibilities of the school in relation to safety.

Plans activities for staff and children to teach safety.

The director builds and maintains good community relations:

Interprets the school and its goals to visitors.

Maintains an effective public relations and advertising process.

Represents the school at community functions.

Establishes contacts with community agencies.

Involves self and staff in professional and legislative activities.

FIGURE 1-1 ■ Responsibilities of a director (continued).

DIRECTOR SKILLS AND CHARACTERISTICS

From the preceding description of what a director does, it is obvious that a variety of skills and personal characteristics are required. **Management skill** is probably the most important.

The manager is the person charged with direction of an institution and who manages all the resources of that institution. In a child care setting, the resources are the people involved, the financial base, and the physical facility. The director's management abilities are the key to ensuring that these resources are used effectively to provide a quality program. Staff, children, and parents need to have a sense of belonging and feel that individual and group goals are being met. The financial base should allow for adequate compensation for staff members, maintenance of the facility, and purchase of needed materials. The physical setting should be well planned to meet the needs of the program and then be maintained in a safe condition.

As manager, the director is also a *leader* who affects everyone involved in a child care facility and forms the character of the program. The leader creates what Bloom (1988) has called the "organizational climate" or a global perception of an organization; in other words, the attitudes, beliefs, perceptions, and values of the individuals in a work setting brought together into a whole through the leadership of the person responsible for guiding them. Being a leader also means being out in front, helping others to become better at their jobs, and inspiring them to meet new challenges. Staff members must be encouraged to try new ideas, learn new skills, and take on new tasks. A leader also sets an example for others to follow by continuing to upgrade his or her own skills.

Directors must have a knowledge of good *educational practices* and an understanding of how children grow and develop. Many were teachers before assuming administrative positions and already have teaching skills. Those who come from other work experiences must acquire that knowledge through college courses. These are minimum requirements for planning and supervising a program. However, few states require educational preparation for teachers or directors. According to the Center for Career Development at Wheelock College, as of May 1996 only 18 states required any specialized pre-service training for teachers in early childhood programs. Pre-service training for a master teacher, head, or lead teacher is required in only eight states. A more positive sign of rising standards for child care personnel is that more states are requiring in-service training than was so in the past.

Directors must like *interacting with people*. Unfortunately, some directors find doing paperwork much easier and tend to avoid people interactions. To be effective, they have to spend much of the day talking to parents, teachers, children, repair people, food and equipment vendors, and school board members or corporation personnel. They need to be able to listen without judging and maintain a respect for the other person's feelings. Sometimes they have to listen to complaints without feeling threatened. Most important, they have to know when and how to respond.

Directors need *self-confidence* because they do the job without a lot of help. Probably the most difficult part of being a director of a school is the isolation from others doing the same tasks. Teachers in a school have each other to talk to, complain to, and work with to solve problems. Although some schools have an assistant director, in most schools directors work alone. In some situations, such as in the multisite corporation school, other directors are available by telephone when the going is rough. In other kinds of schools, opportunities to meet with fellow directors have to be arranged.

THE DIRECTOR AS MANAGER
Management Style

The director's management style forms the character of a child care center. When prospective parents or others visit they may say to themselves, "This is a good place for children, parents, and teachers." They may also have an opposite reaction and think, "I am not comfortable here. I wouldn't want to work here or place my child here." It is sometimes difficult to analyze what makes one center different from another because it is more a feeling or an atmosphere. In Bloom's (1988) words it is the "organizational climate."

What is it that creates a positive organizational climate? One of the primary characteristics is that all the adults work together as a team to reach a common goal. This is achieved through the kind of relationship the director has with staff members. Clear expectations are communicated to teachers; they are given support and encouragement to reach those goals. Further, the relationship between director and staff must be built upon a sense of trust in the competence of teachers. There must also be open, honest feedback followed by direction for further professional growth. In this kind of setting, teachers can provide support and encouragement to one another.

A second dimension of organizational climate is the degree to which staff members are included in decision-making processes. Some directors use a management method that encourages staff involvement, whereas others see themselves as the primary decision maker. Some use one method most of the time; others choose a method to fit a particular situation. One way of classifying management is *authoritarian, permissive,* or *democratic.* **Authoritarian managers** make the decisions and determine policies. These people tell others what is to be done and allow no choices. **Permissive managers** remain passive, leaving decisions to others. These managers give suggestions but do not participate or provide leadership. **Democratic managers** involve others in decisions and policy-making processes.

Authoritarian managers usually believe they have greater knowledge and experience and, therefore, have the responsibility for making decisions for others. They set goals for the school, tell staff how to implement them, and devise a schedule for each day's activities. They purchase materials and equipment to support goals and conduct all parent activities. This style of management does not take into account the needs of

The director wears many hats: organizer, manager, and communicator.

others, but decisions are made on the basis of what seems "right" to the person making the choice.

In an authoritarian environment, staff members have little opportunity to gain new skills or to attempt new ways of doing their jobs. For some teachers, this kind of setting is easy and comforting. When they are told what to do, they are relieved of any responsibility for trying new things. For others, this kind of atmosphere is stifling and leads to early teacher burnout or boredom.

The permissive manager takes a less active role than either of the other two types. This kind of manager may allow teachers to do whatever they want in their own classrooms without any concern for an overall cohesiveness of goals for the school. Teachers may do a lot of the purchasing for their own classrooms, again without concern for the good of the whole school. Parent education activities and conferencing may be done totally by the teacher.

Strong, experienced teachers usually can function well and be quite happy under a permissive manager. They know what to do and carry out their jobs without needing support or leadership. In fact, some teachers prefer to have as little interference from a director as possible. On the other hand, inexperienced or unsure teachers may find they need more direction and support. They need a director who will give them new ideas for classroom activities or help them deal with a difficult child. Inexperienced teachers often have a great deal of difficulty working with parents and need a director who will guide them or who will take some of the responsibility.

The democratic director involves staff members in many aspects of the operation of the school. Staff may take part in developing or revising goals for the school. They may plan curriculum together and jointly decide on large purchases of equipment. Teachers may do a lot of parent education work, help in writing a newsletter, participate in parent meetings, and conduct parent conferences. The democratic style of management is the most people oriented, but it is also the most difficult and time consuming.

A similar way of looking at management methods is to use the three categories described by Baumrind (1971, 1989, 1991). Her studies show the relationship between parenting styles and their effect upon children's independence, self-control, and confidence. Baumrind's categories are *authoritarian, permissive,* and *authoritative.* The *authoritarian parent* establishes rules that are not to be broken or punishment follows. Many demands are made of children, and parent-child communication is rather low. These children are likely to be compliant, but unhappy. *Permissive parents* make few demands and hide their own feelings about children's behavior. Discipline is minimal, but these parents are nurturing and communicate with their children. Children in these families are even less happy than in authoritarian families and also lack self-control. *Authoritative parents* set limits and hold children responsible for infractions, but they also communicate well with their children. They listen, discuss requests, and make compromises. Family rules are more democratic. An important aspect of authoritative parenting is that high maturity demands are made upon children. Growing up with an authoritative parent results in individuals who are happy, are successful, and feel competent.

It is not difficult to transpose these categories to a child care center. The authoritarian and permissive directors described in previous paragraphs are similar to the parenting styles seen by Baumrind. An **authoritative director** would be one who establishes rules, but is also willing to discuss compromises with staff members. This director would have good communication skills, listening to others and including them in decision-making processes. This director would also be expected to increase professional competence.

Newer Approaches

Another current approach to management includes a heightened awareness of the importance of participation by everyone involved. In *Workplace 2000*, Boyett and Conn (1991) see the workplace of the future as a caring community. They point to the importance of finding the right "fit" between employer and employee and then helping each person fulfill his or her potential. They expect that the "I just work here" syndrome will no longer exist when all workers feel they are a part of the organization and are contributing to its success. They also point to the importance of information sharing in helping employees understand decisions. Without that information there tends to be distrust and suspicion, or employees may misinterpret management decisions. On the other hand, when employees know why decisions have been made, they are empowered and motivated.

Average directors' salaries differ greatly from one state to another. In some states, salaries are figured as an hourly rate; in others, directors receive a yearly salary. In Maryland directors receive an average of $26,571 per year. In South Dakota and Arkansas they receive an average hourly rate of $7.91 and $8.37, respectively.

Source: National Child Care Information Center, Vienna, Virginia, 1998.

Collegiality is a term that is used to describe a management method or organizational climate in academic settings. In this kind of environment administrators and teachers work together. They consider one another colleagues, with a variety of skills to contribute to the functioning whole. Members cooperate rather than compete and are mutually supportive. In this kind of system each person is valued and deserving of respect. An important dimension of a collegial atmosphere is that members participate in decision making. When teachers share in decisions, particularly those that affect them directly, they are more likely to implement them. Decisions about goals, which children to include in a group, organization of space, and ways to help particular children are examples.

THE DIRECTOR AS ORGANIZER
Delegating Responsibility

In order to accomplish the many tasks required, directors must be good organizers. This means they must make the best possible use of the resources available to them. The first step is to learn to delegate responsibilities to others. By doing so they will not only accomplish more themselves but also achieve greater participation from staff members. Many directors find it difficult to delegate responsibility to others, feeling that it puts an unnecessary burden on their staff or that they cannot be sure the job will be done right. In *The Early Childhood Super Director*, Sue Baldwin (1991) cited the following reasons directors reported for not being able to delegate:

- unable to let go of control
- staff does not measure up to expectations
- fear of repercussions if delegating occurs
- perfectionist
- concerned about the quality of the job to be delegated
- staff perception that the director may be pushing work onto the staff
- caretaking personality
- fear of imposing on people
- staff that will not say "no" to any requests because of the director's position
- not being able to explain why others should do the tasks
- lack of organization to get help in time

Directors in all-day centers may have an assistant director who is already doing some administrative tasks. When a program is open long hours of the day, one person may open the school in the morning, get schedules set for the day, and talk to parents as they drop off their children. The other may be there at the end of the day to close the school and help parents and children reunite after the long day. In between they may divide other administrative tasks.

The division of labor between the director and assistant should be based on an assessment of their skills and interests. Some people like to do the myriad of paperwork that is necessary in the day-to-day conduct of a school; others like to interact with the people involved. Both should decide which jobs each is more comfortable with and does best. Each will have primary responsibility for those tasks. Once primary responsibility is assigned, the assistant should be free to do the job without interference. The director still bears ultimate responsibility for the functioning of the assistant; therefore, communication between them is important.

Responsibilities can be delegated to other staff members as well. The cook can order supplies, compile information on new equipment to be purchased, or plan schedules for serving snacks and meals. The maintenance person can set up the cleaning schedule, or be asked to suggest ways to recycle or reuse throwaway materials. A secretary may assume responsibility for scheduling classroom field trips that have been suggested by teachers or call a qualified substitute from an approved list.

The director should decide which person can best accomplish the task. This requires an assessment of the skills that are needed and then finding the best person to carry it out. The person who will do the task needs to gain something from doing it. No one should be asked to perform extra duties just to help the director with administrative functions. Having delegated a task does not mean the director can just forget about it and expect it to be done. It is important to set up a schedule and procedure for maintaining overall supervision of delegated responsibilities. The director may wish to meet with the staff person once a week or once a month, or just have that person provide updates through written information.

When first attempting to delegate responsibilities, some directors may find that it takes more time than if they had done the job themselves. However, as employees learn and gain confidence, directors find that their time is freed for those tasks that only they can do. They also discover from repeated experience that both they and their staff will benefit immeasurably from the team effort.

Organizing Time

Time is a precious commodity to busy directors. They will find that they can accomplish much more each day if they make a list starting with either jobs that must be done immediately or jobs that must be done each day; these should take top *priority*. Next come jobs that should be done as soon as possible or need to be done once a week. Last are the jobs that they would like to do or only have to do infrequently.

The director should set aside a specific time to do jobs that have to be done every day. Sometimes it helps, for instance, to get to work a half-hour earlier so that certain jobs can be done before the rush of the day. Some of the daily jobs can be done later in the day. It may be difficult to hold to a schedule for doing the tasks, but if done with persistence, other staff members will begin to honor the commitment.

It is helpful to schedule one day a week or specific days during the month to do tasks that need to be completed less frequently. Ordering materials, compiling financial reports, and writing a newsletter are examples. The director should mark the day on the calendar, block out some time, go into the office, close the door, and get to work. It is surprising how quickly it will be finished when there are no interruptions.

Directors should plan for those tasks they would like to do when they have time. Reading professional materials, writing an article, or making long-range plans may all fall into this category. These are all important and directors should not feel guilty about setting aside an afternoon each month to accomplish any of these.

Emergencies will arise—by definition, at the most inopportune times—but if one is prepared they can be managed. What kinds of emergencies come up in a school for young children? The same kinds that happen in a busy household: the plumbing stops working or leaks occur; the licensing worker is coming to visit and two teachers call in sick; a child falls and is bleeding from a cut on his forehead. No one will panic at any of these if procedures have been thought out ahead of time.

For possible building and equipment emergencies, it is useful to keep an up-to-date list of repair persons. When new equipment is purchased, repair information should be put on the list immediately. For staff emergencies, a list of reliable substitutes is essential. Qualified persons can often be found by advertising in a local newspaper. Students may be found through the local community college or university. If a desirable teacher applies for a position at the school and there is no opening, he or she should be encouraged to be placed on the substitute list. A written procedure to care for children's injuries should be posted in a prominent place so that any staff member can follow the correct procedure. Training in the procedure should be part of orientation. In addition, several staff members should know first aid—Red Cross certified, if possible. Other kinds of emergencies arise, depending upon the area of the country. In southern California, schools are required to have an earthquake disaster plan. In some hillside areas, schools have also developed a plan for evacuating children in case of a brush fire. A tornado drill for schools in the Midwest, Texas, and New England is appropriate. States along the southeastern seaboard may need plans for managing children in case of a severe storm.

A *computer* will save the director an incredible amount of time. Although it takes time to learn to use one and to input data, it will be an enormously useful tool for keeping financial records and budgets up to date along with records from previous years. A quick comparison of this year's income and expenses is immediately accessible. Many personnel records can be kept on a computer file: dates of employment, attendance, and additional academic work are a few examples. A computer word processing program will make any secretarial task faster and easier. All correspondence, newsletters, memos, and notices can be done faster and with greater possibility for interesting variations such as graphics. Programs for developing address lists are available. Ample databases are useful for lists of addresses of parents, staff, community organizations, food and equipment vendors, or persons who have visited the school. Within the last few years, some software manufacturers have developed programs specifically for preschool management. These programs and systems vary considerably in quality and price. Although specific references to computers appear in later chapters, Appendix A contains a lengthy discussion.

Planning

Faced with the pressures of everyday activities, it is easy to overlook any kind of planning, and yet it is an essential part of managing a child care center. Each day is filled with so many occurrences that must be dealt with immediately that it is difficult to find time to focus on what should happen the next day, let alone the next month. However, both short- and long-term planning are necessary for the smooth operation of the facility. Short-term planning ensures the smooth running of each day and provides contingency plans when the unexpected occurs. At the beginning of each day and each week, the director must know what has to be done and then see that those tasks are finished. However, there will be inevitable emergencies. It is important to think ahead about the kinds of emergencies that have occurred in the past and are likely to happen again, and then develop backup plans. This will not eliminate temporary disruptions caused by emergencies, but they will be easier to manage.

Long-term planning will help the director to provide the kind of environment and services that are set forth in the goals for the center. The director decides which goals should be addressed at a particular time and then sets a schedule for implementation. For example, one of the program goals might be that The Child Learning Center will offer a variety of experiences designed to help children acquire the skills needed for kindergarten entrance. To implement that goal, staff members need to know which skills are included, when it is developmentally appropriate to introduce experiences to teach those skills, and how to evaluate children's progress. The director should carefully plan a series of learning experiences to inform the teachers. This kind of in-service may take place over several months or even a year.

The most effective planning will involve the staff as much as possible. Everyone should have a copy of daily and weekly schedules as well as changes for rainy days. In addition, they should identify long-term goals to work toward during a particular period of time. The director should solicit their suggestions for implementing the goals and provide a method for obtaining feedback to evaluate progress.

THE DIRECTOR AS COMMUNICATOR

Directors spend a great deal of time talking to people. It is important to develop communication skills to prevent problems as well as to provide a model for other staff members. All of us experience some difficulty in communicating clearly with others. We know what we mean, and we are sure the other person understands clearly. Often, though, we are surprised at how others interpret what we have said. We think, "How could they have gotten that meaning out of what I said?"

Verbal Messages

Words are a coding system and the means by which our thoughts are conveyed to others. Although each word in a language has a meaning, coloration of that meaning comes from our own experiences. One of the problems is that we cannot all share the same experiences. Words may have different meanings to each of us based on our past. When we use words, what we mean comes from our own experiences. People hearing our words bring their own interpretations. As a result, the message being conveyed may be misunderstood.

Sometimes a particular word triggers an emotional response based on a past experience or association. This causes us to stop listening to the rest of the communication and focus on that one word. The speaker's tone of voice or the emphasis on one word may result in a similar response. "How are you today?" can convey a variety of messages depending on the way it is uttered. It can be merely a polite contact, a real concern, or an irritated inquiry meaning "Are you really all right today since so often you are not?"

Nonverbal Messages

Another reason for problems in communication lies in the fact that we communicate nonverbally as well as verbally. **Nonverbal messages** are the facial expressions, movements, and posture we use while speaking. In addition, we maintain eye contact or we look away. We sit or stand close to the listener or we maintain a distance between us. Each of these behaviors communicates a meaning, and we are not always aware that our words are saying one thing and our behavior something quite different. (It is interesting to note that different cultures also interpret these behaviors differently.) Not everyone notices these subtle expressions, but others see them clearly and react accordingly. The nonverbal message gets in the way of their hearing our verbal message clearly.

Preventing Problems in Communication

Since so much of a director's work is done through communications with others, it is important to develop methods that avoid as many problems as possible. The first step is to decide *what* you want to relay. Are you merely giving information without expecting a response? "There will be two prospective parents visiting your classroom today." Are you stating a problem and do you expect a response from the listener? "I'm wondering if you have any suggestions about how we can make cleaning up the playground at the end of the day any easier?"

Second, consider *when* to convey the message. If the content is important, do not do it when the listener is busy and cannot give full attention. For example, a director should not tell a teacher something important when she is busy in the classroom. It is better to wait until the children are gone or when the teacher can take a few minutes away from the children.

Third, allow *enough time* to get some feedback. "Words said on the run" are likely to be misunderstood. If your message is not grasped, your listener can ask for clarification or you can question whether your message was clear.

Fourth, decide *where* a message should be conveyed. When talking to a teacher in an office with the door closed, an atmosphere of confidentiality or perhaps seriousness is conveyed. When the conversation takes place on the playground or in the staff lounge, the message will seem more casual. Each place may be appropriate for different kinds of communications.

Fifth, decide *how* to present the message. Is it something that can or should be written? Sometimes it is important for others to see something stated clearly in written form. When information needs to be distributed to all staff members, this may be the most efficient way. Remember, though, the written message does not allow for immediate feedback so statements have to be clear. A written communication is always impersonal.

It is often necessary to *follow up* on a message. For example, it is apparent that a teacher has misunderstood what was said or is still confused when the expected response is not forthcoming. It will help to consider the way in which the message was conveyed. Sometimes body language conveys one meaning and words another. Is there another way the message can be stated? Did some of the words cause an emotional reaction? It is also helpful to ask for feedback. "You still seem confused. What is it you do not understand about what I have said?" or "Let me say it in a different way. What I meant was . . . " If the atmosphere encourages open discussion, staff members will likely ask for further clarification when they do not understand. A healthy give-and-take discussion usually clears the air. This can go a long way toward preventing misunderstanding.

Listening

Part of being an effective communicator is the ability to listen while others speak. Sometimes we only partly listen, letting our minds wander to other topics that seem more urgent. At times, we listen only until there is a point at which we can respond with information, sympathy, a solution, or a denial. One of the most important communication skills a director can develop is to really listen to what others have to say and to allow them to express their thoughts fully before responding. The following list describes the process of active listening.

1. Stop talking. That sounds obvious, but it is often forgotten. Do not interrupt.
2. Be mentally ready to listen. Put other thoughts out of your mind and give your full attention to the speaker.
3. Listen to the content of the message. Do not get distracted by the speaker's method of delivery or his or her appearance.
4. Use body language that conveys your interest. Maintain eye contact and assume an attentive posture. Sit or stand in an alert position. Do not slouch or turn away.
5. Try to determine the speaker's intent. Why is the speaker telling you this? If you can answer that question, it will help you to focus on what you hear.
6. Listen for the main ideas. What are the most important concepts or pieces of information, and which are irrelevant?

7. Listen for what is *not* said. You can sometimes learn a great deal from what the speaker leaves out or avoids.

8. Give feedback. Nonverbal feedback, such as a nod or a smile, encourages the speaker to continue. You can also use encouraging phrases. Some examples are "go on, tell me more," or "I understand."

9. Check your own understanding of the message. "I hear you saying . . . Am I hearing you correctly?"

10. Summarize the message. "So the main points of what you have been telling me are . . . "

When directors have developed both their speaking and listening skills, they will find that their interactions with people will change. They gain in understanding others and demonstrate that they are truly interested in others' concerns and problems. Their relationships with staff members, parents, and even children will be enhanced. Problems will not disappear, but be more easily resolved because each party has a greater appreciation of what is involved.

Written Communications

It is sometimes difficult to decide when to convey a message orally and when to write a report, a memo, or a note. If the message is important and affects more than one person, it probably should be written. A written record is permanent and far less likely to be misunderstood.

One type of written communication a director must prepare is a report concerning finances. A board of trustees should have a monthly report of cash flow including income and expenses as well as to-date expenditures compared to the budgeted amount. There should be a schedule for submitting preliminary budgets and then a final budget for the next year. Although this kind of information can be compiled manually, a computer will allow financial reports to be prepared fairly quickly and easily.

A monthly newsletter to parents is another written communication that many directors find effective for disseminating information. Parents want to know what their children are learning, what they have for lunch and snacks, or plans for field trips. A newsletter will give them a sense of belonging and help to establish a bridge between home and school. As with financial reports, a computer makes it fairly easy to generate a good newsletter.

It often helps to distribute written memos or notices to teachers and parents when changes are to take place. Shifts in staff assignments, alterations of schedules, substitutions of menu items, or change of plans for celebrating holidays are examples of information that should be conveyed in writing. Everyone receives the same information, so no one will be surprised or feel they have not been included. Also, a written message is less likely to be forgotten because it can be reread.

Written messages can be used to give positive reinforcement. Everyone likes to be told their efforts have been appreciated, and a written message is a tangible reminder that they are valued. A teacher will appreciate a note recognizing an especially effective project. "I heard many comments from parents about how the children really enjoyed the lessons on different artists. The parents said they, too, learned some things they hadn't known before. Thanks for making school an exciting place for our children."

Ethical Practices

The stresses and strains directors experience on almost any given day are exacerbated by lack of guidelines to help them confront difficult situations. What should they do when a demanding parent wants her child spanked for hitting other children? Or what should they do when they are asked by a board member to enroll his child while others are first on the waiting list? The decisions they make are frequently based upon their sense of **morality,** their view of what is good or right. Morality also includes beliefs about how people should behave and the kinds of obligations we have to one another. **Values** also are a part of the decision-making process when faced with a dilemma. Values are the qualities that we believe are intrinsically desirable and that we strive to achieve in ourselves. The difficulty, however, is that not everyone agrees on issues of morality and not everyone has the same values. There needs to be a link between personal morality and values and a professional code of behavior. **Ethics,** the study of right, wrong, duty, and obligation, attempts to provide that link. *Ethics* and *morality* are closely related and are often used interchangeably. However, ethics implies a conscious deliberation regarding moral choices.

The National Association for the Education of Young Children (NAEYC) responded to the question of "What should the good early childhood educator do when faced with this situation?"(Feeney & Freeman, 1999). Insights were gathered through surveys, and from focus and professional groups and were compiled as the NAEYC Code of Ethical Conduct, first published in 1989 and revised in 1997 (Feeney & Freeman, 1999). The code focuses on the daily interactions with children from birth through age eight and their families. It is divided into four sections: (1) children, (2) families, (3) colleagues, and (4) community and society. Each section addresses responsibilities, ideals, and principles. The intent of the code is to show exemplary professional behavior and define practices that are required, prohibited, and permitted. Each section has statements of ideals that reflect the aspirations of practitioners and principles that are intended to guide conduct and assist practitioners in resolving ethical dilemmas. The following is a sample of the code.

Section I: Ethical responsibilities to children

Childhood is a unique and valuable stage in the life cycle. Our paramount responsibility is to provide safe, healthy, nurturing, and responsive settings for children. We are committed to support children's development, respect individual differences, help children learn to live and work cooperatively, and promote health, self-awareness, competence, self-worth, and resiliency.

Ideals

I–1.1 To be familiar with the knowledge base of early childhood care and education and to keep current through continuing education and in-service training.

I–1.2 To base program practices upon current knowledge in the field of child development and related disciplines and upon particular knowledge of each child.

Principles

P–1.1 Above all, we shall not harm children. We shall not participate in practices that are disrespectful, degrading, dangerous, exploitative, intimidating, emotionally damaging, or physically harmful to children. This principle has precedence over all others in this code.

Section II: Ethical responsibilities to families

Families are of primary importance in children's development. (The term *family* may include others, besides parents, who are responsibly involved with the child.) Because the family and the early childhood practitioner have a common interest in the child's welfare, we acknowledge a primary responsibility to bring about collaboration between the home and school in ways that enhance the child's development.

Ideals

I–2.1 To develop relationships of mutual trust with families we serve.

I–2.2 To acknowledge and build upon strengths and competencies as we support families in their task of nurturing children.

Principles

P–2.1 We shall not deny family members access to their child's classroom setting.

P–2.2 We shall inform families of program philosophy, policies, and personnel qualifications, and explain why we teach as we do, which should be in accordance with our ethical responsibilities to children (see Section I).

Section III: Ethical responsibilities to colleagues

In a caring cooperative work place, human dignity is respected, professional satisfaction is promoted and positive relationships are modeled. Based upon our core values, our primary responsibility in this arena is to establish and maintain settings and relationships that support productive work and meet professional needs. The same ideals that apply to children are inherent in our responsibilities to adults.

A. RESPONSIBILITIES TO CO-WORKERS
Ideals

I–3A.1 To establish and maintain relationships of respect, trust, and cooperation with co-workers.

Principles

P–3A.1 When we have concern about the professional behavior of a co-worker, we shall first let that person know of our concern, in a way that shows respect for personal dignity and for the diversity to be found among staff members, and then attempt to resolve the matter collegially.

B. RESPONSIBILITIES TO EMPLOYERS
Ideals

I–3B.1 To assist the program in providing the highest quality of service.

Principles

P–3B.1 When we do not agree with program policies, we shall first attempt to effect change through constructive action within the organization.

C. RESPONSIBILITIES TO EMPLOYEES
Ideals

I–3C.1 To promote policies and working conditions that foster mutual respect, competence, well-being, and positive self-esteem in staff members.

Principles

P–3C.1 In decisions concerning children and programs, we shall appropriately utilize the education, training, experience, and expertise of staff members.

Section IV: Ethical responsibilities to community and society

Early childhood programs operate within a context of an immediate community made up of families and other institutions concerned with children's welfare. Our responsibilities to the community are to provide programs that meet its needs, to cooperate with agencies and professions that share responsibility for children, and to develop needed programs that are not currently available. Because the larger society has a measure of responsibility for the welfare and protection of children, and because of our specialized expertise in child development, we acknowledge an obligation to serve as a voice for children everywhere.

Ideals

I–4.1 To provide community with high-quality (age and individually appropriate, and culturally and socially sensitive) education/care programs and services.

I–4.2 To promote cooperation among agencies and interdisciplinary collaboration among professions concerned with the welfare of young children, their families, and their teachers.

Principles

P–4.1 We shall communicate openly and truthfully about the nature and extent of services that we provide."

SOURCE: National Association for the Education of Young Children.

Every director should be familiar with the code and use it as a guide when making decisions or interacting with others. In addition, all staff members should have copies and there should be training workshops to discuss the content and its application to daily experiences. Discussions at staff meetings often center around the challenges teachers meet, and these are additional opportunities to consider solutions based upon the code. Further discussion of training staff members is found in Chapter 8.

PROFESSIONAL DEVELOPMENT

Beginning directors often express their frustration about their jobs and their ability to perform them adequately. Bloom (1997) found that only 32 percent felt confident and self-assured when they first became directors. Many had been coaxed and coerced into becoming leaders after success in the classroom, and most felt they were not prepared for the kinds of situations and problems they encountered. Eventually they learn by doing, but the journey is a difficult one.

Bloom quotes some of their comments about their experiences. They said being a director was like ". . . going on a trip—lots of surprises, a few roadblocks and detours, but never a dull moment; . . . going through a large maze without a map to guide me—I encounter many twists and turns, often unsure where I am going exactly"; "riding a roller coaster—the ups and downs are exhilarating and usually unpredictable." Bloom found that directors go through several career stages that correspond to career stages of teachers as delineated by other researchers (Fessler & Christensen, 1992). The stages are survival, competence building, enthusiastic and growing, career frustrations, reflective and inspiring, and career wind-down. The survival stage just means getting through each day, with feelings of extreme inadequacy. By the second year or more of administering, directors begin to feel competent having learned how to perform the basic tasks required of them. Bloom uses a wonderful phrase to describe this shift, "from struggling to juggling." An important realization at this stage is that the qualities that made them good teachers are not always the same qualities that lead to success in their leadership role. The third stage, enthusiastic and growing, is typical of a master director. These persons feel confident, while still juggling the many demands made on them. At the reflective and inspiring stage, directors have reached a high level of competence. They are often seen as leader by colleagues and a mentor to others. The last stage, career wind-down, is reached as directors prepare for retirement or a career change.

Bloom's research indicates the need for a plan to prepare persons to move into administrative positions. Some states already have requirements that include specific courses for directors and site supervisors in publicly funded programs. However, professionals feel there is a need for a credential specifically designed for directors or supervisors. (One such credential program is discussed later in this chapter.) This would go a long way toward helping to prepare beginning administrators.

 THE DIRECTOR'S EVALUATION

Competencies

Assessing director competencies is a difficult task since the job is multifaceted. Bloom (2000) believes that the difficulty also stems from the fact that there is not a clear definition of what competence is. Many educators use a statement put forth by Fenichel and Eggbeer (1990) that competence "is the ability to do the right thing, at the right time, for the right reason." According to, Fenichel and Eggbeer (1990), competence requires ability to analyze a situation and consider alternatives, then evaluate the outcome and state a rationale for the process. How one measures any of these criteria is purely subjective and therefore impossible to quantify.

Additional problems assessing competency stem from the fact that different programs require different abilities from their leader. The director of a small center may have limited administrative tasks to perform and may even teach in a classroom part-time. This person must have an extensive knowledge of child development and curriculum planning. On the other hand, the director of a large program with several sites requires quite different skills. The ability to interact with people effectively and to organize a diversified workload would be essential here. The director of an on-site center at a business must work within the corporate structure with persons who have business rather than education backgrounds. In addition to a background in early childhood education, this director must have a strong grounding in business methods.

Bloom (2000) believes that competence is comprised of three components: (1) knowledge competency in areas such as group dynamics, organizational theory, child development, teaching strategies, and family systems, (2) skill competency encompassing technical, human, and conceptual skills that are needed to do a variety of tasks from formulating a budget to solving problems, and (3) attitude competency that includes personality and emotional components such as beliefs, values, dispositions, and emotional responses that support the best performance from others.

Directors can evaluate themselves, but that is always difficult since it is hard to be objective. A place to start is by listing all the things that are done well. That should be followed with a specific list of things that should be improved. As an example some directors feel they have not done enough to encourage staff to increase their skills. It is important that they answer the questions of why not. Was it lack of time? Was it lack of knowledge about what is needed? Once these questions are answered it becomes easier to figure out a way to change.

Another method is to make a list of goals at the beginning of each year and periodically check to see if the goals are being met. If not, how can they be implemented? At the end of the year it is important to check the list and mark those things that didn't get done. Why not? Was it a lack of skills, of knowledge? Were there other reasons that prevented the attainment of goals? The answers will give directors valuable information about what to change.

Self-Evaluation Tools

Written evaluation tools can be used to analyze the director's performance. These will be similar to those used to evaluate other staff members. There are basically two types: an evaluation sheet containing a list of questions and a rating scale.

The *evaluation sheet* asks questions about specific areas of the job. It should be based on either the job description or the goals that have been set for that year. It will ask, "Have I . . . ?"

Some sample questions are the following:

■ Have I created an open climate for discussion among staff members?

■ Have I used my time efficiently?

■ Have my contacts with parents sufficiently conveyed my understanding of their problems and pressures?

A *rating scale* can also be used. It addresses specific skills such as organization, planning, or initiative. It also includes a way of rating the skills comparatively, such as good versus unsatisfactory, or on the frequency of occurrence. It might look like the following example:

I show consideration for the feelings of my employees.	Often	Sometimes	Never
I try to praise rather than criticize.	Often	Sometimes	Never
I welcome suggestions from others.	Often	Sometimes	Never

A *numerical scale* asks individuals to rate their own abilities on a scale of 1 to 5, with 1 being the highest. It might look like this:

Schedule and organize work	1	2	3	4	5
Plan for future needs of the school	1	2	3	4	5
Communicate clearly with staff	1	2	3	4	5
Resourceful in resolving problems	1	2	3	4	5

Evaluation by Staff Members

A more recent trend is *peer rating,* where directors are evaluated by staff members. This is best accomplished through periodic attitude surveys of how employees view the organizational climate of the child care center. A general survey of a variety of aspects can be included in one survey or individual surveys can focus on specific parts of the work environment. In the example on page 24, teachers are asked to determine whether the following conditions exist most of the time.

Many other items could be added to fit the needs of a particular setting. There should also be a place at the end of the document for comments or suggestions to improve the organizational environment.

Evaluation by a Board of Directors

In a child care center governed by a board of directors, periodic evaluation of the administrator is essential. However, this kind of evaluation has some drawbacks that need to be addressed before proceeding. Board members may not have frequent contact with the day-to-day functioning of the center. They may also be laypersons with limited knowledge of either early childhood education or of organizational management. The director does not always have advance information about the criteria to which he or she is being held accountable.

These problems can be avoided and the process can be done in such a way as to enhance the director's effectiveness. One of the first issues to be addressed is the frequency of evaluation. A usual period is once every 12 months although a board may

Check all the questions that apply.

OPEN COMMUNICATION

Does your director . . .
— encourage questions and discussions of problems?
— allow staff members to express feelings?
— create a team feeling among all staff members?
— solicit ideas for improving working conditions?

PROFESSIONAL DEVELOPMENT

Are you encouraged by the director to . . .
— attend workshops to learn new skills?
— share resources with other staff members?
— visit other classrooms?
— attend college classes and be reimbursed for tuition?
— read professional journals and books?

LEADERSHIP CHARACTERISTICS

Which characteristics apply to your director?
— is supportive
— gives frequent feedback
— is often critical
— is willing to share information with others
— very seldom visits classrooms
— is fair when evaluating staff
— is usually available when needed

choose a six-month period for a new employee. Next, the board and director should agree upon the criteria to be used in the assessment. Two broad categories are standard practice. First, how is the director furthering the overall goals of the program? Second, how effective are the director's leadership and managerial qualities?

The board and director should work together to decide upon the criteria to be evaluated. The director's job description is a good place to start since it is important to know if specific tasks were done and how well they were done. Some criteria will be easy to assess whereas others are more difficult. For instance, it is easy to determine whether enrollment information is being kept up to date and whether reports are presented on time. It is more difficult to decide whether the director communicates effectively. In this case, a rating scale is useful.

Usually a committee comprised of several board members works out the actual wording of the rating instrument, which is then approved by the entire board. Whenever possible the same persons who developed the scale should be involved in conducting the evaluation. Before beginning they should review the criteria and agree upon how to assess them. The director should submit a written report on his or her compliance accompanied by any specific materials that support the report. The committee can then seek further information from others: parents, fund-granting agencies, other directors. It is debatable as to whether to gather information from staff members. Some professionals feel this undermines the relationship between the director and employees.

When all the information has been collected the committee meets with the director to discuss each item. At this time, there can be a discussion about ways to improve performance or to respond with further information. The report is signed by the committee members and the director and is presented to the board. The final step in the evaluation process is to plan for the next evaluation. The following are some sample items that might be included in an evaluation.

ACHIEVEMENT OF CENTER GOALS

Circle the appropriate measure of achievement.

The director:

1. maintained at least an 80% full-time equivalent enrollment.
   Seldom   Often   Always

2. ensured the safety of children by scheduling periodic safety checks.
   Seldom   Often   Always

3. worked with licensing agency to comply with regulations.
   Seldom   Often   Always

4. planned and implemented a staff training program to upgrade the quality of the program.
   Seldom   Often   Always

5. publicized the center by speaking to community groups about the center philosophy.
   Seldom   Often   Always

ACHIEVEMENT OF LEADERSHIP GOALS

Circle the appropriate measure of achievement.

The director:

1. communicates effectively with board members, staff, and parents.
   1 . . . . .2 . . . . .3 . . . . .4 5
   Incompetent   Excellent

2. is available to provide information to board members.
   1 . . . . .2 . . . . 3 . . . . .4 5
   Incompetent   Excellent

3. is viewed by other directors as a leader and a mentor.
   1 . . . . .2 . . . . .3 . . . . .4 5
   Incompetent   Excellent

4. is viewed by parents as knowledgeable and supportive.
   1 . . . . .2 . . . . .3 . . . . .4 5
   Incompetent   Excellent

5. follows through with board directives.
   1 . . . . .2 . . . . 3 . . . . .4 5
   Incompetent   Excellent

Administrative Credential

The state of Illinois has developed a credential that would address the concerns of professionals for director competency. After much consideration of the requirement the developers outlined a Director Credential that is earned through demonstrating accomplishments in five competency components:

■ general education
■ early childhood/school-age knowledge and skills: fundamentals of development and care and education
■ management knowledge and skills: delineates 10 management knowledge and skill competencies
■ experience: on-the-job experience
■ professional contributions: contributions to the profession in six leadership and advocacy situations

The cred ential is awarded at three levels at which the individual must have attained an associate degree for level I, a baccalaureate degree for level II, and a master's degree or other advanced degree for level III. At each level, the candidate must demonstrate the five competency components.

Individuals can achieve the credential in two ways: (1) the entitled program route, by completing an approved program at an Illinois Director Credential Commission-entitled institution of higher education or (2) the direct application route by completing the Illinois Director Credential requirements and submitting documentation to the Illinois Director Credential Commission. For option 1, the individual enrolls in an approved program or an entitled institution of higher learning and completes the coursework requirements for the credential. The institution verifies the attainment of each of the requirements. For option 2, the individual makes direct application to the commission by submitting a portfolio that includes transcripts, verification of experience, and documentation of professional contributions. The credential is conferred by the Illinois Network of Child Care Resource and Referral Agencies on the recommendation of the Illinois Director Credential Commission.

Although there has been no universal acceptance or adoption of a special credential for administrators of programs, there may well be more movement in that direction in the future. For more information about the Illinois model, contact:

INCCRRA
207 West Jefferson, Suite 503
Bloomington, IL 61701
(309) 829–5327 or (800) 649–1884
(309) 828–1808 (fax)
E-mail: inccrra@ilchildcare.org
Web site: http://www.ilchildcare.org

THE DIRECTOR'S RELATION TO BOARDS OF DIRECTORS
Boards of Directors

In the past, the largest number of board-governed schools were nonprofit ones sponsored by churches, community organizations, or social agencies. Also in this category are the programs funded by some level of government: Head Start, migrant worker centers, child care centers, and facilities for children with special needs. More recently, there has been a significant rise in the number of profit-making corporation schools governed by a board. These are the multisite enterprises that operate as few as 10 schools or more than 1,000. In addition, corporate businesses now operate on-site child care centers or participate in a consortium that is set up as a corporation. In order to work effectively in any of these settings, it is necessary to understand the function of boards and their makeup.

Basically, there are two kinds of boards: governing and advisory. A *governing board* makes and enforces policy that is then implemented by the program administrator. An *advisory board* has no power to enforce; instead it suggests policies and procedures or provides information to those who administer a program. The bylaws of an organization should clearly state the purpose and functions of a board of directors.

The composition of a board will vary according to the type of center it administers. A nonprofit board will include members who are chosen from the population it represents. In many cases, these will be parents of the children who attend the school or are members of the sponsoring church. In addition, the board may include professionals in early childhood education and community leaders. A great deal of consideration is usually given to making the board diverse, based on the members' backgrounds, occupation, ethnic groups, ages, gender, and points of view. Board members may be appointed or elected, and membership is contingent upon the individual's willingness to serve.

The board of directors of a for-profit corporation is selected by the shareholders or investors. This type of board usually consists of persons who have business expertise, but it may also include others. In some situations, parents may also be shareholders and therefore eligible for board membership. The board may decide to include nonshareholder parents, early childhood professionals, or community representatives.

There is no ideal number for a board of directors, although some state laws specify a required number. Some boards have as few as three to five members while others have 20 to 25. A small board is more manageable and makes it easier for members to get to know each other and to learn to work together effectively, but there are fewer people to carry out the tasks that may be needed. On the other hand, a larger board may be unwieldy but provides greater diversity of ideas and expertise. In addition, there are more people to assign to committees.

Board members may serve terms of one to three years. One year may not allow an individual enough time to become a fully functioning participant. However, some persons may not be able or willing to serve for a longer period. Many boards choose to have three-year terms in order to maintain continuity. This is particularly effective on large boards where terms can be staggered. At all times, a portion of the board has seasoned members while the remainder are newcomers.

The number of times a board member can be reelected or reappointed should be stated in the bylaws. When vacancies need to be filled, there should also be a clear statement of the method to be used. Some provision should be made to remove board members. Sometimes individuals no longer wish to participate, but removal can also be requested by center personnel, parents, or fellow board members.

Board Duties

One of the first duties of a new board of trustees is to research, draft, and publish an appropriate set of bylaws. In an existing school, bylaws should be periodically reviewed to determine if changes or updates need to be made. The bylaws constitute the basic charter of the school and should include the following:

■ official name of the school
■ purpose
■ composition of the board
■ terms of office and procedure for selection or replacement
■ officers and procedure for selection
■ participation by staff members
■ board duties
■ standing committees and their duties
■ guidelines for regular or special meetings
■ procedures for amending bylaws

A typical set of bylaws is shown in Figure 1-2. Some programs may require additional items to be added.

When the bylaws have been completed, the work of the board can begin. Its first task should be to state the philosophy of the program. Philosophy is discussed in a later chapter, but basically it is a condensed version of the ideas, beliefs, and values held by those formulating the statement. The philosophy statement is used as the foundation for all policies. Policies are general instructions for future actions and should be broad enough to allow personnel to make day-to-day decisions. Broad statements will allow the center director to develop procedures for implementation that fit new or unpredicted situations. When policies are too limited, the director may have to request policy changes at frequent intervals. Most directors would balk at that kind of restriction.

Standing committees usually are charged with the responsibility of developing policies that must then be approved by the entire board. Members of these committees are appointed by the board chairperson and are selected because of their interest or expertise. They should also provide a balanced representation of the board membership in terms of gender, race, and points of view. Although the types of standing committees may vary from one program to another, there are some that appear most frequently. They are:

Executive committee: comprised of officers plus the program administrator as ex officio member. Meets more often than the full board as emergencies arise or as changes need to be made.

(Official Name and Address of School)

Article I. Board of Trustees

Section 1. The board of trustees shall consist of not less than _____ nor more than _____ persons.

Section 2. Members of the board of trustees shall be elected at the membership meeting in _____ (month) and such trustees shall be elected for terms as hereafter provided.

Section 3. The terms of office shall be for _____ years, beginning _____.

Section 4. The board of trustees shall meet at least _____ times a year. A special meeting may be called at any time by _____.

Section 5. A quorum shall be constituted by _____ of the membership.

Section 6. A vacancy on the board may be filled by the board, pending the next meeting of the membership.

Article II. Officers

Section 1. The officers shall consist of _____.

Section 2. All officers shall be elected for a term of _____.

Section 3. Officers shall be elected at the membership meeting in _____ (month).

Section 4. The chairperson shall have the following duties: _____.

Section 5. The vice chairperson shall have the following duties: _____.

Section 6. The treasurer shall have the following duties: _____.

Section 7. The following officers may be elected if desired: _____.

Section 8. The director of the school will serve as an ex officio member of the board.

Article III. Standing Committees

Section 1. The following standing committees shall be appointed by the _____.

Section 2. The function of the (curriculum, finance, personnel, building, etc.) committees shall be _____.

Article IV. Membership Meetings

Section 1. The regular annual meeting of the membership may be held during the month of _____.

Section 2. Special meetings of the membership may be called by _____.

Article V. Amendments

These bylaws shall be subject to amendment by _____ vote of the membership.

FIGURE 1-2 ■ Sample board bylaws.

Finance committee: responsible for the budget and soliciting funding sources. The committee may meet with the center director to gather information for budget preparation, but may also merely approve a budget prepared by the director.

Personnel committee: hires the director, but may also help in the preparation of job descriptions for all staff members. It participates in interviewing job candidates and makes final recommendations to the board.

Program committee: responsible for the children's program, staff in-service, and parent education activities. Frequently, the center director and staff determine the specifics, but the committee formulates overall policies regarding these areas. It may also make recommendations to the director.

Building committee: finds a building appropriate for the type of program and plans for future additions or remodeling as needed. It also oversees maintenance, plans preventive measures, and approves emergency repairs.

Nominating committee: screens potential new members and prepares a slate for election by the board. This committee may also plan and conduct orientation activities for new members.

Grievance committee: After a reasonable period of time to allow the director to resolve problems, this committee may serve as a mediator. Parent complaints and staff differences with the director are examples of situations this committee might handle. Care should be taken, however, not to undermine the authority of the director, thus creating even greater problems.

Communication with Boards of Directors

Responsibility for the operation of an early childhood center is shared by the board and the center director. Effective communication between the two levels is essential to achieve a sense of unity. Ineffective communication can lead to distrust, disagreements, and unresolved problems. It may be necessary to provide training so everyone involved can learn to express their ideas clearly and discuss problems in a way that is nonthreatening and leads to solutions.

Communication has to be two-way, from the board to the director and from the director to the board. The board must inform the director of policy changes and provide reasons for making those changes. A well-functioning board will even seek information from the director before suggesting policy changes. The director must keep the board informed as well. There should be open sharing of problems that arise at the center that might require personnel changes or revisions of job descriptions. The board needs to be informed when parents or staff request changes or additions to the center's program. The board must also be aware of changing community needs that could be addressed by additional services. Communication can take place either through direct contact or by written reports. Both have their place. Often, directors keep closest direct contact with the chairperson of the board of trustees, either through frequent telephone conversations or by scheduled meetings. Sometimes a great deal can be accomplished over a lunch away from the distractions of administrative responsibilities. As an ex officio member of the board, the director also attends board meetings and at that time can present information, discuss problems, or make suggestions. Periodic written reports to the board are also required: enrollment reports, personnel changes, and budget information are examples.

The Corporation

In some corporate settings the director does not have direct contact with a board. In national corporate chains such as Children's World Learning Centers or KinderCare, communications go first to an area supervisor. That person will send the information to the next administrative level. It gets passed on from that level until it finally reaches the person who takes it to the board. Correspondingly, in business settings, the director usually works with an executive such as the director of personnel or a vice president. Some directors find this kind of structure frustrating and impersonal. Others accept the challenge, even finding it easier to be responsible to one person rather than several. Working with a supervisor or business executive takes practice, but it can be done. It is important that both director and supervisor have similar goals and philosophy, and that each respect the other's competency. Here again, communication skills are absolutely essential! Directors must be able to state their ideas clearly, discuss problems openly, and give concise information when required. They must be able to write complete and easily understood reports. In this kind of setting, written information takes on added importance since it may be the primary means to gain access to the board. Being part of a large corporation or business has many positive benefits. Directors can call on resources that are not usually available in single schools. They can profit from the experience and knowledge of specialists who plan curricula. There are others to help resolve problems with staff or parents. Even more important, there are often opportunities to move to higher levels of management within the organization. In national child care chains, directors can advance to area supervisor, specialist, or consultant. In these corporations, or in businesses, there is the possibility of becoming an executive as well.

Throughout this chapter, we have reviewed the characteristics of an effective director, and discussed a wide variety of skills and knowledge that are needed. The director's job is challenging, but it has many rewards. The rewards are different from those of teaching but retain some similarities. The following chapters explore the similarities and differences.

 ## SUMMARY

A director needs some specific skills to be successful. Management skills enable the director to coordinate all the parts of an organization to meet individual and group goals. In addition, directors must have a knowledge of good educational practices and an understanding of how children grow and develop. Certain personality characteristics are necessary for the effective director: ability to lead others, a liking for interacting with people, and self-confidence.

A manager is the person charged with the direction of an institution and who manages all the resources of that institution. In a child care setting, the resources are the people involved, the financial base, and the physical facility.

The director is also a leader who affects everyone who is involved in a child care facility and forms the character of the program. This is sometimes called the "organizational climate."

Directors use a variety of methods. One way of classifying management methods is *authoritarian, permissive*, or *democratic*. A similar set of categories based on Baumrind's categories of parenting styles is *authoritarian, permissive*, and *authoritative*. Collegiality is a term that is used to describe a management method or organizational climate in academic settings.

In order to accomplish the many tasks required, the director must be able to delegate responsibilities. Many managers find that difficult to do. Organizing time is another essential skill. Much more can be accomplished each day if one sets priorities and sets aside time to complete specific tasks. Both short-term and long-term planning also make the director's task manageable.

Since much of a director's day is spent talking to people, he or she must be a good communicator. Both verbal and nonverbal messages must be clear and unambiguous. There are ways to prevent problems in communication. Consider what is to be conveyed and when is the best time. Allow enough time for feedback. Decide whether the message will be verbal or written, and then follow up to be sure the message has been understood.

Written communications are appropriate for periodic reports to a board or to report financial information. A monthly newsletter to parents keeps them informed. Memos to staff members give the same information to everyone at the same time. An effective use of written messages is to reinforce a teacher's accomplishments. Directors go through several stages in their professional development: survival, competence building, enthusiastic and growing, career frustrations, reflective and inspiring, and career wind-down. There is a need for programs to prepare persons to move into administrative positions as well as programs to help directors as they move through the stages.

Directors face many situations during any given day that call for difficult decisions. They use their own sense of what is right or wrong, but they need firmer guidelines to help them make decisions that are based on ethics and professionalism. NAEYC has developed a Code of Ethical Conduct designed to help. Assessing director competencies is a difficult task since the job is multifaceted. Bloom believes that competence has three components: knowledge, skills, and attitudes.

The state of Illinois has developed a credential specifically designed for persons in administrative positions that addresses competencies needed for that position.

 ## REFERENCES

Baldwin, S. (1991). *The early childhood super director*. Mt. Ranier, MD: Redleaf Press.

Baumrind, D. (1971). Current patterns of parental authority. *Developmental Psychology, 4* (Monograph 1), 1–103.

Baumrind, D. (1989). Rearing competent children. In W. Damon (Ed.), *New directions for child development: Adolescent health and human behavior*. San Francisco: Jossey-Bass.

Baumrind, D. (1991). The influence of parenting style on adolescent competence and substance use. *Journal of Early Adolescence, 11*, 56–95.

Bloom, P. J. (1988). *A great place to work: Improving conditions for staff in young children's programs*. Washington, DC: National Association for the Education of Young Children.

Bloom, P. J. (1997). Navigating the rapids: Directors reflect on their careers and professional development. *Young Children, 52* (7), 32–38.

Bloom, P. J. (2000). How do we define director competence? *Child Care Information Exchange, 132,* 13–18.

Boyett, J., & Conn. H. (1991). *Workplace 2000: The revolution reshaping American business.* New York: Penguin Books USA.

The Center for Career Development in Early Care and Education. (1996). *Child care licensing: Training requirements for roles in child care centers and family child care homes.* Boston: Wheelock College.

Feeney, S. & Freeman, N. (1999). *Ethics and the early childhood educator: Using the NAEYC Code.* Washington, DC: NAEYC.

Fenichel, E. S., & Eggbeer, L. (1990). *Preparing practitioners to work with infants, toddlers, and their families: Issues and recommendations for educators and trainers.* Arlington, VA: National Center for Clinical Infant Programs.

Fessler, R., & Christensen, J. (1992). *The teacher career cycle.* Boston: Allyn & Bacon.

SELECTED FURTHER READING

250 management success stories by child care center directors. (1995). Reprinted from *Child Care Information Exchange.* Redmond, WA: Exchange Press.

Jones, E. (Ed). (1993). *Growing teachers: Partnerships in staff development.* Washington, DC: National Association for the Education of Young Children.

Kagan, S. L., & Bowman, B. T. (Eds.). (1997). *Leadership in early care and education.* Washington, DC: National Association for the Education of Young Children.

Wolery, M., & Wilbers, J. S. (Eds.). (1994). *Including children with special needs in early childhood programs.* Washington, DC: National Association for the Education of Young Children.

Snow, C. W., Teleki, J. K., & Reguero-de-Atiles, J. T. (1996). Child care center licensing standards in the United States: 1981–1995. *Young Children, 51*(6), 36–41.

STUDENT ACTIVITIES

1. Visit a school for young children. With permission, follow the director for an hour or so. Count the number of people spoken to and note any follow-up actions.

2. Think of your most flagrant failure in communicating with someone. What caused it? Is such failure common? How can it be remedied?

3. Who has the ultimate authority at your school? How does this power most often make itself felt? Suggest improvements.

4. Attend a board of trustees or advisory committee meeting. What topics were discussed? If decisions were made, how was this accomplished? Share with classmates your perception of the function of these bodies.

5. Discuss how directors might resolve the following problems. Cite the statement in the NAEYC Code of Ethical Conduct that could be used as a basis for the resolution.

   a. A parent comes into the director's office to say she is upset because her child doesn't want to come to school. The child says his teacher doesn't like him.

   b. A teacher comes in late for her morning shift, leaving 18 children with only one teacher for 15 minutes.

   c. During the coldest winter months, some parents wanted their children to play indoors and not go outside. The teachers felt they should have time outdoors.

   d. One parent is chronically late in picking up her child. She always seems to have a good reason, but a staff member must stay overtime to be with the youngster.

   e. The budget for art materials is being used up much too quickly. At this rate there will no paper, paint, or glue by the end of the year.

   f. The teachers are complaining that the bathrooms are not cleaned thoroughly enough by the evening cleaning crew. There is always an unpleasant smell, and they are afraid the area is unhealthy for the children.

 REVIEW

1. Compare a permissive management style with a democratic style. How does each affect teachers?

2. Describe the workplace of the future as envisioned by the authors of *Workplace 2000*.

3. List five reasons directors cite for not delegating responsibility to others.

4. In what ways can a busy director organize time so that necessary tasks are completed?

5. Why are verbal messages often misinterpreted by the listener?

6. List things you can do to prevent problems in communicating.

7. Part of being a good communicator is the ability to listen. State five suggestions for being a better listener.

8. Describe two methods directors can use to evaluate themselves.

9. Compare membership on a board of a nonprofit early childhood center with one that is part of a profit-making enterprise.

10. Standing committees develop policies that are then approved by the full board of directors. List the committees and briefly describe their functions.

CASE STUDY

Jill and Lisa are co-teachers in a classroom for 20 three-year-olds. Both are experienced teachers, with their own classroom management styles and beliefs about how a program should be run. Jill recently talked to the director about her frustrations with Lisa. According to Jill, there are far too many transitions from one activity to the next and not enough time is allowed for cleanup. Consequently, the room is usually disorganized and messy. In addition, Jill was embarrassed recently when a prospective family visited. The room was scattered with materials, the children were undirected, and several arguments broke out between children.

When the director asked Jill how Lisa responded to her concerns, Jill replied, "Well, I haven't mentioned it. It's hard for me to confront someone and I don't want to hurt her feelings." The director responded, "Please talk with her about it. You can be gentle and respectful, but you are really the one who should discuss your feelings with her." Jill was upset with this reaction and felt that it was the director's job to talk to Lisa.

1. What do you think is the problem between these two teachers?

2. What would you suggest that Jill do to resolve the problem?

3. What can the director do to prevent future difficulties between these teachers?

4. If you were the director, how would you follow up on this situation?

HELPFUL WEB SITES

NAEYC Code of Ethical Conduct:	http://www.naeyc.org
Illinois Director Credential Information:	http://ilchildcare.org
National Child Care Information Center:	http://nccic.org

For additional resources related to administration, visit the Online Resource® for this book at www.EarlyChildEd.delmar.com

2

Choices: Schools and Programs

KEY TERMS

child care resource and referral networks
church-sponsored program
cooperative school
corporate child care centers
employer-sponsored programs
family child care home
for-profit proprietary school
laboratory school

OBJECTIVES

After reading this chapter, you should be able to:

- State the differences between a half-day school and one that is in session all day.
- Describe the characteristics for each type of private and publicly funded program.
- Discuss the advantages and disadvantages of each type of program.

A Day In The Life Of ...

A Director of a Church-Affiliated School

Each class in our school goes to chapel once a week. Our pastor knows sign language and teaches the students to sign some of the songs. Christina's mother was picking her up after chapel time and I heard Christina say, "Mommy, Pastor John knows how to do the macarena, and he's teaching it to us."

According to the Children's Defense Fund report *The State of America's Children 2001*, in 1995, 12 million children younger than six were cared for by someone other than a parent. Of these, 38 percent were in center-based care and 21 percent in family child care homes. The others had in-home care or were with relatives.

The number of working mothers in two-parent and single-parent families continues to increase. The U.S. Census Bureau reports that based on data from 1998, 51 percent of married couples had children and both parents had jobs. In addition in 1999, 71.5 percent of single mothers had jobs. Passage of the 1996 Personal Responsibility and Work Opportunity Reconciliation Act increased the number of welfare recipients in the workforce. In 1995, about 40 percent worked at sometime during the year. This figure increased to 58 percent in 1999. It is already difficult for families to find affordable low-cost child care, and it will likely become worse.

Older children often care for themselves after school, but an increasing number are enrolled in group programs. Boys and girls clubs, recreation programs, and community organizations offer some excellent before- and after-school activities for these older children. Many early childhood centers are extending their offerings to include programs for children's out-of-school hours, including special summer sessions.

The quality of care given to children not only determines whether these children are safe and well cared for each day, but also has some long-term effects as well. Studies show that children who have been in quality programs tend to have fewer behavior problems, get along better with their peers, and have better academic skills. Quality care can be provided by individuals who care for a single child in a home or by a family child care provider with a small group of children. However, because of the knowledge and expense required to design and operate a quality program, it is more often found in group-based settings. Later chapters in this text include extensive information concerning the components of quality child care. A summary is outlined as follows.

Quality child care includes:

- a well-trained staff able to provide interactions with children that meet their developmental needs.
- low staff turnover so children can maintain consistent relationships with caregivers.
- health and nutrition practices that promote good health.
- a physical environment that is safe, well maintained, and adequately supervised.
- activities that are developmentally appropriate for the age level of the children.
- collaboration with parents concerning the introduction of cultural activities and information.
- involvement of parents through open access and sharing of decisions that affect their children.
- sensitivity to cultural differences and a commitment to preserve each child's cultural uniqueness.

As a director, it is important to know the possibilities or limitations of the various types of child care arrangements. Although all share many common attributes, each type has some unique features. The characteristics are determined by the hours of operation each day, by the philosophy upon which their goals are based, and by the sponsorship of each program.

 ## TYPES OF PROGRAMS

Half-Day Schools

Half-day schools have sessions of four hours or less. Their primary purpose is to provide an enriched educational experience for children before they are old enough to attend elementary school. They are called preschools, learning centers, or early childhood education centers. They usually serve children between the ages of two and six years. Some schools have extended their offerings to include infants and toddlers.

Fewer half-day schools are available now than in the past. There are basically two reasons for the decline in their number: (1) Parents need all-day care for their children, and (2) the expense of operating a school cannot be met with a half-day session. Among those that are left are church preschools that function as an adjunct to the church's educational program. Cost of space and some services may be covered by the church. Cooperative schools with their decreased cost due to high parent participation are usually half-day programs. Colleges or universities may operate a half-day school as part of their early childhood education curriculum. Private proprietary schools may meet expenses if they schedule a morning class and an afternoon class.

A good preschool will provide for all parts of the child's development: social, emotional, cognitive, and physical. There are many opportunities for interaction with both adults and children so the child can develop social skills and language. Responsive adults encourage independence, self-confidence, and control of impulses. Learning centers or individualized activities allow the child to explore and develop cognitive skills. Outdoor play with wheel toys, climbing equipment, sandboxes, and large blocks will develop large muscles. Cutting, painting, and manipulatives materials indoors help the child develop fine muscle coordination. Since the primary focus of this type of school is the education of the child, the staff should have an especially strong background in early childhood curriculum.

Teachers should have knowledge to plan stimulating activities for children and take advantage of the many spontaneous learning experiences available in the environment. Both the director and staff will be motivated to continue to learn by attending workshops and special classes.

All-Day Schools

All-day schools are in session for more than 4 hours each day, many as long as 10 or 12 hours. Their primary purpose is to provide safe care and a stimulating, age-appropriate environment for children while their parents work. They are called day care or child care centers. They operate 12 months of the year, closing only for a few holidays. A large proportion of child care centers are operated by profit-making corporations, some of which have schools throughout the United States. The largest, KinderCare Learning Centers, has over 1,000, while La Petite Academy and Children's World Learning Centers have over 500. Other corporations have been established within the last few years, some with as few as 10 sites, and others with 50 or more. Individually owned "for-profit" schools also offer child care, providing space for infants as well as preschool and school-age children. Churches and community organizations may also provide all-day care. Many businesses, hospitals, and governmental agencies have begun to offer child care for their employees.

FYI

Head Start has immediate positive effects on children's socioemotional development, including self-esteem, achievement motivation, and social behavior. By the end of the year Head Start children score higher in all three categories than their non–Head Start peers.

Source: The Impact of Head Start on Children, Families, and Communities: Head Start Synthesis Project (1985): U.S. Department of Health and Human Services, Administration for Children, Youth, and Families, Head Start Bureau.

National Head Start Association http://www.nhsa.org

The daily schedule of the child care center must meet the total developmental needs of children since a large portion of their day will be spent there. Time must be allowed for the same kinds of enriched learning activities that take place in a half-day school. But, in addition, enough time must be allowed for children to take care of their own health needs: brushing their teeth, getting enough rest, and eating a nutritious diet. Children must be encouraged to develop independence and language skills. A developmentally appropriate program will allow time for children to be by themselves and to be involved in activities that can be done alone. The pace of the day in an all-day setting should be slower than in a half-day center, alternating quiet times with active times to avoid overstimulation and fatigue (see Figures 2-1 and 2-2 for a comparison of a typical schedule).

The director of a full-day child care center will have different management problems from those of a director of a half-day school. One administrator cannot be present during all the hours the program is open. An assistant director is needed to share administrative tasks. This can be either a separate position or a head teacher who performs administrative tasks when not teaching. One person may work an early shift, from the opening of the school until early afternoon. The other will be there during the middle of the day and assume responsibility for the late afternoon to closing time.

An all-day school needs additional staff. Each group of children will have two shifts of teachers, some who arrive early in the morning and others who stay until closing. Most all-day schools have at least a part-time person who works in the kitchen. Many hire drivers to pick up children at home or at their elementary schools. A secretary and a bookkeeper might also be on the staff.

A daily schedule for any group of children will vary according to their age level. The following is one way of scheduling a morning for a group of three-year-olds.

8:00–8:15	arrival, greeting, free choice of activities
8:15–8:30	group greeting, group activity, explanation of learning activities available
8:30–10:15	free choice of learning activities
10:15–10:30	cleanup, toileting, wash hands
10:30–10:45	snack
10:45–11:15	outdoor play
11:15–11:30	indoor story
11:30	greet parents, dismissal

FIGURE 2-1 ■ Sample schedule for a half-day program.

Schedules will vary for different age levels and according to the weather. This is one possiblity for a group of four-year-olds.

6:30–7:45	arrival, greeting, time with parents or friends, free play indoors or outdoors (weather permitting)
7:45–8:00	group greeting, story
8:00–8:30	wash hands, breakfast
8:30–8:45	clear breakfast dishes, toileting, wash hands, brush teeth
8:45–9:30	outdoor play
9:30–9:45	group music, language, or learning activity
9:45–11:30	free choice of learning activities
11:30–11:45	cleanup, toileting, wash hands
11:45–12:15	lunch in small groups
12:15–12:30	brush teeth, toileting, wash hands
12:30–2:00	rest or naps, soft music
2:00–2:30	toileting, wash hands, snack
2:30–3:30	outdoor play (weather permitting)
3:30–5:00	indoor play: art, music, dramatic play, block building
5:00–5:30	preparation for departure, group story

FIGURE 2-2 ■ Typical daily schedule, full day.

Staff members in an all-day school should have special qualities that help make school a secure and happy place for children. Each person should like being with children. The cook who welcomes children into the kitchen or makes sure that good cooking smells permeate the school does a lot to create a pleasant atmosphere. Since drivers often must help children separate from home, they should be warm and reassuring people. Even a secretary will have contact with children and should be able to respond appropriately. Teachers should be able to allow children to develop at their own pace, not rushing them to perform at unrealistic levels. They also should be nurturing and responsive to children's needs. Everyone involved in an all-day school should have good health and lots of energy.

Communication becomes extremely important in an all-day school when so many people are involved. The director and assistant have to talk to each other every day. The morning teacher must let the afternoon teacher know about anything unusual that happened. The cook, driver, and secretary all need to be a part of the "communication loop," focusing on what is happening to children. Parents, too, want to know what their children did at school during the day and should be encouraged to let the school know about home occurrences.

One of the biggest problems for the staff in a child care center is fatigue. The long hours with children with few days off can put a tremendous burden on the staff. This results in low morale or, in the extreme, burnout. If directors are sensitive to the needs of adults, they will provide time for teachers to be away from children each day. Varying responsibilities for planning outdoor supervision and for naptime duty

A private proprietary school.

can help overcome fatigue. Staff meetings at which teachers can air problems and find solutions will also help. Social activities may be scheduled to promote staff cohesiveness.

TYPES OF PROGRAMS—CHARACTERISTICS

Private For-Profit Schools

Private for-profit school

The private **for-profit proprietary school** is owned by one or more individuals and is established to provide a community service while also making a profit for the owners. Tuition is the primary source of income and must be adequate to meet expenses and allow a profit margin. Many times the owner, or owners, are active participants, alternating administrative tasks with teaching a group of children. These schools can be half-day programs, but increasing numbers are offering a full-day session.

Two factors are important to the director/owner of this kind of school. First, there is the freedom to initiate a program based on the owner's ideas. The program can be designed to emphasize cognitive development of children or can focus on the child's creative expression. Some owners may want to develop a program using the Montessori method and materials. The opportunity to have "the kind of school you've always wanted" has great appeal to a lot of people.

The second factor is a disadvantage. There is likely to be a constant financial worry about making ends meet. Each school is licensed for a specific number of children, so the amount of possible income is limited. Child care is expensive, and it is difficult to keep tuitions high enough to pay expenses but not so high that parents cannot pay. Many schools meet this challenge by adding programs. One can add before- and after-school care of older children, filling in the time slots when enrollment of other children may be less. If most of the preschoolers do not arrive until 8:30 or 9:00, there can be a group of elementary children before they go off to school. The same will be true at the end of the day when some of the younger children have already gone home. The additional outlay for materials and staff can be outweighed by the additional income generated. Having children who come two or three days a week can also add income. The total income from two part-time tuitions can be greater than that gained from one child five days a week.

In the current economic climate, directing a for-profit school must be approached as for any small business. Costs must be controlled as far as possible without jeopardizing quality. Income must cover all expenses and allow for a profit. However, many director/owners do not expect to make a profit beyond their own salary. If they own the building that houses their school, additional compensation may come from equity in the real estate.

Family child care home

Another form of for-profit program, which enrolls the largest number of children of all types of child care, is the **family child care home.** These are also called family child care, home-based child care, or in-home child care, and are usually licensed for six to twelve children. Some states do not require a license, but when they do, certification is done through the same agency responsible for child care centers. Each state has its own requirements, with different specifications for infants, preschoolers, and school-age children. Regulations most often cover the physical environment, but some states have statements regarding the qualifications and training for the caregivers. Guidelines for this type of care will not be the same as for a group setting.

Tuition is the main source of income. The advantage of this kind of program is that operators can earn an income while staying home with their own children. They are also free to design their own curriculum to meet the needs of a particular group of children. It is important, therefore, that family child care operators or directors avail themselves of education and training opportunities through weekend workshops sponsored by professional organizations or classes offered by local educational entities. The disadvantage of this kind of setting is that the owners work alone or with only one other adult. This limits their ability to gain through professional stimulation with colleagues. It is difficult to find the time to take courses or attend conferences to increase their skills and knowledge. Also, the workload is heavy since the owner must do the bookkeeping, order supplies, prepare meals and materials, clean, and plan educational activities for the children.

Many parents choose family child care because of the homelike atmosphere and the small group size. This kind of setting is especially suited to the needs of infants or toddlers. A family child care setting can offer the same kind of stimulating environment that a center might offer. The small group, though, will allow greater interaction between child and adult, more individual attention, and less need for restrictive rules. The day's schedule is likely to be more flexible to meet the needs of an individual child. Another advantage is that a family child care home can usually be found near the parent's work or residence. In addition, when a child is only slightly ill, the home can often provide care, whereas at a center the child would be excluded. The disadvantage for the parent may lie in the fact that there is little supervision of the program. Licensing visits are made only once a year, if that often. During the rest of the time, the operator is free from any kind of monitoring.

Child care corporations

As a business, child care corporations operate multiple facilities at many different sites, often in different states. Income comes primarily from tuition. The **corporate child care center** functions like any big business with a board and a chief executive officer. Ideas may or may not be developed at corporate headquarters, in some cases resulting in a great deal of similarity from one child care center to another. Building, curriculum, and teacher training may be the same in a center in Oregon as in a center in Georgia. In others, much more local autonomy is allowed. General guidelines may be proposed by corporate headquarters, but implementation may be done at the discretion of director and staff at each center.

The thinking behind these corporations is the traditional aim of selling a trusted product to the public. They spend effort and money to create a recognizable image, either a name or symbol. The originator of KinderCare's red tower has said he wanted that symbol to be as familiar as the McDonald's arches.

There are advantages to the director of a corporate child care center. Financial problems for an individual center are lessened because of the greater resources of the corporation. When one center is underenrolled for a period of time, there is financial support until enrollment increases. More money for materials and equipment is available since the company purchases in large quantities. Maintenance and repair people are often available. Area supervisors provide extra support. They help the director plan in-service training, resolve problems, and develop recruitment strategies. Other corporate directors in the area are available by telephone to share ideas, problems, substitute teachers, and even materials. Directors are sometimes able to move to another child care center within the corporation if they change their residence. For many, the greatest advantage is the ability to move up the "corporate ladder." Advancing to area supervisor, and then into other positions within the corporation, is a possibility.

There are also some disadvantages. Directors of corporate child care centers report there is a tremendous amount of necessary paperwork; everything has to be accounted for, sometimes minutely. They may find some constraint on planning curriculum if this is preplanned at the corporate office. A business orientation and making a profit for the corporation are stressed. Costs must be kept within specified budget limits. This can have a definite influence on salaries.

Employer-sponsored programs

Employer-sponsored programs have proliferated in recent years in response to the needs of working families. Only a few companies offer direct assistance and those that do often focus on care for very young children. However, a wider focus is emerging. Some companies now extend their work/family coverage to include elder care, special activities for school-age children and adolescents, and care for children who are mildly ill. Diane Harris, in a 1993 article in *Working Woman* magazine, stated that only one-tenth of 1 percent of companies offer these kinds of direct care, but the ranks swell to 60 percent when counting corporations that offer indirect services. These include free access to child care information services, tax breaks, and time off to take care of family needs. Today, work/family issues are very much a part of the workplace.

In 1993 about 600 companies in the United States supported *on-site* or *near-site centers*. If you add hospitals, the number increases to 1,400. These centers are open during hours that meet the needs of the employees. The primary advantage is location at the work site, or near enough, to eliminate transportation time.

Another advantage is that parents can drop in any time. Parents can visit their child at lunch time or during breaks. Parents are also accessible if a child needs some extra comfort. A director of this kind of center may find this advantage can also have some problems. One director said, "The eyes of the whole company are looking at us all the time." She related that a parent may come to visit a child and observe a teacher trying to manage a problem with someone else's child. When that parent goes back to a work station, the incident might be reported with a possibility for misunderstanding. For some directors without business experience, another disadvantage is having to work within a hierarchy.

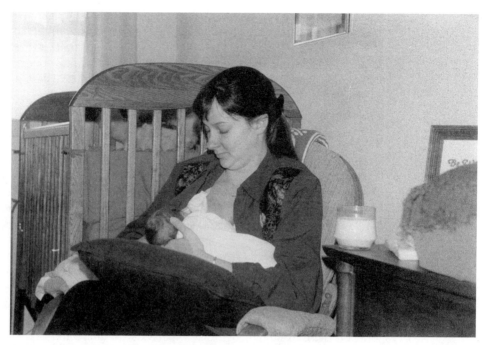

At an on-site center, a mother can still breastfeed her baby.

A company may use family child care homes as *satellites* to a center program. The homes are usually located near the business or near elementary schools. The operators of the homes may receive some salary support and benefits from the company. A few companies have a staff person who works with the home operators to provide training or a toy loan service.

Some companies support child care without operating a center by using indirect methods. In 1980, Merck & Co. in New Jersey *provided a grant* to start a center in a nearby community. The center was run by a local group as a nonprofit enterprise. Space was made available for infants and preschoolers of Merck employees. Continued income for the center comes from tuition, fund-raising activities, and in-kind services. A similar kind of arrangement is the *voucher,* whereby some companies allow their employees to use the child care setting of their choice. The company pays part of the tuition. A variation of the grant method is being tried by some companies. Several form a *consortium* to provide funds to build a child care center.

Some companies have instituted a resource and referral service rather than operating an on-site child care center. Either a person within the company or someone outside the company establishes an information service for parents seeking child care. Xerox Corporation has contracted with Work/Family Directions, a community-based agency, to provide this service to its employees throughout the United States. The service allows parents a wide variety of child care options from which to choose. An agency employee visits each of the approved child care centers or family child care homes before it is placed in the directory. Parents are given guidelines to help them in choosing the appropriate care setting for their child. A list of baby-sitters, especially those who can be available to care for a sick child, is often included in the directory. In addition to information about child care, some companies offer *flexible benefit plans* in which a parent can choose support for child care over dental coverage, for instance.

Child care for mildly ill children

As the number of children in out-of-home child care situations rises, so does the risk of an increase in the number of times a child may be sick throughout the year. For every working parent with a child under the age of five years, it can be expected that each child may have approximately six to nine illnesses per year, which can last three to seven days in length. On the average, working mothers or fathers can miss up to five to twenty-nine days of work due to a child's illness. Employee absenteeism resulting from child care–associated illnesses is estimated to cost businesses in the United States between $160 million and $400 million each year. Because of these statistics, child care centers for mildly ill children have increased in need over the last few years. According to the National Association for Sick Child Daycare (NASCD), only 36 sick-child care facilities existed in 1986. Today there are at least 324 nationwide. Of these existing programs, 50 percent are hospital-based programs (created for hospital employees and community members), 25 percent are child care center infirmaries (attached to a licensed, child care facility), 17 percent are free-standing facilities, 12 percent are in-home care programs, and 2 percent are affiliated with family child care homes. Licensing regulations have already been developed in many states for mildly ill child care programs, and many other states are in the process of developing standards.

The daily schedule for children in a quality, mildy ill child care program is very similar to a day in a regular care center. Teachers and staff will need to carefully monitor and document the child's symptoms while under their care and follow stringent hand washing and cleaning policies. Children are often involved in relaxing and low-key play experiences such as art activities, stories, board games, and dramatic play. Children's videos and computer games—which may not be appropriate for quality, early childhood programs—can be appropriate for the more restful play a sick child may need for the day.

Most programs developed for mildly ill children cannot operate or sustain the business on parent fees. This is because the number of children attending can be highly variable day to day, and staffing requirements are generally more restrictive. Successful programs rely heavily on corporate partnerships, grants, and/or adjoining child care facilities where costs can be shared on the same premises. Research suggests that for every dollar an employer invests in providing a resource for sick child day care, there is a savings of at least three dollars that comes back to the company in productivity and savings in not replacing the absent employee. Companies are becoming more aware of these benefits and are helping to resolve the problem for worried parents. Some provide the resources for care and others are covering the full cost of care for their employees. According to the Families and Work Institute (FWI), only about 5 percent of all employers (9 percent of those with 1,000 or more employees) offer some type of care for children with mild illnesses. This number is expected to steadily increase as many companies begin to be more sensitive to family and work life balance issues.

Nonprofit Schools

Cooperative school

The **cooperative school** is privately owned but operated as a nonprofit enterprise. These schools usually have half-day sessions. A co-op, as it is often called, is owned by all the parents who currently have children enrolled in the school. Ownership ends when school enrollment ends. These schools may be incorporated and have a board of trustees elected by the members. Tuition is the primary source of income; additional income may come from fund-raising activities. Tuition is usually lower than in profit-making schools.

The co-op employs a teacher/director with dual responsibilities for teaching and directing. Parents perform many of the administrative tasks such as purchasing supplies and overseeing finances. Parents also assist in the classroom on a regular basis. The number of co-op schools has decreased in the last decade because few working parents can spare the time necessary for participation.

The cooperative school is a good place for a director who likes working with adults as well as children. There is a lot of interaction with parents on a daily basis as they participate in the classroom. This provides many opportunities for parent education activities. In addition to time in the classroom, parents often spend time building and maintaining equipment, or making materials for the school. The director spends a lot of time in meetings, discussing administrative matters and conducting parent education activities. One director of a co-op reported that the children in her school often "played meetings" because that was what their mothers did. The children got dressed up in high heels and long dresses, took their purses, paper, and pencils, and sat at a table "having a meeting."

Some early childhood educators find that having to share administrative and teaching responsibilities with parents is a disadvantage. It is difficult at times to mediate all the differences of opinions and ideas. Also, there is limited income to purchase equipment or materials. Few co-ops can afford their own building, so they may be housed in a community center, a church building, or a park. Facilities for storage may be minimal.

Church-sponsored programs

A **church-sponsored program** may be a half-day preschool, a kindergarten, or an all-day center. These are set up as an extension of the church educational program or as a service to its members. Enrollment might be limited to church member families or be open to the community. These schools are expected to pay for their own expenses with income from tuitions, although some costs may be shared by the church. Space is usually given to the school free or at minimal cost, maintenance service may be provided, and insurance may be covered through the church policy.

The church board or a committee appointed by the board determines the general policies for the program. They may specify the inclusion of religious teaching along with traditional early education activities. They may also set guidelines for hiring staff or setting up a budget. Directors can decide how those policies will be implemented in the program. It is important in this setting to learn to work cooperatively with the board or committee members.

Directors may be faced with other special challenges in a church-sponsored program. The center often has to share space with church activities during the week or on weekends. The classroom may be used for Sunday school or social functions. Directors and their staff have to develop creative ways to use space or to store equipment at the end of the day.

Laboratory schools

Colleges and universities often operate **laboratory schools** as part of their instructional program in early childhood education, teacher training, or psychology. Some of these schools are half-day programs, but others care for children all day. Enrollment includes children from student or faculty families, but may also include children from the wider community. Although tuition is charged, one or several departments of the college or university supplement operational expenses.

The laboratory school has several purposes. It is designed to demonstrate to students the materials and techniques appropriate for working with young children. It provides a setting for students to do practice teaching under the supervision of a master teacher. The school often is a site for research studies conducted by campus personnel in various disciplines. Lastly, the school might serve as a model for other programs in the community.

Because they serve as models, laboratory schools usually have high standards, well-planned facilities, and a wide variety of materials and equipment. The curriculum will vary from school to school, often based on a particular philosophy or approach. Some design a curriculum using developmental psychologist Jean Piaget's ideas in which children are allowed a great deal of freedom to explore and construct their own knowledge. Another school will base its methods on behaviorist theory with emphasis on more structured learning experiences and a system of rewards for reinforcement. Still another will adopt the ideas of Maria Montessori and use the materials developed by her. Montessori materials are graded in difficulty and the procedures for using the materials have self-correcting features. Some model laboratory schools are now using an approach disseminated by the High/Scope Educational Research Foundation. The content of the High/Scope curriculum supports children's development and learning through key experiences in an active learning environment (Hohman & Weikart, 1995). The curriculum stresses active participation of the child in learning centers with a variety of developmentally appropriate materials. The children are encouraged to actively problem solve as they plan out their day, carry out the plan, and finally, review what they have done. Key experiences include creative representation, language and

Mother and child in a co-op school.

literacy, initiative and social relations, movement, music, classification, seriation, number, space, and time.

The High/Scope curriculum is closely related to Piagetian theory but also strongly supports Lev Vygotsky's theory of social interaction. According to Vygotsky, children learn when they interact with people and materials in their environment. Both Piaget and Vygotsky stressed the importance of encouraging children to construct their own knowledge from a wide variety of activities along with adult support to help them move to higher levels of cognition.

The director of a laboratory school has at least two distinct responsibilities. One is to the instructional program of the college or university. This means that the adult students are the primary focus. Their needs for learning experiences must be met. The children's program has to allow students to plan activities, implement them in a day's schedule, and have an opportunity to evaluate their lessons. The second focus is to foster and maintain a good educational program for the children. This means a delicate balance between the adult students' needs for experimentation with activities, and what is acceptable and appropriate for the children.

It is also important to become part of the campus community. Directors have to learn to work within the campus administrative structure. Sometimes this means selling the program to either administrators or faculty to maintain or increase the budget. They should be active in the wider community, participating in conferences, speaking to groups, and generally informing others of the program. These activities are essential to recruiting new students.

Publicly Funded Schools

Children's centers

Children's centers, also called state preschools, are sponsored by public agencies and maintained primarily to meet the needs of working mothers or one-parent families with limited incomes. Today's centers are an outgrowth of the child care centers started during World War II to care for the children of women working in the war industries. They are all-day programs, open 10 or 12 hours a day, five or six days a week. Funding comes from federal, state, county, or city sources or a combination of these. Tuition may be charged on a sliding scale according to family income. Responsibility for operating the school usually rests with the local school district. The centers are often housed on the school grounds and are sometimes referred to as child development centers.

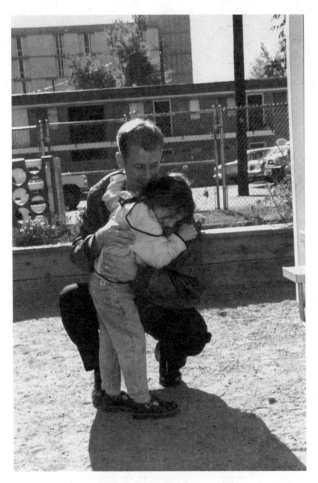

A father brings his daughter to child care.

Hired by the local school board, the director of a child care center carries out the policies of the board. Guidelines and regulations for parent fees, curriculum, staff qualifications, salary scales, purchasing, facility plan, and maintenance procedures may all be covered by board policy. Federal and state guidelines may include additional restrictions on administrative procedures and program requirements.

The director of this kind of center is part of the school district and as such must work within the "system." A distinct advantage is that income does not depend upon tuition; therefore, there is usually more money for materials and equipment. Standards for teachers may be higher than in other schools, and salaries may be proportional. There may be resources through the school district such as psychologists, nutritionists, and curriculum specialists as needed. A disadvantage may be that directors are not totally free to design their own curriculum but must implement the guidelines that come with the funding source. For some people, the restrictions of working within a public school system may be difficult.

Head Start

Head Start is one of the compensatory educational programs begun in 1965 by the Office of Economic Opportunity. It was the outgrowth of political and social decisions to break the cycle of poverty by providing a comprehensive preschool program for young children. It is now administered by the Administration for Children, Youth and Families, Office of Human Development in the U.S. Department of Health and Human Services. Funds go directly to an agency that operates the various centers or to a delegate agency that disburses funds to nonprofit organizations who then operate centers.

When Head Start began in 1965 it was a half-day program and included breakfast and a hot lunch. Over the years that format has changed with additional programs to meet the needs of families. Among them are Early Head Start and Wrap-Around programs that serve children from birth to three years of age and all-day care for children of working parents.

Early Head Start was begun in response to growing bodies of research that showed care for infants and very young children in centers is inadequate. In one study ("Cost, Quality & Child Outcomes Study," 1995), the researchers found that only 8 percent of the centers met the children's needs for "health, safety, relationships and learning." Even within this 8 percent, two in five centers were judged to be minimal. In poor quality settings, basic sanitary conditions were not met, children did not have supportive relationships with adults, and there was a lack of appropriate learning materials. New guidelines were developed to meet the needs of these youngest children in group settings. Some Early Head Start programs also work with parents to help them develop better parenting skills.

Head Start has several clearly defined program goals as stated in their Performance Standard guidelines (DHHS Publication No. 84-31131):

> The overall goal of the Head Start program is to bring about a greater degree of social competence in children of low-income families.

To accomplish this goal, Head Start objectives and performance standards provide for:

1. The improvement of the child's health and physical abilities, including the family's attitude toward future health care.
2. The encouragement of self-confidence, spontaneity, curiosity, and self-discipline, all of which will assist in the development of the child's social and emotional health.
3. The enhancement of the child's mental processes and skills with particular attention to conceptual and communication skills.
4. The establishment of patterns and expectations of success for the child, which will create a climate of confidence for present and future learning efforts and overall development.
5. An increase in the ability of the child and the family to relate to each other and to others.
6. The enhancement of the sense of dignity and self-worth within the child and his family.

Head Start achieves its goals through providing a wide variety of medical and social services to families and through requiring active involvement of parents in the functions of the centers. Parents serve on policy boards, assist in the classroom, and are active in a variety of support committees. In addition to fostering parent participation, Head Start encourages staff to upgrade their skills constantly. Teachers receive financial support to attend classes at local colleges or universities. Some go through a structured training program leading to a Child Development Associate credential administered by the National Association for the Education of Young Children.

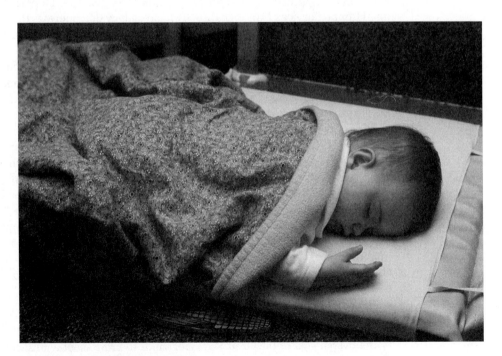

In child care, rest time is needed.

Since many Head Start centers are single-classroom schools, a head teacher is in charge of the center. This person supervises all other staff in addition to teaching. Responsibilities include coordinating all activities at the center, receiving and distributing information from the Head Start office, ordering supplies, and setting up staff meetings. This position is not the same as that of director in other kinds of schools, but does offer a good opportunity for someone with a background in early childhood education.

The head teachers in these centers need to be sensitive to the needs and interests of the community they serve. They should be able to work with families of diverse ethnic and cultural backgrounds. It helps if they can speak the language of the parents, but it is not a requirement of employment. An advantage to working in this kind of program is a higher pay level than would be found in private schools. Staff also enjoy benefits such as health coverage and retirement. One of the most noteworthy disadvantages is the tremendous amount of paperwork required; records must be kept and reports submitted on all aspects of the center's functioning. Guidelines for curriculum are fairly specific and must be followed, although how they are implemented is left to the staff.

Each preschool or child care setting has its own characteristics, advantages, and disadvantages. As shown in Figure 2-3, there is a great variation between types of schools. Directors must understand the differences. They must know the characteristics of the specific school in which they serve to be effective leaders. Knowledge of the differences may also allow prospective directors to choose the kind of program best suited to their particular personality, interests, and experience.

MILITARY-BASED CHILD CARE

Current military populations are comprised of many young families having approximately 500,000 children under the age of five years and 440,000 children from six to eleven years of age. About half of all military families have one or more children below school age and in 60 percent of these families, both parents are working. The Department of Defense reports that 200,000 children, about 58 percent of military families needing care, are being served by military child care programs. The military has set a long-term goal of increasing the coverage of care to 80 percent of the need by the year 2005.

The military child care system has undergone many changes in the last decade and is becoming a national model for child care reform. Their programs are known for their quality of care, availability, and affordability. The Military Child Care Act of 1989 allocated funding for child development centers, set fees based on family income and government matches, and created subsidies for family child care. It also looked at caregiver salaries, linked training requirements to rate of pay, and made accreditation a goal of every center. With continuous and updated research showing how quality child care positively affected recruiting, retention, and military readiness, Pentagon policy makers and military commanders began working together to make child care a top priority for their military communities.

The current program is comprised of a supportive web of more than 800 child development centers (including school-age programs), over 9,000 family child care homes, and many available resource and referral services. The next step is to work with the civilian sector to help improve child care while expanding the availability of quality care for military families. A recent study report developed by the

TYPE	SPONSORSHIP	INCOME	CHARACTERISTICS
Private Schools			
For-profit	One or more individuals	Tuition	Profit making. Freedom to initiate programs. Limited resources for income. Must use good business practices.
Family child care home	Individual	Tuition	Same as for-profit school. **Advantages:** Small number of children. Homelike atmosphere. Suited to infants. **Disadvantages:** Operator works alone. Infrequent monitoring.
Corporate	Group of people	Tuition	Goals set by corporation. Director must be business oriented. **Advantages:** Shared resources for purchasing, maintenance. Financial problems shared. Support from area supervisors. Director can be promoted to other jobs. **Disadvantages:** Many aspects preplanned at corporate headquarters. Need to show a profit. May pay lower salaries.
Employer-supported	Business, hospital, government agency, building developer	Tuition	Set up as fringe benefit for employees. Close to parents' work. **Advantages:** Parents can visit during day. Parents nearby if needed by child. **Disadvantages:** Must work within business hierarchy. "Eyes" of company may be on school.
Nonprofit Schools			
Cooperative	Member families	Tuition Fund-raising	Intense parent involvement. Less costly to operate. **Advantages:** Opportunity for parent education. Opportunity to work with adults as well as children. **Disadvantages:** Work with untrained staff. Lots of meetings. Have to share administrative tasks with parents. Limited income. May not have own building.
Church	Church	Tuition, Fund-raising, Supple-ments	Policies determined by church board. Share church facilities. Is part of church educational program. **Advantage:** Support from the church. **Disadvantages:** Must work with church board. Share space with other church programs.

FIGURE 2-3 ■ Types of schools.

Laboratory	College or university	Tuition Supple-ments	Model program design. Used for practice teaching placements. **Advantages:** Well-planned facility. Good equipment. **Disadvantages:** Must balance needs of children and adult students. Must work within administrative structure of college or university.
Publicly Funded Schools			
Child care centers	Local school district	Government funds Tuition–sliding scale	Director hired by school district. School board sets policy guidelines. **Advantages:** Not dependent on tuition. More money for equipment and materials. Standards for teachers high; salaries better. Resources of school district available. **Disadvantages:** Not totally free to design own curriculum. For some, working within school district is restrictive.
Head Start	Public or private nonprofit agencies	Government funds	Designed to prepare child for school. Parent involvement. Community participation. Director must be sensitive to diverse ethnic and cultural backgrounds. **Advantages:** Higher pay levels. Opportunity to work with parents. **Disadvantages:** Lots of recordkeeping necessary. Segregated according to income.

FIGURE 2-3 ■ Types of schools *(continued)*.

National Women's Law Center, entitled *Be All That We Can Be: Lessons from the Military for Improving Our Nation's Child Care System*, provides six key lessons from the military for state and federal policy makers.

1. Do not be deterred. It is possible to create dramatic changes in the child care system.
2. Recognize the seriousness of the child care problem and the results of inaction.
3. Improve quality by setting standards and rigorously enforcing those standards.
4. Keep parent fees affordable through subsidies.
5. Expand the availability of all kinds of care.
6. Commit the resources needed to get the job done.

The report from the National Women's Law Center can be downloaded at http://www.nwlc.org under Child Care.

Child care in rural areas

In most rural areas there is a shortage of high-quality child care. There are few centers and most child care is done by unregulated, informal arrangements. Several conditions exist to make it difficult to deliver adequate child care services in rural areas. Funding is probably the biggest challenge. Areas of low population often receive far less federal money than do urban communities, and there are few large employers who can contribute to child care services. Families must travel long distances to child care programs, and providers must also travel long distances to training activities. Demand for child care often fluctuates in rural areas along with seasonal jobs. This makes it almost impossible for providers to stay in business.

One solution to the problem has been to use **child care resource and referral networks** (CCR&Rs) (Bailey & Warford, 1995). These networks help parents find child care and provide support and training programs for providers. CCR&Rs operate at the state level and coordinate with local organizations and programs. The passage of the Child Care and Development Block Grant funds in 1991 brought about an increase in the number of these networks. In 2003, there were 756 Resource and Referral agencies across the United States, including satellite and affilliate offices (National Association of Child Care Resource and Referral Agencies, 1994). A state network with large pooled resources makes it possible for smaller CCR&Rs to offer services to rural residents. Employers find they can afford to contribute to a lending library, subsidize a newsletter, or support a small family child care network. The problem of distance can be overcome through the use of new technologies: telecommuting, telephone conferences, and public television broadcasts. States where these innovations are in place find that they can improve the quantity and quality of services to rural communities and use their available child care dollars more efficiently.

CHILD CARE IN OTHER COUNTRIES

As more and more women enter the workforce, countries throughout the world are recognizing the need for child care facilities. In some countries, child care has been available for a long time, but in others the need has only recently been recognized.

China is a prime example of a country in which child care has been available for a considerable time. Since the communist revolution, women have been expected to work in order to contribute to the economy. In modern China, many women also work to add to the income of the family. Although grandparents care for many young children, many attend child care centers at their parents' work site or in a neighborhood facility.

China passed a one-child policy in 1979, mandating severe penalties for families who had a second child: denial of medical and educational services for that child plus a fine or possible loss of their jobs. This often leads to overindulgence of the single child from parents and grandparents. Growing concerns about children's social competence even prompted the producers of *Sesame Street* for Chinese audiences to adapt their format to coach children in how to get along in groups or with playmates (Tung, 1997). Teachers are pressured to help children overcome the effects of "spoiling" and learn the skills they might otherwise develop in a large family of siblings.

Teachers plan activities during the daily routines that teach social skills such as sharing, cooperation, and caring for themselves as well as others.

Children are divided by age group, with 20 to 40 children per class. Each day begins with organized exercises, and group activities continue throughout the day. All children participate in the same activity at the same time. The classrooms are sparsely equipped with toys in stark comparison with a Western classroom where there will be an abundance, including duplicates of some toys. Chinese children have to learn to share, wait for their turn, or negotiate with their peers for an opportunity to play. Teachers even remove some materials as the school year progresses, forcing even more cooperative behavior from the children. When children want to speak in class, they must raise their hand and wait to be recognized. They stand when speaking since it is believed that this helps to overcome self-consciousness. The Chinese child care settings are a good example of how cultural values and practices are reflected in the education of young children.

The Scandinavian countries have also supported child care for many years. Under the Ministry of Education, Finland administers the 1973 Act on Children's Day Care. The act funds preschools and kindergartens to offer education and care for children up to the age of six. These now serve almost all Finnish children under the age of seven. Primary school children have after-school and holiday programs. The curriculum of Finnish centers focuses on fostering all aspects of children's development: cognitive, psychomotor, and affective. Teachers use the basic principles outlined by Piaget. Cognitive concepts are taught through visual and performing arts: painting, music, drama, puppetry, and literature. The physical settings are built specifically for children and often are located in neighborhoods or near community centers, libraries, or youth centers. Space is well planned and attractive. Child-sized work areas invite children to participate in a variety of activities. Overall, Finland's child care centers are exemplary models of public-supported care.

Denmark's preschool programs are similar to those in Finland; however, there is an interesting difference. By law, preschool children are not allowed to be taught formally. There is a pervasive belief that very young children should be allowed to be children. Learning takes place in informal groups or through cooperative play. Adults read to children or the children gain what they can from looking at books. They take field trips to their parents' workplaces or to one anothers' homes. Time is set aside to prepare children for school. They learn to sit still and listen to the teacher. Most facilities are separate from the primary school or at least are housed in a special place within the building.

Another innovation in the Danish system is the establishment of discovery playgrounds. These are places where children can raise vegetables, keep chickens, and house ponies. Within the child care/kindergarten network there are also clubs for young people up to age 18 or 20. Many school-age youngsters and teenagers come to the clubs after school or in the evening to participate in sports, arts, and swimming.

France, too, has an extensive child care program serving most three- to five-year-olds. The French system dates back to the beginning of the 20th century, but there has been a tremendous growth since the 1950s. The programs are under the auspices of the public school system. Some of the centers are free-standing, but others are housed on the campus of a primary school. Every child over the age of two years and three months is eligible although space is still limited for this age level. More than 90 percent of three-year-olds are in school. The hours correspond to the usual school day, 8:30 a.m. to 4:30 p.m. The curriculum stresses cognitive development, but it is implemented with developmentally appropriate practices. Group size is large, 25 to 30 children.

Italy has provided education and care programs for children between the ages of three and six for many years. In 1971, infants and toddlers were included. These programs combine both education and social services concepts. One program begun in Reggio Emilia has become a model for others in Italy, in the United States, and in other countries. The principles embodied in the Reggio Emilia centers rely upon the ideas of John Dewey, Jean Piaget, and Lev Vygotsky.

One of the basic principles of the system is that children should be viewed in relation with other children, with their family, with their teachers, and with their environment. Parents are seen as an essential and active part of their children's learning. The design of each school encourages choices, problem solving, and discoveries as children learn. Thoughtful placement of furniture and materials increases the possibilities of encounters with their teachers and with other children. One of the most important aspects of Reggio Emilia is that the curriculum is not planned. There are general goals, but the curriculum emerges from the children's activities and projects. Children's progress is carefully documented through photographs, videos, and written transcripts. This recordkeeping serves several functions. It allows parents to maintain their involvement because they have an opportunity to share their children's experiences. Teachers can understand children better, thus enhancing their own professional development. The records also allow educators to share information. Possibly the most important is that children become aware that their efforts are valued.

 ## SUMMARY

According to the Children's Defense Fund report *The State of America's Children 2001*, someone other than the parent cares for more than half of children under the age of six. The others have in-home care or are with relatives. In addition, an increasing number of school-age children are enrolled in before- and after-school programs.

The quality of care given to the children keeps them safe and also has long-term effects. Children who have been in quality programs have fewer behavior problems, get along better with their peers, and have better academic skills.

Half-day schools are in session for four hours or less. Their primary purpose is the education of the child.

All-day schools function more than four hours per day. They must provide for the full care of the child. Different management problems are encountered. Additional staffing is also necessary. Communication must be complete for the school to function successfully.

A private, for-profit school is owned by one or more individuals and is expected to show a profit. This type of school has the freedom to experiment and the constraint to operate efficiently.

A family child care home is usually licensed to supervise six to twelve children. This environment is especially suitable for infants and toddlers and probably has a flexible schedule.

Corporate child care centers are relatively new. They are expected to show a profit and have many different locations. They are marked by some similarities with each other, a recognizable "style," and often an interchangeable curriculum. Advantages are their financial strength, increased resources, and the opportunity for staff to advance professionally.

Employer-sponsored programs are increasing in number. The parent company may furnish a building and/or capital for an on-site child care center. Some employers support satellite programs near the workplace or where employees live.

Other companies offer a voucher program where employees are given a fixed amount for child care. Another form of support is a resource and referral service where parents seeking child care may get reliable information.

Employers are also beginning to respond to another need of working parents, care for their mildly ill children. In 1986 only 36 sick child programs existed. Today there are 324 programs nationwide, 50 percent of which are in hospitals. The others are in child care centers, free-standing facilities, or in-home care facilities. Employers are finding that these programs are meeting the needs of families and are decreasing absenteeism of their employees.

The cooperative school, an enterprise somewhat on the decline, is operated as a nonprofit center. The director is also the teacher. Parents fill in as staff, and coordination emerges as a major factor.

Churches characteristically offer a half-day program. It may or may not be religiously oriented. Most of these must be self-supporting, with little or no help from the larger organization. Space may be a problem here as the school often shares facilities with other church-related functions.

Many colleges and universities operate laboratory schools. These serve at least two functions: training and demonstration, and research. Various orientations may be found; standards are generally high.

Child care centers are often publicly funded and are usually adjuncts to the local school system. They have the many strengths and weaknesses of public education, including bureaucratic rules, but offer relatively higher salaries and adequate funding.

Head Start is a federal program begun in 1965 primarily for the disadvantaged child. It is generally a single-classroom school aimed at bringing the child up to grade level before entering elementary grades. It has been generally successful.

The U.S. military has developed a model program for caring for the children of their personnel. The system is comprised of a supportive web of more than 800 child development centers, 9,000 family child care homes, and many resource and referral services.

There is often a shortage of child care in rural areas. One solution is to use resource and referral networks, some of which receive grants through the Child Care and Development Block Grant of 1991.

Countries throughout the world are responding to the need to provide child care for working mothers. China has many centers attached to the workplace. The Scandinavian countries have also supported child care for many years. Centers in Finland serve almost all children up to the age of six. Denmark cares for young children as well as providing after-school programs for older children and clubs for teenagers. France has an extensive system that dates back to the beginning of the 20th century. Every child over the age of two years and ten months is eligible although space is still limited. More than 90 percent of three-year-olds are in school however. Italy provides education for children from infancy on. A program was begun in Reggio Emilia that has become a model throughout Italy as well as in other countries. The design of each school furthers the principles upon which the system is based: learning through encounters, making choices, problem solving, and discovery.

 ## REFERENCES

Bailey, S., & Warford, B. (1995). Delivering services in rural areas: Using child care referral-and-resource networks. *Young Children, 50*(5), 86–90.

Children's Defense Fund. (2001). *The state of America's children 2001*. Washington, DC: Author.

Helburn, S., ed. (1995). *Cost, quality, and child outcomes in child care centers*. Public report. Denver: Department of Economics and Public Policy, University of Colorado at Denver.

Herman, R. E., Koppan, D., & Sullivan, P. (1999). Sick child daycare promotes healing and staffing. *Nursing Management, 30*(4), 45–47.

Hohman, M., & Weikert, D. P. (1995). *Educating young children: Active learning practices for preschool and child care programs*. Ypsilanti, MI: High/Scope Press.

National Association of Child Care Resource and Referral Agencies. (1994). *Child care resources and referral: The shape of things to come*. Washington, DC: Author.

Tung, L. (1997, August 20). How to get to (China's) Sesame Street. *The Wall Street Journal*, p. A12.

United States Department of Commerce, Bureau of the Census. (1996). *Current population survey*. Washington, DC: Author.

 ## SELECTED FURTHER READING

Campbell, N. D., Appelbaum, J. C., Martinson, K., & Martin, E. (2000). *Be all that we can be: Lessons from the military for improving our nation's child care system*. Washington, DC: National Women's Law Center.

Cartwright, S. (1999). Early childhood care and education in China. *Child Care Information Exchange, 126*, 22–25.

Click, P. M., (2002). *Caring for school-age children*. (3rd ed.) Clifton Park, NY: Delmar Learning.

Cordell, R. L., Waternlan, S. H., Chang, A., et al. (1999). Provider reported illness and absence due to illness among children attending child-care homes and centers in San Diego, California. *Archives of Pediatrics & Adolescent Medicine, 153*(3), 275–280.

Gandini, L. (1993). Fundamentals of the Reggio Emilia approach to early childhood education. *Young Children, 49*(1), 4–8.

Gordon, A. M., & Browne, K. W. (2000). *Beginnings and beyond* (5th ed.). Clifton Park, NY: Delmar Learning.

Kennedy, D. K. (1996). After Reggio Emilia: May the conversation begin! *Young Children, 51*(5), 24–27.

Marmer Solomon, C. (2000, December/January). Sic daze. *Working Mother, 40,* 26–30.

Montessori, M. (1967). *The Montessori method* (A. E. George, Trans.). Cambridge, MA: Robert Bentley.

Nielson, D. M. (2002). The journey from baby-sitter to child care professional: Military family child care providers. *Young Children, 57*(1), 9–14.

Sciarra, D. J. & Dorsey, A. G. (2003). *Developing and administering a child care center* (5th. ed). Clifton Park, NY: Delmar Learning.

Sussman, C. (1998). Out of the basement: Discovering the value of child care facilities. *Young Children, 53*(1), 10–17.

STUDENT ACTIVITIES

1. Visit a half-day school and a full-day school. Return to the full-day school at the end of a day. Observe the similarities and differences during the morning hours of each of the schools. What happens at the end of a day at the all-day school? Report your findings to the class.

2. Make an appointment to visit a family child care home. Choose a time when the operator will be able to talk to you. Observe the number of children, the kinds of activities that are provided, and the routine of the day. Talk to the operator about the satisfactions and difficulties of conducting this kind of program.

3. Meet with the director of a corporate child care center. Before the meeting, prepare a list of questions to ask. After the visit, summarize your findings and report to the class. Some suggested questions are the following:
    a. How is your budget prepared?
    b. Is there someone within the corporation you can call on when you have problems?
    c. How is the curriculum of your center planned?
    d. What is the process for hiring new staff members? Are you free to determine the salary for that person?
    e. What are the advantages for you in working in this kind of center?
    f. What have you found difficult about working for a corporate child care center?

4. Visit two other different types of schools. Do you observe differences in the character of the job of director in each? Ask the directors to describe the most important aspects of their job. Are they different or the same in each school? Is the role of a director the same or different from what you expected before your visit?

REVIEW

1. According to the Children's Defense Fund report *The State of America's Children, 2001*, who are the caregivers of the greatest number of children under the age of six?

2. List the components of quality child care.

3. Although an all-day program offers many of the same activities you would find in a half-day program, there are differences. What are they?

4. What is the primary source of income for a for-profit school? In what ways can income be increased?

5. What are the advantages and disadvantages of operating a home-based child care?

6. Discuss the advantages and disadvantages of directing a school that is part of a national corporation.

7. List the types of work/family services businesses are offering to their employees.

8. The laboratory school has several purposes that are usually not found in other programs. What are they?

9. What are the advantages and disadvantages of being the director of a child care center that is part of a public school district?

10. The overall goal of Head Start programs was cited in this chapter. What is it?

CASE STUDY

Andrea is the director of a large church-sponsored preschool and is preparing for the new school year. She has met with the returning teachers to assess their abilities and preferences for group assignments. She needs four new teachers to accommodate the increased enrollment for this year. Because the center is church affiliated, she is committed to recruiting candidates for the positions who have a religious belief close to that of the church. She has run advertisements in the local newspapers and has 11 possible candidates to interview.

1. What questions would you ask the candidates if you were Andrea?

2. Think for a moment about the question "What is your personal educational philosophy?" How would you state it to another person?

3. What information could an interviewer gather from your response to the above question?

HELPFUL WEB SITES

Day Care Provider's Beginner Page:	http://www.oursite.net/daycare/home/htm
Military Child Development Program:	http://dticaw.dtic.mil.milchild
Military Children and Youth Programs:	http://military-childrenandyouth.calib.com
National Association for Sick Child Daycare:	http://www.nascd.com
National Head Start Association:	http://www.nhsa.org

For additional resources related to administration, visit the Online Resource® for this book at www.EarlyChildEd.delmar.com

Part II

Planning: Program and Environment

3

Setting Goals

OBJECTIVES

After reading this chapter, you should be able to:

- Tell what is meant by the philosophy of a school.
- Distinguish between goals and objectives.
- Discuss how goals are developed.
- List methods of evaluating program goals.

A Day in the Life of …

A Director of a Church-Affiliated School

A Jewish family came to visit. They really liked our school, but were worried about the conflict in religious beliefs. I told them their son would come home singing, "Jesus loves me." Because of the look on their faces, I suggested they enroll in a different program and listed several to visit. In a few weeks, they were back saying, "We really like your school." After several more visits and an agonizing decision, they enrolled their child. We wait until October before going to chapel because it gives the students a whole month to adjust to school before adding another transition. By this time we had grown very fond of the family, and I was afraid they would pull their son out when he started talking about chapel after his first experience there. My office is next to his classroom so I heard him talking to his mother when she came to pick him up that day. He was exclaiming excitedly, "Mom, we went to chapel today!" When she asked him what he did in chapel, he replied, "We saw the Rabbi!" Our pastor considered it an honor that the boy thought he was a Rabbi.

Every early childhood center has its own unique characteristics based on the ideas of the original developers, refined by each of the succeeding directors, and implemented by current staff members. At the core are a philosophy and a set of goals that are used for planning and implementing all aspects of the school's operations: the facility design, hiring policies, equipment purchases, and activities that are offered. There is wide variation from one school to the next, for there is no consensus as to what is best for the children who attend these centers. Our ideas about what should be included change as research studies reveal more about how children learn, as social conditions change, as the needs of the children change, and even as political forces exert pressures. Some of the resulting changes are not always based on knowledge of the developmental needs of young children.

The National Association for the Education of Young Children (NAEYC) has been in the forefront of establishing guidelines for quality early childhood education. In 1984 a commission was created for the purpose of developing a statement of appropriate educational practices for young children. The result of the commission's deliberations was first published in 1986, then expanded to book form edited by Sue Bredekamp in 1987, titled *Developmentally Appropriate Practice in Early Childhood Programs Serving Children from Birth Through Age 8.* The book has been widely read and is a frequently used measure of the quality of early childhood programs. Bredekamp and co-editor Carol Copple published a revised version in 1997, *Developmentally Appropriate Practice in Early Childhood Programs.*

The contributors to this new edition felt that the previous material was perhaps too narrow in scope and had found that readers tended to interpret the information as being a prescription for correct practice. The latest edition clarifies what is meant by "developmentally appropriate practice." **Developmentally appropriate practice** results when professionals make decisions based on three areas of their knowledge about children. The first is what is known about how children develop and learn—the predictable stages of children's development and an understanding of age-related skills and capabilities. The second is what is known about children's "strengths, interests, and needs of the individual children in the group." This second statement implies an ability of professionals to be responsive to children's differences as well as similarities. The third area of knowledge is of the social and cultural environment in which children live. This last area ensures learning experiences that are meaningful for the children and their families as well as respectful of their cultural background. Thus, developmental appropriateness has two dimensions: an understanding of the universal sequences of growth and change that occur in children, and the recognition that each child is unique with an individual pattern and timing of growth.

It is the responsibility of the director of an early childhood program to see that the philosophy and goals of the center are implemented effectively. In an ongoing program, someone else would already have developed the philosophy and set of goals. These should be compatible with the director's own professional and personal beliefs and values. In a new facility the director works with others to develop a philosophy statement and then a set of goals.

PHILOSOPHY

The need to formulate a *philosophy statement* for a new school is intimidating to some directors and teachers; however, it should not be. A **philosophy** is a distillation of ideas, beliefs, and values held by a group or organization. There are three areas that are reflected in a philosophy statement: assumptions about how children learn, values held by program planners and parents of the children involved, and ideas about education and the function of a school. There will rarely be a consensus on these areas, but discussions will engender a great deal of thought about the importance of each.

The process begins with an exploration of assumptions about how children learn.

■ Some educators believe that children learn best when they are given extrinsic motivations in the form of rewards such as tokens or gold stars. This is called the *environmental* or *behaviorist approach*. What the child learns is determined by adults and can be observed or measured. The behaviorists Skinner (1953) and Watson (1924/1967) are associated with this approach.

■ Others believe that there is an inner force that activates cognitive systems as children grow and mature. When children are *developmentally ready,* they will choose activities and experiences that they can accomplish. Their satisfaction at mastering tasks provides intrinsic rewards. Gesell (1940) and Erikson (1963) are the theorists most often associated with this approach.

■ Another belief is that learning results from an *interaction* between children and their environment. Children construct their own knowledge through repeated interactions with people and objects. They experiment, test their errors or misconceptions, arrive at new conclusions, and thus, construct new knowledge. Piaget (1952) is the theorist associated with this approach.

■ Finally, some may believe that cognitive abilities result from an interaction of children with more mature members of their society or culture. The social environment provides the support system that guides children from one intellectual level to the next. Adults carefully structure a series of learning experiences so that children gradually move from assisted performance to individual learning. This process is successful only to the extent that adults are sensitive to each child's level of competence. Vygotsky (1978) is the theorist associated with this approach.

The next step is to consider the values held by those involved in planning the program of the center: board members, administrative personnel, teaching staff, and parents. The basic question here is which is more important: social/emotional or cognitive development of children? The following questions should be asked:

■ Which is more important, children's self-esteem or what they learn?

■ Should children develop autonomy in order to enable them to participate fully in a free society, or should they learn to obey adults?

- Do children have a right to make their own choices, or should they accept adult decisions?
- Should families be more a part of school activities, or should school be the exclusive domain of professionals?

Nearly everyone has ideas about education and the function of the school. A thorough exploration of this area must be a part of developing a philosophy statement. For example, the planners may consider the following thoughts about education and a school:

- A preschool center should prepare children for kindergarten.
- A school should teach children to be better disciplined.
- The environment of a school should be nurturing and protective.
- School should prepare children for life, not just for the next phase of education.
- The teaching of moral values should be left to parents.
- The school curriculum should provide an opportunity for students to retain aspects of their own cultural background.

As the planners discuss these beliefs and issues, they will probably find many more ideas and thoughts to include. One person should be designated to compile a list for each of the three areas of a philosophy statement: how children learn, parents' values, and ideas about the function of a school. Committee members can then review the list and rate the items in order of importance. A lot of discussion and negotiation will take place during this process, but debate helps each member to clarify thinking and refine ideas. The dialogue will probably take many weeks. At the end of the process there should be a clear statement of philosophy. A set of goals can now be written. The following are examples of philosophy statements.

EXAMPLE 1

The curriculum of the Child Learning Center is based on the belief that children learn best when they are rewarded for their accomplishments. For the youngest children, rewards are concrete and specific. As children grow, the emphasis shifts to encouraging children to take pride in their own accomplishments without expecting extrinsic rewards. The Child Learning Center also teaches children discipline and a respect for authority in preparation for later experiences in life. Staff members are expected to be positive role models for children.

EXAMPLE 2

Each activity at Golden Preschool is carefully matched to coincide with universal stages in all areas of children's development: physical, cognitive, social/emotional, and creative. Therefore, when children move to new levels of ability, there are always experiences they can choose in order to gain new mastery. There are many opportunities for children to practice physical skills, learn problem solving, gain knowledge of their environment, and practice interacting more effectively with others. We also believe that parents are an important part of children's learning experiences and are partners in the education and care of the children.

EXAMPLE 3

Basic to the philosophy of Green Oaks School is the recognition that children are continually learning, both in school and out. Children are given many opportunities to choose their own activities and to explore their own interests. All classroom experiences actively involve children in their own learning process.

We also believe that their educational development extends beyond the classroom and is influenced by what happens in their home and their neighborhood. Although the school has primary responsibility for the child's academic training, the support and cooperation of parents and others outside the school are necessary in creating an environment in which children can reach their full potential.

EXAMPLE 4

Staff members at the Hanover House Preschool Program and After-School Child Care are committed to including all children and their families. We believe that all children have the right to live in a community where they are valued for their own special qualities. This means we accept children who have special needs or who come from a minority culture. Although we have an overall curriculum model, we are constantly aware of the needs of individual children whether for educational experiences or ways to maintain aspects of their culture. Our professional staff members are capable of assessing individual child characteristics and needs, planning educational and personal goals cooperatively with parents, and implementing appropriate learning activities and instructional techniques.

FORMULATING GOALS
What Are They?

There must be a clear distinction between goals and objectives even though many people use these words interchangeably. Both a goal and an objective can be defined as a change at the end of a specified period of time. However, a **goal** indicates changes that take place over a long period of time. A month and a school year are the typical periods that are specified. When doing overall planning for a school, goals may even extend over several years. Use of the word **objective** is appropriate when referring to short-term changes. A day or a week may be the time period for the attainment of an objective. Teachers use objectives as the basis for daily lesson plans. A director might set an objective of accomplishing a specific task during a particular week. A chart for idea development relating to goals and objectives is found in Figure 3-1.

When discussing goals, people frequently confuse which kind of goal is appropriate: overall, curriculum, or individual. Teachers sometimes make the mistake of thinking only in terms of overall school goals when planning curriculum. A typical overall goal might read "The Child Learning Center will provide a stimulating environment in which children are free to explore." That kind of goal does not say anything about what happens to the child. A curriculum goal should reflect the expected change in the child. This is discussed in greater detail later in this chapter.

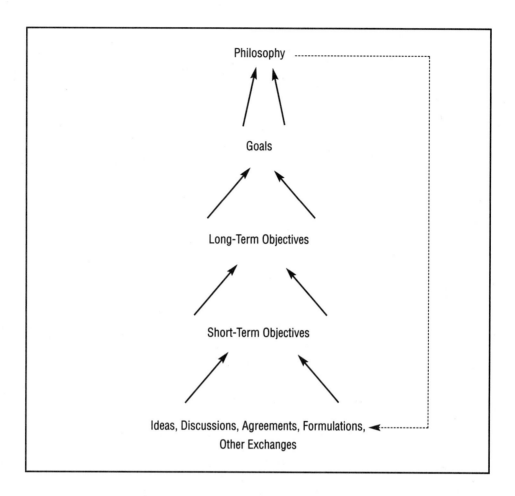

FIGURE 3-1 ■ A chart for idea development.

Who Sets Them?

Directors do not always have an opportunity to develop new goals for a program. They must often refine or renew existing goals when they assume leadership of an ongoing entity. They also have the responsibility to see that goals are implemented effectively and evaluated on a regular basis. Therefore, every director must have a clear knowledge of the process of developing and implementing goals. Goals can be developed by individuals or groups. The process is largely determined by the kind of school for which the goals are formulated. In a singly owned program such as a proprietary school referred to in Chapter 2, the owner usually decides goals. In a corporate school, such as KinderCare, goals often come from the corporate office. However, even in that setting someone with an early childhood education degree needs to provide input.

As can be seen in the preceding examples, overall goal setting starts at the top of an administrative structure. One person sets down a list of goals. School personnel are expected to use these goals to plan and implement all parts of the program. This method of goal formulation has the advantage that it is usually accomplished quickly. Its disadvantage is that those who are responsible for implementing them may not understand or be committed to those goals. At an extreme, teachers may be unaware of their existence.

A preferred method of setting overall goals uses a committee or group of people. Director, parents, teachers, and even community representatives may be involved. This method is likely to be used in nonprofit schools such as cooperatives or church schools. The decided advantage in this method of goal determination is that users of the goals are more likely to implement them. With input comes an inducement to implement those goals. On the other hand, the committee method often takes a long time to produce results. The diverse opinions of each member must be discussed and then negotiated until the final product satisfies all members.

It should be noted here that it is extremely important to include parents when this method of goal setting is undertaken. According to Gonzalez-Mena (2000):

> Child-rearing practices and the beliefs, goals, and values behind them are deeply tied to culture. As long as parents can find people to care for their children who agree with them about child-rearing practice, there's no problem. Cross-cultural issues don't come into play when child-rearing practices are similar. Or if people choose to give their children a cross-cultural or multicultural experience, that's a different matter. However, a potential conflict exists when there is no element of choice, and a person of one culture cares for children of another culture whose value system is very different.

Therefore, the committee approach should include parents representative of the cultures within the center population in order to ensure some synchrony between the home and the school.

Directors can use a third method of setting overall goals. They can circulate a list of goals among staff and then gather opinions, changes, and further suggestions at staff meetings. From these, they can formulate a new list. That list, too, may be subject to revision until all staff members are reasonably satisfied with the results.

A final method might be to use a set of existing goals from another source. Goals can be found in many books and pamphlets. One of the best sources is NAEYC. The association has developed a set of goals for high-quality early childhood programs to be used by schools and child care centers as the basis for a voluntary accreditation system. A kit for self-study is available through the National Academy of Early Childhood Programs, 1509 16th Street, NW, Washington, DC 20009.

Writing Goals

Before starting to write goals, there are several considerations to keep in mind. First, it is better to have a few goals that can realistically be accomplished than a long list that can never be attained. Five to ten goals is a reasonable number. Second, it may be helpful to categorize goals into the areas of a child's development: physical, social/emotional, and cognitive. Lastly, goals should be stated in terms of changes that will occur in children as a result of their school experiences.

Key words in the philosophy statement may be used as the starting point for writing goals. In Example 3 of the philosophy statements, key words might be the following:

1. *choose their own activities and explore their own interests*
2. *involve children actively in their own learning process*
3. *development is influenced by what happens in their home and neighborhood*
4. *environment in which children can reach their full potential*

Based on the first two statements, a goal might be the following:

Children will choose their own learning experiences in order to stimulate their curiosity about the world and develop confidence in their own abilities as learners.

The third statement might refer to the fact that children today live in neighborhoods where violence is a daily occurrence. A goal for a school might be the following:

Children will learn to resolve problems without resorting to violence and will acquire techniques for mediating disputes.

The fourth statement might yield the following goal:

Children will learn to appreciate their own unique characteristics and abilities and strive to reach their own level of excellence.

Goals are sometimes categorized by the areas of children's development. Example 2 of the philosophy statements speaks of children gaining mastery in all areas of their development. Those writing goals for this preschool might categorize them.

Physical: Children will become competent in managing their bodies and acquire basic gross motor and fine motor skills.
Cognitive: Children will be able to acquire cognitive skills that lead to lifelong learning.
Social/emotional: Children will develop a positive self-concept and a genuine concern for others.
Creative: Children will develop an appreciation for artistic and cultural experiences.

As can be seen from the preceding examples, goals are merely statements of what we hope the children will achieve as a result of being in a preschool, school, or child care center. Each facility will have its own separate and unique goals. There are many variations, but each goal represents a commitment to help children "be the best they can be."

DEVELOPING OBJECTIVES
From Goals to Objectives

Goals are broad statements, and it may seem difficult to get from there to the daily activities of a school. Actually, it is not too hard. Think of objectives as paths or steps that lead to the goals. Many directions or many different steps can be pursued before reaching the final goal.

It is helpful to write down the end-behavior, attitudes, or abilities that will indicate the achievement of a goal. It is easier to describe this for goals that are about actions. Actions can be observed. It is usually possible to picture the kind of behavior that will indicate a child has achieved the ability to choose and carry through an activity. It is more difficult to envision the behavior that will indicate a child has a positive self-image.

An example will help to illustrate how to go about this task.

EXAMPLE

GOAL: The child will be able to choose, carry through, and take pride in a variety of learning experiences.

What observable behavior would lead a teacher to decide that a particular child had indeed achieved this objective? Many situations could be used, but a child's use of blocks is a good example. The teacher might observe the following incident:

> When free choice time is announced, John goes to the block shelf and begins taking down a pile of long blocks. He lays them out in a square, goes back to the shelf, and chooses four more blocks the same size. He continues in this manner until he has a structure that is three blocks high. He looks around to find suitable materials for a roof. He decides against using blocks and chooses a square piece of plywood. It fits.
>
> John now tries to park some small cars on the roof of the building. To get the cars up on the roof, he attempts to build a long ramp with several inclines and square blocks to lift the inclines to the right height. It is a difficult problem, but after several tries, he does it. As he drives the first cars up the ramp and parks them, he sits back with a look of pleasure on his face. At snack time, he asks his teacher if his building can be saved to show his mother when she comes to pick him up.

John chose his own activity without any help from the teacher. He solved the problems that arose as he carried his project to the end. His pride in his accomplishment was indicated by his request to save it to show to his mother.

What steps were necessary to reach this result? There would have been many over a long period of time. A few will serve to illustrate the process. As you will see from the examples, a series of carefully planned challenges led John to the achievement of this goal.

CHOOSING

When the teacher suggests an activity, John willingly takes part.

When three activities are suggested, John is able to choose one of them.

When told that it is free-choice time, John is able to choose an activity without help from the teacher.

CARRY THROUGH

John is able to complete a 15-piece puzzle with some help from the teacher.

John is able to put together a 20-piece puzzle by himself.

TAKE PRIDE

John complains to the teacher that he cannot build a garage for his cars and wants some help. His teacher shows him how to start, and he continues to build.

John is able to start his building but gets frustrated when he cannot figure out how to make a ramp for the cars. He knocks down the building and goes off to paint. His teacher suggests that next time he could ask for help in solving his problem rather than knocking down the whole building.

John is able to build the kind of structure he wants and asks to save it for his mother to see.

Each of these already described behaviors is a step leading to the achievement of the goal. The same kind of steps might have been observed in art activities, outdoor play, or any number of situations during the school day. They all were paths leading to the achievement of the goal. If the teacher has in mind what the end behavior will be, it will be possible to observe the behavior in many situations.

It is a little more difficult to describe the end behavior when the goal involves feelings or attitudes. Take the goal: "The child will have a positive self-concept, valuing her- or himself as a unique individual." Each person will probably have different ideas about how a child will show those characteristics. So each teacher will have to decide what evidence suggests that a child has a positive self-concept. Consider some of the following attitudes and behaviors:

■ The child is clear about being a boy or a girl.
■ The child walks with an appearance of self-confidence.
■ The child enters the room in the morning saying, "Well, here I am, Teacher."
■ The child says, "I have brown hair, and my sister has blonde hair."
■ The child often says, "I don't need any help. I can do it."

Many more attitudes and behaviors could be added to this list. Some may be ways in which most children show how they feel about themselves. Others may be specific to individual children. But each will constitute a step or path that leads to the attainment of the goal of a positive self-concept.

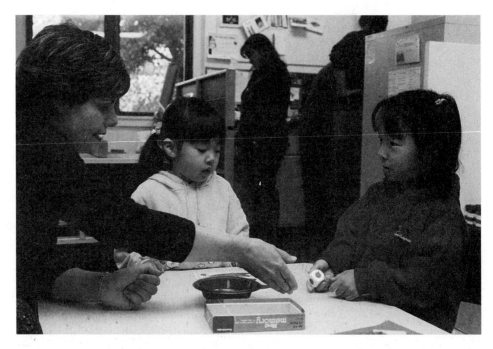

It's fun to learn and play at the same time.

Behavioral Objectives

Behavioral objectives can be formulated when the steps leading to the achievement of a goal have been outlined. There are traditional ways in which this is done. An outline should provide further help:

- State the objective in terms of the child's behavior.
- Include the conditions for learning in specific terms.
- Verify that the behavior is observable.
- State the amount or extent of expected behavior.

Certain words are helpful in clarifying objectives.

TO DESCRIBE CONDITIONS FOR LEARNING

When asked . . .

When shown . . .

When completed . . .

Having used . . .

TO DESCRIBE OBSERVABLE BEHAVIOR

The child will select . . .

The child will place . . .

The child will express . . .
The child will return . . .
The child will identify . . .
The child will match . . .

Another example of a goal and the behavioral objectives that might lead to its attainment should help to clarify the process.

GOAL: The child will be able to attend to and appreciate music, poetry, and stories.

BEHAVIORAL OBJECTIVES:

- When reading a list of six words, the child will be able to say correctly a word that rhymes with three of them.
- When reading three lines of a four-line poem, the child will be able to state the final line.
- When hearing the sound of six hidden objects, the child will be able to identify five of them correctly.
- When hearing a recording of "Peter and the Wolf," the child will be able to name three of the instruments correctly.
- When alone with the teacher, the child will be able to attend to and identify 60 percent of the objects in a picture book.
- In a group story time, the child will be able to listen to a short and simple storybook.

Each step reflects weekly or monthly objectives. There will be many more than those listed here. The teacher carefully plans the kinds of activities and experiences that the child needs from the beginning of the school year to the end. Daily, weekly, and monthly activities are not haphazardly put together but are put together in an organized manner. Figure 3-2 provides a sample plan for the goal and objectives in a week.

 ## IMPLEMENTING GOALS AND OBJECTIVES
General Principles

After objectives have been formulated for each goal, the teacher takes steps to implement them by following some general principles.

Implementing objectives begins with setting up the environment. The teacher organizes the environment and structures the learning experiences in ways that stimulate the kind of reaction desired in the children. When implementing the goal of developing their ability to make choices, the classroom must be set up so that this is possible. A variety of activities and materials should be available. Children should be free to choose whatever they wish.

The child must have opportunities to practice the kind of behavior implied by the objective. Changes in behavior are achieved slowly. Therefore, for any objective, the children must have many experiences in which they can meet this objective. Often this means repeating the same activity many times. Young children will build up a tower of blocks and knock it down many times. Others will paint 10 pictures, each time experimenting with brush strokes or mixing colors. Each of these experiences provides an opportunity to practice a skill, leading eventually to the achievement of an objective.

GOAL: The child will develop habits and attitudes that promote and maintain his or her physical health and well-being.					
Behavioral Objective: When presented with a new food, the child will taste it.					
Activity	Monday	Tuesday	Wednesday	Thursday	Friday
Learning Centers	Vegetable Lotto Game	Taped reading of *Carrot Seed*	Videocassette on food and nutrition	Categorize foods—cut and paste pictures	Seed collage
Story	*Carrot Seed*		*Stone Soup*		
Play Activity	Prepare carrot and raisin salad for lunch		Cut up vegetables for lunch soup		
Lunch	Throughout the week, the children will set the table and serve their own portions from serving dishes.				
Outside	Throughout the week, the children will be getting soil ready and then planting a vegetable garden.				

FIGURE 3-2 ■ Sample plan for a week.

The child must gain a feeling of satisfaction from carrying on the behavior expected to result from the experience. Each learning experience should give the children satisfaction from having participated in it. Unpleasant experiences will cause children to avoid the same or similar experiences in the future.

The child must be able to achieve the behavior expected to result from the learning experience. Teachers must have a good knowledge of child development. With that knowledge, they are less likely to set unrealistic expectations for children. When a learning experience is designed to produce behavior in children that is far beyond their level of functioning, they become discouraged. If the experience is far below their level, they will not be challenged.

The child should have a choice of experiences that can result in the desired behavior. Any group of children will have a wide range of interests and abilities. Even individual children will vary from one time to another. Choices will allow alternate ways of achieving an objective.

The child should be able to repeat familiar activities in order to achieve the desired behavior. Every learning activity has many possible outcomes as children change. At age three, children use clay to explore how it feels or how it changes under different conditions. They will cut it, roll it, pound it, and squeeze it. By age five,

Preparation for kindergarten.

children use clay to express an idea. They may make a figure, a rocketship, or an animal, for example.

Many teachers get bored with the same activities or materials. With freedom to explore, children seldom get bored. At each age level, children find new possibilities in the use of familiar materials.

Overall Curriculum Design

It may be difficult for beginning teachers to put into practice all the guidelines outlined here. At the start of their teaching career many are unable to envision how a few goals and their related objectives can be put together to form a curriculum for a semester or a year. One method is to begin with one goal and the objectives that will lead to successful attainment of that goal. The teacher plans a variety of activities for each of the objectives. This may cover a period of days, weeks, or even several months. Next, the teacher keeps a log of the learning activities offered each day, including comments about how the children responded to the experiences or any variations the children themselves brought to the activity. It is important to add to the log notes any suggestions for presenting the activity in another way, since a different arrangement of the activity may lead to an earlier attainment of the goal. Over a period of months, the record of activities and reactions related to a particular goal will yield a great deal of information that can be used for planning for additional goals.

Each of the theories of development discussed earlier in this chapter includes general statements about how children learn. Those designing the curriculum should develop a list of their beliefs and then decide which of the theories most closely matches those beliefs. Activities can then be planned that are commensurate with those beliefs and that are appropriate for the age level of the children involved. In practice, many teachers use an eclectic approach, taking methods from each of the theorists for different activities or age levels. However, the environmental approach associated with behaviorists Thorndike, Skinner, and Watson will serve as an example of how to use one theory. According to their ideas, children are like clay ready to be shaped by adults. Activities are planned and controlled by adults through direct teaching of small units of learning broken down from larger tasks. Extrinsic motivations are given to reinforce learning.

A teacher who uses this approach would determine what children need to learn and then outline a series of small steps leading to that outcome. Specifically, a long-term goal might be for children to acquire the skills needed for later academic achievement. One of those skills is learning to read and therefore can be used to formulate a series of objectives. This might begin with helping children to recognize their own name. The teacher could start with flannelboard letters to teach them to identify the first letter of their name, then the last letter. When they can do that, they can distinguish the shape of their name. For example, Beth looks like this, but Elizabeth has a different configuration. Children are rewarded with a gold star, praise, or a treat as each step is achieved. Additional activities can be planned to lead to recognition of printed words.

The *developmental approach described by Gesell and Erikson* leads to a very different kind of curriculum. They believed behavioral changes result from physiological maturation along with environmental situations that encourage the achievement of developmental tasks. In this kind of situation the teacher would provide a wide variety of materials suited to the general developmental level of all the children. Each child could choose those that suit his or her particular developmental level. Learning activities can be designed in the form of units or broad themes using the children's interests as a starting point. The children should be allowed a great deal of freedom to sample activities as they wish. Motivation comes when children are praised for their efforts and they feel pride in their own achievement.

An example of this approach to curriculum design may be seen in the many varieties of activities that help three-year-olds develop the use of their fine motor coordination. The ability to use the fingers to hold small objects and to manipulate the objects is essential to the later ability to write words. Therefore, in a classroom for three-year-olds there may be some or all of the following activities. At the art table there are many kinds of materials that can be used for a collage: small bits of fabric, beads, yarn, and buttons. In addition, on the table are blunt-end scissors, some paper punches, and a stapler. At a math table, objects of different sizes can be picked up, counted, and placed into a numbered container. Tweezers and tongs are included for those children who want to use them. A science table may contain small flower pots, packets of seed, and planting mix. Children can pick up several small seeds and put them into a filled pot. These activities encourage children to use their thumb and fingers to manipulate small objects.

A *Piagetian cognitive model* is based on the belief that learning results from an interaction between the child and the environment. Piaget believed that as children reach each stage of development, they are able to reorganize their learning in new ways. Through constant interaction and experimentation they reach new levels of understanding.

If teachers use this model, they would need a roomy environment in which children can be actively involved. They should plan learning centers that contain multidimensional materials to encourage children to explore and problem solve in sequential steps. Materials for the centers are concrete so children can use more than one sense to learn. Adults help children to conceptualize information, but are not involved in direct teaching. Motivation comes from children's own joy at discovery and achievement.

A math center in a classroom for four- and five-year-olds can be used to exemplify how Piagetian activities are planned. There might be a simple activity for the younger children that involves matching a quantity of small objects to a number written on a heavy card. An activity in which the weight of an object is guessed, then the object is weighed would challenge older children. Children doing this activity could also be asked to record their predicted weight, then compare it with the actual weight. This adds the dimension of having to write numbers. In between these two different activities there could be others with varying degrees of difficulty. Children can choose the level for which they are ready.

The *social cognitive approach associated with Vygotsky* is based on the belief that cognitive abilities result from interactions between children and more mature members of their culture. Through carefully orchestrated instruction and specially designed play activities, children develop the capacity to manipulate and control symbol systems required by their particular culture. Interactions may be between adult and child or between children of different levels of competency and understanding. Vygotsky envisioned a classroom as a community of individual learners who work cooperatively to develop understanding and acquire the skills expected of them by the society in which they live.

Activity centers that are part of a larger study unit are an integral part of a Vygotskian classroom. These are based on children's evolving interests and competencies rather than on long-term plans formulated by the teacher. Centers are designed to permit children to work together or with an adult on various culturally based projects leading to the achievement of individual and group goals. The teacher may have in mind some general goals to be met by a particular unit. The children give their input into selecting and organizing the tasks to meet those goals.

An example is a unit on the importance of plants in our environment for an after-school classroom that includes children ranging in age from six to ten. Two computers comprise one center in which children can research what is happening in the rain forests. They work together to map the areas in which rain forests are found, list the animals that are endangered, or research the effect on global weather conditions. At another center, an adult plays 20 questions with the children. When presented with a box containing one vegetable, the children are encouraged to ask a variety of questions until they are able to identify what is in the box. A small group of children work together in another area to plan the kinds of vegetables to plant in their garden. They refer to gardening books and discuss the kinds of vegetables that are their favorites. They have to make compromises since some culturally based favorites may not be adaptable to their particular area of the country. They list the vegetables, then draw a plot plan of the garden. A local farmer is scheduled to meet with the children to discuss farming in their community.

Regardless of the approach teachers use, it is also helpful to keep a log of learning activities offered each day. The log should include any comments about how the children responded to the experiences or any variations they might have brought to them. Children often think of new ways to use materials that teachers have never considered.

The log notes may also include suggestions for setting up the activity in another way. With a different presentation, the objective may be achieved more easily. Over a period of months, the record of activities and reactions related to a particular objective will yield a great deal of information. It should certainly help in planning for other objectives.

EVALUATING OUTCOMES

To determine whether goals are being met, they must be evaluated continually. Evaluation of a director was discussed in Chapter 1, and evaluation of teachers appears in Chapter 8. The NAEYC accreditation process has its own method of evaluating the overall program of a school or child care center. This section focuses on assessing curriculum goals.

Evaluation Process

If objectives have been stated clearly the process of evaluating outcomes will be much easier. The objective should contain a statement of the behavior that is expected. Some examples follow:

- The child completes a puzzle.
- The child shares a toy.
- The child unbuttons the sweater.
- The child returns the books to the shelf.

When the behavior is clear, the next step is to set up standards for judging an acceptable level of performance. Should the child perform the expected behavior all the time or only part of the time? Must the child be able to complete a series of tasks or only part of them? Some illustrations of this kind of statement follow:

- Shown five name cards, the child will correctly pick out his own name 75 percent of the time.
- Shown the colors yellow, red, and blue, the child will correctly name each of them.

The evaluation process should also include a determination of where to look for evidence that the objective has been met. This is especially true of the social areas of the child's development. The teacher should look for these in situations where children are interacting, not during times when children are alone. It is helpful to list the possible situations in which the expected behavior is likely to occur.

Methods of Evaluation

Methods of evaluation are the ways in which the achievement of objectives is tested or judged. Regardless of the method teachers use, evaluation will yield valuable information. As teachers focus on each child, they will become more aware of all children's abilities. The resulting information may force teachers to change their curriculum or the ways they present materials. Evaluation also helps teachers plan more effectively for individual children. When a particular child's strengths and weaknesses are known, teachers can plan to foster or increase them. Finally, if teachers thoroughly understand a child's capabilities, they will be able to report more accurately to parents. Most parents want to know how their child is doing. Specific information is more helpful than generalities.

Although some methods of evaluation may be valuable, they may not be practical for daily use. Teachers simply may not have time to carry through complex testing methods with each child and to do it well. In this case, it is better not to do it at all since the results will not be accurate. It is important that the methods suit the particular school and the staff available.

Observation

The most frequently used evaluation method in preschools is the *observation* or *anecdotal record*. Basically, these are notes made by teachers as they observe children's behavior. Teachers often keep these records on index cards or in a log. What is written down is what teachers choose as being important. They usually include what the child does and says. Sometimes teachers add their own conclusions about the behavior.

Many teachers choose to record information about each child on a weekly basis. Others find it is easier to focus on part of the group one week and the other the following week. In the conduct of a busy day, teachers often have little time to sit back, watch, and then record what is happening. Less frequent observations may still yield plenty of information. However, teachers must guard against coming to any conclusions about a child based on only one observation.

The difficulty with anecdotal records is that only a small portion of what the child is doing or saying can be recorded. Therefore, what teachers actually write may present a skewed picture of the child's behavior. It is also true that two people looking at the same situation may see two entirely different actions. Still, with practice, teachers can learn to be more accurate in their reporting and can choose what is important.

The anecdotal record is only one form of observation that can help teachers. A video camera, tape recorder, or movie camera can provide more permanent records of what children are doing. These methods might be especially helpful when considering how to help a child who is having some difficulty. Rather than trying to deal with the child and observe at the same time, teachers can look at what happened during leisure time. Also, having more than one person look at the record may yield further information.

Commercial Tests

Today, tests that have been developed specifically for use in assessing young children's development are available. If they have been developed by experts, they usually have been tested with children of varying backgrounds. It is important to choose only standardized tests from reputable companies and to follow the directions for administration and interpretation.

Unfortunately, these ready-made tests have some drawbacks. First, administration can be time-consuming and inconvenient. Teachers seldom have the time to spend an hour alone with each child. Some of these tests require the administrator to have special training or to be a psychologist. Few schools have that type of person on the staff or can afford to hire one.

An even more serious problem with commercial tests is the question of quality. Many tests are biased in favor of white, middle-class children and, therefore, are inappropriate to use in all situations. Children who come from poor families or who are bilingual will not be assessed accurately.

Before using commercial tests, the teacher should get as much information as possible. It may be possible to find personnel from another school who have used the test and ask how they would rate it. Another alternative is to check with college or university staff in the community to find out if they know of the particular test. If the teacher is part of a school district, the school psychologist can probably help.

NAEYC developed a position statement on standardized testing of young children in 1987. The developers have cautioned that standardized tests are possibly inappropriate since they seldom provide information beyond what teachers and parents already know. However, since some programs still choose to use this type of evaluation, the purpose of the position statement is to help educators make informed decisions. NAEYC believes that the most important issue in evaluating and using standardized testing is utility criterion. The purpose of testing must be to improve the services for children and be sure that they benefit from educational experiences.

The following guidelines can be used to determine the appropriate use of testing:

■ All standardized testing in early childhood programs must be reliable and valid according to the standards of test development set by the American Educational Research Association, American Psychological Association, and National Council on Management in Education (AERA, APA, NCME, 1985).

■ Decisions that impact children (enrollment, retention, or assignment into classes) must be based on several factors and never be based on a single test score.

■ It is the responsibility of teachers and administrators to critically evaluate standardized tests for the purpose that they are intended, to be knowledgeable about the testing, and to interpret the results accurately and cautiously to parents, school personnel, and the media.

■ Selection of standardized tests to evaluate a program must be based on how well a given test matches the determined theory, philosophy, and objectives of the program.

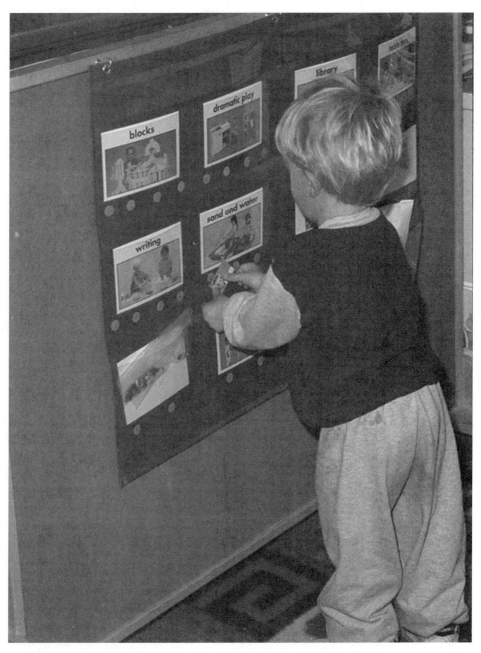

Children choose their own activity.

■ Children must be tested by educators who are knowledgeable regarding testing and are sensitive to the developmental needs of young children. Additionally, these educators must be qualified to administer the tests.

■ Lastly, testing of young children must recognize and be sensitive to individual diversity.

Checklists

Checklists are a quick and fairly easy way of assessing a child's capabilities. They can be constructed to cover almost any aspect of development. They can also be designed to match specific objectives. A checklist may have items that can be merely checked off, or it may include a rating scale indicating degree or frequency of accomplishment.

An example from one of the goals already discussed should help to clarify the process.

GOAL: The child will choose, carry through, and take pride in a variety of learning experiences.

From the behavioral objectives listed for the attainment of the particular goal, the following checklist could be developed.

ACTIVITY	Usually	Sometimes	Never	No Opportunity to Observe
Chooses one of three activities				
Initiates own activity				
Completes 15-piece puzzle with help				
Completes 20-piece puzzle with no help				
Uses words to express pride				
Shows completed task to others				

Each school or center should develop its own checklist to suit its set of goals. It can be helpful to gather lists from other schools for ideas, but each checklist should be specific for the program it is evaluating. Another word of caution: The checklist should not be so long that the evaluator begins to guess at items. It is easier to observe and then check off a short list than to do a list of 30 or 40 items. Several short lists can be used during a school year to get an idea of a child's progress. An example of an evaluation sheet used at one center is shown in Figure 3-3.

Parent Information

Parents are an excellent source of information about children's progress and should be included in assessment procedures. It is helpful to develop a questionnaire using a short list of questions that can be answered with a "yes" or "no" or with a brief statement. The questions should be specific, such as "Can your child recognize his name?" or "Does your child speak clearly and in sentences? Give an example."

PRESCHOOL EVALUATION SHEET

Name: _____   Date: ___/___/___

COLOR RECOGNITION

❑ red   ❑ blue
❑ yellow   ❑ green
❑ purple   ❑ orange
❑ black   ❑ brown

LETTER RECOGNITION

❑ a	❑ n	❑ A	❑ N
❑ b	❑ o	❑ B	❑ O
❑ c	❑ p	❑ C	❑ P
❑ d	❑ q	❑ D	❑ Q
❑ e	❑ r	❑ E	❑ R
❑ f	❑ s	❑ F	❑ S
❑ g	❑ t	❑ G	❑ T
❑ h	❑ u	❑ H	❑ U
❑ i	❑ v	❑ I	❑ V
❑ j	❑ w	❑ J	❑ W
❑ k	❑ x	❑ K	❑ X
❑ l	❑ y	❑ L	❑ Y
❑ m	❑ z	❑ M	❑ Z

❑ writes name
❑ knows telephone number
❑ knows address
❑ fine motor activities
❑ gross motor activities
❑ listens attentively in groups
❑ participates in groups
❑ accepts & respects authority
❑ offers good suggestions
❑ follows directions
❑ makes good use of time
❑ listens while others speak
❑ speaks clearly & in sentences
❑ works & plays cooperatively
❑ takes good care of materials
❑ helps clean up

SHAPE RECOGNITION

❑ square   ❑ circle
❑ rectangle   ❑ triangle

COUNTS TO: _____

Comments: _____

_____

_____

_____

_____

Teacher: _____   Date: ___/___/___

FIGURE 3-3   Preschool evaluation sheet.

A face-to-face interview with a parent or guardian will provide even more information. During a conference, teachers have an opportunity to compare the way children function at home and at school. Children sometimes are quite different in different situations, and the disparities can provide clues to their development that might not be evident only in the school setting. Even more important, an interview will allow parents to reinforce their goals for their children and to judge if those goals are being met.

Time Samplings

Sometimes, time-interval sampling of the presence or absence of behavior is helpful in understanding a child. This is a record taken at periodic intervals. The kinds of behavior that lend themselves to time-internal sampling are language development, interest span, and incidences of aggression. If teachers want to know how long a child stays at an activity, they can do a time sampling every five minutes, say for half or three quarters of an hour. During that time, they will be able to see how often the child changes activities. It provides a better picture of the child's interest span than trying to record the number of minutes spent at each activity.

Portfolios

Elementary school teachers traditionally use homework and seatwork papers to judge how well children are doing. In preschools and child care centers, a similar technique can be employed. Teachers can save children's artwork over a period of time. As children get older and start to write their name or numbers, some of those efforts should be saved. Pictures of their block buildings can be placed in a file. If a video camera is available, short vignettes of play situations can also be a valuable record.

Assessment Information Summary

Once sufficient information about a child has been gathered, the teacher should put it together in an organized form. This *profile* is a picture of the child's development at a particular time. It should be organized according to goals that were set at the beginning of the evaluation period. If the goals have been categorized into the three areas—physical, cognitive, social/emotional—these may be the broad areas. The teacher should summarize the information gathered from all sources supporting the child's achievement of each goal or area. This information can then be used to plan further for each child.

Clear goals and objectives, along with an effective evaluation process, can make a school a model for others to follow. However, neither goals nor objectives may be formulated or achieved in a short space of time. Both take thought, planning, and cooperation to reach worthwhile ends.

 ## SUMMARY

Every early childhood center has its own characteristics that are articulated in its philosophy and goals. A philosophy is a distillation of ideas, beliefs, and values held by an individual, a group, or an organization. There are three areas that are reflected in a philosophy statement: assumptions about how children learn, values held by program planners and parents, and ideas about education and the function of a school.

Although the words *goals* and *objectives* are often used interchangeably, there is a difference. Goal is used to indicate changes that take place over a long period of time—a month or even a year. Objective is used to describe changes that take place during a short period of time—a day, a week, or a month. Goals may be formulated by individuals, a group, or a committee. The process of writing goals begins by underlining key statements in the philosophy statement. These are used as the basis for a goal that indicates changes in children's behavior as a result of their school experience.

Objectives are used by teachers to plan daily activities for children. Objectives can be thought of as steps or paths that lead to the eventual achievement of goals. The teacher begins by writing down the end behavior and then lists all the steps that will lead to the goal. These become the objectives.

Once objectives are specified, the teacher can implement them by

- organizing the environment in ways that stimulate the expected reaction.
- giving children ample opportunity to practice.
- allowing children to feel satisfaction.
- determining that the child is developmentally able to achieve the objective.
- providing a choice of experiences.
- allowing children to repeat familiar experiences.

Putting together an overall curriculum design is sometimes difficult for beginning teachers. One way is to start with one goal and the objectives that lead to it. It is helpful to keep a log and use it for later planning.

Teachers should decide which of the developmental theorists is closest to their beliefs about how children learn. This information can be used to plan the curriculum.

An evaluation process is facilitated when a standard for judging achievement is established. Methods of evaluation include observation, commercial tests, checklists, parent interviews, time samplings, and collection of end products.

Goal achievement for each child can be summarized by compiling a profile, a picture of the child's development at a particular time. This can be used for planning individualized instruction for each child.

REFERENCES

Bredekamp, S., & Copple, C. (Eds.). (1997). *Developmentally appropriate practice in early childhood programs* (Rev. ed.). Washington, DC: National Association for the Education of Young Children.

Erikson, E. H. (1963). *Childhood and society* (2nd ed.). New York: Norton.

Gesell, A. (1940). *The first five years of life: The preschool years*. New York: Harper & Row.

Piaget, J. (1952). *The origins of intelligence in children* (M. Cook, Trans.). New York: International Universities Press.

Skinner, B. F. (1953). *Science and human behavior*. New York: Macmillan.

Vygotsky, L. S. (1978). *Mind in society: The development of higher psychological processes*. Cambridge, MA: Harvard University Press.

Watson, J. B. (1967). *Behaviorism* (Rev. ed.). Chicago: University of Chicago Press. (First edition published 1924)

SELECTED FURTHER READING

Bredekamp, S., & Rosegrant, T. (Eds.). (1992). *Reaching potentials: Appropriate curriculum assessment for young children* (Vol. 1). Washington, DC: National Association for the Education of Young Children.

Gestwicki, C. (1999). *Developmentally appropriate practice: Curriculum and development in early education*, (2nd ed.) Clifton Park, NY: Delmar Learning.

Gonzalez-Mena, J. (2000, July/August). High-maintenance parent or cultural differences? *Child Care Information Exchange, 134* 40–42.

Kagan, S. L., & Neuman, M. J. (1997). Highlights of the quality 2000 initiative: Not by chance. *Young Children, 52*(6), 54–62.

Katz, L. G., & Chard, S. C. (2000). *Engaging children's minds: The project approach* (2nd ed.): Norwood, NJ: Ablex.

Williams, K. C. (1997). "What do you wonder?" Involving children in curriculum planning. *Young Children, 52*(6), 78–81.

STUDENT ACTIVITIES

1. Review Example 1 of the philosophy statement for the Child Learning Center. Write three curriculum goals for this school. Remember to state them in terms of what happens to children.

2. Write to, or visit, four different kinds of schools: a corporate school, a privately owned center, a Head Start unit, and a business-sponsored child care center. Ask for a list of their goals and inquire as to how they were formulated. Are there similarities, or are they all different? What accounts for any differences?

3. State one goal for a group of four-year-olds. Write three behavioral objectives that would lead to achievement of that goal.

4. Use one objective to plan five activities that lead to its achievement.

5. Discuss your beliefs regarding parents' roles in setting goals for a school.

REVIEW

1. Define a philosophy of early childhood education.

2. How does a goal differ from an objective?

3. Three methods for setting goals were discussed in this chapter. What are they?

4. How many goals is considered a reasonable number?

5. List the six general principles for implementing goals and objectives.

6. What is the most frequently used method of evaluating goal achievement?

7. State the drawbacks of using a commercial test to evaluate children's progress.

8. What kind of information about a child's progress can be obtained from a parent interview?

9. Describe a time sampling.

10. What is a profile? What information should be included?

CASE STUDY

Wendy has been a teacher in several centers that are part of a large child care corporation. Advertising for the chain highlights the "academic" approach, indicating that children who are enrolled in the program will begin to read as early as age two. Wendy has always agreed with this idea, but is beginning to wonder if there isn't a better way to help children learn. This is partly the result of a course she took at the local community college and also attendance at several conferences on child care. So she decides to start looking for a new job.

Her first interview is with Ulma, the director of a private proprietary school. As they visit classrooms, Wendy observes that the children are all busy with what Ulma calls "hands-on experiences." She is introduced to a parent who is volunteering in a classroom. The mother tells her how excited her child is about coming to school and how much he has learned. Wendy and Ulma talk about their differences in approach to learning. The more they talk, the more certain Wendy is that she won't be hired.

1. Would you hire Wendy and hope that she could adjust to your philosophy of teaching?

2. What questions might you ask Wendy to determine whether she would fit into your school?

3. What would you do to help Wendy fit into your program?

HELPFUL WEB SITES

ERIC Clearinghouse on Elementary and Early Childhood Education (ERIC/EECE):	http://ericeece.org
National Center for Early Development & Learning:	http://www.fpg.unc.edu/~ncedl
I Am Your Child Public Engagement Campaign:	http://www.iamyourchild.org

For additional resources related to administration, visit the Online Resource® for this book at www.EarlyChildEd.delmar.com

4

Planning: Infants and Toddlers

KEY TERMS

attachment
developmentally
appropriate infant-toddler
program
flexibility
psychosocial area
sensorimotor period
sensory diversity
synchrony
trust versus mistrust

OBJECTIVES

After reading this chapter, you should be able to:

- Describe the steps in human development occurring between birth and two years.
- State the components of a developmentally appropriate program for infants and toddlers.
- List and describe the essential areas to be included in an environment for infants and toddlers.
- Discuss the inclusion of children with special needs.
- State the characteristics of a caregiver for infants and toddlers.

A Day in the Life of ...

A Director of an Employer-Sponsored Program

During our Halloween parade, one of the two-year-olds excitedly told me that the bumpkin was orange. To encourage appropriate language skills, I corrected him. I told him it was a pumpkin. He said, "Yeah, bumpkin." I again said, "Pumpkin." He said, "I heard you. Bumpkin."

An increasing number of infants and toddlers are placed in child care while their parents work to support the family. In addition, more single women and teenagers are having babies. The growing need for places to care for all young children is acute and the supply is limited. Even more scarce are quality programs that are designed specifically to meet the needs of infants and toddlers and are not just adaptations of preschool practices. In order to add an infant-toddler program, planners must have an understanding of the characteristics of children under the age of two. This chapter will present an overview of developmental stages, then discuss appropriate programs.

 ## INFANT-TODDLER DEVELOPMENT

Most children go through universal patterns of development in a predictable way. Children crawl before they walk and understand some words long before they speak a single one. By understanding the pattern, it is possible to know what a child will probably be doing at some future time.

That does not mean that all children are going to follow an exact pattern. They do not. So along with understanding the universal characteristics, it is important to be aware of each child's uniqueness. Children have their own timing of growth so they go through the stages at different rates. They have different ways of approaching new experiences and different ways of interacting with others. Each may have special needs that have to be addressed when planning a program.

The period between birth and age two is a time of startling change, probably more rapid than in any other stage of children's development. During these two short years, they reach half their adult height and move from a state of helplessness to being able to walk around freely. Once totally dependent on others for all their care, they learn to do things for themselves. They start to communicate their needs, thoughts, and feelings. Through exploration, they develop an understanding of the world around them. The following is an overview of developmental characteristics.

During infancy the brain has the greatest capacity to grow, developing synaptic connections that affect lifelong development. Research (Newberger, 1997) shows that there are critical periods when certain kinds of learning take place. The neurons for vision are most active between about two and eight months, while those for speech begin activity at about six months. At birth children have many more neurons than they need. When they experience positive interactions with adults, their brains are stimulated, causing the neural synapses to grow and connections to be strengthened. As the synapses continue to be used, they become permanent while those that are not used are eliminated. If babies are given the proper stimulation during these periods of synaptic growth, their ability to learn is greatly enhanced.

Children under the age of two learn by experiencing their environment with all their senses. They taste, touch, look at, listen to, and smell whatever they contact. Piaget called this stage the **sensorimotor period.** Even infants, who cannot move around, use their senses to absorb the world around them. They can stare at objects for long periods of time, attend to an adult's voice, and even wave their arms to touch things

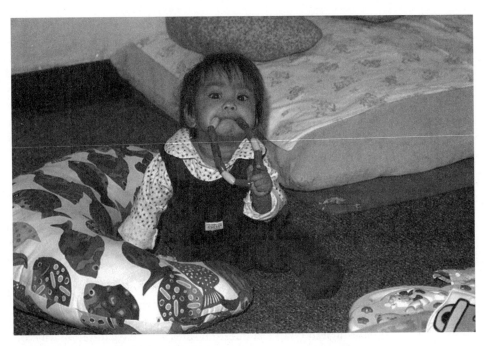

Infants explore the world through their senses.

within their reach. As they begin to crawl—somewhere between five and twelve months—their explorations become broader.

Mobile toddlers continue their active exploration of their environment using their senses, but a new dimension is added. They can also think symbolically. They are able to combine their sensory experiences and come to new conclusions about what they have learned. They remember some past events, can imitate previous experiences, and even think ahead to what will happen next. In this way, they begin to accumulate and organize information about their world.

Motor skills develop quickly and in an orderly sequence. In the first few months, babies are able to lift their heads, then roll over. Gradually they can sit, then crawl. Most children take their first steps at about age one and can walk and run well by age two. Their ability to use their arms, fingers, and hands progresses through several steps as well. At first, movement of their arms is random, then it can be controlled to touch an object. When they first grasp something, they do it awkwardly, for they use their whole hand. Later, they can use their fingers to manipulate or pick up small objects.

Infants are learning to trust themselves and others. Erik Erikson called this stage in an infant's development **trust versus mistrust.** Erikson observed that through repeated experiences babies learn that adults will be there when needed and that they will provide food, warmth, and comfort. This results in a feeling of trust in the world outside themselves. When adults are not always available or do not respond consistently to infants' needs, babies develop a sense of mistrust. They perceive that others are unreliable and cannot be depended on to provide their needs.

Along with developing trust in others, babies develop a secure sense of self. "If my needs are met fairly often, then I must be a worthy person." This is the beginning of later self-confidence and a positive self-image. As they move into the toddler stage, a secure sense of self allows them to act independently at times, but seek comfort from adults when they are tired or frightened.

Infants and toddlers are developing strong attachments to others. It was once thought that babies could develop this kind of relationship only with the mother. More recent research shows that babies are capable of forming strong **attachments** to several people. However, the strongest attachments are to the parents. Attachment is a vital part of children's development. It provides them a safe haven from which to go out and explore their environment. Those with the strongest attachments to parents or caregivers are the most comfortable in moving away from their caregiver, while still returning at intervals for reassurance.

At around nine months, many infants express some anxiety over separation from their parents. They cry and cling when they are left with the caregiver. During the next year or so, one of the primary tasks is to find ways to manage separation anxiety. Reaction to separation is not always consistent. Sometimes infants or toddlers separate easily from their parents. A few weeks or a month later, they may cry or cling desperately when left. Eventually, by about age three, most children are able to manage separation more easily.

Along with this separation from others comes an awakening awareness of themselves. They realize they are not a part of others, but separate with certain skills and capabilities of their own. They learn the power that comes from being able to get others to respond to them. They gradually find out they can do things on their own. All these things combined form their sense of self. This begins a lifelong process of developing and refining an identity.

Competence and independence are acquired during the first two years. As children's ability to control their bodies increases, they have a growing sense of mastery. The more they can do, the more competent they feel. Typically, toddlers go through a time of "I can do it myself." This is their way of saying they want to be capable and to be less dependent on others for help. They often get so engrossed in perfecting their skills that they resent any attempts to direct their energies elsewhere.

Part of the striving toward independence involves learning to control their body eliminations. During the second year, toddlers become more aware of what is happening to their bodies; they begin anticipating the need to urinate or defecate. Soon, they are able to control their sphincter muscles long enough to get to the toilet. When they are able to do this, they usually have a tremendous feeling of power.

Language begins to appear during the second year and develops rapidly. Infants can communicate by crying or fussing. Parents and caregivers learn to interpret the cries, though some adults are more adept at this than others. But the ability to tell others exactly what is needed does not develop until the second year. With the advent of

A study published in the August 2000 issue of *Pediatrics* indicated that 20.4 percent of sudden infant death syndrome (SIDS) deaths occurred while infants were in the care of a nonparent. The deaths were more likely to occur between 8 a.m. and 4 p.m. to older, white infants with well-educated parents. Recently, efforts to have babies placed on their backs have resulted in an overall decrease in SIDS deaths, but babies in child care settings are still likely to be sleeping on their stomachs. The study recommends that parents discuss with caregivers the importance of placing babies on their backs for their naps.

Source: American Academy of Pediatrics. Retrieved 2002 from http://www.aap.org

words, children can begin to say what they mean. At the same time, they find that words have tremendous power; they love to test out their effect on others. An example of this is a toddler's frequent use of "No." With that one word, they can often control what happens to them and, sometimes, control what others do.

Infants and toddlers are learning how to get along with other children. Put two babies on the floor together, and they will look at each other intently. When they are mobile, they may move toward each other, then investigate with pokes and pats. It takes a long while for them to learn that the other "object" is another person who has feelings or may react. As they near the age of two, they begin to play together for brief periods of time. Still, the ability to share and play cooperatively will not be fully developed for another year or so.

CHARACTERISTICS OF A DEVELOPMENTALLY APPROPRIATE INFANT-TODDLER PROGRAM

Goals

A **developmentally appropriate infant-toddler program** is based on knowledge of the physical, emotional, social, and cognitive abilities of the children served. Program planners use this knowledge to develop goals that form the basis for planning for this age level. Goals are guidelines for choosing activities that allow children to explore their environment freely and use all of their senses to absorb information. Goals imply the kinds of caregiver-child interactions that promote trust and attachment. Goals should also address the development of language and opportunities to learn to interact well with others. Guidelines for developing goals were discussed in Chapter 3. Some additional considerations that must be kept in mind when writing goals for an infant-toddler program follow:

- Do the goals reflect current research on development at this age level? New information is being disseminated each year as more is learned about the earliest years.

■ Are the goals developmentally appropriate for this age level? Often, goals for infants and toddlers are a diluted version of preschool goals and may not be appropriate.

■ Do the goals take into account the unique ways that infants and toddlers learn? Goals should allow children to explore using all their senses while developing their gross and fine motor skills.

Interactions with Caregivers

A developmentally appropriate program for infants and toddlers should allow for maximum interactions between children and caregivers. During the early months of life, children are learning about themselves and others. They learn through their interactions with the people who care for them. To allow time for this kind of interaction, the teacher/child ratio must be kept low. The typical number is four children to one adult. Three children, or even two to one, is a better ratio. This level of staffing will add to the expense of an infant-toddler program, but it will ensure quality care.

It also helps to assign primary responsibility for two or three children to each caregiver. That person is the first to care for those children's needs. When the primary caregiver is occupied with feeding or diapering one child, other adults can share responsibility for the remaining members of the group. The pace of each day should be slow and based on the children's requirements, not the adults'. There should be time to hold babies and get to know each infant's way of expressing distress. A leisurely, flexible schedule will allow infants to explore their environment at their own pace. In addition, there should be time for babies to adjust slowly to new situations and gradually learn to anticipate the next step.

The way caregivers respond to infants is important. Sometimes the word **synchrony** is used to describe the coordination between infants and their parents or caregivers. It means simply a back-and-forth interaction that is responsive to the baby's needs. The baby coos; the adult responds. The adult tickles the baby; the baby laughs. The baby turns away; the adult waits quietly for a return of interest before responding again. From these kinds of play, babies learn about relationships, how to sustain them, or when to withdraw if they become overwhelming. They also learn how they can get a response from others when they wish, and how to respond themselves.

Toddlers develop feelings of competence and independence as their interactions with caregivers change. They move away from their caregivers at times to explore their environment, although they may return at intervals for comfort or encouragement. They test their new abilities by attempting tasks on their own, sometimes even angrily rejecting adult help. Frequently heard words during this period are "No" and "Do it myself." However, they also want the security of knowing that adults will "set limits" when their behavior overwhelms them or becomes dangerous.

Routines

A large portion of caregivers' time will be spent on routines: changing diapers, washing, dressing, and feeding. These children need to be on their own schedule rather than one imposed by adults. Each routine activity should be perceived as an integral part of the curriculum, as they are just as important to infants and toddlers as examining a toy, building with blocks, or looking at a book. When caregivers give their undivided attention to children during routine functions, they are satisfying babies' needs for security, attention, and closeness. When adults talk to infants during diapering about what is happening, or what might happen next, they are teaching concepts of present and future. When caregivers quietly wait while one-year-old toddlers struggle to get food into their mouths, they are teaching the children to do things for themselves.

Sometimes caregivers' needs interfere with understanding babies' needs. While concentrating on their own needs for a response, caregivers may not recognize that babies sometimes are getting too much stimulation. At other times, caregivers want freedom from the demands of the children in their care and again, fail to recognize what the demands mean. A typical example is feeding a fussy baby because it is fretting, while what the baby really needs is some comforting. It helps if caregivers take time to listen, to look, and to try to feel what babies are communicating. This sets up a two-way communication pattern.

Routines can be used by caregivers to judge children's development. For instance, resistance to diapering or to using the toilet may be a sign of growth, a push toward independence. Children's ability to anticipate and cooperate in a routine can show the development of a cognitive ability. When children can anticipate the next step, they are beginning a long process that eventually leads to logical thinking.

Parent Involvement

Parents need to be involved in order to manage their anxiety about placing their infant in child care. Some experience overwhelming feelings of guilt while others are afraid their babies will no longer be as strongly attached to them. They also worry that others will not be as responsive to their babies' needs as they are. They frequently experience strong separation anxieties.

Parents are sometimes faced with other disturbing feelings. If their babies seem to get along well in child care and don't fuss much when they are left, parents feel left out. If, on the other hand, the babies cry when left, parents feel just as terrible. In either situation, there is a possibility for jealousy and competition with the caregiver. If left unrecognized, these may turn into complaints and dissatisfactions.

Many of these problems can be prevented or alleviated when parents and caregivers work together. Good parent-caregiver relationships are based initially on an understanding of the importance of each in the child's life. Then both must work together in a spirit of cooperation for the optimal development of the children. This happens when

- caregivers recognize that parents are the most important people in children's lives.
- child care staff create an open environment in which parents feel welcome and included.
- procedures are established for frequent communications between parents and caregivers through daily conversations or notes, telephone calls, conferences, or meetings.

- caregivers are sensitive to cultural differences in child-rearing practices.
- parents and staff members discuss and mutually determine ways to manage major changes in children's development such as toilet training, weaning, and sleeping patterns without creating excessive conflicts caused by cultural differences.

Attachment and Separation

A **developmentally appropriate infant-toddler program** should foster the development of attachment to caregivers and begin the resolution of separation problems. Developing attachment and managing separation are primary tasks of children during the first three years. Research by Mary Ainsworth (1973) pointed to the importance of the bond between a developing infant and an adult. She defined attachment as the affectional tie that binds one person to another and that endures with time. Infants want to be close to or maintain eye contact with the person to whom they are attached. Infants' first attachment is to their parents, but attachment can be developed with a caregiver. In a child care setting, this allows the infant to feel secure when separating from the parent.

Attachment develops when caregivers are totally involved with the infants. This means that there is a lot of touching, holding, interaction, and verbal responsiveness. The adult is truly with the child on the child's level. When stimulation is needed, the adult responds with appropriate suggestions or materials. When the infant needs comforting, the adult is there with hugs, holding, or stroking.

Attachment between infant and adult can take place only if there is consistency from one day to the next. Each child should have one or two caregivers who are there every day. As attachment strengthens, separation becomes easier but still may be difficult for the infant. It is hard for parents and caregivers to realize that children who are expressing separation distress are behaving quite normally. When children cry or cling to the parent, they show they are attached. If they can transfer to the caregiver when comforted, they are also developing attachment to the caregiver.

The following procedures will facilitate both parent and child adjustment:

- Discuss the separation process with parents before the child enters the program.
- Greet parent and child upon arrival.
- Encourage parent to stay all or part of the first day, then part of the next few days.
- Allow child to have a favorite object: Teddy bear, blanket, or Mom's purse.
- Be sensitive to the needs of each child. This may mean rocking a baby or allowing a toddler to play alone.
- Maintain close communication with parent. Telephone at work during the day if necessary, or report on child's progress at the end of the day.
- Be empathetic to parents' feelings about leaving their child.
- Encourage friendships among the parents. Introduce them to each other, or plan social activities.
- Remember that children's separation anxieties may be greater at naptime or when they are tired.

Records

Good recordkeeping is essential to an infant-toddler program. Daily notes kept by both parent and caregivers provide a record of children's development during this period of rapid change.

Caregivers should keep daily notes of the routine activities of each child as well as any pertinent comments about behavior or development. These should be kept in a specific place so they are accessible to each caregiver who shares responsibility for the child during the day. Guard confidentiality so that these notes are not available to anyone who is not concerned with the child.

Consistent contact with parents is necessary so that caregivers know of any changes in the children that occur at home. Caregivers should know about babies' sleeping, eating, and eliminating patterns. Any changes in behavior such as fussiness or lassitude should also be shared with caregivers. Information that is shared should also include changes that indicate babies are moving to a new stage of development. Signs of greater acceptance of solid foods or drinking from a cup are examples. See Figure 4-1 for a sample daily information sheet to be completed by parents.

DAILY INFORMATION SHEET FOR CAREGIVERS
To Be Filled Out Each Day by Parents

Date_____

Child's Name_____

When was child last fed?_____ What?_____
                                             (Time)   (Type of food)

How much did child eat?_____

How long did child sleep last night?_____

When did child awaken this morning?_____

Did child sleep well?_____ If not, what seemed to be the problem?_____

_____

Did child have a nap before arriving today? If so, please note the time.

From_____ To_____

Has child had a bowel movement today? Yes_____ No_____

What is child's general mood today?_____

_____

Is there any other information that will help us take better care of your child today?

_____

_____

FIGURE 4-1 ■ Sample daily information sheet for caregivers.

Caregivers should provide parents with a record of children's eating, sleeping, and eliminating behaviors during the day. Information for parents may also include new things the children are learning. Caregivers should be cautious, though, about telling parents about important milestones such as first steps or first words. Sometimes it is best to let parents find out these things for themselves at home. See Figure 4-2 for a sample daily information sheet to be completed by caregivers.

INFANT/TODDLER DAILY INFORMATION SHEET

Parent Report

Parent's Name _____

Child's Name _____ Date _____

Last fed, time, what _____

Last slept from _____ to _____

Medication needed: dosage _____ time _____

Physician's note on file _____

Additional comments _____

_____

Staff Report

Your child slept   From _____   To _____

　　　　　　　　　　 From _____   To _____

　　　　　　　　　　 From _____   To _____

　　　　　　　　　　 From _____   To _____

Your child ate   Amount/Type

　　　　　　 _____   _____

　　　　　　 _____   _____

　　　　　　 _____   _____

Diaper changes: time, BM or wet _____ _____ _____ _____

_____ _____ _____ _____

Needs: Diapers wipes clothing sheet blanket

Medication given to your child at _____

_____

_____

Disposition/comments _____

Daily activities or special events: _____

_____

Staff member reporting _____

FIGURE 4-2 ■ Infant/toddler daily information sheet.

With good records, parents and caregivers can make better plans for each child. Decisions about when to introduce solid foods, when to start toilet training, or when to introduce new challenges to the children are more solidly based.

Environment

The environment of an infant-toddler program should be safe while allowing the maximum possibility for exploration. There should be distinct and separate areas for the various activities that take place: diapering, eating, sleeping, and playing. The diapering area must have accessibility to running water. The table where the children eat should be free from distracting toys, and the sleeping area should be quiet so that children will not be disturbed.

Vinyl tile and soft carpeting can provide a variety of surfaces for crawling babies. Ideally, the area should be large enough so that babies can explore freely and safely out of the traffic pattern of toddlers. There should also be specific areas where activities take place. All toys and activities should reflect children's interests and capabilities, neither too simple nor too complicated. For example, at six months, babies can usually sit up and use their hands and arms to manage objects. They will enjoy having toys they can poke, bang, and shake. Manipulative boards, push toys, and pop-up toys are also popular. If the toys make sounds, that is even better. At 15 months, most children are walking and love to push or pull toys as they wander around. At this age, children are also ready to climb simple structures. Vinyl-covered cubes or other shapes of different sizes can provide a safe climbing experience.

Outdoors there should also be areas and equipment that are appropriate for the age level. Babies need soft areas where they can explore freely and safely. Simple soft ramps allow them to use their large muscles. Hammocks and fabric swings and tunnels might offer additional interest areas. More active toddlers need to have separate places to play. Low fences can be used to provide areas where they can ride trikes, run, and play ball. Low climbing equipment and a sandbox might also be in this area.

Within this environment there must be constant vigilance to maintain the health and safety of the children. Staff members must be able to anticipate problem areas and eliminate them before any child is hurt. They must be able to see a tiny object on the floor that babies might put in their mouths or judge that a space is such that a baby might get stuck in it. They should be able to guess the kinds of explorations toddlers will make as they try to understand their environment. It helps to get down to the children's eye level and see the kinds of things that might attract them. If there is a potential danger, it should be changed or removed.

Play

A developmentally appropriate infant-toddler program should allow for many kinds of play. Children should have choices of things to do that are appropriate for their age level and interests. Caregivers should observe the children to determine what they are capable of doing or what they currently want to be doing. They should then provide toys or materials to foster those interests. It may help to consult books or talk to other

Toddlers love to practice language.

caregivers to get ideas for play materials. However, constant variety is not necessary. Children enjoy familiar toys and will often find many new ways to use them.

Caregivers should encourage play interactions between children. If babies are placed on the floor near each other, they can look at, or maybe even touch, each other. Rather than always providing two of the same toy, caregivers should let two toddlers play together with the same toy. Obviously, this must be the kind of toy that lends itself to use by two children. A pegboard and large pegs or a shape box are examples.

Children need a variety of play materials so they can find those that meet their own particular interests. It is a good idea to include the current favorites of children in the group, but also add new things. Some will use the familiar toys to perfect new skills. Others will find new materials that provide an opportunity to develop additional skills. There should be a balance between new situations and familiar things. Too much novelty, and some children become frightened and will withdraw. Not enough novelty, and they won't be interested and won't learn.

Language

A developmentally appropriate infant-toddler program should encourage children to use language skills. The first step is choosing caregivers who have good language skills themselves. They should be people who will talk to babies and not feel silly doing so. Toddlers need caregivers who will allow them to exercise the power of words without feeling threatened. Both infants and toddlers need caregivers who will

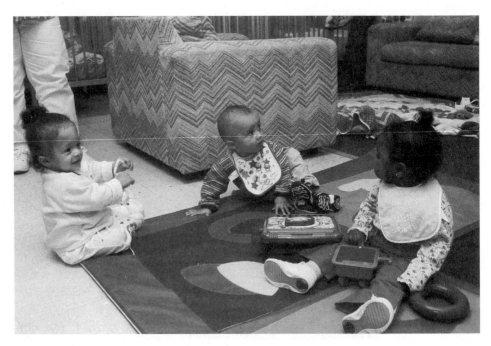

Toddlers often play on the floor.

listen when they try out their newly acquired skills. Caregivers should model a balance between talking and listening so that children learn they need both skills.

Caregivers should be able to adjust their communication styles to suit the children in their care. Short, simple sentences are best to use with toddlers. Quiet children need caregivers who listen more than talk. Talkative children must learn to listen to others.

Activities during the day should allow children many opportunities to hear language and to try out their own. Caregivers talk or sing to babies as they carry out routines. Back and forth "conversations" in which the baby makes a sound and the caregiver responds encourage the development of language. Toddlers love to hear words in simple stories or finger plays.

Caregivers should foster children's language use to solidify what they are learning. Adults should use appropriate words to describe daily events and activities, serving as a model for the children. Children should be encouraged to put ideas into words or to describe objects. Whenever possible, children should be motivated to relate past experiences or explain concepts.

Staff

The core of a developmentally appropriate infant-toddler program is an educated, stable staff. It takes special people to withstand the tremendous demands on infant-toddler caregivers. It is important to choose personnel carefully. Directors should look for people who are

- physically healthy, with lots of energy.
- able to be nurturing, providing comfort when needed.
- flexible and able to change routines to meet the children's needs.
- patient and willing to wait while inept toddlers struggle to be competent.
- able to anticipate and plan for times a child may need extra attention or help.
- able to provide an interesting and varied environment.
- good listeners who also will encourage language development.
- willing to continue learning about children's development.

And staff members should be able to

- help children learn to get along with others.
- include parents in decisions affecting their children.

Consistency of caregivers is especially important to infants and toddlers. Therefore, the director must do everything possible to retain staff. This includes being a strong advocate for adequate salaries, planning training sessions that help them improve their skills, and allowing them opportunities to discuss problems and voice frustrations. The director should encourage caregivers to see themselves as professionals who make an important contribution to the center and include them in decisions that affect them.

It is important to encourage good relationships between the adults who work together in the infant-toddler room. Caregivers should be chosen carefully. It is helpful if caregivers share common goals and do not have too many conflicting ideas. They should be encouraged to develop a mutually dependent relationship. There will be times when each will have to rely on another. While one diapers a baby, the other has to assume responsibility for all the other children. They will have to plan activities together so that the needs of all the children are met.

 PROGRAM: INFANT AND TODDLER ACTIVITIES

The following are some suggested activities for planning a program for infants and toddlers. They are roughly arranged in developmental order. The first activities are appropriate for young infants; the later ones, for toddlers.

SENSORY ACTIVITIES

Touch
caregivers wearing different textured clothing
stroking, touching, holding
warm baths
tub filled with different textured materials: rice, sand, spaghetti, small beans, plastic balls, cotton balls
assorted rattles, soft toys
nylon net balls, soft rubber balls, bean bags

textile books, textile cards

squish bags: zip-lock bags filled with Jello, whipped cream, shaving cream, small beans

fingerpaints: starch and tempera paint, applesauce, shaving cream, chocolate pudding

sand and water play

Hearing

listening to music, singing

clapping patterns

making pretend sounds, imitating baby's sounds

recording baby's sounds, playing back

hide-and-seek with a squeaky toy

toys that make a sound: bells, rattles, ball with bell inside

metal pans, objects to pound or drop into to make a sound

stories and finger games

experimenting with sounds shoes make on different surfaces

Seeing

caregivers wearing different colored clothing

pictures at child's eye level

hanging a beach ball from the ceiling

opening and closing curtains

bright scarves

adding a fish tank and pets to room environment

changing objects in the room to add new colors: rug, vase and flowers, pillows on floor

adding toys with a variety of colors

unbreakable mirror at floor level

cloth or cardboard books

Motor Activities

soft, low crawling ramp

placing a toy just outside the reach of baby on the floor

putting baby on a large towel, pulling across the room

holding baby under stomach to encourage arm and leg movements

pull toys

large ball to encourage rolling and following

wagon, simple riding toys

hanging a mobile over baby's crib; lowering it so baby can reach it

providing containers into which balls, large pegs, spoons, or other objects can be dropped

stacking and nesting toys

simple puzzles, large pop beads, sorting box

cups, spoons, plastic glass, bowl

blocks, large and small

shape boxes

Social Activities

imitating sounds baby makes

mirror

toy telephone

dress-up clothes, housekeeping equipment

dolls, small dishes, spoons

water play

 ## SPACE: INFANT AND TODDLER ENVIRONMENT
Licensing

Some states may not have added regulations for infant and toddler programs to the guidelines for preschools and child care centers. Directors should check to determine if regulations exist and what they are.

In areas that have implemented infant and toddler program guidelines, there are usually some general categories of requirements. One category may cover the sanitation of the building, playground, bedding, food areas, and toys or equipment. Concern for health may be reflected in requirements that all surfaces, including flooring, be washable. Specifications might stipulate that all toys be washable and free of small parts children might swallow. There may also be suggestions for cleaning and sanitation procedures for caregivers to follow.

Regulations will likely cover the arrangement of indoor space. It might be necessary to provide sleeping space separate from indoor activity space. There may be statements requiring safe places for babies to crawl and explore. Guidelines might suggest that the environment contain pictures, books, and other objects that invite children to explore.

Requirements for outdoor space may also be covered in the regulations. Outdoor space should be fenced and safe from anything that is a potential hazard. Specifications may require a shaded area and a sunny one. Crawling babies may need to be in an enclosed area safe from the more vigorous activities of the toddlers.

Safety

Extra precautions must be taken to ensure that the infant-toddler environment is safe and free from all hazards. This age level is known for its active exploration, poking, pushing, and pulling on objects to find out what will happen. Therefore, the elimination of all possible dangers is extremely important. Heavy pieces of furniture or

The furniture fits the size of the infant.

equipment should be secured so they don't topple over. All electrical outlets must be covered, and the sharp edges of furniture should be padded. It is important to check all furniture to be sure there are no braces on legs that might entrap a baby's head. Babies must be protected from injury under the rockers of a rocking chair by keeping toddlers out of these chairs. (They may not notice crawling babies underneath.) Toddlers should have their own child-sized rockers. Another way to have rockers in the room, but protect the babies, is to place the rockers outside of the babies' crawling area or purchase glider rockers.

Gates or grates can be used to close off any areas that might be hazardous to infants or toddlers. It is also imperative to secure stairways, air conditioning or heating vents, and kitchen areas. Half-doors into the classroom may be a useful safety measure. The upper half can be left open so that anyone entering the room can see whether a small child is close by before opening the door. A telephone or intercom in the room will also allow help to be summoned in case of an emergency.

Rest, Solitude

The infant-toddler environment should provide areas where children can rest or where they can retreat to be alone. There should be a separate sleeping area for the babies who nap frequently during the day. A walled-off area within the classroom will serve this purpose. By using clear Plexiglas for large areas of the wall, staff can view the babies, or babies can watch activities in the room if they wish. Within the classroom, hiding areas can be provided behind low screens, under tables, or in large boxes. Crawling babies or walking toddlers can withdraw there when group stress gets too much for them. Outdoors, a sandbox, large packing boxes, tunnels, and climbing structures can offer hiding areas. Another way to provide privacy for children, either indoors or outdoors, is to respect their right to play by themselves. A toddler may want to play in the small sandbox all alone for a while or to be the only one in a large crate.

Ethnic and Cultural Relevance

During the first three years of life, children lay the foundation for their sense of identity. Their cultural or ethnic heritage is an important part of "who they are." Therefore, the infant-toddler room should encourage and support the cultural background of each child's family. Parents should be consulted to find out the kinds of furniture or play objects the children might have at home. Where appropriate, those should be included in the infant-toddler room. It is also helpful to provide books and display pictures of babies and families from different backgrounds, decorate the room with colorful objects or fabrics that are culturally based, and play ethnic music or sing folk songs.

In addition, using unbreakable mirrors in the infant-toddler room will foster children's self-image. These should be secured to the wall, at a crawling baby's eye level and extend upward to a level that can be seen by toddlers. Some equipment supply companies also feature a wall mirror that has a wooden bar across the center. This allows beginning walkers to watch their own progress while holding onto the wooden

The sandbox encourages toddlers' play.

bar. In this way, they are able to see a new image of themselves as an upright person. A display frame attached to the wall at floor level can feature pictures of families and children of different ethnic backgrounds. Crawling babies can see others like themselves or their own pictures.

Sensory Input

Infants and toddlers use all their senses to explore their environment and to organize information about the world around them. Therefore, they need an environment that is rich in **sensory diversity.** There should be things they can look at, listen to, smell, feel, and taste.

Some ways to add sensory stimulation to the environment of these youngest children are the following:

FOR LOOKING

Provide windows so that children can see outside.

Optionally provide skylights in the room for added brightness.

Choose pleasant colors for walls of the classroom.

Add colorful curtains, objects, blankets, and toys.

Place pictures at the children's eye level.

Attach an unbreakable mirror to the wall at eye level.

Place an enclosed fish tank on a low shelf.

Hang a mobile over a crib; change at frequent intervals.

Include books with brightly colored pictures.

Hang a large ball, balloon, or mobile from the ceiling.

FOR LISTENING

Provide pieces of crumpled, heavy foil, parchment paper, tissue paper, and colored paper used for wrapping produce.

Play soft music at rest time.

Hang wind chimes near the door.

Include a music box or jack-in-the-box.

Include squeeze toys that squeak, and rattles.

FOR TOUCHING

Use both carpet and vinyl flooring.

Have grass or a wooden deck outside.

Place soft pillows in a corner.

Include cuddly toys.

Include large plastic beads or plastic keys.

Include a collection of fabric pieces with different textures and pieces of fur.

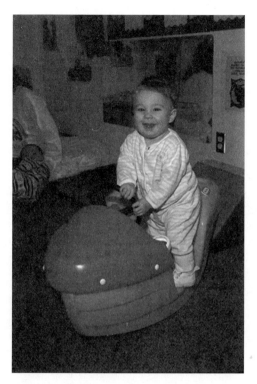

Pretending to drive a car like Daddy does.

Provide a sensory enclosure large enough for a baby or toddler to sit in and fill with plastic or cotton balls.

Provide a large tub for holding cooked spaghetti or warm, soapy water.

FOR TASTING AND SMELLING

Serve foods with pleasing odors and tastes (avoid the strong odors and tastes that most children dislike).

Place fruit or flowers that have intense fragrances in the room.

Make sure the room always smells clean and fresh.

Choose cleaning and disinfectant materials that have a mild odor.

Flexibility

Because infants and toddlers are growing and changing so rapidly, they need **flexibility.** Moveable partitions with Plexiglas windows can be used to change the configuration of the room as needed. All indoor equipment should be on large casters for easy moving. Large mats, cubes, and ramps can be used for building indoor climbing equipment. Tables that can be raised or lowered easily can be used as low as six inches off the floor for the babies and then raised to fit the toddler-sized chairs when needed.

SPECIFIC AREAS

Routines

A large portion of the day in an infant-toddler room will be filled with routine tasks: feeding, changing diapers, or sleeping. The areas for these activities must be planned so they can be both used and maintained easily by staff members, and also meet the needs of the children.

Food Preparation and Eating

The eating area of an infant-toddler room has two parts: a place where food can be stored and prepared, and a place where babies can be fed and toddlers can feed themselves. Babies and toddlers seldom eat at regularly scheduled times, and therefore, staff must be able to provide nourishment quickly without waiting for food to come from a kitchen. Also, many babies have their own formulas or special foods that parents bring from home. These need to be close at hand.

The food storage and preparation area should include

■ a counter and sink.

■ a refrigerator and microwave oven.

■ utensils for preparing food (pans, spoons, tongs).

■ unbreakable dishes, bottles, and nipples provided by parents.

■ equipment used for washing and sterilizing dishes and area—these must be kept in a locked cupboard.

■ a bulletin board for posting instructions for each child's food intake and schedule—it should also include a place for recording actual amounts each child consumes each day.

When babies and toddlers are eating, social interactions can take place. Children can see each other; adults and children can talk or listen. The eating area should foster as much interaction as possible. Some ways to do this are to

■ provide high chairs or low tables and chairs—chairs with curved backs are ideal for toddlers and babies who are able to sit up.

■ arrange tables and/or highchairs so children can see each other.

■ have rocking chairs so adults may nurture bottle-fed babies during feeding— add large, soft pillows for babies who attempt to hold their own bottle while being assisted by an adult.

Sleeping

The sleeping area should be partitioned off from the play area. It should also be easily supervised by staff members. The furniture needed will depend on the age of the children. It is important to check licensing regulations for specifics of spacing or equipment. This area might include:

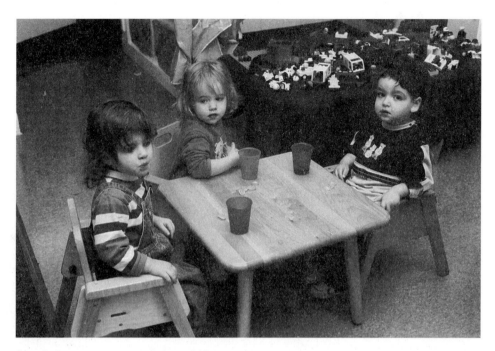

Snack times can encourage social interaction.

- bassinets for the youngest infants; cribs for older infants.
- cots or individual mats for toddlers—each child should have a separate sleeping place not shared with others.
- a rocking chair or other comfortable chair.
- at least one crib on wheels for transporting babies in case of an emergency.
- shades on windows so the room can be darkened.
- clean sheets and blankets for each crib (some centers may ask parents to supply and launder these).
- space of at least 24 inches between each of the cribs to protect against transmission of germs.

Diapering

A well-set-up diapering area will allow the task to be accomplished easily but will also foster a lot of social play and interaction. The diapering area should be equipped with

- a table that is a good height for the adults and with some type of barrier so children will not fall off.
- a cupboard for all the supplies that are needed: lotion, ointment, wipes, paper covers for table, paper towels, and germicidal spray.
- a sink with a foot-operated faucet.

- a storage can for storing used diapers.
- a mirror where babies can see themselves and the caregiver.
- mobiles hung from the ceiling near the area.
- a sign reminding staff to wash hands.
- a step stool for older toddlers to walk up to the table, eliminating the need for staff to lift heavy children.

Toileting

During the second year, some toddlers begin to indicate they are ready to use the toilet. Facilities should be provided away from the play area for the children to develop independence in caring for their own needs.

- low toilets, potty chairs, or toilet seat adapters (disinfect after each use)
- low sinks
- steps for toilets or sinks if needed
- soap dispensers and paper towel holder
- covered pail for used disposable diapers
- low mirror over the sinks

Cognitive Area

A section of the room should provide a safe and interesting environment where both infants and toddlers can develop their cognitive abilities. The youngest babies need to be in a protected area where they can see and hear activities in the room or explore a few simple toys. As they get older, they want to be able to crawl about freely and explore wider sections of the room. Toddlers are mobile and need space to move about and to engage in social interactions. Therefore, depending on the the age levels of the children involved, an infant-toddler room might have two cognitive areas.

For Infants to One Year

- a soft-sided pool for safe viewing of activities or playing with plastic balls
- a space partially enclosed with low barriers and filled with textured pillows
- pictures at floor level
- texture boards, texture quilts, or wall quilts
- mobiles—some that make sound, some that move—or balls hung from the ceiling
- unbreakable mirror mounted at floor level
- a few colorful, soft, washable toys—make sure there are no small parts that may come off and be swallowed
- cloth or cardboard books
- rattles, nesting toys, balls
- mechanical toys that make sounds: jack-in-the-box, pounding toys

For Toddlers

- vinyl flooring or large plastic sheets to cover the carpet
- low table and chairs
- large trays or tubs for floor activities
- low shelves containing a variety of manipulative materials: large beads, stacking cones, large Legos, simple puzzles
- tubs to fill with dry rolled oats, rice, beans, soapy water, and cooked spaghetti—add scoops, measuring cups, pans, sponges, or dolls as needed
- variety of mechanical toys that can be pounded, poked, or pushed
- kitchen sets, pots and pans, hats, purses for dramatic play

Fine Motor Area

This area should include a variety of materials children can use to strengthen their fingers and hands. Many commercial materials are designed specifically for this purpose. Many items that are found at home can also be used for infants and toddlers to manipulate. The following list contains items that can be found in most households. Before these items are introduced to the classroom, they must be washed in a standard bleach solution and rinsed thoroughly. (The standard bleach solution can be made with 1/4 cup bleach to a gallon of water.)

- shelves for conveniently storing a selection of materials
- clear plastic boxes or bins to hold the materials
- a selection of materials: large pop beads, nesting cups, small blocks, large Legos, simple puzzles, form boards, stacking toys, linking loops, large pegs and pegboard, form box, pounding toys, plastic lock box
- large plastic curlers, plastic clothespins, plastic containers
- large plastic or metal mixing bowls, wooden spoons
- plastic bread baskets that can be used for putting things in and dumping them out

The work area may be defined by using a low table. If children prefer to work on the floor, large trays may be placed on the floor. The children can take their material to a tray and work there. A mat or large piece of cloth can be placed nearby to indicate that this is where the materials are to be used.

It is a good idea to look at catalogues from companies that supply educational toys. They contain a wide choice of materials.

Large Motor Area

One of the main tasks for children during the first two years is to develop their motor skills. They are eager to try new things and to repeat or practice things they have already learned. So the large motor area will be a much-used part of both the

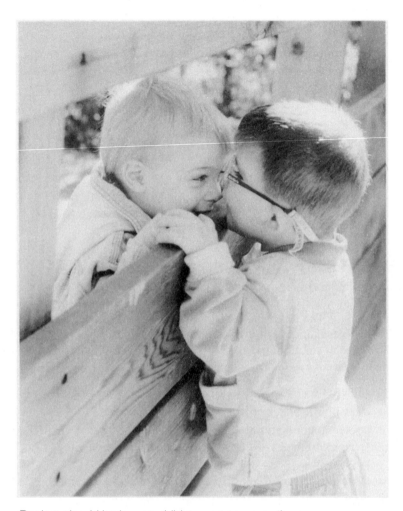

Barriers should be low so children can see over them.

indoor classroom and the outdoor play area of an infant-toddler program. Through large muscle play, these children have an opportunity to develop their posture and balance. They gain a sense of security as they learn to control their own bodies. They can learn to integrate both sides of their body, sometimes using alternate sides for tasks.

There should be planned activities to maximize the safety of all the children in the room. Crawling infants must be protected from any equipment that might injure them, but they should be allowed access to any that are safe. For instance, if there is a rocking boat in the room or outside, infants should not be able to crawl nearby. On the other hand, if large foam mats and cubes are used for a climbing activity, some babies may be able to manage safely.

Indoors, this area might include

■ large vinyl-covered mats, cubes, and ramps.
■ rocking boats, rocking chairs, a rocking horse, and rolling trikes.
■ vinyl-covered foam tunnels.
■ low climbing structures with a low slide and steps.
■ large pillows, bean bags, and buckets.

Outdoors, this area might include

■ low climbing structures.
■ large boxes, either wooden or cardboard.
■ buggies, wagons, bikes, large trikes, cars, and push toys.
■ wide walking boards, steps, large boxes, and ramps.
■ bounce mattresses, barrels, and tunnels.
■ large blocks and hollow blocks.
■ rubber tires and inner tubes.
■ a sandbox, shovels, pails, cups, pots, and pans.
■ low sand/water tables.
■ large balls.
■ a wading pool or large tub for water.
■ tire swings, and swings with safety belts.
■ push toys and buggies.
■ a variety of surfaces, such as wood, grass, and sand.
■ hilly and flat areas for walking, running, or rolling.
■ low slides.

Language Area

By the end of the first year, infants are able to understand a great deal of the language they hear. During the second year, they learn to use words themselves to express ideas, thoughts, and feelings. An infant and toddler program should encourage language skills as adults speak and listen to children. A language activity area can provide additional stimulus for language development.

The language area should

■ be in a secluded area, away from distractions (for example, an enclosed corner with shelves).
■ have large, soft pillows or a low couch where children can sit.
■ provide a collection of soft puppets.
■ include a collection of cloth, cardboard, or plastic books that the children can look at and touch.
■ include tape recorders, record players, and musical instruments.

- include albums with photos of the children and their families.
- include pictures at the children's eye level.
- include books that adults can read to or share with children.

Psychosocial Area

A **psychosocial area** of an infant-toddler room should provide for interactions between adults and children and among the children themselves. This area should allow children to learn about themselves and to develop relationships with adults and with their peers.

An area for learning about themselves might include

- nonbreakable mirrors attached to the wall at both crawling and standing height.
- small unbreakable mirrors that children can pick up and use.
- pictures of babies and children displayed at eye level.
- places for being alone—tunnels, blocked-off areas, or large boxes.
- individual storage spaces for their belongings.

An area for developing relationships with adults might include

- comfortable, low places for adults to sit while observing or interacting with children.
- rocking chairs where an adult can comfort an infant, and soft chairs where an adult and toddler can sit together.
- low barriers—some of Plexiglas™—so adults and children can see each other.
- changing tables and feeding areas that are comfortable for adults and children, thus fostering interaction.

An area for developing relationships with peers might

- include low tables where toddlers can stand to play.
- provide enough duplicate toys so toddlers can play near each other with the same toy.
- have low barriers, shelves, or equipment so infants and toddlers can be together.
- provide padded areas where toddlers can jump and play together safely.
- provide safe places where babies can crawl together.
- provide a place for dramatic play—table, chairs, stove, dishes, pots, pans, dress-up clothes, dolls, and mirror.

ADAPTATIONS FOR INFANTS AND TODDLERS WITH SPECIAL NEEDS

Infants and toddlers with special needs can benefit from being mainstreamed into regular child development programs. Part-time participation will benefit these children, although some working parents may need all-day care. A quality program can provide the kinds of activities that these children need to optimize their development. In addition, parents will find help and support for the sometimes difficult task of caring for their children. When a decision is made to accept these infants or toddlers, the director should seek out community resources and consultation before planning an environment or program.

A basic need for all children during the first two years, and especially important to children with special needs, is to gain control over themselves and their environment. In order to achieve mastery, the environment should

- be appropriate for each child's capabilities.
- offer challenges while also ensuring some successes.
- be safe and free of any objects or obstacles that could be harmful.
- provide appropriate sensory stimulation—the infant with a visual disability provided assortments of tactile materials, the child with a physical disability provided visual or auditory materials, and so on.
- include orthopedic chairs, table, or other specially designed structures for making infants comfortable.

 ## SUMMARY

Directors of infant-toddler programs need to understand the stages of children's development during the first two years. There are universal patterns of development that most children go through, although not at the same pace.

Children under the age of two experience their environment with all their senses. Piaget called this the sensorimotor period. During the stage that Erik Erikson called trust versus mistrust, most children learn that adults will be there when needed to provide food, warmth, or comfort. Attachment to others develops during the first two years, but it also results in anxiety over separation from parents or caregivers. Language begins to appear during the second year and toddlers learn the power of words to tell people what they mean or what they want. During this period children also learn to get along with others, to share, and to play cooperatively.

Developmentally appropriate programs are based on a set of goals. The way in which routines are conducted should be considered part of the curriculum. Other aspects of developmentally appropriate programs include interactions between adults and children, good recordkeeping, provision for many kinds of play experiences, and an educated and stable staff.

The environment should meet all licensing requirements and ensure the safety of the children. Infants and toddlers need places where they can rest and be alone, and where they can explore using all their senses. Materials should be representative of their cultural or ethnic background in order to lay the foundation for their identity.

Specific sections for an infant-toddler room should include space for routines, cognitive activities, fine motor and large motor development, a language area, and a psychosocial area.

REFERENCES

Ainsworth, M. D. S. (1973). The development of infant-mother attachment. In
  B. M. Caldwell & H. N. Riccuiti (Eds.), *Review of child development research*
  (Vol. 3). Chicago: University of Chicago Press.

Newberger, J. J. (1997). New brain development research—A wonderful window
  of opportunity to build public support for early childhood education. *Young
  Children, 52*(4), 4–9.

SELECTED FURTHER READING

Bredekamp, S. (Ed.). (1997). *Developmentally appropriate practice in early childhood programs serving children from birth through age 8.* (Rev. ed.) Washington, DC: National Association for the Education of Young Children.

Gonzalez-Mena, J. (2001). *Multicultural issues in child care* (3rd ed.). Mountain
  View, CA: Mayfield Publishing.

Gonzalez-Mena, J., & Eyer, D. (2001). *Infants, toddlers, and caregivers* (5th ed.).
  Mountain View, CA: Mayfield Publishing.

Miller, K. (2001, July/August). Sleep issues in infant and toddler programs. *Child
  Care Information Exchange, 140,* 50–61.

Ramsey, P. G. (1998). *Teaching and learning in a diverse world* (2nd ed.). Columbia
  University: Teachers College Press.

Robertson, C. (2003). *Safety, nutrition, and health in early childhood education.*
  (2nd ed.) Clifton Park, NY: Delmar Learning.

Ross, H. W. (1992). Integrating infants with disabilities: Can 'ordinary' caregivers
  do it? *Young Children, 47*(3), 65–71.

Zeavin, C. (1997). Toddlers at play: Environments at work. *Young Children,
  52*(3), 72–77.

STUDENT ACTIVITIES

1. Make an appointment to visit a child development center that serves children from birth to school age. Spend some time in a preschool classroom
   and then visit the infant-toddler room. Compare the kinds of toys and
   materials that are available in each. Are the materials in the infant room
   appropriate for the age level? If not, why?

2. Interview a caregiver in an infant-toddler program. Find out what is most
   difficult about the work. What is most enjoyable? What are the most
   important characteristics for an effective infant-toddler caregiver?

3. Make a list of 10 pieces of equipment that might be included in an infant-
   toddler room. Defend each of your choices based on developmental appropriateness.

4. Observe a group of toddlers for at least an hour. List and describe any
   sensory activities they engaged in during this time.

REVIEW

1. Piaget called the period between birth and two years the sensorimotor period. What is meant by the term?

2. What is meant by the word *synchrony* in reference to infants and their caregivers?

3. It takes special adults to withstand the tremendous demands made on infant-toddler caregivers. List the characteristics a director should look for when choosing these personnel.

4. List five materials that will help infants or toddlers learn by using their sense of touch.

5. Describe three activities that will encourage babies to use their motor abilities.

6. Licensing requirements for infant-toddler programs have some specific areas of focus. What are they?

7. List some ways the environment can provide visual stimulation for an infant.

8. Describe a cognitive area suitable for infants to one year.

9. List furniture and equipment that might be in a psychosocial area to promote development of relationships with peers.

10. In what ways can the environment support mastery in children with special needs?

CASE STUDY

Lien and Chen Wang, twins, are enrolled in Emily's infant-toddler group. Chen goes to sleep fairly quickly in his crib at naptime, but Lien screams loudly. Emily rubs Lien's back, hoping that it will help her to relax. But, Lien persists and doesn't stop until she is finally so exhausted that she falls asleep. The other children grow increasingly agitated over the crying and some of them are unable to fall asleep.

Emily is beside herself trying to figure out what to do. She has tried all the things that help other children who are afraid to fall asleep in the child care setting, but none have worked with Lien. She has spoken to Lien's mother, but Mrs. Wang has limited understanding of English and hasn't been able to help.

1. What do you think is the problem?

2. How could you find an answer to Emily's dilemma?

3. If you were the director of Emily's program, what would you suggest?

HELPFUL WEB SITES

Baby Center (helpful information for parents
about development and behavior management):   http://www.babycenter.com

Council for Exceptional Children: http://www.cec.sped.org

Parents Place (resource for parents on
development and health, plus a forum
for sharing information):   http://www.parentsplace.com

Zero to Three (mission is to support families,
practitioners, and communities to promote
the healthy development of infants and toddlers):   http://www.zerotothree.org

For additional resources related to administration, visit the Online Resource® for
this book at www.EarlyChildEd.delmar.com

5

Planning: Preschool-Age Children

Objectives

After reading this chapter, you should be able to:

- Describe the major developmental characteristics of three- and four-year-old children.
- State the components of developmentally appropriate practices in an early childhood program.
- List and discuss general considerations for organizing space.
- Describe adaptations of the environment for children with special needs.

A Day in the Life of ...

A Director/Teacher of a For-Profit School

During our annual "Presidents' Day" discussion, I explained to the four-year-old class that the president of the United States lives in the White House. The lesson was going well and the children were interested. One little boy asked me, "If the president lives in the White House, who lives in the brown houses?"

It is the responsibility of the administrator of an early childhood center to help staff provide an optimum setting in which children can develop physically, socially, emotionally, and intellectually. The best preschool programs provide developmentally appropriate experiences for the children they serve. This means, simply, that learning experiences are based on a knowledge of what most children are capable of doing and where their interests lie. Therefore, this chapter provides a brief overview of the development of children in the preschool years, then some guidelines for planning a curriculum.

Note that when speaking of staff in this chapter and in other chapters in this text, two words are used: teacher and caregiver. *Teacher* has long been understood by nearly everyone to designate a person who teaches or instructs. More recently, with the proliferation of child care settings, *caregiver* has appeared in the vocabularies of early childhood professionals. It is most often used to describe adults who care for infants and toddlers but may also designate an adult in after-school care. The use of this term implies nurturing and concern for the physical well-being of the children. The two terms are sometimes used interchangeably since a teacher also cares for children while a caregiver also teaches children. A teacher should not be seen as more valuable than a caregiver. Each has an important function in furthering children's development. *Educarer* is a more recent term that has been proposed, but is not in wide use at this time.

 ## PRESCHOOL DEVELOPMENT

Preschool period designates the years before a child enters elementary school. Some people include children two to five; others term three- to six-year-olds as preschoolers. In the context of this chapter, *preschooler* means three- and four-year-olds. Two-year-olds are discussed in the previous chapter on infant-toddler development. Five-year-olds are usually in a prekindergarten or kindergarten program and, therefore, are not included.

Three- and four-year-olds each have their distinct characteristics that must be considered when planning an appropriate program for them. The threes are no longer toddlers, but they often have some of the same characteristics. At other times, they show the motor skills and language abilities that are usually seen in four-year-olds. Similarly, four-year-olds sometimes function at the level of the previous age period. At other times, they display abilities to learn, think, and reason that would be expected of kindergarten children. Preschool teachers and caregivers must understand the continuum from toddlerhood to school age and judge each child's development accordingly. Although the scope of this chapter cannot present a highly defined differentiation between these two age levels, where appropriate, the distinction will be made.

During the preschool years, physical growth slows down. By two, most children have achieved adult body proportions. That is, the percentage of their height apportioned to the head, the torso, and the legs is similar to that of an adult. Two-year-olds look like children rather than round, roly-poly babies. This development continues in the preschool years, but the physical changes are less noticeable because they are slower. If you had not seen a three-year-old for several months, you would probably not detect changes in physical appearance. This slowdown in growth is important because it means children need fewer calories per pound of body weight than they did in the previous years since birth. As a result, their appetites are noticeably smaller.

Along with changes in body height and weight, changes are taking place in the brain. By age five, most children have attained about 90 percent of their full brain weight. As the brain matures, specialization of function takes place. During this period, children must have the opportunity to maximize these functions as well as increase the coordination between functions.

During the preschool period, children have an extremely high activity level. This is a period in which children are mastering their gross motor skills. They recklessly practice running, climbing, jumping, and so on. They test out what they can do and attempt to overcome fears of new activities. It can be a time when the accident rate is high unless preventive measures are taken.

Three- and four-year-olds are perfecting their fine motor skills as well. Threes have great difficulty managing complex tasks such as cutting with scissors or tying their shoelaces. They still tend to use their whole hands and cannot manipulate objects easily with their separate fingers. By age four, most children have mastered scissors, and many can tie their own shoes. Fours can use their fingers to pick up and manipulate small objects.

The difference between the physical development of boys and girls during this period is minimal. Boys may be slightly taller and more muscular. Girls may mature a little more rapidly. Their bone age may be ahead of boys, and they lose their baby teeth sooner. However, these physical differences do not seem to cause differences in abilities. The amount of practice children engage in has a greater impact on differences in abilities.

Children's play changes in the preschool years. During infancy and toddlerhood, play allows children to use all their senses and motor abilities to explore their environment. In the preschool period, children use play to master new skills. Block building provides an opportunity to learn how to control the hands while placing one block on top of another. Riding bicycles outdoors allows children to develop the ability to control their legs and arms.

Although three-year-old boys and girls often play together, by age four there is a decided preference for same-sex playmates and a difference in choice of play activities. Researchers explain this by suggesting that the innate biological differences become more prevalent, causing this disparity. Others suggest that the explanation lies with the impact of how parents and culture shape children's gender identity, and therefore, their play preferences. Whatever the cause, a decided shift to same-sex playmates at age four accompanies a corresponding preference for certain kinds of play activities.

Dramatic play becomes an important part of children's play during this period. In this kind of play, children act out familiar or fantasy scenes. Most children employ standard plots. Three-year-olds typically play out scenes reminiscent of home experiences. There may be a "mommy," a "daddy," and a "baby." The scenario includes all the experiences that are part of a child's day at home, from eating to going to bed, from administering punishment to giving rewards. On the other hand, four-year-olds

Preschool children are learning to work independently.

branch out to characters and situations outside the home. They may play out scenes involving favorite TV people or people they see in their neighborhood. They become the current TV "monster" or the neighborhood gas station attendant or firefighter.

Through dramatic play, children have an opportunity to test out what it might be like to be the person portrayed. This kind of play also provides them with an opportunity to perfect physical skills as they carry out the tasks assigned to each role. To be included in others' dramatic play, children must develop social skills and learn to cooperate to prolong the play. Finally, dramatic play allows children a chance to work out feelings they may have about their own experiences. Children who give "shots" with glee to other children during "doctor" play are reliving what it felt like to have an injection themselves.

Aggressive acts become more frequent during children's play in the preschool years. Two-year-olds often bite other children. This kind of aggression is not really directed toward the other child but is a way of expressing frustrations. During the preschool period, deliberate aggressive acts begin to appear. Sometimes these are poorly executed approaches to other children. They may not be meant as aggressive acts, but in their execution they seem so to the child who is being approached. During this period children do begin to hit when they are angry or to shove children who are in their way. This should be seen as a healthy sign of developing assertiveness in the pursuit of their own goals. However, children need to learn to use language as a way to express their feelings and that physical acts of aggression are unacceptable. By the time children reach four, aggressive acts begin to diminish.

Children are able to fantasize but may also develop fears during the preschool period. By age three and later, children are able to imagine but may still have difficulty knowing what is real and what is not real. Some children develop elaborate constructions of a fantasy friend who is with them throughout the day. They talk to the friend, include the friend at the dinner table, and blame the friend for any transgressions. Other children develop fears. A typical example is fear of dogs, even though there has never been an unpleasant encounter with one. Some children have nightmares. Each of these developments comes from the ability to think about things that cannot be seen or may not have been experienced directly. Because children's understanding is still limited, some of their thoughts may frighten or overwhelm them. Both a fantasy friend and fears or nightmares are normal for this age level. With support from adults, most children manage to move beyond this stage.

During the preschool years, children are trying to define their self-concept. They begin to understand some of their own characteristics but have unrealistic ideas about others. They develop quite general and usually positive impressions of themselves. But they also have unrealistic ideas about what they are capable of doing. They may think they can build the biggest block building or run faster than anybody. This is vastly different from the elementary school child who says he is "good" in reading but is "terrible" in math.

Preschoolers are trying to solidify their understanding of gender. At about age three, most children become aware of differences. They are curious about other children's bodies and explore their own. Gradually, they begin to understand "I am a girl" or "I am a boy." But not until close to the age of five do children know gender is irreversible, that they will always be the same. Until that time, they sometimes believe changing clothes or hairstyles will also change their gender.

Self-concept in the preschooler also depends on what Erik Erikson called "initiative." Because of higher activity levels, children are eager to initiate new experiences. Children enthusiastically enter into new play activities and try new things. When these efforts end in failure or criticism, children may feel guilt or that they are worthless. A certain amount of guilt is necessary to learn to control impulses and behaviors that interfere with others, but too much guilt paralyzes children's ability to function to their fullest.

As children develop their own sense of self, they also begin to have a greater awareness of others. This enables them to give up some of their strong attachment to their parents and to begin to move out into their wider environment. They begin to see that not everyone has the same needs, thoughts, and feelings that they and their families do. With help, they can learn to accept and appreciate those differences.

Children's thinking changes during the preschool years. The ability to imagine and think symbolically begins to emerge at about age two. Two-year-olds can pretend to play out scenes from their own experiences but require concrete objects to support their play. With a tiny cup in hand, they can feed their doll or Teddy bear. By age three, children can pretend without props or can use any object to represent what they want. If a car is not at hand to add to their block play, they can pretend that a particular block is one. If they do not have an airplane, they use their hands and appropriate sounds to simulate a plane flying over their building.

Their ability to think has some limitations, however. They tend to be **egocentric,** being able to see things only from their own point of view. They cannot imagine reversing processes. As an example, children may understand that 3 plus 1 is 4 but will not be able to see that 4 minus 1 is 3. This kind of thinking interferes with their ability to think through processes in a logical way.

Language develops rapidly during this preschool period. Some children will learn as many as 10 new words a day, usually following a predictable sequence. Nouns seem to be learned most easily by all children. They seem to have some understanding of grammar, but often apply the rules incorrectly. For instance, children learn that adding an *s* makes a noun plural. They may say "foots" until they learn the correct plural form. Similarly, they learn that adding *ed* to words makes them past tense. They will say "he goed" instead of "he went." During this period, many children also try out the power of words. They learn that certain words bring intense responses from adults or other children.

Differences in language skills are often evident during these preschool years. Girls, first-borns, and single-borns tend to be more proficient in language than boys, later-borns, and twins. Middle-class children often have more advanced communication skills than lower-class children. Family communication patterns also affect children's language skills. Parents who talk to children, listen to their children's communications, and encourage further conversation produce children with greater ability in language skills.

A developmentally appropriate child care center can foster optimum growth in all areas of children's development. Environment, activities, and adult-child interactions must be based on a firm knowledge of what children are like at this stage of their development. In addition, adults must understand the characteristics of a good program, then adapt these ideas to fit the needs of their particular school.

CHARACTERISTICS OF A DEVELOPMENTALLY APPROPRIATE PROGRAM

Grouping Children

Imagine being a child in a classroom full of other children, materials, and strange adults. In addition, imagine a lot of noise, confusion, and people moving around. All but the most independent child might be overwhelmed. In order to facilitate each child's adjustment to a group setting, group sizes must be manageable. The National Association for the Education of Young Children (NAEYC) recommends that a group for three- and four-year-olds be no larger than 16, and should be staffed by two adults. When staff members are highly qualified, groups can contain up to 20 children with a teacher/child ratio of 1:10. However, group size and teacher/ child ratio are also affected by other factors.

Licensing requirements usually specify the number of children allowed in a particular physical space. The regulations typically state that there must be 35 to 50 square feet per child in indoor space. So the size of the classrooms will determine how many children can be accommodated there. The classroom may have fewer children but it cannot exceed that limit.

The *philosophy and goals* of a program may also dictate the number of children in each group. Some people believe that children do best when they have the opportunity to develop close, interactive relationships with adults. This requires a small group of children so that teachers or caregivers can develop a close bond with children. Others believe that children do best when they work independently of adults. In this kind of situation, a larger group of children can be managed.

The *needs of children* may dictate the best group size. When a group contains children who have special needs, consideration should be given to limiting the total number of children and decreasing the teacher/child ratio. Children who have any of the disabilities discussed later in this chapter may require additional time and attention. In some situations, this can best be accomplished in smaller groups.

Directors must also decide what *ages* of children to put together in each group. The most frequent grouping puts children who are close in age in the same group. This is called *peer* or *chronological grouping*. Many directors and teachers feel this configuration allows for better programming. They can plan materials and activities more easily when children are close together in age. An alternate way of grouping children is in "family groups." Here, children may differ in age as much as two or three years. A typical group might have a few two-year-olds, some threes and fours, and possibly even some five-year-olds. Rationale for this kind of group is that children can help each other and learn from each other. Another argument points to the closer resemblance to a family.

Staff qualifications may also determine the size of preschool groups. When staff members are highly qualified and have had experience planning and implementing programs, they can usually manage a larger group. Preprofessionals who are in the process of learning to be qualified teachers should either be under the supervision of experienced teachers or be assigned to a limited number of children. (Specific staff qualifications are discussed extensively in later chapters.)

Schedule

The daily schedule should allow alternate periods of quiet and active experiences. There should be a pattern that minimizes the possibility that children will become overstimulated or overtired. If quiet times are interspersed with others that allow children to move around vigorously, children will not become exhausted.

The schedule should provide what is best for the group as well as the needs of individual children. Many children benefit from the stimulation of group activities. Others cannot stay with a group for long periods and should be allowed to leave and go to something else. Some children get engrossed in an activity and deeply resent having to leave to go on to something else. Others want to spend a longer time at a particular activity and, whenever possible, should be allowed to do so.

Child-initiated activities should be balanced with teacher-directed ones. Children need large blocks of time in which they can choose from a variety of activities or even do nothing if they wish. At other times, there should be group learning activities led by the teacher. Children need to develop both abilities—to be self-directed and to function in a teacher-structured situation.

The schedule of a day should provide for both indoor and outdoor play. Some schools have an open indoor/outdoor program in which children can move freely from one to the other. This requires an adequate number of staff to supervise, and a mild climate. Other schools set times when all children in a group move outdoors and then back inside again. This is the more usual approach since it allows more than one group of children to use the outdoor space. In areas where winter weather prevents children from being outside, they will need plenty of opportunities to engage in active play. Indoor climbing equipment, active games, or music activities can substitute for outdoor play.

Goals

Goals provide the framework for designing a developmentally appropriate preschool program. In its publication *Accreditation Criteria & Procedures,* NAEYC recommends that staff provide activities and materials that help to achieve the following goals:

- Foster positive self-concept.
- Develop social skills.
- Encourage children to think, reason, question, and experiment.
- Encourage language development.
- Enhance physical development and skills.
- Encourage and demonstrate sound health, safety, and nutritional practices.
- Encourage creative expression and appreciation for the arts.
- Respect cultural diversity.

Assessment

A program for three- and four-year-olds should be realistic, that is, based on an assessment of what children are capable of doing. The most frequently used assessment tool is observation: watching the children to find out what they can do. Simple tests can also be used to evaluate children's abilities. Games that require physical agility can become tests for those abilities. Checklists are an easy way to assess other abilities. It is possible to find out individual or group interests by listening to the questions children ask or what they talk about. These will provide clues to their interests.

Developmentally appropriate learning experiences should be designed based on children's capabilities and interests. Materials and learning activities should fit the age of the children. Some should be easy for most of the children so they will have a feeling of competence. It is important to include some experiences that will challenge children to move to a new level of functioning.

Activities should be planned to fit the needs and interests of the gender makeup of the group. As indicated in the overview of development at the beginning of this chapter, a group of three-year-olds seldom divides along gender lines. But by age four, children show decided sex preferences in playmates and play activities. Teachers and caregivers should provide for those differences and encourage children to cross strict gender lines in their play.

Variety

Children should be provided with a wide variety of materials and activities so they can select their own experiences. This fosters the development of initiative and also allows children to choose what is best for them. Some classrooms have a selection of materials available on shelves at all times. There may be puzzles, manipulatives, art materials, construction kits, and block accessories. Children are free to take down what they want, use it, and then replace it before moving on to another area. In other classrooms, teachers select a variety of materials to put out each day and allow children to move from one to the other. The first method allows children a wider choice, but requires a lot of storage space for the materials. Another drawback is that occasionally teachers fail to change or add to the selection, and the children become bored. The second method allows children a smaller number of choices each day, but may offer more choices in the long run.

Cognitive Development

The preschool program should be designed to foster children's cognitive development through the use of **concrete materials** that children can touch, taste, smell, hear, and see. There should be blocks, cars, trucks, and planes for building; dolls, dishes, and dress-up clothes for dramatic play; puzzles, Legos™, and other small manipulative materials; and real tools for real tasks such as cooking. Children can manage knives for cutting food and blenders or frying pans for preparing food when they are closely supervised. All materials should be relevant to the children's own lives, things they either know about or have previously experienced. In this way, each new experience builds on the base of previous experiences.

Materials and activities should *foster children's self-confidence and independence*. One typical way in which this is accomplished is through learning centers. In specific areas of the room, teachers set up materials that children can explore either with a few friends or by themselves. The activity must be designed so children can participate with a minimum of help and supervision from adults. The best learning centers are set up so that children can immediately see what might be done there and can proceed entirely on their own.

Cognitive activities should *encourage children to think, question, and experiment*. Open-ended activities that have more than one answer do this. An example is a collection of spoons for children to categorize. The collection should include small and large spoons; silver, plastic, and wooden ones; and soup ladles, stirring spoons, and teaspoons. Children can categorize this collection according to size, material used to make the spoon, and use for the spoon. There may even be additional categories such as color, kind of decorations on the spoons, and slotted or unslotted.

Cognitive activities should *encourage children's language skills*. Children should be able to add new words to their vocabularies through their play activities. They should have many opportunities to practice language to explain what they have learned, to ask questions, or to solve problems. Gradually, the development of language skills may include the ability to recognize some written words. Children learn to recognize their own names during the preschool period, some as early as age three. A few children learn to read other words during this period.

Cognitive activities should *emphasize the development of physical skills*. There should be ample opportunities to enhance both large- and small-muscle development.

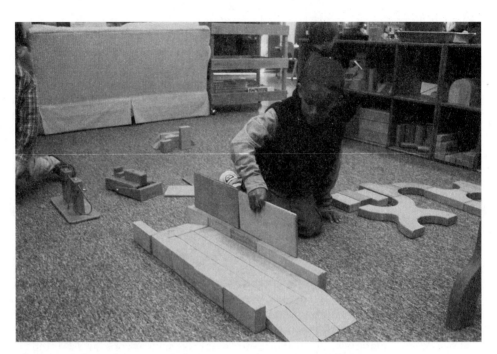

Play is work for children and their way to construct knowledge.

Scissors, paintbrushes, collage materials, and puzzles are some examples of materials that require small-muscle coordination. Music and movement activities and outdoor play encourage children to use their large muscles. Both are necessary for the development of preschool children.

Creativity

The preschool program should provide children opportunities to be creative. In the context of this chapter **creativity** means a unique way of reacting to a situation, not just imitating what others have done. Unique ways of reacting call for behaviors that include intuition, originality, divergent thinking, and flexibility.

Opportunities for creativity can be provided in many of the activities of the preschool. The one that is thought of first is art. Children should be given materials to use as they wish. Patterns and prepared models stifle creativity. There should be selections of paint, paper, brushes, collage materials, scissors, marking pens, and so on. From these tools, children can use their imaginations to produce whatever they want.

Creativity can be fostered in the dramatic play area of a classroom. The kind and variety of props that are available to the children will dictate the subject for their play activities. They will enjoy a selection of clothes, jewelry, hats, shoes, brushes, combs, hair curlers, razors (without blades), and so on. Anything children may have in their own homes will encourage play in this area.

Diversity

Early childhood professionals stress the importance of including *concepts concerning diversity* in the early childhood curriculum. Two terms are used to describe these ideas. **Multiculturalism** is the most widely used, and its focus is on introducing children to the similarities and differences among different cultures and ethnic groups. The goal of a multicultural program is to provide opportunities for children to develop a positive self-concept, including an acceptance of their own differences, and the differences of others. **Anti-bias curriculum** is the term used to describe a broader approach that includes not only cultural aspects, but also gender and physical ability differences. Those using this approach stress the importance of freeing children from gender stereotyping, and preventing the development of biased attitudes toward persons who are differently abled. The additional goal of an anti-bias curriculum is to encourage children to develop critical thinking skills that will enable them to counteract injustices that are directed toward themselves or others.

Whichever approach one chooses, all activities should be part of an integrated curriculum, not just added onto the existing curriculum. Too often, an attempt to introduce diversity into an early childhood program becomes what Louise Derman-Sparks (1989), writing in *Anti-Bias Curriculum*, labeled the "tourist" curriculum. Cultural concepts are introduced through holiday celebrations such as Chinese New Year, or Cinco de Mayo. When this is done, children learn only about the more exotic aspects of a culture. She recommends that children learn about the everyday aspects of life in other countries starting with those cultures represented in their neighborhood.

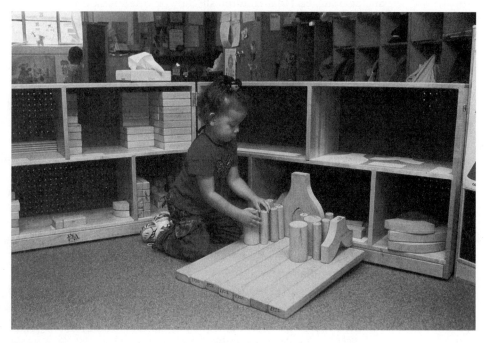

Children learn many concepts during the process of block building.

Friendship develops early.

She also suggests that children should "be free to ask questions about any subject, to engage in real dialogue with adults, to make choices, and to have some say in their daily school life. If we are to facilitate children's sense of self-esteem, critical thinking, and ability to 'stand up' for themselves, then our methodology must allow them to experience their intelligence and power as having a constructive effect on their world."

The following materials can be used to create a diverse environment:

- images of people of different color; women and men doing work in the home or outside the home, elderly people, differently abled people, different family configurations
- books that show a diversity of gender roles, people from different cultures or backgrounds doing ordinary tasks, various families
- dramatic play materials that reflect a variety of gender roles, including everyday objects used in different cultures, tools and equipment used by people with special needs (crutches, canes, etc.)
- art materials that include a wide variety of skin-tone colors, papers and fabrics that suggest different cultures, paintings or sculptures done by artists from different backgrounds
- tapes or CDs that reflect various cultures, opportunities for children to sing or dance to ethnic music
- dolls that represent ethnic groups, both male and female dolls, dolls that reflect different kinds of disabilities
- foods of different cultures

Staff

Staff interactions with children should convey warmth and acceptance of each child's worth and uniqueness. Teachers and caregivers do this by touching and holding children and by speaking to them at eye level. This is especially important at the beginning of a day when children may be feeling anxious about separation from their parents. A warm good-bye at the end of the day will also help to bridge the gap to the following day.

Staff should use positive management tools that empower children to resolve their own problems. When these techniques are used, children learn to take control of their own actions and feel good about themselves (Nelson, Lott, & Glenn, 1993). One method is to anticipate problems and make suggestions for alternative behaviors from which the child can choose. An example is: "Evan, your freeway is about to get in the way of Kathy's house. Can you make an off-ramp or change the direction so that it won't knock down her building?" Another method is to ask questions and let the children decide how to resolve the problem. Example: Two girls want to wear the same costume from the dress-up box. The teacher can help them resolve the conflict by saying, "I can see you both want to wear that pink dress. What can you do so that both of you can have fun playing in the dramatic play area?"

Staff interactions with children should foster the development of self-esteem. According to Eaton (1997), "The goal in using discipline is to guide children's behavior in such a way that they will internalize expectations and develop the self-control that they need to function securely in life." Young children do not have the cognitive skills to understand why they should consider others when trying to satisfy their own needs. Management strategies should help them to problem solve while taking control of their own actions. The first step is to calm the children and help them focus on the problem. The next step is to give each party to the conflict an opportunity to relate what happened. It helps to clarify the problem by restating what the children have said. Finally, the adult can encourage the children to find a resolution that will satisfy all those involved. Certain behaviors in children such as messiness, crying, resistance, and aggression are part of normal development. Adults should accept these behaviors as indications of the child's developmental stage while guiding them to more acceptable behaviors. Adults must never respond to children in ways that will destroy or decrease their self-esteem. This includes yelling in anger, blaming, teasing, accusing, insulting, threatening, or humiliating children.

Staff should encourage children to be as independent as they are capable of being at each stage of their development. Three-year-olds can work with an adult to put away some of their toys and to wipe up spills at snacktime. A reminder will encourage them to care for their personal belongings and wash their hands after toileting. Four-year-olds will probably be able to do some of these tasks without reminders and adult help. Fours take pride in getting out their own materials and in putting them away at the end of a play period. They can participate in preparing snacks, serving them, and then cleaning up afterward. Four-year-olds are pretty independent in caring for their own personal needs. They can manage their clothes in the bathroom and put on their own jackets.

Staff should be responsive to children, ready to listen as children communicate their ideas, thoughts, and feelings. They should encourage children to share their experiences. All adults should allow children to put their feelings into words, to talk about things that make them angry or frightened. Each communication from children to adults should be treated with respect. Children's thoughts and feelings should not be belittled or passed off as unimportant. In this way, children learn to understand themselves better and to accept their own feelings.

Parents

Children learn more effectively when parents participate in the school. A good preschool program includes parents whenever possible. Parent involvement begins with an orientation process in which parents learn about the goals of the school and its operating procedures. Preenrollment visits may be scheduled for parents and children. It is helpful to ask parents to stay with their child during the first few days of school. Parents should be involved in plans for bringing about separation from their child.

Once separation has taken place, the teacher should keep parents informed about their child's progress. Frequent informal reports as well as parent conferences let parents know what is happening at school. Daily written communications are an established procedure in many schools. Newsletters, telephone calls, and bulletin boards also keep parents informed.

The teacher should encourage parents to visit whenever possible. In some situations, parents can have lunch with their child or visit briefly at the beginning of naptime. Some parents can volunteer time in the classroom. If parents cannot be involved because of working hours, other family members should be encouraged to be a part of the school activities. Grandparents or older siblings may stand in for parents.

Peer Relationships

A quality preschool should foster the development of friendships between children. The group makeup should allow most children to find someone on their own level with whom they can talk and play. This usually means having a mix of ages, gender, and abilities. A group of 14 boys and one girl will not work as well as one in which gender is more evenly distributed. A group of 15 three-year-olds may not offer a counterpart for a capable four-year-old.

Activities should be designed to encourage social interactions among children. When some learning centers are set up, they should accommodate more than one child working there at a time. Double-sided easels allow two children to work in close proximity, possibly encouraging interaction. Activities that are set out on tables should accommodate several children at a time so that they can talk about what they are doing.

Staff interactions with children should foster relationships and cooperation. Children should be encouraged to play together and to talk to each other. They should be allowed to work out their own problems whenever possible without undue adult interference. When adults do step in, it should be to help children find their own solutions.

Children enjoy preparing their own snacks.

 PROGRAM: GENERAL CONSIDERATIONS

When planning an early childhood education program, it is important to keep in mind two other considerations. One is the *addition of computers* to the classroom materials. Today's generation of children will probably need skills to manage many kinds of technology when they become working adults. Therefore, perhaps it is appropriate to begin children's education early. The second consideration is how best to *incorporate children with special needs* into the regular activities of an early childhood environment. The answers are not easy to find and cannot be thoroughly explored within the scope of this text. A brief discussion follows, but it will be necessary to do additional research and reading, and discuss theories before making program decisions.

Computers

The use of computers in early childhood classrooms is still the topic of a great deal of controversy. Although they are becoming more common, many professionals question the appropriateness of including computer activities in the early childhood curriculum. They point to the belief that children learn best by hands-on experiences with concrete objects. They ask, "if children learn best what a square is by handling a square object, can they really learn the same concept by drawing one on a computer screen?" The answer that seems to be emerging from research is that it depends on the type of software programs that are used. Open-ended programs do help children to make significant gains in several areas: intelligence, nonverbal skills, structural knowledge, long-term memory, complex manual dexterity, and self-esteem (Haugland, 1992).

There are some specific areas in which computers are particularly effective. When preschool children have plenty of time to practice, computers can aid them in increasing prereading or reading skills. This requires the use of an easy-to-use word processor program, not just sight-reading practice programs. In order to integrate computer work into a whole-language approach, children should be encouraged to work together to plan stories, revise them as needed, discuss how the story is presented, and consider the spelling of words before using the spell-checker. Children can take risks when putting their thoughts into words because the text can be so easily revised on the computer.

Open-ended programs such as Logo can also increase children's problem-solving skills. Research studies show that preschool and primary grade children can use Logo to perform some higher level thinking tasks (Clements, Nastasi, & Swaminathan, 1993). They can plan an approach to a problem; break the solution into small, understandable tasks; write a set of instructions to perform each task; construct a program to perform all the tasks in the right order; and evaluate the program.

Logo is easily used for developing mathematical concepts, but can also fit into other areas of the curriculum. The Logo Web site reports the following uses of the program.

■ "First graders in New Hampshire use a single-stroke version of Logo™ to move the turtle and explore shapes and lines."
■ "Fourth graders in California program a miniature golf game in Logo™."
■ "Fifth graders in Massachusetts learn the geography of their state by drawing a map in Logo™."
■ "Paralyzed students in Pennsylvania use a single-switch device with Logo™ to move the turtle and create designs." (http://www.terrapinlogo.com)

In 1996 NAEYC developed a position statement on computer use in early childhood programs. This was in response to the growing use of technology throughout society, from home computers to schools to businesses. Research points to the benefits of technology on children's learning and development. Clements (1993) found that computers are most often used to supplement rather than replace the usual early childhood activities and materials. Shade and Watson (1990) learned that although computers can be used in developmentally appropriate ways, they can also be misused. NAEYC cautioned that educators must use care and knowledge when evaluating the introduction of computers into early childhood classrooms. The NAEYC Position Statement on Technology and Young Children—Ages 3 Through 8, lists the following criteria:

1. It is up to the teacher to use professional judgement to determine if a specific use of technology is developmentally appropriate.
2. When used according to principles of developmental appropriateness, technology can increase children's cognitive and social abilities.

3. Computers or other technical equipment should be integrated into the total learning environment and should supplement other learning experiences.

4. There should be equitable access to computers for all children and their families, including children with special needs.

5. Software programs or other related materials must be free of stereotyping of any group and of violence as a problem-solving method.

6. Technology should be recognized as an important tool for professional development and continuing education.

SOURCE: National Association for the Education of Young Children.

Children with Special Needs

With the passage of PL 101–476, the Individuals with Disabilities Education Amendment of 1990, the question for early childhood administrators is no longer one of accepting, or not accepting, children with special needs. The question now is "How can we best meet the needs of these children in our program?" The law requires that an individual education plan (IEP) be prepared for each child. In most cases, a multidimensional assessment is done by a team made up of physicians, psychologists, teachers, child care workers, parents or guardians, and the child. This should provide information needed to develop a comprehensive intervention plan. General goals for including children with special needs should be to support families and promote children's mastery and independence. In addition, children should be encouraged to develop skills that will allow them to have normalized life experiences. Lastly, goals should be established that prevent the emergence of future problems or disabilities (Wolery & Wilbers, 1994).

Attention Deficit Disorder

Description. Attention deficit disorder is a condition characterized by an inability to sustain attention, lack of perseverance, impulsivity, inability to suppress inappropriate behavior, overactivity, and excessive talking.

Teaching methods. These children do best in a loosely structured environment in which they can be actively involved. It is also important to provide materials and activities that are developmentally appropriate. Behavioral treatment should include giving rewards for appropriate behavior, providing brief and specific directions, and being consistent in methods of discipline used.

Developmental Delay

Description. Levels of delay are often determined by testing, but teachers should use their own observational abilities to further assess children's abilities. They should look at motor, language, and social abilities; notice how much help is required from adults or how much the children can do themselves; and note attention span and comprehension of concepts.

Teaching methods. Low staff/child ratios will provide maximum individualized attention that will be needed. Tasks should be broken down into small components and allow for many repetitions. Teachers should use a lot of positive reinforcement and be consistent in routines and presentation of experiences.

Physical Disabilities

Description. Physical disabilities may range from poor coordination to severe limitations of mobility. Some children show difficulty when attempting tasks that require fine motor skills and become easily frustrated. Other children have trouble climbing, riding bikes, or doing other large-muscle activities.

Teaching methods. There should be easy access ramps in all areas of the physical environment. Children should be encouraged to participate in a wide variety of activities requiring physical skills. Teachers should investigate innovative materials that will enhance physical skills and offer positive reinforcement for successes.

Hearing Disabilities

Description. Limited communication is a frequently seen result of a hearing disability. In addition, these children often do not understand or respond when others talk to them. They may be inattentive at group times.

Teaching methods. The teacher should face children with hearing disabilities when talking to them and articulate clearly. In group times, these children should be seated close to the adult. The teacher should talk to these children to provide language stimulation and use tapes for additional listening opportunities.

Speech and Language Disabilities

Description. Many children exhibit articulation problems as they develop language. Some children continue to have difficulties beyond the expected period of time. They may omit, substitute, and distort sounds of words and letters. Other children exhibit language problems by using gestures or only single words when you might expect them to use sentences.

Teaching methods. Teachers and caregivers can assist children in developing language by using simple phrases or short sentences. In addition, daily activities that include singing, talking, and word games provide help. Listening activities such as stories read by the adult or on a tape allow children to hear the use of correct language. Above all, adults should listen and respond to children's attempts at communication.

Emotional or Behavioral Problems

Description. In preschools, teachers often see either overly aggressive children or those who are extremely passive. The overly aggressive children are competitive, hostile, defiant of authority, and combative. They are easily distracted and often disrupt classroom activities. Passive children are often forgotten in a classroom, for they are withdrawn and afraid, seldom talk to others, and frequently do not even look at other people.

Teaching methods. Both passive and aggressive children may benefit from an atmosphere in which they can receive individualized attention. Both need help in verbalizing their feelings. Most important to these children's development is consistency in routines, in what is expected of them, and in how adults respond to their behaviors.

Visual Disability

Description. Children who have been diagnosed as having a visual disability may be categorized as either partially sighted or blind. Children who have visual problems may be observed rubbing their eyes, squinting, and blinking. They may also hold objects far away or too close. Their heads may tilt when they try to focus. A few will complain of headaches or dizziness.

Teaching methods. The teacher should provide a variety of materials and activities that require the use of other senses. Children's independent movement in the classroom is fostered by orienting them to where things are and then keeping the arrangement constant. Sometimes other children can be encouraged to help by offering guidance when needed and by stimulating social interactions.

The most important task of a director is to provide a quality, developmentally appropriate program for the children enrolled. It not only benefits the children by allowing for maximum development, but also makes good business sense. The school will build a reputation for being "a good place for children and their families." That makes it easier to fill the enrollment. An added bonus is that staff will probably take greater pride in their jobs and there will be less staff turnover. All of these advantages are worth the time and effort it takes to work with staff to create a good program.

SPACE: GENERAL CONSIDERATIONS
Reality

Every director and probably most teachers have a picture of the ideal school. It has lots of open space with rooms that are clean and bright. Each room has a bathroom and sinks with hot and cold running water. There are spaces where teachers can relax and where they can prepare materials. Other space is available to provide privacy for parents and staff to talk. For most, that is just a dream.

The reality is that most directors and staff find themselves in space that has either been planned by someone else or that has been used for another purpose. That space has to be adapted to fit their school's requirements. In an existing school, the kinds of changes that can be made may be limited. Renovating a residence or commercial building may be costly. So the ideal school always has to be weighed against what is possible and the demands of the budget.

It may be impossible to make drastic changes in an existing school where rooms and supporting space have already been designated. However, it may be feasible to make changes within rooms or even consider using rooms for new purposes. The director should start by asking the teachers to make detailed plans of their indoor and outdoor space. The plans should locate indoor electrical outlets, doors, windows, and any fixed objects. Outdoors, they should include placement of trees, walkways, and gates. In a series of meetings, the staff can consider ways their space can be changed, keeping in mind the considerations listed in the following sections.

A director who is starting a school in space that has been used for another purpose will have to visualize how the space can be divided. It may be possible to add or take out walls, add bathrooms, or cut new doors. To minimize the cost, it is important to get as much information as possible before deciding on a final plan. The director should visit other schools to see how they utilize space, talk to other directors, refer to child development textbooks that deal with planning space, and consult an architect.

Regulations

The director should check licensing requirements for any regulations that might affect plans for the environment of the program. There will probably be statements regarding the amount of space required for each child, the number of bathrooms, space for isolating sick children, and areas for adults. There may also be specifications for outdoor fences and the kinds of surfacing used.

City departments may also have regulations governing child care facilities. Building codes may specify the kinds of changes that can be made to indoor space. Health departments may have requirements for storage of food or cleaning supplies. The fire department may require firewalls and doors.

Goals and Objectives

Both indoor and outdoor space should reflect the goals of the school. The director and staff should examine the basic educational purposes of the program and consider ways in which they can be furthered through a planned environment.

As an example, one of the goals of a program may be to encourage children to take responsibility for themselves and their belongings. There are many ways this can be accomplished, such as the following:

- cubbies for each child's belongings
- areas for performing real tasks such as woodworking and cooking
- child-sized tables and chairs
- learning centers that require no assistance from adults
- faucets and drinking fountains at children's level

One of the goals might be to encourage children's social skills. If so, space might be provided for the following:

- spaces where children work together on a common project
- a block area that will accommodate a group of children
- a housekeeping center

- an art area where several children can work together
- outdoor dramatic play area (playhouse, store equipment, gas pumps, and signs)

Program Type

The type of program will have an impact on the overall design of space. An all-day center must provide areas for the physical care activities that are less important in a half-day school. There must be space for children to eat their meals, take a nap, and care for their physical needs. Few centers have the luxury of a separate room for naps or meals. These functions must be carried on in the same classroom where all other activities take place. If meals are served, there must be enough space to seat each child comfortably. It is helpful to have additional small tables so that children can serve themselves buffet style or clean up their dishes when finished. Cots must be stored in a manner that makes it easy to take them out when needed. Bathrooms need places for children's toothbrushes and washcloths.

An all-day school should plan areas where children can be alone. The stimulation of being in a group for long hours during a day can be stressful for some children. They need a quiet place where they can be by themselves or where they can work individually.

A parent cooperative or a laboratory school must consider a place for adults as well as for children. Rooms have to be large enough to accommodate the adults

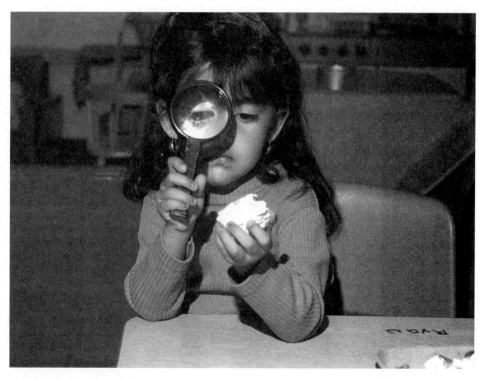

The environment is planned for independence.

who participate during the course of the day. A laboratory school will be enhanced by the addition of an observation room and a place where students and instructors can meet.

Age Appropriateness

Environments should be appropriate to the age level of the children who will use them. Very young children have different requirements than do older children. For instance, two-year-olds seem to feel more secure if their indoor and outdoor space is not too large or does not have too much equipment in it. On the other hand, four-year-olds need lots of space for strenuous physical activities. They need places to ride their trikes, climb, and run.

If the age level is mixed, the problem is a little more difficult. The environment must provide challenges for the oldest children while still being safe for the youngest. In this kind of setting, equipment should be changeable and movable rather than fixed in place. Indoors, there should be enclosed spaces with partitions for some of the youngest children. Children need places to play on the floor rather than always at tables. Outdoors, the use of movable barriers will allow some children more active play while protecting the younger ones. Equipment such as boxes, boards, tires, and inner tubes can be used by many different age groups.

Traffic Flow

When planning space, the director should consider traffic flow. This includes examining where doors are placed and imagining the ways children and adults are likely to move through the room to enter and exit. Next, the director must decide whether to allow direct access or to divert the flow somewhat. Large pieces of furniture or equipment will change the way people move from one place to another.

Furniture can be placed so that activities are not interrupted by children moving about the room. A reading corner can provide a cozy place for quiet contemplation if others are not tramping through it. A block area will be used more extensively if buildings that the children make are protected from traffic paths.

The director must consider the safety of children when planning the placement of outdoor equipment. Children are more active outside, running or riding their bikes. They can be oblivious to possible safety hazards, so swings and climbing equipment should be placed away from the traffic flow. It is important to check licensing regulations since some states prohibit swings in child care centers. Interesting walkways will invite children to explore their environment on foot or on bikes. A path with a slight incline or a bridge is much more enticing than a straight, flat one.

Noise Level

A room full of preschoolers can get pretty noisy at times, causing tension and irritation to both adults and children. When planning space, the noise levels of different activities must be considered. It is best not to have two noisy activities side by side.

Learning centers allow children to explore.

Block play and dramatic play are examples. They should be separated into different areas of the room. (Sound-absorbing materials such as carpeting, drapery, and acoustical tiles will help to modify sound level.)

Noisy activities should be separate from those that require the children to pay attention and concentrate. Science activities should take place in a quiet area of the room. A reading or music area may be enclosed with shelves or cupboards. A quiet area might also be designed into a structure within the room. For instance, some schools build a loft structure inside. In the upper level, children can play without interruption from activities below. In the lower level, there might be cozy spots where children can be alone.

Outdoors, children need areas where they can run vigorously, jump, or climb. Other areas should accommodate more quiet play with sand, dolls, and manipulatives. Hills, plants, large boxes, and pieces of equipment can be used to separate these areas.

Storage

Adequate storage should be provided in all areas of the school. A central storage area is essential. It should allow for storage of supplies such as paper, paint, and glue. In addition, there should be room for teaching materials that can be shared by more than one classroom. Boxes that contain special science or math projects can also be placed here. Extra props for dramatic play might also be included. This should be a place where teachers can come to find new materials to enrich their daily classroom activities.

Outdoors, there should be a place to store bikes, sand toys, and other movable equipment at the end of the day. A large outdoor shed, where dramatic play and art materials can be kept, will be a tremendous asset to any school.

Each classroom should have space for curriculum materials. Teachers should have closed cupboards where they can store materials that they take down as needed. Open shelves can be used for materials that children are allowed to get out for themselves. These should be placed close to where the materials will be used. Children will not carry a puzzle across the room to a table. If there is no table nearby, they will use the floor. Often the result is that puzzle pieces get lost.

Hard and Soft Areas

The preschool classroom should include both hard and soft spaces. Children respond to tactile stimuli, so the classroom should have some objects that are soft and pliable to the touch. Rugs, pillows, soft furniture, fingerpaints, and clay are some examples. Kirtchevsky, Prescott, and Walling (1977) of Pacific Oaks College studied the effect of environments on children and concluded that soft objects "provide experiences where the environment responds to the child." Children can roll around on a rug, pound clay, and spread fingerpaint. Each object does what the child wants it to do.

In contrast, hard surfaces provide a different kind of experience. Tiled floors, wooden furniture, and asphalt playgrounds tell children that they must do what the environment requires of them. Prescott feels that young children are not ready to abide by that message for long periods of time during the day. She says that, especially in a full-day program, inhibiting children's behavior through a hard environment is fatiguing and will lead to tension.

There should be hard and soft areas outdoors as well. Children need soft areas for playing in sand and water, digging in the dirt, or gardening. Wood chips and grass are another way to provide soft play areas. Cemented or asphalt areas are hard surfaces where children can ride bikes, build with blocks, or play ball.

Aesthetic Appeal

Play areas for young children should have **aesthetic appeal**. Children may not comment on the appearance of a room, but they do react to a pleasant environment. Attractive colors should be used in the classrooms, with well-designed basic furniture. The environment should be simple and uncluttered. The children's eye level is very much lower than adults', so furniture lines should be low so children can see over them. Bulletin boards should be at the children's level so they can see them.

In outdoor play areas, trees, shrubs, and flowers add to the pleasure children get from their environment. Natural woods used in play equipment add another scope. Surfaces such as grass, dirt, redwood chips, and sand add to the interest of outdoor areas.

Statistics concerning America's children are disheartening. According to the Children's Defense Fund, as of December 2001 (based on estimated need) the following numbers of children were on waiting lists for quality, safe child care.

California	280,000
Florida	46,800
North Carolina	25,363
Texas	36,799

Three in five preschoolers have working mothers.

One in three is born to an unwed mother.

One in four lives with only one parent.

America's poor young children are more likely to live in a working family than a family on welfare. Of these children,

three out of five are White.

one in three is African-American.

one in four is Latino.

Source: Children's Defense Fund, *The State of Children in America's Union: A 2002 Action Guide to Leave No Child Behind.*

Diversity

Earlier in this chapter, the importance of diversity in the early childhood curriculum was discussed. One goal is to introduce children to differences and similarities of ethnic and cultural groups. The second goal is to stress the importance of freeing children from gender stereotyping and preventing the development of biased attitudes toward persons who are differently abled. Activities and materials were suggested to create a diverse curriculum. In addition to the materials, the total environment of an early childhood classroom should reflect an attitude of acceptance of diversity as well as provide spaces for activities.

Furnishings and equipment in the classroom should include articles from different cultures. Examples are the following:

- a child's chair from Mexico
- a bedspread from India
- tatami mats from Japan
- a Chinese wok
- baskets from Guatemala

Pictures displayed at activity areas should show the following:

- persons of different ethnic/racial groups doing everyday tasks
- a balance of men and women doing jobs both inside and outside the home
- images of elderly persons of various backgrounds doing different activities
- images of children and their families, showing a variety of configurations and backgrounds
- images of differently abled persons from different backgrounds doing work or in recreational activities

Artwork displayed in the classroom should reflect the culture of the artist.

- sculpture, wood carvings
- woven textiles
- ceramics
- paintings or prints
- folk art objects

Diversity should be considered in the planning of outdoor areas as well.

Flexibility

An environment for young children should be **flexible,** not set in one pattern. Periodically, staff must assess what is happening within that environment and decide whether to change it.

The director should ask the staff to consider how the environment either fosters or deters goals. They might ask themselves the following questions:

- Are children using the environment in ways that are achieving my goals?
- Are children using the environment in ways I hadn't thought of?
- Are there other ways I can arrange materials or equipment to further my goals?

Teachers can include children in a discussion of the environment. They can talk about the ways the space is being used and any problems that occur and question whether any changes can be made. Some brave teachers have even taken all the furniture out of a room and then asked the children to bring it back in and arrange it. It is certainly worth trying to stimulate new ways of looking at physical space.

 ## SPECIFIC AREAS

Aside from the general considerations used when planning space, the director and teachers might wish to consider ways to plan for specific activities. Most schools for young children have specific areas for blocks, dramatic play, creative activities, learning, and music or reading. The goals of each school may call for the inclusion of some additional areas.

Dramatic Play

The dramatic play area is often called the housekeeping center because the first play usually focuses on activities the children have experienced at home. They cook, put babies to sleep, clean the house, go off to work, and discipline the children. They may talk to each other on the telephone or visit for meals. It is an area where children can role-play being an adult or a baby. They can use small-muscle skills to prepare meals or do cleaning chores. They also have many chances to increase their social skills and language abilities.

As children get older, dramatic play areas may include a doctor's office or hospital. Sometimes a restaurant, fire station, or gas station appears. This kind of play gives them additional opportunities to role-play jobs and situations they have witnessed. Some of the play in these areas mimics situations they have seen on television.

To make dramatic play as satisfying as possible for children, they must have an appropriate setting and adequate props. The teacher should select props to put out at various times to further play already in progress or to stimulate new play.

The setting should

- be in a place free of traffic interference.
- have enough space for several children.
- include convenient storage space.
- allow some privacy but also allow for adequate supervision.
- be near related activity areas or be large enough so that the play can accommodate more than one dramatic theme (inside and outside the house, bike riding and gas station, cooking and sleeping).

Props for dramatic play can include the following:

FOR HOUSEKEEPING

child-sized furniture (stove, sink, refrigerator, table, chairs, beds, mirror)

dishes, pots and pans, utensils, brooms, and mops

dolls representing a variety of ethnic groups: African-American, Latino, Asian-Pacific, Native American, White (dolls can be homemade or bought, but should be reasonably authentic-looking)

dolls that are both male and female, with an assortment of appropriate clothing articles

dolls with different kinds of disabilities (can be bought or homemade)

dishes, pots, pans

empty food containers, including some that are typical of specific ethnic groups

food models (plastic fruit or vegetables, meats, breads, eggs)

dress-up clothes for both males and females, and representing both work and play activities

costume jewelry

cleaning equipment (broom, mop, sponge, bucket)

tools that are used outside the house (rake, wrench, wooden hammer, flashlight)

unbreakable mirror at children's eye level

two telephones

tools and equipment used by persons with special needs (canes, braces, heavy glasses, crutches, wheelchair, hearing aid)

FOR DOCTOR OR HOSPITAL

cot or doll bed, blankets, small pillow

stethoscopes

white jackets, surgical masks

Band-Aids, pill bottles (use small cereal for pills)

cotton balls, elastic bandages

FOR GAS STATION

gas pumps, short hose lengths

signs

ramp for repair area

tools and toolbox (wrench, screwdriver, flashlight)

FOR FIRE STATION

short fire hose lengths (1/2-inch hose)

firefighters' hats

firefighters' jackets

fire-fighting tools (plastic hatchet, flashlight)

HAIRDRESSER

curlers, hair clips

combs, brushes, hand mirror

makeup (face powder, lipstick, eyebrow pencil)

soft whisk

electric trimmer (remove cord)

razor (remove blade)

cloths for shoulder covers

The possibilities for dramatic play props are almost endless. Materials should be available as children's interests call for some new accessories to their play. These can be stored in the school's central storage area and shared by all the classrooms.

Block Area

Many teachers have said that if they had a limited budget to spend for equipment, they would still include a good set of unit blocks. This is because of the versatility of blocks. They can be used in many different ways and by widely divergent age groups. Blocks allow children to develop their fine and gross motor skills while working out problems of replicating their own experiences. Block play encourages the use of social skills as children work toward a common goal. They can learn mathematical concepts as well as increase their understanding of balance, spatial relations, size, and shape.

The setting should include

- a large enough set of unit blocks to accommodate several children at the same time; arcs, ramps, and cylinders are included in these sets.
- shelves that are wide enough to accommodate the largest blocks.
- as needed by the children: cars, trucks, boats, planes, trains, road signs, and rubber or wooden animals.
- a variety of hats.
- flat boards, hollow blocks, colored blocks, trees, rocks, and pieces of driftwood.
- people, both male and female, from different ethnic groups.
- to stimulate ideas, pictures of buildings, freeways, train tracks, boat dock, airport, farm, forest with wild animals, and men and women working at a variety of jobs.
- dollhouse furniture.

Dramatic play needs the right clothes.

Art Center

The freedom to explore and experiment in an art area affords children an opportunity to develop a variety of skills. Children can acquire fine motor skills as they manipulate paintbrushes, cut with scissors, use a paper punch, or paste small pieces on a collage. They use their whole arms when playing with clay or fingerpaints or when painting at an easel. This develops large motor skills. Art materials allow children to feel successful at an activity of their own choice and so increase their self-image. An art area can be set up so that children work together strengthening their social skills. Some children use creative activities to express their feelings about themselves, their experiences, and their environment. Lastly, art experiences help children to develop an appreciation for color and form or, perhaps in a broader sense, beauty.

The setting should include

- easels and brushes of different sizes.
- paints, including tan, brown, and black paint.
- crayons that include skin-tone colors.
- mirrors so children can look at their own appearance.
- paper of different colors, textures, and sizes.
- scissors, rulers, paper punch, stapler, tape, and glue.
- felt pens, crayons, and chalk.

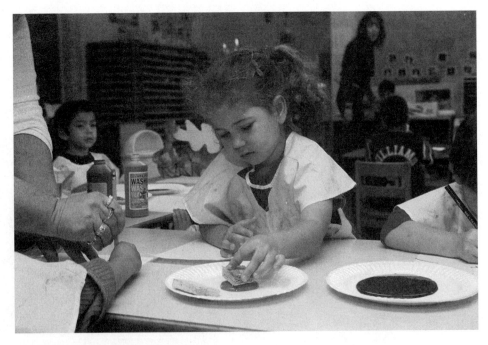

A child explores with art materials.

- collage materials: fabric scraps, ribbons, glitter, beads, wood pieces, wrapping paper, and so on.
- Styrofoam pieces and toothpicks.
- textured materials—sandpaper, rubber, and plastic.
- sewing equipment—burlap, tapestry needles, buttons, embroidery hoops, and yarn.
- magazine pages, wallpaper pieces, and tissue paper.

The teacher should add any other materials of interest to the children. The variety is endless.

Math and Science Center

This area should provide children many opportunities to explore and to test their own knowledge or skills. They should be able to increase their vocabulary of mathematical and scientific words. They can learn to count, sort, and classify objects. Children can judge and understand size, shape, and texture of objects. They should be able to learn about their physical environment, about matter and energy, and about living things. Activities in this area should provide many opportunities for children to use all their senses to consolidate their learning.

A math and science center can be set up in two ways. It can be arranged at a table so that several children can work at the same time on separate projects or together at a single project. It can also be placed in an area where children can work alone. Either way, it is important to place this center in a place where the children will not be distracted by noisy or active play from others. Some science projects may require the use of electricity, which further dictates where the center should be located.

The teacher should plan carefully how a science table or individual workplace will be set up. The use of large trays is one way to delineate each work space. If the setup is attractive, children will be motivated to explore this area. The arrangement should tell children what to do with the materials.

The setting should include

- materials for counting, sorting, weighing, and measuring (beads, beans, small blocks, wood shapes, pegs and pegboard, empty egg cartons, measuring cups).
- scales, a magnifying glass, color paddles, a thermometer, a prism, and magnets.
- growing plants and animals.
- large-dimensional numbers and letters of varied textures (sandpaper, cardboard, felt).
- collections of birds' nests, eggs, insects, feathers, shells, rocks, and crystals.
- small pets, such as a fish, hamster, or gerbil.
- pictures and books on science-related topics.
- books that require counting objects.

As with each of the areas described here, the variety of materials that can be included are not limited to those listed here. Many different kinds of materials can be used for counting, weighing, and measuring. The physical world provides countless objects and ideas for exploration.

Reading and Writing Center

This area should provide opportunities for children to acquire skills they will need to read and write. That includes an appreciation of books and the development of language skills and fine motor skills. Activities in this area should also help children to develop the ability to put events in proper order and to relate a story from beginning to end.

The setting should include a selection of storybooks that

- reflect diversity of racial and cultural backgrounds, ages, gender roles, and physical abilities.
- show people of all groups working at daily tasks.
- show different lifestyles based on income level or family configurations.
- reflect different languages (alphabet books, stories in different spoken languages, stories in Braille, or sign language).

The setting should also include

- large picture-card stories reflecting diversity.
- a puppet stage and puppets (both male and female, different ethnic groups, special needs).
- a tape recorder and recorded stories (earphones for individual listening are recommended).
- both soft places to sit and a small table and chair for writing.
- writing materials (pencils, felt pens, paper of different sizes and colors).
- feltboard stories and a feltboard.

Music and Listening Center

The purpose of this center is to encourage children to listen for information and for enjoyment. Activities should increase their language skills as well. Children should have opportunities to create rhythms and their own dance movements.

The setting should include

- a CD player.
- CDs, including music that reflects different cultures.
- musical instruments, both homemade and commercial, including some that are typical of different cultures.
- a tape recorder, cassettes, and earphones.
- tapes of children in the class singing, talking, or playing instruments.
- pictures of instruments and musical games.

Circle and Game Center

There are times during each day when most teachers schedule an activity involving all the children. Conversations can take place and children can share experiences. Group lessons can be given or plans can be made for future activities.

This setting should include

- ■ a quiet comfortable area, large enough for all the children.
- ■ carpet or another soft surface for sitting.
- ■ a bulletin board and flannelboards.
- ■ freedom from other distracting materials.

Cooking Center

Cooking can be seen as a science activity, but it also incorporates many other learning opportunities; therefore, it is treated here as a separate center. Young children enjoy the real tasks involved in preparing their own snacks or meals. While doing so, they have an opportunity to use real tools, playing a role they have observed many times. In addition, cooking gives them a chance to see how matter changes under different circumstances. Social skills develop as children wait their turn or share tasks with others. Cooking activities can also provide children with some basic information about where food comes from and about nutrition.

This center should include

- ■ a table—the number of children at this center can be limited by the size of the table.
- ■ an electrical outlet—the table should be placed so that children will not trip on the cord.
- ■ a portable oven, frying pan, ice cream maker, popcorn popper, blender, mixer, and food processor.
- ■ mixing bowls, spoons, measuring cups, and knives—children can safely use short serrated knives with rounded ends.
- ■ large trays, chopping boards, and baking pans.
- ■ recipe picture books, flip-card recipes, and pictures of food and food products.
- ■ sponges, buckets, and soap for cleaning up.
- ■ aprons for children—for especially messy projects.

Computer Center

Computers can be used as another learning center in a preschool classroom. They should not replace the concrete, hands-on kinds of experiences, but they can supplement and reinforce learning activities. The key is in choosing appropriate software to achieve the goal the teacher has in mind. Some programs allow a great deal of creativity and imagination, while others are designed to teach specific, limited skills.

What can preschoolers do with computers? They can use the direction keys, joysticks, or a mouse to move objects right, left, up, and down to solidify their sense of direction. They can compare and match objects or discriminate between them. They can create shapes and then change them. Some programs require problem-solving skills or memory. They can play games that test their eye-hand coordination or the speed of their reactions. Programs like LOGO™ allow children to assemble their own figures on the screen, then move them in any direction.

Aside from the physical and cognitive skills that computer use can develop, there are some emotional and social benefits. Children will often stay at a computer center for long periods of time, exhibiting a high level of motivation. They obviously enjoy the sense of control over this adult tool. Researchers have also noted that rather than isolate young children, computers become a drawing point for social interaction among children. This social interaction leads to acquisition of new words and increases in language ability almost as a by-product.

This setting should

- be in an area away from light sources that will reflect on the monitor screen.
- be in an area that is away from heat, dust, and magnetic fields created by television monitors, telephone bells, and vacuums.
- be placed on a static-resistant mat if the area is carpeted.
- contain a child-sized table with at least two chairs.
- include a central processing unit, a monitor, and either a keyboard, mouse, or joystick.
- be near an electrical outlet and include a power strip (a multi-outlet strip that includes a surge suppressor to protect from surges of electrical power).
- be placed so the on/off switch is easily reached.
- have pictorial labels on switches and disk drives showing the sequence of actions to be followed. (It may be helpful to include a chart of the sequence of steps.)
- include a place to store and display software conveniently. (Software programs should be labeled with a picture for children who cannot read the name.)

Outdoor Space

Outdoor space should be planned as carefully as indoor areas. Outdoor time should allow children to explore freely and to experience the sights, sounds, and smells of the outdoors. They should be able to run, jump, climb, swing, and ride bikes. In addition the outdoors can stimulate new kinds of dramatic play incorporating widely separated areas. It can move from the playhouse to the bike-riding area to the sandbox. Some educators (Henniger, 1994) even believe that outdoor play should allow children to take healthy risks as they try to master progressively more difficult physical tasks.

Most playgrounds typically include nonmovable equipment such as swings, slides, a jungle gym, and sandbox. These are certainly well used by children, but children lose interest in them after a while or their play themes may remain static. They also do not provide children with new challenges to their physical abilities. The following list contains suggestions for making the playground an exciting, ever-changing place for children to play. The setting should include

- pathways for running or bike riding.
- clearly defined areas for each activity.
- different surfaces: sand, grass, cement, dirt, and wood chips.
- shaded and sunny areas.
- hilly areas and flat surfaces.
- natural areas for trees, bushes, and plants.
- large boulders or logs for climbing on.
- an easily accessible source of water and a drinking fountain.
- a sandbox with storage for sand toys.
- spaces for woodworking, art activities, and dramatic play.

Equipment should include

- a multilevel climbing structure.
- accessories for the climbing structure: boards with cleats, a rigid ladder, a rope ladder, and a pulley.
- innovative additions to basic equipment: tires, inner tubes, plastic-covered pillows, planks, sawhorses, large boxes, and a hammock.
- things that can be used for dramatic play: hoses, signs, hats, tools, and housekeeping furniture.
- prop sets collected in crates or boxes: gardening tools, house painting materials, and transportation toys.
- a collection of different sizes and kinds of balls.
- tricycles, wagons, and scooters.
- storage areas for outdoor equipment.

 ## ADAPTATIONS FOR CHILDREN WITH SPECIAL NEEDS

Many early childhood centers now incorporate children with special needs into regular classrooms. More will do so in the future. Some adaptations to the environment must be made to accommodate these children. The safety of the children should be of primary concern to those planning an environment that includes children with special needs. There should also be every attempt to remove any barriers that prevent the children from participating as fully as possible in all the school's activities. The following list provides some ideas. Refer to the reading list at the end of this chapter if you wish to obtain further information.

INDOOR ADAPTATIONS

Build ramps into the room and out to the playground.
Widen doors to 32 inches or install offset hinges.

Remove any barriers to free movement around the room, especially for children in wheelchairs.

Install grab bars beside toilets.

Provide easy access to cubbies from a wheelchair—position them at proper height for a seated child.

Install a smoke alarm with a flashing light.

Store materials where they can be easily seen or reached.

Label areas in Braille, with different textures of fabric, or with pictures.

Set up areas in such a way that children easily recognize the routine—place bright aprons at the entrance to the art area to remind children to put them on before painting.

Provide easels, tables, and a water table that can accommodate a child in a wheelchair.

Purchase wheeled equipment (**scooter boards,** wagons) for children who navigate by crawling.

Most children enjoy swinging.

Provide adaptive equipment that assists children to stand.

Display books on slanted shelves or hanging in clear plastic pockets—more easily read by children with visual disabilities.

Build a low platform or use futons or low couches in the reading area—children on scooter boards or in motorized carts can easily move to them for comfortable reading.

Provide tabletop easels for children who wish to read seated in their wheelchair.

Secure any loose rugs or use carpet and nonskid floor covering.

Purchase an overhead projector for enlarging pictures.

OUTDOOR ADAPTATIONS

Provide wheelchair-accessible pathways from one area to another.

Build a table-high sandbox.

Place extra railings and handles on climbing equipment.

Provide bucket seats with safety belts on swings.

Include grassy areas where children who use wheelchairs can be out of their chairs and feel the grass.

Include plants that have a fragrance and bamboo or trees that make sounds in the wind.

Delineate pathways with low-growing plants that have interesting textures.

Include plants that attract butterflies or birds.

Use planter boxes or containers for vegetable gardens.

The environment "tells" both children and adults how to behave there. To have a well-functioning, effective program with reasonably content inhabitants, it is important to start with a well-planned physical plant. It should be assessed periodically to determine whether it continues to meet expectations. If not, it should be changed. The physical space, equipment, and materials of the school are the most important asset. Visitors notice and assess the environment long before they understand the intricacies of the curriculum or the skill of the staff. An environment that is as attractive as possible will help to convey what the program is all about.

 SUMMARY

The best early childhood centers provide developmentally appropriate experiences that are based on a knowledge of the capabilities and interests of most children. Several changes take place in children during the preschool years. The body changes size and shape, and the brain reaches 90 percent of its full weight. Play changes as children choose playmates and develop their interests. Children also try to define their self-concept, and they change the ways they think.

There are 11 components of a developmentally appropriate program, ranging from group size to parent involvement. The ideal environment for an early childhood center is one in which children feel calm, competent, and cooperative. Physical space in most facilities is subject to licensing regulations, but also must be commensurate with the goals of the program. Additional considerations when planning space include providing a variety of areas and surfaces and setting aside special areas for some activities. Outdoor space should be planned as carefully as indoor space. It should include pathways, water, areas for specific activities, hilly and flat sections, basic equipment, and storage facilities.

REFERENCES

Clements, D. H. The uniqueness of the computer as a learning tool: Insights from research and practice. In *Young children: Active learners in a technological age*, eds. J. L. Wright & D. D. Shak, 31–50. Washington, DC: NAEYC.

Clements, D. H., Nastasi, B. K., & Swaminathan, S. (1993). Young children and computers: Crossroads and directions from research. *Young Children, 48*(2), 56–64.

Derman-Sparks, L. (1989). *Anti-bias curriculum tools for empowering young children*. Washington, DC: National Association for the Education of Young Children.

Eaton, M. (1997). Positive discipline: Fostering self-esteem of young children. *Young Children, 53*(6), 43–46.

Haugland, S. W. (1992). The effect of computer software on preschool children's developmental gains. *Journal of Computing in Childhood Education, 3*(1), 15–30.

Henniger, M. L. (1994). Planning for outdoor play. *Young Children, 49*(4), 10–15.

Kritchevsky, S., Prescott, E., & Walling, L. (1977). *Planning environments for young children: Physical space* (2nd ed.). Washington, DC: National Association for the Education of Young Children.

Nelson, J., Lott, L., & Glenn, S. (1993). *Positive discipline: A to Z*. Rocklin, CA: Prima.

Shade, D. D., & Watson, J. A. (1990). Computers in early education: Issues put to rest, theoretical links to sound practice, and the potential contribution of microworlds. *Journal of Educational Computing Research*, 6(4): 375-92.

Wolery, M., & Wilbers, J. S. (Eds.). (1994). *Including children with special needs in early childhood programs*. Washington, DC: National Association for the Education of Young Children.

SELECTED FURTHER READING

Bunnett, R., & Kroll, D. (2000, January/February). Transforming spaces: Rethinking the possibilities. *Child Care Information Exchange,* (131), 26–19.

Caesar, B. (2001, March/April). Give children a place to explore. *Child Care Information Exchange,* (138), 76–80.

Delaney, E. (2001). The administrator's role in making inclusion work. *Childhood Education, 56*(5), 66–70.

Haugen, K. (1997). Using your senses to adapt environments: Checklist for an accessible environment. In Beginnings Workshop, "Environments for Special Needs." *Child Care Information Exchange,* (3), 50–56.

Nabhan, G. P., & Trimble, S. (1994). *The geography of childhood. Why children need wild places.* Boston: Beacon Press.

Neugebauer, B. (Ed.). (1992). *Alike and different: Exploring our humanity with young children* (Rev. ed.). Washington, DC: National Association for the Education of Young Children.

Rivkin, M. S. (1995). *The great outdoors: Restoring children's right to play outside.* Washington, DC: National Association for the Education of Young Children.

Schoen, T. M., Auen, J., & Arvantis, M. (1997). Children blossom in general education integration plan: A private child care center and a public school collaborate. *Young Children, 52*(2), 58–63.

STUDENT ACTIVITIES

1. Visit a preschool. Observe a play area for at least half an hour. Observe the activities of two boys and two girls. Guess their ages as either three or four and write down what they do. Try to find a common thread of behavior. Confirm their ages with the teacher.

2. Collect several lesson plans. Analyze each to find whether they agree with the developmental level of the children for whom they are written.

3. Plan a playground for a group of three-year-olds. Draw the plans, placing all equipment in appropriate places. Indicate any movable or changeable equipment.

4. Examine the outdoor environment of your center. List the ways it would have to be changed to meet the needs of children who use wheelchairs or children who are blind.

REVIEW

1. What is meant by the term *developmentally appropriate practice*?

2. Unless preventive measures are taken, the accident rate among preschool children can be high. Why?

3. As children develop language skills, they sometimes apply rules of grammar incorrectly. Indicate how children might configure the following:
   a. change *go* to past tense
   b. make *goose* plural

4. What is the maximum group size for preschool children recommended by NAEYC?

5. NAEYC recommends that staff provide materials and activities that help children achieve specific goals. List the goals.

6. What factors affect achievement of an ideal physical setting for young children?

7. How are space requirements of an all-day program different from one that is in session only four hours each day?

8. Give some examples of how pictures can be used in the environment to convey attitudes toward diversity.

9. List props that can be added to a dramatic play area to expand children's awareness and acceptance of diversity.

10. Describe a cooking center for a group of three-year-olds.

CASE STUDY

Maria teaches in a new center that is part of a corporate child care chain. She is assigned to a classroom of 11 three-year-olds. The children seem to be particularly interested in the new outside play equipment.

Maria enjoys watching the children explore their new environment, but is experiencing some anxiety about the almost daily accidents on the large, colorful, twisting slide. The most recent occurred when Miguel started down before Mary was finished. They bumped together but weren't hurt. A more serious accident occurred when Aimee fell from the top and landed on the wood chips covering the ground below. The director of the program purchased the slide from a large child care equipment distributor, and it was very costly. She justified the expense feeling that it would clearly be a selling feature for parents and it could be used in the after-school program in the late afternoon.

1. How can directors and teachers determine whether equipment is age appropriate?

2. How should Maria communicate to the director her concerns about the slide?

3. What can Maria do to see that the equipment is safe for the children in her group?

 HELPFUL WEB SITES

American Academy of Pediatrics
(data for optimal physical, mental,
and social health of all children):   http://www.aap.org

National Network for Child Care
(publications and resources relating
to child care, support and assistance
from experts):   http://www.nncc.org

 For additional resources related to administration, visit the Online Resource® for this book at www.EarlyChildEd.delmar.com

6

Planning: School-Age Children

OBJECTIVES

After reading this chapter, you should be able to:

- Describe children's development between the ages of six and twelve.
- List the components of a developmentally appropriate program for older children.
- Describe the characteristics of a caregiver for school-age children.

A Day in the Life of ...

A Director of a Church-Affiliated School

We recently added a terrarium containing three newts to our science center. The teachers and children debated a long time before coming up with the names: Sir Isaac Newt, Wayne Newt, and Fig Newt.

Parents and professionals sometimes refer to the middle childhood years as a period of relative quiet between the difficulties of the early years and the storms of adolescence. Changes take place, but they seem to proceed more smoothly than during earlier or later times. Physical growth slows down, cognitive development helps children to learn quickly, and social development allows them to relate easily to their peers and teachers. However, not all children pass through this stage without problems. Those who lack physical skills, those who are not successful in school, or those who have difficulty making friends may pass into adolescence with feelings of inferiority or rejection that will affect them the rest of their lives. Before- and after-school programs can contribute a great deal to help children meet the challenges they face during middle childhood, but to do so requires a knowledge of the developmental stages during that time span. This chapter will give you an overview of development during the years between six and twelve that can be used as a guide for planning a program for school-age children.

SCHOOL-AGE DEVELOPMENT
Physical

In contrast to the rapid growth spurts of the preschool period, during middle childhood children grow much more slowly. The next rapid change does not take place until the approach of adolescence. However, if you observe children on any elementary school playground, you can see wide variations in height and weight. Some of their differences can be attributed to heredity, but nutrition also plays a part. Another cause of variation is the different growth rate of boys compared to girls. Girls grow faster and are often noticeably taller than boys during part of this stage. However, girls stop growing earlier than boys, and by adolescence the boys catch up and soon surpass the girls.

Motor abilities develop rapidly during middle childhood, and both boys and girls are usually equal at most tasks. However, there are some differences. Girls develop small-muscle control earlier than boys and thus, are more adept at writing tasks. Boys have greater forearm strength and may do better at games like baseball. Girls seem to excel at gymnastics. However, neither sex nor body size is as important as experience. These children need to be active, and both boys and girls benefit from practice. When they have ample opportunities to perfect their skills, differences lessen.

During middle childhood, children's cognitive development allows them to be much more aware of others than during the previous years. Therefore, any differences in appearance are noted as they judge themselves and others. Children who are obese often are teased or rejected. Early- or late-maturing youngsters may feel they do not belong. Many sixth-grade girls already have maturing breasts, and some even begin their menstrual cycles. These girls may suffer because they contrast themselves to their peers and are embarrassed by menstruation. Late-maturing boys also have difficulty. They compare themselves with boys who are beginning to show signs of puberty, such as facial or pubic hair and greater height. They worry that they will never catch up to their peers in appearance.

Language

During the preschool years, children's vocabulary, grammar, and pragmatic language skills develop rapidly. By the time they reach middle childhood, they are ready to use language in new ways. They enjoy experimenting with words and use them as the subject of jokes, changing words around, or playing with the ambiguity of words. They test the power that certain words have to evoke reactions in others by using slang or profanity. Groups of children coin their own words. Those who use the words are accepted as part of the group, and those who do not are excluded. During this period, children also learn to use words to achieve more positive ends. They learn to express feelings and to resolve conflicts through discussions.

Approximately 13 million children under the age of six and 31 million between ages six and seventeen have both parents or their only parent in the workforce and are in need of child care.

29% are cared for in child care settings.

25.2% are cared for by a relative.

15.3% are cared for in a nonrelative provider's home.

1.1% are cared for in other arrangements.

24% are cared for by the parent who works in the home.

Source: Bureau of Labor Statistics, March 1998.

Middle childhood youngsters are adept at changing from one form of speech to another, a process called *code-switching*. When they talk to their parents, for instance, they omit profanity or the words used by their peer group. The most obvious example of code-switching occurs when children use one form of speech in the classroom and another when they are on the playground with their friends. When addressing the teacher, they use complete sentences, attempt to speak grammatically, and eliminate slang. On the playground they lapse into "street" talk, "Black English," or include words specific to their own native languages.

Thinking

Children's thinking abilities change dramatically during the period between five and seven. They have a good memory for concrete ideas and can remember facts and events. They are able to sustain interest in an activity over a long period of time, enabling them to plan ahead and postpone the achievement of a goal until a future time. They are sometimes able to apply logic to practical situations and can give thought and judgment to decisions or problems. They weigh cause and effect, consider alternatives, and choose appropriate actions or solutions.

One change that is particularly important in a child care setting is children's increasing ability to understand and abide by rules. At age five or six, they begin to accept that rules are for everyone, that rules are guidelines for play, and that rules must be followed. This comprehension allows them to engage in organized sports and games, activities that were difficult or impossible a year or so earlier. It is well to remember, however, that not all five- or six-year-olds will be ready to play by the rules. Some will still need flexibility when they engage in organized activities.

Independence

Middle childhood brings about children's greater independence from their families. They spend a large portion of their days outside the home, either at school, in child care, playing in neighborhood parks, or on the streets. In doing so, they broaden their horizons, meeting new people and new ways of life. They form clubs, **cliques,** or "gangs" to strengthen bonds with their peers and to free themselves from adult supervision. They feel more secure as part of a group while they learn how to find their own way in the world outside their families.

However, the groups often impose their own rigid standards on their members. Each group has its own social codes, its own games, and its distinct manner of dress. To be a member of the "in" group, members must adhere strictly to the rules. Those who do follow the group rules have a sense of belonging, while others who are left out suffer. The group influence is powerful and can induce children to engage in behaviors they would not attempt by themselves. This can be a positive influence, encouraging children to develop new skills and gain new experiences. However, sometimes the behaviors encouraged by the group are socially unacceptable ones such as shoplifting, smoking, or drinking. In the case of gangs, behaviors may include some that are even more dangerous.

Peers

Friends are extremely important to school-age children. Although they still depend on parents for some kinds of support, they begin to rely more heavily on their **peers.** Their self-esteem is closely related to how their peers perceive them. If other children like them and seek them out, they feel good about themselves. Friends also provide a sounding board for weighing parental values, deciding which to keep and which to discard. A good friend can help with the emotional "ups and downs" of development. There is comfort in being able to talk to a friend about one's worries and fears, and to find that others have similar feelings.

Children tend to seek out friends who are like themselves in regard to age, sex, race, socioeconomic status, and interests. Friendships are intense and usually last for many years. Many children, especially girls, acquire one "best friend" on whom they depend a great deal while they negotiate new experiences and environments. Temporary setbacks in the friendship, or its dissolution, may cause severe suffering in some children.

Skills

Erik Erikson called middle childhood the stage of **industry versus inferiority.** During this period, children acquire the skills they will need as adults in their particular environment or culture. Children acquire many of these skills in school, so curriculum planners try to predict what children will need as future workers. Consequently, today's children not only learn to read, write, and compute; they also learn about complex technology. In addition to work-related skills, children need to learn practical, everyday skills: how to use tools, how to build and repair objects, how to cook, and how to care for babies or animals. In the past, it was parents who taught children to perform those tasks. At present, as more and more children spend their out-of-school hours in child care, those kinds of experiences need to be included in group programs.

Children also need to develop social skills such as helping, cooperating, negotiating, and talking to others to resolve problems. Group settings are ideal situations to learn new ways of interacting with others. Caregivers can help children through difficult encounters with individuals or can plan specific activities to enhance social skills.

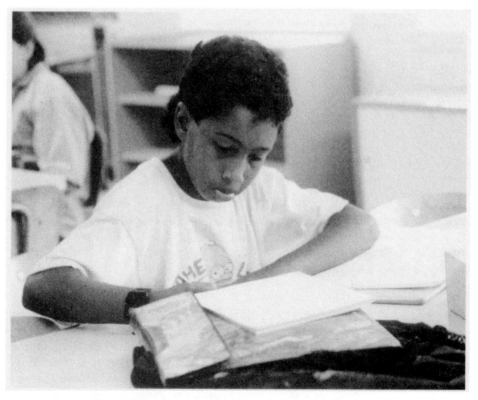

Children need time and a place to do homework.

Self-Esteem

The most important key to success and happiness is a positive self-concept. As children pass the preschool period, they begin to develop theories about who they are. These ideas change based on a combination of past experiences, the opinion of others, and, as yet, untested assumptions about themselves. Past experiences with *success* contribute to a *positive self-image,* while *failures* can add to a *lack of self-worth.* Children who perform well in school or are competent at other activities such as sports, music, or art feel good about themselves. When peers, parents, or teachers praise or reward them for their achievements, their esteem is boosted. In addition, children test their assumptions about themselves. They look at themselves with greater cognitive awareness and become more accurate in assessing which are true and which are false. As an example, some children will say, "I know I am not very good at math, but I'm getting pretty good at music."

Children look to role models to help them shape their own identity. During the preschool period, children modeled their behavior after the people closest to them, their immediate family members. In middle childhood, they have a broader circle of role models from which to choose. Although they continue to imitate some of the behaviors they see at home, they can now take on the characteristics of friends, teachers, or caregivers. They may also admire and try to emulate the people they see on television or in films. Sometimes family cultural values conflict with the other role models in children's environments.

CHARACTERISTICS OF A DEVELOPMENTALLY APPROPRIATE PROGRAM

Goals

The National Association for the Education of Young Children (NAEYC) has developed guidelines for *appropriate practices in the primary grades.* Although those guidelines are written as curriculum goals for academic programs, they are still pertinent to before- and after-school programs. They state that appropriate practices should be

- designed to develop children's knowledge and skills in all developmental areas—physical, social, emotional, and cognitive.
- designed to develop children's self-esteem, sense of competence, and positive feelings toward learning.
- responsive to individual differences in ability and interests.

Bredekamp (1987) discussed two components of developmental appropriateness: age appropriateness and individual appropriateness. The first refers to knowledge of universal, predictable growth and changes in all children. One example is that all children go through predictable changes in their motor skills. Another example is that during middle childhood, children strive to achieve independence. Individual appropriateness describes each child's unique patterns and timing of growth. Although all children go through similar changes, each may do so at very disparate

Best friends are important during school ages.

times. It can be observed that two children of the same age can vary tremendously in appearance, abilities, use of language, and thinking processes. Two school-age children can look very different. One might be tall, having already gone through a growth spurt. Another may be much smaller, still having the appearance of a much younger child. Children may vary in their ability to think through problems logically. One child may be able to resolve a problem by imagining the solution, while another is still dependent upon concrete objects. A developmentally appropriate program must address both components to meet the needs of all children.

Albrecht and Plantz (1993) expanded the NAEYC guidelines for Project Home Safe to more specifically fit before- and after-school programs. They were guided by input from child care experts and also reviewed research studies on the development of school-age children. They recommend that the schedule of child care offer a change of pace from the day at school. Each day should have some structured time in which the whole group meets together. Project Home Safe guidelines also suggest that schedules be flexible and that required participation in activities or experiences is limited.

Developmentally appropriate programs should offer children many different ways to enhance their ability to function independently. They also need many opportunities to develop cognitive and physical skills. Friends are important to school-agers so an after-school program should have times when children can be with one or two special friends. There should also be times when they can enlarge their circle of friends by participating in a group project or in group games. Parents should be kept informed of their child's progress and be included in special events.

Pace

An after-school child care program for older children must offer a *change of pace from the day at school.* Children spend long periods of the school day sitting down. They need an opportunity to work off some of their pent-up energies. They should be allowed to actively participate in games or sports or to use outdoor equipment. Each day should have some structured time in which the whole group meets together. Typically, this is at the beginning of the afternoon session. This is a time for discussions, planning, reading a story, or singing together. After the group time, children should be free to choose among the activities that are available. The Project Safe guidelines recommend that "schedules allow great flexibility" and that "required participation in activities and experiences is limited."

Some children may want a quiet time by themselves, away from the pressure of group activities. They should have places where they can work on an individual project, read, or "just do nothing" for a while. Some children need a short rest period, occasionally falling asleep. Other children look for an adult to help them make the shift from school to child care. A brief period of time talking with a caregiver allows these children to move into more active participation.

Independence

After-school programs should offer children *many different ways to develop their need for independence.* A wide variety of materials should always be available so they can initiate their own activities. Materials for creative activities should be easily accessible. Different kinds of paint, paper, collage materials, fabric, and the like will encourage children to devise interesting art projects. Materials for dressing up can encourage impromptu dramatic play or more planned and structured productions. A CD or tape player, and a variety of instruments can lead to experimentation with music. Some adults are successful in getting children to do some creative writing.

Children can develop independence by planning and preparing their own snacks. The director may allow them to decide on snacks for a week, let them make a shopping list, then send them with a caregiver to purchase the supplies. Simple cooking activities can be part of each day's program.

Participation in planning and decision making also increases children's feelings of independence. They should have opportunities to plan their own program, including special events. They should be able to decide what kinds of activities will be scheduled next week or next month. Children really get involved when they set out to plan a special day for parents or a trip to the zoo or park.

It is important to foster independence by allowing children to resolve their own problems. This means that caregivers should not be quick to step in when two children are involved in an altercation unless there is danger that one will get hurt. Encourage children to work out their differences in ways that are satisfying to each of them. When a group has a common problem, caregivers can encourage independence by leading a discussion. The children should clarify the problem, offer solutions, and institute a plan of action.

Activities should fit the age level.

Skills

A developmentally appropriate program will *allow many opportunities for the development of skills.* A wide variety of activities should encourage children to think, reason, experiment, and question. Participating in science activities, classifying collections, and performing magic tricks all further the development of skills. Many games require reading and math. Time should be set aside for children to do homework, with tutors provided as needed.

Both individual physical activities and organized sports offer additional ways to develop skills. Some children just want to practice "shooting baskets," for instance, while others need the competition of a game. Some children want to increase their skills by using gymnastics equipment, while others want organized competitions. There should be opportunities and equipment for both individual and group activities.

Children can develop needed skills when they are involved in planning and maintenance of their play areas. They can learn how to do simple repairs using real tools. They can learn that materials must be put away after use so they will be available when needed at another time. At times, they will also have to use their problem-solving skills as they perform these tasks. Children should be encouraged to see these as real jobs that they take responsibility for, not just something to occupy their time. In that way, they will not only learn the skills involved, but also increase their sense of independence.

Friends

A quality child care setting will provide *opportunities for children to make friends*. There should be times when children can choose to participate in an activity with one or two "best friends." These should not be used by the children as times to exclude others but as a way of solidifying friendships.

There should also be times when children are encouraged to include a larger circle of peers in a play activity. These times can be used to emphasize accepting differences and learning to compromise. Activities such as producing a newspaper or putting on a play can draw on the talents of many children. These joint efforts can benefit from the diversity. Group sports are another time when a larger number of children can be included. Those children who feel inadequate at sports may need help to find a place in the game. However, if some children do not want to be involved in competitive sports, their wishes should be respected.

Children should have opportunities to develop friendships with their caregivers. There should be times when adult and child can sit and talk, or times when they can work together at a needed task. Some children miss the comfort that a parent traditionally provided at the end of a day at school and need to find that same kind of comfort in their child care worker.

Parents

By the time children reach middle childhood, parents do not need to be as closely involved in their child's school and child care center as in earlier years. However, parents should be kept informed about the child's progress. They need to know that the transition from school to the child care setting is going smoothly. They certainly want to know about the kinds of activities in which their child participates. They want to be included in special events. They need to know about any signs of illness the child might show during the day.

PROGRAM: ACTIVITIES

The following are some activities most children between five and twelve seem to enjoy. There are many more to be found in curriculum books. Teachers can add their own ideas or ask the children to suggest activities.

CREATIVE ACTIVITIES

painting with brushes, hands, string, marbles, sponges

clay, play dough, papier-mâché

collages from leaves, flowers, fabrics, buttons, ribbons

crayon etchings, chalk drawing, textile painting

basket making, sewing, knitting, crocheting

tie-dyeing, batik

puppets, puppet shows

making and playing musical instruments

painting to music

writing a play, making costumes, producing the play

dancing to popular, classical, or ethnic music

GAMES

Mother may I?, Simon says, charades

tic-tac-toe, memory games, card games, dice games

gossip, 20 questions, guess the number

jump rope, hopscotch, leapfrog race, obstacle race

FIELD TRIPS

beach or zoo

print shop, computerized office, newspaper

local radio or television station

artist's studio

museum, children's museum

SCIENCE AND MATH ACTIVITIES

care for animals such as fish, bird, gerbil, guinea pig, hamster, kitten, rabbit, snake, lizard, tortoise (Some areas may prohibit one or more animals on this list.)

cultivate a garden outdoors, keep potted plants indoors

collect shells, rocks, fossils

experiment with magic

chart the weather, make predictions

weigh a variety of objects, weigh themselves

play table games that require counting

cook a snack using a recipe that requires measuring

 CHARACTERISTICS OF TEACHER/CAREGIVER

The adults who care for children in before- and after-school programs have a variety of titles: aides, teachers, assistants, caregivers, leaders, guides, and recreational supervisors. This text uses the term **caregiver** because it implies an essential function of these adults: the ability to provide a caring, nurturing environment for children who must spend their out-of-school hours away from home. Whatever the director chooses to call the staff members hired for the school-age program, they should have certain characteristics. The director should look for people who

- like being with school-age children.
- can allow children to be independent.
- have a knowledge of the developmental stages during middle childhood.
- are good role models for children to emulate.
- have a lot of interests they can share with children.
- can allow children freedom to be independent while also setting limits.
- have good communication skills, including the ability to listen.
- enjoy physical activity such as active games or sports.
- care about families and can accept each family's uniqueness.
- understand the role of caregiver, a blending of teacher and parent.
- are able to work as a team with other staff members.

Beyond these personal characteristics, there are two broad areas of education and experience that are usually required in school-age child care. Some directors want adults who have *completed courses in early childhood education,* including human development and curriculum planning. Other directors lean more heavily toward persons who have backgrounds in recreation. Those staff members will have *taken courses in physical education* and may have had experience in supervising playgrounds or working in summer camps. The ideal staff member for a school-age program would have both, but there is an alternative. The staff can be balanced with some having an *early childhood education* background *and* others with *recreation experience.* Further balance may be achieved by including both men and women so that children have additional role models.

 ## SPACE: GENERAL CONSIDERATIONS
Licensing

Just as with infant programs, regulations in some areas may not have caught up with the trend toward adding school-age child care to existing preschools. It is important to check with the state licensing agency to find out if guidelines exist.

Where school-age regulations have been adopted, several categories may be covered. One may require the separation of older children from younger ones within the preschool setting. Outdoors, this can be accomplished by using low fences, establishing a separate play area, or scheduling use of outdoor space at different times. Indoors, older children should be separated from preschoolers for unstructured play activities. Movable walls and partitions can be used to create separate areas for older and younger children. Each can use a room at different times. During structured activities, older children and preschoolers can often work together effectively.

Regulations will probably specify toilets with separate stalls for individual privacy, or even separate bathrooms for boys and for girls.

Even in areas where regulations for school-age child care have been adopted, they are likely to be less stringent than for younger children. Older children are less vulnerable to physical hazards than infants and preschoolers. This does not mean that a director should not be concerned. Regulations are minimum standards only, and every center should provide the best possible setting for the children they serve.

Goals

Throughout this text, you have read that goals are the basis for planning all aspects of a facility for young children. School goals must be reviewed before deciding how to plan space in the school-age section. Although the overall goals for the school may include statements that can be applied to the school-age program, there will probably need to be others that are specific for that age group. Some examples will help to illustrate. Children should be able to

■ sustain cooperative efforts and involvement in activities over a long period of time.

■ gain greater control over their bodies through participation in individual activities and organized games.

■ develop independence in caring for themselves.

Safe Yet Challenging Environment

The school-age period is a time when children are rapidly developing their physical skills. They are capable of performing almost any motor skill and can challenge themselves and each other to reach higher levels of mastery. Some of this testing can put them into dangerous situations. Picture the eight-year-old walking along the top of a narrow, high wall to test his balance, or an eleven-year-old plunging off a ramp on his skateboard. The physical skill that allows children to perform these feats is there; the judgment to assess the danger may be lacking.

Children should be able to test their physical abilities as far as possible in after-school programs, but they should be protected from serious injury while doing so. The child care center should provide space only for those activities that the children are developmentally capable of performing. Areas for active play should be separated in distance from quieter pursuits. All playground areas and equipment should be inspected and maintained periodically. Children must be taught ways to use equipment safely and supervised closely at all times. There should also be space and opportunity for sewing, knitting, painting, or preparing food.

Homelike Atmosphere

The setting for after-school child care should be quite different from the typical schoolroom environment. At school, children have to sit on hard chairs at desks or tables. The environment tells them how to behave. In child care, they should be able

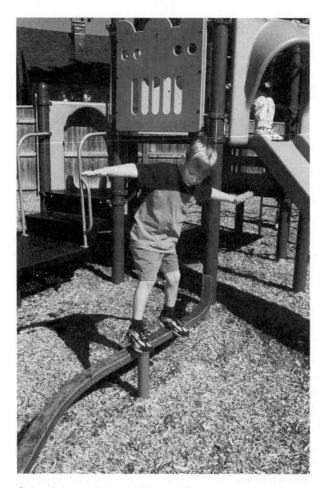

School-age children build on skills.

to sit in soft chairs, lie on a couch, or loll on the floor. Therefore, the child care environment for older children should be more like home than school.

A homelike atmosphere can be accomplished by including some of the following:

- couches or soft, easy chairs
- large pillows, bean bag chairs, soft mats
- appropriately sized tables and chairs
- places for children to store their school books, lunch boxes, and jackets
- places to store their ongoing projects such as stamp collections or woodworking projects
- places to store games children bring from home
- places to be alone—boxes, lofts, tents, screening
- broom, dustpan, bucket, mop, sponges for cleanup

Both preschoolers and older children can use this playground.

Flexibility

Space for school-age children should be flexible and easily modified. Children change over a period of time, so what was suitable in September may not fit their needs in May. Also, the age span in an after-school program may be from six to twelve years. Physical space must accommodate the different interests of children at these widely diverse ages. There are many ways to make space flexible such as

- providing a variety of spaces—large open ones, or small ones designed for specific functions.
- having mobile dividers to create work spaces.
- having plenty of things that can be moved around to create spaces the children can design themselves—boards, crates, large building blocks, ladders, platforms, blankets, tires, and ropes.
- providing a variety of surfaces that can be used for different activities—blacktop, grass, sand, hills, and dirt.
- allowing access to water for sprinkling on hot days, playing in water, gardening, and playing in the sandbox.
- creating spaces for privacy for individuals or small groups—loft, tree house, hammock, or rocking chair.

Size

School-age children need furniture and equipment that is appropriate for their size. If they must use a classroom that is used by preschoolers at other times of the day, there should be at least one larger table with proper-sized chairs. Older children can use the table for working on projects, doing homework, or eating snacks. Some areas can be used by both age levels. The preschool classroom may have large pillows or bean bag chairs in a reading area. Older children can use this area as well. Additions for the older children might include a workbench for woodworking and an adjustable easel for painting. Trays or mats can designate places for games or other activities to be done on the floor.

Outdoor equipment should allow for the kinds of activities older children enjoy. Examples include trees to climb, swings, a high jungle gym, and a horizontal ladder. A blacktop area will provide space for organized games.

Aesthetically Pleasing Space

Space for all ages should be pleasing to the eye. The use of color on the walls or furniture, pictures, and interesting objects will make the environment cheerful. Children's artwork should be framed and displayed.

The children will be able to suggest ways to make the environment cheerful. They may wish to paint posters, put up signs, or bring objects from home to add interest and beauty. Where it is possible, they should be allowed to paint a mural on a wall. The most important thing to remember is that the *environment should be pleasing to the children.*

Storage

If storage of equipment is convenient, children will have more time to spend at activities and play. There should be plenty of space for the ongoing projects school-age children enjoy. At this age, children have the attention span to work on long-term projects. They like to put together collections of stamps, insects, rocks, shells, and so on. They may start a woodworking project that will take a week or two to finish. They must have safe places to store these materials from one day to the next. If they share space with younger children, these cupboards should be secured from interference.

These children should have a place to put their school belongings—their books, lunch boxes, and jackets.

 ## SPECIFIC AREAS
Quiet Corner

After a long day at school, many children need to have a quiet time to "unwind" before being involved again in group activities. Some may want to rest, read, or just sit by themselves. Others may want to sit quietly and do their homework. Some children will use this space for meetings of "secret clubs" or as a place to talk to a special friend.

This kind of area can be created by providing

■ corners enclosed by shelves or dividers—furnish with rugs, large pillows or bean bag chairs, or sofa.

■ extra space for being alone such as stairways, closets, or offices.

■ a book corner with a selection of appropriate books.

■ a music corner where a child can listen to music with earphones.

■ a comfortable table or desks and proper lighting where children can do their homework.

Creative Area

Creative materials can provide children a release from some of the tensions left over after a day at school. A variety of materials should be available to children along with an adequate place to work. This area can be furnished with some of the following:

■ paint—fingerpaint, tempera, watercolors, brushes of all sizes

■ wide variety of paper—colored, parchment, oatmeal, etc.

■ play dough, clay, papier-mâché

■ crayons, chalk, marking pens

■ colored sand, glue

■ scissors, paper punches, staplers

■ ice cream sticks, coffee stirrers, Styrofoam pieces

■ weaving materials, small looms

■ yarn, knitting needles, crochet hooks, tapestry canvas

■ tissue paper, struts for kite making

■ fabric and materials for tie-dyeing, batiking

■ collections of materials for collage—wood pieces, fabric, ribbons, beads, shells, rocks

■ fabric markers, puff pens

■ large pieces of fabric for making costumes

Games and Manipulatives

School-age children enjoy the challenges provided by games, puzzles, and other kinds of manipulative materials. Many of the materials that are used in the preschool can also be fun for this age level. These activities can take place either at a table or on the floor. Children can get the materials from a shelf and return them when finished. Some things to include in this area are

■ playing cards for games such as concentration, go-fish, war, rummy, hearts, and solitaire.

■ board games such as Monopoly™, Scrabble™, Life®, Clue®, checkers, Chinese checkers, jackstraws, bingo, tic-tac-toe, and dominoes.

- marbles and jacks.
- magnetic marbles, magnetic building sets, magnetic designers, and magnetic mazes.
- Legos™ and Lego™ accessories.
- parquetry-design blocks, and design cards.
- large jigsaw puzzles and small 100- to 500-piece jigsaw puzzles.
- plastic building sets and Tinker Toys.™

Woodworking, Cooking

School-age children enjoy the independence that comes from being able to use real tools to perform real tasks. These activities should be set up in an area free from traffic flow and away from any quiet areas. Safety precautions must be taken to make sure that children don't trip on electrical cords or get burned by hot appliances. An adult must explain to the children safety rules for the use of woodworking tools.

A woodworking area should be equipped with

- a sturdy workbench.
- safety goggles.
- saws, hammers, screwdrivers, drills, pliers, clamps, level, and tape measure.
- a variety of sandpapers, nails, screws, nuts, and bolts.
- sheets of wood, small wood pieces, wooden spools, and wheels.
- varnish, paint, and brushes.

A cooking area should be equipped with

- a table to work on, either at sitting or standing height.
- pot holders and aprons.
- water and cleaning supplies nearby.
- a variety of cooking tools—mixing and measuring spoons, measuring cups, cookie cutters, graters, and rolling pins.
- a cutting board and knives.
- several size pans and mixing bowls.
- cookie sheets, muffin tins, baking pans, and pots.
- a hand or electric mixer and a blender.
- a popcorn popper, electric frying pan, ice cream maker, small oven, waffle iron, and toaster.
- cookbooks written for children or other cookbooks containing "easy to prepare" recipes.
- a fire extinguisher.

Dramatic Play

Through dramatic play, children can imitate adult role models, play out their fantasies, or relive childhood experiences. Some children will use dramatic play to relieve stresses they encounter at school or at home. As children in this age range get a little older, they use dramatic play materials for producing their own plays or skits.

A dramatic play area should be equipped with

- a full-length mirror.
- a variety of clothes for dress up and an assortment of hats.
- washable face paint or makeup.
- scarves, jewelry, and plastic or silk flowers.
- a puppet theater and an assortment of puppets.
- a stethoscope, gauze, splints, and Band-Aids.™
- a tool carrier, tools, old shirts, and flashlight.
- theatrical or Halloween costumes and wigs.

Block Building

Children at widely different age levels can use blocks. If the after-school program is housed in a preschool classroom, the children can use the blocks that are already there. The block area should be placed where buildings will not be toppled by other children moving about. Having a hard surface to build on is ideal, but children can also build on a carpeted floor. The children can be encouraged to add to the basic materials to create their own play activities.

Some of the things that might be in a block area are

- wide shelves to hold the blocks—if the shelves are on casters, they can be moved if needed.
- containers for accessory materials such as dolls, cars, trucks, boats, trains, airplanes, and animals.
- colored blocks, sheets of Masonite,™ or thin plywood.
- large hollow blocks and large cardboard blocks.
- giant lock bricks, waffle blocks, and giant Legos.™

Discovery Center

A discovery center for school-age children should supplement the kinds of learning children are exposed to at school. However, activities should be presented in such a way that children do not feel pressured to participate, but can follow their own interests. This area can promote children's natural curiosity and ability to pursue topics over a period of time.

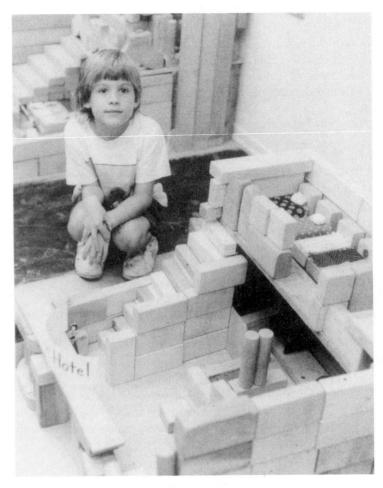

School-age children can create elaborate block structures.

The discovery area should be equipped with

- magnets and an electromagnetic kit.
- a simple microscope and a collection of prepared slides.
- magnifying glasses and insect collections.
- an aquarium and books on tropical fish.
- an ant farm and ants.
- a bug house, bug-catching containers, and a butterfly net.
- collections of shells, rocks, and fossils.
- sun-sensitive paper.

- prisms, gyroscopes, and color wheels.
- small animals, cages, and an incubator for hatching eggs.
- seeds, potting soil, and small pots.
- binoculars and bird books.
- a selection of books with project ideas and science information.
- things to take apart—clocks, small appliances.

Language Center

Even though language development is very much a part of the elementary class-room, children can also enjoy participating in this kind of activity in the child care center. As with the discovery center, there should be no pressure to participate, and the activities should be fun.

The language area might include

- a table and chairs or soft pillows and bean bag chairs.
- a selection of books.
- a tape recorder, recorded stories, earphones, a microphone, and blank cassettes.
- stamp pads with letters—both uppercase and lowercase.
- poster boards of different colors.
- word puzzles, crosswords, and games such as Scrabble.™
- word-matching games, word lotto, and letter dice.
- individual chalkboards, chalk, a wipe-off board, and marking pens.
- paper, pencils, and pens.
- a typewriter.

High-Tech Center

School-age children enjoy the challenge of operating equipment that is part of contemporary society. They get excited when they can master a computer, use a calculator, or write on a typewriter.

This center could include

- a table and chairs at a comfortable height.
- a computer, rack for software, bulletin board or manuals with instructions for use, and printer.
- a calculator, paper, and pencils.
- a typewriter and paper.
- a filmstrip projector and filmstrips.
- a VCR and selected cassettes.

Clubroom

During the school-age period, children develop strong relationships with their peers and begin to group themselves according to shared interests. These friendships and interests are fostered through the formation of clubs, allowing groups to pursue topics in depth or sustain an interest over a period of time. Typical topics that appeal to children are photography, calligraphy, ceramics, computers, cooking, magic, collecting (rocks, shells, stamps), dance, drama, ecology, stitchery, space, sports, and woodworking.

A clubroom might include

- a table and chairs or bean bag chairs and soft pillows.
- shelves or a cabinet for storing materials.
- a sign and decorations made by the children.
- a bulletin board for posting rules, outlining plans, or presenting a display.
- specific materials or equipment needed for special interests.

Sharing Indoor Space

Not every school has the luxury of having a separate room for school-age children. This group may be required to share space with another age level, or use space that was designed for another purpose. With a bit of imagination, it is possible to create an environment that fits their needs. The following are suggestions for the director and staff.

- Set up interest centers each day. Store all the materials necessary for an activity in large boxes, shoe boxes, baskets, or five-gallon ice cream cartons. Label each container, and list the materials contained in each.
- Put large casters or wheels on cupboards, bulletin boards, or dividers that can be used to designate activity areas. Label the cupboards according to contents and apply locks.
- Choose furniture that can be used in more than one way. Examples are cupboards with doors that can also be used as bulletin boards or chalkboards. Attach hooks to the side of cupboards so that a screen or divider can be attached to create an enclosed space.
- Use large pegboards, framed and mounted on casters, for hanging woodworking tools, art supplies, or cooking equipment.
- Have large pillows or bean bag chairs to create a quiet corner, or for being alone.
- Involve the children in setting up the environment each day or in finding new ways to use the area. They are the ones who will use the space and often have creative ideas about ways to adapt it to their own needs.
- Purchase adjustable equipment that can be raised when used by older children—tables and easels are examples.
- Utilize extra space such as hallways or special rooms for small group projects.
- Place stackable containers on a wheeled platform for use as individual cubbies for the children.

- Provide carpet squares or mats for designating areas for floor activities.
- Use large cork boards or foam boards mounted on wheels to display children's artwork or project displays.
- Most important, encourage all staff members who share space to work together to make the arrangement mutually satisfying. It will take patience, flexibility, and time to develop ways to share space without problems.
- Before the program begins, meet together to plan.

Outdoor Environment

After being confined in the elementary school classroom all day, children need the opportunity to be outside, engaging in active play. Also, their physical development is changing rapidly during the middle childhood years. They are able to run rapidly, throw a ball fairly accurately, and climb more easily than they did at an earlier age. They want to be competent at any of the physical activities they try and need to have places and opportunities to practice their skills.

A sandbox stimulates a wide variety of play activities.

While the outdoor environment should be safe, it should also offer some challenges. This can be accomplished by adding new equipment when children reach higher levels of agility. Most school-age children can swing themselves, climb a jungle gym, go up a ladder, and slide down a slide. It takes greater agility to cross a swinging bridge strung between two structures or to traverse a horizontal ladder. An outdoor environment for older children should include the following:

- single-purpose equipment: swings, parallel bars, ladder, slide, climbing rope, swinging bridge
- **multipurpose equipment:** sandbox, large boxes, jungle gym with different levels
- an **adventure play area** where children can build their own structures using large blocks, cartons, cable and spools, sawhorses, tires, inner tubes, logs, pieces of wood or cardboard

Parallel bars are an example of single-purpose equipment.

- areas where children can talk with friends or be alone: a playhouse, park bench, tree house, or a secluded corner under a tree
- space for special activities: hard surfaces for skateboarding or roller-skating; covered areas for creative activities; blacktop for dodgeball, kickball, jump rope; basketball court; baseball diamond or soccer field; swimming pool
- different levels for climbing or hiding under: hilly area, ladder, tents, benches, large pipes, low tree branches, a fallen log
- shaded area for resting or reading: a large tree in a grassy area, a hammock, large plastic-covered pillows
- area where children can learn about and gain respect for their natural environment: unmanicured grass, bushes, plants, some rocks, a birdbath or feeder, plants that attract butterflies or birds, a garden for planting flowers or vegetables
- storage area for additional equipment as needed: balls, racquets, hoops, hockey sticks, jump ropes, tumbling mats, horseshoes, yo-yos, batons

Sharing Outdoor Space

It is often difficult for staff members in school-age programs to plan shared outdoor space with younger children. Many directors solve the problem by scheduling groups to use the play areas at separate times, but that does not completely address the needs of children at disparate age levels. The following suggestions may help.

- Provide adequate supervision of all areas of the playground.
- Establish clear rules so that older children know what they can and cannot do when younger children are present.
- Encourage older children to help younger children.
- Use movable equipment (see suggestions in the previous section) that can be brought out when younger children are not present.
- Set aside some areas for the exclusive use of older children, using movable barriers or fences.
- Schedule times that older children can use community facilities such as a park, a baseball diamond, a basketball court, or a swimming pool.
- Plan joint activities with another school-age program that has its own outdoor area.

 ## SUMMARY

Middle childhood is often referred to as a period of quiet since changes take place more slowly and smoothly than in early childhood. Physical growth slows down, while cognitive growth moves forward rapidly. Children become independent from their families and form strong bonds with their peers.

NAEYC drafted a statement of characteristics of developmentally appropriate programs for children during middle childhood. They include the following:

- opportunities for children to develop skills in all developmental areas
- a program designed to enhance children's self-esteem
- a responsiveness to individual differences in ability and interests

Project Home Safe redrafted the NAEYC guidelines to fit the needs of after-school programs. Space for school-age children, both indoors and outdoors, should be designed specifically for their needs. Ideally, this means having "dedicated" space, not shared by other parts of a program. General considerations for planning space for older children are similar to those used for younger children, but they are implemented differently. Basics for planning space include the following:

- safe yet challenging
- homelike atmosphere
- flexibility
- size
- aesthetically pleasing
- storage

Specific areas are listed as well as suggestions for how to share space with other programs.

 ## REFERENCES

Albrecht, K. M., & Plantz, M. C. (1993). *Developmentally appropriate practice in school-age child care programs* (2nd ed.). Dubuque, IA: Kendall/Hunt.

Bredekamp, S. (Ed.). (1987). *Developmentally appropriate practice in early childhood programs serving children from birth through age 8.* Washington, DC: National Association for the Education of Young Children.

 ## SELECTED FURTHER READING

Clemens, J. B. (1996). Gardening with children. *Young Children, 51*(4), 22–27.

Click, P., & Parker, J. (2002). *Caring for school-age children* (3rd ed.). Clifton Park, NY: Delmar Learning.

French, M. A. (1999–2000). Building relational practices in out-of-school environments. *The Wellesley Centers for Women Research Report, 20*(1), 8.

Katz, L. G., Evangelou, D., & Hartman, J. A. (1990). *The case for mixed-age grouping in early childhood education.* Washington, DC: National Association for the Education of Young Children.

Lewis, B. (1995). *Kid's guide to service programs.* Minneapolis, MN: Free Spirit Press.

STUDENT ACTIVITIES

1. Observe a group of school-age children on a playground or in your child care group. Are there some children who are much taller or much smaller than the others? How do they seem to get along in the group? Are there children who are excluded? Why do you think they have difficulty joining the activities?

2. Obtain several catalogues from companies that supply materials for school-age children. Choose three items that you would use in a classroom and three for outdoors for a group of 18 children ranging in age from six to eleven. Defend your choices in terms of what you learned from reading this chapter.

3. Plan and conduct one indoor and one outdoor activity for a group of six eight-year-olds. Evaluate the success of the activities. How long did the children stay involved? What comments did they make? Would you change either the materials you provided or the way in which the activity was conducted? If so, in what ways?

4. Write several paragraphs describing the kinds of play activities you enjoyed during middle childhood. Which of the interests inherent in these experiences have you continued to pursue at the present time?

 REVIEW

1. What changes take place in children's thinking during the period between ages five and seven?

2. During middle childhood, children form clubs, cliques, or gangs. What are the purposes of these alliances?

3. What are the bases for children's self-concept?

4. How can caregivers provide opportunities for children to make friends?

5. List three field trips and three games that would be of interest to school-age children.

6. State one goal that is applicable to a school-age program.

7. How do licensing requirements for school-age programs differ from those for younger children?

8. List several ways to make space flexible.

9. State six ways to adapt indoor space when it must be shared with younger children.

10. Describe ways that outdoor space can be successfully shared with other groups.

CASE STUDY

Ignacio is the site supervisor of a school-age program and has experienced a high turnover in staff. In an attempt to discover the reason, he distributed a supervisor review form for the staff to complete. Among other things, he has learned that the employees are unhappy with his management style and programming skills. The employees do not feel valued and are not included when important decisions have to be made. He sends them written directives about what to include in their program without considering their interests and abilities or the interests of the children.

1. What can Ignacio do to improve morale in this program?

2. How do you feel about staff reviews of supervisors?

3. How would you react if your staff had these complaints about you?

 HELPFUL WEB SITES

Afterschool.gov:	http://www.afterschool.gov/health.html
National Institute on Out-of-School-Time (NIOST):	http://www.wellesley.edu/wcw/sac
National SAFEKIDS Campaign:	http://www.safekids.org
National School Age Care Alliance:	http://www.nsaca.org

 For additional resources related to administration, visit the Online Resource® for this book at www.EarlyChildEd.delmar.com

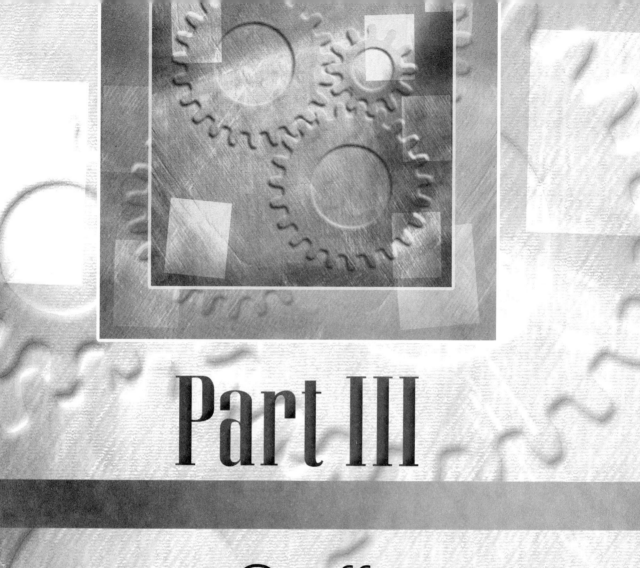

Part III

Staff

CHAPTER

7

Staff Selection/Personnel Policies

KEY TERMS

contract
knowledge
probationary period
skill
statement of personnel policies

OBJECTIVES

After reading this chapter, you should be able to:

- State the procedures for finding qualified staff.
- Plan the steps in recruiting employees.
- Describe the process of selecting a staff member from qualified applicants.
- List the kinds of information contained in a personnel policy statement.

A Day in the Life of …

THE DIRECTOR OF A CHILD CARE LEARNING CENTER

Our center recently went through some staff turnover due to several employees returning to college. I was feeling very stressed because of the changes, the parent complaints, and the realization that the applicants did not live up to my expectations. I must have interviewed 20 candidates and would have considered only a few of them for a position. I was becoming very depressed. It seemed as though all the wonderful teachers were now leaving the field of early childhood education and the persons applying had no ambition to work with children.

192

I always have my staff participate in evaluating any applicant I am considering for a position since they must work together positively on a daily basis. It is important that I receive their input. During these interviews my staff members were also getting depressed since they too did not care for the people who were applying.

A dedicated employee who has worked with me since the center opened walked into my office after spending the day with three applicants. She patted me on the back and said, "Don't worry Karen, you can count on some of us." She then offered to do anything I needed or wanted her to do to help out.

A beautiful building and the best equipment cannot make a good school. It takes well-trained teachers to make the environment come alive. Directors want the most qualified staff members possible and that means choosing personnel who fulfill the requirements of that setting.

 ## STAFF QUALIFICATIONS

Before beginning a recruiting process it is important to understand what makes an excellent teacher. Researchers have been interested in finding out if teachers with higher levels of education are better in their interactions with children or in their ability to provide a learning environment since many teachers in early childhood programs begin with little or no specialized education.

Whitebrook, Howes, and Phillips (1990) found that education was a good predictor of sensitive, caring interactions with children. More recently, a study done by the National Institute of Child Health and Human Development (1996) found no relationship between the teachers' educational level and their positive caregiving interactions. Both of these studies looked at general educational level. Specialized education experiences, on the other hand, do seem to matter when judging teacher effectiveness. A follow-up of the Howes, Whitebrook, and Phillips 1990 study (1992) showed that specialized education at the college level was an important factor, particularly with infants and toddlers.

Several studies have shown that there is a relationship between teacher education and the quality of the learning environment as measured by the Early Childhood Environment Rating Scale (ECERS) (Harms & Clifford, 1980). Whitebrook et al. (1990) found that there is a positive correlation between "appropriate caregiving," a category of the ECERS, and overall classroom quality. Epstein (1993) found general education of caregivers was associated with higher scores on the Harms scale and the Infant and Toddler Environmental Rating Scale (ITERS) (Harms, Cryer, & Clifford, 1990). It must be noted, however, that a higher level of education does not guarantee that caregivers will design a better learning environment. Educational level is a starting point from which to investigate caregiver qualifications.

Education

Check your state's licensing requirements for the academic background of teachers of young children. Specifications are usually minimal. The educational requirement may be as low as 12 postsecondary semester units in early childhood education or child development. A teacher in an infant-toddler room is sometimes required to complete an additional course in infant studies. Teachers in a before- and after-school program for older children might be able to substitute credits in recreation, physical education, and elementary teaching for early childhood education courses. The director should set standards for the school as much beyond the minimum as possible.

Publicly funded programs have different requirements for teachers. In public school early childhood education programs, teachers must have teaching certificates for the primary grades. They must also meet any other requirements set by the local school board. Head Start teachers have four-year degrees in early childhood education or elementary education. Degrees in psychology or child welfare may also prepare someone for Head Start teaching. Head Start teachers who do not have a four-year degree are encouraged to work toward the Child Development Associate credential sponsored by the National Association for the Education of Young Children (NAEYC).

Nonteaching staff in a school also must meet minimum standards stated in licensing requirements. They must be in good physical health and free of diseases that might be transmitted to children. A background check should indicate that they have not been convicted of a crime other than a minor traffic violation.

Experience

The director decides how much and what kinds of experience staff members should have. Licensing guidelines in each state will specify a minimum amount, but the director can decide to require more. In some states, teachers are required to have as little as a year of classroom experience with children while assistant teachers need none. In a new school, it is best to look for experienced teachers who will be able to function without initial training or supervision. The first year of operation will be smoother, and although it may increase the percentage of the budget allocated to salaries, it may be worth it.

Personal Characteristics

The success of a school depends largely on the adults who work there and the kind of relationships they establish with each other and with children. In order for that to happen, staff members must be chosen carefully based on a clear picture of the kinds of characteristics needed. The following characteristics are those that are cited most often by experienced directors. They say they look for staff members who

■ like being with children (some adults prefer being with infants while others prefer preschool or older children).

- are able to be nurturing (especially important for infants and toddlers).
- are able to be flexible.
- are patient and willing to wait while children accomplish tasks themselves.
- are good role models for children to follow.
- have good communication skills, including writing and the ability to listen.
- can allow children to be independent and resolve their own problems.
- can accept individual differences in both children and adults.
- are able to work as a team with colleagues and with parents.
- are healthy and energetic, and enjoy physical activity.
- have lots of interests that can be shared with children and adults.
- are willing to continue learning.

Required Skills

Next the director should make a list of the skills each position requires. According to the dictionary, a **skill** is an ability that comes from knowledge, practice, or aptitude. It simply means the ability to perform certain tasks as part of a job. A word that is currently used is *competencies*. It is applicable to all positions.

Teachers need to be able to do a variety of things as part of their job. The choice of which ones to include in job requirements depends on the type of school. The following list is a compilation of skills that might fit several settings. It can be used as a guide to develop a more specific list.

A teacher should be able to

- set up an environment that motivates children to participate.
- design activities that stimulate children to think, solve problems, and make choices.
- encourage children to use language by listening and respond to their communications.
- promote children's physical development.
- help children feel successful.
- create an environment that helps children accept ethnic differences.
- assess and measure children's achievement.

For further help, NAEYC has a useful pamphlet that lists the competencies for several levels of educational personnel. It is pamphlet No. 530, entitled "NAEYC Position Statement on Nomenclature, Salaries, Benefits, and the Status of the Early Childhood Profession." You can obtain a copy by writing to the association's Washington, DC, office.

Knowledge

Knowledge is a familiarity with a particular subject or branch of learning. It can also mean an acquaintance with facts, truths, or principles. Knowledge provides the information that allows workers to do their jobs. Should the teacher have a knowledge of child development? Should the cook need to know something about nutrition in order to plan meals? Will the secretary need to know public relations techniques? To make these decisions, the director must know the functions and needs of each job and then consider the knowledge necessary to perform those functions.

Some examples of what teachers need to know are

- stages of development, with special emphasis on cognitive, language, physical, social, and emotional development.
- atypical development.
- how young children learn.
- positive guidance strategies.
- ways to present materials and activities so children will want to get involved.
- how the family influences the child's development.
- ways to form a partnership with parents for the education and care of the child.
- communication and conference techniques.

Some examples of what a secretary needs to know are

- how to type or use a computer.
- how to set up and maintain a filing system or computer database.
- how to perform bookkeeping tasks either manually or on a computer.
- how to set up and maintain a schedule.

A food preparation person may need to know

- the food group pyramid.
- recommended serving sizes for children.
- how to prepare and store food for maximum health and safety.
- the kinds of food most children enjoy.
- how to present food in appealing ways.
- health regulations.

 STAFF RECRUITMENT

The search to find qualified personnel can begin after a clear statement of the qualifications for each job has been formulated. A concise announcement should be prepared for each position. As shown in Figures 7-1 and 7-2, the following information should be included:

- name of school
- address of school
- job title and brief description
- contract period (September to June or the calendar year)
- salary range

RECRUITING NOTICE

The Village Child Care Center at 8126 West 8th Street is seeking a Head Teacher for a group of 18 four-year-olds. Responsibilities include planning and conducting the program for the group, working with parents, and participating in staff planning and decision making.

The applicant selected will be given a one-year contract with a salary ranging from $18,000 to $24,000. The school is in session all year, with each staff member entitled to 15 days paid-leave each year. Starting date for this position is August 1. Deadline for applying is July 1.

Applicants should have a B.A. degree in child development or related fields and have had at least two years' experience in a preschool program. We are an Equal Opportunity Employer.

An application, résumé, and three letters of reference are required. The application form may be requested by calling:

Mary Anton

555-8659

FIGURE 7-1 ■ Sample recruiting notice for a head teacher.

- brief statement of qualifications
- name and phone number of person to contact
- application process
- deadline for applying
- affirmative action statement
- starting date of position

This notice does not have to be fancy or costly. With a computer, it is easy to put together an attractive notice by varying the type font, using bold letters, or adding a border. With a typewriter, capital letters or underlining can be used for emphasis. Brevity is the key. Most people will not read a lengthy notice with "wordy" sentences.

Job information should be distributed as widely as possible. The more people who see it, the greater probability of finding the right person. If there are several positions to be filled, there may be many applicants. In that case, it may be better to eliminate

---

ASSISTANT TEACHER WANTED

Teacher Assistant for infant-toddler room in a church-sponsored school. Responsibilities include all aspects of daily care of children, planning appropriate activities, and maintaining children's records. Must have at least 15 college units in Early Childhood Education including a course on infant-toddler development. Experience preferred. Job available immediately. Send résumé to P.O. Box 1320, Thousand Oaks, CA 91359 or FAX to 815-222-3487. We are an Equal Opportunity Employer.

FIGURE 7-2 ■ Sample newspaper advertisement for an assistant teacher.

the telephone number from this information, but request that applicants write for application materials.

If the school is already in operation and there is only one position to fill, those already on staff should be notified. An assistant teacher may feel ready to apply for a position as teacher. A secretary who has taken some early childhood courses may be ready to move to an assistant's job.

Further distribution sources are

- public and private schools.
- unemployment service offices.
- college and university placement offices.
- civic groups, clubs, and special interest groups.
- professional organizations.
- churches.

The director can also place an ad in local newspapers. The ad needs to be much shorter than the recruitment notice. It should be only a few lines long and contain the following information:

- name of school
- position being filled
- required background and experience
- contact—address or telephone

Many directors find the search for qualified staff a difficult and frustrating part of their job, and the high turnover in early childhood centers causes the search to be a constant one. Although turnover of employees cannot be entirely eliminated, it may be significantly decreased by creating a climate in which staff members feel valued. This will go a long way toward retaining staff. A good personnel policy statement is also important, as you will read later in this chapter.

 APPLICATION INFORMATION

The director should develop an application form that can be used each time a position is to be filled. There may be one basic form for all jobs or one for teachers and one for other categories. Forms should be simple and short. Questions should be clear and related to the job.

The application form might include the following:

- date the application is made
- name of applicant
- address of applicant
- telephone number of applicant
- Social Security number
- position applied for

- job or volunteer experience (include dates and type of work)
- educational background
- hobbies or special interests
- references (include name, address, telephone)

In addition, the application for a teaching position may include the following:

- credentials and/or academic degrees
- professional affiliations
- published works

Some applicants may need help in filling out an application form. Language differences, inexperience with forms, or limited education should not deter a potentially qualified person from applying. The secretary or another staff member should be available to help.

Additional information can be obtained by observing an applicant's response to children. With the teacher's permission, the director should ask the applicant to sit in on an activity, participate in a snacktime, or read a story to the children. How does he or she interact with the children? Are the applicant's responses appropriate for the age level of the children? Does he or she ask to see lesson plans or resource materials? Some center directors ask the top three candidates to spend half a day being actively involved in the classroom. However, it may be unrealistic to expect that a stranger to the children can perform in exactly the same way he or she would do in a familiar setting. Observing a candidate's interactions with children should yield useful information that can be added to the verbal interview information.

SELECTION PROCESS
Screening

After the application deadline has passed, the screening process begins. An advisory committee member or a teacher may be asked to help. Although the director or the board of trustees will make the final choice, others can make recommendations. When staff members participate in this process, they have a chance to learn some new skills. Having some "say" in choosing their colleagues can promote staff solidarity as well.

The director should look through each of the applications for those who meet the minimum requirements. This usually includes academic background, experience, and credentials or licenses. The applications should be sorted into three groups. One will be for those who meet all the minimum requirements. The second will be for those who meet some. The last will be for those who meet none.

The last group can be eliminated immediately.

It is important to check references. A reference can be in the form of a letter submitted along with the application, or it can be the name of a person to contact.

The director should read written recommendations carefully or telephone the personal contacts. It helps to have some specific questions to ask. "What are ___ 's greatest strengths working with children?" "In what areas do you think ___ needs additional knowledge or experience?" "Would you hire ___ to work with a group of three-year-olds?"

Once the field of applicants is narrowed down to a few likely candidates, it is time to schedule interviews. Usually three to five applicants who meet all the requirements will yield a satisfactory new hire.

Interviewing

The interview portion of the application process is the most difficult, but it can be the most valuable. When meeting with a prospective staff member, there is an opportunity to explore the "fit" of the person to the school. This is a two-way process. The applicant needs to find out if the school is "right," and the director needs to find out if the applicant will suit the program.

At least a half hour should be allowed for the actual interview, with 10 or 15 minutes between candidates for jotting notes about each person. It is best not to rely on memory. When several interviews in a row have been completed, the applicants will begin to "blur" together. Notes will refresh one's memory when trying to make a final decision.

The interview should be preceded with a tour of the school if time permits. This will allow the applicant to get some information about the school. It will also provide a chance to see how the person responds to children. Comments or questions during the tour can provide important insights about the applicant.

In some settings, several people will compose an interview committee. The director, a board member, a parent, a supervisor, or a teacher may be included, depending on the organization of the school. If several people are to be involved, some directors schedule separate interviews for each. Others do it as a group. Too large a committee may overwhelm some candidates.

For purposes of later evaluation, the interview should have some structure. This applies whether one person interviews candidates or a committee is involved. Each applicant should be asked similar questions that are written out before the interview. In this way there will be no question of preferential or prejudicial practice. In a committee, one person should be designated to lead. To avoid repetition of information, each member should choose an area to question. For example, one might ask about curriculum skills, while another asks about previous experience.

The procedure is still the same if committee members conduct separate interviews. The group should agree ahead of time about the questions that will be asked. Each may pursue particular areas, or they may all ask similar questions. For a sample interview questions worksheet, see Figure 7-3.

Questions that require only a one-word answer should be avoided because they provide very little information. "Did you decide to become a preschool teacher because you like children?" is an example. Also to be avoided are questions that already imply the kind of answer that is expected. "What kind of punishment would

---

INTERVIEW QUESTIONS

_____   _____

Name of Applicant   Date of Interview

_____

Position applying for

_____

Interviewer

1. Briefly state your teaching philosophy.
2. What are your strengths as a teacher of young children?
3. What are your weaknesses?
4. You have a child in your toddler class who is biting other children. How would you respond?
5. What would you do if a child kicked you?
6. A parent tells you she is very upset over an incident that happened the day before. What would your first response be? What else would you do to help that parent?
7. Briefly describe three activities that would be age appropriate for three-year-olds.
8. What would be your primary focus as a teacher in an infant program?

_____

Signature of Interviewer

Rate applicant on a scale of 1 to 10, 10 being an outstanding applicant and 1 being someone you would not consider for this position.

_____

Rating

FIGURE 7-3 ■ Sample interview questions form.

you use for a child who hits others?" Here the implication is that punishment is the only way to handle that kind of behavior.

The interview should be conducted in a quiet place, free from interruptions. It is important to make sure the applicant will be comfortable. The applicant should not be asked to sit facing a row of committee members or an interviewer who is barricaded behind a desk. A circle configuration is the most effective.

Each committee member will need time to review the application material. This way they can familiarize themselves with the applicant's academic background and previous experience. This will save time by eliminating direct questions about that kind of information in the interview.

The director should begin the interview by introducing him- or herself, and others, if more than one person is participating. If the applicant has not had a tour of the school, the director can describe the school briefly and talk a little about the specific class in which there is an opening.

PART 3 ■ **Staff**

It is best to ask an easily answered question first, mainly to help the applicant start talking. For example "I see by your application that you have worked at . . . Tell us what you liked best about the job." Or "Describe any aspects of that job that might be applicable to the position here." Questions should begin with words like the following:

■ Tell me . . .
■ Describe . . .
■ List . . .
■ Outline . . .

To find out about personal qualifications, it is helpful to pose a question that might show the person's feelings or attitudes:

■ *Enthusiasm for teaching*: "What do you like best about working with young children?"
■ *Attitudes toward differences in people*: "Suppose you had a child in your class who was blind. What are some things you would do to integrate that child into the classroom activities?"
■ *Ability to manage problem situations with children*: "You have a child in your class who refuses to participate in any of the group activities you plan. She either won't come to the group area, or if she does, she never says anything. What would you do?"

To get information about specific skills, the director might ask the applicant to plan a specific learning activity for a particular age group. For example:

■ "Describe one science activity that would be appropriate for a group of four-year-olds."
■ "List three things you might do to encourage parents to get involved in the education of their children."
■ "Plan a cooking activity that would be appropriate for a group of children in an after-school program."

To find out the applicant's knowledge of child development:

■ "Briefly describe how you would design an indoor environment for a group of four infants and six toddlers."
■ "Name three art activities that most two-year-olds should be able to do successfully. Name three that might be a little difficult."

To elicit unstructured information, applicants should be encouraged to talk freely about themselves:

■ "What else would you like to tell us about yourself that might be important as we consider you for this position?"
■ "Tell us what you feel your strengths are. What are the kinds of things you would like to do?"
■ "What kind of job do you expect to be doing 10 years from now?"

There are some areas of inquiry that should be avoided, and some information that should not be requested either in an interview or on an application. The following are some guidelines:

- The interviewer can ask for place of residence, but not whether the person owns or rents.
- It is legal to require an applicant to provide proof that he or she meets a minimum age requirement, but it is illegal to seek any information that identifies someone over age 40.
- The interviewer can ask the name and address of a parent or guardian of a minor, but cannot ask questions that indicate applicant's marital status, number and ages of children, or provisions for child care.
- It is illegal to ask any questions regarding the applicant's race or complexion, color of skin, eyes, or hair.
- It is acceptable to state that employment is contingent on passing a physical exam and ask if there is any physical condition that would limit his or her ability to perform the job. It is unacceptable to inquire about the applicant's general physical and mental health.
- A prospective employer can require references, but may not directly ask those persons questions about the applicant's race, religion, national origin, medical condition, marital status, or sex.

During the interview there will be an opportunity to observe many things about the applicant. Depending on what is important, the director might look for the following:

- Ability to communicate: How clear are the answers?
- Organizational ability: Does the applicant organize answers logically and in a way that is easy to understand?
- Sense of humor: Does the applicant see some difficult situations from a humorous viewpoint?
- Tense or relaxed: Does the applicant's body language communicate extreme tenseness or relaxation?

The applicant should have an opportunity to ask questions at the end of the interview. The questions asked will give valuable clues to the person's ability to understand the job being filled. They may also provide insight into the person's particular interests or even biases.

This interview format can be used for employees other than teaching staff. The same kinds of questions can be asked; however, the content should be modified so that they are specific to the job. The following are some examples:

- *To find out how the maintenance person will react to children*—"The children have been playing in the sandbox with water from the drinking fountain. You arrive just in time to see a child using a very sandy bucket to get some more water. What would you say?"

- *To find out whether the cook can plan nutritious meals that children will like—* "What would a typical lunch for a group of four-year-olds consist of?"
- *To find out whether the secretary has good public relations skills—* "Some irate parents tell you there is a mistake on their bill and that you have overcharged them. You know the bill was correct and that a payment was missed. What would you say?"

The interviewers should record their information and impressions as soon as the interview is concluded. They should not talk to their co-interviewers first. (Caution: *The interviewer should not write notes during the interview.* The applicant may spend so much time worrying about what the interviewer has chosen to write down that an accurate picture of the person's abilities is not presented.) Some situations may require rating each candidate on a numerical scale. This should be done following the interview. The interviewers' notes should include a recommendation for hiring or not hiring.

Evaluating

Evaluation of applicants is the final step of the selection process and is sometimes the hardest. The evaluation will be based on several sources of information: the applicant's background and experience, responses to questions, and image. It is important to be as objective as possible.

It is not too difficult to evaluate an applicant's background and experience. If a specific degree or credential is required it will appear on the application. The applicant's experience will also be listed there. However, the only way to judge the quality of a person's background or experience is in an interview. Someone can take a course in human development, but not really have an understanding of the stages of development. Someone else may have many years of teaching experience, but it may have been in a very different kind of program. Evaluating answers to questions posed in the interview sometimes seems an almost impossible task, but if interviewers have a clear understanding of what they are looking for, the task is manageable.

Some very well-qualified applicants may not perform well in an interview. The opposite is also true. Someone who comes across well in an interview may turn out to be a poor choice for the school. There is a way to give an applicant a further chance. The finalists can be asked to spend a day working in a classroom. They should be paid the going salary rate for their time. Even though this procedure has some drawbacks, it will certainly provide additional information for making the final choice.

Finally, there is no foolproof way to find the exact person who will do well. It is necessary to listen, to watch, and evaluate each candidate. The more often directors go through this process, the more accurate they become in choosing the best staff.

 ## NOTIFICATION OF EMPLOYMENT OR NONSELECTION

When a new staff member has finally been selected, most directors are eager to finalize the process. One way is to telephone the person, then follow that with a letter. The letter should give the starting date of employment and the salary offered. If the center uses a contract, that should also be included.

The following is a comparison of mean hourly wages in different child care jobs:

- family child care provider: $4.82
- child care worker: $7.43
- preschool teacher: $8.16
- administrator: $15.92

Source: Childcare Services, United States Department of Labor, 2002, http://stats.bls.gov

The successful candidate should be given a time to return the contract or to come to the school to complete the process. This may include submitting the required credentials or transcripts and completing payroll and personnel forms.

When the hiring process is completed, the director should send information about the new employee to any interested persons. This may include board members, advisory committee members, or existing staff. The director will also want to tell parents about the new staff member. The children, too, need to know who their new teacher is going to be.

Those who were interviewed and not hired should also be informed. This is never a pleasant task, but they should not be left wondering. If possible, the director should telephone the people who were interviewed, thank them for their time, and tell them the position has been filled. The director may wish to ask whether they can be called for substitute jobs, or if future openings become available. If a telephone call is too difficult, it is acceptable to send a letter like that in Figure 7-4 to these people. In addition, a simple note to each person who sent in an application would be both courteous and professional (see Figure 7-5).

VILLAGE CHILD CARE CENTER

(Date)

Dear_____:

Thank you for your interest in Village Child Care Center and your desire to become a member of our staff. We wish to inform you that we have made a selection from the applicants for the recent opening.

Your application will be kept on file, and should an additional opening become available, you will be notified. If you are still interested in working with us, we hope that you will reapply.

Sincerely,

Mary Anton, Director

Figure 7-4 ■ Notification of nonselection.

VILLAGE CHILD CARE CENTER

(Date)

Dear_____:

    Because of the large number of requests to our recent recruiting efforts, we were unable to interview all applicants. However, we wanted to notify you that the position has been filled. Your application will be kept on file, and you will be notified when we have other openings.

                                     Sincerely,

                                   Mary Anton, Director

FIGURE 7-5 ■ Notification of applicants who were not interviewed.

PERSONNEL PRACTICES

In some preschools and child care centers, staff members stay for years. In others, turnover occurs frequently. What accounts for the difference? Sometimes people leave a job looking for higher pay. Others stay in a job in spite of low salaries. Teachers who stay in a school when they could get more money elsewhere say they stay because "It's a good place to work." Directors can make theirs that kind of school by treating the staff as professionals, providing job security, developing fair personnel practices, paying the best salary possible for each job, supporting fringe benefits and retirement plans, and offering employees a contract.

Contract

A **contract** or personnel agreement is a written commitment between employer and employee that promotes job security. A contract states that during a specified period of time, each has an obligation to the other. The employer agrees to employ the person for that period at a designated pay level. The staff member agrees to carry out the functions of the job (see Figure 7-6).

A contract is essential for good morale in any teaching staff. Young children need to have the security of teachers or caregivers who are predictable and who are there for a long period of time. It is hard for a child to learn to trust that school is a good place if adults disappear frequently, never to be seen again. Working parents, too, feel better if they know the adult who cares for their child will stay for a while. Learning to trust their child's caregiver takes time. Teachers need time, too, to find ways to work together. Teachers sometimes say that working together in a classroom is a bit like a marriage. It takes "working at" and does not happen overnight.

The contract should be a statement of all the conditions of employment. The following points should be included:

■ *time period of the contract*—the date when the contract goes into effect and the termination date

PERSONNEL AGREEMENT

Employee: Name: _____

Address: _____

_____

Phone: _____

JOB TITLE: Head Teacher

JOB DESCRIPTION:

I. Basic Functions: The head teacher is responsible for supervising the development and implementation of a daily program which will promote the children's physical, cognitive, social, and emotional growth.

II. Responsiblities:

1. Reports to the executive director of child care center
2. Ensures that written class plans are prepared in a timely fashion and posted prominently
3. Provides ongoing direction to staff as needed
4. Confers with director about changes, programming, and/or problems
5. Refers individual children to the director, who may need services from outside agencies
6. Provides opportunities for staff to develop
7. Shares pertinent information or concerns about individual children with assigned staff
8. Confers with staff on a weekly basis to discuss planning, individual children, and concerns of individual staff
9. Prepares performance appraisals of staff according to policy
10. Ensures communication between staff and parents through daily informal contact and semiannual scheduled conferences with written progress reports
11. Arranges conferences with parents whenever deemed necessary
12. Ensures a physically safe environment
13. Ensures daily attendance and health logs are maintained
14. Approves break-time
15. Assumes responsibility for continued professional growth in the areas of early childhood education
16. Substitutes for the director during periods of director's absence
17. Complies with personnel policies

Conditions of employment.

1. Salary: $24,000 for a 12-month calendar year
2. Health insurance program when permanent status is achieved
3. Paid holidays: New Year's Day, Memorial Day, Fourth of July, Labor Day, Thanksgiving Day, and Christmas Day
4. Paid annual vacation days, 10 (5 after 6 months, 5 additional after 1 year)
5. Paid annual sick days: 6
6. There is a probation period of three (3) months after which the full contract is in effect. This agreement may be terminated after due process if it is determined that you have not fulfilled the responsibilities of the position as described above. Termination by either party must be preceded by a notification period of thirty (30) days.

Approved by: _____   Employee: _____

Dated: _____   Dated :_____

FIGURE 7-6 ■ Sample personnel agreement.

- ■ **probationary period**—the time before the full contract goes into effect, usually from one to three months
- ■ *salary*—pay for the period covered by the contract
- ■ *fringe benefits*—the number of days of vacation and sick leave, and the medical and retirement benefits
- ■ *termination*—conditions for termination of the contract (would include termination by either the employer or employee)

Orientation of New Employees

The center director is responsible for ensuring that each new employee is given the information necessary for a smooth introduction to the work environment and the specifics of the job. All staff members, including supporting staff, need to be given a statement of personnel policies as soon as the hiring decision is made. This is a written document, described in the following section, detailing all facets of the employee-employer relationship. Employees should be told to read it and ask for clarification of any items they do not understand.

Their first day on the job, new employees should be given a tour of the entire physical plant and introduced to all staff members. They should know where materials are stored, where the adult rest rooms are, and where their personal belongings can be kept. Teachers should be introduced to the parents as soon as possible. Some directors notify families of staff changes by mail; others post notices on the parent bulletin board or include the information in a newsletter. Wherever possible, however, parents should have a personal introduction when they bring their child to school. The director must be available at arrival time to introduce the teacher and parents to each other. When the timing can be synchronized, a new teacher can be introduced to parents at a meeting. During the first weeks of employment, the director must check with the new employee frequently to answer any questions, help with problems, and build a supportive relationship. This is also a time when the new employee can become familiar with the performance standards the director expects. In some situations it is not always possible for the director to spend a lot of time with each new employee. In this circumstance, a senior staff member can be asked to be available to support the person until he or she feels comfortable. The director should still find time to meet with the new employee during the early weeks or to visit the classroom. It is important to establish the kind of relationship that lets the new staff member know the director is available to give support and help when it is needed.

In addition to the statement of personnel policies, some directors provide handbooks for new staff members. This document contains guidelines for situations ranging from how many children can play on an outdoor structure at one time to who is responsible for daily cleaning. A handbook should certainly include any rules that govern conduct in the classroom or ensure safety on the playground. A staff handbook may include these items:

- ■ philosophy of the center
- ■ statement of goals
- ■ bylaws of the board (where applicable)

- classroom procedures
- playground rules and restrictions
- suggestions for interacting with children
- copies of forms used for children's records
- information about the community the center serves
- directory of staff members

When this kind of information is made available to all staff members they have a common reference point. If questions arise they can refer to the written information.

One final method for orienting new employees is through an initial training session. This is especially effective if more than one new staff member has been hired at any given time. General information can be distributed, questions can be answered, and confusions clarified. This is also a good opportunity for senior staff members to get to know new members and begin to share with them strategies or materials that will be useful.

Statement of Personnel Policies

A **statement of personnel policies** is a written document covering employer-employee relations. It spells out the conditions of employment. Given to new employees, this kind of document will convey information about the job in a concise manner. Even though some employees may not read it from cover to cover, the information is there for reference as needed. It will not eliminate problems, but when they do arise, the statement may provide a solution or prevent misunderstandings. If employees are required to read the entire document, they may be asked to sign a statement indicating they have done so.

A written statement of personnel policies should be

- short and to the point.
- clear.
- organized into logical sections.

Many directors say they do not have a written policy statement because conditions change each year. Some do change, but many stay the same. It is fairly easy to redo a few pages to meet any changing circumstances in a school. This is another time-saving use for a computer. When information must be added, this can easily be done with a computer. The pages can be photocopied and put together into a looseleaf booklet.

The director must decide what is appropriate to put into the school's statement of personnel policies. An overview of the sections to include is presented in the following paragraphs.

Details of Employment

One section should be devoted to the details of employment: the number of hours per day, holidays, and vacations. A calendar showing holidays and starting dates of the school year is helpful. The length of the probationary period and what is to take place during that period could be outlined.

EXAMPLE

The probationary period is three months. During that time you will be observed by the director at least once a month. A conference will be scheduled at the end of that time to evaluate your performance. If performance has been satisfactory, the full contract will go into effect. Once the contract is in effect, each employee will be evaluated once a year. The observation and conference will be scheduled at a mutually agreed upon time between the director and the employee.

New employees should know the lines of responsibility in a school. When problems arise, they should know whom to go to first. They should also know who will be directly responsible for supervising them. An organizational chart included in the personnel policies manual will show these personnel relationships.

If the school provides payment for—or requires—continuing professional training, that information should be included. Some schools pay for conferences and professional dues. Some offer full or part tuition payments for staff to attend classes.

Physical Environment

A personnel policies statement might include a section on managing the physical environment. In some situations, staff members need to know where to get keys to the classroom or where to park. Parking may not be an issue in some areas, but in crowded urban settings it could create problems. Assigned spaces help to alleviate the hassle and possible expense. Personnel also need to know if there is a safe place for them to leave their belongings. Many centers forget this while concentrating on making the environment a good one for children. There could also be a statement concerning teachers' responsibilities for maintaining their classrooms and equipment. Although there may be a regular cleaning service, teachers usually must do a certain amount of cleaning and straightening in their own classrooms.

Health and Safety Matters

Every employee should be *fingerprinted* for use in completing a background check. Records will show whether this person has ever been convicted of a crime that would be detrimental to the safety of the children. *Health examinations* should be required, including a tuberculosis test. The director should also consider requiring that staff members be immunized for hepatitis B or receive booster measles immunizations. Another issue to clarify is whether the employee is expected to pay for the health exam or whether this is covered by the employer.

How many "sick leave" days does each employee have? Can the days be carried over from one year to another? What are the conditions under which employees will be excused from work due to illness?

The statement of personnel policies should outline procedures for *reporting employee accidents*. If a form is required, an example should be included with instructions for where it can be obtained. There must be clear procedures for dealing with disasters such as fires, earthquakes, or tornadoes.

Employees will need details about the fringe benefits the school offers. If a medical plan is included, it is important to spell out the procedures for enrolling and the kinds of services covered

Some programs offer free or reduced-cost child care for children of employees. A few are beginning to offer a broad family benefit package that allows choices such as child care, elder care, maternity leave, or family leave. If there is a retirement plan or if the center pays into Social Security, that information should be included. Any other types of benefits such as group life insurance, unemployment insurance, and workers' compensation should be outlined.

It is appropriate to include in this section information about employee relief periods. Each staff member should have at least 10 minutes of relief during every four-hour period. If a staff member works more than four hours, a 30-minute break should be scheduled for rest and lunch away from the children. Some schools allow staff members an hour while children are napping as long as they stay on the premises. In that way, they are available if needed in an emergency.

Termination of Employment

The personnel policies statement should include procedures for *terminating employment*. How much notice is required when the employer or the staff member ends employment? It is customary to have a two-week notification. The causes for termination should be clearly stated.

It is important to have a grievance process that can be followed when problems arise. Such a procedure might prevent termination of employment, increase staff morale, and decrease turnover. One church school has the following statement:

> In the event of disagreements between members of the teaching staff, the Director will make the final decision. When there is a disagreement on procedure between members of the teaching staff and the Director, the Director may ask the Vice-President, Education, to arbitrate. Both parties, Director and staff member, will abide by the decision.

This statement provides for most disputes to be settled by working through the chain of command from staff member to director to church board. In some cases, staff members might have such serious disagreements with a director that some other method needs to be in place. It may be necessary to designate some person within the school organization that staff members can contact when problems cannot be resolved by going through the usual channels.

Job Description

A *job description* should be included for each position. This is a list of duties and responsibilities. A teacher's job description should include all activities related to teaching, communicating with parents, and attending staff meetings. The job description should include minimum legal and local qualifications for the position as well (see Figure 7-7).

JOB DESCRIPTION: CLASSROOM TEACHER

The person in this position is responsible for the general management of a group of 15 children between the ages of two and five.

QUALIFICATIONS

The person selected for this position must have successfully completed at least 12 postsecondary units in early childhood courses. In addition, this person must have had two years' experience as a teacher in a preschool classroom. Personal qualifications for this position include the ability to interact effectively with both children and parents, the ability to work cooperatively with other staff members, and the ability to be flexible. Good health would be beneficial.

RESPONSIBILITIES

The teacher will be responsible for planning and conducting a program for a group of children and all activities relating to that program. Duties will include, but are not limited to:

- planning and conducting daily experiences for the children based on the goals of the school.
- preparing all materials required to implement the program.
- planning and maintaining a physical environment that meets the goals of the school, is safe and free of health hazards, and is attractive.
- planning for the needs of individual children in regard to their interests, special needs, pace, and style of learning.
- including materials and experiences in the classroom that foster children's cultural or ethnic identity.
- attending and participating in staff meetings, training sessions, and planning activities.
- participating in recommended courses, conferences, or other activities for professional growth.
- participating in ongoing assessments of children's development and progress.
- planning and participating in activities designed to include parents in the education of their children.
- conducting ongoing parent contacts and conferences to notify parents of their children's progress.
- assisting in public relations events sponsored by the school.

FIGURE 7-7 ■ Sample job description for a teacher.

Job descriptions for personnel other than teachers will have information related to the particular position. As an example, a cook's job description may include statements about planning menus, preparing food, purchasing food items, storing food, and maintaining kitchen cleanliness (see Figure 7-8).

Advancement Opportunities

The school may offer opportunities for staff to *advance to higher pay levels or to other positions*. If so, that information should be included in a personnel policies manual.

JOB DESCRIPTION: COOK

The person in this position will be responsible for the general planning and implementation of all food services of the school.

QUALIFICATIONS

This person must have had experience in quantity cooking and have shown an ability to plan for economical purchases of foods. This person should be able to plan, prepare, and serve nutritious and appetizing meals under the supervision of the school's nutritionist. This person should have good personal cleanliness habits and should be able to maintain an orderly and hygienic kitchen. Lastly, this person should like being in an environment with young children and be able to work well with other adults.

RESPONSIBILITIES

- using menus planned by the nutritionist, purchase, prepare, and serve two meals and two snacks each day to all the children

- reviewing the food service periodically with the nutritionist and the director

- coordinating food services with other activities of the school

- incorporating foods for special celebrations into the regular menus

- maintaining a clean and orderly kitchen and storage area

- storing foods in such a way as to minimize waste

- participating in periodic training sessions with other staff members to increase knowledge of child development

- attending training sessions as required to upgrade knowledge of nutrition and food preparation

---

FIGURE 7-8 ■ Sample job description for a cook.

It should state the conditions for advancement, either further education or time of service. A salary scale showing the steps, the requirements for each step, and the salary at each level is an easy way to furnish this information.

 ## PERSONNEL RECORDS

Licensing guidelines usually require each school to maintain up-to-date records on each employee. So it is important to complete each file as soon as possible after hiring and to update it as necessary. The contents of the file may vary from school to school but generally will contain similar kinds of information. The following paragraphs describe the categories of records in a personnel file.

Application Materials

Each file should contain an application form that is usually completed even before the person is hired. The form should have a place to record the employee's name, address, Social Security number, and a person to contact in case of emergency. Application records may also contain

- records of education and relevant experience.
- transcripts and/or credentials.
- reference letters or forms.

Health

Health records should be maintained on each employee. If the school requires a pre-employment physical examination, a summary of that exam is placed in the file. Many states require periodic tuberculosis testing for preschool and child care personnel. The test results should be in the file. Immunization against hepatitis B is recommended. The health record should be included in each personnel file.

Any on-the-job injuries should certainly be recorded in the employee's file. The record should include the treatment given and the outcome. Figure 7-9 provides a sample staff injury report. It is also important to keep a record of each person's absences due to illness. Frequent illness may indicate that some measure needs to be taken to ensure better health in that employee.

Employment Record

An employment record form should be included in each file. This should show the starting date, any leaves that might have been granted, and the final day of employment.

It should also allow space for salary levels during the time of employment and include any promotions or transfers to another school within the organization.

Staff should be allowed to add to their own files if they wish. Special awards or commendations are examples of additional information to add to an employment record.

Evaluation

If the school has a system of evaluation, the record of each rating should be placed in the employee's file. A series of assessments over a period of time will provide a good record of each individual's job performance. A periodic review of evaluations may point to the need to provide more, or different kinds of, in-service training.

Conferences

The director should record any conferences scheduled with staff members and place the information in each employee's file. This will include routine conferences that follow each evaluation. But it should also include conferences that the director or the employee request to discuss a problem. The record should be brief and to the point. It is enough to state the problem that was discussed and briefly describe any resolution.

STAFF INJURY REPORT

Name	Position
Address	Phone Number
Date of Injury	Time

Location Where Injury Occurred

How Injury Happened

Description of the Injury

Witnesses

Physician's Name	Phone Number

Type of Treatment Required

FIGURE 7-9 ■ Sample staff injury report.

Termination of Employment

When employees leave a job or are fired, the director should place a record in their file. A brief note stating the reason should be enough. It must be objective and factual.

Recommendations

Employees who leave a center may ask for a reference letter for a new job. If the director cannot write a positive letter, the employee should be told so. If the director does write a reference letter, a copy should be placed in the employee's file. Future requests can be filled easily by copying the first letter unless specific new information is requested. The file should include a record of the dates and to whom copies have been sent.

The creation of a professionally oriented atmosphere in a center is a challenge. It often means a delicate balance between economic pressures and personnel requirements. The center should offer the best salaries that can be managed within the budget and include some fringe benefits. Beyond that, personnel policies that convey to staff members that they are important will go a long way toward making any center a good place to work. These efforts should result in less employee turnover and greater harmony among staff.

 ## SUMMARY

The director of a child care center should develop and follow systematic procedures when seeking new staff members. Important factors to look for are education, experience, personal characteristics, skills, and knowledge.

A statement listing full requirements for each specific position can be used to advertise for positions both inside and outside the school.

The selection process should be standardized. The first step is to screen applications for minimum requirements, check references, and note special talents.

Next, the director prepares an interview schedule. This includes setting up the interviews and notifying the interviewing committee. A chairperson designates uniform question areas to be covered. Everyone on the committee should record impressions of each candidate immediately after the interview.

The director should notify the person selected as soon as possible and also inform those not selected. Personnel selection is not an easy process, but careful procedures pay big dividends.

Once the personnel are hired, they should be inducted into fair and consistent employee practices. A written contract is one of the best ways to do this. Procedures spelled out in a policies statement should include their physical environment, health and safety conditions, terms of employment, job description, and advancement opportunities.

Personnel records are vital and often required by law. A permanent file should include the original application, health records, dates of employment and duties involved, evaluations and conferences, and date and reason for termination (if needed).

Everything considered, open, frank, and reasonable personnel practices lead to happier employees and reduced turnover.

 ## REFERENCES

Epstein, A. S. (1993). *Training for quality: Improving early childhood programs through systematic inservice training.* Ypsilanti, MI: Hightscope press.

Harms, T., & Clifford, R. (1980). *Early childhood environment rating scale.* New York: Teachers College Press.

Harms, T., Cryer, D., & Clifford, R. (1990). *Infant/toddler environment rating scale.* New York: Teachers College Press.

Howes, C., Whitebrook, M., & Phillips, D. (1992). Teacher characteristics and effective teaching in child care: Findings from the national child care staffing study. *Child and Youth Forum, 21*, 399–414.

National Institute of Child Health and Human Development, Early Child Care Research Network. (1996). Characteristics of infant child care: Factors contributing to positive caregiving. *Early Childhood Research Quarterly, 11*, 299–306.

Whitebrook, M., Howes, C., & Phillips, D. (1990). *Who cares: Child care teachers and the quality of care in America. Final report of the national child care staffing study*. Oakland, CA: Child Care Employee Project.

 ## SELECTED FURTHER READING

Blood, P. J. (1993). But I'm worth more than that! *Young Children, 48* (3), 65–68.

Bloom, P. (1988). *A great place to work: Improving conditions for staff in young children's programs*. Washington, DC: National Association for the Education of Young Children.

Bredekamp, S., & Willer, B. (1993). Professionalizing the field of early childhood education: Pros and cons. *Young Children, 48* (3), 82–84.

Goffin, S., & Lombardi, J. (1988). *Speaking out: Early childhood advocacy*. Washington, DC: National Association for the Education of Young Children.

Manfred-Petitt, L. (1993). Child care: It's more than the sum of its tasks. *Young Children, 49* (1), 40–42.

Manning, D., Rubin, S. E., Perdigo, H. G., Gonzalez, R. G., & Schindler, P. (1996). A "worry doctor" for preschool directors and teachers: A collaborative model. *Young Children, 51* (5), 68–73.

National Association for the Education of Young Children. (1990). NAEYC position statement on guidelines for compensation of early childhood professionals. *Young Children, 46* (1), 30–32.

Phillips, C. (1990). The child development associate program: Entering a new era. *Young Children, 45* (2), 24–27.

 ## STUDENT ACTIVITIES

1. Write a statement for recruiting an applicant for your job.
2. Get application forms from three different schools. Note the different kinds of information each asks. What does this tell about the school?
3. Role-play an interview with a prospective teacher. Alternate the roles of teacher and director. Ask for subjective feelings involved in each role. What insights does this give in this process?
4. Write a job description for child care assistant.
5. Invite several teachers and directors to discuss salaries and fringe benefits with your class.

REVIEW

1. List five sources for recruiting teacher applicants.
2. This chapter listed characteristics most directors look for when recruiting staff members. How many can you recall?
3. List the skills teachers need in order to fulfill their job responsibilities.
4. What information should be included in a recruitment statement?
5. Describe the process for screening applicants for a staff position.
6. Who should be included in the screening process for new staff members?
7. Formulate questions to be used in an interview to obtain the following kinds of information:
   a. attitudes toward differences in people
   b. specific skills
   c. knowledge of child development
8. What points should be covered in a contract?
9. List the kinds of information that are contained in a statement of personnel policies.
10. What kinds of information should be included in a personnel file?

CASE STUDY

Angela Suarez is a first-year director of a large child care center. The beginning of the school year was approaching, and she had several teaching positions to fill. She placed ads in the local paper, notified the job placement office of the nearby college, and told as many people as she could that she was looking for staff members. Several teachers applied and she interviewed each of them. Finally, she made some decisions, checked references, and offered jobs to several people. During the first day of employment, Angela distributed the necessary personnel paperwork and then mailed the required information to the Department of Justice (DOJ) on her "new hires." She was pleased that the new school year seemed to be off to a great start!

Four weeks into the semester, Angela received a notice from the DOJ that a new employee, Amanda Anniston, had a criminal record. The information she received is limited, but after gathering further information, she discovered that Amanda had a history of alcohol abuse, including one DUI conviction. The children and parents seem to like her and her teaching performance is satisfactory.

1. What would you do in this situation?

2. What would you say to Amanda?

3. Are there laws or regulations covering this kind of situation? If so, what are they?

4. Is there a way that Angela could have avoided this problem?

HELPFUL WEB SITES

Center for the Child Care Workforce:	http://www.ccw.org
Center for Career Development in Early Care and Education:	http://ericps.crc.uiuc.edu/ccdece/ccdece/html
Bureau of Labor Statistics:	http://www.bls.gov

For additional resources related to administration, visit the Online Resource® for this book at www.EarlyChildEd.delmar.com

CHAPTER **8**

Staff Supervision and Training

KEY TERMS

critical job elements
evaluation
mentor
supervision

OBJECTIVES

After reading this chapter, you should be able to:

- Discuss the components of effective supervision.
- List the steps in an evaluation process.
- Cite methods and sources for staff training.
- Discuss strategies for preventing burnout among employees.

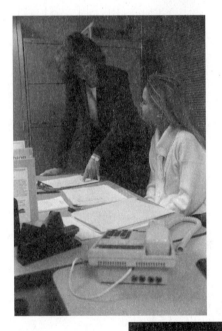

A Day in the Life of ...
A DIRECTOR OF A CHILD CARE LEARNING CENTER

A four-year-old child walked into my office one morning concerned about what we would be serving for lunch. I informed her and her mother that it was spaghetti and meatball day. Her little face lit up and she said, "Yes, I love the way Miss Linda makes her meatballs. I don't like the way my mommy makes hers. I am going to ask Miss Linda to teach my mommy right now. Come on Mom, let's go to the kitchen."

Staff members in early childhood programs come from a variety of backgrounds. Typically, there are *three different paths* taken by those who become teachers or caregivers: the traditional path of *academic preparation*, the parent path of *firsthand experience*, and the accidental path beginning with *an unrelated job*. In the first group are persons who set out to prepare for an already chosen profession in early childhood education. They attend college and do supervised teaching. In the second group are persons who learn from firsthand experience of caring for their own children. They may gain additional experience through becoming home-based child care providers or participating in Head Start. In the third group are persons who prepare for a career unrelated to teaching but by luck or chance find themselves in a setting where there are children. The work is rewarding and they decide to change careers.

Almost every child development center or child care center will have on the staff individuals who fit the three categories. The reality is that directors cannot afford to recruit only persons with extensive academic preparation in early childhood education to fill the positions in their school or center. One reason is that the supply is so limited that untrained persons are desperately needed to care for all the children who are in group settings. Another reason is that there is a great need to staff early childhood centers with persons who reflect the backgrounds of the children who are enrolled. The children need teachers who come from their own communities, who understand their culture, and who speak their language. Some of these adults may not have extensive academic backgrounds.

Directors who view individual differences of staff members as an asset will value every staff member regardless of their training or credentials. These directors will also help each to continue to grow as professionals. This can be accomplished through effective and fair methods of supervision and evaluation, followed by training activities that motivate staff members to increase their skills. The Council for Early Childhood Professional Recognition is addressing differences in staff

States differ in requirements for prekindergarten teachers in state-funded programs. As of 2001–2002

California required 24 college credits in early childhood education plus 16 credits in general education.

Georgia required a Child Development Associate (CDA) credential.

Illinois required a bachelor's degree and an Early Childhood Education certificate.

Source: A Study in Staffing and Stability in State-Funded Pre-K Programs. Center for Child Care Workforce, 2002.

education and training on a national level through its Child Development Associate (CDA) program. The program is administered by the CDA National Credentialing Program in Washington, DC. Teachers in Head Start, early childhood centers, and child care programs can participate. To qualify for a CDA credential, teachers must show evidence that they are competent to do the following:

- Plan and set up a safe and healthy learning environment.
- Cultivate physical and intellectual competence.
- Support social and emotional development.
- Ensure positive participation of children and adults in the learning environment.
- Establish and maintain close coordination between school and families.
- Sustain a commitment to professionalism.

Participants in the CDA program go through *three steps* before the credential is awarded. They do *field work*, *take courses*, and are *evaluated* by a person appointed by the council. There are approximately 41,000 CDAs in the United States, with the largest percentage in Head Start. About 15 percent are in private sector early childhood centers. To receive a copy of *CDA Competency Standards*, write to: Council for Early Childhood Professional Recognition, 2460 16th Street, NW, Washington, DC 20009-3575, or telephone 800-424-4310. Additional information can be found at http://www.cdacouncil.org.

 ## SUPERVISION OF STAFF

The director of an early childhood center will probably be responsible for supervising all employees, although in Head Start or in large corporate organizations, another employee may fulfill this function. In its narrowest sense, supervision means overseeing staff members during the performance of their jobs. But from a broader perspective, **supervision** is a constantly changing relationship between employer and employee that is based on mutual respect. Daily contact with employees and the many hours spent talking together facilitate that kind of relationship. This is the basis of an essential support system in which employees can try out new ways of fulfilling job responsibilities.

The director establishes rapport with each staff member by being available as often as possible. A good place to start is greeting staff members when they arrive and planning to be free for a short chat. Some directors do relief teaching for short periods while a teacher takes a break, prepares materials, or meets with a parent. They also help out in classrooms when there is an emergency such as a sick or injured child. Staff members may need the director to be available at the end of the day as well. This is a time when teachers are often tired or discouraged and a willingness to listen may relieve some of the negative feelings. These strategies will be effective in developing a relationship of mutual trust only if the director's attitude expresses genuine caring and willingness to help.

An important part of supervision involves seeing that policies and procedures are carried out. In some instances, administrators issue directives and expect their staff to comply. Safety rules, health procedures, schedules, and methods for ordering materials are all examples. It is important to communicate expectations clearly to every employee and then do a follow-up to see that they are being carried out. Are the teachers in the infant room following the health procedures when they change diapers? Is the cook following guidelines for ensuring the safety of food during cooking and while serving? In other instances, there is room for differences in interpretation of guidelines. Curriculum goals are a prime example. Each teacher will implement a school's goals somewhat differently. Here, supervision involves assessing whether each teacher's method of implementation follows the guidelines closely enough, or if there is a need for change. The director will need to spend time observing in each job setting and then discussing these observations.

When an employee needs to change, the director's job becomes one of helping to bring about that change. This is one of the most difficult aspects of being a director because it demands a great deal of time and extensive expertise in communication. The director becomes a coach, providing ideas, encouragement, and feedback. At times, it means observing; at other times, it calls for modeling behavior. Inexperienced teachers will need more time and coaching. Teachers who have a lot of experience require less time, but still benefit from support. They need constructive criticism at times and positive reinforcement at others. As staff members become more accomplished and learn to work within the framework of a particular setting, there is another way in which administrators provide supervision. These staff members can be helped to evaluate their own performance and to discover ways to perform their jobs more effectively. Finally, these persons can be helped to develop the skills needed to take on responsibility for supervising aides, assistants, student teachers, or volunteers.

 ## EVALUATION OF STAFF PERFORMANCE

Evaluation is a process that determines if the goals of an early childhood center are being met. Teachers are evaluated on their ability to implement the educational goals of the center. Support staff are assessed on their ability to perform their jobs in ways that supplement the educational function. In most education settings, all staff members are evaluated at least once a year. Teachers will often welcome and benefit from more frequent reviews.

Although most teachers and directors see evaluation as a means of professional growth and the basis for improving performance, evaluation has some inherent problems. First, the process creates anxiety in both the person to be evaluated and the one who will do the evaluating. As a rule, few teachers are completely comfortable having someone judge their performance. And many directors are uneasy about judging their staff members.

The second problem is that two different levels of performance are evaluated. On one level are things that are obvious. Performance can be seen and sometimes measured or counted. The secretary types ten letters a day with great accuracy or only eight with quite a few errors. The teacher keeps the room in order or leaves it an absolute mess. On the other level are factors that cannot be seen, touched, or heard. How does the director evaluate the ability of a teacher to encourage decision making in children or the secretary's ability to create an accepting atmosphere for visitors? If only one performance level is used, it may result in an incomplete or skewed picture of the staff member's ability.

The third dilemma is deciding who is to be responsible for evaluation. The final responsibility is the director's. The actual rating may be done by any of a number of people in a school. Sometimes evaluations are more meaningful when more than one person is involved, each one having a specific part in the procedure.

In a small school, the director will probably evaluate all the employees. Staff and director develop the procedures cooperatively and the director carries them out. In a larger school, the director may work within a more complex organization for evaluating performance of employees. Staff members at different levels may be responsible for those under their immediate authority. The head teacher evaluates the assistant teacher(s) and the head cook evaluates the assistant cook, for example.

In a very large system or organization, one person may evaluate all employees. This evaluator works with the director and possibly a few other staff members to design and facilitate the process. In some situations, people on a specific job level might evaluate others on the same level. As an example, one teacher might evaluate another teacher. This is called evaluation by one's peers.

Some evaluation systems may include self-evaluation by the employee. This would not replace other evaluations but would supplement them.

The director usually decides if all employees should be evaluated, or if only those in certain job categories should be rated. Should only teachers and aides be evaluated, or should the performance of all employees in the school be examined? If a school is to create an atmosphere in which children can grow and change, no staff member can remain static. All employees must be aware of their own strengths and weaknesses and be helped to find ways to improve. If the atmosphere is one in which real learning is encouraged, the dynamics must apply to every staff member.

The Evaluation Process

Obviously, evaluation cannot focus in great detail on all areas. An overall evaluation in some specific areas may be enough at certain times. Whatever the focal point, the decision of when and what to evaluate should be a cooperative one between the evaluator and the person to be evaluated. No employee should be formally rated without knowing about it in advance.

Objectives

The procedure for evaluation should begin with an agreement between the director and the staff member concerning what is to be accomplished during a stated period of time. These expectations should flow from the statement of goals for the entire school or the job description for that position. For example, one of the school's goals might be the development of decision-making skills in children. The director and the teacher may list as many ways as possible this can be done. The evaluation will determine how effectively these were actually carried out.

Standards

The director and the staff member should also agree on the standards to be used in judging achievement or nonachievement. The staff member should know what will be considered a satisfactory level. In the example just given, the teacher should know whether all possible ways of developing decision-making skills must be implemented or whether a certain percentage will be acceptable. A refinement of this is the establishment of various levels of achievement: outstanding, superior, average, below average, and inferior, or like terms. Each of these should be defined as precisely as possible if they are to be used. A "pass" and "fail" standard is easier to understand, but it is sometimes more difficult to use.

The director and the staff member should decide when the rating will take place. There should probably be a written understanding that the evaluation will be done at a certain time and will cover a specified period. For instance, the rating will be done on March 8, and will cover the period from September 1 to March 8.

Both the evaluator and the person to be rated should agree on the form of the evaluation. Each one should understand that a checklist will be used, or that there will be two observations on certain dates (October 11 and March 8), followed by a conference. If the evaluator is going to observe, the staff member should know what the objectives are. If a checklist is to be used, the teacher should be given a copy well in advance of the first visit.

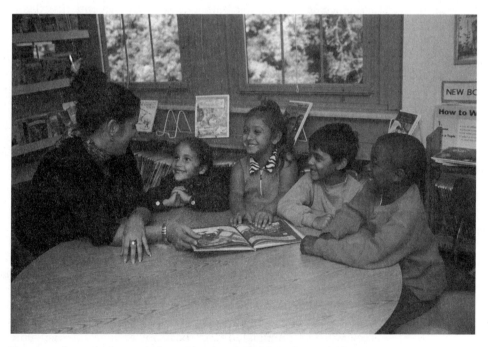

Teachers have their own styles of implementing learning activities.

Methods of Evaluation

In an earlier chapter, methods of evaluating curriculum were listed and examined. Similar procedures are used for evaluating staff members. Figure 8-1 contains a sample rating form for evaluations.

Tests

Tests are primarily an entry-level screening device. However, they can be used to gauge staff development, especially in subject matter areas. Colleges and universities offering teacher-training programs are a good source for locating appropriate test materials. Educational testing services are another source for prepared tests.

Knowledge of child development, curriculum construction, main points of nutrition, and first aid are topics that lend themselves to a prepared test. Professional organizations and universities are trying to develop teacher competency tests, but, in general, they are no substitute for direct observation.

Performance Elements

A newer approach to evaluation begins with the listing of the most important elements in the total job of teaching. This is a joint effort initiated by the director and executed by the teacher. From this list, both choose a number (usually three to five) of **critical job elements:** things that, if they were not done, would seriously impede the total teaching practice. Or both can agree to elements that this particular teacher wishes (or needs) to focus on for the next period. These elements would form the basis of evaluation for the next rating cycle. These elements will very likely be unique to each teacher. When these are agreed upon and written down, the director and teacher may try to agree on a rating scale of, again, three to five points (outstanding through unsatisfactory). The scale is far less important than is agreement on the major critical elements.

The performance elements methodology is an ongoing process. It probably should be for rather limited time periods and a restricted number of elements. One benefit of this method is that the director gets to know each teacher much more intimately than would be possible using almost any other rating method.

Observations

Once the staff member and director have agreed on objectives to be met, it is time to schedule observation visits to each classroom or work site. The staff member should know when the visit is scheduled. The director should plan to spend an adequate amount of time. It is important to record the visit as accurately as possible. (The director should use abbreviated words in order to record more information.) Some staff members may be open to the use of videotapes or a tape recording, but many will feel intimidated. It is best not to tape the visit unless the person is comfortable with it since it will not be an accurate record of performance anyway. The director should plan more than one observation at different times of the day or

---

RATING SHEET

Date _____

Name _____   Rated by _____

PERFORMANCE CHARACTERISTICS	Often	Sometimes	Never
Personal Qualities			
Has a sense of humor			
Is friendly, cheerful			
Assuming Responsibilities			
Is independent in assuming responsibilities			
Initiates solutions to problems			
Working with Children			
Determines and plans for each child's needs			
Creates a stimulating learning environment			
Working with Adults			
Cooperates with other staff members			
Includes parents in plans for their children			

Specific strengths _____

_____

Areas for improvements_____

_____

I have read this evaluation.

Signed: _____

(Employee and Title)

Further comments by either employee or supervisor _____

_____

FIGURE 8-1 ■ Sample rating form.

several over a period of a month. Examples should be recorded to substantiate the ratings. In that way, an evaluation will be more objective.

Sampling of Behaviors

Another method of evaluating teacher performance is to record samples of specific kinds of behavior. For example, a teacher might decide that one objective or critical element would be to encourage language development. One way to measure success in meeting this would be to count the number of words spoken by the teacher and by the children at a particular time. This count would be repeated at intervals. Analysis of the results would show whether the children were encouraged to talk. The evaluator can also make samplings of other behavior at specified intervals.

Another way to evaluate performance is to collect products made by the children. An increase in the number or changes in the quality would determine whether an objective or critical element had been achieved. As an example, if a teacher's objective was to develop more extensive use of art materials, a comparison of the number and quality of paintings at the beginning and the end of the semester would yield some information.

Questionnaire or Checklist

The evaluator may complete questionnaires or checklists privately or in the presence of the teacher in a colleague-like way. Self-designed lists may be constructed to be answered by a simple "yes" or "no," but these are often overly simplistic. Lists requiring longer answers or multiple responses are usually preferred. An example might be, "Does this teacher encourage the children to take care of their own physical needs?" The question may be answered *yes* or *no*, but it may also be answered on a scale such as *often, sometimes*, or *never*.

Use of Evaluations

Every evaluation should be followed by a conference between the evaluator and the staff member. The evaluator should focus first on the strengths that person exhibited during the assessment process. It is important to be specific, pointing out the ways in which teacher behaviors support the goals of the school. If there are areas that need improvement, the evaluator should be objective, relate all observations in a nonjudgmental manner, and then ask the staff member whether his or her perception is the same. If not, how is it different? Good questions to ask are "Why did you do it that way?" or "What was your reason for doing it that way?" A great deal can be learned by listening carefully to responses. There is seldom a "right way" in any teaching environment. What a teacher does should reflect sound educational practices, and there are many ways to do that.

Whatever the method or combination of methods of evaluation, there should be a permanent record of the results. The personnel file of each staff member should contain the periodic evaluations. Each staff member may then see the total picture of development, and the evaluator has a record of past performance.

A written copy of the evaluation should be given to each person evaluated. This can be a written copy of the rating or a summation of notes of the conference. There should be no doubt as to the outcome of the evaluation or the areas in which improvement is recommended. It is just as important to reward excellent performance with due praise. The employee should sign the evaluation form after reading it.

When a staff member gets an unsatisfactory or borderline rating, the director should make a great effort to bring about improvement. The director and employee must agree as to the specific steps to be undertaken. There are few things so discouraging as to be rated unsatisfactory without being told how to improve. Lists of things to do with milestone dates are sometimes helpful. Simple encouragement often works. Above all else, every attempt should be made to end on an optimistic note.

As will be seen later in this chapter, the evaluation process can reveal strengths and weaknesses in the teaching staff. A good many of these weaknesses, insofar as they involve lack of knowledge, may be remedied by various means of staff training.

Evaluation is an effective and powerful tool to be used with great care and sensitivity. It can be an instrument for change and self-growth. It can also produce profound discouragement if not done well. The following are suggestions for the evaluator:

- *Be objective*—Describe specific incidents to illustrate behavior being discussed. (Count them, if possible.)
- *Be gentle*—Discuss the positive things you have observed before going on to the negative.
- *Establish a climate for discussion*—Let staff members know what you are criticizing, but allow time to listen to their points of view. Try to look at the behavior from the teacher's view.
- *Be constructive*—Help teachers or other staff to find alternatives. Provide resources for further information where applicable. Offer help and continued support.
- *Be professional*—Do not discuss evaluations with other staff members unless they share evaluation responsibilities.

 STAFF DEVELOPMENT

Staff development is a broad term that refers to all the processes that encourage personal growth in employees in any work environment. In an early childhood setting it usually refers to procedures that help the teaching staff achieve greater professionalism. Earlier in this chapter, you read about the supportive relationship between a director and staff members that enables staff to try new ways of carrying out the various functions of their jobs. In addition, changes in teacher behaviors can be brought about through specific training activities.

Purpose of Training

All personnel in an early childhood facility come to the job with a certain level of skills and knowledge. Training activities should help them move to new levels of effectiveness in carrying out their jobs. Some beginning teachers, for instance, are at a "survival level." They just try to get through the difficulties of each day. In-service instruction can help them interact with children in ways that not only minimize their frustration, but also increase their enjoyment. Experienced teachers sometimes feel "stale" and in need of new ideas or challenges. Training can give these people curriculum ideas that will spark a new enthusiasm for teaching.

Another purpose of staff training is to help those who want to move to new job categories. Assistant teachers may dream of having their own class. A teacher may feel ready to assume some administrative tasks. A secretary may want to assist in the classroom. Training activities can give these employees opportunities to gain the skills necessary to move to those new positions.

Another important purpose of staff training is to develop professional identity. Teachers sometimes have difficulty defining who they are and relating the importance of what they do. Consequently, others also regard early childhood education as less important than other levels of schooling. As teachers gain knowledge and add to their skills, they will be able to take pride in their work and project a more professional image.

An additional reason for promoting staff development is that parents are much more demanding of their child's caregivers than they were in the past. Parents know more about child development and what their children should be learning. They ask teachers questions about their child's stage of growth. They want to know about the school's curriculum and to discuss issues of child rearing. Teachers must have the background to respond knowledgeably.

Stress and burnout are often a fact of life for those who staff all-day, year-round centers. Working with children is exhausting at best. It is even more difficult for the person who has minimal skills to deal with the problems that arise. Staff training can furnish some new strategies that minimize stress and decrease burnout.

Planning Staff Development

The director may want to offer staff training but not know how to get started. There is always so much new information available. Research studies and pilot programs reveal more and more information about children's development, curriculum, and family influences. By attending conferences or meeting with other professionals, directors gain new insights. It is difficult to choose from such a wide variety of training topics. So the director has to identify the areas the staff needs at a particular time. There are several ways to do this.

Staff-Needs Assessment

One of the simplest ways to find out the areas in which staff members need additional training is to establish an *open-door policy*. This means being available to listen to both staff members and parents, encouraging suggestions and discussion of issues, and being open to questions and ideas for change. In this kind of atmosphere, there is an opportunity to hear where teachers feel they need help or what parents want stressed.

Teachers can also be asked to do a *self-evaluation*. A rating scale or questionnaire are the simplest forms, but an evaluation can be as simple as asking staff members to indicate the areas in which they feel the need or the desire for additional training. Evaluation should be seen as an instrument for growth, not as a means for criticism.

Observations of staff members, both teaching and nonteaching, as they perform their jobs will also provide some ideas about training needs. In order to do this, the evaluator needs to have a good knowledge of each job. What are the basic tasks a person in this job must be able to do? In addition, what will make an "acceptable" performance and an "outstanding" one?

Information from professional sources will also provide data to use when planning staff training. Organizations such as the National Association for the Education of Young Children (NAEYC) have lists of competencies that teachers should acquire. College and university child development programs may also have compiled information about teaching skills.

The director should *get regular feedback* from employees about their own progress. Are they using information from previous training sessions? If not, what is standing in their way? It is possible they were not ready to use that information, but needed to "fill in some gaps" before doing so. It is important to give positive feedback when they are striving to be more capable.

The director should also *make a list* of topics individuals have indicated are training needs and circulate the list among all staff members. Nonteaching staff should be included because they, too, may want to know more about child development or how to manage child behaviors. The employees should rank the topics from most important to least important. Figure 8-2 is an example of a staff interest survey.

A staff-needs survey often highlights the fact that staff members have different levels of needs. Some people want only to add to the very basic information that all persons who interact with children need to know. Others want practical information such as planning a more exciting and challenging curriculum. Still others may be ready to explore theoretical issues such as learning theory or the influence of environment on children's development.

Size of Groups

Next the director decides if staff training will be for all personnel or for small groups at a time. When staff members are extremely diversified in their levels of knowledge, it sometimes is more feasible to divide them or even to provide individualized training for some. On the other hand, people learn from others. So sometimes a group with mixed abilities allows for learning from peers.

If the number of employees is large, meetings for the entire staff may be unwieldy for certain kinds of training activities. A discussion is difficult if there are more than 10 people. A workshop can accommodate as many as the space allows. Conversely, a small group sometimes needs outside stimulation and ideas. When the number of employees is small, the director might consider using films, lectures, or field trips.

Time

Finding the time for staff training is very difficult in an all-day school. Many schools resolve this problem by scheduling meetings while the children are napping. Teachers can rotate nap room duty, allowing the others to attend. The director should not make the mistake of always assigning one person to nap room duty, thus excluding that person from training sessions.

STAFF INTERESTS SURVEY

I need information concerning topics for upcoming staff training sessions. The following is a list of some suggestions that have been made in discussions with staff members. Choose six and rank them in importance to you with "1" being the highest priority.

_____ Ways to enhance children's language development

_____ Using computers in our classrooms

_____ Stimulating more creative outdoor play

_____ Involving children in snack preparations

_____ Individualized music activities

_____ Rearranging our environments to achieve our goals

_____ Carpentry skills for teachers

_____ Easy to plan and implement science activities

_____ Kits for stimulating dramatic play

_____ What are babies really learning?

_____ Conducting more effective parent conferences

_____ Avoiding burnout

Suggestions or comments:_____
_____
_____
_____

Please return your form to me by the end of the month so I can begin to plan upcoming sessions.

Thanks,

Betty Beaumont
Director of Country Day School

FIGURE 8-2 ■ Staff interests survey.

Another alternative is to schedule training meetings before or after school hours. A small group meeting could be held early in the morning before the children arrive. It is also possible to hold meetings right after the last child leaves in the evening. The staff could have a potluck dinner and have the meeting while they eat. This serves two purposes. It provides staff social time and avoids the fatigue that comes when staff must return later in the evening. When people are actively involved in discussion or an interesting workshop, they tend to overcome any fatigue they may have felt at the beginning. So if the activities are exciting, staff will be "recharged" rather than tired out at the end. Schedules for meetings should be set at regular intervals, preferably covering at least a six-month period. In this way, all staff members can plan their time to be available.

Place

The director must select an appropriate setting for the chosen kind of training activity. For a workshop, there must be enough space for everyone to work. Teachers who sit on child-size chairs all day will appreciate comfortable tables and chairs. For a discussion, it is important for everyone to be included. There should be no "back row sitters," for they will not really feel a part of the proceedings. For a sample staff meeting agenda, see Figure 8-3.

Attendance

A question many directors ask is whether attendance at training sessions should be required or voluntary. Staff will be there "in body" if it is required as a condition of

---

STAFF MEETING AGENDA

Thursday, February 19
7:00 p.m. Teachers' Lounge

   I. Discussion of individual children
     Patty will discuss Jerrod
     Suggestions

  II. Discussion of individual children
     Annemarie will discuss Emily
     Suggestions

 III. New children who have entered or will be entering
     Donna will give brief background information on each child

 IV. Report on recent professional conference attended by Donna and several
     teachers.
     Display new materials and resources
     Discuss new ideas

  V. Adjournment

FIGURE 8-3 ■ Sample staff meeting agenda.

employment, but they cannot be forced to learn. On the other hand, a purely voluntary training policy may result in avoidance by the people who need it most. It is probably best to require staff to attend and then make the training provocative and practical.

Skills Application

When a training session has been completed, staff will need to practice their new skills as soon as possible. The director should provide them with the materials they will need and allow them time to plan and prepare lessons. Following a science workshop, for instance, it is important to see that teachers have the kinds of equipment they need to put their new ideas into effect. Many teachers feel really anxious about offering science lessons and need a lot of encouragement. If they have the right equipment, they may feel a bit more secure.

Learning Styles

Just as children learn in very different ways, so do adults. Some people can learn by seeing or hearing information. Others need to be actively involved in doing before they learn. The director should ask staff members how they learn best and then choose training activities to meet those needs. For some, a workshop will be the best way to help them learn. For others, films, discussions, or even reading will turn out to be the most effective.

Popular Training Methods

Orientation

Training begins as soon as a new employee is hired. The director should start by giving the new worker the employee handbook and then sit down with that person to answer any questions. Next, the person should be taken to the work site (the classroom or the kitchen, for instance), shown where materials are and how to operate the equipment, and introduced to other staff members.

Orientation for teachers has some added dimensions from those of other employees. Teachers can read the philosophy and goals in the handbook, but they may need to understand how to implement them in the classroom. So, the director should spend extra time with all new teachers during the early weeks of employment. It is helpful to visit their classrooms briefly and get to know their teaching styles. (Visits too frequent or too lengthy may overwhelm or frighten some new teachers.) The director will need to meet more frequently with new teachers than with experienced staff. These can be brief meetings before or after school to answer questions or clarify problems. Additional effort in the beginning will often prevent difficulties down the line. Refer also to Chapter 7 for more extensive information on orientation.

Mentoring

A mentor program is one way to help new teachers or to upgrade the skills of more experienced teachers. In the context of education, a **mentor** is one who serves as a trusted counselor helping a teacher to perform more effectively. Program developers have identified requirements for mentors (Whitebrook, Hnatiuk, & Bellm, 1994; Bellm, Hnatiuk, & Whitebrook, 1996). A mentor should have a solid background in early childhood education and have spent time in a classroom or in family child care. Personal qualifications include good interpersonal skills, the ability to develop a supportive and trusting relationship with others, and experience or education in working with adults. They should also have a willingness to continue their own learning since many mentors say they learn as much from their trainees as they teach because they are forced to reevaluate their own methods. The mentor must also be committed to helping adults and have the time to devote to the process. Needless to say, the mentor should be paid for the time. This responsibility should not just be added to other duties without extra compensation.

A mentoring relationship differs from supervision. A supervisor has responsibility for evaluating the trainee; a mentor guides, supports, and encourages without being judgmental. Confidentiality is essential in this relationship in order to establish trust. The trainee must feel secure that whatever is discussed within the working relationship will not be shared with others. An exception, of course, would be if the protégé's actions in some way jeopardize the safety of children.

Professionals who adopt this kind of training use a variety of methods that seem to have positive results. They

- establish a relationship of trust with the protégé.
- observe for a whole day, then consider what changes are doable and which are not.
- model behavior.
- start an activity with children and ask the trainee to finish.
- give frequent and immediate feedback.
- ask questions that lead to thoughtful discussion. "What gave you the most difficulty today?" "What would have made it easier?" They discuss the responses.
- provide resources for information or materials as needed.
- are sensitive to the fact that adults have different styles and rates of learning just as children do.

Mentoring has proved an effective method of improving the quality of educational settings for children.

Those interested in starting a mentoring program can contact the National Center for the Early Childhood Work Force (NCECW) to receive training materials for mentors. Write to: National Center for the Early Childhood Work Force (NCECW), 733 15th Street, NW, Suite 1037, Washington, DC 20005–2112. Telephone 202–737–7700; fax 202–737–0370.

Team Teaching

Another way to provide informal and ongoing training is to set up a partnership style of training. In this method, two teachers work closely together as equal partners. They function as a team, with common aims. Each learns from the other, as they come to recognize their own strengths and weaknesses. To make this kind of relationship work, they must be able to overcome the competitiveness many teachers feel. They also have to spend time talking with each other, planning, learning, and resolving problems. The director should meet with them periodically to assess their progress and perhaps suggest resources for learning.

College and University Classes

Colleges and universities offer another source for training staff. The advantage of using this resource is that the courses are often taught by well-qualified persons with wide experience. In addition, other students from varied backgrounds offer stimulus for learning. The campus setting often offers facilities such as a laboratory school, a library, and even remedial help for those with learning or language difficulties.

It is important to weigh the disadvantages of college courses for staff training before choosing this method. The philosophy of the instructor may differ markedly from that of a particular director. It is disruptive when staff come back to school and want to carry out ideas that differ from the goals of their employer. The cost of tuition may be prohibitive for the student and more than a school can support. An added difficulty is that many college courses are scheduled during the day. Teachers who work all day cannot attend.

Staff Meetings

Staff meetings are a time for all staff members to communicate with one another, perhaps the only time during their busy days with children. This can be a fruitful time to clarify issues and brainstorm problems. In order to be effective, the director must create a climate in which each person's ideas and opinions are valued and where it is safe to express feelings. A skilled director who can accomplish this will foster a collegial climate as was discussed in the beginning of this text. He or she will also serve as a model for other staff members to emulate in their dealings with one another, with children, and with parents.

Each meeting should be planned to take into account concerns, needs, or questions of the director and staff members. The director should write out an agenda and distribute it to staff members at least a week ahead of time, add any information that needs to be read before the meeting, and post the schedule or place a copy in staff mailboxes (see Figure 8-3). The biggest mistake many directors make is trying to do too much at any one meeting. It is best to set limited objectives so there can be more thorough coverage. Whatever the topics, staff meetings should be an opportunity for everyone involved to learn something. A meeting might be devoted entirely to discussing several children who are creating problems for staff members. The primary teachers can present information about the children, with additional information from any other teachers who have contact with them. Another meeting might be devoted to some new curriculum ideas along with an opportunity to look at actual materials. Another kind of meeting might be one in which a major decision has to be made, for instance the purchase of some new playground equipment. Information about the options can be distributed, followed by a discussion of the pros and cons of each choice, then culminating with a decision.

Portfolio

Writing a portfolio can be a meaningful way for teachers to evaluate their own abilities and to upgrade their skills. It is a written documentation of what teachers do, why they do it, and how it relates to competency as a professional. Portfolios are used as a self-study vehicle and as the basis of discussions between teachers and supervisors. They are the primary means for assessing competency of Head Start teachers who are candidates for the CDA credential. However, portfolio writing is an effective instrument for staff development in any early childhood setting. An important benefit teachers will gain from portfolio writing is practice describing the teaching processes in their own words. As they learn to refine and clarify their writing, they will be able to view differently what they do. They will gain insight into their own strengths and weaknesses plus an awareness of where changes need to be made.

Directors should schedule time to discuss portfolio entries with teachers. This can be a time to focus on teachers' strengths and show genuine interest in their progress. A dialogue about recorded incidents will also provide a greater understanding of how each teacher functions in the classroom. At times, directors will need to answer questions or to be a resource for finding information.

Portfolio entries can be supplemented by videotapes of teachers as they work in the classrooms or on the playground. Obviously, one needs to have a good camera and someone with time to operate it. Introduction of this device as a method of training needs to be done with a great deal of sensitivity to people's feelings. Many people do not like to see themselves portrayed in photographs, and a video is even more revealing. The staff member to be taped must be included in the decision to do so and allowed to decide when and where the taping will be done. Following the taping session there must be time for the staff member to view the tape and to discuss it with the person responsible for training. The discussion should include ways to change or improve performance. If done carefully, videotaping can be a powerful tool for increasing staff competencies and self-esteem.

Workshops

A workshop is sometimes called a "hands-on experience." Participants get actively involved in doing or in making something to broaden their practical skills. In a workshop, teachers can learn songs, make curriculum materials, and practice reading or telling stories. A workshop could just as easily be planned for other job categories as well. Cooks from several schools could get together to try out new recipes that children might like.

Again, planning is the key to the success of a workshop. It is important to provide a comfortable setting and make sure that the task to be accomplished can be done in the time allotted. The director should have enough materials for everyone to use, distribute copies of directions or any information needed to complete the task, and be available to offer help or give encouragement as participants work.

Group Discussions

The format of a group discussion can range from open discussion during the entire meeting, to a short interchange following a presentation. Group discussion is one of the most effective ways to help adults learn. One of the tremendous advantages of this format is that often the whole staff can be included, not just teachers. Some of the same problems are encountered whether a staff member works in the kitchen, drives the bus, or manages a classroom. Each frequently has the same kinds of reactions to children's behaviors and needs to have an outlet for expressing those feelings.

Group discussions are an effective way to pursue a specific topic. As an example, discipline is a commonly requested topic for discussion. Ask any group of adults who are around children all day, and they will tell you that discipline is their biggest problem. It is possible to just give them a list of techniques to manage difficult children. But a more effective way of helping them is to encourage a discussion of their own feelings about children's behavior. They may find that their own reactions contribute to the trouble. Once they have gained that kind of insight, they will be more open to trying new techniques for managing children's behavior.

Role-Playing

Role-playing is a drama in which the participants put themselves into a designated situation. It is an informal type of meeting that can be adapted to many kinds of problems.

Role-playing is an excellent tool for resolving interaction problems between adults. Several participants act out the problem or situation. The audience watches, listens, and then discusses what happened. The "actors" can contribute how they felt as the play progressed. The final result may be a discovery of alternate ways of behaving, or just the insight gained from understanding the feelings involved. When two staff members are having a problem, it helps to ask them to role-play, reversing their parts. When each is asked to "assume the role" of the other, the situation may look quite different.

Exchange Observations

Exchanging observations between teachers within a school is another way of encouraging new ideas. By mutual agreement, two teachers observe each other in the classroom. After the visits, they meet to discuss their observations.

Obviously, this kind of staff training can work only when teachers trust and respect each other. It is not appropriate at the beginning of a school year, or with new or insecure teachers.

Films, Slides, and Tapes

Audiovisual materials add other dimensions to training sessions. Public libraries have many materials that are free. Some schools allow money in the yearly budget for renting or purchasing materials. It is also a good idea to watch the local television schedule for programs that can be used. (Copyright laws forbid keeping taped materials longer than 45 days.) If the director or a staff member owns a video camera, the school can make its own tapes. Slides or tapes are frequently available at professional conferences. NAEYC is an excellent resource for training materials. Some of their videos that can be used for staff training are the following:

- Building Bridges to Kindergarten: Transition Planning for Children
- Child Care Administration: Tying It All Together
- Culture and Education of Young Children
- Appropriate Curriculum for Young Children: The Role of the Teacher
- Designing Developmentally Appropriate Days
- Daily Dilemmas: Coping with Challenges
- Painting a Positive Picture: Proactive Behavior Management
- Partnerships with Parents
- Child Care and Children with Special Needs

This is only a partial list of videos available through NAEYC. Call 866-623-9248, fax 770-442-9742, or visit their Web site, http://www.naeyc.org, to receive their latest catalogue.

Field Trips

Field trips are another way to broaden staff members' learning. Some visits can be made as a group in the evening or on weekends. Others will have to be made by individuals when they can be relieved from duties at school. Visits to other schools always give teachers new ideas for curriculum or arranging their environment. Often, just the opportunity to talk to other teachers in different settings renews enthusiasm for teaching. On a weekend, the group could visit a supplier of learning materials. Many of these places have employees who are knowledgeable about children and can offer new ideas for learning activities.

Guest Speakers

It is often helpful to invite guest speakers to attend training meetings. The director should provide the speaker with information to use in determining the focus of the presentation and share any questions or interests staff members have communicated. The speaker should also know how much time is to be allowed and whether there will be time for

---

STAFF MEETING AGENDA

Thursday, May 28
7:00 p.m. Teachers' Lounge

  I. New enrollments
     Background information and assignment of new children

  II. Introduction of guest speaker
     Dr. Martha Emrin, Pediatrician
     She will discuss the inclusion of a child with AIDS.
     Ample time will be allowed for discussion and questions.

  III. Adjournment

You will find an article on pediatric AIDS in your mailbox. Please read it in preparation for this meeting.

FIGURE 8-4 ■ Sample staff meeting agenda which includes a guest speaker.

questions and discussion following the talk. Staff members should be provided with reading material if that is appropriate and asked to come prepared with questions they might want answered. After a meeting of this type, it is the director's responsibility to follow up with staff members to help them implement any new ideas they have gained from the session. See Figure 8-4 for a sample staff meeting agenda which includes a guest speaker.

Professional Meetings

Staff should be encouraged to attend meetings and conferences of professional organizations. Chapters of NAEYC are found in many areas of the United States. Everyone on staff will benefit from membership. Meetings and conferences offer a wide variety of speakers, workshops, and displays from which teachers can learn. Publications are also available through the organization.

Reading

It is worthwhile to provide employees with books, pamphlets, and magazines that will help them develop their skills. The director can encourage them to use the materials by bringing some to a staff meeting and pointing out some of the interesting articles or parts of a book that they might want to read. The collection should be expanded as often as possible. If the budget is limited and does not allow for the purchase of books, the director can make a list of what is available in the public library and distribute copies to the staff.

Format for Training Sessions

It may be helpful to have in mind some principles for effective training sessions that can be used for several different methods. They can be varied to fit each method of training. The following are some guidelines:

- Arrange the setting for the purpose of the session.
- Provide participants with an agenda, including objective.
- Prepare the setting ahead of time.
  a. Put out materials, arrange chairs, provide coffee or other beverages.
  b. Check audiovisual equipment if to be used.
- Carry out the procedure as planned.
  a. Begin and end at the time planned.
  b. Stay as close as possible to the objective.
- Ask participants to evaluate the meeting.
- Follow through.
  a. Provide materials so participants can practice new skills.
  b. Get feedback after staff put new ideas into practice.

 ## STAFF RELATIONSHIPS

A discussion of staff development would not be complete without considering how the people in a school get along with each other. They spend long hours together each day. Nerves become frayed with the constant demand that young children make on their patience and energy. Bickering, competitiveness, or burnout may result. The director, is the key person in changing destructive patterns of interacting to ones that are positive and cooperative.

Communication

The director should start by helping the staff to develop good communication skills. One way is to plan a workshop on effective communication using Thomas Gordon's "I" messages. The staff is asked to practice stating problems or concerns by starting a sentence with phrases such as "I feel sad," "I get upset," or "I am discouraged." The group discusses how the listener might react when this approach is used. It is important to consider nonverbal communication as well. What type of message is conveyed by a clenched jaw, tightly folded arms, lack of eye contact, or raised eyebrows? This discussion can be followed with a role-play. The participants are asked to note whether "I" messages were used and whether what was said was congruent with the body language used.

After this kind of workshop, staff members should be encouraged to resolve some of their own problems. Rather than having them expect intervention each time a difference arises, the director should send them back to talk to each other. They will probably find they like the feeling of competence that comes from dealing with difficulties themselves. They will also develop closer rapport with one another.

At staff meetings, it is important for each member to participate. In any group of people, some speak out whether they have something meaningful to say or not. Others seldom say anything. The director should limit the participation of the "big talkers" and encourage the nonparticipants to contribute.

Decision Making

When there is a democratic atmosphere in a school, staff will want to be included in important decisions that affect them. Effective directors will encourage this kind of participation. The purchase of expensive pieces of playground equipment is an example. Some staff members will request one kind and others want another. If the director chooses, part of the staff will be happy and the other part disgruntled. It is better for them to go through a decision-making process and make the choice themselves. They will learn from the process and will probably be more satisfied with the result.

To decide which playground equipment to purchase, the staff could go through the following steps.

1. *Gather information.* In this case, they will want to find out as much as they can about the possible choices. What do the pieces look like and how long are they expected to last? What is the cost of each piece? What possible uses can children make of each? Is there a good place on the playground to put all the pieces?

2. *Set priorities.* The next step is to list their priorities based on the goals of the school. One piece may lend itself to imaginative play, while the other will develop children's physical abilities. Which will more closely fit the school's goals?

3. *Make a choice.* A consensus should be reached among staff about which one to choose.

4. *Decide how to implement the choice.* Is the equipment to be purchased immediately? Will it be installed during school hours so the children can watch, or on weekends so the children can be surprised?

5. *Evaluate the choice.* For future learning, the staff should evaluate the decision after a period of time to determine whether the choice was a good one. In this example, are the children using the equipment as expected? Are there other ways it is used that weren't expected? Should a different choice have been made?

This process of decision making has been described in terms of a concrete object, the piece of equipment. The same steps can be adapted to other kinds of decisions.

 ## BURNOUT

Stress and burnout are problems that plague many people who work in jobs that require a lot of emotional energy. The very character of early childhood programs contributes to the likelihood of staff burnout. Several causes of burnout can be identified.

Causes

Lack of recognition as a professional is one cause that is often listed by teachers. Their low status is reflected in the minimum salaries that many schools pay their staff. Along with low pay, few have fringe benefits such as a medical or retirement plan. Low status is also seen in the reaction of some parents to early childhood teachers and caregivers. They may comment "You only play with the children all day," or they refer to the child care center teacher as their child's "babysitter." Few parents have a real idea of the curriculum of their child's school and, thus, little appreciation of what is being taught. All these things contribute to feelings by teachers that they are not worth very much.

Time pressures also lead to fatigue and burnout. Child care teachers spend six to eight hours a day with children. During that time, children's demands leave little opportunity for any planning or preparation. Few schools pay teachers for time away from the children. Any work they might do to enhance classroom activities must be done at the end of a long day. Consequently, planning may be haphazard, further contributing to dissatisfaction with their job.

An unrealistic view of their role may be another cause of burnout in teachers. In their book *Planning and Administering Early Childhood Programs*, Decker and Decker, (2001) write that teachers are "unable to maintain a detached concern" because they see themselves as surrogate parents. These authors also feel that teachers are so indoctrinated with the importance of the early years that they are let down if they don't achieve what they expect. Preschool teachers do often feel personally responsible for the development of the children in their care. Any achievements the children make confirm their own value as teachers. Any failures to move forward are considered evidence of the teachers' failures.

Classroom management problems sometimes cause extreme stress, and then teacher burnout. One difficult child in a group can create chaos for all the others if the behavior is not curbed. Inexperienced teachers who have not developed ways of managing these children have an especially difficult time. More experienced teachers, who still have difficulty being firm, may also find this kind of child "trying."

Administrative incompetence and insensitivity should certainly be mentioned in a discussion of burnout. This refers to directors who fail to take into account the needs or feelings of employees. Sometimes this happens when directors make decisions that affect staff without consulting them. Other times, directors are unaware of how teachers feel. When asked, teachers will describe a variety of behaviors that fall into this category. "I came in one morning to find that I had two new children in my group." "I was told that I couldn't take the time off to go to my daughter's school play because they couldn't pay a substitute." "My director does not really understand how much that one child disrupts my group. She says I should be able to control him." All these examples are indications that the directors did not take the time to consider their employees' feelings. The result could be built-up resentment and then burnout.

Prevention

A variety of sources offer suggestions for alleviating stress and preventing burnout. The following have been culled from several of these sources. For more in-depth reading, look to the Selected Further Reading at the end of this chapter. Among the items on the following list, there are some that the director can facilitate. The others can be passed on to employees as suggestions to help themselves.

1. Deal with problems as they occur. Don't let them build up. Discuss problems in a nonconfrontational manner.

2. Find an outlet for tension that works for you. Try walking, gardening, games, crossword puzzles, and so on. Stay away from the things that work for only a short time, such as eating or drinking too much.

3. Learn more about child development. When you know what to expect of children at different age levels, you will be neither surprised when some behaviors appear, nor disappointed when others don't.

4. Be prepared each day with lesson plans, but be flexible and willing to adapt or change those plans as needed.

5. Keep records on children so that you can really see they have made some progress.

6. Try to detach yourself from situations that can't be changed. There will always be some children you cannot change or some families you cannot help. Learn to accept this.

7. Keep in good physical health. Get enough sleep; eat a balanced diet.

8. Get away from the children for brief periods during the day. A 10-minute break can definitely help.

9. Try to avoid getting caught up in the daily "gripe sessions" with fellow employees. It does little good and only makes you feel worse.

10. Become an advocate for recognition of early childhood education as a profession with adequate and competitive compensation.

The challenge as a director of a school for young children is to help the staff become the very best they possibly can be. This is admittedly more formidable than trying to help children change. Adults are less malleable and are more set in their ways. They resist any change with reactions of anger or anxiety. But when the director begins to see the results of a good staff training program, it will be clear that all the efforts have been worth it.

 ## SUMMARY

Staff members in early childhood programs take different paths to become teachers: the traditional path of academic preparation, the parent path of experience, and the accidental path beginning with an unrelated job. All are needed to care for the children who are in group settings.

Directors who value individual differences will be faced with the task of helping each to grow as professionals. This can be accomplished through fair and effective methods of supervision and evaluation, followed by training activities. Another way that teachers can become more professional is to participate in the Child Development Associate credential program.

Supervision means overseeing staff members during the performance of their jobs. It is also a constantly changing relationship between director and employees.

Evaluation is a process to determine if the goals of an early childhood center are being met. The evaluation process should begin with an agreement on goals to be reached during the time period being assessed and include standards of measurement. Methods of evaluation may be a combination of tests, observations, samplings of behavior, questionnaires, and checklists. A record of evaluation results should be placed in personnel files and a written copy given to the teacher. Every evaluation should be followed by a conference between the director and the staff member.

Staff development is a broad term that refers to all the processes that encourage personal growth in employees in any work environment. In an early childhood setting, it refers to procedures that help teaching staff achieve greater professionalism. Staff training needs are revealed during supervision and evaluation activities. Other sources of information include staff self-evaluation and information from professional sources.

The director should plan training activities by grouping staff appropriately, finding a time that fits staff schedules, choosing a place that fits the activity, and deciding whether attendance is voluntary or mandatory. When a training session is completed, staff should be encouraged to practice their new skills.

Popular training methods are orientations, mentor relationships, team teaching, college classes, staff meetings, portfolio writing, workshops, group discussions, role-playing, exchange observations, audiovisual materials, field trips, guest speakers, professional meetings, and reading.

Staff development must include helping staff get along with one another. They will benefit from practice in communication and decision making.

Burnout may occur among persons who work in early childhood settings. It is important to identify the cause and to provide staff with suggestions for preventing or alleviating stress.

REFERENCES

Bellm, D., Hnatiuk, P., & Whitebrook, M. (1996). *The early childhood mentoring curriculum: A trainer's guide and mentor handbook.* Washington, DC: National Center for Early Childhood Work Force.

Decker, C. A., & Decker, J. R. (2001). *Planning and administering early childhood programs* (7th ed.). New York: Prentice Hall

Whitebrook, M., Hnatiuk, P., & Bellm, D. (1994). *Mentoring in early care and education: Refining an emerging career path.* Washington, DC: National Center for Early Childhood Work Force.

SELECTED FURTHER READING

Abbot-Shim, M. (1990). In-service training: A means to quality care. *Young Children, 45* (2), 14–18.

Bloom, P. J. (1988). *A great place to work: Improving conditions for staff in young children's programs.* Washington, DC: National Association for the Education of Young Children.

Bredekamp, S. (1992). Composing a profession. *Young Children, 47* (2), 52–54.

Caruso, J. J. (1991). Supervisors in early childhood programs: An emerging profile. *Young Children, 46* (6), 20–24.

Eiselen, S. (1992). *The human side of child care administration.* Washington, DC: National Association for the Education of Young Children.

Epstein, A. (2002, January/February). Early childhood professionals: Current status and projected needs. *Child Care Information Exchange, 243,* 45–48.

Feeney, S., & Freeman, N. K. (2002, January/February). Early childhood education as an emerging profession: Ongoing conversations. *Child Care Information Exchange, 143,* 38–41.

Forrest, R., & McCrea, N. (2002, January/February). How do I relate and share professionally? *Child Care Information Exchange, 143,* 49–52.

Goffin, S., & Lombardi, J. (1988). *Speaking out: Early childhood advocacy.* Washington, DC: National Association for the Education of Young Children.

Hildebrand, V. (2003). *Management of child development centers* (5th ed). New York: Merrill.

Levine, M. (1992). Observations on the early childhood profession. *Young Children, 47* (2), 50–51.

Washington, V. (1996). Professional development in context: Leadership at the borders of our democratic, pluralistic society. *Young Children, 51* (6), 30–34.

Whitebrook, M., & Bellm, D. (1996). Mentoring for early childhood teachers and providers: Building upon and extending tradition. *Young Children, 52* (1), 59–64.

 ## STUDENT ACTIVITIES

1. With permission of the director, survey the staff members of a child care center. Ask the following questions:
    a. How long have you been a teacher/caregiver?
    b. Where did you work before your present position?
    c. What kinds of academic preparation or experience qualified you for this job?

    Summarize your findings. Compare the profiles of staff members at this center with the three paths leading to a teaching profession that are described in this chapter.

2. Interview a director of a child care center. Ask about the methods used to evaluate teachers. Are support staff evaluated as well? If so, what methods are used?

3. Plan a staff training workshop. State specifically what will be accomplished, materials needed, and room arrangement. If possible, implement your plan at the school where you work. How successful was the session? Are there things you should have done differently?

CASE STUDY

Eva has been a preschool teacher for the last 15 years. Over these years she has worked in toddler, two-, and four-year-old programs. Generally speaking, she works well with children, families, and staff. As of late, she seems to be in a "slump." Her lesson plans have been lacking creativity, and she has been impatient with the children and other staff members. Late one evening, the director of the center received a complaint from one of the children's mothers. According to Mrs. Guirreza, Eva was angry with Angelita because she had refused to participate in an activity and was poking other children during circle time. Eva yelled at the child and Angelita began to cry. Mrs. Guirreza is concerned because her daughter does not want to return to the center. She did not like the way Eva handled the situation and feels that perhaps Eva shouldn't continue working with children.

1. How should the director respond to Mrs. Guirreza? What is appropriate information to share with her about "burnout" in the child care industry?

2. What can the director do to help Eva and other staff members to prevent or overcome burnout?

3. How could the director plan a staff development day to further educate and rejuvenate the staff members?

 REVIEW

1. There are three different paths that lead to becoming teachers or caregivers. What are they?

2. Teachers must show evidence that they are competent in six areas in order to qualify for a Child Development Associate credential. List the six competencies.

3. Define the words *supervision* and *evaluation*.

4. Briefly describe the following methods of evaluation and the ways they are used:
   a. tests
   b. performance elements
   c. sampling of behaviors
   d. observations
   e. questionnaire or checklist

5. State two purposes of staff training.

6. Finding time for staff training is often difficult in an all-day school. What suggestions were made in this chapter?
7. List seven popular training methods.
8. Discuss the use of portfolio writing as a staff training method.
9. Describe the steps in setting up a training session.
10. List the steps in a democratic decision-making process.
11. What are the causes of professional burnout?
12. List the suggestions for preventing burnout.

HELPFUL WEB SITES

Council for Early Childhood
Professional Recognition: http://www.cdacouncil.org

Center for Career Development
in Early Care and Education: http://institute.wheelock.edu

Center for Child Care Workforce: http://www.ccw.org

For additional resources related to administration, visit the Online Resource® for this book at www.EarlyChildEd.delmar.com

9

Student Teachers/Volunteers

KEY TERMS

master teacher
student teacher
volunteer

Objectives

After reading this chapter, you should be able to:

- Describe the role of director regarding student teachers.
- List the criteria for choosing a master teacher.
- Discuss how children may react to student teachers.
- Explain how volunteers may most effectively be used.
- List several sources of volunteers.
- Define what qualities make volunteers most valuable.
- Describe how volunteers may be trained.

A Day In The Life Of ...

A Coordinator of a College Laboratory Center

7:30 A.M. Arrive and greet the staff. Check voice mail. Messages from students who cannot work today. Adjust staffing accordingly. Greet children who are arriving. Gather materials for college course later in the day. Counsel a walk-in student about classes for summer and fall.

8:30 A.M. Confer with practicum students, observe their activity setups. Set up video camera and turn on microphones in observation room.

9:00 A.M. Greet parents who are leaving children for room #1 morning program.

9:15 A.M.   Begin videotaping student's group time.

9:40 A.M.   Return phone calls; one from a dean who wants me to proof next fall's schedule of classes. Walk through both classrooms to observe today's teacher, students, and children.

10:00 A.M.   Greet Practicum 1 students and clarify assignments.

10:40 A.M.   Selectively videotape another student project.

11:00 A.M.   Return two more phone calls. Rush to dean's office to proofread schedule. Rush back. Write an accident report for a child with a minor bump. Administer first aid to another who has been accidentally hit on the head with a shovel. Write an accident report. Walk outside to observe Practicum 1 and 2 students on the playground.

11:30 A.M.–12:20 P.M.   Videotape a student, greet parents, evaluate students who have done projects today.

12:20 P.M.   Lunch—whew!

12:50 P.M.   Gather my thoughts and material and prepare to teach a college course.

1:00–3:00 P.M.   Teach Practicum 2 course—lecture, discussions, hands-on experiences.

3:00 P.M.   Scan mail, gather staff for meeting. Today's agenda includes: staffing for expansion, materials to order for expansion, and further discussion about changes in program philosophy.

4:00 P.M.   Staff leaves for the day. Back to the mail, sort, read some information, put some on secretary's desk for filing, enter meeting dates on calendar. Work on the computer: two student recommendation letters and new ideas for parent handbook. Grade student lesson plans.

5:30 P.M.   Go home, taking student language assignments from Practicum 1 to grade tonight.

Life? What's that?

Many postsecondary institutions offer a course in early childhood education or related fields. Often, degree requirements for these fields include some time spent in practical experience with children. Practice teaching, sometimes called field experience, provides that exposure.

Although some of these institutions have their own laboratory schools where students get their practical experience, many do not. To fill the need for field experience, they use schools and child care centers in their communities. Even when there is a lab school, many use outside placements to provide additional experience for students. Community schools are seen as a step into "the real world." Thus, if a center is chosen to be an outside placement for the local college, both director and staff members should be fully informed before accepting. They should know what will be expected of them in terms of supervision of the students and how much classroom experience the students will have had, if any.

CHARACTERISTICS OF STUDENT TEACHERS

Student teachers, like volunteers, are unpaid. However, they differ from volunteers in some significant ways.

Before they come to a school, student teachers will have taken some courses in early childhood development. They usually have a basic knowledge of the stages of growth. In curriculum courses, they have been taught how to plan learning activities. They may have some understanding of children's behavior from formalized opportunities to observe children.

Student teachers receive college credit for their field experience so they are likely to have a commitment to completing the required number of hours. As part of their teaching assignment, they must plan lessons and then present them. They usually are eager to use the skills they have learned in their course work.

Student teachers know they will be evaluated on their work in the classroom. This brings about a certain amount of anxiety in some, but it also causes them to work harder to do well. They are aware that future jobs may depend on their success in student teaching.

Many student teachers are quite young, in their early twenties or younger. They may have chosen this field because they enjoyed caring for younger siblings at home. Their age and experience place these young people somewhere between adolescence and adulthood in their own development. Sometimes their interactions with children are more like that of siblings than teacher to child. On the other hand, their youth and energy enable them to interact with children enthusiastically. They often bring a sparkle to the classroom that is missing when teachers are becoming burned out.

Today, more and more older women are returning to college. They, too, liked being with their children, so they turn to early childhood education as a career. But their performance in student teaching is different from that of the young students. Because of their maturity and experience, they play more of a parental role in their interactions with children. They tend to accept children's behavior more easily since they have been through it all at home.

Some student teachers may be young men. Although the low salary level keeps many from entering this field, a few choose to do so in spite of the low income. Their presence is particularly valuable in today's schools where many of the children do not have fathers living with them. "Psychological fathers" is the term David Giveans, producer and narrator of the film *Men in Early Childhood Education*, uses to describe these teachers. He views the male teacher of young children as a balancing role model in the traditionally female world of the preschool.

ROLE OF THE DIRECTOR

Directors usually have limited direct participation with student teachers. Their main responsibility is to see that the partnership with the college or university is a positive one for all involved. A secondary responsibility is to support **master teachers** as they work with the students. This may involve resolving problems, providing suggestions, or acting as a liaison with the student's institution.

Each student teacher is assigned to a classroom under the direction of a staff member, who is often called a master teacher. Students may spend one or several days a week in this placement. The master teacher and student should meet after each day of practice teaching, so teachers will need extra time for this purpose. Because of the extra time and energy needed, they should be relieved of some other responsibilities. The director should acknowledge their efforts by praise or a salary differential if possible and be prepared to give support or help to resolve any problems that arise.

All master teachers should be notified well in advance of the time a student will be starting an assignment. Teachers should have plenty of time to prepare for the arrival of a new person in the classroom. They will want to let parents know about the student. Children should certainly be told. Teachers can tell children, "Melissa will be coming to our room tomorrow and will be here every Tuesday. She is learning how to be a teacher at her own school. She will be one of your teachers on that day and will read stories, help with art, and do a lot of other things with us."

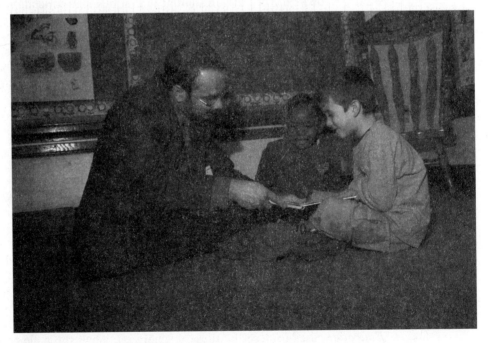

Male teachers make good role models.

An adviser or supervisor is usually appointed by the students' institution to work with their off-campus placements. Directors and master teachers should meet with the adviser before the placement starts in order to clarify goals and discuss expectations for the students. This is also a good time to determine when and how often the college supervisor will visit.

 ## CHOICE OF A MASTER TEACHER

Several teachers in a school may indicate their willingness to accept student teachers into their classrooms. It is up to the director to decide whether each of these staff members will be able to offer a good learning atmosphere for the students.

The first determinant should be *willingness* to accept a student teacher. Some teachers may not feel ready to work with student teachers. The director should respect their judgment and not try to change their minds. It is important to discuss their reasons with them but they should be allowed to decline. They may feel more capable later.

Teachers must be amenable to *sharing* children and teaching tasks with student teachers. Most teachers are accustomed to being in charge of all the day-to-day planning and execution of activities. They cherish and jealously guard their close relationships with children. When they decide to accept a student teacher, they must be able to give up some of this autonomy. They will need to step back while student teachers learn how to manage children, and watch while student teachers carry out lessons. At first many find it painful, but later they take pride in the increasing competence of their student teachers.

Master teachers must have enough *self-confidence* to withstand the kinds of questions student teachers are likely to ask. From their curriculum courses, student teachers often have formed their own ideas about how lessons should be planned or presented. They may have learned methods of teaching or ways of interacting with children that are different from the master teacher's. They often ask "Why?" when they see things that are unlike what they have been taught. Their questions give them the opportunity to test out their knowledge, but it takes a strong teacher not to feel intimidated.

Master teachers must be able to *allow others to make mistakes*. Many can excuse children but are intolerant when adults make mistakes. When student teachers plan a lesson that turns out to be a fiasco, they get terribly upset. A good master teacher will help the student teacher see what went wrong and make suggestions for changes the next time.

Just as with children, *positive feedback* works with student teachers. The master teacher who can be liberal with praise and positive feedback will give the shaky student teacher more confidence. A good laugh about the disaster of the day helps to put things in proper perspective. Reassurance that the ability to be a good teacher takes time will do wonders.

The most obvious characteristic needed by master teachers is to be good *role models* themselves. Student teachers will observe and often copy what their master teacher does. The director should choose only the best teachers to help student teachers.

ORIENTATION OF STUDENT TEACHERS

Orientation for student teachers is similar to the introduction given to paid staff members or volunteers. In this case, though, some will take place on the student's campus and some in their off-campus placement. Often the campus coordinator prepares a handbook for student teachers in addition to presenting information in a preplacement seminar. The director and master teachers should have a copy of the handbook and other information presented to the student teachers by the coordinator. Orientation at the school should then supplement campus orientation.

A student teacher should know the following:

- *Details of the placement*—hours, number of weeks, holidays. A calendar will clarify dates.
- *Evaluation procedures*—who will evaluate, when it will be done, how a grade will be given.
- *Supervision*—when college adviser will visit, what will be observed.
- *Requirements*—written lesson plans, daily log, additional papers.
- *Extra activities*—attendance at staff meetings, parent meetings, parent conferences.
- *Absences*—procedures for reporting to school and making up the time.

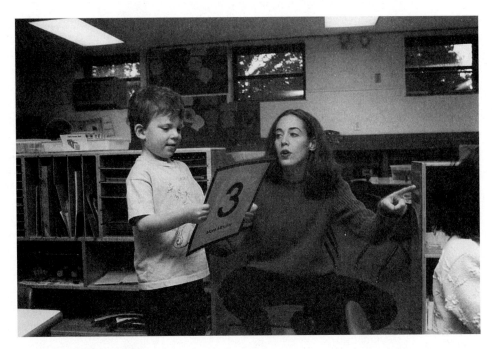

Student teaching is hard work.

- *Organization of school*—lines of responsibility.
- *School characteristics*—goals, grouping of children.
- *Curriculum*—overall curriculum of class where student teacher is assigned.
- *Discipline*—school policies for disciplining children.
- *Children*—general information about children in student teacher's class. (Further information about children should be left to the director discretion.)
- *Problems*—procedures for reporting and resolving any problems student teacher might have.
- *Professionalism*—professional conduct and attitude.

It is important that the director and master teacher expect student teachers to have respect for the diversity of the children in the program. If they have not had that preparation in their college course work or have developed a narrow perspective on multiculturalism and anti-bias, it is the responsibility of the director and master teacher to include this in an orientation process (Neuharth-Pritchett, Reiff, & Pearson, 2001). Student teachers need to participate in discussions of what diversity means and how it should be implemented in the classroom. They should have an opportunity to explore their own attitudes and ways of interacting with persons from cultures other than their own. In the classroom, they should have an opportunity to observe models of multicultural implementation.

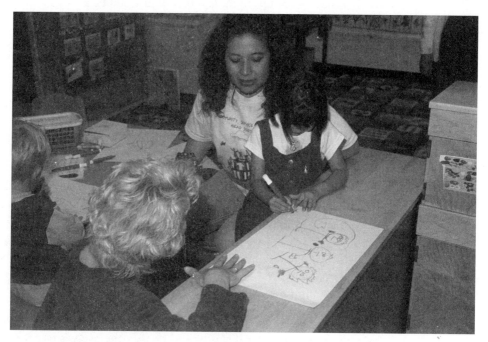

A student teacher begins by observing.

RESPONSIBILITIES OF THE MASTER TEACHER

The master teachers are key persons when student teachers are placed in community schools. It is they who have daily contacts with the student teachers and who make it either a positive or negative experience. The following are some practical suggestions for master teachers.

- Learn as much about the student teacher's background as possible. Often the college will supply information concerning the courses the student teacher has taken and kinds of experience completed.
- Introduce the student teacher to children, parents, and other staff members. Treat the student teacher like a colleague.
- Allow time for the student teacher to become familiar with the total school environment, the assigned room, and the storage areas.
- Allow the student teacher time to observe before taking over any part of the program.
- Discuss school goals with the student teacher, indicating how these are implemented on a day-to-day basis.
- Plan a calendar for the student teacher to gradually assume teaching responsibilities.
- Pace the student teacher's teaching responsibilities according to readiness to do so. Some student teachers are ready to "plunge in" immediately, but others need time to get acquainted with the setting and the children.
- Let the student teacher know that failure can be a way of learning. Suggest changes and encourage the student teacher to try again.
- Allow the student teacher to try out new ideas. Student teachers often bring a fresh approach to teaching. However, discuss lesson plans before they are presented. Slight changes may forestall problems.
- Schedule time for regular conferences. After each teaching day is the best time. Discuss lessons the student teacher presented as well as interactions with children. Make suggestions for changes if needed.
- Be generous in providing materials and resources to the student teacher.
- Evaluate the student teacher's performance midway in the assignment. This allows time for improvement in any areas that need it.
- Maintain continual communication with the college adviser concerning the student teacher's progress. Immediately discuss any problems. Don't let difficulties build up until they cannot be resolved.
- Be objective when writing the final evaluation. Remember the evaluation may affect the student teacher's future job opportunities.

REACTIONS OF STUDENT TEACHERS

Student teachers often arrive at an outside placement with mixed feelings. If directors can remember what it was like when they themselves faced a group of children for the first time, they will be able to avoid some problems. It will be helpful to review some of the concerns expressed by student teachers.

Student teachers often say they are unsure of their role in the classroom. During their practice teaching period, they take on many of the teaching tasks. But they often do not know how far they can go to make changes in the classroom environment or activities. Children sometimes say, "You're not my real teacher," making it even more difficult for the student teacher.

Student teachers may be afraid that the children will not like them. When the children do not respond immediately to student teachers, they often interpret it as dislike. Student teachers get the same feelings if the children refuse an activity they have prepared.

Gaps in their knowledge may make some student teachers uneasy. They may have learned that two-year-olds often bite other children, but they do not know what to do when confronted with this behavior. They may be afraid that if they ask for help they will be considered inadequate.

Some master teachers push student teachers into assuming too many responsibilities too soon. As a result, the student teachers feel exploited. They work while the master teacher takes it easy.

"Tell me what to say when . . ." is a frequently heard plea from student teachers. When the answer isn't readily available, they feel frustrated. They sometimes think experienced teachers have found the magic formula but are withholding the information from them.

Young student teachers sometimes identify more closely with the feelings of the children than with adults. They may become upset when the master teacher disciplines a child or at the way a parent reacts. It is hard for them to see the situation from the viewpoint of the adult.

When first confronted with the intensity of their own feelings, they may become afraid of their reactions to children. The first time they get really angry at a child, they worry they will never become good teachers. Or conversely, they often fear becoming too attached to children because they know that parting from them will be painful.

Student teachers are being graded, so there is a tremendous pressure to perform well. They often feel that their every word and action are being judged. They are certain that every mistake or lapse is noted and will be criticized.

Welcoming student teachers into a school can be a rewarding adventure for everyone. It can bring new life to a program and give teachers an added dimension of experience. They can feel proud to be able to foster the professional growth of a

In 2002, 44 percent of adults report they volunteer regularly, once a month or more. Women are more likely to volunteer than men, and 59 percent of teenagers volunteer an average of 3.5 hours per week. The volunteer workforce represented the equivalent of 9 million full time employees or a value of 239 billion dollars.

Source: 2002 news release of a survey by the Independent Sector organization. From: http//www.independentsector.org, 2003

neophyte teacher. But it can also be difficult and time consuming. If one follows these logical and progressive steps, the chances for success are good. Time and patience are rewarded.

VOLUNTEERS

Volunteers share some of the characteristics of student teachers. Generally, however, volunteers have less theoretical background in child development. Both groups are normally enthusiastic and eager, but the basic motivations differ. Student teachers have made a commitment to early childhood education as a career. Volunteers may be equally sincere, but they generally have different goals and experiences.

All that considered, volunteers may add a whole new dimension to a school. They are almost always filled with vigor and energy. Used with perception and care, they may supplement areas of a school that may badly need bolstering. Two criteria are foremost: selection and training.

A PLAN FOR VOLUNTEER SERVICES

Before deciding to include volunteers, it is important to establish needs. The director should distribute a questionnaire to teachers, asking if they need help, the times that would be most helpful, and the kinds of services they need. This may yield the information that the need is varied, ranging from supervising while a teacher takes a short break, to long-range planning for a parent event. There may even be some staff members who do not want volunteers at all. Their wishes should be honored. The next step is to consult others in the child care organization, board members, or higher-level administrators. It also makes good public relations to ask nonteaching staff and parents of the children. There should be some consensus of opinion that volunteers would be welcome and useful.

The Volunteer Coordinator

Someone on the full-time staff should be appointed as the coordinator of volunteers. This usually will not be a full-time position. In a small school, the director will probably be chosen. But one person must have the responsibility of selecting, training, assigning, and evaluating each volunteer. The stakes are too high to have unsupervised volunteers at large in a school. After the program has been successful for a period of time, it may be possible to use a volunteer as a coordinator.

The coordinator should know each person in the program as intimately as possible. The school should be able to use the volunteers' strengths wisely and avoid their weaknesses. The coordinator should know training methods and which ones to apply to each volunteer. But mostly, the coordinator must be "inspirational" and be able to praise sincerely. Although praise may be the only reward most volunteers will get, directors can also verify their efforts in reference letters.

RECRUITMENT OF VOLUNTEERS

Very likely, the best volunteers are recruited from people already known to the staff. These are parents, grandparents, and other relatives, primarily. In general, it is far better to seek a volunteer than to accept one casually.

Senior citizens' groups are an often-overlooked source. The American Association of Retired Persons (AARP) has a special section of members who have volunteered to work in the community. If there is not a local chapter of the AARP in the neighborhood, they may be reached at 601 E. St., NW, Washington, DC 20049. Retired executives are often eager to give help in business problems and budgeting. Counselors and other retired professionals may be available. If a school has an infant program, older persons are often helpful in nurturing situations.

Some older people enjoy reading stories to children. Art specialists who have retired are useful. Seniors have been known to staff telephone hotlines for "latchkey" children. The benefits are not entirely one way. Seniors seem to benefit greatly by their contacts with young children. However, screening of individuals is

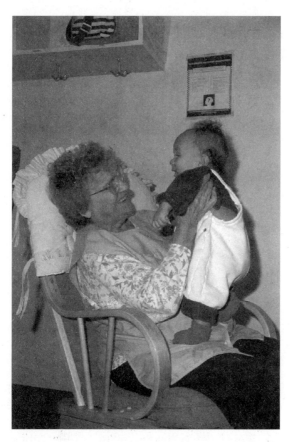

Senior volunteers do many jobs.

important here. The director must be aware of health considerations, including a chest X-ray for participants.

An increasing number of high schools are offering child development courses. Students from these courses, screened by the director and the high school teacher, may be used productively. Exemplary high school students are known for their high energy level. Their vitality and interest can bring renewed vigor to teachers.

Some cities or localities may sponsor volunteer bureaus. These may be the source of miscellaneous personnel. Usually very little screening is done, and the job of evaluating the volunteer's personality and health requirements becomes that of the school.

If the need for volunteers is really acute, and all other sources fail, the local newspaper may carry a feature article on the school and its requirements. Or, of course, placing an advertisement is an option.

Some schools have prepared a simple brochure focusing on volunteers: standards, jobs needed, rewards, school policy, and so on. This can be a simple $8\frac{1}{2} \times 11$ folded colored paper, with one basic art caption. It can be handed out or mailed to those seeking volunteer positions.

 ## SELECTION OF VOLUNTEERS

The rigorous screening of volunteers is vital to the success of the program. Selection should have two major objectives: fitting the right person to the job and eliminating the obviously unfit. It is important to the success of the school that those who volunteer but are not accepted be helped to find other outlets for their enthusiasm.

Volunteers should first file a written application. Suggested information to request follows:

- name, address, phone number
- educational background
- interests and hobbies
- car, license, insurance coverage
- special skills (dance, art, music, etc.)
- work experience
- health record
- kinds of volunteer work preferred

In a few cases, the director may want to include arrest record, but without cooperation of the local police department for checking, this may produce more ill will than not.

The coordinator of volunteers should interview each volunteer, keeping in mind good relations with children. The main thrust of the interview should be to determine the applicant's special skills in the interests of the school. The applicant may meet with children in the classroom so that the volunteer coordinator can observe the results.

Many volunteers on first contact will say they want to be with children, but may become interested in other options if described to them. The volunteer coordinator should pay close attention to the experience of each volunteer and how it will fit in with school needs. It is important to determine the unique background of each and find ways these persons can extend the program. Some may have business, secretarial, educational, medical, or other training that may help immensely. They might enrich curriculum, plan field trips, or help in decorating the building. The list is almost endless.

Sometimes, the requests of the volunteer and the needs of the school are not congruent. Then, the best skills of the coordinator are required to channel the volunteer either into school needs or outward into other activities.

Once the volunteer has been tentatively chosen, a schedule can be agreed upon. The coordinator must impress upon the volunteer the need for promptness and attendance. This is particularly true if the projected work involves the children. Children adjust more easily to the presence of "outsiders" if they know that they will appear at specific times.

Volunteers who are to work with children should also be assigned to one group and one teacher. It is too difficult for an untrained person to learn to work with several teachers and large numbers of children.

 ## ORIENTATION OF VOLUNTEERS

All new volunteers should be given a thorough introduction to the school and its policies. This should be systematic and may involve a checklist. It is both unkind and unwise to throw a new volunteer into service without an orientation. The overview may be one intensive day or extended over a week or more with shorter periods of training.

This activity should include as many of the permanent staff as possible. It is helpful to introduce them by name and repeat their names often. Sometimes, wearing name tags is advisable. Each volunteer should be introduced to everyone possible.

A volunteer assigned to office work should become familiar with the teaching routines. Parents doing physical labor should know each other and the teachers. Most important, the children should learn to accept the volunteer. Basic, also, is an understanding of the goals of the school and what each teacher is attempting to accomplish.

Because there is seldom time for extensive training of most volunteers, on-the-job learning is vital. This can most easily be accomplished by assigning the volunteer to one particular person. The volunteer should have the opportunity to ask questions as soon as possible so that misunderstandings are not allowed to develop. Informal breaks are important in learning, too. There should be times available to socialize with the staff.

In summary, the following general areas should be covered during the orientation period:

- *school organization*—structure of the school, names and functions of each staff member, different children's groups
- *educational beliefs*—program goals and objectives, and how they are being implemented
- *developmental information*—ages and age-groups of the children, general information regarding children, and what to expect (or not expect) from them
- *volunteer responsibilities*—general expectations, overall schedules, and written assignments
- *volunteer supervision*—to whom they will be responsible, to whom they can direct questions, who will evaluate them, and to whom they can go for help

HANDBOOK FOR VOLUNTEERS

A short, concise handbook should be made available to all volunteers. In addition to the information already listed, it might contain

- rules and regulations of the school.
- a sample time sheet with instructions for signing in and out.
- a sample evaluation sheet (if used).
- suggestions for dealing with children in problem situations.
- safety rules for staff and children.
- procedures for field trips or excursions.
- simple "dos" and "don'ts" in working with children.

The more condensed and simple this information, the better. Volunteers cannot be expected to spend great amounts of time with this material.

There should be continued on-the-job training for all volunteers. They should be given ample opportunity to attend workshops, films, discussions, or visits to other schools. Volunteers can be included with regular teachers for in-service training activities. If they are working with children, workshops in art, science, or other specialized fields will help. Persons involved with fund-raising will profit from discussions with professional fund-raisers. Anything at all that will add to the effectiveness of the volunteer may be used, especially intermingling with regular staff.

SUPERVISION OF VOLUNTEERS

The activities involved in training and supervising volunteers are really inseparable. In the beginning, it is important to assume nothing about any volunteer, no matter how extensive the background. This, of course, must be done without "talking down" to the person. But it takes time for even the most adept person to fit into a school. Gentle guidance and suggestions will accomplish a great deal.

The same principles of supervision that apply to the regular staff are just as valid for the volunteer. Insofar as possible, the director should get to know the individual and be sure that the volunteer knows what is expected in the particular job assigned. The limits of each job should also be made very clear. Written schedules are imperative.

When new tasks are assigned, the director or coordinator should run through each routine once with the volunteer. As with everyone, volunteers learn at different rates. When the volunteer has mastered the new task supervision can become minimal.

Positive reinforcement is a rewarding technique for training and supervising. Achievements should be immediately recognized and praised. A small "reward" will make the volunteer feel appreciated. The supervisor should not dwell on failures but steer away from them discreetly by emphasizing the positive in all actions. All volunteers should feel that they have made a contribution each day. Volunteers should also assume the status of co-worker and equal. On the other hand it is not appropriate to grant elaborate privileges in lieu of pay.

The director or coordinator may want to use written evaluations similar in form to those used with regular staff members. Special abbreviated procedures may fit the situation better. Each observation or evaluation should be followed with a conference in which plans are made to improve skills, techniques, or knowledge. Volunteers should feel that the evaluation is a real learning experience.

If there are many volunteers in the school, it is most efficient to hold periodic meetings with the entire group. This is a time to discuss problems and introduce items of general interest to everyone. It is also an opportunity to implement a group feeling of sharing and contribution. Identification with the school is important, as is sharing common goals.

 ## RECOGNITION STRATEGIES

For many volunteers, some tangible evidence of service is important. This can take the form of a "Certificate of Service." A one-time contribution may be acknowledged by a personal letter. For longtime service, a small token emblem in the form of a plaque or statuette may be presented by members of the board of trustees at an appropriate ceremony. The director should send ample publicity to local media sources. Some schools have an annual party for volunteers, coupled with a fund-raiser.

It may be possible to acknowledge everyone at a party, with or without the children. An evening affair along more formal lines is sometimes indicated. In other situations, an informal picnic is more fun. Following the trends of industry, some schools even award a pin for so many years or hours of service.

Newspaper or media coverage of volunteer service is another way to show appreciation. The director can call the newspaper or radio office and explain the program and the important work that volunteers do. It may be possible to arrange a photo session or radio interview. The children can also plan a form of thanks to their volunteers. They can

- write individual notes.
- draw pictures of favorite activities they do with the volunteer.
- prepare a plaque honoring the volunteer.
- put together a booklet describing all the things the volunteer does with the children.
- give a framed photograph of all the children.
- prepare a special lunch.

 ## KEEPING RECORDS

A permanent record of all volunteer service will help to ensure continuity in the program. After a period of recordkeeping, it is also easier to view the program in perspective and reevaluate it. Volunteers, themselves, on entering the program may find the record invaluable. Also, any extra time and effort expended in the volunteer program may be justified by such a record.

Although they may vary somewhat from school to school, some major points to include in volunteer records follow:

- overall plan and objectives
- kinds of work open to volunteers
- sources for recruiting volunteers
- applications for volunteer work
- beginning and ending dates for each volunteer
- jobs successfully filled by volunteers
- major points of orientation sessions
- evaluations of volunteers
- evaluations of the total program
- minutes of meetings concerning volunteers
- records of awards given for service
- correspondence file

Although the use of volunteers requires considerable start-up time, it is generally repaid fully in extensive and beneficial returns to a school. The best way to get full return from the services of volunteers is by careful planning and thoughtful administration.

Several organizations can provide information. Those listed here have publications with information on aging and guides for intergenerational programs.

American Association of Retired Persons
    601 E. Street, NW
    Washington, DC 20049
    800-424-3410
    http://www.aarp.org

The Gray Panthers
    733 15th Street, NW, Suite 437
    Washington, DC 20005
    800-280-5362
    http://www.graypanthers.org

National Council on the Aging
    409 Third Street, SW, Suite 200
    Washington, DC 20024
    202-479-1200
    http://www.ncoa.org

Teachers who work with senior volunteers will need to understand the aging process and to recognize the benefits of intergenerational programs. The following films or videos can help:

"Across the Ages: A New Approach to Intergenerational Learning" (video), 1980.
Temple University Institute on Aging
1601 N. Broad Street, Philadelphia, PA 19122
28 min., color, 3/4″

"Generations Together—SCARP" (slide/tape), undated.
University Center for Social and Urban Research
University of Pittsburgh
600 A Thackery Hall, Pittsburgh, PA 15260
7 min.

"Old Mother Goose Ain't What She Used to Be" (video), 1983.
College Avenue Players
546 Crofton Avenue, Oakland, CA 94610
30 min., color, 3/4″ and 1/2″

"One to One: The Generation Connection" (film or video), 1989.
Terra Nova Films
9848 S. Winchester Avenue, Chicago, IL 60643
24 min., 16 mm., 3/4″ and 1/2″

"Partners in Education: Teachers and Volunteers" (slide/tape), undated.
National Association of Partners in Education
601 Wythe Street, Alexandria, VA 22314
10 min.

The following films are available through
University of North Texas Film Library
http://www.library.unt.edu/media/aging.htm

"Surrounded With Love: Grandparents Raising Grandchildren."
Chicago, IL: Terra Nova Films, Inc. (1999)
University of North Texas Film Library
23 minutes VHS format

"The Story Lady"
Salt Lake City: BWE Video (1997)
120 minutes VHS format

"The Granny Myth"
Seattle, WA: KCTS Television
57 minutes, VHS format

 ## SUMMARY

Student teachers have a good deal of theoretical knowledge of child development but limited practical experience. Also, their characteristics are becoming more varied.

The director's role is one of a stage manager.

The appropriate choice of a master or supervising teacher is vital.

If the school accepts student teachers, there should be a well-organized orientation schedule.

Support of student teachers will ensure a flow of quality persons into the profession.

A majority of schools find some way to use unpaid persons to perform staff functions, often part-time. The director should consult everyone in the school when volunteers are used; everyone on staff should agree.

One person should be designated volunteer coordinator, with the responsibility for their recruitment, use, and evaluation. Very likely the best source of volunteers is a recommendation from someone already associated with the school. However, senior citizens, high school and college students, people within the local neighborhood, and advertising are other sources if careful screening is done.

A carefully planned program of orientation for volunteers is necessary. It is closely related to later supervision.

A concise manual for volunteers could be very helpful because much of the training will be on the job.

It is important to use techniques of positive reinforcement and to give praise promptly when due.

Supervision and evaluation of volunteers are important. Public recognition for service rendered is vital. A certificate, a party, or a long-service pin are ways a school may show appreciation.

A permanent record of volunteer activities is necessary for continuity and total evaluation of the program. The use of volunteers should yield very positive results over a span of time.

REFERENCES

Neuharth-Pritchett, S., Reiff, J. C., & Pearson, C. A. (2001). Through the eyes of preservice teachers: Implications for the multicultural journey from teacher education. *Journal of Research in Childhood Education, 15*(2), 256–269.

SELECTED FURTHER READING

Abbot-Shim, M. (1990). In-service training: A means to quality care. *Young Children, 45*(2), 14–18.

Barhyte, D. M. (2000, November/December). Keep volunteers invested in your program. *Child Care Information Exchange, (136)*, 12–14.

Brand, S. (1990). Undergraduates and beginning preschool teachers working with young children: Educational and developmental issues. *Young Children, 45*(2), 19–24.

Peterson, K., & Raven, J. (1982, September/October). Guidelines for supervising student teachers. *Child Care Information Exchange*, 27–29.

Porter, P. (2001, July/August). Intergenerational care in action. *Child Care Information Exchange*, (140), 66–69.

Shirah, S., Hewitt, T., & McNair, R. (1993). Preservice training fosters retention: The case for vocational training. *Young Children, 48*(4), 27–31.

Wallach, L. B. (2001). Volunteers in Head Start: How to strengthen your program. *Young Children, 56*(5), 37–40.

Watkins, K., & Durant, L. (1987). *Preschool director's staff development handbook.* West Nyack, NY: Center for Applied Research in Education.

STUDENT ACTIVITIES

1. Discuss your experience as a student teacher. How did your reactions compare with those discussed in the text?
2. Observe a master teacher. List several reasons this person was chosen for the job.
3. Interview several directors, each from a different type of school. How does each see the school's relation to training teachers?
4. Visit a school that uses volunteers. Observe what volunteers do that benefits the school.
5. Discuss the role of the director as coordinator of volunteers.
6. Use role-playing to interview a prospective volunteer.

REVIEW

1. Why is it important to have the director take an active interest in the "utilization" of student teachers?
2. List a few major characteristics of an ideal master teacher.
3. What are the chief responsibilities of the master teacher regarding the student teacher?
4. Do student teachers have fears in common? What are they?
5. How can the concerns of student teachers be most easily handled?
6. What are some safeguards to observe when recruiting volunteers?
7. What are some acceptable sources of volunteers?
8. Why are selection and training vital when using volunteers?
9. Who should supervise volunteers?
10. How can volunteer service be compensated?

CASE STUDY

Ricardo is retired from a stressful job in a computer-related business. He thought he would just relax, play golf, and visit friends. Instead he found that he was restless and wanted to be doing something. He decided to volunteer at a nearby after-school program. He loved being with the children, but found that working with the teachers was difficult at times. He wanted to play with the children as he did his grandchildren, but the teachers had other ideas about his role. Sometimes the teachers seemed to feel he was a disruptive influence rather than a help. Ricardo was getting discouraged and was about to decide this was not the place for him and that he should find some other place to volunteer his time.

1. Could this problem have been avoided? If so, how?

2. If you were the director what would you do?

3. What suggestions would you make in order to use Ricardo's expertise?

HELPUL WEB SITES

American Association of Retired Persons:	http://www.aarp.org
Independent Sector:	http://IndependentSector.org
Volunteer Today:	http://www.volunteertoday.com

For additional resources related to administration, visit the Online Resource® for this book at www.EarlyChildEd.delmar.com

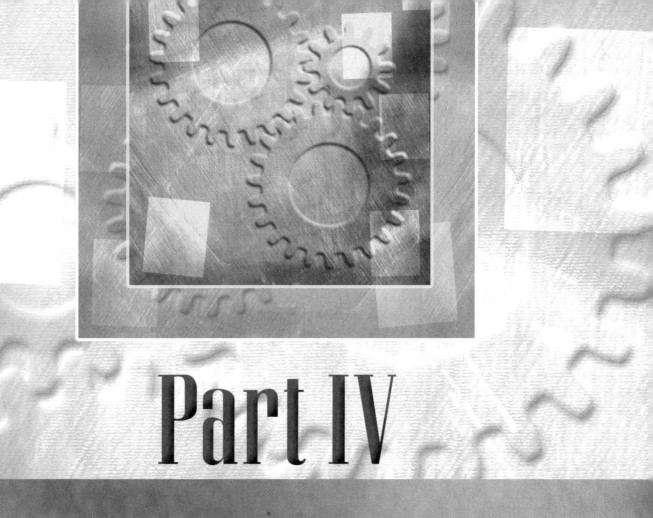

Part IV

Management

CHAPTER

10

Budget

KEY TERMS

budget
budget calendar
fixed expenses
fringe benefits
variable expenses

OBJECTIVES

After reading this chapter, you should be able to:

- Define a budget.
- List the major categories of expenses.
- List the sources of income.
- Describe a budget process.

A Day In The Life Of ...
A Director of a Church-Affiliated School

One day a mother of one of our preschoolers poked her head into my office and said, "Just thought you'd like to know, my son refers to you as Mrs. Office."

The budget is very likely the most important written document a school will have. A **budget,** in the simplest terms, is a statement of goals for one year expressed in financial terms. It is not mysterious or difficult. It involves nothing more than elementary arithmetic, logic, and some experience. The first budget will be the most difficult one by far.

Although at the time it may seem more demanding, the more people involved in the budget-making process, the easier and more satisfactory will be the final result. The trustees, assistant director, teachers, secretaries, cooks, and even maintenance person can contribute to the budget. By doing so, each will have a stake in its success and fulfillment.

The budget must be viewed realistically. A child care center, of almost any type, is a small business. It has all the strengths and weaknesses of this kind of enterprise. It cannot lose money and continue to function. Laudatory and high-sounding aims should not obscure this fact.

DEVELOPMENT OF THE BUDGET

Budgets are based on the goals of a school. If there are special objectives to be reached during a particular year, they should be listed in order of their priority. As the budget process continues, it may be necessary to eliminate some items from the list, but as many people as possible should agree on what these will be. Sometimes it is wise to seek the help of an accountant when preparing this first budget. Although accounting and legal fees may seem high, they are well worth the price if they help in making sure that all necessary expenses will be covered and the year will end without a deficit. Occasionally, a center has the luxury of having an accountant or attorney on the board of trustees who can perform this service.

Time is an important consideration in planning any budget. Most organizations have a budget cycle that is really endless. When one budget is finished, planning for the next year begins. A standing committee of the board, or of the staff, may concern itself primarily with the budget. The process consists of gathering reasonable requests from all concerned. Considerable guidance is sometimes needed for the staff to define "reasonable" in achievable terms. Experience does help. It is the director's responsibility to keep the budget process moving forward.

So, after (re)stating goals and objectives, the most common activity is to prepare a **budget calendar.** This will consist of dates that are essentially deadlines that must be met. This document should be circulated to all concerned. It is important to establish a "tickler" file that will be a reminder of important budget milestones. The director must hold meetings and make decisions as the process unfolds.

A justification must accompany budget requests from various areas of the school. This is a reason for being, not just a statement like "this would be nice" or "I've always wanted one." The justification must be goal and objective linked as nearly as possible. It should withstand independent scrutiny, or it should not be included. This should be clear to everyone who has a hand in making the budget.

Once all budget requests have been assembled, it is time to put together a working budget. A computer and a data management software program will make the budget process much simpler. (Appendix A lists several that are designed specifically for early childhood centers.) If a computer is not available, the director must decide on a form for the budget at this point. Corporate or government-sponsored schools often have a predetermined budget form. The director of a for-profit entity will have

SAMPLE BUDGET FORM

INCOME

Registration fees _____

Books and materials fees _____

Tuition _____

Gifts and contributions _____

Fund-raising _____

Investment income _____

Grants _____

Total Income _____

EXPENSES—Personnel

Staff salaries _____

_____

_____

_____

_____

Total _____

Fringe benefits _____
(10–15% of total)

Workers' compensation, FICA,
health insurance _____

Discounted staff tuitions _____

Total Salaries & Fringe Benefits _____

EXPENSES—Controllable

Consultant services _____

Equipment _____

Educational _____

Housekeeping _____

Office _____

Supplies & materials _____

Educational _____

Housekeeping _____

Office _____

Discounted sibling tuitions and vacancies _____

Food _____

FIGURE 10-1 ■ Sample budget form.

Transportation	_____
Advertising	_____
Uncollected tuitions	_____

EXPENSES—Fixed

Space costs	_____
Utilities	_____
Insurance	_____
Taxes	_____
Marketing	_____
Other costs	_____

TOTAL EXPENSES

Cost per child (total expenses ÷ number of children)	_____

NET (income minus expenses) _____

Download a printable version of this form at http://www.EarlyChildEd.delmar.com

FIGURE 10-1 ■ Sample budget form *(continued)*.

to develop a form for the first budget. Figure 10-1 shows a sample. There are two major sections in a budget: *income* and *expenses*. Expenses are divided into two sub-categories: *variable* and *fixed*.

EXPENSES—PERSONNEL
Staff Salaries

Salaries comprise the largest proportion of a budget, on average 65 percent, but in some schools as high as 75 to 80 percent. This budget category includes administrative personnel (director and assistant director), teaching staff (teachers, assistants, substitutes), and nonteaching staff (secretary, cook, janitor, bus driver, maintenance person). Decisions concerning salary levels for all employees will be influenced by several factors. The first is the education and experience of the teaching staff. Teachers with bachelor's or master's degrees and previous experience will expect higher pay than those without degrees. A second consideration is the going rate of pay in the school's community or area of the country. Salaries tend to be the highest in the northeastern states and lowest in southern states. Third, employers must comply with minimum wage laws and tax laws. One last factor may affect the pay level of

BUDGET FOR A SINGLE FOR-PROFIT SCHOOL

INCOME

Tuitions

Infants: 6@700/mo.	50,400	
Toddlers: 8@650/mo.	62,400	
Preschool: 50@550/mo.	330,000	
School-age: 25@300/mo.	90,000	
		532,800
Vacancy: 5%	<26,640>	506,160
Registration fees: 89@50	4,450	
TOTAL INCOME		**510,610**

EXPENSES: PERSONNEL

Director	26,500	
Teachers:4@17,800	71,200	
Teachers: 4@16,000	64,000	
Teachers: 4 PT@10,000	40,000	
Assistants: 5@8,000	40,000	
Substitutes	4,000	
Secretary	17,500	
Cook: PT	8,000	
		271,200
Benefits (FICA, workers' compensation, unemployment, medical): 13%	35,256	
Total Personnel		**306,456**

EXPENSES: VARIABLE

Equipment		
Educational	4,000	
Supplies & materials		
Educational	5,500	
Office	1,500	
Housekeeping	1,000	
Food	27,000	
Staff development	4,000	
Advertising	3,500	
Petty cash	1,800	
Total Variable		**48,300**

EXPENSES: FIXED

Building lease	60,000	
Utilities	12,000	
Insurance	10,000	
Taxes	800	
Other	500	
Total Fixed		**83,300**

TOTAL EXPENSES		**438,056**
Cost per child (89 children)	4,921	
NET (income minus expenses)		**72,554**

FIGURE 10-2 ■ Budget for a single for-profit school.

employees. Some may be members of a union that has a mandated pay scale. The center may also be part of another entity, a public school or community agency. Each of these will have a predetermined pay scale.

Unfortunately, salaries for child care personnel tend to be low. The sample budget shown in Figure 10-2 reflects a realistic budget based on current salary levels. Chapter 15 contains a discussion of the Worthy Wage Campaign undertaken by the National Center for the Early Childhood Work Force in 1994. The chapter also includes an editorial that appeared in the National Association for the Education of Young Children (NAEYC) publication *Young Children* suggesting ways directors can improve staff compensation and quality.

Personnel costs include taxes that must be paid to various governmental agencies and the **fringe benefits** offered to employees. Required payments include the percentage of an employee's salary for Social Security, workers' compensation, and unemployment insurance. A growing trend in early childhood centers is to offer fringe benefits as a means of keeping qualified staff. Although benefits may seem expendable, they will reduce turnover and the resulting cost of finding and training new staff members. Fringe benefits may include health insurance, sick leave and vacation pay, reduced-cost child care, or retirement plans. Fringe benefits can comprise 10 to 15 percent of the total salary amount. When doing a first budget estimate, that figure can be used as a guideline. A computerized budget form will facilitate budget formation allowing the director to figure fringe benefit costs accurately and to ensure that no essential items have been left out. Refer to Appendix A for information about the software programs that are available.

EXPENSES—VARIABLE

Variable expenses are those over which the director has some measure of control. They will vary depending on how much is spent for supplies and equipment, which services are used or eliminated, and how much is spent for food or transportation.

Consultant or Contract Services

Not all schools will require the services of a consultant or someone who contracts for a service. In this category are persons who perform specific services, sometimes on a one-time-only basis. Included are educational consultants, accountants, lawyers, dentists, doctors, nurses, social workers, psychologists, and nutritionists. In public school systems or in large organizations, these persons may be considered regular employees rather than consultants. In other situations, they work for a fee, agreeing to provide specific services to the school.

Fees for consultants are usually on a per diem basis, including any expenses they incur while working under their contracts. The rate will include food, transportation, and lodging if the consultant is not local.

Equipment

Equipment is usually defined as nonexpendable items, ones that are not consumed in a short period of time. Three to five years is the usual time allocation. Tricycles, typewriters, garbage cans, and desks are all examples. Traditionally, it is easier to subdivide equipment into several types: educational, office, maintenance, and kitchen. The director should keep a chart of the state of repair of each major item and schedule replacement at regular intervals. Each item usually has a "period of obsolescence." If this can be ascertained, the piece should be replaced well ahead of complete breakdown.

Supplies and Other Materials

Readily expended items are placed in this group. They are naturally consumed and used up. Art materials, floor wax, office supplies, and tissues are supplies. The same categories are used as with equipment: educational, office, maintenance, and kitchen. Food is considered separately.

Transportation

This item varies with the services a school furnishes. Bus service is expensive and includes the cost of gas, maintenance on the vehicle, and insurance. The budget should include any planned field trips, journeys to other schools, conferences, and workshops if the school vehicle will be used to transport children or staff members.

Food

This item includes all meals and snacks served at the school. If the director has some experience in food service or can tap the resources of another school, it is fairly easy to calculate the average cost per child per day. A small margin should be added each year for inflation. For a first budget, it is best to estimate on the high side.

Marketing

Every business needs to be marketed to the particular client community in which it will be situated. Potential clients need to know of its existence and what its product is. In the case of a child care center, the product is the kind of educational program that is being offered. Marketing is done through various forms of advertising. This can range from newspaper and telephone book ads to brochures, flyers, and local radio or TV spots. Some of the large corporate schools design an easily recognized logo that is used on signs, T-shirts, coffee mugs, stationary, and business cards. Future marketing will be done through Web sites that provide information about the center. A marketing budget for a center that is just being established should be larger than for one that has been in existence for a long time. Even then, marketing should be an

ongoing process that keeps the public aware of the presence of the school and knowledgeable about what is being offered.

 EXPENSES—FIXED

Fixed expenses are those that either do not vary or change very little over long periods of time. The director has limited or no control over them.

Space Costs

Space costs cover rent or mortgage payments on a building. In either case, this cost
must be analyzed carefully since this is a long-term commitment. Since most states
or localities specify the maximum number of children that a particular space can
accommodate, the amount of income generated from the total square footage is limited. The income that can be generated from tuitions must be enough to carry this
cost.

Utilities

Utilities include water, gas, electricity, telephones, and trash removal. In some areas
it may also be necessary to include sewer charges. If these costs are included in rent
payments, they should not be duplicated here.

Insurance

In recent years, liability insurance has become an increasingly high-expense item.
The only advice that is sound is to shop around for insurance before starting the
budget and try to get the best coverage for the least money. Fire insurance and some
incidental coverages can be purchased at the same time. A reduction in rate is sometimes given if all insurance is purchased as a "package."

Taxes

Tax implications vary according to the type of school. Not-for-profit schools may
have significant tax advantages over profit-making ones in some states. It is important to make adequate inquiries of a certified public accountant or tax authorities:
local, state, and federal.

Audit

A yearly audit by an independent auditor is a necessary part of operating any business. An audit is done for the purpose of overseeing the general accounting practices
and protects the financial personnel by making sure the job is done according to procedures. It also provides assurance to a board or an agency that funds are being
recorded as planned.

Other Costs

This miscellaneous area covers fees, licenses, advertising, petty cash, and other one-time expenditures. There is a growing trend to also include some kind of reserve or contingency fund here.

 ## INCOME

Tuition

The first operating budget must estimate income from all sources. Tuition will be a major source. The director should check with neighboring schools to determine current practice. Any one school cannot charge too much more than other schools in the area, or it will not be able to compete for business. On the other hand, tuition has to be high enough to cover expected expenses if a school is to stay in operation. Therefore, this first tuition must be figured with extreme care.

Once the tuition rate has been determined, it would seem straightforward to multiply the fee by the number of children the center can be licensed to enroll. In practice, however, it is not that simple. First, many schools do not want to enroll the maximum number of children they are allowed or cannot attain full enrollment. To fill enrollment and to accommodate parents, many schools accept children two or three days a week. In addition some schools have children who attend only before they leave for elementary school and then again after school. All these charges must be figured in the estimated income for the year.

Some Other Sources

In general, any fees charged beyond tuition are meant only to cover expenses. It is traditional for private, church, and corporate schools to require a *registration fee*. This may range from $25 to $75 and is payable each year before school begins. Fee payment is included in the process of enrolling a new child or reenrolling a child. Since traditionally this fee is nonrefundable, it is a method of partially ensuring enrollment for a future period.

A *materials fee* is levied when special curriculum materials or books are required. It should include the cost of the articles plus handling and storage charges.

A *transportation fee* may, or may not, be charged. Some (usually more expensive) schools include this in the tuition. Some parents prefer to deliver the children personally. It is important to include this factor if the school is providing bus or other transportation, since this item can become very expensive.

Although it is not too general, some schools do charge a *food fee*. Many schools today find it too costly to serve school-prepared meals, preferring to confine their food service to snacks and perhaps milk at lunch. Children bring their own lunches from home. A few schools, though, still serve a meal as a convenience to parents. It then may be necessary to charge an extra fee for this service. Generally, it is probably better to include food under tuition charges if at all feasible. Some parents may object to a number of isolated fees.

Special activities such as dance and swimming are expensive; these activities should be charged separately. In fact, any activity that only a few children require should be examined for its fiscal implications and charged for appropriately.

Fund-raising and contributions vary tremendously as sources of income. Very few schools start with an "endowment," or a free gift of investment capital. However, as time goes on and the school prospers and gains in reputation, the possibility of a fund-raiser or a request for contributions may be considered in the planning. Annual dinners, picnics, parents' days, award banquets, or any festive occasion may be converted into a fund-raiser. And if the school is certified as nonprofit by the Internal Revenue Service (IRS), contributions may be tax deductible.

Federal, State, and Local Items

There are other sources of income, occasionally of great value, that are not covered in detail in this text. One of these is federal grants, both direct and given through states. Generally, a school must be IRS-certified nonprofit to qualify, although there are exceptions. The *Catalog of Federal Domestic Assistance* is issued yearly by the Government Printing Office in Washington, DC. However, the bulk of government aid is allocated through the State Departments of Education (SDE), located in the various state capitals. Directors should write to their SDE for pertinent information.

The techniques and procedures of application, and of being eligible, for all types of grants are quite complex. The whole field is often referred to as "grantsmanship" and is one that requires special study.

Often as fruitful in a search for funds, especially when launching special projects, is the local service club or area philanthropy. Rotary Clubs and other service groups, the United Way, private donors, and even the department of social services are sometimes interested in things that benefit the community. The local library and a consultation with the librarian may unearth unexpected resources.

Some Intangibles

When computing income for the first operating budget, one of the most uncertain areas of income is estimation of the "shrinkage," or vacancy and dropout factors. These may vary widely according to school location, economic factors, tuition cost, and many others. Only experience can be a reliable guide here. The school year will not end with exactly the same number of children with which it started. Therefore, tuition estimates should allow for less than full enrollment.

A final caution is to provide for uncollected or uncollectable tuitions. For various reasons such as when families move or are unemployed, it may be impossible to collect some money that is owed. An efficient secretary can be helpful in keeping this amount at a minimum by reminding parents when tuitions are overdue. Some centers levy fines for overdue payments or require payment of tuition before services are rendered. Parents pay at the beginning of a month rather than at the end. Figure 10-3 shows a computer-generated accounts receivable spreadsheet.

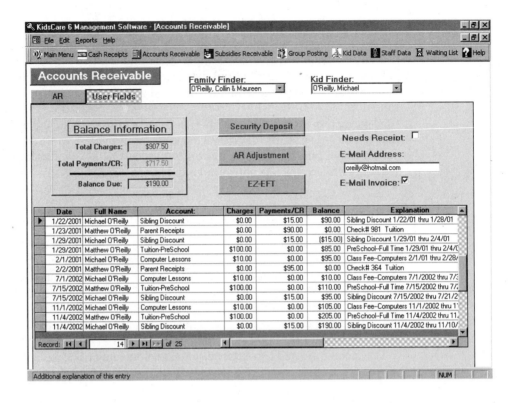

FIGURE 10-3 ■ Computer-generated accounts receivable spreadsheet.

 TRIAL BUDGET

When all *Income* and *Expenditure* items have been assembled, the hardest part of budget making begins. The trustees, corporate headquarters, or other higher authority should be told of the results. A special meeting of the trustees may be solely devoted to budget, or the budget committee of the trustees may meet, or the data may go in to corporate headquarters according to schedule.

Needless to say, there must be no deficit apparent in the budget balance. At this time, it is necessary to ensure a small surplus balance, either for reserve funding or for unexpected additions before the budget is finalized. If the center is a for-profit business, now is the time to calculate the amount of that profit.

The director should hold a staff meeting where everyone concerned may make comments on items submitted. Almost without fail, some entries must be curtailed or eliminated. This is painful. But throughout the budget process, it is important to keep everyone involved with it informed. The watchword is "no secrets!" The staff should be able to agree on trade-offs, substitutions, and the establishment of priorities that extend from year to year.

Next the director should set a date for the accomplishment of the publication or summary budget, solicit final input, and again send the budget for final approval to the next level of administration (if any).

Finally, by the last day of the fiscal year on the budget calendar (or considerably before), the final budget should be completed. This is the working financial outline for the coming year. Beyond this date, the budget cannot be altered. Some changing among categories of expenditure may be made, but this practice is not recommended.

After a year or so in operation, enough data should have been collected to ascertain at what particular month of the year specific expenditures should most advantageously be made. For example, where *Equipment Rental* and *Parent Communications* do not vary during the year, spending for *Educational Supplies* and *Maintenance* change to fit the calendar. Maintenance projects are often done before the heavy enrollment in September, during Christmas (billed in January), and at the close of the fiscal year in September. With a computer, it is possible to compare current expenditures in a timely manner on a month-by-month basis. The computer compares actual versus allocated values and imposes tighter budget controls in a timely way.

 ## SUMMARY OF BUDGET CYCLE

The following are suggestions for the director who is planning a budget:

1. The budget is a cyclical process. Begin a new one when the current one is completed.
2. Start with your goals for the year. List them.
3. Seek outside help if necessary on a first budget.
4. Assign one person central authority for the budget.
5. Publish budget deadlines and what is expected of each staff member.
6. Try to include as many people as possible in planning.
7. Ask for written budget requests on a standard form.
8. Ask for a justification for each major request.
9. Assemble a trial budget and establish priorities.
10. Be sure positive budget balances or profit is calculated.
11. Consider using computerized methods.
12. Publish the trial (preliminary) budget and circulate it for written comments.
13. Keep major divisions of Income and Expenditures.
14. Get committee approval at board, staff, or other level.
15. Submit final budget for approval by higher authority after incorporating last comments and discussion.
16. Publish final budget.
17. Begin new budget.

Of course, this list is an idealized schedule. It does not include the traumas and drama of any real budget. Yet, it is important to have an agenda and stick with it.

BUDGET ANALYSIS

Before the budget is finalized, the director should make sure every item is included and that this document will achieve the goals that have been set for the year. Keeping notes in a budget folder is a valuable practice as the year progresses. It is a rather frightening experience to "run out of budget" before the close of a fiscal year. Good planning and analysis will eliminate this.

The following are a few hints to use in analyzing the budget:

- Is every item necessary to meeting the goals of the school included? Have obsolete goals been abolished and new ones provided for?
- Has every cost been included? Part of the review process is to ensure inclusion of every vital factor.
- Are there marked differences between this budget and last year's? If so, what has changed? Are the changes necessary? Have changes been fully justified?
- Has any single item shown a marked increase or decrease? If so, have objectives changed? Marked increases may signal need for cost-control measures.
- Was there great difficulty in reconciling differences between Income and Expenditures? If so, major equipment, maintenance, or other items may have to be postponed.

It is a major test of administrative skill to have everyone reasonably satisfied with the final budget. No one gets everything; everyone should get a little bit.

 According to the Children's Defense Fund publication, *The State of America's Children 2001*, the average salary of a child care worker is only $15,430 a year, less than salaries for funeral attendants, bellhops, and garbage collectors.

 IMPLEMENTING THE FINAL BUDGET

The approved paper budget is only the road map; a skilled driver is necessary to arrive safely at the destination. That person is the director. The director implements the budget during the year by using skillful management techniques.

- Only one person should have purchasing authority. Requests for budget expenditures must be submitted in writing.
- One person has the responsibility for disbursing money. The bank should honor the signature of only one (or at most two) authorized people.
- Each person involved with the budget should have an overview copy as well as a detailed subsection for particular expenditures.
- Monthly progress reports of budget income/outgo should be issued to all vitally concerned. This is especially easy to do with a computer.

- Overspending should be curtailed early. Underspending should be investigated at the end of the year. There may need to be some "corrective" factors if this is a first budget.

 KEEPING BUDGET RECORDS

Future budget preparation is easier if accurate records are kept. Budget tracking information for each month is shown in Figure 10-4. As a minimum, the following are included as permanent file entries.

- current cost of all budget items
- budget forms used by school or other agencies

MONTHLY FINANCIAL REPORT FOR BUDGET TRACKING

Period covered: From _____ To _____

	This month	Year to Date
INCOME		
Tuition		
Fees		
Donations		
Total Income		
EXPENSES		
Salaries and wages		
Taxes and benefits		
Staff training		
Lease payment		
Food purchases		
Utilities		
Supplies		
Equipment		
Insurance		
Advertising		
Total Expenses		
Previous Balance		
Income for (month)		
Expenses for (month)		
CURRENT BALANCE		

Download a printable version of this form at http://www.EarlyChildEd.delmar.com

Online Resources

FIGURE 10-4 ■ Monthly financial report for budget tracking.

	OCT	NOV	DEC	JAN	FEB	MAR	APR	MAY	JUN	JUL	AUG	SEP	TOTAL
VARIABLE EXPENSES													
* * *													
Educational supplies	484	484	1,166	497	506	870	524	510	1,155	494	494	1,176	8,360
Equipment rental	123	123	123	123	123	123	123	123	123	123	123	123	1,476
Maintenance	2,500	800	875	1,350	875	1,125	800	850	875	900	875	1,250	13,075
Parent communications	150	150	150	150	150	150	150	150	150	150	150	150	1,800

Download a printable version of this form at http://www.EarlyChildEd.delmar.com online Resources

FIGURE 10-5 ■ Sample budget detail, month by month.

- copies of taxes, insurance, licenses, and assessments
- copies of budgets for last three years
- copies of cost control practices used
- budget correspondence
- minutes of budget review meetings
- copies of the annual report for three previous years

Figure 10-5 shows how monthly variable expenses can be tracked for an entire year to help prevent overspending.

SUMMARY

A budget is the statement of goals for one year given in financial terms. The director should begin to compile it with lists of services to be provided, programs to be included, and goals to be reached.

The following items are included as major headings of budget expenditures.

- Staff salaries
- Fringe benefits
- Consultant services
- Equipment
- Supplies and materials
- Transportation
- Insurance
- Cost of space
- Utilities

- Food
- Taxes (if any)
- Other costs

The following are listed as major income items.

- Tuition
- Materials fee
- Transportation fee
- Food fee
- Special activities fee
- Fund-raising and contributions
- Possible federal, state, or private sources

The budget should allow for "shrinkage" factors and for uncollected tuitions.

A budget calendar includes deadlines for meeting each milestone in budget development. The director is responsible for *estimating Income and reconciling Expenditures*. Everyone involved in the budget process must be kept informed.

Once a trial budget is outlined, it is important to request further input. The budget should be analyzed for omissions and unneeded items. The final steps are to make compromises, reconcile budget income with outgo and establish profit (if any), achieve final approval, and publish the final budget.

Authority for budget administration is centralized. The director should examine the budget continually and make every attempt to stay within budget bounds. Good recordkeeping will ease future budget preparation.

 ## SELECTED FURTHER READING

Campbell, N. D., Appelbaum, J. C., Martinson, K., & Martin, E. (2000). *Be all that we can be: Lessons from the military for improving our nation's child care system.* Washington, DC: National Women's Law Center.

Cantrella, G. (Ed.). (1999). *National guide to funding for children, youth, and families* (5th ed.). New York: The Foundation Center.

Geever, J. C., & McNeill, P. (1997). *The Foundation Center's guide to proposal writing* (Rev. ed:). New York: The Foundation Center.

Mitchell, B., Stoney, A. L., & Dichter, H. (2002). *Financing child care in the United States: An expanded catalog of current strategies.* (2nd ed.). Kansas City, MO: Ewing Marion Kaufman Foundation.

National Association for the Education of Young Children. (2001). Financing child care facilities. *Young children, 56*(2), 56.

 ## STUDENT ACTIVITIES

1. Contact several child care directors. Ask for an estimate of their cost per child per year. How does it compare with the amount shown in Figure 10-2? What accounts for the difference?

2. Prepare a questionnaire to distribute to your fellow students. Tell them their answers will be anonymous. Ask the following:
   a. Are you currently teaching in an early childhood center?
   b. How many hours a week do you work?
   c. What is your weekly pay?
   d. Do you receive any benefits other than those required by law? If so, please list them.

   Summarize your findings and report to the class regarding working conditions for early childhood teachers.

 ## REVIEW

1. Define a budget.
2. List at least six items of expenditure in a budget.
3. What should one of your first actions be in beginning a budget?
4. Who has responsibility for budget preparation?
5. What single item constitutes the largest budget expenditure?
6. What are some of the major steps in the budget cycle?
7. What is a reasonable percent of profit for a preschool? Defend your statement.

CASE STUDY

Lido, Nathan, and Monica's mothers are among the 12 parents at a center who have been laid off from a local retailer due to a mild recession in the area. Eleven of the 12 families withdrew from the program with little or no notice. All contracts require a two-week written notice, but under the circumstances, these families could not comply.

The director developed her budget based on 95 percent enrollment of the center, which has a capacity of 70 full-time enrollments. She is now expecting approximately $4,700 less per month than planned. In addition, she is staffed for these 11 children, all in different programs because their ages range from two through three and a half.

1. How could the director attempt to reconcile the budget?

2. How could the director avoid layoffs in her own staff? Is that possible?

3. Do you think the director's aim of 95 percent enrollment is realistic? Why?

4. What could you learn from this case study?

8. Specify some methods of budget review.
9. Tell how a budget can be controlled. Why is this important?
10. What items should be included in budget records as an aid to planning?

 HELPFUL WEB SITES

Bureau of Labor Statistics:	http://www.bls.gov
Families and Work Institute:	http://www.familiesandworkinst.org
Federal Grant Sites and the Catalog of Federal Domestic Assistance:	http://www.dhhs.gov/progorg/grantsnet

 For additional resources related to administration, visit the Online Resource® for this book at www.EarlyChildEd.delmar.com

11

Maintenance, Health, and Safety

OBJECTIVES

After reading this chapter, you should be able to:

- Differentiate between maintenance and operations activities.
- Tell how maintenance, cleanliness, and safety are related.
- Discuss the components of a safe environment.
- Describe how to deal with an emergency.
- State goals for a health plan in a childhood center.
- Discuss ways to implement health goals.

A Day in the Life of ...

A Director of a Church-Affiliated School

There can be anxious days in the life of a director. One day Patrick's mother arrived to pick him up from "lunch bunch," and we couldn't find him. He had been with two teachers and a group of children on the playground. One minute he was there, and the next he was gone! Our playground is fenced but has one gate that can be opened by the students. A teacher is always near the gate to supervise children who may have to go down the hall to the bathrooms. We checked the bathrooms first, then every classroom, then the parking lot.

By now my heart was racing and Patrick's mother started to panic. I'll never forget the look on her face as long as I live. We were close to calling 911. I kept thinking how hard it would be for a child to leave our playground or school without being noticed, so I decided to check the playground one more time. I looked in the bushes and the playhouse. I walked around the sand area where we have a large tractor tire. I spotted Patrick curled up inside the cozy, warm curve of the tire, sound asleep! Whew! Patrick had been "missing" no more than 10 minutes, the longest 10 minutes of this director's life.

When so much emphasis is put on other aspects of an early childhood program, it is easy to overlook the physical environment. This can be a costly error both psychologically and financially. Teachers and children spend their day either in pleasant and safe surroundings or in a mess. Order and safety have logical connections, and a regard for healthful conditions is both a legal and parental concern. It is the responsibility of the director to ensure orderliness and security in the school.

A safe and healthy environment requires careful and continuous maintenance. In an unkempt environment there is the possibility that either children or teachers may be injured or become ill. Orderly, clean rooms create an atmosphere which is more pleasant and conducive to learning than one that is constantly disordered. There are naturally occurring hazards in a play yard as well as the possibility of injury on play equipment. However, with a well-managed schedule of maintenance, injuries can be kept to minor ones.

 ## MAINTENANCE OR OPERATIONS?

Many schools distinguish between maintenance and operations. **Maintenance** consists of major repairs and projects such as repainting exteriors and interiors, repaving, and reroofing. **Operations,** however, is concerned with day-by-day housekeeping such as sweeping, dusting, cleaning, emptying, and other seemingly endless tasks that go into making up a tidy and attractive school. The difference may be especially important at budget time. Most maintenance efforts are scheduled at yearly (sometimes longer) intervals. Maintenance tasks are often costly, and money must be set aside each year to cover the expense when it finally occurs. Operations take place each day and are essentially short range. This kind of expense must be part of each month's expenditures.

Maintenance

Aside from high cost, a major problem with maintenance projects is scheduling. Repainting is very difficult to do when school is in session. Weekends are a possibility, but a better solution is to group all major maintenance for times when children are not present for at least a few days. Although there are increasingly more year-round schools, there are sometimes a few days or a week during the year when rooms are vacant. It helps to plan a year or so ahead for this and keep a log of when major maintenance tasks are due.

In addition to charting due dates of all projects, the director should keep a list of local maintenance services and make notes about their cost and reliability. Such services as plumbing and electrical are sometimes needed in an emergency. Figure 11-1 gives a suggested format for keeping a record of phone numbers and comparative prices.

Proper maintenance may also include periodic replacement of some furniture or equipment. A child care center, open 10 or 12 hours daily, will need a larger budget for maintenance and operations than one that is in session only a few hours. Active, young children are physically demanding on their environment. "Things" wear out rapidly. Figure 11-2 is a sample equipment maintenance card, and Figure 11-3 is a repair and replacement record form.

Operations

Seldom can a child care center afford an in-house custodial staff. Some corporate schools do have crews that clean and repair, but this is not the norm at most preschools. There must be some other means of routine cleaning. The aim should be the maximum health and safety of the children. To give optimum results, an outside cleaning service, hired on a part-time basis, is about the only solution economically possible.

REPAIR AND MAINTENANCE SERVICES				
Name	Address	Telephone	Rate	Comments
Plumbing				
Carpentry				
Painting				
Paving				
Roofing				
Electrical				
Gardening				
General Repairs				
Other				

FIGURE 11-1 ■ Sample repair and maintenance service form.

EQUIPMENT MAINTENANCE RECORD			

Item _____ Date Purchased _____ Price _____

Purchased from _____

Warranty No. _____ Manufacturer_____

Warranty Expiration Date _____

Maintenance Record

Service Date	Description	By whom	Charge

FIGURE 11-2 ■ Sample equipment maintenance record.

There are many such cleaning services, and they perform at all levels of efficiency. The director should prepare a list of essential tasks that must be done before beginning negotiations with any of them. One way is to list specifications and ask for bids. The next step is to examine the two or three lowest bidders and interview the owners or managers. Pertinent questions to ask are who they employ, how long they have been in business, what hours they will work, their cost per hour, and how long their contract will run. They must be available on a schedule to fit the school's needs.

Figure 11-4 provides some suggestions as to frequency of cleaning and general housekeeping. The initial contract for services should be short so that the performance of the cleaning service can be assessed.

The director must be especially alert when adding new programs. In addition to the cost of the room and equipment, there must be sufficient money to provide a safe, clean, and comfortable environment. Although this is especially true when adding an infant-toddler room to a school, it is important to any addition. The staff, parents, and children will notice the difference. In some surveys, cleanliness (in rather broad terms) is the most requested and looked-for item when parents are seeking child care.

Teachers question the degree to which they should be involved in routine cleanup procedures. There is no doubt that, if teachers keep their rooms tidy during the day, cleaning needs will be significantly less. In the normal course of the day, teachers should not feel that their first duty is orderliness in the classroom. A short period of tidying up at the end of the day or the lesson helps. (A discussion of the special requirements in an infant-toddler room is found later in this chapter.) Children should participate in putting away materials. Learning to store objects in their proper

REPAIR AND REPLACEMENT RECORD					
Item	Repair	Replace	Repaint	Date Requested	Date Completed
Classrooms					
Tables					
Chairs					
Shelves					
Book cabinet					
Hollow blocks					
Floor blocks					
CD player					
Sand table					
Play Yard					
Swings					
Sandbox					
Sand					
Wheel toys					
Planks					
Boxes					
Jungle gym					
Playhouse					
Storage					
Office					
Typewriter					
Duplicator					
Adding machine					
Paper cutter					
Desk					
Chairs					
Bookshelf					
Computer					
Printer					
Grounds					
Driveway					
Parking lot					
Walks					
Garden					
Lawn					
Other					

FIGURE 11-3 ■ Sample repair and replacement services form.

HOUSEKEEPING SCHEDULE					
Task	Daily	Weekly	Twice Weekly	Monthly	Comments
Bathrooms					
Toilets sanitized	X				
Washbowls cleaned	X				
Floor mopped	X				
Mirrors cleaned			X		
Towels refilled					As needed
Walls wiped				X	
Classrooms					
Floors wet mopped	X				
Floors waxed				X	
Carpets vacuumed			X		
Clean tables and chairs	X				
Sanitize cots and mats	X				
Wastebaskets					
Emptied	X				
Washed			X		
Windows washed				X	
Shelves dusted		X			
Stove cleaned				X	
Refrigerator					
Cleaned			X		
Defrosted				X	
Hallways					
Vacuumed		X			
Offices					
Vacuumed		X			
Dusted		X			

FIGURE 11-4 ■ Sample housekeeping schedule.

EQUIPMENT INVENTORY RECORD			
Item: _____ Date Purchased _____ Price _____			
Dates Inventoried	Accumulated Depreciation	Depreciation Current Year	Insurance Value

FIGURE 11-5 ■ Sample equipment inventory record form.

places is part of the maturing process. Extreme disorder is not conducive to learning or pleasure for most children or teachers.

INVENTORY

The director should prepare an inventory of all physical equipment in the school over a specified dollar value. This list should be created when the school begins and be updated yearly. Recordkeeping of this type is necessary for tax purposes, if for no other reason. Each piece of equipment should be depreciated on a fixed basis. A tax adviser can recommend the precise time span. There are computer inventory programs, or this information can be tracked on 3 × 5 cards as shown in Figure 11-5. These cards should be kept permanently in a safe place.

SAFETY

Environment

Creating a safe environment should be a top priority in any setting for groups of children. As children proceed through various stages of development, they test their physical skills, sometimes doing things that may be potentially harmful. All equipment and materials both indoors and outdoors should allow children to develop their skills safely without risk of injury. To do so takes a knowledge of potential hazards and constant vigil to prevent deterioration of the environment. The director should have a thorough knowledge of how to create a safe environment. In addition, teachers must be alert to potential hazards and know how to prevent injuries to children.

Prevention measures should begin with a weekly check of both the classrooms and the playground. Teachers should check a classroom other than their own. They may notice something that is overlooked in the day-to-day functioning in the area. The director should look for places in the school where young children may be hurt, arrange for repair of any equipment that needs it, and remove any that cannot be repaired. It is helpful to develop a checklist for the particular environment so that nothing will be overlooked during a walk-through. Figure 11-6 is a suggested checklist for assessing the safety of the environment.

SAFETY CHECKLIST

\

Classrooms
____ Furniture is free of sharp corners.
____ All furniture is an appropriate size for the children using it and has been tested for safety.
____ Safety devices are on all electrical outlets.
____ Childproof locks are on cupboards containing cleaning supplies.
____ Hot water is set at 120°F.
____ All toys less than $1\frac{1}{2}$ inches in diameter have been removed. Staff has been trained to use the "choke tube" measuring tool.
____ No small objects such as pins, thumbtacks, nails, or staples are available to children.
____ All broken toys or parts of toys have been removed.
____ Art supplies are free of toxic ingredients.
____ There are no loose or torn carpet areas.
____ Vinyl flooring is not slippery.
____ Each classroom has a working smoke detector.
____ An emergency evacuation plan is posted in a visible place in each classroom.
____ Directions for emergency shutoff of gas, electricity, and water are posted in a visible place.
____ The infant-toddler room has one clearly marked crib on wheels for quick evacuation of nonwalking children.

Outdoors
____ All equipment has an adequate fall zone with safety-certified ground cover.
____ All moving parts on equipment have been checked for defects.
____ All equipment meets licensing requirements.
____ There is adequate spacing between pieces of equipment.
____ Platforms have sturdy guard rails.
____ Play equipment is sturdy and free of sharp edges or splinters.
____ There are no loose nuts or bolts on equipment.
____ Play equipment is anchored securely to the ground.
____ There are no tripping hazards such as raised concrete on walkways or warped surfaces on climbing equipment.
____ Grass has been cut; walkways are free of debris.
____ The playground is free of broken toys, glass, or any objects that may have been thrown into the area.
____ All fences are at least 4 feet high and have securely latched gates.
____ Sandboxes are clean and have been raked at least once a week.
____ Riding toys have a low center of gravity and are well balanced.
____ The riding area for wheel toys is separate from other play areas and away from traffic patterns.
____ The riding area for wheel toys is smooth and not slippery.
____ Children and staff members are aware of the rules regarding use of equipment.

FIGURE 11-6 ■ A sample safety checklist.

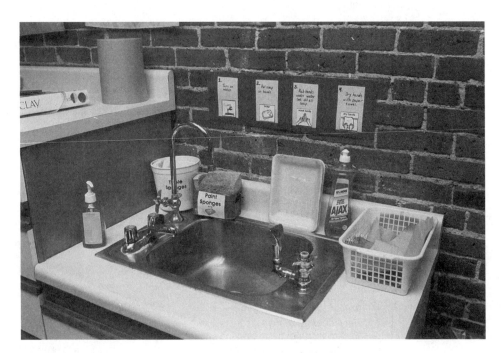

A clean school.

First Aid

Every school should have at least one major well-stocked and freshly renewed first aid kit. There should also be at least one adult who has taken the American Red Cross First Aid course. If possible, smaller first aid kits should be stored in each classroom, with antiseptic and Band-Aids as minimal contents.

A list of emergency telephone numbers for fire, police, and utilities should be permanently affixed near the first aid kit and in each room as needed. The school physician's (or nurse's) phone number should be readily available. The number of the nearest emergency room, hospital, or paramedic unit should also be posted. All other information should be centralized so that staff can deal with emergencies expeditiously.

The central first aid kit should be stocked with items such as the following:

adhesive tape (¼″ and 1″)	hot water bottle	splints
alcohol	ice pack	thermometer
Band-Aids, assorted	needle, sewing	tongue blades
blanket	safety pins	towels
cotton balls	scissors, blunt	triangle bandage
flashlight	soap, liquid	tweezers
gauze pads, assorted	spirits of ammonia	Vaseline

Accident Management

Every school or child care center needs a standard procedure for managing any accidents that happen at school or when children are in transit. The following are some recommendations for the director.

- Each child's file should contain a form signed by the parents authorizing emergency medical treatment.
- Have a standard form on which pertinent accident information can be recorded. Complete it as soon as possible after the accident (see Figure 11-7).
- Call paramedics or take the child to the nearest emergency room as required by the nature of the accident.
- *Telephone the parents* as soon as possible. If the child is to be taken out of the school, ask that the parents go directly to the hospital.
- If the injury seems minor and does not require emergency care, the parents should *still be notified*. A joint decision can be made if the child should stay at school or be taken home.
- If the child stays at school, make sure that teachers watch for any further signs of difficulty during the day.
- Answer any questions the other children may have as completely and honestly as possible. Reassure them that the injured child is receiving care.

Outdoor equipment must be sturdy and solid.

ACCIDENT REPORT FORM

Name of School _____ Date of Report _____

Child's Name _____ Sex M   F   Birth Date _____

Parent Name _____ Phone Number _____

Home Address _____

Date of Injury _____ Time _____ AM   PM

Location Where Injury Occurred _____

Teacher in Charge _____

Present at the Time of Accident _____

Type of Equipment Involved _____

Description of How Accident Happened _____

_____

_____

_____

Action Taken: _____

First Aid Treatment _____
                         (Name of person administering)

Taken to Doctor _____
                         (Name of doctor)

Taken to Hospital _____
                         (Name of hospital)

Refused Treatment _____
                         (Name of person refusing treatment)

Parent Notification:

Was Parent Notified?   Yes   No   Time of Notification _____

How Was Parent Notified? _____

Comments from Parent _____

_____

_____

Witnesses to Accident _____

_____

Director's Signature _____

FIGURE 11-7 ■ Accident report form.

Disaster Plans

Your state's licensing regulations may require a **disaster plan.** Even if not mandated, *preparation for disasters* such as fire, flood, hurricane, tornado, and earthquake should be made *before* any children enter a child care facility. Every staff member must be familiar with procedures for evacuating children or moving them to safe places in the building. *An evacuation route plan* should be displayed prominently in each room and at the entrance of the school. Fire alarms, fire extinguishers, and emergency exit lights should be clearly visible and checked regularly. *Drills should be scheduled frequently* so that children have a chance to practice and staff have an opportunity to evaluate whether the plan needs any changes. *Parents must be aware of disaster plans*, including alternative shelters where children might be taken.

One staff person should be designated to summon emergency help and see that the building has been completely emptied. That person will also contact parents. A final check of the building should be made to turn off any equipment, shut off gas lines (important in earthquakes), or take any other measures that are necessary in a particular facility.

It is important to store emergency supplies in evacuation areas within the building, packed in easily movable containers so they can also be taken to the alternative shelter when necessary. An emergency kit should include

- first aid supplies.
- blankets.
- water for at least one day's supply.
- nonperishable food.
- flashlights.
- a battery-operated radio.
- children's books, games, crayons, paper, and small toys.

Transportation

A discussion of safety would not be complete without considering measures to be observed when transporting children by car or bus. This is especially important today when many child care centers or preschools provide a pickup service. Even schools that do not offer that convenience occasionally take children on field trips.

The driver of any vehicle must be properly licensed. The person should also be responsible and able to manage a group of children. Some training may be necessary to provide that capability. Parents should know the person who transports their children to school in order to feel more confident. A written permission form should be on file at school.

Sometimes teachers may be used as substitute drivers. The director must be particularly sure in such cases that the teacher has been given the same training and is licensed the same as the regular vehicle driver. People operating in a different environment are often susceptible to accidents.

All vehicles used to transport children should be equipped with restraints appropriate for the age of each child and approved for the make of the car. Infants should be placed in rear-facing seats. Preschoolers who are at least 1 year of age and weigh at least 20 pounds can use front-facing seats with a full harness restraint (lap and shoulder belt). When children reach the top weight for their car seat or if their ears reach the top of the seat, they can use a booster with lap and shoulder belts. A few cars and vans are equipped with built-in seats and may be used by preschoolers. Each child must be buckled in for every trip, no matter how short.

Maintenance of all vehicles used for children is extremely important. Periodic inspections should be followed with any necessary repair work. A fire extinguisher should be placed near the driver so that it is easily available when needed. Adequate liability insurance must be purchased to cover the vehicle, driver, and the maximum number of passengers.

In some schools, parents transport children on field trips. It is necessary to take precautions to ensure children's safety at these times as well. There must be a safe place for cars to park when loading and unloading children. Parents may need to be reminded to use restraints and watch when closing doors. Although the school is not liable when parents transport their own children, it may be liable when they carry other children on a field trip. The director should make certain insurance will cover such an eventuality. A last precaution is to use parents for field trips as infrequently as possible. It is risky.

 ## HEALTH

The United States Department of Health and Human Services' Child Care Bureau and Maternal and Child Health Bureau have launched a campaign to promote healthy children. The campaign revolves around a Blueprint for Action encompassing 10 steps. Communities can either use existing sources or create new services to assess child care and health care resources and implement the goals.

The 10 steps were outlined in a January 1998 issue of *Young Children*.

1. Promote safe, healthy, and developmentally appropriate child care environments for all families.
2. Increase immunization rates and preventive services for children in child care settings.
3. Assist families in accessing key public and private health and social service programs.
4. Promote and increase comprehensive access to health screenings.
5. Conduct health and safety education and promotion programs for children, families, and child care providers.
6. Strengthen and improve nutrition services in child care.
7. Provide training for and ongoing consultation with child care providers and families in the areas of social and emotional health.

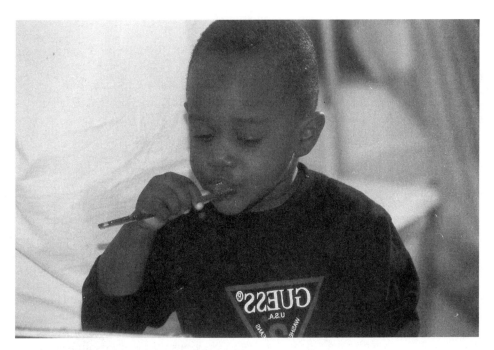

In a child care center, children brush their teeth.

8. Expand and provide ongoing support to child care providers and families caring for children with special health needs.
9. Use child care health consultants to help develop and maintain healthy child care.
10. Assess and promote the health, training, and work environment of child care providers.

A fuller description of the campaign and information about implementation can be obtained from: The National Center for Education in Maternal and Child Health, 2000 15th Street North, Suite 701, Arlington, VA 22201–2617; phone 703-524-7802; fax 703-524-9335; or visit http://www.ncemch.org.

HEALTH GOALS

The Healthy Child Care Campaign is an effective way to make families and child care providers aware of the importance of promoting child health. Each child care center should have a set of health goals and methods for implementing those goals. The result will be healthier children with fewer illnesses. That should be a bonus for working parents who will miss fewer work days because their children are ill. If the policy also includes health and safety education for families, the impact of the program will extend even further to all family members.

The following are some sample goals.

■ Assess the child's current health status and recommend treatment of existing problems.
■ Suggest treatment for conditions that are progressive.
■ Identify and suggest treatment for conditions that may interfere with how the child functions in school.
■ Institute practices that prevent future illnesses.

Assessing Current Health Status

When a child first enters a school, whether for part of the day or all day, it is important to know the status of the child's health, particularly whether the child is capable of participating in all the activities of the school or if there should be some restrictions. Most schools require a preenrollment physical examination. The physician's report will certify that the child is free of communicable diseases, describe any abnormal conditions, and include a record of immunizations.

Further assessment may include a discussion with the child's parents in which a brief developmental history is taken. In some cases, it may be important to know about the mother's pregnancy and the circumstances of delivery. Additional information may include allergies, previous illnesses, hospitalizations, and any accidents the child has experienced.

Health screening tests are used in some schools, especially those that receive government funds such as Head Start. Children may receive hearing or vision tests in addition to medical and dental screening. Some may receive general motor coordination tests.

Observations by teachers are also useful in discovering a child's health problems. They see children for many hours during a week and can often detect problems that

- Immunization of children increased to 80 percent in 1999.
- The number of deaths due to AIDS in children under 13 has decreased from 582 in 1994 to 76 deaths in 1999.
- Asthma is one of the most common chronic conditions among young children, affecting 4.4 million children under 18.
- The number of overweight children has more than doubled within the past 10 years and now represents almost 11 percent of all children between the ages of 6 and 19. Sixty-seven percent of these children have a higher than recommended intake of fats per day and fewer than one out of five eat the recommended number of servings of fruits and vegetables.

Source: U. S. Centers for Disease Control as reported in *The State of America's Children,* Children's Defense Fund, 2001.

may not have been previously noticed. They may notice behavior that points to hyperactivity, hearing and vision impairment, or poor motor coordination. Poor nutrition may be seen as a reason for the child's listlessness or withdrawal from group activities.

Treating Progressive Conditions

Certain health conditions will become progressively worse if left untreated. They may have a lasting and irreversible effect upon the child's health and ability to function in school. Examples are excessive tooth decay or strabismus (crossed eyes) and amblyopia (lazy eye). Malnutrition may permanently disturb the child's growth pattern. Behavior problems may affect learning and may become increasingly difficult to treat successfully as the child grows older. Often, though, it is hard to find the best sources of help, and they are likely to be expensive when found.

Comprehensive health care provided by some publicly funded preschool and child care programs covers the cost of treating progressive conditions. In Head Start centers, a health coordinator works with the community involvement worker to facilitate health referrals for medical or dental care when necessary. A Head Start Nutrition Committee, made up of parents, plans monthly menus and assists in conducting nutrition activities for children. This committee also plans and conducts nutrition activities with the parents.

Schools that do not have the support of public funds must find other ways to work with families to treat progressive conditions. They must tap the resources of communities or seek out help from national organizations. Health departments sometimes have low-cost clinics or treatment centers. Service and research organizations such as the American Academy of Pediatrics, the American Lung Association, or the American Cancer Society have up-to-date information for staff and parent education. They may also be able to provide information about treatment facilities.

Individuals within the school may also be helpful in providing information. Parents can often tell the director which pediatricians are best when interacting with families and children. They may know dentists who manage children sensitively as they treat their dental problems. Other directors in the community may know of sources of psychological help for families.

The director of an employer-sponsored school may have another option. The business or industry that supports the center may be associated with a health care organization that can provide health services. The role of the director is to be knowledgeable about those benefits and suggest that parents make appointments with appropriate departments or health organizations. Hospitals that support child care obviously have their own built-in services that are probably available to families.

Identifying Conditions That Interfere with Learning

Often, conditions that interfere with learning never become identified until the child reaches elementary school. By then, a lot of time in which the difficulties could have been corrected has been lost. The preschool or child care center can be instrumental in preventing this delay.

The most obvious *vision* problems usually are recognized, but only a very alert adult will recognize other conditions. Teachers should watch for the child who has difficulty with eye-hand coordination or is awkward in games. The child who avoids close work or assumes an abnormal posture when doing it may also have poor vision. Complaints about inability to see or lack of curiosity about visually interesting objects may indicate vision problems.

Children's speech is often a good indicator of *hearing disabilities.* The teacher may be the first person to recognize a difficulty because parents are so accustomed to understanding the child's particular speech pattern. Hearing loss in young children is fairly frequent, sometimes due to the recurring middle-ear infections suffered at this age. Some indications of hearing problems that teachers should be aware of are listed here.

1.   limited use of speech
2.   lack of response when spoken to
3.   consistent lack of attention during group activities
4.   talking very loudly or very softly
5.   asking for a repetition of what has been said
6.   watching intently when being addressed

Speech difficulties may occur without hearing loss but will have an equally severe impact upon a child's learning. Language skills are intimately related to the development of cognitive skills. These problems range from *delayed speech* to *indistinct articulation.*

Delayed speech may stem from a wide range of causes. A neuromuscular disorder such as cerebral palsy or simply shyness and lack of environmental stimulation may lead to limited speech.

Articulation deviations are common in young children. Many children find it easier to say "b," "d," and "g" at the beginning of words and often end words with "p," "t," and "k." Double consonants such as "sp" and "tr" are difficult. If only a few words are unintelligible, the child will probably be able to say words more clearly with time. On the other hand, if all the child's words are unintelligible and the child is older than three or three and a half, professional help is indicated. A speech therapist should evaluate the child and possibly institute a remedial program.

Children who have delayed speech may be helped through special activities at school and at home. Both teachers and parents can encourage children to talk by listening carefully to what they have to say. Adults should ask questions that encourage children to use sentences rather than a single word. Most important, children should have interesting experiences they can talk about.

Certain *behaviors* may interfere with the child's ability to take advantage of the curriculum of the school. These may range from very mild patterns to severe disabilities.

Mild patterns of behavior that limit the child's learning capability sometimes go unnoticed by parents. In school, though, the behavior is usually noted. In this category are such things as extreme shyness that prevents the child from participating in group activities or making friends. Also included is the limited ability to stay with an activity long enough to finish. Then, there is the child who only wants to play with one toy or one activity. Each of these behaviors interferes little with other children's rights, but if left unchanged, that behavior will limit what the child will gain from a preschool experience.

More severe patterns of behavior are easily identified by both parents and teachers. These are the behaviors that infringe upon others' rights. The child who hits or bites is noticed by everyone around him, at home or at school. The child who constantly moves around, creating havoc everywhere he goes, also does not escape notice. Severe temper tantrums long past the time when most children have found other ways of expressing frustration can also be considered serious.

Behavior deviations can often be assessed correctly by experienced teachers. They will know that some behaviors are part of a child's normal developmental progression. Others are personality characteristics. Children with other behaviors, particularly those that persist or severely limit the child, should be referred to appropriate professionals. A detailed discussion of behaviors is not appropriate here, but suggested sources for further information appear at the end of this chapter.

Some children with special needs can profit from participating in programs designed for children without special needs. This process is called *mainstreaming*. Additional staff, materials, and perhaps modifications in the physical environment may be required. Although the Americans with Disabilities Act prohibits discrimination in enrollment policies, private schools can decide if they can provide the necessary environment. Before accepting a child, both director and staff should make an honest assessment of the child's needs. The director should observe the child, discuss needs with the parents, and confer with staff members about the ways the environment and/or curriculum can be changed to accommodate the child. The experience for both adults and children should be a positive one, so careful consideration ahead of time is essential.

Children with special needs such as mental retardation, visual or hearing limitations, and physical difficulties can be managed fairly easily in the regular classroom. On the other hand, a child with emotional problems may be a disruptive influence in the classroom that many teachers do not have the skills to manage. One disruptive child can make it impossible for all the other children in the group to gain as much as they might from their preschool activities. The school should enroll children with special needs only if it can be a positive experience for the children, other children in the group, and the teachers.

Preventing Future Illnesses

Each person involved in an early childhood program should be concerned about the problem of illnesses in children in their care. Young children are especially vulnerable to a variety of infections and communicable diseases. This vulnerability is due to some special characteristics of this age level. Young children

1. have not developed immunity.
2. have a small body structure. The distance between the nose and throat area and the middle ear is especially small. Respiratory infections are the result.

3. are in close contact with other children while playing, eating, toileting, and diapering.

4. use their mouths as an additional way to find out about the world around them.

5. fall frequently, getting bumps and scrapes that can become infected.

6. do not know how to protect themselves and have not developed routine hygiene procedures.

One way to minimize occurrences of illness in a school is to develop procedures for care of the *environment*. Since the requirements for infants and toddlers are somewhat more extensive than those for older children, it is helpful to look at these separately.

General precautions to prevent the spread of diseases in a child care environment are the following:

1. Clean rooms on a regular basis, including floor scrubbing and carpet cleaning.

2. Wipe tables with detergent and water after a play activity.

3. Clean and disinfect toys, utensils, or any objects that children handle or put in their mouths at least once a week. Wash in a dishwasher or dip in a bleach solution ($\frac{1}{4}$ cup household bleach and 1 gallon of water prepared fresh each day).

4. Clean and sanitize bathrooms daily using a bleach solution.

5. Clean and disinfect the entire play area on a daily basis.

6. Clean sleeping cots or mats at least once a week. Each child should have a cot or mat with a sheet or blanket. Wash sheets or blankets each week.

7. Whenever possible, clean with paper towels rather than cloth towels.

8. Encourage children to wash their hands after toileting, before eating, and before participating in a cooking activity.

9. Establish a policy for exclusion of children whose condition is highly contagious.

10. Encourage children with runny noses to use a tissue and then wash their hands afterward.

The incidence of **AIDS** and other serious infectious diseases that affect children makes it necessary for staff members to take additional precautions when handling any body fluids (urine, feces, vomit, blood, saliva, or discharges from the nose, eyes, or draining sores). Important measures are the following:

1. Staff should wear latex gloves when cleaning up any body fluids. Gloves should be used once, for only one incident, then discarded.

2. Staff should wash their hands after handling any body fluids, whether they were wearing latex gloves or not.

3. For spills of vomit, urine, or feces, staff should clean and disinfect the area, including floors, walls, bathrooms, and tabletops.

4. Blood-contaminated material should be disposed of in a plastic bag with a secure tie and placed out of the reach of children.

5. If any staff member has any known sores, or breaks in the skin, on his or her hands, particular care to wear gloves should be taken when handling blood or body fluids containing blood.

6. Staff who may be exposed to hepatitis B or to contaminated blood should be informed about immunization.

The requirements for an *infant and toddler room* are more stringent because of the kinds of activities that go on there. Children crawl on the floor, are diapered, and put almost all objects in their mouths. So, in addition to the general room cleaning that is done, some special procedures can increase the safety of this area of the school. They are the following:

1. Cleanliness is important in this area of the school but should not present an obstacle to interactions with children. Cleanliness should become so automatic that children can be attended to while also having as safe and disease-free an environment as possible.

2. Vacuum carpeting daily and wet-mop vinyl floors with detergent and disinfectant. Clean all floor surfaces thoroughly on a regular schedule.

3. Wipe cribs and mattresses with a disinfectant regularly. Change the sheets whenever wet or soiled. Wash sheets weekly, or as needed.

4. Cover the diapering table with paper towels when being used; however, wipe it with a disinfectant after each use.

5. Dispose of soiled diapers or hold for a laundry in a closed container.

6. Rinse the potty chair cup after each use, and spray the seat with a disinfectant.

7. Wash all toys with a disinfectant at the end of each day. Put them in a mesh bag, dip them in a disinfectant solution, and hang them to dry.

8. Spray with disinfectant and wipe any large pieces of equipment that children climb.

9. Disinfect food containers and utensils regularly.

10. A solution of $\frac{1}{4}$ cup of chlorine bleach in a gallon of water is an adequate disinfectant for most cleaning purposes.

11. All caregivers in the infant-toddler room should automatically wash their hands after diapering and before feedings or preparing food for children.

A discussion of preventing unhealthful conditions should include *management of the sick child*. Each school should have a child inclusion/exclusion policy statement stating when children should be kept at home and under what conditions a child will be sent home. Such a policy might state that children will not be denied admission nor sent home unless

a. their illness prevents them from participating in activities.

b. their illness results in need for more care than the staff can provide without jeopardizing the health or safety of other children.

Children should be sent home and kept home as long as the following conditions exist or until medical evaluation deems it safe for the child to return.

1. oral temperature 101°F or greater; rectal temperature 102°F or greater; armpit temperature 100°F or greater, accompanied by changes in behavior or other signs of illness

2. symptoms and signs of a severe illness: coughing, wheezing, lethargy, irritability, crying

3. vomiting: two or more episodes in the previous 24 hours

4. uncontrolled diarrhea

5. rash, along with a fever or change in behavior

6. mouth sores accompanied by drooling

7. purulent conjunctivitis (pink eye)

8. tuberculosis

9. strep throat or other streptococcal infection

10. scabies, head lice, or any other infestation

11. impetigo

12. chicken pox, until six days after onset of the rash or until all sores are dry and crusted

13. mumps, until nine days after the onset of gland swelling

14. pertussis, until five days of antibiotic treatment have been completed

15. hepatitis A virus, until one week after the onset or as directed by health authorities

16. rubella, until six days after onset of rash

17. measles, until six days after onset of rash

The first step is to train teachers and caregivers to recognize early signs of a sick child. The most obvious symptoms are a runny nose, red throat, sneezing, and coughing. Diarrhea and vomiting also are quickly associated with a possible illness. Less apparent signs may be "glassy" or watery eyes and a general listlessness. Irritability, fatigue, or loss of appetite might also not be recognized as portending an illness. Several staff members should know how to take children's temperatures and to interpret the reading. (An oral temperature over 99.4°F or an axillary reading over 98°F accompany many childhood illnesses.)

The next step in managing a sick child is to decide what to do when the illness is first recognized. If it is at the beginning of the day during morning inspection, the child should be sent home. If the illness only becomes apparent as the day wears on, other decisions may have to be made.

The ideal would be to have a portion of the school environment set aside for the care of sick children. Here children could stay and be taken care of until the end of the day when the parents can come to pick them up. Some programs do offer this kind of service. The school must have a planned environment that allows the children to be in a less stimulating setting than their regular classroom. There also should be medical services available by telephone as needed. The Fairfax–San Anselmo

Children's Center in Fairfax, California, provides this kind of service. One of the classrooms is called the "get well" room. Staffed by regular child care workers who have had specialized training, the room can accommodate six children. Parents let the staff know about the child's evening and morning symptoms. Staff keep careful records of the child's day for parents' information at pickup time.

Some child care centers provide care for a sick child within the regular classroom. The Frank Porter Graham Child Development Center in Chapel Hill, North Carolina, has operated such a program for more than 10 years. Children with minor illnesses are allowed to attend school and stay in their regular classrooms. Children with contagious diseases such as measles and chicken pox are excluded, but because so many children are immunized, few have been kept home. The usual caregivers take care of the children, but medical assistance is nearby when necessary. The designers of this program reason that the child is most contagious long before recognizable symptoms appear, so there is little reason to exclude children once the illness has been identified. Children in this program do not become ill more frequently than in other programs, and the diseases are no more severe.

Another kind of service for sick children is a child care center totally devoted to their needs. An interesting child care center aptly named Chicken Soup in Minneapolis, Minnesota, is the first school in the United States licensed to care only for children who are moderately ill. The program accommodates children from six months to twelve years who have colds, flu, or even chicken pox. Children are separated according to their illnesses, and nurses are available to care for them. Although this is a relatively expensive kind of child care, it is probably a bargain to the parent who might otherwise miss a full day's pay by staying home to care for the child.

Including sick or recovering children in the regular classroom may mean that staff will have to be responsible for *giving medication* during the day. This should be done only with signed permission from both parents and the children's physicians. Medicines must be kept in a separate place, either on a high shelf or in the refrigerator. It is absolutely necessary to maintain careful records of the time a dosage was given, the person who gave it, and the amount given. Parents and caregivers should confer daily as to the continuance of the medication.

One further way to prevent future illness is *immunization*. This practice protects children against many of the preventable childhood diseases including rubella, mumps, measles, polio, whooping cough, diphtheria, and tetanus. Many parents have their children routinely immunized from an early age. Others are seemingly unconcerned because they do not recognize that some of these conditions are life-threatening to young children. Others think these diseases have been eliminated and, therefore, their children need not be subjected to the procedure. A few worry about the side effects of immunization.

Immunization is required before entering public school in all states and the District of Columbia. In states where the requirements for preschools and child care centers are not similar, many teachers, directors, and others responsible for policies have opted to require immunization as a condition of entrance. Visit http://www.cdc.gov/nip to view the recommended immunization schedule for children.

When, in spite of all preventive measures, a child in a school has contracted one of these illnesses, it is the director's responsibility to see that the parents of all children who might have been exposed are notified. A simple form can indicate that their child has been exposed to such-and-such illness. The form should include information about the incubation period and possible signs and symptoms.

Children should not be allowed back into the classroom until their physician certifies that they are free of contagion. This will protect staff, children, and parents in the best possible way.

Including Children with HIV/AIDS

Although reports from the Centers for Disease Control (CDC) indicate that the number of children with AIDS has declined since 1994, there are still many who are infected. Despite the fact that evidence indicates these children can attend child care programs without harm to other children, many child care professionals are concerned. In actuality, HIV children themselves are at risk of contracting other childhood diseases because their immune systems do not develop antibodies to combat them. In order to relieve anxieties by staff members and parents, it is important to become educated about what the disease is, how it is transmitted, and what precautions can be taken to prevent spread.

Children with HIV have been infected by their mothers during pregnancy or through receiving a contaminated blood transfusion. Adults acquire the disease by sexual contact involving secretions and sperm, infected blood, and contaminated needles. It is *not* transmitted by casual contacts such as sharing food, dishes, drinking glasses, toilets, pools, clothing, or toys. You cannot get it from hugging, kissing, or touching. Children with HIV can go to school, play with friends, and participate in out-of-school recreational activities without risk to other children. The CDC and the Pediatric AIDS Foundation of Santa Monica, California, recommend that children be kept out of group activities *only if they have bleeding or open sores* that might expose other children to risks. When children are included in school, the precautions listed in this chapter should be strictly adhered to, especially when cleaning up any blood or blood-contaminated fluids. It is recommended that schools and child care centers *draft a policy on infectious diseases, including HIV*, which is distributed to all staff members and parents. For further information about HIV, contact the Centers for Disease Control of the U.S. Public Health Service and the Pediatric AIDS Foundation.

Centers for Disease Control & Prevention (CDC)
  http://www.cdc.gov
  301-458-4636

Pediatric AIDS Foundation
  1311 Colorado Avenue
  Santa Monica, CA 90405
  310-314-1459
  http://www.pedaids.org

Another excellent source of information regarding health and safety of children in group care can be obtained from the National Association for the Education of Young Children (NAEYC). It is called *Model Child Care Health Policies* and is available on a computer disk, either IBM-compatible or Apple/Macintosh. Topics covered include admissions policies, supervision, discipline, care of ill children, health plans and services, emergency plans, transportation of children, sanitation and hygiene, food handling, sleeping, and staff policies. The publication can be obtained by writing to:

NAEYC
1509 16th Street, NW
Washington, DC 20036–1426
202-232-8777; 800-424-2460; fax 202-328-1846

Recordkeeping

Although the matter of adequate records of children's health has been touched upon, it is important enough to be covered more extensively. Adequate records are the basis for planning for individual children, for developing policies and procedures, and for checking the attainment of health goals. Each child should have a file that contains information about health before entering school and during the time of attendance.

Each child's file should contain the following information.

HEALTH

physician's examination prior to entrance including general health status, any conditions that might interfere with functioning at school, immunizations, conditions the school should be aware of, such as seizures and allergies

health screening tests or observations by teachers

continuing health care—illnesses, surgery, injuries, current medications

CHILD DEVELOPMENT

information concerning the mother's pregnancy

developmental history from birth to school entrance

profiles done by teachers on a periodic basis

FAMILY INFORMATION

application form including residence, place of work of both parents, family members

emergency information including persons to contact in case the child is hurt or ill

release for emergency medical treatment

persons authorized to take child from school

authorization for use of child's photo or voice recording for educational purposes

permission to take child on trips away from school

financial arrangements for payment of tuition

Health and safety of their children when being cared for by someone else is probably the greatest concern of working parents. A well-maintained, safe, and healthful environment is worth all the staff effort and time that it takes. The parents will be grateful and there may be a financial benefit as well. A safe, well-maintained, and attractive school will bring a more stable enrollment and a more consistent income.

SUMMARY

The physical environment of the school should be planned carefully because it bears equal weight with educational programs.

Maintenance consists of major projects; operations are the day-to-day tasks required to keep the school functioning hygienically and attractively.

The director should take an inventory of all buildings and equipment at least annually and keep accurate records.

Licensing guidelines and local building and safety codes are designed to ensure the safety of children in group settings. It is important to know what is required and comply at all times. Regular safety checks of all equipment both indoors and outdoors are required.

Every school should have a well-stocked first aid kit. At least one person on staff at all times should be Red Cross certified to administer first aid.

It is important to develop a disaster plan for meeting emergencies such as fires, floods, hurricanes, tornadoes, or earthquakes. An evacuation route should be posted in each classroom and in entry areas. Frequent drills will prepare staff and children for what to do in the event of a disaster.

Every early childhood center should have a set of health goals designed to promote the health and well-being of children. These goals should be the basis for health policies that guide preventive practices.

Health goals should address children's health status and include means for alleviating conditions that prevent children from learning. Health goals should also address the prevention of future illnesses.

Prevention of future illnesses is facilitated by maintaining a clean and sanitary environment. In addition, staff must take additional precaution when handling body fluids.

Each school should have a child inclusion/exclusion policy stating when children should be kept at home and under what conditions children will be sent home.

The inclusion of children with HIV/AIDS is an issue that needs to be addressed in child care. All staff members and parents should become educated about the causes of AIDS, how it is transmitted, and what precautions can be taken to prevent its spread. It is important to keep accurate records of children's health. Records should include information regarding the child's general health status, developmental information, and family information.

SELECTED FURTHER READING

American Public Health Association and American Academy of Pediatrics. (1992). *Caring for our children: National health and safety performance standards for out-of-home child care programs*. Elk Grove, IL: American Academy of Pediatrics.

American Academy of Pediatrics. (2002). *National health and safety performance standards for out-of-school child care programs* 2nd ed. Elk Grove Village, IL: Author.

Children's Defense Fund. (2001). *The state of America's children 2001*. Washington, DC: Author.

Healthy child care America: A blueprint for action. (1996). *Young Children, 51*(5), 57–58.

Kendrick, A. S., Kaufmann, R., & Messenger, K. P. (Eds.). (1995). *Healthy young children: A manual for programs–1995 edition*. Washington, DC: National Association for the Education of Young Children.

Mickalaide, A. (1994). Creating safer environments for children. *Childhood Education, 70*(5), 263–266.

Robertson, C. (2003). *Safety, nutrition, and health in early childhood education*: (2nd ed.). Clifton Park, NY: Delmar Learning.

Werner, P., Timms, S., & Almond, L. (1996). Health stops: Practical ideas for health-related exercise in preschool and primary classrooms. *Young Children, 51*(6), 48–51.

STUDENT ACTIVITIES

1. Draw the floor plan of a classroom you know. How would you replan it after having read this chapter? What are your reasons for the changes?

2. Visit a school for young children. Observe the playground for an hour. What changes would you make if you were in charge? Why?

3. What methods are used to clean your school? Are they adequate? Why?

4. Visit the health department of your community. What services are available to children? Who can use them?

5. Look in the telephone book under the listing for physicians. How many pediatricians are there?

6. Where is the closest emergency hospital to your school? Is the phone number posted? Do you know the most direct route?

REVIEW

1. Why is the physical appearance of a school more than cosmetic?

2. List safety precautions that should be taken when transporting children.

3. What kinds of information are included in a disaster plan?

4. List items that should be included in a disaster kit.

5. List five general precautions to prevent the spread of diseases in a child care environment.

6. What special precautions should be taken when handling any body fluids?

7. How do physical disabilities interfere with a child's ability to learn?

8. Under what conditions should children be sent home and be kept at home?

9. What are the current recommendations for including children with HIV/AIDS in child care?

10. What are the three categories of information that should be in a child's health file?

CASE STUDY

Ryan Walsh is three years old and was diagnosed with hemophilia when he first began to walk. At home the family has been able to restrict his activities somewhat so that he has had few problems. However, now his mother feels he needs to be with other children and would like for him to be in a good preschool. She visited several in her community and none of them had openings. She finally called a small school owned and operated by Maria Guiterrez. Maria said they did have an opening and would be willing to discuss Ryan's enrollment.

Mrs. Walsh visited the school and liked what she saw. Maria seemed willing to discuss Ryan's enrollment further and asked what special accommodations would be needed to keep Ryan safe. Outdoors at home Ryan wears a helmet, elbow pads and knee pads, and could do so at school. Additionally the school would need to have ice packs available at all times; these would be provided by the family. Mrs. Walsh would also see that the school had all necessary emergency telephone numbers. They agreed to pursue Ryan's enrollment further by having him come for a visit.

1. How would you feel about enrolling Ryan if you were Maria? Ryan's teacher?
2. What should Maria do to educate her staff members about managing a child with hemophilia?
3. If you were Maria, would you enroll Ryan in your program? Why or why not?

 ## HELPFUL WEB SITES

Americans with Disabilities Act (ADA) Home Page:	http://www.usdoj.gov/crt/ada/adahoml.htm
CDC National Prevention Information Network:	http://www.cdcnpin.org
Council for Exceptional Children:	http://cec.sped.org
National Program for Playground Safety:	http://uni.edu.playground
National Resource Center for Health and Safety in Child Care:	http://nrc.uchsc.edu
National SAFEKIDS Campaign:	http://www.safekids.org

 For additional resources related to administration, visit the Online Resource® for this book at www.EarlyChildEd.delmar.com

12

Food and Nutrition Services

allergens
Food Guide Pyramid

OBJECTIVES

After reading this chapter, you should be able to:

- Explain why good nutrition is important in an early childhood center.
- List several principles of menu planning.
- Describe some of the mechanics of food service.

A Day in the Life of ...

A Church-Affiliated School

Slices of watermelon were served at snacktime. One teacher saved the seeds to use for gluing on to construction paper cut in the shape of a slice of watermelon. Some of the seeds were still slippery when the activity began. When one little boy tried to pick them up between his thumb and forefinger, they would shoot away from his hand. After several tries with the same result, he sighed, "These are just too quick for me."

Proper nutrition is vital to the development of young children. What children eat during the years of rapid growth between birth and five years can affect their development for years to come. Improper nutrition may delay or permanently stunt physical growth. A child who is ill or lethargic because of poor nutrition will certainly have less interest in learning. An irritable child is likely to have problems in social situations. So, as more children spend longer hours in group settings, the adults who care for them must assume greater responsibility for seeing that they get an adequate diet.

 ## CAREGIVER'S ROLE

The caregivers or teachers who are with children during most of their waking hours must closely observe their eating patterns. They should be aware of children's food likes and dislikes, the amount each child consumes, and any changes in food habits. At times, this information can be used to reassure parents that their child is eating well at school. At other times, parents must be alerted to changes in a child's eating patterns.

Caregivers must also know what changes to expect in children's food consumption at each stage of development. During periods of rapid growth, children eat well. When growth slows down, they automatically consume less. Unless the adult is knowledgeable enough to see this as a normal change, adults may be needlessly anxious or pressure their children to change.

Current recommendations for good nutrition should be a part of the caregiver's knowledge. As research reveals more about what the body needs, ideas about what constitutes a proper diet have also changed. For instance, in the past, solid foods were introduced to infants as early as five to six weeks. In 1981, the American Academy of Pediatrics recommended that breast-fed babies do not need supplementary foods until six months of age. Formula-fed babies may need some vitamin supplements. At about six months, the ability to chew, swallow, and process solid foods is more developed. At that time, parents can gradually add cereal, fruits, vegetables, meat, and fish. By the end of the first year, children should be consuming a variety of foods from the four food groups.

Caregivers should know how to encourage children to make appropriate food choices, yet be sensitive to cultural differences. What children eat while in child care has the potential for conflicts with parents that are then communicated to the children. Some families eat little meat, for example, or may even be strict vegetarians. Other families avoid pork or use only foods that have a kosher mark. It is important that caregivers are aware of these differences and that the food served accommodates those preferences. Another area of possible conflict with parents is over self-feeding. Professionals agree that it is important to encourage even babies to start feeding themselves as soon as possible, but in some cultures children are fed by an adult until age four or later. This may be true in cultures where neatness is stressed, such as Japan. The same attitude may be true in American families where food cannot be wasted. Young children who are just learning to feed themselves may also "play" with the food before consuming it. Many experts advise leniency in allowing children to touch their food. Some teachers even use food as a sensory experience. Parents who have experienced deprivation may be offended or angered at this kind of waste.

MENU PLANNING

The director's responsibility will be either to plan menus or to oversee someone else who does the planning. If a school is open all day, it may be necessary to serve breakfast, lunch, and two snacks each day. This constitutes a large portion of the child's daily intake. Therefore, it is important to plan meals that include as much of the child's daily requirement as possible.

Licensing requirements will vary from state to state but are based on the number of hours a center is in operation. In general, guidelines specify the following:

- If a center is open three to four hours, it should serve a midmorning or afternoon snack no closer than two hours before the next meal.
- If a center is open five to eight hours, food service should provide one third to one half of the daily requirement.
- If a center is open nine hours or more, it should serve at least two thirds of the total daily requirement.
- If a center includes infants, they will have individualized eating plans and schedules.

Some child care programs receive funding under the Child Care Food Program. This provides reimbursement for meals in child care centers and for the cost of labor and administration. Money comes from the Food and Nutrition Service of the U.S. Department of Agriculture and is administered through state departments of education. Guidelines specify nutritional standards and serving sizes for children from birth to age 12. Head Start centers also have their own nutritional standards and serving-size regulations.

There are many ways to organize menu planning so that it is efficient. Marotz, Rush, and Cross (2001) recommend the following materials to help in menu planning.

- menu forms
- a list of foods on hand that should be included
- a recipe file
- old menus with notes and suggestions
- a calendar
- grocery ads for short-term planning

The main dishes to be served for lunch should include protein foods or substitutes. Vegetables and fruits should also be served. These can be as salads, with the entrée, or as dessert. Enriched or whole-grain breads or cereal products come next. The meal should include a beverage, usually milk. Snacks and breakfast can be planned to round out the daily requirements.

Many schools have cyclic menus. The first step is to make out several weekly menus and test them out to see if the children will eat the food. After making any necessary changes, the menus can be recycled every month or so. This has a decided advantage since it is possible to order larger quantities of some foods, thus saving money. It will also save the time it can take to prepare new menus every week. Children like familiar foods and do not mind having the same things every few weeks or so. It is easy to make changes to some basic menus using seasonal fruits or vegetables.

Including some ethnic or regional foods will help children from different backgrounds feel more comfortable. It will also introduce all children to the concept of cultural differences or similarities.

Some schools have instituted the idea of "special day foods." These foods do not appear on the cyclic menu but are served on special occasions. The "party" atmosphere of a day such as this may encourage children to try foods they would ordinarily reject. Examples might be a "smorgasbord" of out-of-the-ordinary fruits or vegetables that the children can taste-test at snacktime. Another might be an "upside-down day," such as whole-wheat pancakes with fruit toppings for lunch or cheese sandwiches for breakfast. The idea is to make tasting foods an adventure.

Some schools provide snacks in the morning and afternoon, but they expect parents to supply lunches for their children. If this is the case, it is still the responsibility of caregivers to see that children's lunches are as nutritious as possible. Parents can be educated about proper nutrition for their children and how to make appealing meals that will not end up in the trash can. It might be helpful to schedule a parent meeting with a nutritionist who can make suggestions for appealing brown-bag cuisine, or make a list of suggestions to be included in a parent newsletter.

 ## GUIDELINES FOR MENU PLANNING

Some further guidelines may be helpful in developing a series of menus to use in a school. The person responsible for planning meals should work within the framework of the **Food Guide Pyramid** developed by the U.S. Department of Agriculture's Human Nutrition Information Service. The pyramid (see Figure 12-1) shows four levels of choices and is easily understood by both adults and children. The widest part of the chart indicates those foods that should make up the largest proportion of the diet. At the highest level are the fats and sugars which should be consumed in small quantities. The number of servings for each level is also indicated and reflects the total intake for a single day. If a school provides two snacks and lunch to children, the menus should cover at least a third of the children's daily requirement.

Some centers may have children who are eligible for free or reduced-price meals from the United States Department of Agriculture (USDA), Child and Adult Care Food Program (CACFP). Children's eligibility is based on family income and providers are reimbursed at specific rates that are readjusted each year. Providers in the following categories may qualify: public or private nonprofit centers, profit-making centers that receive Title XX compensation for at least 25 percent of enrollees, Head Start programs, settlement houses and recreation programs, and family child care homes. All participating agencies must serve meals that meet the standards set by the USDA. Figures 12-2 and 12-3 show the kinds of foods to be served and the portion sizes. Further information about requirements and children's eligibility can be obtained by contacting a regional office of the USDA or by calling the National Food Service Management Institute's "Help Desk" that is funded by the USDA. The phone number is 800-321-3054.

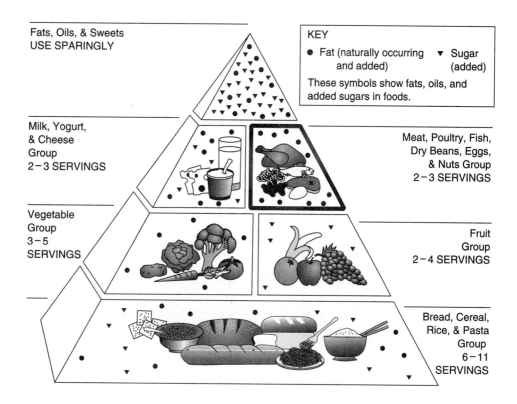

FIGURE 12-1 ■ Food Guide Pyramid.

It is important to choose foods children like. Children are sensitive to the four basic tastes—salty, sweet, sour, and bitter. Because of this enhanced taste awareness, they are more conservative in their approach to foods. Most have a very limited number of foods they like. They will often reject foods that are strong in flavor or heavily spiced. They often reject new foods before they even taste them. Children do not like their foods mixed in casseroles or stew. Most want their food to be easy to manage, in bite-sized pieces or as finger foods. A list of the proven favorites can be used to plan basic menus. New foods can gradually be added to broaden the children's diet.

The person who plans the menus should take into consideration the kitchen equipment that is available. When preparing food for large numbers of people, one of the problems often incurred is that there is not enough oven space or large pans. It is important to know what is in the kitchen and anticipate what will be needed to prepare and serve the food. As an example, a finger food can be prepared for dessert if all the small bowls are to be used for the meal.

The director should consider the number of personnel available for preparing and serving food. If a school is very large, there may be both a cook and an assistant. Meals are likely to be different in this kind of school than in one where there is only a part-time

MEAL PATTERN	CHILDREN 1 TO 3	CHILDREN 3 TO 6	CHILDREN 6 TO 12
BREAKFAST			
Milk	1/2 cup	3/4 cup	1 cup
Juice or fruit	1/4 cup	1/2 cup	1/2 cup
Bread or	1/2 slice	1/2 slice	1 slice
Cereal: cold, dry or hot, cooked	1/4 cup	1/3 cup	1/2 cup
SNACK (select 2)			
Milk, meat, or meat substitute	1/2 cup	1/2 cup	1 cup
Bread or substitute	1/2 slice	1/2 slice	1 slice
Juice, fruit, or vegetable	1/2 cup	1/2 cup	3/4 cup
Cereal, cold, dry or hot, cooked	1/4 cup	1/3 cup	1/2 cup
LUNCH OR SUPPER			
Milk	1/2 cup	3/4 cup	1 cup
Meat or alternative—One of the following combinations to give equivalent quantities.			
Meat, poultry, fish	1 ounce	1 1/2 ounce	2 ounces
Egg	1	1	1
Cheese	1 ounce	1 1/2 ounce	2 ounces
Cooked dry beans	1/4 cup	3/8 cup	1/2 cup
Peanut butter	2 tablespoons	3 tablespoons	4 tablespoons
Vegetables and/or fruit (2 or more to total)	1/4 cup	1/2 cup	3/4 cup
Bread or alternate	1/2 slice	1/2 slice	1 slice
Butter or margarine	1/2 teaspoon	1/2 teaspoon	1/2 teaspoon

Figure 12-2 ■ Child and Adult Care Food Program, meal pattern for children.

cook. In a family child care home, where the owner-operator does all the cooking, meals must be extremely simple and easily prepared.

Foods should provide appetite appeal. Remember the old saying "We eat with our eyes as well as our mouths." It helps to vary the color of foods served. A meal of mashed potatoes, fish, and cauliflower will hardly be appealing. The cook should occasionally change the shape of familiar foods. Sandwiches may be cut in triangles, circles, or slim rectangles. Meals should include several different textures: crunchy, soft, chewy.

A new food should be introduced along with a familiar and accepted food. As an example, if the goal is to have children try a new vegetable, it could be served with their favorite chicken. An unfamiliar carrot salad could be served along with the fish sticks most children love.

Menus For Week Of ______________

	MONDAY	TUESDAY	WEDNESDAY	THURSDAY	FRIDAY
BREAKFAST	½ orange ¼ cup shredded wheat cereal ¾ cup milk	½ cup tomato juice 2 4" pancakes 2 Tbsp. applesauce ½ tsp. margarine ½ cup milk	½ cup sliced peaches ¾ cup milk bagel half low-fat cream cheese	½ banana ¼ cup shredded wheat cereal ¾ cup milk ½ slice toast ½ tsp. margarine	½ cup orange juice French toast ½ slice bread milk egg powdered sugar ½ cup milk
SNACK	½ cup milk 2 graham crackers melon cubes	½ slice cheese 4 small whole-wheat crackers apple juice	½ cup yogurt with fruit 2 whole-wheat crackers banana slices water	½ slice cheese ½ apple water	½ cup apple juice 2 graham crackers low-fat yogurt
LUNCH	½ cup milk 2 fish sticks 4 carrot sticks ½ slice bread ½ tsp. margarine ⅓ cup applesauce	½ cup milk 1 oz. meat loaf ¼ cup peas ¼ baked potato ½ tsp. margarine 2" square of spice cake made with whole-wheat flour	½ cup milk ½ cup spaghetti ¼ cup meat sauce ¼ cup green salad 2 orange wedges	½ cup milk ½ cup macaroni & cheese ¼ cup string beans ¼ cup Apple Betty w/ wheat germ topping	½ cup milk ½ tuna sandwich ¼ cup carrot & raisin salad ½ cup ice cream
SNACK	assorted raw vegetables sour cream dip ¼ slice whole-wheat bread ½ tsp. margarine water	½ cup yogurt with fruit 1 graham cracker water	½ peanut butter sandwich ½ cup milk	whole wheat raisin cookies ½ cup milk	½ cup milk ⅓ warm tortilla ½ tsp. margarine or grated cheese

FIGURE 12-3 ■ Weekly menu in a child care center for a group of three-year-olds.

In a study on serving and food intake, Baylor College of Medicine researcher Dr. Jennifer Fisher found that preschool children ate 25 percent more when given a larger portion of food, increasing lunchtime calorie count by 15 percent.

These findings suggest that regular exposure to "supersized" portions encourages overeating among children. The study also produced a surprisingly positive result. When children were allowed to serve themselves from serving bowls, the amount they served themselves was appropriate. As Dr. Fisher reported, "We found that large portions lost the power to promote overeating when the children were allowed to serve themselves."

Source: Baylor College of Medicine, 1999.

Dessert should be an integral part of the meal, not a special treat when other foods are eaten. Desserts should contribute to the daily food requirement. Fruits, cakes made with whole-wheat flour, cookies with nuts or raisins, or milk puddings are all examples. Children also enjoy ice cream or fruit sherbets, which contribute to good nutrition.

Children learn when they help plan their own meals and snacks. When given limited choices, preschoolers and school-age children can plan some of their own meals and snacks. Obviously, they cannot be given total freedom since they might well choose a meal of potato chips, ice cream, and chocolate cupcakes. But if they are given information about the food groups, they should be able to plan a meal using foods from each. Children should be allowed to plan lunch once a week, once a month, or as often as possible.

INCLUDING PARENTS

It is important to keep the parents of children in the school informed about the foods to be served. One of the first questions many parents ask when they arrive to pick up their child at the end of the day is "Did my child eat well today?" Parents are concerned that their children eat the right foods in adequate amounts.

Weekly menus should be posted in an easily seen place so parents know what was served that day. When they see a food they know their child likes, they can feel more confident. At home, the evening meal can then supplement whatever the child had at school.

A parent newsletter is a great way to provide information about appropriate food choices for young children. Information can be obtained from articles in nutrition jounals or from the local library. The articles can be summarized or reprinted in totality for parents. If the children bring breakfast or lunch from home, parents can be given suggestions for choosing nutritious foods and advice about how to avoid the "television

Lunch is a time to socialize.

advertising trap"—those appealing ads that make children demand the foods in their lunch boxes. Only clever substitutes will satisfy many children (see Figure 12-4). A newsletter might also give suggestions for nutritious birthday treats that parents may bring to school.

Instead of whole milk: use dry low-fat milk, cottage cheese, mild cheddar cheese, ice milk.

Instead of expensive cuts of meat: use less tender cuts, stewing chickens, fresh fish in season, home-cooked meats.

Use dried beans, peas, lentils, peanut butter.

Fruits and vegetables: buy fresh fruits and vegetables in season.

Breads and cereals: use whole-grain or enriched flour, homemade cakes and rolls, whole-grain crackers.

Use brown rice and enriched spaghetti and noodles.

FIGURE 12-4 ■ Inexpensive substitutes with more food value.

Teachers should keep parents informed about their child's food intake. Some schools have a form that is filled out by teachers each day indicating how much the child ate. If the school does not use a form, teachers should be alert to each child's consumption so that parents' questions can be answered.

The school should develop a partnership with parents of infants and toddlers to plan food choices. The diets of these young children need to be carefully thought out to avoid food allergies, digestive upsets, and poor nutrition. Pediatricians have traditionally worked with parents to avoid these problems. Now the school must be included in the planning. Compounding the difficulty is the fact that babies react in different ways to new situations, including new foods. Caregivers need to be aware of those habits so they can avoid rejection of food the child needs. Many toddlers have particular ways in which they want their food prepared or presented. No other way will do. So it is essential that the school have a close alliance with the parents to ensure that these youngest children are eating an adequate diet.

All parents must inform the school of their child's allergies. A large number of preschool children have allergic reactions, although not all are to food. The common food **allergens** are chocolate, milk and milk products, wheat, and eggs. When planning a menu item using these foods, there must be a substitute that can be served to the allergic child. Some schools ask parents to supply alternate foods on these days. Other schools keep foods on hand to use at these times.

Parents should be offerd recipes of school foods that children especially like. Many children talk about a popular menu item and want Mom to prepare it at home. Quantity recipes can be translated to smaller portions so that copies are available when parents ask. Just as serving homelike foods at school brings home and school closer together, the opposite will bridge the gap as the child reenters the home routines.

 ## FOOD SERVICE FOR CHILDREN

The best-planned menus are of no use unless children eat the food. The atmosphere in which food is presented should encourage the children to consume an adequate amount.

The classroom should be straightened before mealtime. Many teachers involve children in this task. It can also be done while the children are outdoors or having a story in another area. The teacher should put toys that might create a distraction out of sight and clear away any clutter on shelves or floors.

Tables should be as attractive as possible. A centerpiece of flowers or something made by the children will add interest. Children can make their own personalized placemats. The mat can be covered with clear contact paper for durability. The table should be set in an orderly manner with napkins, utensils, and plates carefully placed and convenient to the children's reach. Special occasions such as holidays or birthdays call for special table decorations.

Mealtime furniture should be appropriate for the age level of the children. One consideration is whether to use tables or highchairs for toddlers. According to Magda Gerber (1991), Director of Resources for Infant Educarers, highchairs are confining.

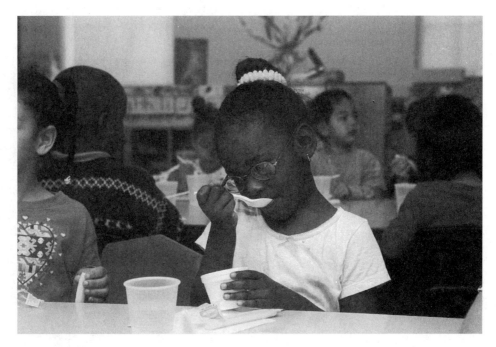

Snacktime.

As soon as babies can crawl and sit up, Gerber says they can get themselves to a table that is only a few inches off the floor. At the other extreme, school-age children need larger chairs and higher tables than preschoolers.

Children should participate as much as possible in the routines of mealtimes. They can certainly set the table before the meal begins. Children can serve themselves from serving bowls rather than having each plate already "dished out" before it comes to the table. At the end of the meal, children can scrape leftovers from their own plates and put their utensils in a container.

Teachers and caregivers should eat with the children at mealtimes. Seeing adults enjoying food serves as a role model for the development of appropriate attitudes and behavior in the children. Mealtimes should also be a time when children and adults have a chance to talk quietly to each other. It certainly should not be a time when table manners are stressed or pressure exerted for "clean plates."

 COOKING EXPERIENCES FOR CHILDREN

Cooking experiences can be planned for children as part of the overall process of food service. Children are quite capable of preparing some of their own meals or snacks as part of the curriculum of each classroom. Directors should be the motivating force to encourage teachers to become involved as well as provide the equipment and materials to do so. Some teachers love to cook and enjoy sharing their skills,

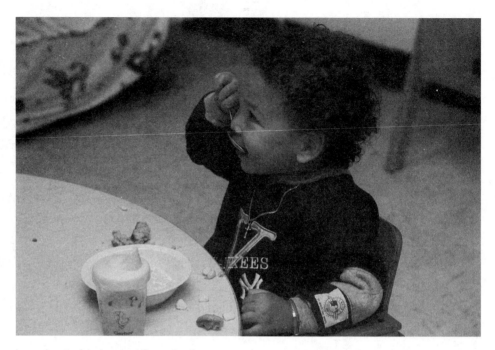

Learning to feed yourself can be fun.

interests, and knowledge about food with children; others see it as a chore. Those who see it as a chore may need a little extra help and encouragement.

The director should include the staff in discussions of menus and invite their suggestions for things they can prepare with the children. Starting with snacks is the easiest, since many can be done without much preparation or cooking. Even two-year-olds can spread peanut butter on a cracker with a plastic knife. Preschoolers can make a fruit shake in a blender or cut their own hard-cooked eggs with an egg slicer. School-age children, obviously, are capable of preparing a variety of nutritious snacks for themselves.

At staff meetings, it is important to discuss how teachers can set up a cooking experience so there is little danger that children will get hurt. Many adults shudder at the thought of three- and four-year-olds using a knife or an electric frying pan. Careful planning is essential. If an activity is set up properly and supervised adequately, teachers should have few problems. The following books can help teachers plan cooking in the classroom.

Catron, C., & Parks, B. (1986). *Cooking up a story*. Minneapolis, MN: T. S. Dinison and Company.

Cook, D. (1995). *Kids' multicultural cookbook*. Charlotte, VT: Williamson Publishing.

Jenkins, K. (1982). *Kinder krunchies*. Pleasant Hill, CA: Discovery Toys.

McClenahan, P., & Jaqua, I. (1976). *Cool cooking for kids: Recipes and nutrition for kids*. Belmont, CA: Fearon Pitman.

Nissenberg, S. (2002). *Everything kid's cookbook*. Avon, MA: Adams Media Corporation

Nissenberg, S. (Ed.). (1994). *The healthy start kid's cookbook: Fun and healthful recipes that make themselves*. Hoboken, NJ: John Wiley & sons.

Stori, M. (1980). *I'll eat anything if I can make it myself*. Chicago: Chicago Review.

Wanamaker, N., Hearn, K., & Richarz, S. (1979). *More than graham crackers: Nutrition education and food preparation with young children*. Washington, DC: National Association for the Education of Young Children.

Wilkes, A. (2001). *The children's step-by-step cookbook*. New York: Darling Kindersley.

Wilms, B. (1984). *Crunchy bananas*. Salt Lake City, UT: Gibbs M. Smith.

Zeller, P. K., & Jacobson, M. F. (1987). *Eat, think, and be healthy!* Washington, DC: Center for Science in the Public Interest.

The following is a list of children's books that help children understand the various types of food.

Ahlberg, J., & Ahlberg, A. (1978). *Each peach, pear, plum*. New York: Viking.

Babcock, C. (1995). *No moon, no milk*. New York: Scholastic.

Brown, M. (1947). *Stone soup*. New York: Scribner.

De Paola, T. (1992). *Jamie O'Rourke and the big potato*. New York: Scholastic.

Degen, B. (1986). *Jamberry*. New York: Scholastic.

Fowler, A. (1995). *Thanks to cows*. Danbury, CT: Children's Press.

Fowler, A. (1995). *We love fruit!* Danbury, CT: Children's Press.

Gibbons, G. (1993). *The milk makers*. New York: Scholastic.

Krensky, S. (1993). *The pizza book*. New York: Scholastic.

Littledale, F. (1988). *Peter and the north wind*. New York: Scholastic.

McDonald, M. (1996). *The potato man*. Danbury, CT: Children's Press.

Minuchkin, F. (1994). *Latkes and applesauce: A Hanukkah story*. New York: Scholastic.

Nelson, J. (1990). *Neighborhood soup*. New York: Modern Curriculum.

Robbins, K. (1982). *Make me a peanut butter sandwich and a glass of milk*. New York: Scholastic.

Rose, A. (1979). *Akimba and the magic cow: A folktale from Africa*. New York: Four Winds.

Scheer, J. (1964). *Rain makes applesauce*. New York: Holiday.

Westcott, N. (1987). *Peanut butter and jelly: A play rhyme*. New York: Dutton.

Nutrition Education in the Classroom

The act of preparing food is fun and exciting for young children and can be an incredible source of knowledge as well. They learn many things by planning, shopping for, preparing, and serving food. They can also learn a great deal by growing and harvesting food. Many children have no idea what corn looks like before it ends up in the supermarket or in a can. Probably few know that carrots and potatoes grow under the ground, celery grows above the ground, and peas grow on vines. In many families, there is little opportunity for children to help prepare food. In fact many families do not frequently sit down to a meal together. They stop at the fast food place on the way home, use prepackaged foods, or call for home delivery.

Although there is a lot of information available in magazines and newspapers about good nutrition, not everyone reads and absorbs that information. In addition, there is a lot of misinformation and conflicting theories that can confuse even the most sophisticated reader. Children need to have straightforward facts that they can understand at their level. They also need knowledgeable adults who will discuss this information with them.

The child care center, then, has a unique opportunity to educate children about what good nutrition means, what their bodies need to keep healthy, and how to select and prepare nutritious, good tasting food. The following are some suggestions:

- Display the Food Guide Pyramid along with posters of foods included in each group.
- Prepare and display posters showing seeds, plants, and food end products.
- Include pictures of food preparers in the cooking area.
- Show different ethnic groups along with their methods of cooking and food served.
- Discuss concepts of good nutrition using words such as vitamins, protein, and carbohydrates.
- Collect and sprout seeds in the classroom.
- Prepare a garden plot and then grow vegetables such as carrots, lettuce, radishes, pumpkins, peas, and green beans.

Cooking Activities

The following are some simple activities that can be used with children as young as three.

Easy Pizza

Purposes: learn that familiar foods can be prepared from alternative ingredients

practice measuring

increase small-muscle coordination by spreading and sprinkling

Ingredients and Procedure

English muffins	table knives
tomato sauce	tablespoons
oregano	baking sheets
salami or other meats	oven
mozarella cheese slices	

Spread one half of an English muffin with 1 tablespoon of tomato sauce. Sprinkle a pinch of oregano on top. Place one slice of salami, then a slice of cheese on top of the sauce. Place on a baking sheet and bake at 425°F for 10 minutes.

Food Group Sandwiches

Purposes: reinforce knowledge of foods from the Food Guide Pyramid

                      expand experiences with different foods

                      communicate information about choices to others

Ingredients and Procedure

bread: whole-wheat, wheat pita bread, whole-wheat tortillas

fruits and vegetables: cucumbers, tomatoes, bananas, raisins, apple slices, and sprouts

meat and meat substitutes: peanut butter, hard-cooked eggs, sliced turkey, hummus

milk: low-fat Swiss cheese, low-fat cheddar cheese, low-fat cottage cheese

fats: low-fat mayonnaise, margarine, whipped butter

Group the foods on trays labeled with their food group. Allow each child to make a sandwich using as many food groups as possible. During snacktime, have each child describe the sandwich and name the groups.

Baking Powder Biscuits

Purposes: measure accurately

                      develop small muscles by sifting,

                      blending, kneading, and cutting

Ingredients and Procedure

2 cups flour	measuring cups
2 teaspoons baking powder	measuring spoons
1 teaspoon salt	sifter
2 tablespoons shortening or margarine	mixing bowl
2/3 cup milk	pastry blender, fork
additional milk as needed	breadboard, rolling pin
	biscuit cutter or knife
	baking sheet, oven

Measure and sift flour, baking powder, and salt into mixing bowl. Add shortening or margarine and cut in with pastry blender. Add milk and stir in quickly with fork. Add more milk, little by little as needed, until dough is soft and light but not sticky. Turn out on floured board and knead with floured hands until smooth. Roll lightly $\frac{1}{2}''$ to $\frac{1}{4}''$ thick. Cut out with biscuit cutter or cut into squares with knife. Place on ungreased baking sheet and bake 12 to 15 minutes at 450°F. Makes 12 to 15 biscuits. Variations: Add $\frac{1}{2}$ cup grated cheese or 2 tablespoons peanut butter.

Yogurt Smoothie

Purposes: measuring accurately

                   cutting, spooning, pouring

Ingredients and Procedure

$\frac{1}{2}$ cup yogurt   knife

$\frac{1}{2}$ banana   cutting surface

$\frac{1}{4}$ cup other fruit: canned pineapple,   measuring cups
fresh apricots, berries, etc.   blender
dash cinnamon   spatula, spoon

                                                             glasses

Blend all ingredients for a few seconds. Pour into glasses. Makes one cup, but can easily be multiplied.

MECHANICS OF FOOD SERVICE

With the cost of food constantly rising, directors need to be wise shoppers when buying food for a large school. The goal is to serve high-quality meals at a cost the budget can afford.

Purchase

The director should check the community for food service companies that supply restaurants and institutions. They offer large-quantity packaging, often at a lower cost than the local supermarket. If the school is a nonprofit institution, they may even give an additional discount. Some deliver, but it is important to check on the cost of that service. The cost may be too high, or completely justified when weighed against the time required to shop for the food.

Newspaper ads are a good source for the weekly specials and also for fruits and vegetables that are in season. Markets feature items that are in large supply and lower the cost to attract buyers. The school can save money by filling out cyclic menus with whatever fruits and vegetables are on sale.

The quality of food chosen should be best suited for its purpose. Top quality, and probably a higher price, is not always necessary. It is important to read labels and check grades of food before deciding. A can of peaches to be used in a cobbler for dessert does not have to be the best but can be a lesser grade, for instance.

Perishable foods should be bought in a quantity that can be used quickly. Meats, fruits, vegetables, and milk products fall into this category. The quantity ordered should correspond to how much children are eating at meals.

Preparation

The best-planned meals will not be eaten if they are not prepared properly. Food can be overcooked or undercooked. Nutrients can also be lost in the cooking process so that the food contributes little to the children's health.

It is the director's responsibility to see that appropriate guidelines are followed by whoever prepares food at the school. This includes teachers in the preschool or after-school care rooms who help children with cooking. It also covers the person in the kitchen who puts together meals for the entire school. The following precautions shoule be taken.

- Prepare ahead only those foods that can safely be held under refrigeration: puddings, Jello™, and spaghetti sauce are some.
- Plan so that all foods finish cooking at about the same time so that none are held too long or reheated.
- Use cooking methods that preserve as many nutrients as possible. Do not soak vegetables for long periods of time in water or cook them in large quantities. Do not overcook vegetables.
- Prepare foods in ways that will be appealing to children. Add a touch of color sometimes with a sprinkling of paprika or parsley. Put a dab of jelly on vanilla pudding to make it more appetizing.
- Prepare food that is easy for children to manage. Cut meat into small pieces. Quarter sandwiches or cut them into interesting shapes. Vary the way fruits and vegetables are cut: Oranges can be in slices or wedges; carrots can be sticks or "pennies." Figures 12-5 and 12-6 list foods that will appeal to children and are easy for them to manage.

Safety

The safety of food served to children in a preschool or child care setting should be of primary concern to all. Food must be stored properly and prepared safely. All preparation and serving areas should be clean. Teachers, kitchen staff, and any others who handle food should observe good hygienic practices.

Food handlers must maintain the strictest standards of health practices. They should undergo periodic medical evaluations to determine their general health status and that they are free of tuberculosis. Anyone suffering from an illness should stay at home until recovered.

Food handlers must maintain strict standards of personal hygiene. This includes wearing clean clothes and washing hands frequently. Hair should be tidy or contained under a net. Food preparers should refrain from smoking.

Food handling should ensure that food is clean and free of contamination or spoilage. When food is delivered, it should be inspected for spoilage. Fruits and vegetables should be washed thoroughly. Foods that need refrigeration or are frozen should be put away immediately. Bulk foods such as flour or rice should be stored in airtight containers.

Food storage should provide optimum conditions for preserving the safety and nutritive value of food. Refrigerators should maintain a temperature of 38°F to 40°F.

Blender Beaters

yogurt, fruit, honey

yogurt, banana, canned crushed pineapple

milk, nonfat dry milk, berries

yogurt, frozen fruit (berries or cherries), honey

Yogurt Yummies

plain yogurt with any combinations of the following:

maple syrup, honey, brown sugar, molasses

wheat germ

applesauce, apple butter

raisins, nuts

peaches, pineapple, blueberries, strawberries

chocolate syrup, vanilla, cinnamon

Pancake Parade

whole-wheat pancakes with any of the following:

applesauce, apple butter, peach butter

crushed berries, sour cream

maple syrup, honey, molasses

mashed bananas with lemon juice, honey, cinnamon

mashed canned apricots combined with applesauce

berries, plums, or pears blended with pineapple juice

crumbled cooked bacon mixed into batter

Snazzy Sandwiches

grilled cheese

grilled cheese and tuna

open-faced: pizza sauce, grated cheese

refried beans, cheese in a soft tortilla

pita bread stuffed with chopped tuna

pita bread, scrambled egg, mild salsa

FIGURE 12-5 ■ Better breakfasts.

A freezer for long-term storage should be at 0°F. Foods on the shelf should have an even, cool, dry temperature. All containers should be stored off the floor.

Leftover food that has been served but has not been eaten should not be saved. The only exception might be fruits and vegetables. These can be washed and saved for serving at a later time. Food that has been left in the kitchen and held at a safe

Peanut butter with
    raisins or dates
    apples or banana
    applesauce
    chopped celery or shredded carrots
    graham crackers
    nonfat dry milk and honey
Cheese balls—form balls with softened cheese and roll in chopped nuts
Nut bread with cheese spread
Celery stuffed with peanut butter, cheese spread
Pizza—use pizza dough or English muffins
Tacos or burritos—fill with cheese, leftover meat, or finely shredded carrots or zucchini
Cottage cheese with fruit
Yogurt with fruit
Ice cream in milk shakes, with fruit, or in make-your-own sundaes
Deviled eggs
Wheat toast topped with tuna salad or cheese, broiled to melt
Tiny meatballs on toothpicks
Orange sections
Banana slices—dip in honey, roll in nuts
Watermelon wedges—try seedless melons
Peaches
Apple slices, dip in orange juice to prevent browning
Granola or cereal sprinkled on yogurt
Assorted raw vegetables with seasoned cottage cheese dip
Fruit shakes—blend fruit and nonfat dry milk in blender with a few ice cubes
Fruit kabobs—banana wheels, pineapple chunks, cherries, strawberries, orange wedges
Fresh fruit juice gelatin cubes

FIGURE 12-6 ■ Scrumptious snacks.

temperature can be covered and put into the freezer for later use. These foods will still be safe if hot foods have been held at 160°F; cold foods must be held at below 40°F.

Seeing that children in a school are well nourished, healthy, and developing positive attitudes toward eating is just as important as making certain that they acquire appropriate cognitive skills. Sadly, though, some directors see it as far less critical. Staff, parents, and children will benefit if it is a goal of the school.

SUMMARY

Caregivers or teachers must have an adequate knowledge of nutrition that enables them to be sensitive to children's dietary needs and behaviors.

Menu planning or supervision is an important part of a director's schedule. There are several principles to observe in planning menus.

- Use the four basic food groups.
- Choose foods children like.
- Plan menus within the capabilities of the kitchen.
- Fit menus to personnel available to cook and serve.
- Include food that has appeal.
- Introduce new foods along with familiar ones.
- Consider a nutritious dessert as an important part of the meal.
- Integrate meal planning into part of the child's learning.

Ordinarily, parents are very concerned with their child's eating habits. It is important to communicate with parents about the food served and the child's eating habits.

The eating environment and atmosphere are important. Classrooms used as dining rooms should be neat and attractive, furniture should be comfortable, children should participate in setting and serving, and teachers should eat with their charges.

Children should be exposed to cooking experiences that are appropriate to their developmental level.

The director should give a good deal of thought and enterprise to the mechanics of food procurement and preparation. Purchasing must be done along thrifty lines. Food poorly prepared is often wasted. Food should be easily handled and appealing to children.

Food must be prepared and served under strict sanitary conditions. All food handlers should be free of infectious disease. Care must be taken to prevent spoilage in handling and storage.

The development of good attitudes toward food is as worthy a goal as the acquisition of any other socially desirable trait. The preschool has an important role to play here.

 REFERENCES

Gerber, M. (1991). *Manual for resources for infant educarers.* Los Angeles: Resources for Infant Educarers.

Marotz, L., Rush, J., & Cross, M. (2001). *Health, safety, and nutrition for the young child* (5th ed.). Clifton Park, NY: Delmar Learning.

Shinnamon, F. *Childhood: A multicultural perspective.* Unpublished manuscript.

 SELECTED FURTHER READING

American Academy of Pediatrics. (1993). *Pediatric nutrition handbook.* Elk Grove, IL: Author.

Bomba, A. K., Oakley, C. B., & Knight, K. B. (1996). Planning the menu in the child care center. *Young Children, 51*(6), 62–67.

Briley, M., Roberts-Gray, C., & Rowe, S. (1993). What can children learn from the menu at a child care center? *Journal of Community Health, 18*(6), 363–377.

Cosgrove, M. S. (1991). Cooking in the classroom: The doorway to nutrition. *Young Children, 46*(3), 74–76.

Dahl, K. (1998). Why cooking in the classroom? *Young Children, 53*(1), 81–84.

Drake, M. A. (1992). Menu evaluation: Nutrient intake of young children and nutrition knowledge of menu planners in child care centers in Missouri. *Journal of Nutrition Education, 24*, 145–148.

Fuhr, J. E., & Barclay, K. H. (1998). The importance of appropriate nutrition and nutrition education. *Young Children, 53*(1), 74–80.

Nutrition programs for children. (1994). Champaign, IL: ERIC Clearinghouse for Elementary and Early Childhood Education.

Robertson, C. (2003). *Safety, nutrition, and health in early childhood education* (2nd ed.). Clifton Park, NY: Delmar Learning.

Rogers, C., & Morris, S. (1986). Reducing sugar in children's diets. *Young Children, 41* (5), 11–16.

Weiser, M. G. (1990). *Group care and education of infants and toddlers.* Columbus, OH: Merrill/Macmillan.

STUDENT ACTIVITIES

1. Prepare a poster for school-age children that shows the Food Guide Pyramid. Include suggestions for snack foods from each of the groups.

2. Plan a series of three lessons designed to teach four-year-olds about nutrition. Present the lessons to a group, then evaluate its effectiveness. Did the children understand the concepts you presented? Were there any perceptible changes in their attitudes toward any of the foods you discussed?

3. Observe two meals in a child care center. Evaluate them using the following rating:

	Excellent	*Good*	*Fair*	*Poor*
Attractiveness of setting	____	____	____	____
Cleanliness of setting	____	____	____	____
Comfort of seating	____	____	____	____
Appearance of food	____	____	____	____
Child-size portions	____	____	____	____
Teacher participation	____	____	____	____
General atmosphere	____	____	____	____

4. List the foods you liked as a young child. Why do you think these particular foods were favorites? Was it the taste, color, or ease of eating? Or were they favorites because of some association with pleasant experiences? What does this tell you about serving food to children in a child care setting?

REVIEW

1. Why is it important to see that young children receive adequate nutrition in child care?

2. If a center is open nine hours or more, what proportion of a child's daily minimum nutritional requirement should be provided?

3. Which foods are at the bottom of the Food Guide Pyramid?

4. Which foods are at the top of the Food Guide Pyramid?

5. State five suggestions for encouraging children to eat nutritious foods.

6. In what ways can a school establish and maintain a partnership with parents regarding their child's nutritional needs?

7. How can a director encourage teachers to plan cooking experiences for children?

8. Suggest some ways to decrease the cost of purchasing foods.

9. List several snacks that can easily be prepared for a group of preschool children.

10. Food storage should preserve the nutritional content of food and ensure safety. At what temperature should the refrigerator be kept? What is the optimum temperature for long-term storage in a freezer?

CASE STUDY

Arroyo is four and enrolled full-time in a pre-K program. She has a healthy appetite, and her mother sends a large lunch plus several snacks to the center each day. Most of the food consists of starchy foods high in sugar and fat. Arroyo has gained more weight during the semester than would generally be expected, and the other children are beginning to notice. She is teased and taunted by her classmates, especially during lunch.

While visiting the classroom, the director overhears a conversation between Arroyo and several other children. One girl calls Arroyo "fatty" and another calls her "lard butt." Arroyo attempts to defend herself, but becomes upset and finally begins to cry.

1. What might the director have said to the children? What could the teacher say?

2. How could the director implement a reasonable physical education program for the pre-K group?

3. Suggest ways to educate this group of children about appropriate food chocies.

HELPUL WEB SITES

Child and Adult Care Food Program (CACFP):	http://ww.fns.usda.gov/cnd/care
Food and Nutrition Information Center:	http://www.nal.usda.gov/finic
National Center for Health Statistics:	http://www.cdc.gov/nchswww

For additional resources related to administration, visit the Online Resource® for this book at www.EarlyChildEd.delmar.com

13

Beginnings: A New Program/A New Year

KEY TERMS

business plan
expendable supplies
family group
nonexpendable items
ongoing costs
peer group
start-up costs

OBJECTIVES

After reading this chapter, you should be able to:

- Discuss factors affecting the location of a school.
- Discuss costs of starting a new school.
- Identify additional requirements a school should meet before beginning operation.
- Develop procedures to facilitate routine opening-of-school tasks.
- Identify tasks that are necessary to begin a school year.

A Day In the Life Of ...
A Director of a Church-Affiliated School

It is always fun to come back to school in September after a long summer and see the smiling, tan faces of the returning students. Last September, on the first day of school, a little girl came running toward me with arms outstretched and fell into my waiting arms. "Oh, Mrs. Channels! You missed me so much." I started to say "I missed you, too" when it registered just exactly what she had said. I simply answered "I sure did."

Plans for opening a school must be thought out and considered as carefully as for any business. Depending upon the size of the facility, the initial investment can be large and no one wants to lose money because of poor planning. It may take as long as a year to research the issues that will affect the operation. It is important to put together a realistic business plan for start-up and ongoing operation, including budgets for both phases. Project KickStart, a computer software program listed in Appendix A, allows the planners to lay out the steps necessary for beginning and helps to organize the process.

Whether done on a computer or without one, a **business plan** is essential. It is a written document that describes in detail a proposed venture. Its purpose is to reflect projected needs and expected results of a new business. It helps planners to think out the viability of the project, assess resources, and make it possible to borrow money.

The components of a business plan are the following:

■ a short description of the project, including unique characteristics and the target population

■ marketing methods: how information about the venture will reach the target population

■ available resources such as expertise of participants, accessible cash for initial expenses, knowledge of reasonable costs of operation

■ summary of research into the need for the proposed center

■ assessment of realistic risks, including potential problems and plans to resolve them

■ financial forecast of income and expenses

■ time line from planning stage to financial stability

 LOCATION
Community Survey

Before making the investment of time and money, the needs of the community should be assessed. This involves collecting information on the number of families with children, income level of parents, number of working parents, transportation available to families, and number of child care facilities already in the neighborhood. Some of this information can be obtained from U.S. Census data, labor and employment statistics, school district counts, and child care organizations. Directors of existing schools may be willing to discuss whether their schools are full or if there seems to be a need for additional places for children. The local public library is a good source to check for census and employment data.

There are various ways to survey a community with a *needs assessment questionnaire*. On a college campus an article can be placed in the campus newspaper, with a request for reply by telephone or in written form. Within a business, a questionnaire can be sent to all employees. In an apartment complex or densely populated residential area, door-to-door canvassing may be an effective way to determine the need for a school.

In general, the questionnaire should be as simple as possible, yet it should ask all the questions that need to be answered. The sample company assessment questionnaire on the next page may provide a beginning.

This preliminary information should indicate whether there is a need for another school. It will probably also help when considering the kind of school to plan. If there are more school-age children than younger ones, then an after-school program with provision for summer and holiday care for children may be needed. If there are more infants, toddlers, and preschoolers, a preschool with an infant room should be successful. A large number of working parents will probably rule out the possibility of a co-op and point to the necessity for an all-day center.

COMMUNITY HOSPITAL
5329 Center Way
Emerson, PA 16112

In response to a request by employees, we are assessing the need for a child care center on the premises of Community Hospital. It may become part of your work/family benefit package. Please complete the questionnaire and return it to your supervisor before December 15.

Name_____ Employee Number_____

Department_____Location_____Shift_____

Number and ages of your children_____

Do you have a child who needs special care?_____

Describe his/her special needs_____

Where are your children cared for now?

    Preschool or childcare center: cost/hr_____   per week_____

    Caregiver in your home: cost/hr _____   per week_____

    Family child care home: cost/hr _____   per week_____

    Relative's home_____   Home alone_____

What kind of child care service do you need?

    Part-time_____(hrs) Full-time_____(hrs)

    Evening_____(hrs) Weekend_____(hrs)_____

Would you enroll your child in a quality child care center on our premises?

Please rank (1-most, 2-somewhat, 3-next, 4-least) the following benefits in importance to you and your family.

    *Prepaid medical and dental_____   *Child care_____

    *Elder care_____   *Maternity/family leave_____

Comments:

_____

_____

*These items may need to be altered to fit specific benefit packages.

Licensing

Licensing regulations will have an impact upon many aspects of an early childhood or child care center. Regulations provide the baseline for acceptable care of children and are meant to be minimum standards below which no program should operate. All states within the United States have licensing requirements, but they vary widely in scope. Therefore it is important to be familiar with the regulations in the area before proceeding further with planning. State licensing offices are listed in Appendix D.

Why Regulation?

Licensing requirements should achieve their primary purpose of ensuring adequate, safe care of children. Each state, though, determines what the actual acceptable level should be. Variation from state to state comes from differing community needs. Some differences, however, result from disparate perceptions of what children need or lack of official recognition of the importance of quality care. Over the years, licensing agencies have worked with professionals in early childhood education to raise the standards of acceptable care.

A good regulatory system will benefit those who provide care as well as the children they serve. A license carries with it an official recognition of the importance of the job. It can also be an advantage when recruiting children. Families will feel more secure placing their child in a licensed facility. Parents may benefit in another way because of licensing. Licensing agencies can provide parents with helpful information about standards for quality care when they choose a place for their child. On the other hand, facilities can more readily justify the high cost of quality care when parents understand the standards.

Who Is Covered?

Not all programs are covered by licensing. There are some exceptions. In general, those programs that are covered by other regulations do not have to be licensed. Exempted programs might include those covered by state education codes such as the children's centers within public school systems. Laboratory schools in public colleges or universities also fall into this category. Head Start and other federally funded programs have their own standards that are usually higher than the licensing requirements.

Licensing regulations also do not apply to those who care for children of family members in their home. Even family child care homes that care for nonfamily members may not be regulated. Some states register family child care homes rather than include them in licensing procedures. Where this is true, inspection is not required before registration, and the programs are not monitored. Parents are informed of standards and are encouraged to inspect or monitor for themselves.

All other programs must obtain a license before they can begin operation. When operating a private for-profit school, a church-related program, an employer-sponsored child care center, or a cooperative, a license is required. Each school within a corporate chain must have its own license. Licenses are awarded for a specified period of time and must be renewed before their expiration date.

The first step in planning a new school is to contact the state's licensing agency. They will send an application packet and a copy of licensing guidelines. The guidelines include information necessary when designing a school or choosing an appropriate building. The application packet also includes all the paperwork that must be completed.

The application process entails obtaining clearances for the building, getting staff fingerprinted, and compiling records. It may take three to six months to complete these tasks. Once the application is completed and returned to the licensing agency, an appointment can be scheduled. Inspectors will determine whether all specifications have been met. If not, a period of time will be allowed to do so.

Licenses are usually awarded for a year. Another on-site visit will be made before a new license can be given. In addition to renewal, most licensing regulations include methods of enforcement. If the licensing agency makes an unannounced visit to a school and finds infractions, a notice of noncompliance will be sent. The licensee will be given a period of time to rectify the problems. If they have not been rectified when another inspection is made, a fine can be levied. Schools that do not obtain a license or operate with an expired license may be closed by legal means.

What Is Covered by Licensing?

In general, licensing regulations are directed toward conditions that affect the health and safety of children. Statements tend to be broad and general in content to fit a variety of situations. Schools and child care centers can be found in converted warehouses, storefronts, churches, or residences. It is unrealistic to expect that requirements that are too specific could apply in all these settings. With general statements, those who monitor programs can interpret the regulations to fit the needs of each school.

Licensing regulations may cover some or all of the following topics.

- *admission procedures and enrollment records*
- *general administrative procedures*
- *amount of physical space*, both indoors and outdoors
- *equipment*—usually general statements requiring that it be appropriate for the age and number of children and that it provide for their developmental needs
- *food services and nutrition*—requiring that children be served nutritious meals that are prepared under safe conditions
- *health procedures*—requiring that preadmission health reports of children be on file, that health records are maintained, that sick children be isolated, that emergency medical care of children is provided
- *safety procedures*—providing for the safe storage of cleaning supplies or any other harmful materials, safe maintenance of equipment and building, fire and disaster procedures

- *program*—requiring that the daily schedule offer opportunities for children to engage in activities that promote their growth and development, that there be time for rest and taking care of their physical needs
- *staff*—specifying the number of staff required for the number of children served, the qualifications of all staff members, personnel procedures and records
- *discipline*—prohibiting certain kinds of punishment, encouraging the use of positive means of disciplining children
- *transportation*—requiring safe maintenance of vehicles used to transport children, methods to ensure children's safety while in transit, and the qualifications of drivers
- *parent involvement*—requiring that parents be included in planning for their children, serve on advisory boards, be given materials and information about the program's goals and policies, have contact with staff through conferences

Some states have now included additional guidelines for those who care for infants and elementary school children. Many of the same topics as those already listed will be covered, with specifications suitable for these age levels.

For infants, the following areas may be added.

- specifications for sleeping equipment
- provision for storage, preparation of food, feeding procedures
- provision for diapering, including equipment needed and procedures to follow
- specifications for general sanitation procedures
- procedures for meeting children's developmental needs—toilet training, introduction of solid foods
- inclusion of parents in planning

For older children:

- specification of a play area separate from the younger children in a school
- special equipment or furniture appropriate for older children
- safety procedures for swimming pool activities and field trips

Licensing requirements specify the number of square feet needed both indoors and outdoors. This will limit a school to certain communities where there is enough space to accommodate the required footage. In some states, 35 square feet per child is a minimum recommendation for indoor space. To provide for maximum play space and freedom of movement, 40 to 60 square feet per child is preferable. Space used by children usually constitutes 60 percent of a school's total area, with an additional 40 percent needed for storage, kitchen, offices, bathroom, and so on. A fenced-in yard containing 75 to 100 square feet per child is recommended for outdoors.

In some states, preschools cannot be operated on the second floor of a building, setting further limits on the search for space. A ground floor school is safer since young children have difficulty managing stairs. They should have easy access to outdoor play areas. Meeting requirements for bathroom facilities also can be a challenge when looking for space for a child care center. The bathroom should be close to the classrooms, and there should be enough toilets and basins for the number of children anticipated. Specifications for the number of windows and the kind of heating, kitchen equipment, drinking fountains, and so on, may all affect decisions.

Other Regulations

Early childhood facilities are subject to other regulations besides licensing. Zoning ordinances in many communities specify that child care facilities that are operated for profit can be located only in a commercial or business zone. In some cases a zoning variance can be granted to allow a center in a residential area if the operation will not create undue disturbances to the neighborhood. Nonprofit programs sometimes have greater latitude in choosing a location. Zoning regulations may also require provision of off-street parking for staff and visitors, further limiting locations to where there is enough space.

Before choosing a location, it is important to drive through the neighborhood where the school would be located. Is it a place where parents would want to bring their children? Does it have the right kind of environment for a school? The site should be easily visible to street traffic since the sign and school building will be the best advertising. There should be no barriers preventing easy access to the school entrance. The ultimate consideration is whether this is a safe place for children to spend their day.

Multi-use playground equipment.

A child care building must also meet strict codes that relate to the health and safety of occupants. Before a facility can be licensed, the city will send representatives from the building, fire, and sanitation departments. It is necessary to be familiar with these regulations, including any special requirements for children with disabilities.

Buy, Build, Remodel, or Rent?

Building a school on a convenient lot is a dream of many potential owners. It is probably the only way to have most of the things they want in their school. But as costs of both land and building have increased in the last few years, this option is less and less feasible. One way to estimate the cost is to find a school that has been built recently, and find out what it cost to build. If that is not possible, builders or architects in the area should be able to estimate the cost of building. Realtors can estimate the cost of purchasing land.

If building a school is a hopeless dream, there are other options. Many attractive schools for young children are housed in *renovated residences*. If it is possible to find a large, older house at a reasonable price, this may be a good choice. Unfortunately, some communities prohibit schools in residential areas. In addition, the cost of renovation is often very high. Usually, there must be additional bathrooms and bathroom fixtures. Hallways, stairs, porches, heating equipment, outdoor fences, and gates that meet safety standards also add to the cost.

Another possibility is to rent unused classrooms in a public school. Dwindling populations of families with young children have left some school districts with space that is not being used. This can be a viable solution for a child care center, but there will likely be several problems to be solved. Bathrooms may not be adjacent to classrooms, or playgrounds are not easily accessible from the indoor space. There may be restrictions on changing walls or adding plumbing. In addition, there may be no extra space for offices or other supporting uses. With careful planning, however, the space often can be adapted.

Churches often provide space for preschool programs as part of their own educational program. Sometimes they will rent space to a separate organization. Laws do not allow renting for profit-making purposes, but they may allow rental to nonprofit organizations. The main disadvantage of this kind of arrangement is having to share space with church functions. In addition, church space that was planned for religious classes may not have the kind of outdoor area needed by a preschool. Often, though, there is enough space on the church grounds where a playground can be installed.

Storefronts have been used for early childhood programs. In the author's community there are currently three child care centers in shopping centers. Each has a large playground enclosed by a six-foot wall behind the school. In areas that cannot accommodate an attached playground, storefront schools use nearby parks where the children go for outings. An advantage to this type of site is the high visibility of the center as people come to shop. That in itself may provide sufficient publicity to attract initial enrollees and to maintain enrollment. A disadvantage may be the cost of installing bathrooms, dividing indoor space, and building a playground.

Making good use of cramped quarters.

Industrial sites such as a factory or warehouse can also be used as a school when a little imagination is applied. These sites may be near where parents work, allowing them to visit during the day. The rent may also be low. A factory, with its high ceilings, might be converted with a two-level design, allowing for climbing, delineation of spaces, and nooks or corners in which children can be alone. On the negative side, industrial areas are sometimes noisy and may be subject to various kinds of pollutants. The Great Pacific Iron Works Child Development Center in Ventura, California, had to spend thousands of dollars removing soil beneath a playground when the soil was thought to be polluted by toxic wastes from a previous industrial tenant. It is important to ensure that the surrounding environment is safe for children.

If the planners already own some land, putting *pre-fab buildings* on the site may be the best solution. One California school in Santa Monica used two "temporary" bungalows unused by a school district. The buildings were attached, then divided inside to make two classrooms, offices, bathrooms, and a conference room. This choice is somewhat limiting because of the adjoining walls and the structure of the buildings, but it is possible to use the space creatively.

A final possibility is to *buy an existing school*. Each year some schools change hands for one reason or another. It is a good idea to watch real estate ads, check with directors in the area, and talk to realtors. Chances are a school will come up for sale. A potential buyer should check carefully, though, as to why the school is being sold. Is it because the area already has too many schools or just that the owners no longer want to run a school? Just as when buying a house, it is important to investigate the building and find out all the things that will need to be repaired. Buying a school may

The high cost of child care makes it difficult for many families to find quality care for their children. Tuition for a four-year-old averages $4,000 to $6,000 a year, reaching as much as $10,000 in some centers. Low-income families are especially impacted by these costs and have few choices. Consequently, they are often forced to place their children in lower quality care.

Source: Schulman, K., & Adams, G. (1998). *Cost of child care.* (ERIC Document Reproduction Service No. ED426785)

be a good decision especially for a profit-making school since it can be seen as a real estate investment as well as a business investment.

When it is time to make a decision about where to house the school, it is helpful to list the advantages and disadvantages of each proposed site, remembering that few schools have ideal environments. Most school personnel learn to make creative adaptations of the space they have. Start-up costs will certainly figure in the decision. However, the least expensive may not always be the best choice, for minimal facilities may make a poor and unsuccessful school.

When a site for a school has been tentatively chosen it is time to contact all the other regulatory agencies that control the operation of a child care facility. The buyer should ask for an inspector to tour the site. Building and safety regulations specify that buildings must be free of hazards such as asbestos or lead paint, and electrical wiring must meet current standards. There must be adequate air circulation if windows cannot be opened. There may also be specifications regarding the kinds of carpeting used or the number and type of exits. Exits may be required to have lighted signs and locks that can be easily opened in case of an emergency. Fire codes include requirements for the number and location of fire extinguishers, smoke and/or fire alarm systems, and the location of furnaces and water heaters.

Federal regulations that directly affect child care centers are the 1990 Americans with Disabilities Act (ADA) and The Occupational Safety and Health Act of 1970 (OSHA). ADA requires that equal access to all facilities and services be provided to individuals with disabilities. This means that ramps must be provided where there are stairs, that doorways be large enough to accommodate a wheelchair, and that bathrooms be accessible. OSHA specifies that an environment should be free of any hazards that could cause death or injury to any employees. Where both local and federal guidelines overlap, the facility must be in compliance with each.

FINANCES

Start-Up Costs

Before making a final decision, the **start-up costs** of opening a school at the chosen site must be considered. Start-up costs are those expenditures that must be made during the initial stage of planning before opening and before any enrollment money comes in. Renovations may need to be made, equipment must be purchased, and staff must be hired to take care of licensing, order materials, and interview parents. These costs can be considerable for a large school since the cost per child can run as high as $2,000 to $5,000. Figure 13-1 shows a start-up budget for a school for 70 children to be housed in a renovated school building.

Capital costs include the purchase of land and an existing school or a building to be renovated. When purchasing property, the down payment must be considered in start-up cost. Repayment of the loan is then amortized over the ensuing years and included in each following year's budget. Even when renting a building, an initial outlay will include the first and last month's rent and any security deposit required (see Figure 13-1).

Everything needed to begin operation of a school must be purchased before opening day. Equipment, furniture, and learning materials all entail a fairly large investment. Planners can use catalogs from the various companies to estimate the cost. (Information about equipment companies can be found in Appendix C). Some companies will send a sales representative out to the school to assist in the task. Lakeshore Learning Materials in California offers further help by publishing a list of suggested learning materials and furniture for age levels from infants to school-age, plus classroom layout planning grids. This information is available on the Internet at lakeshore.learning.com. Click on the Free Resources on the left-hand bottom of the page. Not all schools can start out with ideal environments but add to the equipment once the school gets started. It is also possible to make many things or purchase used furniture.

The director should allocate money to cover the probability that enrollment will not be filled immediately after opening the school. There may not be full enrollment for several months or even a year. During that time, expenses will not be decreased proportionately. California licensing laws require three months operating expenses to be set aside before a license is issued. Even if a state does not have that requirement, providing a "cushion" to fall back on during the early stages of getting a school started is a good idea.

Personnel costs have to be considered as well, when figuring start-up costs. Someone has to go through the lengthy process of obtaining a license; in urban areas, this can take as much as six months. Someone must order materials and equipment and then unpack them after delivery. The building has to be readied, and any renovations must be made. Anyone who has done house remodeling knows how long that can take. It is recommended that the director be on salary full-time at least two months before opening. A part-time secretary during this time can help to get paperwork done.

A core staff should be hired before the opening of a school and the remainder of the staff as enrollment requires it. The core staff members should be on salary at least two weeks before the opening day. During that time the director can have an orientation/training session. This time together helps staff to develop a good working relationship. Teachers can also set up their rooms and plan their curriculum for the first few weeks. The costs for salaries during this time should be included in the start-up budget.

Some of these personnel expenses can be met through in-kind contributions. When directors are also owners of schools, they sometimes forgo salaries during the

---

SAMPLE START-UP COSTS

Capacity: 70 children
            Purchased school building to be renovated

Start-up personnel costs

Director—$35,000/yr. (3 months)	$8,750
3 Teachers—$22,000/yr. each (2 weeks)	2,538
2 Asst. teachers—$19,000/yr. each (2 weeks)	1,462
Secretary—$16,000/yr. (1 month)	1,333
	$14,083
Employee benefits (estimated 15%)	2,112
Total personnel cost	$16,195
Renovation	$50,000

Contract services and consultants

Architect	$3,000
Lawyer (3 hours @ $250/hr.)	750
Contractor (10 hours @ $35/hr.)	350

Supplies

Office (computer, paper, etc.)	2,500
Cleaning & paper goods	500
Food (breakfast, 2 snacks)	900
Classroom materials & supplies	2,000
Advertising (phone book, flyers, newspaper)	1,000

Occupancy

Down payment on building	75,000
Utilities	1,000
Furniture, equipment, vehicles	45,000

Other

Business license	500
Insurance (quarterly payment)	1,500
Miscellaneous expenses	1,000
Payment into cash reserve	35,000
TOTAL START-UP COSTS	**$250,178**
START-UP COST PER CHILD	$3,574

Download a printable version of this form at http://www.EarlyChildEd.delmar.com

Online Resources

FIGURE 13-1 ■ Sample start-up costs.

start-up period. In other situations, a parent who has time and energy may take on some of the start-up tasks. Teachers may also be willing to volunteer a day or so getting their rooms set up. Some equipment cost can be decreased through renovations done by a skilled volunteer or donations. But the director should proceed with caution when expecting people to work without pay, taking care not to exploit those who are willing or who need to have a job.

Some expenses can be amortized over the first year of operation. It may be possible to delay paying some bills until tuition fees begin to arrive. Renovation costs can sometimes be handled in the same way. If the landlord in a rental property does improvements, the director may be able to pay off the cost over the first year. It is important to add these costs into the operating budget and be sure that income will be able to sustain them.

Contract services and consultants may be necessary in some settings. Legal advice is especially important when two or more people own a school. When organized as a simple partnership, either partner is liable for all partnership debts. The private assets of either one may be charged for payment of indebtedness. When the school is set up as a corporation, the corporation assumes responsibility for any debts. The individual is protected from personal liability.

Although attorneys are expensive, they are indispensable in drawing up incorporation papers or assisting in the establishment of partnerships. It is better to have sound legal advice early than to flounder in indecision later. Legal requirements vary from state to state. The owners of the school should consider the advantages of incorporation over a partnership at tax time and in relation to liability for debts.

It may be wise to have an architect draw up renovation plans needed for building-safety approval for zoning. An accountant can help to set up a bookkeeping system. A pediatrician or child development specialist can offer advice when setting up an infant room. All these services are expensive, some costing hundreds of dollars per hour. Some of these services might be provided free of charge by a parent or a friend. Low-cost legal services can sometimes be obtained from a legal service agency.

Advertising and publicity are essential to a new school. Families with children have to know about the school if the enrollment is to be filled as soon as possible. Some methods are relatively expensive for the start-up period, but there are others that cost little. One form, without cost, is an article in the *local newspaper*. The director can contact a reporter and describe some unique feature of the program. There may be enough interest to warrant some publicity. Telephone advertising is excellent since parents often look there first when trying to find child care. The timing may not always fit the school's need during start-up, however, since telephone books are printed only once a year. Listing is included in the cost of service installation, but a display ad can cost close to a hundred dollars a month. Next to advertising in the phone book, the radio seems to be the most effective way to publicize child care. The *local radio station* can run ads during morning drive times when parents might be listening. Cost of an ad will vary depending on the time the promotion is aired.

The director may wish to purchase a mailing list of prospects for the center. Companies that supply lists can be found in the Yellow Pages under "Mailing Lists." Lists can target a geographic area, residences in which there are children and those in which the parents earn a certain income. For a fee of about $50, the company will provide a list that can be used on a one-time basis, and may even send the address labels. They will also rent the list for a one-year period. It is a good idea to compare prices from various companies to get the best service for the least cost. The list should be used to send an eye-catching *flyer* to announce the opening of the school and invite recipients to come for a visit.

Direct mail marketing is costly and the success of the mailing depends on whether the target market has been reached. The average response from this form of advertising is 1 to 5 percent. More people will open and read the mailings if they

- are sent by first-class mail.
- are hand addressed.
- have been creatively designed.
- begin with a "teaser" to urge the recipient to respond.
- are consistent with recognizable color schemes and logo.
- are sent more than once, especially at peak enrollment times of the year.

A director may include a discount offer on registration or tuition as part of the mass mailer. This may motivate prospective families to call for an appointment to tour the facility and provides a golden opportunity to "sell" the program. The director should greet parents and children warmly, explain the program, answer all questions, and offer a business card upon the close of the tour for any further questions that may arise.

An attractive brochure is an effective tool for selling a school. However, it can be expensive if the layout includes photographs or it is printed on heavy paper. It might be prudent to employ some of the less costly methods of advertising during the start-up period but develop a brochure that can be used for continuing recruitment once the center has opened. The contents and makeup of a brochure are discussed in Chapter 14.

There are several ways to publicize a new school. An open house can be held just prior to the opening. The classrooms should be attractive with materials set out as though waiting for children to arrive. The director can conduct tours of the school, telling visitors about the program, the teachers, and the philosophy. Community groups might welcome a presentation about the school. If brochures are available, this is a good time to distribute them. Pictures, slides, or a video would be an effective addition to a talk. The director should meet with the personnel directors of large businesses in the vicinity. They may be looking for places to refer employees for child care. Local professional organizations may have newsletters to which the director can submit an article. It is a good idea to attend professional meetings and talk to other directors about what has worked for them. Lastly, the director should notify a local resource and referral agency if there is one in the community. All of these can be effective ways to let a community know of the service being offered.

Another form of advertising that will help to recruit students is an attractive sign outside the school. It should be in keeping with the neighborhood but should be clearly visible from the street. Once a school is in operation, the outside of the school and the playground will help sell it to prospective families. The appearance of a school is an ever-visible advertisement to any parent driving by on the way to work.

Insurance costs are typically divided between start-up costs and the first-year budget. Usually, a portion of the insurance must be paid even before the school opens and the balance is paid during the year. Insurance for schools has become a problem in recent years because the cost has gone up astronomically. Checking around is the best way to find adequate coverage at a reasonable price. The National Association for the Education of Young Children (NAEYC) offers a good insurance package. Write to them for information. Most schools have the following kinds of insurance:

- liability and property damage—to provide legal protection for the owner/operator of the school
- fire damage—to cover buildings and contents
- fire, extended coverage—to protect against vandalism and malicious mischief
- automobile—for any vehicles used in transporting children
- accident—for children and staff
- workers' compensation (required by law if 10 or more persons are employed)—to cover on-the-job injuries

The following kinds of insurance should also be considered:

- burglary and robbery—on the contents of the building
- business interruption—payment for lost income while damaged property is being repaired
- fidelity bond—to protect against theft by employees

Ongoing Costs

Before going further in the decision-making process, the director should make a tentative estimate of **ongoing costs.** Budget is discussed in detail in Chapter 10, but at this point it is important to compare potential income with expected costs of operating the school.

Potential income is determined by the number of children enrolled in the school. That figure is found by dividing the total amount of indoor space in a building by the requirements set by the state's licensing agency. The next consideration is the amount of tuition being charged by other schools in the area. Tuition should be set near that amount. It would seem logical, then, to multiply the number of children by the amount of tuition. However, schools seldom will have 100 percent enrollment, even after the school has been established for a period of time. Most successful, established schools average 95 percent capacity. During the first year, allowing for a slow first few months, capacity may not reach more than 60 to 75 percent capacity. It is better to figure low when estimating income rather than having a shortfall at the end of the year. After the first year, there will be a better baseline of information to make the second-year budget.

Tuition income may be less than expected for another reason. During some months, children tend to become ill more frequently than others. Parents see no reason to pay for school when the child is not attending. The expenses go on, though, despite decreased attendance. A policy requiring tuitions be paid even when children are ill for short periods of time will decrease low cash flow times. Most schools excuse tuition only when a child is ill for several weeks or more.

Another factor that affects the ability to project income is that the school will always have uncollectable tuitions. For one reason or another, families fall behind in payment of fees; some even leave the school without paying. The budget should allow 10 to 15 percent of the expected income as uncollectable. Procedures for following up on late fee payments will eventually decrease that amount.

Costs should be estimated by starting with salaries since that will take the largest proportion of total revenue. Salaries may take 50 to 75 percent of total income. The director should figure the number of staff members needed during the times when the school has the most children. In an all-day school, peak hours of enrollment may be from 8:00 in the morning until 4:00 in the afternoon. There must be enough teachers to maintain the ratio of adults to children required by licensing. The director should also estimate the number of children and teachers needed to cover the times before and after the peak times. Before actual enrollment of children begins, it is impossible to know how many children will be present before 8:00 a.m. and after 4:00 p.m. After estimating the number the director can make a chart of children and staff as shown in Figure 13-2.

Hours												
		Morning					Afternoon					
	7	8	9	10	11	12	1	2	3	4	5	6
Number of Children	15	45	60									30	20

Teachers
#1
#2
#3
#4
#5
#6
#7
#8
#9

Download a printable version of this form at http://www.EarlyChildEd.delmar.com

FIGURE 13-2 ■ Sample teacher assignment chart.

The cost of the building will probably be the next largest budget expenditure. This usually takes about 15 percent of total income, but it should not exceed 25 percent. This expenditure includes the cost of repaying a loan to purchase property and renovate or of making the ongoing rental payments on the property. In 1990, the U.S. General Accounting Office (GAO) issued *Report on Early Childhood Education: What Are the Costs of High-Quality Programs?* which offered guidelines for determining the real costs of providing quality early childhood programs. The estimates of costs show that personnel costs are the largest portion of a budget.

All personnel	70%

The breakdown of nonpersonnel budget items in the GAO report are as follows:

Rent or mortgage	27%
Food	20%
Educational materials/equipment	8%
Other*	45%

*Other includes telephone and utilities, repair, maintenance, office supplies and equipment, insurance, health and social services, and other miscellaneous costs.

STAFF SELECTION

The entire process of staff selection was discussed more fully in Chapter 7. However, some guidelines for staffing the new school are helpful here.

Staff can be recruited through advertisements in the local newspapers or flyers sent to teacher organizations and local colleges and universities. In many programs it is necessary to follow affirmative action guidelines. The ad or flyer should state the education and experience required for the position and the method of application. If time is short, the director may request that replies be made by telephone. However, if there is time, written applications should be returned by mail or fax.

The first teachers should be chosen carefully since during the first year the reputation of a school is being formed. Teachers are an important part of that process. The director should be sure that teachers know the goals of the school and that there is time to help them implement the goals.

WORKING CHECKLIST

Each of the tasks necessary for opening a new school may entail many weeks of work. There may be delays when trying to meet licensing requirements. Bad weather may delay building or renovation plans. It is important to allow a realistic amount of time and add extra time for unforeseen events. A checklist of tasks with a time line will help to ensure that everything is getting done. An example is seen in Figure 13-3.

Task	Expected Completion Date	Date Completed
1. Prepare needs assessment		
2. Contact licensing and zoning agencies		
3. Seek legal advice if needed		
4. Survey available sites		
5. Figure start-up costs		
6. Choose building or decide to build		
7. Supervise building or renovations		
8. Meet with representatives from all licensing agencies		
9. Obtain building permits and clearances		
10. Start licensing process		
11. Establish a bank account		
12. Obtain insurance		
13. Prepare first-year budget		
14. Order supplies and equipment		
15. Prepare a brochure		
16. Advertise for students		
17. Write job descriptions		
18. Advertise for staff		
19. Interview and select staff		
20. Set personnel policies		
21. Prepare forms for children's files		
22. Meet with children and parents		
23. Conduct orientation for staff		
24. Conduct orientation for parents		
25. Prepare for opening day		

Download a printable version of this form at http://www.EarlyChildEd.delmar.com

FIGURE 13-3 ■ Checklist of tasks needed to open a new school.

PLANNING FOR OPENING DAY

The opening of the school should be planned for a time that will fit the needs of the community or a particular situation. In an employer-sponsored program, for instance, the time will probably not be important. When opening a private school in a community, the director needs to think about the optimum time to open the doors. Traditionally, families make plans for their children's education during the summer. Changes in child-care arrangements are often made at this time. A September opening that coincides with the school calendar often works best. It is necessary to allow at least two months before the opening date to complete all the preparations.

Existing programs, too, find that changes often take place during the summer. Families move or children go on to elementary school. After summer vacation is the time many families decide to make a change in child care arrangements. So even in managing an existing year-round school, there will be some of the same tasks as in opening a new school.

At the beginning of a new academic year, schools receive a flurry of telephone calls from parents frantically looking for places for their children. During this time, it is also necessary to order materials and prepare the classrooms. The playground may need new sand, and equipment must be inspected for safety. If the director develops organized procedures for managing all these tasks, life will certainly be easier.

ENROLLMENT

During the several weeks before opening day, the most important task is to enroll children. Parents usually make their first contact by telephone. It is important to keep a record of each call and to have a procedure for follow-up. Printed cards or a report form will provide an organized method of getting information. Figure 13-4 shows a form that can be used to record inquiries about the school. Each call should be followed with a mailed brochure or information sheet about the school. Even if the parents do not enroll their child, they may pass the information on to other families. An application packet containing the application form, brochure, fee schedule, and medical forms should be sent to those parents who seem ready to enroll.

A computer will make the task considerably easier. The names and addresses of anyone inquiring about the school are entered in a database. When new programs or changes that would affect these inquiries are added to the school, it is simple to notify these people. A form letter can be personalized with the name of each person on the list. This list should be updated periodically.

Before finalizing any application, the director should meet with the parent and child. Some parents want to visit the school even before sending in an application. Others already know about the school and schedule a visit after they send in their application. Figure 13-5 shows a sample registration form. Whichever order is chosen for the visit, it is important that the director and the family have a chance for a leisurely visit. No child should be enrolled without it. In fact, some states require visits as a part of licensing. These visits usually take half an hour or longer so they should not be scheduled too close together.

INQUIRY REPORT

NAME _____   DATE _____

ADDRESS _____   PHONE _____

_____

Child's Birthdate _____

Month-Day-Year

How did you hear about our school? _____

Brochure sent _____

Date

Application packet sent _____

Date

Additional comments: _____

_____

_____

Download a printable version of this form at http://www.EarlyChildEd.delmar.com

Online Resources

FIGURE 13-4 ■ Sample inquiry report form.

The purpose of these visits is to provide information to the director and the parent. If possible, the visit should take place in the classroom where the child will be placed after enrolling, with the teacher present. The child should have some toys to play with during the visit. This is an opportunity to observe the child informally and to get an impression of the parent-child relationship. The parents will be able to ask questions about the school and express any concerns about the child's adjustment. If the parents decide to enroll the child, this is a good time to get some of the forms filled out for the child's file.

Enrollment Decisions

The maximum number of children the center can accommodate will be determined by the size of the physical space and specified on a license. It is possible to enroll every applicant up to the maximum allowed or decide to limit the number of children accepted. The total number of children must then be divided into manageable groups. Group size will vary depending on the skill of the teacher, the age of the children, and the licensing specifications in the state.

As children are placed in groups, there is another decision to make: should the children in each group be approximately the *same age*, or should the groups have a *range of age* level? The first method is called a **peer group** and includes children who are near the same age, usually with about a six-month to one-year difference. The

CHILDREN'S REGISTRATION FORM

General Information

Child's Name_____ Date of Birth_____

Social Security #_____

Parent/guardian(1)_____ Social Security #_____

Home Address_____ Home phone_____

_____

Employer_____ Work phone_____

Work address_____ Hours of employment_____

_____

Parent/guardian(2)_____ Social Security #_____

Home Address_____ Home phone_____

_____

Employer_____ Work phone_____

Work address_____ Hours of employment_____

_____

Other person(s) authorized to pick up child

Name_____ Phone_____

Name_____ Phone_____

Medical Information

Pediatrician's name_____ Phone_____

Address_____

Dentist's name_____ Phone_____

Address_____

My child has the following allergies and/or special needs:_____

_____

Enrollment Information

First day of enrollment_____

Arrival time_____ Departure time_____

Registration fee paid_____ Deposit paid_____

Materials fee paid_____

_____   _____

Parent/guardian(1)   Parent/guardian(2)

_____   _____

Date   Date

Download a printable version of this form at http://www.EarlyChildEd.delmar.com

FIGURE 13-5 ■ Sample application form.

second method is called a **family group** and includes children with a wide age span. Children in this group may differ in age as much as several years. Teachers and administrators who prefer peer grouping point to the advantage when planning curriculum activities. It is easier to include materials that most of the children will be able to use successfully. Those who like the family group will extol the advantage of children learning from others who are older or younger than themselves. They also feel that, especially in child care settings, this kind of group more closely resembles the home and, therefore, is more familiar to the children. The director has to decide what suits the school, goals, and teachers.

Another important consideration is the inclusion of *children with special needs*. Under the ADA enacted in 1990, discrimination against persons with disabilities is prohibited. This measure has an impact on early childhood education programs since it requires all public and private schools, child care centers, and family child care providers to make reasonable accommodations to include children with special needs. Each child's needs must be evaluated on an individual basis and then an equal, nonsegregated educational program provided. A primary legal reason for refusing admission to a child with special needs is that doing so would place an undue burden on the provider and that there is no reasonable alternative. An additional reason for denial of admission is that the child's condition would pose a direct threat to the health or safety of that child, other children, or staff members.

There are many other questions to be answered in relation to accepting children with special needs into a school. Some communities have resources such as a "Health Hotline." California has one with a toll-free number: 800-333-3212. The local resource and referral agency may provide information and materials. Every director should have a copy of *Caring for Our Children, National Health and Safety Standards: Guidelines for Out-of-Home Child Care Programs,* a joint project of the American Public Health Association and the American Academy of Pediatrics. The California Child Care Law Center publishes *Caring for Children with Special Needs: The Americans with Disabilities Act and Child Care.* The booklet covers legal concerns, insurance, and taxes. The Law Center's address is 22 Second Street, San Francisco, CA 94105.

The director should make an *attendance chart* showing the days and hours each child will be attending school. Most children will attend on the same days and at the same hours fairly consistently. Some schools give parents the option of choosing to send a child two or three days a week instead of five. Attendance may vary more radically, for instance, in the case of the parent who works changing shifts. It will be important to record this so teachers will know which children to include in their plan.

An overall *schedule* for the school is used to plan where each group will be during specified periods of time during the day. This prevents all the children from being on the playground at once and allows teachers periodic use of additional spaces in the school building. A daily schedule should allow for snack and meal times, toileting and handwashing, naps, and large blocks of time both indoors and out. The day should have a leisurely pace so that children do not feel they are constantly being rushed from one activity to another. This is especially important in an all-day school since children are there for many hours.

The school should establish a *file* for each child enrolled. Each file should contain the following:

- registration form (see Figure 13-5)
- medical evaluation
- dietary restrictions, if any
- emergency information (see Figure 13-6)
- permission form for medical treatment (see Figure 13-6)
- permission form for field trips (see Figure 13-7)
- financial agreements (see Figure 13-8)

In addition to the foregoing information, California currently requires a form signed and dated by the parents acknowledging receipt of a *child abuse prevention* pamphlet. If the parents refuse to sign the form, the director must note their refusal in the child's record file.

Some directors use a running checklist that shows at a glance what is still needed in a file. Another system is to put the completed files in one place, leaving the incomplete ones in another place until finished. Whatever the system, it is important to see that the task of getting all needed forms on file is accomplished as quickly as possible at the beginning of the school year.

The school must have a procedure for *checking children in and out* so there is a written record of attendance plus arrival and departure times. A few teachers have had panic-stricken moments when they find a child missing and don't know if the parent has picked up the child. One school has a sign at the checkout: "Make certain you only have your own child." They had experienced children slipping out with other parents before anyone realized they were gone. A sign-in-and-out sheet or book posted at the entrance of the school or at each classroom will serve this purpose. There are computer programs that simplify this task. See Appendix A.

There should be a place for *parent messages*. A bulletin board in the reception area will serve for general notices. Some other method should be used to send notes to individual parents. Some schools use something like a shoe bag that hangs on the wall outside each classroom. There are pockets for each family. Others have pigeonhole slots in a cabinet at the entrance to the school. Teachers can use these to send messages to parents about the child's day or some special occurrence that might be important for the parent to know. Some schools use a HappyGram form; others just use an informal note. Another possibility is to communicate with parents by e-mail.

If the school has a before- and after-school program for older children, it may be necessary to arrange for *bus service*. The school can rent the buses from school bus companies or buy vehicles and employ a driver. The director should list the children who will be using the service to pick them up from home and take them to school or pick them up after school; list their addresses and approximate times that fit in with parents' schedules and the school schedules; and use a map to chart a route for the bus driver.

Once a route and schedule have been set, the driver should do a trial run during the hours that would ordinarily be used. That is the only way to see if the schedule is realistic in terms of the traffic and the distances traveled. Some adjustments may be needed.

IDENTIFICATION AND EMERGENCY INFORMATION

To Be Completed by Parent or Guardian

Child's Name _____ Date of Birth _____

Address _____

Street Address

_____

City   Zip   Phone

Parent 1 or guardian _____

  Business Telephone _____ Hours _____

Parent 2 or guardian _____

  Business Telephone _____ Hours _____

Additional persons who may be called in an emergency:

Name   Address   Phone   Relationship

_____

_____

_____

Physician to be called in an emergency:

Name _____ Phone _____

Address _____

If physician cannot be reached, what action should be taken? _____

  Call emergency hospital_____

  Other_____

Names of persons authorized to take child from the facility:

Name   Relationship

_____

_____

Time child will be called for _____

Signature of parent or guardian   Date

_____   _____

Download a printable version of this form at http://www.EarlyChildEd.delmar.com

Online Resources

Figure 13-6 ■ Sample identification and emergency information form.

PERMISSION

I hereby give permission for_____

child's name

to participate in the following activities at_____School.

_____Field trip with the class. I understand that I will be notified prior to a scheduled trip and will be given information regarding transportation, destination, lunch or other food, and arrival and departure time.

_____Pictures taken of my child to be used for educational purposes, teacher training, or school use. I understand my child's name will not be used at any time.

_____Distribution of my address and/or telephone number to other parents of a child enrolled in this school. (Addresses will not be given out for any commercial purposes.)

Signature of parent_____

Date_____

Download a printable version of this form at http://www.EarlyChildEd.delmar.com

---

FIGURE 13-7 ■ Sample permission form.

FINANCIAL AGREEMENT

I agree to pay $ _____per month, payable in advance for tuition for my child. I understand there is no tuition allowance for absences unless my child is ill for more than two weeks.

I also agree to notify the school two weeks in advance of withdrawal, should that be necessary. I understand that without notification, I am obligated for two weeks' tuition or until the place is filled.

I have read the Parents' Handbook and understand the school's policies regarding tuition payment.

Signed _____

Parent 1 or guardian

Signed _____

Parent 2 or guardian

Date _____

Download a printable version of this form at http://www.EarlyChildEd.delmar.com

---

FIGURE 13-8 ■ Financial agreement.

PARENTS

A handbook provides parents with information that will help them become oriented as quickly as possible to their new experiences in the school. It can also serve as a handy reference as needed during the school year. The handbook should contain the following information:

- *Philosophy*—a statement of the program's ideas, beliefs, and values relating to how children grow and learn. "The staff members of the Child Learning Center share a common philosophy that children learn best when they can actively interact with their environment. We also share a common commitment to helping each child develop fully: physically, socially, emotionally, and cognitively. Each child is valued as a unique individual with a particular pattern of growth and manner of acquiring knowledge and skills. In your child's classroom, you will observe learning centers that contain a wide variety of materials that can be used in many different ways. Children can explore the materials, solve problems, develop skills, increase knowledge, or be creative in ways that help them to solidify their abilities at one level and be ready to move on to the next. All activities are developmentally appropriate for the age level of the children using them and take into account the different rates at which children mature." "Staff members will allow children to engage in activities at their own level of development at a particular time. When children demonstrate readiness, teachers will encourage them to move to a higher level of functioning by gently questioning, suggesting, or providing additional materials. Staff members will also foster children's own interests by providing the kinds of materials or experiences that will increase knowledge or feelings of competence and self-esteem. In this way, every child is able to develop fully according to his or her own interests and capabilities."

- *Arrival- and departure-times and procedures for signing in and out*—"The Center is open from 6:30 a.m. to 5:00 p.m. Please notify staff members of the time that you will deliver and pick up your child. If you will be late for pickup, notify the school. There will be an additional charge of $3.00 for every 15 minutes overtime. A sign-up sheet will be posted outside each classroom. Please sign in the time you bring your child and do not forget to sign out at pickup time."

- *Health policies*—guidelines for inclusion or exclusion of children who are ill. "It is our policy to maintain the health of all children and staff members by excluding anyone with a communicable illness. If your child exhibits any of the following signs, please do not bring him or her to the Learning Center. The signs or symptoms as well as the conditions for a return to school are described in the following table" (See Table 13-1).

"If children become ill while at school, you will be notified and the child will be isolated until someone is able to take him or her home. During the time your child is isolated a staff member will make your child as comfortable as possible and provide whatever care is necessary."

TABLE 13-1   Guidelines for Exclusion of Ill or Infected Children

Illness or Infection	Sign or Symptom	Return
Temperature	Oral temperature of 101°F or more; rectal temperature of 102°F; should be accompanied by behavior changes or other symptoms	Until doctor releases child to return to care
Symptoms of severe illness	Unusual lethargy; irritability; uncontrolled coughing; wheezing	Until doctor releases child to return to care
Uncontrolled diarrhea	Increase in number of stools, water, and/or decreased form that cannot be contained in a diaper or underwear	Until diarrhea stops
Vomiting illness	Two or more episodes in 24 hours	Until vomiting stops and child is not dehydrated or doctor determines illness not infectious
Mouth sores with drooling		Until condition is determined to be noninfectious
Rash	Rash accompanied by fever or behavior change	Doctor determines it is noninfectious
Conjunctivitis	White or yellow discharge in eye(s) accompanied by eye pain and/or redness around eyes	Until 24 hours after treatment has begun
Head lice, scabies, or other infestations	Infestation present	Until 24 hours after treatment has begun; no remaining lice on hair or scalp
Tuberculosis	Cough; fever; chest pain; coughing up blood	Until doctor or health official allows child to return to care
Impetigo	Rash-blister to honey-colored crusts; lesions occur around mouth, nose, and on chin	Until 24 hours after treatment has begun
Strep throat	Fever; sore throat; throat drainage and tender nodes in lymph	After cessation of fever or 24 hours after antibiotic treatment
Chicken pox	Sudden onset of slight fever, fatigue, and loss of appetite followed by skin eruption	Until 6 days after eruption of rash or until blister eruption has dried and crusted over
Whooping cough	Severe, persistent cough	Until 5 days after antibiotic treatment to prevent infection
Mumps	Tender/swollen glands and/or fever	Until 9 days after onset of gland swelling
Hepatitis A virus	Fever, fatigue, loss of appetite, abdominal pain, nausea, vomiting, and/or jaundice	Until 1 week after onset of illness or as directed by local health department; immune serum globulin should be administered to staff and children who have been exposed
Measles	Rash, high fever, runny nose, and red/watery eyes	Until 6 days from onset of rash

Illness or Infection	Sign or Symptom	Return
Rubella	Mild fever, rash, swollen lymph nodes	Until 6 days after onset of rash
Unspecified respiratory illness	Severe illness with cold, croup, bronchitis, otitis media, pneumonia	Until child feels well enough to participate
Shingles	Lesions	Until doctor allows child to return to care or if child can wear clothing that covers lesions
Herpes simplex (1)	Clear, painful blisters	Until lesions that ooze, involving face and lips, have no secretions

"Some childhood diseases are undetectable during an early stage when they are highly infectious and able to expose others to the illness. If this should happen to a child at the Learning Center, you will be notified and told of the kinds of symptoms to watch for should your child become ill."

■ *Safety*—what the school will do when a child is injured or needs medical help. "The safety of all children at our center is our primary focus and we do everything in our power to insure that we provide a hazard-free environment. In order to do this we have established the following policy:

1. We always maintain an adequate number of adults to supervise every group of children whether in the classroom or on the playground. No child is ever left in a situation without supervision.
2. Every classroom and the playground areas are inspected regularly to eliminate or correct any equipment or situations that may cause injury to the children.
3. In the case of an emergency, every classroom has an intercom connection so that help can be summoned. Emergency telephone numbers are posted by every telephone in the center.
4. There is an emergency evacuation plan posted in each classroom showing the fastest route to safety.
5. When a child is involved in an accident requiring medical intervention, the parent or guardian will be notified promptly. If the parent is unable to come to the center to transport the child, a staff member will accompany him or her to the medical facility indicated on the child's information form. If help is needed immediately, the nearest response team will be called.
6. An incident report form will be filled out by the attending teacher and the director. One copy will be placed in the child's file and the other given to the parent. The director and staff will review the incident and determine whether some preventive measures need to be taken."

■ *Food*—what kind of food can be brought from home; foods that will be served at school. "Your child will receive two snacks and lunch at school if he or she is enrolled for a full day. Our dietitian follows the Food Pyramid guidelines set by the U.S. Department of Agriculture's Human Nutrition Information Service." The Pyramid is shown in Figure 13–9.

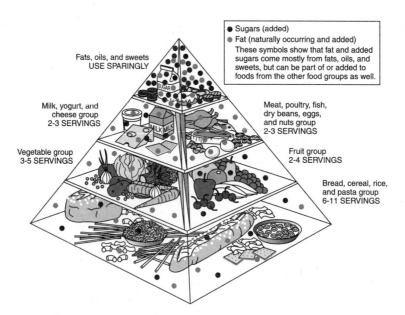

FIGURE 13-9 ■ The Food Guide Pyramid.

SOURCE: (Courtesy Robertson, *Safety, Nutrition, and Health in Early Childhood Education,* 2nd ed., Delmar Learning, 2003).

"We also make every effort to select and prepare foods that appeal to children. We often include the kinds of foods that children may be familiar with at home or are part of the family cultural traditions. Mealtimes are planned as carefully as all other experiences since they are considered part of the overall learning environment of the children. Weekly menus are posted outside the office door."

"Frequently, children are given the opportunity to prepare their own snacks. The dietitian and the teacher plan an appropriate snack and the materials are set up as a learning center. With supervision, children can learn to cut up fruit, prepare pancakes, and make pizzas and many other delicious edibles."

■ *Special occasions*—how the parent can make a birthday a special occasion for the child and his or her class. "Children enjoy celebrating their birthdays with their classmates, and we encourage you to bring a treat either for snacktime or at lunch. Some suggestions for special desserts that are nutritious are cupcakes made with whole-wheat flour and applesauce instead of sugar and fat, frozen yogurt or low-fat ice cream, special fruits or fruit gelatin, and oatmeal cookies. Please check with your child's teacher before bringing food that contains potential allergy-causing ingredients. There may be a child in the class who will have a reaction."

■ *Home toys*—what the child can bring to school. "We discourage children from bringing toys from home and forbid any type of weapon. It is our belief that part of the developmental process involves learning to share, and to this end we provide toys and equipment that children can share or use together. When children bring toys from home, they rightfully feel that they own the toy and should not have to share. This creates problems not only for the child, but for others in the classroom. Therefore, if your child wants to show a new toy to the class, there will be time during the first group time for him or her to share. The toy then must be put into the child's cubby until going home time."

- *Clothing*—what is appropriate for school activities. "Children at the Learning Center will be actively playing during the time that they are in school and need to have clothing that can allow them freedom to do so. They also are developing independence in caring for their own needs. Dress your child in comfortable clothing that can withstand the wear and tear of playing in the sand, climbing, digging in the garden, sliding down the slide, and all the other activities at school. Also, try to choose clothing that allows your child to manage his or her own toileting or putting on a jacket. Put a label in jackets or sweaters so they are easily identifiable. Please bring an extra set of clothes to be kept in your child's cubby in case there is a need to change."

- *Parent visits*—how to be a good visitor. "You are welcome to visit our center at any time. In order to make your visit meaningful to you, we ask that you follow these guidelines:
  1. Stop at the office to let us know you are visiting.
  2. After greeting your child, find a place to sit, close to your child if that is what he or she requests.
  3. Remember that the teacher needs to focus attention on the children and cannot be available for conversations. If you have questions or comments, there is usually time at the end of a session when you can talk to your child's teacher."

In addition, many parent handbooks contain general information to help parents understand their child's school experience better and make the adjustment easier. These kinds of information are the following:

- *developmental characteristics*—brief profiles of expected behavior of children at different age levels
- *separation*—suggestions for making separation between parent and child easier for both
- *progress reports*—methods staff will use to report the child's progress to parents
- *information*—the kinds of information parents can provide teachers
- *parent involvement*—ways in which parents can be involved in school activities

A parent handbook should be a useful and attractive tool to both parents and staff; therefore, a lot of thought should go into its writing and composition. The following suggestions may help the director who is developing a handbook:

- Think about whether some information will vary from one year to the next or if it will always be the same. Be sure that variable information is on a separate page. If changes are needed, choose a loose-leaf or stapled binding for the book so pages can be inserted as needed.
- Arrange information logically, with a table of contents. Try printing each section on a different color paper so that it is easily identifiable. You can also cut each section wider or longer than the previous one, providing a tab for ease in locating.

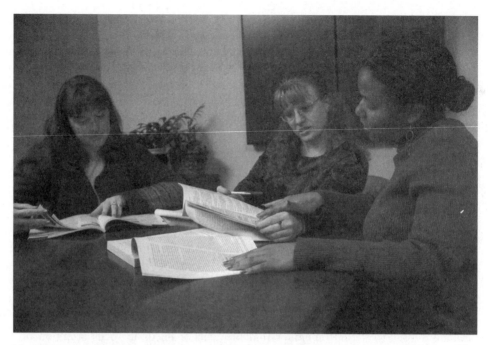

It is important for staff members to establish relationships with one another.

- Information should be concise. Remember that some parents will never read the whole document. Make it possible for them to get specific kinds of information without a lot of searching.
- The writing should be clear and free of poor grammar or misspelled words. Sentences should be easy to understand; they should not contain any professional jargon.
- Make the handbook attractive so that parents are invited to explore its contents. A computer will allow you to vary the print font, add drawings, or alter the format.
- Cost will probably be a consideration, especially if you have it typeset and printed professionally. Get several estimates before deciding to use this method. If it is too expensive, consider using a copier and collating it yourself.

THE NEW SCHOOL YEAR
Staff

It is important that all staff members work one or two weeks before the opening of school. This is a time when each classroom *environment* is prepared. Teachers should have time to

- do last-minute room cleaning.
- clean and organize supply cupboards.
- put away new materials.

- rearrange their classroom furniture.
- set up a schedule for general classroom maintenance.

Staff should have time to review *curriculum materials* available in their classrooms and in the general storage areas. They should also have time to

- order last-minute items as needed.
- prepare lesson plans and curriculum materials for the first week of school.

The time before school is an important one for the establishment of *relationships among staff members*. This is a time to set the tone for the working partnership between the director and staff. It is a time when the director can

- give teachers a list of the children in their classes.
- make children's files available.
- share critical medical information.
- prepare and distribute name tags.
- discuss group schedules.
- review sign-in procedures to be used by parents.
- review emergency procedures for safety of children.
- encourage teachers to schedule and complete home visits.
- plan procedures for the first day of school.

Staff members are included in planning.

Supplies

The beginning of a school year is a good time to do an inventory of supplies and equipment on hand. This can be very detailed or cover only items that are most used. For instance, it may not be necessary to know how many pencils are on hand, but it is important to know if there will be enough paint for the teachers to use.

Paint is an example of an **expendable supply**, things that get used up and have to be replaced. Also included are paper, glue, paper towels, toilet paper, and cleaning supplies. Bikes are **nonexpendable items** for they last a long time before they need to be replaced. Office equipment, outdoor equipment, and many toys are also considered nonexpendable.

Inventory should be divided into the two categories. The director should complete the count of what is on hand and shop around for the best prices before ordering what is needed. Ordering in large quantities often decreases the cost. Many times it will take up to six weeks for an order to arrive, so it is important to allow enough time for delivery.

Setting up a petty-cash fund for each classroom is an additional way of providing supplies. A specified amount is budgeted for the year for each room and teachers are allowed to purchase things they need. This can relieve the director of some of the responsibility and can also give teachers greater freedom to buy what they need.

Finances

Only a few schools can afford the luxury of a bookkeeper. Therefore, some directors have to assume that job. Before school begins each year is a good time to review whether procedures for collecting tuitions, recording income, and paying bills are efficient. There may be changes indicated. The following suggestions may be helpful for the director who is also the bookkeeper:

■ Collect tuition payments promptly each month on the same date.

■ Accumulate checks for a few days at a time, then alphabetize them and post them on individual ledger sheets for each child (see Figure 13-10).

■ When parents pay in cash, issue a duplicate receipt—one for the parent and one for the school.

■ Record all checks and cash in the cash receipts record (see Figure 13-11).

■ At a specified time, usually 10 days, check individual ledgers to see if tuitions have been paid. Notify all families who have not paid the tuition. It is acceptable to charge a late fee for overdue tuition.

■ Record expenditures as they are made and summarize them each month (see Figure 13-12).

■ Prepare a monthly budget summary (see Figure 13-13).

Almost all these procedures can be assisted by use of a computer and computerized methods (see Figure 13-14 for a computerized Plan Expense record).

Name _____		No. of days per week _____			
Address _____		Tuition Amt. _____			
Telephone _____					
Date	Item	Amt. Due	Amt. Paid	Credit	Balance

Download a printable version of this form at http://www.EarlyChildEd.delmar.com

FIGURE 13-10 ■ Sample individual ledger sheet form.

CASH RECEIPTS RECORD				
Date	Item	Cash	Check Number	Amount

Download a printable version of this form at http://www.EarlyChildEd.delmar.com

FIGURE 13-11 ■ Sample cash receipts record form.

EXPENDITURES RECORD				
Date	Item	Check Number	Amount	From Account

FIGURE 13-12 ■ Sample expenditures record form.

MONTHLY BUDGET SUMMARY					
Date	Item	Budget Amt.	This Month (last day)	Year to Date	Balance

FIGURE 13-13 ■ Sample monthly budget summary form.

Facility

The final task before the beginning of the school year is to check the overall appearance and safety of the school. It should be clean and attractive. Often parents say the first thing they look for in a school is cleanliness. Parents' first impressions will be formed by how the school looks. Is the entrance to the school appealing? Is there a bulletin board that will interest parents? Does the environment welcome parents as well as children?

The playground should also look inviting. Often this is what people see as they approach a school. It should look like a place that is safe for children and that children will enjoy. If there are any garden areas around the school, have they been cared for? Is lighting adequate for dark mornings or late afternoons? The director should

| KidsCare 6 Management Software - [Plan Expense] | | | | | | | | | | | | _ 🗗 X |
| File Edit Switch Plans Reports Help | | | | | | | | | | | | _ 🗗 X |

| **Plan Expense** | | 2002 | | | | | | | **Start Over** | | | |

Whole Dollar amount planned for each account — Use Budget Monthly amounts

Account	Jan	Feb	Mar	Apr	May	Jun	Jul	Aug	Sep	Oct	Nov	Dec
Advertising	50	50	50	50	50	50	50	50	50	50	50	50
Auto Expense	195	195	195	195	195	2000	195	195	195	195	195	195
Checking Service Charges	10	10	10	10	10	10	10	10	10	10	10	10
Children's Enrichment	25	25	25	25	25	25	25	25	25	25	25	25
Classroom Expense	100	100	100	100	100	100	100	100	100	100	100	100
Cleaning	125	125	125	125	125	125	125	125	125	125	125	125
Consultant Health Care	25	25	25	25	25	25	25	25	25	25	25	25
Dues and Subscriptions	0	0	0	0	0	50	0	0	0	0	0	0
Equipment Rental	87	87	87	87	87	87	87	87	87	87	87	87
Food Expense	300	300	300	300	300	300	300	300	300	300	300	300
General Supplies	55	55	55	55	55	55	55	55	55	55	55	55
Insurance - Employee Group	500	500	500	500	500	500	500	500	500	500	500	500
Insurance - Liability	300	300	300	300	300	300	300	300	300	300	300	300
Insurance - Workman's Con	130	130	130	130	130	130	130	130	130	130	130	130
Interest Expense	0	0	0	0	0	0	0	0	0	0	0	0
Landscaping	0	0	0	80	80	80	80	80	80	0	0	0
Legal and Accounting	0	0	0	0	0	0	0	0	0	0	0	0
Miscellaneous Expense	0	0	0	0	0	0	0	0	0	0	0	0
Office Expense	20	20	20	20	20	20	20	20	20	20	20	20
Payroll Services	0	0	0	0	0	0	0	0	0	0	0	0
Postal Expense	29	29	29	29	29	29	29	29	29	29	29	29
Rent Expense	1500	1500	1500	1500	1500	1500	1500	1500	1500	1500	1500	1500
Repairs and Maintenance	50	50	50	50	50	50	50	50	50	50	50	50
Taxes - Other	0	0	0	0	0	0	0	0	0	0	0	0
Totals	3776	3776	3776	3856	3856	5711	3856	3856	3856	3776	3776	3776
	Jan	Feb	Mar	Apr	May	Jun	Jul	Aug	Sep	Oct	Nov	Dec

Put cursor in any program box, then press
Control-S to spread amount for remaining months

Forecasted expenses for Nov.   FLTR   NUM

FIGURE 13-14 ■ Computerized plan expense record.

try driving up to the school in the morning and look at it as a parent would. Does it have "curb appeal"? Is it a place a parent would want to stop to investigate as a place for their child? If the answer is "yes," then the school is ready for another year!

SUMMARY

The decision to open an early childhood center must be carefully thought out, for it entails many choices and a variety of tasks. The first step is a *needs assessment* to determine whether there is a pool of prospective clients. Consulting census information about the community is one way to determine whether it will support another child care center.

There are several options for *housing* a school. It is possible to build anew, remodel a residence, rent unused public school classrooms, use space in a church, renovate a storefront or industrial building, use pre-fab buildings, or buy an existing school.

The *start-up costs* of opening a center will include the cost of the land and buildings, equipment and materials, and personnel. Additional expenses will include fees for consultant or legal services, advertising, and insurance.

Before going any further in the decision-making process, it is necessary to make an estimate of *ongoing costs*. Potential income will be determined by the number of children the facility will support. There are some suggested ranges of fixed costs that may help. The chosen site must accommodate enough children to cover expenses.

The school should open at a time that fits the needs of the community. Often the optimum time is at the end of summer. The director should develop *enrollment procedures* that ensure careful attention to each inquiry. Once applications begin arriving, it is time to make enrollment decisions: the total number to accept, whether to group children in peer or family groups, and how to incorporate children with special needs into the program. There are additional tasks that must be completed such as making attendance charts, preparing an overall schedule for the school, establishing and completing files for each child, and organizing a place for parent messages. The enrollment of school-age children may require a bus schedule to take children to and from their schools.

Each new parent should be given a handbook that includes information about the philosophy of the school and specific information about rules and procedures. It is helpful to have a parent orientation before school begins or within the first few weeks. Informal meetings allow time for questions and for a relationship between parents and teachers to be established. Staff members should be working at least two weeks before opening day. This is a time to prepare their room environments and to review curriculum materials.

Some additional tasks to be completed before a school is ready to open its doors include ordering supplies, setting up procedures for collecting tuitions, and giving the facility a *final inspection*. The appearance of the school must be clean and inviting.

SELECTED FURTHER READING

Kagan, S. L., Brandon, R. N., Ripple, C., Maher, E. J., & Joesch, J. M. (2002). Supporting quality early childhood care and education: Addressing compensation and infrastructure. *Young Children, 57*(3), 58–65.

Mitchell, A., Stoney, L., & Dichter, H. (2001). *Financing child care in the United States: An expanded catalog of current strategies* (2001 ed.). Kansas City, MO: Ewing Marion Kaufman Foundation.

National Women's Law Center. (2000). *Be all that we can be: Lessons from the military for improving our nation's child care.* Washington, DC: Author.

Whitebrook, M., & Eichberg, A. (2002). Finding a better way: Defining policies to improve child care workforce compensation. *Young Children, 57*(3), 66–72.

STUDENT ACTIVITIES

1. Visit your local zoning agency. Ask for zoning requirements for a child care center and a home-based center. If there are differences, ask about the reasoning behind them. Share this information with small groups assigned to the task.

2. Obtain a copy of the licensing requirements for your area. Determine the following:
   a. What is the maximum size for a group of toddlers?
   b. What is the teacher/child ratio for a group of four-year-olds?

c. Are there any regulations pertaining to school-age children?

d. What are the minimum qualifications for staff members?

3. Invite a director of a child care center to visit your class. Ask him or her to discuss which sections of the licensing code make a director's job easier. Ask also if there are items in the regulations that should be changed.

4. Collect parent handbooks from several child care centers. Groups can compare them and answer the following questions:

a. Do they contain the same kinds of information?

b. In what ways do they differ?

c. Is the information easy to understand?

d. Do you think essential information has been omitted?

 REVIEW

1. What information should be included in a community survey to determine whether a community can support another child care center?

2. List the possible types of housing for an early childhood center.

3. Discuss the advantages and disadvantages of using the following space for a child care center: a church building, a factory, an existing school.

4. Differentiate between start-up and ongoing costs.

5. List the categories of expenses that are included in a start-up budget.

6. Which expenditure comprises the largest percentage of ongoing costs?

7. What is meant by the terms *peer group* and *family group*?

8. List the completed forms that should be included in a child's enrollment file.

9. What is the purpose of a parent handbook? What kinds of information should it contain?

10. What is meant by expendable and nonexpendable supplies?

CASE STUDY

Amanda has worked for the past six months getting ready to open her own child care center in her community. She located the site, made the required renovations, obtained a license, hired staff, and did all the many other things needed for opening day. That day is fast approaching and she still has only 43 children enrolled. She needs at least 52 full-time tuitions to break even on expenses, not to mention a salary for herself.

1. What should Amanda do to attract additional enrollments?

2. What else can she do to ensure that there will be enough money to pay the first month's expenses?

HELPFUL WEB SITES

America Taking Action:	http://www.americatakingaction.com
Child Care Resource:	http://childcare-resource.com
Early Childhood Education Web Guide:	http://www.ecewebguide.com
ERIC:	http://www.ericps.crc.uiuc.edu/nccic/statepro.html

For additional resources related to administration, visit the Online Resource® for this book at www.EarlyChildEd.delmar.com

Part V

Beyond the
School Itself

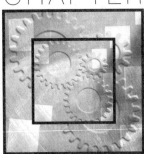

14
Including Families and the Community

OBJECTIVES

After reading this chapter, you should be able to:

- Discuss the changing roles of parents and preschools.
- List some ways that parents may participate in the school.
- State some possible goals for parent education.
- Cite several ways a school may help parents learn.
- Itemize some activities that can publicize a school.

A Day in the Life of ...
A Regional Director, Corporate Child Care

I began my day at one of the four centers I supervise. The director of the center had scheduled a meeting with a group of parents who had expressed serious concerns about the program. We found that their expectations were somewhat unreasonable and their attitudes were hostile. Two parents asked for more of a "voice" in the school. I suggested creating a Parent Association. They were enthused. We arranged another meeting to discuss it further. Following the meeting, I met with the director alone and explained the role of the Parent Association. I told her that parents often feel a sense of ownership if they are actively involved in an organized association. She seemed comfortable with this idea.

A few days later, we met again with these parents and opened the meeting to all other parents. The meeting started out as before with a list of complaints, but the director took control. She explained her decision to establish a Parent Association and asked for volunteers. She got a tremendous response!

Two months later, when I again met with the director, she reported that the association changed the climate of the parent group at the center. The director's life was much more pleasant after this new group was established, and she retained enrollment!

Traditionally, parents have been responsible for rearing children, and schools have had the task of educating them. Recent years have brought about some changes in these two roles.

CHANGING ROLES OF FAMILIES

Changing family life has forced modification of the traditional role of parents. In the United States, more than half the mothers of children under the age of six work outside the home. Children no longer stay home until they go to elementary school at five or six. Many children start in child care as babies and continue until or even through adolescence. As a result, parents no longer have sole responsibility for rearing their children. This task is shared with teachers or caregivers.

Those who are with the child while parents work are forced into new roles as well. Teachers can no longer focus only on teaching. They have to help children through each developmental stage, be concerned about their health, and provide the nurturing that once was done solely by parents.

This merging of responsibilities for rearing and educating the child has caused both parents and teachers to realize that their responsibilities overlap and that they must work closely together. This is especially true when infants are involved. Parents are understandably anxious about placing their baby in someone else's care. They want caregivers who will listen to their concerns and who will follow their suggestions about feeding, sleeping, and toileting. On the other hand, the school needs that kind of input to plan for the appropriate care of the baby. This need to work together changes in character but continues even when the child is a preschooler and older.

PARENT INVOLVEMENT

Even when children are in child care, research consistently shows the enormous influence parents still have on their children. They remain the primary support for the child as teachers and caregivers change. Parent involvement in the school becomes essential for the optimum development of the child. Follow-up studies of children who attended Head Start or those who have been in programs modeled after Head Start show lasting gains through their school years and into adulthood.

One of the crucial factors is the involvement of parents and community (Hayes, Palmer, & Zaslow, 1990; Schweinhart & Weikart, 1993).

Many parents and teachers who took part in the early cooperative schools found their involvement brought unexpected benefits. The parents learned a good deal about their own children. They also learned some basic principles of child development. They gained comfort by finding that other parents had similar problems. In fact, they learned that some problems were merely stages in a child's growth. The school provided a support system sometimes lacking in many communities. A few parents gained enough inspiration to become teachers when their children got older.

Beginning in the 1960s, some parents began demanding a more active role in the education of their children. It was a time of social unrest, marked by the civil rights movement. Some of the demands arose from criticism of schools in general. More specifically, the grievances were aimed at the "failure" of educational systems to understand minority needs. Some people felt schools were unresponsive and bureaucratic. The Head Start Project was one result of all this turmoil.

However, early attempts to involve parents in Head Start projects were difficult for the parents and the schools. Parent participation was "built into" the legislation. But parents sometimes felt insecure in the presence of the authority symbol of the teacher. On the other hand, teachers were reluctant to include parents for fear they might dominate the program. The partnership that was mandated in Head Start guidelines took time to implement.

Family-Centered Child Care: What Does It Look Like?

- Family-centered child care supports the connections between children and their families. It recognizes that children draw their identities from family. A basic belief in the value of families permeates program policies and practices. All family members are treated with respect, warmth, and courtesy.

- A family-centered program speaks the languages and respects the cultures of all families in the program. Staff members are drawn from the community the program serves.

- Family-centered programs build on family strengths. Such programs recognize stages of development in family members and work with them to meet their needs.

- Family-centered child care supports and trains caregivers. It is important to provide training for staff on the basic principles of family-centered child care. Pre-service and in-service training, peer coaching, and mentoring opportunities are provided on a regular basis.

Source: Child Care Bureau, 1996.

Today, in the successful Head Start centers, parents and professionals seem to be working together harmoniously. Parent representatives serve on advisory committees. Parents have a high degree of input into curriculum. Some serve as aides in the classroom helping the teachers directly. Parents are taught how to enhance learning through activities at home.

For some time, nonprofit schools have used parents in fund-raising, recruitment, and public relations activities. However, the attitude that educational aspects should be left to the school staff persisted. Now, schools are finding that parents have many skills they are willing to share for program enrichment.

So, too, have proprietary schools found that parents are willing to take part in many ways. Parents with a profession offer their skills as consultants; others use special abilities to enrich subject matter. Satisfied parents are more willing to help the school broaden its recruitment activities.

As already noted, the steadily increasing number of child care programs has altered the picture. When children spend many of their waking hours in school, the relationship between home and school has to be even closer. Directors must be instruments for change in this situation. Parents and teacher, guided skillfully by the director, share the responsibility for determining the best environment for the child's physical, social, and intellectual growth.

The kind and extent of **parent involvement** depends on the program offered by the school. As in Head Start, parent participation may be mandated with specific guidelines.

The extent of parent participation where there are no specific written agreements will depend on the philosophy and attitudes of the school. In centers where director and staff fully realize the importance of parent presence, the involvement may be broad and almost unlimited.

Parental Roles

Parents may participate in the school in several ways. They may sit on policy-making committees, play a supportive role, act as aides in the classroom, or be trained as teachers of their own children at home.

The rationale for involving parents stems from the belief that people feel a commitment to decisions in which they have had a part. Research shows that parent involvement benefits both parents and children (Becher, 1986; Powell, 1989). Parents feel more a part of their children's education and children are able to achieve more when encouraged by their parents. And, in practical terms, many tax-supported programs depend on active community support for renewal of funds.

Further rationale for involving parents comes from the belief that development of decision making and other skills will help in other aspects of their life. Learning that their personal input can influence the school encourages self-growth and further participation outside the school.

In a *policy-making role,* parents may take part in planning a new program by suggesting goals. They may be asked to join in operational aspects such as hiring or helping to evaluate staff. They may also suggest topics for parent education activities.

Some policy-making functions for parents might be

- serving as members of an advisory committee or council.
- representing parents on the board of trustees.
- helping to set policies concerning finance and personnel.

Some parents may fulfill *supportive roles*. These are tasks the parents can sometimes do at home or outside of the school. They are designed to aid or supplement educational functions. Some tasks parents may perform in a supportive role are to

- provide parts of major maintenance projects.
- act as clerical support.
- plan and carry out fund-raising.
- be responsible for social activities.
- provide baby-sitting or car pool services.

The real purpose of a supportive role for parents is to fulfill a mutual need; the school and parents both want the best for the children. The school may desperately need some services parents can provide.

The supportive role may help some parents begin involvement at a level of their own comfort. Not everyone is ready or able to invest as much time and effort as is necessary to become competent in policy making or serve as an aide.

Fathers should be included!

When they do work as *aides in the classroom,* parents must learn some of the duties and skills of a teacher in order to be effective. As aides, parents may

- perform tasks assigned by the teacher, such as helping with large-group activities or working with individual children.
- prepare materials, arrange the room, and keep records of children's progress.
- supervise small groups of children during specific times.

In some programs, participation of parents as aides is part of the "career ladder" concept. This may be the first rung in the progress toward paid employment. Head Start and many child care centers train mothers for jobs in schools for young children.

Parents may be trained to become *better teachers of their own children.* In this role, parents

- learn to recognize the child's readiness for learning.
- learn the value of a variety of learning experiences to further the child's development.
- make use of common materials found around the home to enhance the child's learning.

Head Start has met this need by providing Home Visitors who work with families in their homes. Together the Home Visitor and parents plan activities for the child and determine what the child is ready to learn. Common and inexpensive household materials are used for activities. All family members are encouraged to participate. Schools other than Head Start can also provide this kind of training in other ways. As parents become more competent, they are encouraged to become more involved in their child's school. Training parents as teachers of their own children is discussed in more detail later in this chapter.

Planning for Multicultural Parent Participation

Head Start programs, begun in 1965, required parent participation. That experience has shown that children do better when parents are involved, not only during the Head Start period, but during later school years. It works because parents are involved at many levels, and their diversity is honored and respected. It has a remarkable record of involvement. In 2002, over 867,000 parents volunteered in local programs, and 29 percent of the staff were parents of current or former Head Start children (U.S. Department of Health and Human Services, 2003).

Although Head Start has the advantage of funds to create a climate for multicultural involvement, all programs can adopt some of the methods that made the program successful. The following are some suggestions to help directors create a welcoming environment.

- Ask parents to assist in ways to introduce children to various cultures through books, special celebrations, art exhibits, or community events.
- Include in any discussions of cultural differences the ways in which family values such as fairness, loyalty, or honesty are shared by all cultures.

- Avoid making sweeping generalizations about children from different backgrounds. Look at the individual child, family, and neighborhood environment before labeling differences as cultural.
- Work to understand differences, but also to find common ground.

Limits on Involvement

Each community and the schools within it have their own particular characteristics. The appropriate kind of parent involvement must be tailored to fit the situation to be effective. Factors to be considered are (1) number of working parents, (2) ethnic group values, (3) stability of the community, (4) size of the community, and (5) physical setting of the school.

The number of working parents, especially mothers, certainly determines the amount and time of involvement. Obviously, in a child care school where almost all the parents are working, few parents can serve as aides. It is possible that some parents may work part-time or on a flexible schedule that would allow them some limited participation. Most parents cannot do this. The school must realize that the working schedule of parents determines involvement.

However, some ways in which fully employed parents can be involved in the education of their children are to

- participate in decision making at convenient times.
- provide support by doing work at home or after work.
- be involved in training as teachers of their own children at home.

Directors must realize, and staff should be reminded, that a working parent often has little surplus energy. Reluctance to become involved in the school may be just plain fatigue, not an indication the parent is not interested.

Values, attitudes, and traditions of the parents in a school may also affect the extent and manner in which parents are willing to participate. It is important that directors and teachers be aware of parents' beliefs when differences arise over issues involving the children. Perhaps the adults' attitudes will not change, but at least they should listen to each other and respect their differences.

> There are many instances where parent and teachers come from the same culture, but have differing values, beliefs, and practices. Teachers must respect these parents even though they do not share the same views on many subjects. It is sometimes easier to understand and explain differences when a cultural label can be attached to them. It's harder to accept and respect diversity when the person looks like us. It is also important not to make assumptions about people's culture based on their appearance (Gonzalez-Mena, 2001).

Directors will be more effective if they consider the following:

- How do the parents feel about being involved in their child's school?
- Do parents and teachers have similar or widely differing attitudes about the education of children?
- Do the families see the school and home as entirely separate entities?

The stability or mobility of the community from which the school draws children also determines the degree of parent participation.

- ■ If the population is largely transient, involvement that takes a long time to develop will not be possible.
- ■ If the community is relatively stable, parents can take the time to develop decision-making and teaching skills.

The size of the community in which the school is based will also determine parent involvement.

- ■ If children are bused to school from distant areas, it may be harder to find ways to involve parents.
- ■ A school located within walking distance may naturally become a center for varied activities.

The physical limitations of the school may restrict involvement by parents.

- ■ If the school is small and space is at a premium, many parents may feel "squeezed out."
- ■ If certain areas can be set aside and scheduled for parents' use, they may feel more welcome and free.

Initial Contact

Parents' first visits to a school after enrolling their children are the most important for setting the tone of future contacts. As parents walk into the school, will they feel welcome? Are there ways in which the environment says "Parents are welcome, too"? Does the director or some other staff member greet parents when they enter? Does the school have an open-door policy in which parents are welcome to visit at any time?

Some schools opt for an open house to set the tone for parent relationships. Often scheduled just before the school year begins, an open house gives parents an opportunity to meet all the staff and get to know other parents.

Every contact staff members have with parents is important. Teachers should be as responsive to the parents as to their children. Even during brief meetings when the child is delivered or picked up in the evening, teachers should be sensitive to parents' feelings. In other words, parents should feel that the school people are as interested in them as they are in their child.

A physical space reserved for parents is important. If a room can be used as a parent-teacher lounge, or a place for the parent to feel at home, big dividends will accrue. A bulletin board for parents used to announce parent meetings, community lectures, fund-raisers, books of interest, and so on is useful. The weekly food menu could also be posted. A newsletter for parents will keep them informed and emotionally involved with the school.

Encouraging Participation

Once the initial contact with parents is made, the task of encouraging continued participation begins. The primary responsibility is the director's. The director must *create the climate* in which staff members work. Staff members who have high morale and who feel secure in their jobs will feel more positive toward both parents and children.

A second task as leader is to *implement a program* that emphasizes home-school relations. Teachers may need encouragement to involve parents in their classroom activities. The director can suggest ways they can use parents as aides or in supportive roles and let them know which parents have talents or skills they might call on for help.

The third important task for the director is to *act as coordinator* for a program of *parent involvement*. Busy teachers may need help in arranging times and other specifics of getting parents to help with classroom activities. The coordinator can also offer positive reinforcement for parents who have participated.

The process of involving parents in the education of their children has some built-in obstacles. Parents and teachers often deal in stereotypes of each other. This makes working together difficult. The parent may see the teacher as an "expert" and, therefore, critical of parents. This may make the parent feel uneasy and unwelcome while visiting the school. As a result, the parent avoids contacts with the school.

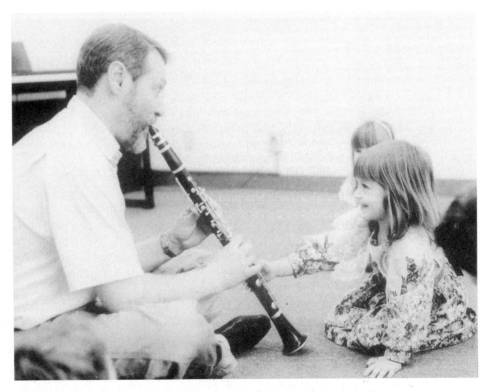

Parents can use their special abilities to enrich the curriculum.

Teachers, on the other hand, may feel the parent has unrealistic expectations for what the school should do. When these expectations are not reached, the teacher feels under attack. Again, there is avoidance, this time from the teacher.

Parents' attitudes toward school are often based on their own experiences. If they hated school, they may need a great deal of encouragement to participate in their child's school. On the other hand, some parents loved school and are only too ready to participate when asked.

Inexperienced teachers often feel they have enough to do learning to work well with children. Having to be concerned about parents is an added burden. Some may have tried to get parents involved but have been unsuccessful. It then is easier to justify not including parents by feeling that these parents do not care enough about their children. Even experienced teachers may be influenced by negative contacts with parents.

Some teachers fear that parents may not regard them as knowledgeable because they do not have children of their own. A few parents do say, "You don't know what it's like being with a child 24 hours a day." Even when it is not said, some teachers feel parents will think it.

Lack of training in working with parents may also create problems. Working with adults does require special skills and adroitness. Teachers often do not understand and, therefore, are critical of the feelings parents have about their children. Teacher training programs often fail to help the beginning teacher develop greater empathy for parents.

Some teachers seem to be able to involve parents more easily than others. These teachers can help other teachers. The director should schedule times when beginning teachers can observe more experienced teachers working with parent volunteers. Their observations can be discussed in follow-up staff meetings.

Incentives for Sustaining Involvement

It is often as difficult to sustain parent interest and participation in a school as it was to acquire it originally. But the most important incentive for parents is, of course, their children. Parents want their children to be successful in school. Feedback on children's progress in the school helps. They also want to know how to be better parents. The school can build upon these needs to foster parent involvement. If they believe they are helping their children, they will freely help the school.

Few schools can pay parents with money. A few publicly funded programs can offer reimbursement for out-of-pocket expenses. But mostly encouragement, knowledge, and positive reinforcement are the coin of repayment. Some employer-sponsored schools may offer limited released time away from the job to help in the school. Or in child care centers, dinner meetings may be arranged just after the close of school with free child care time.

Parents' interest can be aided by promoting personal growth. In some programs, contact with the school is the first or only activity tried by parents outside home or work. If they feel successful, their feelings of worth will increase. It may be the first step to broader community activities.

Social relationships that are developed through parent involvement are also important in continued interest. Single parents, especially, may find friendships that become an important part of their lives. New associations with other adults offer a single parent a broader outlook than a strictly child-centered world. Family-oriented social activities will allow parents to get to know one another. Some suggestions are children's concerts, puppet shows, family spaghetti dinners, picnics, and museum trips.

Some programs should be geared solely to adult needs. Classes in nutrition or family finance might be successful rallying points. If there is room and these classes meet at the school, parents have an additional inducement toward belonging. Even broader excursions such as trips to museums, art galleries, or theaters may broaden parents' experiences and enhance friendships.

Recording Parent Involvement

The director should keep records to show the extent of parent involvement in the school. In some publicly funded programs, this is necessary to stay within guidelines. In any case, the records may prove valuable when attempting to evaluate the program and to determine if changes may be made. The following records may prove useful.

- list of current committee members
- minutes of all meetings involving parents
- attendance records at committee and board meetings
- copies of resolutions involving parents' work
- correspondence relating to parents' efforts
- evaluation of parent involvement
- records of any citations or awards made

To think of the parents as part of a team made up of the school and the home is most productive. The teacher and parents have similar aims that are sometimes frustrated by false impressions. One of the major aims of parent involvement is to break through these barriers in order to give the children a superior education. The teacher, director, parent, and community should be considered as a unit. Without this sense of wholeness, there are sure to be gaps in the child's education and development.

 ## PARENT EDUCATION

While the aim of parent involvement is to establish a partnership for the care of the child at school, **parent education** is designed to help parents be better informed about child-rearing and family life. The director has a responsibility to formulate the structure for a parent education program. Teachers should be encouraged to participate as fully as possible. It might be easier for the director to do all the parent education work, but the staff will gain by taking part.

The place to start is formulating some goals. It is possible to work on several simultaneously or concentrate on one goal for a period of time. Goals, though, should form the base for planning parent education activities.

Goals for Parent Education

Although all the following may not be completely applicable, they may provide some ideas for developing goals. It is most important to have goals that are consonant with the general philosophy of the total school.

Establish a partnership with the family for the education and care of the child. The director should convey the attitude of partnership to each staff member. It begins when a parent first walks into the school and talks to the secretary or director. To convey this attitude is especially important during the time the child and parent are adjusting to school attendance.

Help parents to recognize and respect their own abilities. Most parents do a good job of rearing their children. They sometimes feel inadequate. An important part of parent education is to help them realize their own strengths and trust their own feelings about what is right for the child.

Provide parents with factual information about child development. Many parents have limited experience with young children and may feel that some of the things their children do are unusual. A knowledge of child development will help them to view behavior as developmental stages.

Explain the school curriculum and planned activities. Parents should know why the school provides certain activities and materials. They should understand why the teacher presents the materials in a specific way. They need to understand the value of free play and what is gained in group participation.

Help parents understand the ways that children can learn. Some parents believe that learning takes place only when the instructor is teaching. They may not remember that children are actively learning when they are playing. Children learn in different ways. Parents can be encouraged to recognize experiences at home that may be important.

Introduce the parents to a wide variety of educational materials and experiences. The family can be helped to make use of readily available materials for the child's learning experiences. They may need guidance as to the sources and values of toys, books, paper supplies, puzzles, and other aids such as how-to-do-it books and games. The appropriate materials for the child's age level are recommended to encourage creativity and self-growth.

Activities

An attractive parent education program will have a wide variety of activities and methods from which parents may learn. Some are planned and structured; others occur spontaneously. An effective program may use some of the following formats.

One of the first opportunities for a parent to learn in the school setting is the orientation meeting. This may be held at the beginning of a school year or at various times throughout the year as new families enroll. This meeting should be seen as an opportunity to convey general information about the school and to answer parents' questions. An evening meeting usually works best for parents who have jobs. If child care is offered, more parents may be able to attend.

The director should

- plan the meeting to last about an hour or an hour and a half.
- offer simple refreshments before the meeting starts or at the conclusion. Either an "old" parent or a teacher should be asked to serve.
- send written invitations to parents. If an RSVP is included, it is important to follow up on any who do not respond.
- begin the meeting on time by welcoming the parents.
- introduce staff members, indicating their room assignments.
- distribute a copy of the goals of the school and explain each.
- explain school rules (e.g., clothing for children to wear, bringing toys or snacks from home).
- describe methods of introducing children into their classrooms and managing separation from parents.
- allow time for answering parents' questions.
- set a friendly tone for establishing a partnership with parents in the care and education of their children.

Observation is an important avenue for learning. Parents can see how the school operates and see the interaction between teachers and children.

Observations may be casual and unscheduled. Each time a parent is in a classroom is an opportunity to observe. If a school has one-way screens into the classroom, the parent may observe without intrusion. This type of observation may be especially helpful for parents who are having separation problems with their children. The parent can see that the child almost always stops crying when the teacher diverts or comforts the child. This may help immensely in guilt reduction.

The one-way screen offers anonymity to the parent. Often the child acts differently when the parent is present. This is a rare chance to see the child more objectively. Within the school's child-oriented environment, the child is often different from the person seen by the parent at home.

Casual observation also has its pitfalls. The parent may see something that is not entirely understood. Either the teacher or director should be available to explain the child's part in the total group. Many times parents have questions most easily answered by the director, as a "neutral" observer.

Scheduled observations of demonstration activities also help parents learn. Their attention can be directed to specific activities. They can be coached as to what to look for and what not to expect. They may also be asked to note the way the teacher varies activities of the group and of each child.

If a group of parents observes, there should be time for a discussion after each session to clarify and reinforce learning. As in any endeavor, each person sees slightly different aspects of what happened. Sharing and comparing observations may be an exciting way to learn.

Group discussions are an invaluable tool for parent education, especially when led by a skilled staff member. Groups can either be structured with a particular topic as the focus or unstructured, allowing the topic to be determined by the interests of the group. The structured group begins with a brief presentation of information. The topics might be one of the following: stages of a child's development, aspects of the school curriculum, or how to manage situations that arise at home between the parent and child. Parents have an opportunity to relate their own experiences with the information. Some structured group discussions might be centered around one of the parent training packages such as Gordon's Parent Effectiveness Training (1970) or Dinkmeyer and McKay's Systematic Training for Effective Parenting (1976).

Unstructured group discussions allow parents to discuss topics that may be uppermost in their mind at a particular time. Parents have an opportunity for an informal exchange of ideas and the leader functions as a resource for information as needed. One of the secondary results of this kind of group is that parents find they are not alone in their confusions or frustrations about the best ways to manage their children. They also learn that their child is probably not much different from other children. This is particularly important if they have never had the opportunity to watch their siblings grow up or to be around young children.

When these two kinds of discussion are used at different times along with observations in the classrooms, parents have an excellent opportunity to learn more about their own children and child-rearing in general. Discussions that take place in the meetings often stimulate further conversation between parents outside of the group setting.

Lectures or panels are additional teaching methods. Experts in various fields can be asked to speak at parent meetings. The speaker should be interesting as well as informed. Nothing can be so deadly to a parent education session as a long, dull speech, especially if it is given after working hours. Something of this sort not only can induce sleep, but also can seriously derail the entire effort.

Lecture topics must be chosen with care. Some topics create anxiety rather than promote knowledge. Controversial topics attract interest but should be handled skillfully. Both sides of an issue should be presented.

Films, slides, and tapes help parents learn. Many informative and interesting films and videotapes are geared to parents of young children. The director should preview each tape or film before showing it and make notes while viewing for use during the discussion period that follows.

Films or videotapes made at the school should illustrate the activities and materials used in everyday teaching. Videotapes made at intervals may show language development during the year. The same holds for other kinds of ventures. Art, music, and science all hold developmental promise. Tapes must be edited carefully so that nothing embarrassing to any child will appear.

Workshop participation can offer information about the curriculum. Parents may participate in the same activities as their children do. They may fingerpaint, work with wood or blocks, and sing. This gives them a firsthand feel of what the child is doing.

Another kind of workshop is one in which parents can make learning materials to use at home with their child. This can be a game, a piece of equipment, or a learning kit. This kind of workshop for parents can have a twofold benefit: (1) they have made something for their child, and (2) they have explored the potential of materials.

Parents can learn through participation in the classroom. Many parents have special skills or training that can be useful on a short-term basis in the classroom. It is a welcome change of pace to have a parent read a story, lead a music activity, or share a cooking experience. Some parents may be able to share stories and objects from their own ethnic backgrounds. This can be an effective way of bringing an added dimension to the classroom.

If parents show some desire to serve as aides on a longer term basis, the hurdle of training may appear. This will vary with each individual, but a brief overview followed by on-the-job instruction will probably suffice. Volunteers must understand the special goals of the school, if any. They need to know the rudiments of interacting with young children in a group. They should begin by working under the close supervision of the regular teacher and progressing to individuals or very small groups.

Saturday or holiday sessions of a school give fathers an opportunity to participate. Some schools schedule this kind of activity at least once a year. With both father and mother now working, this type of scheduling is gaining in popularity.

All communications with a parent have an educational potential. Any phone call to or from a parent is part of the parent involvement/parent education program of the school. Phone calls made when a child is home sick are especially important to remember. It tells the parent that the teacher cares. It may also give the parent a moment to talk to the teacher about the child.

Daily contacts, though routine, are important. The way the teacher answers a parent's questions about the child establishes feelings. A simple question such as "Did Johnny eat?" may be answered in some detail or with a colder "Yes." Parents want reassurance that the teacher knows and cares about what the child did during the day. When that kind of feedback is given, the result can be greater trust and confidence in the school. The little things do count.

Conferences are probably the most efficient way a school can help parents learn. They are also an effective means for solidifying their relationship to the school. The following are some general suggestions for the director and teacher to keep in mind for all **parent conferences.**

■ Provide a comfortable setting that is free from any interruptions.
■ Start and end the conference on a positive note.
■ Do not be afraid to tell parents that you do not have all the answers or information, but that you will try to find out.
■ Assure parents that you share their interest in and concern for their child.
■ Allow enough time to cover the topic adequately, but do not let the discussion become too lengthy.
■ Be sensitive to each person's "comfort zone" regarding self-revealing dialogues. The values and beliefs learned as part of growing up in a particular

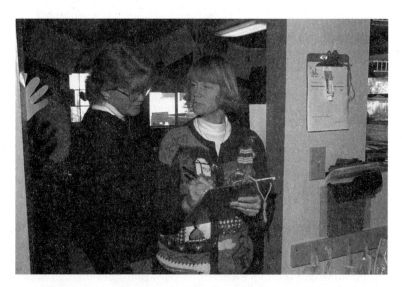

Sometimes parent conferences are informal.

culture may have a powerful influence on communication patterns and child-rearing practices.

■ End the conference with a summary of what has been discussed and future procedures.

■ Schedule a follow-up conference if it is warranted.

When the conference is for the purpose of reporting on a child's progress:

■ Plan conference content before the scheduled time. Be prepared to present information about the child's achievements and to describe incidents that illustrate that information.

■ Be prepared to discuss suggestions for helping the child attain a higher level of functioning if there are areas in which the child needs to improve.

If the conference is for the purpose of discussing a problem:

■ Remember that parents have a strong emotional investment in their child. Empathize with parents about their concerns. "I understand how you could be really upset when that happens."

■ Avoid labeling a child or making broad statements. Instead of calling a child a "troublemaker" tell the parent "At story time he will poke the child sitting next to him" or "She constantly interrupts when a teacher is reading a story to the group. She will ask a question, say she can't hear, or say that she doesn't like the book."

■ Acknowledge that it is not easy to report on problems that occur at school. Describe the behavior or situation without being critical or making the parents feel it is their fault.

- Allow parents to ask questions or to describe how they see their child's behavior.

- Remember that no matter how careful or gentle you might be, sometimes parents are going to be defensive or angry. They will respond with denial that the problem exists. "We never see that kind of behavior at home." They may also respond with an attitude of projection. "It's the school's problem because that teacher doesn't know how to handle my child."

- Remind parents that you have a common concern for their child.

- Avoid using educational jargon, talking down to parents, or using lengthy explanations. Use clear and concise descriptions of behavior and short explanations of developmental stages. Where necessary, use a translator or speak in the parents' native language.

- Guide parents to find their own solutions to problems or be prepared to describe how you will work with the problem at school. "Do you have ideas about how you will respond to his temper tantrums now that we have talked about what precedes them?" Or "Now that I understand more about why she is behaving that way, these are the things that I think will help at school."

- Do not expect a solution to every problem. Sometimes merely letting the child have time to move to another stage of development or find his or her own way will change previously troubling behavior.

- Schedule a follow-up conference in the near future to discuss whether the new procedures that have taken place are working or whether another approach needs to be found. "Let's meet again in two weeks to see how our plan has been working."

- Make notes of the conference (not while parent is present, but when the conference is finished) and place it in the child's file.

Telephone conversations with a parent sometimes become mini-conferences. These can be initiated by either the parent or a staff member to report a change in the child or to better understand the child. Often parents are more comfortable talking on the phone than sitting down with a staff member at a more formal conference. Certain topics lend themselves best to telephone conferences. For example, the parent relates what happened at home before the child came to school or a teacher describes a child's special achievement that day. In other words, the telephone is an opportunity to share information about the child.

Sometimes parents want to talk about a problem and finding time for a sit-down conference is difficult. It is important to address their concerns even when the telephone is the only medium for doing so. If this happens, the same guidelines should be followed as were discussed in previous paragraphs about a conference for the purpose of discussing a problem.

Casual contacts between staff members and parents should also be seen as part of parent education. These usually occur when the parents leave their children at school or pick them up at the end of the day. Short, casual contacts, like telephone conversations, should be used for the purpose of exchanging information, answering questions, or discussing the program. They should not be used for discussing a problem since there is too much opportunity for a misunderstanding. In the morning both parents and staff are rushed and at the end of the day both are tired.

It is also important that the staff person who is present at the end of the day know any important information about the child's day at school. This means that the morning teacher needs to communicate any critical information that should be shared with the parent. If some concern is expressed by the parent or by the teacher, a time for a sit-down conference should be scheduled.

Home visits are another way of helping parents become more effective in the education of their own children. Head Start actually has an entire program called Home Start in which parents are taught to provide educational activities for their own children through visits from a trained professional. Most child care centers do not have the luxury of having a staff person whose main responsibility is to work with parents in their own homes. However, home visits can be used as a way to expand and enhance the educational activities that children are exposed to in the school setting. One advantage of a home visit is that the staff member has an opportunity to learn more about the environment in which the child lives. This can be helpful in understanding both the child and the family. Another advantage is that parents can learn how to use easily available home materials to provide learning experiences for their children. The staff member might also bring materials to be used at home and demonstrate their use. Finally, both parents and children are proud when the teacher takes the time to come to their home. It helps to bridge the gap between home and school.

Information can be conveyed to parents through a parent library, a periodic newsletter, or a bulletin board. Some parents may prefer to increase their knowledge by reading. Others may resist this fiercely. But the school should make available some books on child development—the best in the field. If the budget will not allow outright purchase, a reading list of good resources at the local library may suffice. Already mentioned, the newsletter may keep parents informed of what is happening at the school and in the field of child development. The director and teachers can write articles aimed at parents. A centrally located bulletin board, attractively arranged, can serve as a center of interest near an exit or entrance. The board should be well maintained and up to date.

An integral part of early childhood education is the enlightenment of parents. The school has the children for only a part of each day. For each child's education to be consistent, the parents must carry the same goals into the home. To make this possible, the school must make a concerted effort to present itself to the parents. Parent education is really a cooperative enterprise on the part of the school and parents to make the child's education truly unique and whole.

 THE SCHOOL AND THE COMMUNITY

Schools must actively promote themselves in order to remain competitive. No one requires very young children to go to school. When parents choose to put their children in school, they sometimes make choices capriciously. The school is located near the home or workplace. It is convenient to transportation. It is inexpensive. The motivations are many and varied. The schools with full enrollment and waiting lists have made earnest efforts to promote themselves.

Probably the best form of public relations is good parent education and intense parent involvement with the school. One of the most sincere forms of advertising is word-of-mouth testimony of satisfied customers. Parents who are satisfied are good promoters.

A few schools have adopted easily recognized symbols to promote themselves. KinderCare uses a red tower in all its buildings and as a logo on printed material. It is not necessary to compete on this level, however. There are common, everyday ways of making the school known in the community, and even outside it.

The director usually assumes responsibility for public relations. This self-promotion should be approached in an organized and thoughtful way. It makes sense to pursue areas over which there can be some control before launching something such as a paid campaign. Some things to think about include (1) the exterior appearance of the school, (2) telephone-answering procedures, (3) visitor utilization, (4) brochures and pamphlets, (5) open houses, and (6) community activities.

Appearance of the School

It is easy to become habituated to the appearance of a school. The casual passerby has not. Evaluations are frequently formed from first impressions. Sometimes it is helpful to adopt the attitude of a total stranger. What does the outside of the school look like? Peeling paint and fading signs or an attractive color and well-kept entrance?

Playground areas are often visible from the outside. What kind of equipment can be seen? Is it being used? Does it look sturdy and well maintained? Is the equipment designed to appeal to children or only to adults? Are there open places for children to play?

When visitors enter the building, what do they see first? Is the entrance arranged so that someone will greet them? Is there a place to sit down? Is the reception area pleasant looking? Are there things that interest parents? Is the area clean and free of unpleasant odors? Sensory impressions are important in setting the tone for first visitors.

Telephone-Answering Procedures

Many first contacts and first impressions are made over the telephone. The person answering the telephone becomes a front-line public relations person.

Often this person is the secretary. Parents telephone for information regarding price, hours, age range, and other variables. To ease the burdens on the director's time, the secretary can be trained to give this kind of routine information about the school. The director should provide forms for recording names, addresses, and telephone numbers and establish a procedure for following an inquiry with written information. The secretary should be trained to know when to refer calls. Directors may want to answer questions about policy, curriculum, or goals themselves.

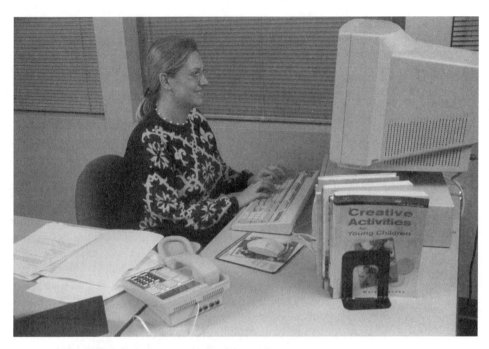

A good secretary is vital to public relations.

The secretary should be pleasant and polite when answering the telephone and use clearly enunciated speech. An unrushed and unhurried manner may reassure a parent who already has a doubt or two.

Visitors

Parents of children already enrolled in the school should feel free to visit at any time. Specific times should be set aside for other visitors. For example, one or two days a week could be planned to accommodate prospective parents, community persons, or others wishing to see the school. There should be a plan for what the visitors will see. Written materials are often helpful. Teachers should be informed that they will have visitors in their classrooms.

After a short orientation, the director should take the visitors to a classroom and introduce them to the teacher. They should be seated well away from the center of activity of the children. Thirty minutes is about the maximum time for visitors to spend in the classroom.

Another half an hour to an hour should be set aside for a discussion after the observation. This is the time to encourage visitors to share what they have seen or to ask questions. If disparate interest groups, such as visiting teachers and prospective parents, are touring the school, it is best to meet with them separately. Their questions and observations may be quite different.

Visitors should be scheduled for times when interesting activities are taking place so they can see children working at learning centers or involved in a group activity. Discussion with visitors can focus on how the lessons further the goals of the school.

The Brochure

An attractive brochure is an effective tool for selling a school and should be a succinct portrayal of the school. It should be attractive and in good taste. Colors may be used as long as they are not gaudy.

The brochure may be sent out in response to a telephone call, given to parents who stop by, distributed at professional meetings, or sent out into the community. It is a small ambassador.

The effectiveness of the brochure depends on how carefully it has been prepared. A poor brochure is worse than none at all. A good one has few rivals for good publicity. Staff members or parent volunteers with special art or writing abilities may be able to help in the production.

Many people don't read brochures carefully. For that reason the information should be condensed, not detailed. The essential facts should be clear when the document is skimmed.

It must contain all pertinent information. It should be of a size and weight that can be mailed for minimum first-class postage. The paper used should have a good "feel." Twenty-weight coated stock is often used in an 8 1/2 × 11 format, folded three times. A brochure that can be mailed without an envelope is less costly.

Although total cost must be considered, it is not wise to count pennies. The addition of cuts for pictures and of some color costs more. But selective bidding by printers and a judicious selection may partially compensate. Perhaps fewer brochures for limited and controlled distribution would be better if quality suffers.

A brochure should include

- the name, address, and telephone number of the school.
- sponsorship (if any) of the school.
- hours school is in session. Days of the week and months of the year might also be helpful.
- the procedure and cost of enrollment. If enrollments are taken only at specific times, this should be stated.
- ages of children served.
- tuition and other fees. (It may be wise to use a separate sheet for tuition and fees. It is less expensive to reprint when costs change.)
- brief statements of philosophy—in terms everyone can understand.
- a short description of the school's program(s).
- a description of unique features.
- the name of person to contact for enrollment.
- affiliations or accreditations.

See Figure 14-1 for a suggested brochure layout.

(Picture of a classroom)

ORCHARD VALLEY CHILD
CARE CENTER
A UNIQUE LEARNING
ENVIRONMENT FOR YOUR CHILD

Orchard Valley Child Care Center
1000 Valley Drive
Orchard Valley

Place stamp
here

(Picture of a classroom)

FIGURE 14-1 ■ Sample brochure *(continues)*.

PROGRAM

Orchard Valley Child Care Center is committed to providing an optimum environment for children while they are in our care. Our philosophy and goals are used to plan and implement all aspects of our program.

We believe:

* Each child is unique and deserves opportunities to make choices, to develop independence, and to receive reinforcement when successful.

* In providing a physical environment in which the child can be safe, can explore, and can be challenged to develop optimum motor skills.

* All teaching staff should be role models for children and should plan learning activities appropriate for each age level.

* Parents are the most significant adults in a child's life and should be included as partners in planning for the child's growth and development while at school.

(picture of a child)

ENROLLMENT

New enrollments are accepted at any time there are openings available. Application must be made in person. For an appointment, please call:

Mrs. Mary Anton
555-3014

A $35.00 nonrefundable registration fee is charged at the time of initial enrollment and at the beginning of each new enrollment year.

AGES

Our infant-toddler program accepts children at six weeks.

Children between ages two and five can be enrolled in our preschool program. A kindergarten classroom is available for those who are ready for a more academic program.

A before- and after-school service meets the needs of children from age six to twelve. If required, our school van will take these children to their elementary school in the morning and pick them up again in the afternoon.

HOURS

Orchard Valley Child Care Center is open from 6 A.M. until 6 P.M. Monday through Friday.

FEES

Fees are payable at the beginning of each month and are based on the number of hours the child attends. A child may be enrolled for a half or full day, two to five days each week.

A fee schedule will be sent to you upon request.

(Picture of a child)

Orchard Valley Child Care Center is a member of the Preschool Owners Association.

In 1988, the school was accredited by the National Association of Schools for Young Children.

FIGURE 14-1 ■ Sample brochure (continued).

Open House

An open house can be the vehicle for publicizing the best features of a school. This can be especially effective when just opening a new school. There are really two parts to it: preparation of the school itself and publicity to lure the community to attend.

As many staff members as possible should be involved in planning and preparing for the open house. The more dramatic and graphic aspects of the educational program should be highlighted. Classroom displays with children's artwork will show creativity. Block buildings, pictures, storybooks, and varied constructions all lend themselves to self-advertisement.

Room arrangements should be attractive. A story corner can be set up as though children were expected. A table set for snacktime shows that proper nutrition is a vital part.

After visiting the classrooms and displays, the visitors should have ample opportunity to ask questions. Staff members should be available to talk about the program or to answer questions. A guest book should be placed near the entrance for guests to write their addresses, telephone numbers, and comments. These names can then be added to the general mailing list.

Brochures should be displayed in a prominent place. If a brochure isn't available, a simple one-page statement of philosophy and goals will suffice. Either document should include school name, address, phone number, and contact person.

The finest open houses are somewhat wasted efforts if attendance is light. Although individual notices may be sent to people on the mailing list, a more general outreach

A school shows its best at open house.

is required. Simple posters may be placed in local stores. The community newspaper may run a feature or place an ad. Local service clubs may make an announcement. One hint is to start early with publicity efforts—several weeks is not too long.

Community Activities

Involvement in community activities is another way to make a school known. Some schools are planned to serve as part-time community centers, with adjacent meeting rooms. Others may gradually evolve into centers because of the variety of services offered. Either way, the school becomes known in the community for its openness and friendliness.

There are many ways to bring the community into the school. Services for parents, older people, and older children are recommended. Lectures, films, and discussions centering on child-rearing will be attended by community folks as well as parents if they are given ample publicity. Rummage sales, art sales, and used book sales attract people of all ages. Saturday art classes and general recreational activities can be offered for older children.

Fund-raisers are a good way to publicize the school as well as to collect funds. The publicity and program should include facts about the school and stimulate further interest.

Staff members should be encouraged to join one of the community organizations open to them, such as the Chamber of Commerce, community child care task forces, women's organizations, and parent groups. Staff members should do this consciously as school representatives. In reality, it often falls to the director to carry the major load of community activity.

Director and staff should also participate in professional meetings, conferences, and workshops. This leads to the exchange of ideas within the early childhood group. Another idea is writing an article for a magazine for parents or a professional journal. Even though these methods do not reach the public directly, they can be a way of letting others know about the school. Other directors and teachers may have opportunities to refer parents to the school.

It may be possible to get free mention or presentation on radio or television if the school has innovative programs, or anything new and different. Media people are constantly searching for human interest stories, and few topics are as intriguing to the public as young children's activities. But the director must go to them and sensitize them to the many possibilities open. A news release to the local media is the first step. A telephone call is often necessary as a follow-up.

Technology and access to the Internet has opened a new avenue for publicizing a school. Schools can now create their own "home page," which is an on-line brochure to convey information about their program quickly and to a diverse audience. A home page may cost $100 to $200 to set up with a small monthly fee for a company to maintain and update the Web site.

The Web site should include pictures of the school. Those who access the site should be invited to send comments or questions and to sign a guest book, including their e-mail address. From these it is possible to generate a large list of contacts. They can be e-mailed newsletters, announcements of events, promotional offers, or short articles of advice for parents. If the list includes contacts such as donors, doctors, or community professionals, the Web site can serve to build community involvement.

SUMMARY

As the role of the parent has changed, so has the role of the school changed to compensate.

Parent involvement in the school yields benefits to the school and to the parent.

The ways in which parents may become part of the school are many and varied.

There are also limits on what the school may expect of the parent.

Techniques for encouraging participation are limited only by the ingenuity of the school; they may begin with initial contact.

Sustaining interest is as difficult as stimulating it. A major incentive and focus is the welfare of the child.

One of the major aims of parent education is better understanding of the child and of themselves.

Specific goals for parent education must be consonant with the total philosophy of the school.

A great many specific activities lead directly to a greater understanding of the child: orientation meeting, child observations, lectures or panels, films and tapes, workshops, and active classroom participation.

Conferences are an effective means for educating parents as well as solidifying their relationship to the school. Sometimes conferences have to be done by telephone or occur when there are casual contacts between parents and staff members. Home visits are another way of educating parents.

One of the best forms of public relations is a group of satisfied parents. However, other methods of advertising may be used effectively.

The physical appearance of the school should be as attractive as possible.

Telephone answering, especially with regard to first contact, must be as pleasant as can be managed.

Preparation for visiting groups should expose them to the best the school has to offer. The open house as a variant on this can be used effectively.

A tasteful brochure can serve as a fact-filled ambassador.

Involvement with community activities works two ways: Staff members should be involved locally and the community should feel at home in the school.

REFERENCES

Becher, R. M. (1986). Parent involvement: A review of research and principles of successful practice. In L. G. Katz (Ed.), *Current topics in early childhood education* (Vol. 6, pp. 85–122). Norwood, NJ: Ablex Publishing Group.

Dinkmeyer, D., & McKay, G. D. (1976). *Systematic training for effective parenting: Leader's manual*. Circle Pines, MN: American Guidance Service.

Gonzalez-Mena, J. (2001). *Multi-cultural issues in child care* (3rd ed.). Mountain View, CA: Mayfield Publishing.

Gordon, T. (1970). *Parent effectiveness training*. New York: Peter H. Wyden.

Hayes, C. D., Palmer, J. L., & Zaslow, M. J. (Eds.). (1990). *Child care choices*. Washington, DC: National Academy Press.

Head Start Program Fact Sheet. (2003). U.S. Department of Health and Human Services, Administration for Children and Families, Head Start Bureau. http://www.acf.hhs.gov/programs/research/2003.htm

Powell, D. R. (1989). *Families and early childhood programs*. Washington, DC: National Association for the Education of Young Children.

Schweinhart, L. J., & Weikart, D. (Eds.). (1993). *Significant benefits: High/Scope Perry preschool study through age 27*. Ypsilanti, MI: High/Scope Press.

 SELECTED FURTHER READING

Coleman, M. (1997). Families and schools: In search of common ground. *Young Children, 52*(5), 14–21.

Comer, J. P., & Hayes, N. M. (1991). Parent involvement in schools: An ecological approach. *The Elementary School Journal, 91,* 271–278.

Gorham, P. J., & Nason, P. N. (1997). Why make teachers' work more visible to parents? *Young Children, 52*(5), 22–26.

Mallory, N. J., & Goldsmith, N. A. (1991). *The Head Start experience*. (ERIC Document Reproduction Service No. ED327213).

Manning, D., & Schindler, P. J. (1997). Communicating with parents when their children have difficulties. *Young Children, 52*(5), 27–33.

Murphy, D. M. (1997). Parent and teacher plan for the child. *Young Children, 52*(4), 32–36.

Sturm, C. (1997). Creating parent-teacher dialogue: Intercultural communication in child care. *Young Children, 52*(5), 34–38.

Wardle, F. (2001). Supporting multiracial and multiethnic children and their families. *Young Children, 56*(6), 38–39.

Wasson, J. (2000, July/August). Power pack your center brochure. *Child Care Information Exchange, 134,* 16–17.

Workman, S. H., & Gage, J. A. (1997). Family-school partnerships: A family strengths approach. *Young Children, 52*(4), 10–14.

 STUDENT ACTIVITIES

1. Discuss the degree of parent involvement that you think is appropriate for your school. What factors are important in determining this?

2. Talk to some parents in a Head Start program in your community. How do they feel about involvement?

3. Plan a parent education activity for your school. Use an evaluation form to check its effectiveness.

4. Interview several directors of different kinds of schools. How do their goals for parent education differ?

5. Obtain brochures from at least three different schools in your community. Compare and evaluate.

6. Write a two-paragraph news release concerning a recent event at a pre-school.

 REVIEW

1. Describe the changing nature of school and home since the end of World War II.

2. What are some of the benefits to the child that parent involvement entails?

3. Are there unreasonable demands that the school may make on the average parents? What are they?

4. What are some of the ways that the school can encourage parent participation?

5. What is the major goal of parent education?

6. What is one of the most tangible forms of public relations?

7. Why is the physical appearance of the school important?

8. List some of the facts to include in a brochure.

CASE STUDY

Consuello, a teacher in the infant-toddler program, decided to invite the parents to participate in a volunteer program. First she obtained the support of her director and then arranged to have several parents read stories, sing songs, and help with feeding. Kylie's mother, Marie, has spent the last two weeks participating in the program. Marie spends most of the time with her own daughter and often talks to and distracts the other staff members in the group. Consuello overheard a conversation between Marie and one of the assistant teachers regarding another staff member. The content of the conversation was purely gossip, so Consuello made an appointment to discuss it with the director.

1. What would you expect the director to do with this information?

2. How would you handle this with Marie if you were either Consuello or the director?

3. How could Consuello motivate Marie to continue her volunteering, and yet be sensitive to center policies?

4. If you were the director, how would you deal with the other caregiver involved?

HELPFUL WEB SITES

Head Start Publications Management Center:	http:/ /www.hskids-tmsc.org
Interracial Voice networking news journal:	http:/ /www.Interracialvoice.com
National Parent Information Network:	http:/ /www.npin.org

For additional resources related to administration, visit the Online Resource® for this book at http://www.EarlyChildEd.delmar.com

15

Maintaining the Quality of Child Care

KEY TERMS

accreditation
Child Development Associate (CDA)
child abuse

OBJECTIVES

After reading this chapter, you should be able to:

- Describe the accreditation process.
- List several categories of child abuse.
- Explain how child abuse may be prevented.
- Cite a few laws pertaining to child care.

A Day in the Life of ...

A Director of a Learning Center

The culminating activity at Thanksgiving time was a "feast" with all of the preschoolers participating. The children ate the traditional foods of the holiday that the classes themselves had prepared (with some help, of course). This feast was held in the center courtyard of the school and the children came dressed as either Pilgrims or Native Americans. It was quite a sight to behold.

I was concerned that a child who had attended our school since age three might be jaded and tired of this feasting so we planned an alternate activity for the first graders. Two first graders were seen watching the banquet and one turned to the other and said wistfully, "Don't you wish you were young again?"

According to the National Association for the Education of Young Children (1995), "Child care at most centers in the United States is poor to mediocre, with 40% of infants and toddlers in rooms having less-than-minimal quality." A Special Research Report published by NAEYC (1995) summarized the findings of a study done at the University of Colorado entitled "Cost, Quality and Child Outcomes in Child Care Centers." That study found only 14 percent of centers offered developmentally appropriate care. As more and more of our nation's children spend their early years in child care it is crucial that the quality of programs be the very best they can possibly be.

 ## UPGRADING THE QUALITY OF PROGRAMS

One of the ways to upgrade the quality of programs is through **accreditation** offered by NAEYC. In addition, teachers must become better trained and their salaries must be commensurate with their professional status.

Accreditation of Schools

The NAEYC accreditation service is administered by the National Academy of Early Childhood Programs. Any group program serving children from birth through the elementary years can be accredited. Programs already accredited or in the process include half-day or full-day church-related programs, parent cooperatives, public school prekindergartens and kindergartens, Montessori programs, Head Start centers, laboratory schools, for-profit child care centers, and hospital-affiliated centers.

The system is voluntary and involves a three-step process: self-study by the director, teachers, and parents; validation visits by trained professionals; and an accreditation decision by a team of early childhood experts. Schools can pace the length of time involved in completing the process, but it usually takes from four to eighteen months.

The self-study step is the critical element of the accreditation process. After paying a fee and receiving the Accreditation Manual, the director, teachers, and parents rate the quality of the program in 10 different categories. Upon the completion of the self-study, a final report is prepared and the results are reported to the academy. Academy personnel review the materials to determine whether the information is complete or whether further material is needed.

The categories of center operations that are covered by the accreditation process are the following:

- interactions among staff and children
- curriculum
- staff-parent interactions
- staff qualifications and development
- administration
- staffing patterns

■ physical environment
■ health and safety
■ nutrition and food service
■ evaluation processes

When the director feels the center is ready, an on-site validation visit is requested. One or more validators appointed by the academy may visit a site depending on the size of the center. The purpose of the visit is to verify that the day-to-day operations of the center are as described in the self-study report. Validators meet with the director, observe in classrooms, and interview staff. At the end of the visit, validators and the director meet to discuss the results of the validation. At this time, the director can submit additional information concerning any nonvalidated criteria.

The final step involves an Accreditation Commission consisting of three people chosen from a diverse group of early childhood professionals. The commission reviews the information provided by validators and can decide to grant accreditation, or to defer it until further improvements are made. If deferment is decided, reasons are given for deferment and specific recommendations are made. Deferred centers can appeal, and if there is just cause, another commission will be assigned. Accreditation is valid for three years. During this time, centers must submit annual reports. Before expiration, centers must repeat the evaluation process.

Those who have already been involved in the accreditation process report that the expense and time involved are worth it. Directors point to the improvement in staff development, morale, and communication among staff members. Parents seem to feel a greater sense of trust in the school after having been involved in the accreditation process. In some situations, accreditation is being used as a selling point for funding requests. Even if a school already has a high-quality program, accreditation can help to achieve recognition in the community.

Information about accreditation can be obtained by writing to:

National Academy of Early Childhood Programs
    1509 16th Street, NW
    Washington, DC 20036–1426
    800-424-2460
    202-328-2601
    fax 202-328-1846
    e-mail NAEYC@naeyc.org
    Web site http://www.naeyc.org

In addition to the accreditation system developed by NAEYC, there are other rating scales that can be used to assess the environment of group programs. The *Early Childhood Environment Rating Scale* is a self-assessment tool for groups serving two- to five-year-olds that was developed by Thelma Harms and Richard M. Clifford at the Frank Porter Graham Child Development Center at the University of North Carolina at Chapel Hill. The scale assesses seven areas of a program's functioning: personal care routines of children, furnishings and display for children, language-reasoning experiences, fine and gross motor activities, creative activities, social development, and adult needs. The result is expressed in quantitative terms that can be used to summarize the process. Information about this tool can be obtained at the following address.

Early Childhood Environment Rating Scale by Thelma Harms and Richard
   M. Clifford
   Teachers College Press
   1234 Amsterdam Avenue
   New York, NY 10027
   212-678-3929
   http://www.teacherscollegepress.com

Harms and Clifford have also developed a rating scale targeted primarily for programs serving infants to three-year-olds. Information about this tool can be obtained from:

Infant/Toddler Environment Rating Scale by Thelma Harms, Debby Cryer, and
   Richard M. Clifford
   Frank Porter Graham Child Development Center
   The University of North Carolina at Chapel Hill
   Campus Box 8180
   105 Smith Level Road
   Chapel Hill, NC 27599–8180
   919-966-2622
   http://www.fpg.unc.edu

Accreditation of Teachers and Caregivers

Upgrading the quality of programs can also come about through the credentialing of teachers and caregivers. The **Child Development Associate (CDA)** credential is a nationally recognized credential for early childhood personnel. It is based on the achievement of a series of competencies and is available to those who work in centers or in family day care homes.

The model curriculum designed by the Council for Early Childhood Professional Recognition contains a set of goals and a series of graduated experiences that lead to the achievement of those goals. The goals are

1. to establish and maintain a safe, healthy learning environment.
2. to advance physical and intellectual competence.
3. to support social and emotional development and provide guidance.
4. to establish positive and productive relationships with families.
5. to ensure a well-run, purposeful program responsive to participant needs.
6. to maintain a commitment to professionalism.

The graduated experiences are achieved through three phases of work. Phase I is fieldwork in which the students participate in the daily activities of a program. They follow written materials prepared by the council that include readings and exercises that help the candidate build skills. An early childhood professional guides and advises the student through hands-on experiences with children.

During Phase II of the program students attend courses or seminars offered through local college, university, or other postsecondary educational institutions. The instructional curriculum covers the basic components of early childhood education, but the institutions may supplement the curriculum with their own resources. Students are encouraged to relate their in-class information to their field experiences.

The final Phase III is directed toward integration and evaluation of the student's experiences. During this period the student returns to working with children and at the same time completes a series of exercises. Council-written materials contain a performance-based assessment of the student's achievement. The last step in the process is a series of interviews with a council representative in which all documents submitted by the candidate are reviewed. If the representative's assessment is favorable, the candidate receives a CDA credential, which is valid for life.

For more information about the CDA credential, contact:

Council for Early Childhood Professional Recognition
2460 16th Street, NW
Washington, DC 2009-3575
202-265-9090
800-424-4310
fax 202-265-9161
http://www.edacouncil.org

Increased Pay for Child Care Professionals

One of the ways to increase the quality of child care programs is to have educated teachers who understand child development and know how to work with children in groups. Unfortunately, the pay level of the average caregiver is very low. One study done by the Economics Department of the University of Colorado at Denver listed the average teacher hourly wage as $7.22, assistant teacher at $5.70, and average administrator at $11.33. Educated teachers move on to higher-paying positions. The result is a high turnover rate of 40 percent according to a national study (Whitebrook, Phillips, & Howes, 1993). No director can run a high-quality program when there is a constant need to find and retrain staff.

The National Center for the Early Childhood Work Force launched a Worthy Wage Campaign in 1994 to improve the economic status of teachers. Their plan was to rally governmental representatives and to showcase the issue using media resources and personalities. Others have also raised public awareness of the need for improved working conditions for child care staff. NAEYC has long been an advocate of well-trained and well-paid teachers. An editorial in *Young Children* (NAEYC, 1997) listed six things directors can do to improve staff compensation and quality.

1. "Use your annual operating budget as a working tool. Most decisions have budgetary implications." Directors should learn to read line items in the budget and track expenses for each category. There are usually alternative spending choices that could increase the amount of money available for salaries.

2. "Recognize that budget is policy: be actively involved in the development of the annual budget." The director should question items in the budget

and give a rationale for any proposed changes, especially including any that would increase quality.

3. "Get support from a financial analyst or business administrator when necessary." Using a cost analysis, there may be ways to eliminate items that are not proving cost effective.

4. "Polish your leadership and negotiating skills to effectively guide the budget development process." In order to guide others into making changes, the director needs to have skills as a leader.

5. "Don't forget strong human resources skills in working with staff." Leaders who are effective provide support to staff, but they also support autonomy and demand a high level of professionalism.

6. "Make sure your program offers a career lattice." When staff members have equal opportunities to move up a career lattice, there will be less turnover. Each person will know that with increased education and competency, there is a possibility of moving to a higher salary bracket.

 ## CHILD ABUSE

Press coverage frequently highlights sensational cases of child abuse, both in child care centers and within families, but many more incidents go undetected or unreported. Those that occur in centers are sometimes the result of poor quality control. Prevention should be a primary concern of every director and can be achieved by choosing the very best staff members, planning training sessions, and adequately supervising all employees. It is the responsibility of the director to see that everything possible is done to prevent abuse in the child care setting and to inform staff of the laws pertaining to reporting.

All states have laws relating to **child abuse.** These are designed to protect both children and adults who care for children. The laws for each state can be found by contacting the attorney general's office.

Several categories of abuse are recognized.

■ *Physical abuse*—a child is physically injured by other than accidental means. Severe corporal punishment may be classified as abuse.

■ *Physical neglect*—failure to provide a child with adequate food, shelter, clothing, protection, supervision, and medical or dental care.

■ *Emotional abuse*—excessive verbal assaults, continuous negative responses, and constant family discord may add up to emotional abuse. These cases are extremely difficult to prove and to prosecute.

■ *Emotional deprivation*—deprivation suffered by children when their parents fail to supply normal experiences that help children to feel loved, wanted, and secure.

■ *Sexual abuse and exploitation*—any sexual activity between an adult and child. When the activity occurs between blood-related persons, it is called incest. Included in sexual abuse is the use of children for making pornographic pictures or films.

Causes of Child Abuse

Although it is often believed that most child abusers are poor, uneducated, or emotionally disturbed, this is not true. Studies show that only one in ten abusers can be classified as "disturbed." Most abusers are not very different from any other parents. They love their children and want what is best for them, but something happens to trigger abuse.

According to several studies, adults are more likely to abuse children when the following factors exist:

- They were abused as children themselves.
- They are young—abuse is more frequent when the parents are under age 20.
- They are isolated from others, with few friends or nearby relatives.
- They are victims or perpetrators of spouse abuse.
- They use drugs or are alcoholics.
- They have experienced stress caused by family problems, divorce, loss of a job, or unwanted pregnancy.
- They live in crowded conditions, with little privacy.
- They have low self-esteem.
- They have difficulty controlling anger.
- They have unrealistic expectations for children's behavior.

Recognition of Abuse

Both parents and early childhood professionals must learn to recognize the signs of abuse. Because the idea of any kind of mistreatment of children is so repugnant, there is a tendency to overlook the indications. Yet, children say and do things that should warn us. Often, though, it is only after abuse is finally recognized that we can look back and say, "Yes, I did see some things that made me wonder." All staff members should be familiar with signs that may indicate a child has been physically, emotionally, or sexually abused. Parent education programs should provide the same kinds of information to parents.

The state attorney general's office or licensing agency can probably supply information about what might be suspicious. If not, the following summary should be helpful.

Physical Abuse

Physical abuse might be suspected when the following injuries are seen on a child:

- *Burns*—burns in places that would not be expected as the result of accident (e.g., buttocks, shoulder blades, abdomen).
- *Linear marks*—wraparound marks made by a strap, belt, or electrical cord.
- *Bruises*—multiple bruises with different colors indicating various stages of healing, bruises on many parts of the body including the genitals.

Over 900,000 children were confirmed as victims of child abuse and neglect in 1998. The highest number were in African-American and Native-American families. Almost 40 percent of victims are under the age of six; infants represent the largest proportion. Domestic violence is also found in 60 percent of families where child abuse occurs.

Source: Children's Defense Fund. (2000). http://www.childrensdefense.org (2002).

- *Lacerations*—multiple wounds or locations of wounds in unexpected places. Mouth lacerations, for instance, may indicate a bottle nipple has been jammed into the baby's mouth.
- *Fractures*—any fracture in an infant under 12 months should be suspect.

One of the most important grounds for further investigation is when a child says "My daddy hurt me" or "My mommy spanks me with a belt." The caregiver should take what the child says seriously.

Physical Neglect

Physical neglect is the failure of a parent or caregiver to provide adequate care and can be suspected when

- there are unsanitary conditions in the home or child care site.
- there is inadequate heat or there are potentially unsafe conditions.
- food is inadequate or not sufficiently nutritious.
- the child lacks proper clothing for the weather, or clothing is unclean.
- the child lacks proper medical or dental care.
- a young child is left at home or unsupervised for any period of time.

Emotional Abuse

Although some of the signs of emotional abuse are the kinds of behavior occasionally seen in all children, the extent, the frequency, or the duration of the behavior should alert an observer. Abuse might be suspected if any of the following behaviors continue for a long period of time or are the only ways that a child behaves.

- The child is withdrawn, depressed, or apathetic.
- The child "acts out" or is often disruptive.
- The child is overly rigid, is afraid to misbehave, or fails to do what is expected.
- The child shows signs of emotional disturbance such as repetitive movements, or lack of verbal or physical communication with others.

Children sometimes reveal emotional abuse when they comment on their own behavior. They may say "My mommy tells me I'm bad" or "My daddy says I can't do anything right." It is important to listen and take the child seriously.

Emotional Deprivation

Emotional deprivation is the most difficult to judge, but should be suspected if the following behaviors are observed.

- The child refuses to eat, or eats very little.
- The child is not able to do things that would be expected of the age level—walking, talking.
- The child may have exaggerated fears.
- The child is frequently aggressive or shows other antisocial behaviors.
- The child is abnormally withdrawn or sad, or does not respond to others.
- The child constantly seeks attention from any adult, even strangers who come into the school.

Sexual Abuse

Children go through periods of being curious about their own bodies and those of others. They have times when they masturbate or ask about how you get babies. Teachers and parents are often embarrassed by this behavior. They don't want to see or hear it. As a result, signs of sexual molestation sometimes go completely unrecognized. Children, too, learn to be secretive about what happens to them when they see how others react. In addition, abusers often frighten children by telling them that terrible things will happen to them if they tell anyone.

Sexual abuse can remain hidden for a long time. It should be suspected, though, if the following signs are evident:

- The child has bruising or inflammation of the anus or the genitals.
- There is a discharge or blood in the child's underwear.
- The child has unusual interest and awareness of sexual activities. Sometimes young children play out sexual scenes in the dramatic play area.
- The child is particularly seductive with adults, touching their breast or genitals.
- The child seems fearful of an adult or is afraid to talk about that adult.
- The child is the victim of other kinds of abuse.

Children probably least often reveal sexual abuse by talking about it. They may not even have the words to express to others what has been done to them. If they have been threatened by the abuser, they will be even more reluctant to tell their secrets. Responsive adults who are willing to let children reveal their stories in their own way can find out a great deal.

When to Report Abuse

Teachers and others who have close contact with children are in a unique position to see signs of abuse. Because of this, they are legally mandated to report suspected incidents. They are not required to prove abuse and, if none is found, are protected from any retribution. On the other hand, if mandated individuals know of abuse and fail to report it, they may be liable for fines or imprisonment.

The law is clear, but the moral dilemma facing a teacher who suspects abuse is not always clear. Suspicion of abuse can be extremely upsetting for parents or for school personnel. The normal reaction is to become angry, to feel guilt, or to want the perpetrator to be punished immediately. Everyone involved must remain calm. When adults overreact, harm to the child may be intensified. The opposite reaction may also occur. Adults can convince themselves that they must have been wrong, that nothing really happened. Nothing is done, and that may lead to further harm to the child.

So how do teachers and caregivers know when to report? They should not report every time they see some signs of disturbance in children. Many times that is normal, transitory behavior. They *should report* when they have enough evidence to convince themselves that there is reasonable suspicion to warrant further investigation. Obviously, if there are signs that a child's life may be in danger, it must be reported immediately.

When there are any of the signs listed in previous paragraphs, the teacher or caregiver should make a record. They should write down what they observed, what the child said, or what the parent said. If they see bruises, burns, or lacerations on a child, they should take a picture of them. Photographs can be taken without the parents' consent as long as they are not used for any other purpose.

If there are injuries that do not quite meet the usual criteria for abuse, it is important to keep a record anyway. Over time, it may become apparent that the same kinds of injuries keep recurring. A pattern of abuse may emerge that can be reported.

In cases of uncertainty, it helps to talk to other professionals. Teachers should talk to their director; directors can corroborate the teachers' observations. Child abuse agencies or hotlines in the area might also be helpful. They can often help to sort out impressions. The child protective agency in an area can help as well. Workers there can often clarify whether there is a reportable offense.

When ready to report, the director or teacher should telephone the local child protective services, the sheriff's department, or the police department. The following information will probably be needed.

- child's name, address, and age
- where the child is at the present time
- observations and descriptions of injuries
- information that led the director or teacher to believe abuse has occurred
- parents' names, address

If the child is in immediate danger, it is important to make that clear to the person who is taking the report. It may be necessary to follow the verbal report with a written report within a specified period of time. Forms for the report will be available from law enforcement or protective services agencies.

Many teachers and directors ask whether they should tell the parents about the report. Opinions vary and some states require them to do so. If someone other than the parents is the abuser, the parents may be relieved that the abuse has been discovered. They will welcome the support and concern for their child. If one of the parents is the abuser, the person reporting the abuse is likely to be the target of tremendous anger. There may also be denial at first and even accusations that the abuse occurred at school, not at home. The parents may immediately withdraw the child from the school. It is realistic to be prepared for any of these reactions.

The discovery of abuse is a traumatic experience for parents, teachers, and child. The director will have to remain calm and sympathetic. It may lessen the trauma for everyone involved. The child will need to know that others understand and that they will be supportive. Whether the parents are the abusers or not, they, too, need to have support through this experience. Also, the director can see that the family gets support from others in the medical, legal, and child advocacy systems.

Staff members will probably need help in dealing with the abuse. They must be cautioned to respect the privacy of the child and family. Information about the abuse should never be discussed with anyone not directly involved in the incident. They should try not to be judgmental toward the parents.

Staff may also need an opportunity to talk about their own feelings of anger or guilt. If the child remains in the school, staff may react by being overprotective. They should be cautioned that the child will recover more quickly if helped to follow regular routines. Sensitive handling of an abuse situation will help everyone involved to recover.

Unfortunately, because of the upheaval discovery causes, a large number of child abuse cases never get reported. The director should encourage staff to see that it is their moral, as well as legal, obligation to protect children. When cases are not reported, there is the possibility that other children will be victimized.

Abuse Allegations at School

Some directors are faced with having one of their staff members accused of abuse. Reports may come from parents or from other staff members. If the report first goes to the licensing agency, it will be referred to the police department. If the police department receives the first complaint, they will report to the licensing agency.

The two agencies will work together to complete an investigation of the report. The staff member should receive appropriate legal representation before being interviewed by the police. Although no one is required to answer questions, it is best to cooperate. In this way, a quicker resolution to the problem can occur.

Prevention

Schools can play a vital role in the prevention of abuse.

First, directors can do a great deal to lessen the possibility of abuse by staff members by

- developing hiring procedures that carefully screen applicants—most states require a fingerprint check.
- checking the person's references carefully.
- planning and implementing in-service training for new employees, and ongoing staff development for others.
- adequately supervising staff and pairing new employees with experienced ones.
- holding regular staff meetings to discuss problems with children and parents, or among staff members.
- developing clear personnel policies regarding methods of disciplining children.
- allowing staff members the means for alleviating fatigue and burnout (e.g., adequate breaks, reasonable staff/child ratios, adequate salaries, positive reinforcement).

Second, a school and its staff can be extremely effective in helping parents manage the stresses of parenthood that might lead to abuse. Teachers and caregivers can

- become part of an "extended family" that provides support.
- educate parents about what to expect of children at different age levels.
- act as models to help parents find more effective ways of interacting with their children.
- provide an outlet for parents to express some of the frustrations involved in parenting.
- share with parents the joys of watching children grow and change.

Third, a great deal can be done to lessen the chances of misunderstandings that lead to accusations of abuse at school. The director should

- educate parents about child abuse—what causes it, signs that may indicate abuse.
- establish an open-door policy and welcome parents' visits at any time, without an appointment.
- share the schools' discipline policies with parents.
- establish a caring relationship with parents by listening to their concerns and answering their questions.

Fourth, teachers and caregivers can educate children about what is and what is not acceptable behavior between an adult and a child. From as early as eighteen months children can learn about body parts. Older children, age three to five, can learn which body parts are unacceptable for others to touch. In addition, children should be encouraged to say "no" to an adult when they feel uncomfortable about any bodily contact. Lastly, they should be encouraged to tell an adult when they have had an encounter with an adult that made them uneasy.

Prevention of child abuse is certainly a preferred tactic to reporting and punishing abuse. As more and more children are in group settings at earlier ages, the role of the school becomes vital to prevention. Directors, staff, and parents must be educated. Although there is no sure cure for child abuse, the knowledge and skills of those who care for children can help.

 ## LAWS PERTAINING TO CHILD CARE SETTINGS

Most child care centers must meet federal, state, and local laws pertaining to employer-employee relations. Some small schools may be exempt, but it is a good idea to comply wherever possible. In that way, it is easier to expand the school in the future. If the school contracts with federal, state, or local government agencies, it may have to comply with some special requirements.

Directors must be as educated as possible about laws with which they must comply. They can write to appropriate agencies for information and consult an attorney to find out about state and local laws. The scope of this book cannot thoroughly address every geographical area. The following information is a broad outline of the issues.

Personnel Policies

Good personnel policies, as discussed in Chapter 7, are necessary to ensure the smooth operation of a school. In addition, personnel procedures may be covered by federal laws such as the following:

- The Equal Pay Act of 1963 requires equal pay for men and women performing similar work.
- The Fair Labor Standards Act of 1938 (1972 Amendment) sets a minimum wage, equal pay, and recordkeeping requirements.
- The Civil Rights Act of 1964—Title VII (amended in 1972) prohibits discrimination because of sex, race, color, religion, or national origin.
- The Rehabilitation Act of 1973 prohibits job discrimination because of a disability. It further requires affirmative action to hire and advance workers with disabilities.
- The Vietnam Era Veteran's Readjustment Assistance Act of 1974 prohibits job discrimination and requires affirmative action to hire and advance qualified Vietnam veterans.
- Executive Orders 11246 and 11375 require an affirmative action program for all federal contractors and subcontractors whose contract exceeds $10,000.
- The Age Discrimination Act of 1967 (amended in 1978) prohibits discrimination against persons 40 to 70 years of age in hiring practices for any employment.
- The Family Medical Leave Act of 1993 entitles employees up to 12 weeks of unpaid leave during a 12-month period. It can be used for the birth or adoption of a child, to care for a family member, or when the employee cannot work because of a medical problem. The employer must maintain existing medical coverage and reinstate the employee when ready to return to work.

Salary Procedures

Some laws require or prohibit certain procedures related to employee salaries.

■ The Federal Wage Garnishment Law restricts the amount of an employee's wages that may be deducted in any one week for garnishment procedures. It further restricts the amount that can be deducted when an employee is discharged because of garnishment.

■ The Social Security Act of 1935 and Federal Insurance Contributions Act provide for retirement, disability, burial, and survivor benefits to eligible employees. They require deductions from salary plus matching contribution from the employer.

■ The Federal Income Tax Withholding requires the employer to collect employees' income tax and deposit it in a federal depository. Failure to comply with this law is a criminal offense.

On-the-Job Safety

Federal law regulates any conditions that might affect the safety and health of employees.

■ The Occupational Safety and Health Act of 1970 requires employers to maintain a safe and healthful work environment, comply with all occupational safety and health standards, keep Material Safety Data Sheets in a conspicuous place, and provide employees with training in safe work practices.

For further information, visit http://www.osha.gov.

■ Most states require employers to carry workers' compensation insurance to ensure injured workers will receive necessary medical care and be compensated for loss of income.

Sources of Information

More information regarding laws that may affect a school can be obtained by writing to the following:

U.S. Equal Employment Opportunity Commission
1801 L Street, NW
Washington, DC 20507

Employment Standards Administration
Office of Federal Contract Compliance Program
200 Constitution Avenue, NW
Washington, DC 20210

United States Government—Social Security Administration
10 North Jefferson Street
Frederick, MD 21701
301-462-6765

U.S. Department of Labor
  Occupational Safety and Health Administration
  Frances Perkins Building
  200 Constitution Avenue, NW
  Washington, DC 20210
  866-4-USA-DOL

California Chamber of Commerce
  Commanon Corporation
  P.O. Box 815
  Danville, CA 94526-0815
  916-444-6670

Posting Employee Information

Certain information must be posted in conspicuous places used by employees. Both federal and state laws govern the kinds of information needed. An attorney can provide advice for compliance within a particular state. Federal laws require the following:

■ Minimum wage and maximum hours—obtain from U.S. Department of Labor, Wage and Hours Division.

■ Equal employment regulations—obtain from nearest branch of Federal Equal Employment Opportunity Commission.

■ Age discrimination laws—obtain from nearest branch of Federal Equal Employment Opportunity Commission.

■ Annual summary of specified injuries and illnesses—obtain information from U.S. Department of Labor, Occupational Safety and Health Administration.

■ Fire prevention and evacuation plan.

■ Safety and health protection on the job.

U.S. Census figures show that within a few years there will be 23 million children under the age of six. As more and more mothers enter the workforce, there must be places to care for these children, yet quality child care is already in short supply. As the nation tries to fill the gap, careful thought must be invested in the issues of regulation. Children must be adequately protected, and quality care must never be sacrificed for other considerations. On the other hand, potential operators must not feel overly constrained with laws and regulations. It requires a delicate balance.

SUMMARY

One way to upgrade the quality of programs is through accreditation, a process initiated by the National Academy of Early Childhood Programs. The voluntary process consists of self-study, a visit by a professional team, and a written evaluation.

Quality is also enhanced when teachers and caregivers have a knowledge of how to further children's development. The Council for Early Childhood Professional Recognition offers a Child Development Associate credential to students who finish a three-phase program. Graduated experiences take students through fieldwork, seminars, and written materials to assess achievement. A council representative also interviews students and reviews all documents submitted by the candidate.

Increased pay for child care professionals will also upgrade the quality of programs. When pay is low, educated teachers move on to higher-paying jobs, causing a huge turnover. The National Center for the Early Childhood Work Force and NAEYC have long been advocates for improved working conditions for child care staff.

Prominent press coverage has highlighted child abuse recently. Abuse can be of several kinds: physical abuse and neglect, emotional abuse and deprivation, or sexual exploitation. There are many causes.

Certain physical or emotional results occur after abuse. Teacher and caregivers should be able to recognize each kind. It is often difficult to determine whether to report child abuse. It is always acceptable and reasonable to keep a record.

Since much emotion is encountered in child abuse situations, the most consistent attitude to take is one of calm objectivity.

There are proven ways to prevent child abuse in a preschool. It is the responsibility of the director to inform the staff.

Many federal, state, and local laws pertain to child care. There are numerous sources, and most of them are listed here. It is, again, the responsibility of the director to inform the staff and parents of these laws.

 ## REFERENCES

Bergman, R. (2000, March/April). Building collaborations between programs and within the community. *Child Care Information Exchange, 132,* 55–57.

National Association for the Education of Young Children, Special Research Report. (1995). Cost, quality, and child outcomes in child care centers: Key findings and recommendations. *Young Children, 50*(4), 41–45.

National Association for the Education of Young Children. (1997). *Quality, compensation, and affordability. Six things directors can do to improve staff compensation and quality.* Washington, DC: Author.

National Center for the Early Childhood Work Force. (1993). *Worthy wage campaign 1994 action packet.* Oakland, CA: Author.

Whitebrook, M. C., Phillips, D., & Howes, C. (1993). *The national child care staffing study revisited.* Oakland, CA: Child Care Employee Project.

 ## SELECTED FURTHER READING

Bredekamp, S. (Ed.). (1998). *Accreditation criteria & procedures of the National Academy of Early Childhood Programs.* Washington, DC: National Association for the Education of Young Children.

Morgan, G. (1983). Child day care policy in chaos. In E. Zigler, S. Kagan, & E. Klugman, (Eds.), *Children, families, and government: Perspectives on American social policy* (pp. 249–265). New York: Cambridge University Press.

Phillips, C. B. (1990). The child development associate program: Entering a new era. *Young Children, 45* (3), 24–27.

Pizzo, R. D. (1993). Parent empowerment and child care regulation. *Young Children, 48* (6), 9–12.

Whitebook, M., Howes, C., & Phillips, D. (Eds.). (1989). *Working for quality child care.* Berkeley, CA: Child Care Employee Project.

STUDENT ACTIVITIES

1. Schedule a visit to an accredited center in your community and an interview with the director. Ask the director to describe the accreditation experience and its effect on staff and parents. Was it a positive experience? What changes were undertaken as a result?

2. Write a short paper on child abuse. Focus on whether media coverage of high-visibility cases has changed attitudes of early childhood personnel. Are they more cautious about how they interact with children? Are they more aware of the signs of abuse in children in their care?

3. Visit an agency in your community that works with families where abuse has occurred. What is the agency doing to help families?

REVIEW

1. Accreditation involves a three-step process. What are the steps?

2. What is the Child Development Associate credential?

3. List the three phases of the CDA program and briefly describe each.

4. According to an editorial in *Young Children,* what are the six things directors can do to improve staff compensation and quality?

5. What are six measures a director can take to prevent child abuse by staff members?

6. What are the causes of child abuse?

7. List the five kinds of child abuse.

8. Describe the procedures for reporting child abuse.

9. Discuss the role of a school in preventing abuse.

10. Name and describe three federal laws that pertain to employees in child care centers.

CASE STUDY

Julia was in her first year as director of a child care center. She was feeling overwhelmed by staffing issues, parent concerns, and curriculum implementation. Reva, a teacher in the four-year-old program, came to her to express a concern about a child. She suspected Dylan was being neglected by his parents. Dylan was rarely bathed and often came to the center in soiled clothes. Additionally, he had bruises on the inner side of his arms and on his upper thighs. Julia asked Reva to document the information and "keep an eye out" for further incidents. Reva left the director's office unsatisfied. As a mandated reporter, she thought that she should report this information to Child Protective Services (CPS). She kept notes as she was asked and continued to keep a watchful eye on Dylan.

Two weeks later, Dylan arrived at the center with a large bruise on his face. Reva asked him what had happened. His response was, "My dad got mad at me and pushed me. I fell down on the stairs, but he said sorry, then I went to bed."

Reva related this to Julia and they telephoned CPS to report the incident. The agency contacted Dylan's family. They vehemently denied any wrongdoing and were angered about the report. The family withdrew from the center immediately and did not even honor the two-week notice required in their contract.

1. How would you handle this situation if you were the director? The teacher?

2. When do you think that this family should have been reported?

3. Could this have been handled differently? How?

HELPFUL WEB SITES

Family and Medical Leave Act
Employee/Employer Advisor Wage
and Hour Division: http://www.dol.gov/elaws/fm/htm

Job Accommodation Network,
a service of United States Office
of Disability Employment Policy: http://www.jan.wvu.edu

National Academy of Early
Childhood Programs: http://www.naeyc.org

National Clearinghouse on Child
Abuse and Neglect Information: http://www.calib.com/nccanch

U.S. Department of Health and
Human Services: http://www.dhhs.gov

U.S. Equal Employment Opportunity
Commission (information regarding
interplay of ADA and FMLA):   http://www.eeoc.gov/docs/fmaada.txt

For additional resources related to administration, visit the Online Resource® for
this book at www.EarlyChildEd.delmar.com

Douglas Schoenberg, Vice President, SofterWare

Computerized Center Administration

Today the vast majority of child care centers are using computers to enhance their administration. Computers have continued to become more affordable and more powerful, and the software available has continued to improve in terms of ease-of-use and functionality. When considering computerization, the first place to start is with the software to be used.

Although there are many wonderful general purpose programs like Microsoft Word, Calendar Creator, Excel, etc., which can be useful in managing a center, they are usually not a complete solution to a center's needs. For most centers it is wise to invest in products that are specifically designed for the child care industry. The end of this section includes a list of products that you may wish to consider. In order to help you evaluate possible solutions, this section will review the possible applications for computers in center operations and suggest important criteria when evaluating software and vendors.

POTENTIAL AREAS OF COMPUTERIZATION

Data Management

This is a general term for storing and reporting on the myriad pieces of information a center must maintain. The principal advantage of storing this data on the computer is the ease with which the information can be accessed, sorted, selected, and reported. In most centers the major applications are as follows:

Enrollment

Information on enrolled children includes family information, child information, medical information, emergency and authorized pickup information, demographic information, etc. Since the information that must be maintained will vary depending on the type of center, licensing regulations, and forms used, you should evaluate a product's *flexibility* in this area carefully. Having to skip nonrelevant fields or not having needed fields is one of the most common complaints among software users.

427

Prospect/Waiting List

It is a good idea to enter information on every family that inquires about your center. This allows you to analyze the effectiveness of your marketing, easily send follow-up letters and newsletters, and maximize enrollment at your center. Since typically the information you want to maintain on a prospect is much less than (and often different from) the information for an enrollee, it is usually best if prospect information is entered into a separate database (file). Well-designed software should still allow you to easily transfer a record from a prospect or waiting list database into your enrollment database without needing to re-enter information.

Staff

As with enrolled children, there is a great deal of data on staff such as employment dates, training and certifications received, medical information, etc., that can be maintained in the computer for easier access and analysis. Here too, flexibility is a critical feature.

Other Types of Data Tracking (Incidents, Inventory, etc.)

Although more secondary, there are other types of data that can benefit from being computerized. Consider how convenient it would be to have all incident records entered in your computer. This would allow you to easily review all incidents involving a particular child, class, time frame, type of incident, etc. What licensing department (or parent) would not be impressed with this level of professionalism?

As you think about your center, review all the paper forms that are produced; each is a candidate for automation. Since not all centers have the same requirements, software that allows you to create additional databases can be a great advantage in accommodating these needs.

Report Writer

All center management software will come with a wide variety of standard reports that can be generated from the databases above; however, very few provide any real ability for the user to create their own "custom" reports. An easy-to-use report writer can be a very powerful enhancement to any system since it will allow you to tap the full benefits of all the data that will be stored on your computer.

Here are a few suggestions. Since some products offer third-party report writers which may be more oriented to programmers, it is a good idea to ask to see a demonstration of just how easily *you* can create a new report. Although it is also useful to be able to modify the selection or sorting criteria of an existing report, don't confuse this with the ability to create a new report. Lastly, be wary of companies who suggest that they will "create" any custom reports you need for a small fee. Not only will this involve extra expense, but it does not address the likelihood that you will want to generate many useful reports that are quick, one-time queries intended to answer day-to-day business questions.

Scheduling Management

Unless all children and staff come for the same hours every day, a center can benefit from computerized schedule management. Typically this involves entering a schedule for children and staff and allowing you to analyze and report on these schedules. Most programs allow you to maintain some form of recurring schedule that repeats each week (or sometimes several weeks). In addition, the more sophisticated products allow you to apply these recurring schedules to a calendar which factors in holidays, vacations, temporary schedule changes, etc.

The main benefit of this function is in the ability to better match staffing levels to anticipated child attendance, thereby more effectively managing the greatest expense in every center: payroll. In addition, for those centers whose fees are based on the child's schedule, the information should also be usable for calculating fees automatically.

Attendance Management

This area can encompass everything from simple attendance sheets that provide an opportunity for parents (or staff) to mark attendance to sophisticated computerized time clocks that allow parents and staff to clock in and out on the computer. This technology might use bar codes, pin numbers, or even touch screens to allow sign-in. Each technology has its advantages, and software that supports a variety of input mechanisms is usually best. Although not cost effective today, soon parents will be identified by fingerprint, voice, or other biometrics.

Effective attendance management utilizing a computer and software can

- increase revenue by ensuring that fees for extra hours, late pickup, etc., are applied consistently.
- provide accurate information for payroll calculations.
- enhance the center's ability to evaluate staffing efficiency.
- support parent communication by displaying messages as part of the check-in process.
- improve center professionalism.

Access Control

By interfacing the time-clock function to an electronic door strike, some products provide a low-cost mechanism to control access to the facility. In order for this technology to be effective, the physical layout of the center must accommodate this type of setup. Usually this works best when the center has an inner and outer door, where the equipment can be located in a vestibule protected from the weather.

Revenue Management

Perhaps the single most important area for automation is the managing of fees and center revenues. Although most off-the-shelf accounting systems provide Accounts Receivable, they are usually very poorly suited to the unique requirements of centers. Centers have many unusual needs such as providing parents with a year-end record of payments, managing parental and subsidizer fees, and automatic posting of recurring charges. Virtually any product design for child care centers will handle these needs; however, they will vary widely in their ability to accommodate various rate structures and the ease with which they allow you to work with ledgers and perform postings. Good products will provide adequate checks and audit trails to ensure that postings are made correctly.

One major innovation in center fee collection is the ability to allow parent fees to be collected automatically by EFT (electronic funds transfer) or automatic credit card billing. This technology offers the potential of more reliable cash flow, less administrative time and cost, enhanced convenience for parents, better security and control of funds, and minimizing the need for directors to act as a collection agent. This technology is widely used by health clubs, Christian schools, and utilities, and is now available to child care centers as a product called EZ-EFT (see listings).

Food Program

The child care food program requires a substantial reporting burden for those centers that participate. Typically this falls into two areas:

Meal Count Management—This allows centers to track children's eligibility for the program and calculate the number of meals served by eligibility class. This information can either come from the child schedules (and then be adjusted) or from the time-clock data.

Menu Planning/Food Production—This allows centers to establish menus and calculate required food purchases based on serving size and unit size data. Although this requires a great deal of initial setup, those centers that are required to document menus and food production reports will find this very useful.

Expense/Financial Management

Managing the center's checkbook and producing financial statements are handled by the Accounts Payable and General Ledger components of accounting software. These functions allow the center to save time in paying bills and analyzing the center's financial results. Although almost anyone can typically use an Accounts Payable system, it is usually best to have a trained bookkeeper or accountant responsible for the General Ledger. If you are unfamiliar with a G/L chart of accounts and the difference between a debit and a credit, you may wish to leave this responsibility to your accounting firm.

Payroll

Calculating wages, taxes, deductions, etc., is a time-consuming process for any business. Many organizations use outside payroll services to handle this process, but payroll software can make this process relatively quick and easy. Centers that use a computerized time clock should be able to transfer staff hours into this component, eliminating almost all additional data entry.

Parent Communications

Perhaps the most basic computer application of all is word processing. In addition to writing letters, today's word processors offer sophisticated font, clip-art, and layout control that allows you to produce attractive newsletters for communicating with parents and prospective families.

Center management software should allow you to use your existing word processor (such as Microsoft Word) to produce merge letters that insert information from your other databases. Products that have their own word processor will typically be limited in features and require you to learn an additional product.

The Internet

No discussion of computers today would be complete without touching on the Internet. Although most centers are only starting to have access to the Internet, there is no question that the majority of centers will have Internet access in the next few years. The major opportunities for a center to use the Internet today are:

Marketing

More and more parents will use the Internet as a way to find child-care providers. A center can either set up its own "home page," which is principally an on-line brochure about your center, or sign up with an independent child care locator service. A home-page will typically cost $100–200 to set up and a small monthly fee for a company to "host" on their computer. There are also several child care site locator services that allow parents to search for centers that have certain characteristics such as location, size, ages served, price range, etc. See the appendix for resources.

Parent Viewing

Several companies have developed products that allow parents to subscribe to a service that allows them to view the activities in their child's classroom via the Internet. Although this may address certain fears that parents have over leaving their children in the hands of others, the principal benefit is to increase parent involvement and provide a convenient (and nondisruptive) mechanism for a parent to observe classroom activity and the opportunity for parents to experience some of the benefits of "on-site" child care.

Electronic Mail

As the number of parents who have access to e-mail increases, centers will find this an inexpensive and convenient way to communicate with parents. Even though parents are in the center every day, their busy schedules do not always allow them to read every notice, and e-mail is fast becoming many people's preferred form of communication.

Source of Information

The Internet is full of resources that can be useful in operating your center. By using a search engine such as Infoseek or Yahoo, you can locate potential vendors, information on operating small businesses, data on health and parenting topics, and more. Additionally, there are a number of child care center discussion groups that allow you to "discuss" topics of mutual interest.

Hopefully this brief overview has opened your eyes to the many potential benefits of computerization of child care administration. Remember, computerizing is not a once-and-done activity; every center can benefit from continually evaluating additional solutions and enhancing its current operations.

APPENDIX A

Computerized Data Management

In order to update this appendix, every software developer was contacted. Those who appeared in the previous edition of this text were sent a copy of the write-up and asked if they wished to revise it. A few new software developers were also contacted and asked to write a summary of their program. Therefore, many of the descriptions are in the words of the developers. They are not meant to be an endorsement by the author of this text.

ADMINISTRATIVE MANAGEMENT COMPUTER SOFTWARE

Childcare Manager Professional Edition

The Professional Edition offers a full-featured child care management and accounting program that gives you everything you need to run your business in one program and at one low price. With Childcare Manager Professional you get a complete contact management system to track your family, child, employee, and agency information. You also get a complete accounting package with everything you'll need to manage your center finances.

Childcare Manager Standard Edition

The Standard Edition of Childcare Manager is designed for child care administrators who use QuickBooks 2002 or 2003 (Pro, Premiere, or Enterprise Editions) for their general accounting needs. Childcare Manager complements QuickBooks by providing a complete system for tracking family, child, other payor (agency), and employee information. In addition, Childcare Manager provides billing and revenue management features unique to child care. These features let you link charges to children, create individual due dates, and perform weekly and monthly billings in a matter of seconds. Add Childcare Manager Standard to QuickBooks and you will have everything you need to run your center in one system (contact management, accounting, payroll) and at a price far below other systems.

College and university administrators can receive a free copy of Childcare Manager to use in their classrooms by contacting

Personalized Software, Inc.
P.O. Box 359
Phoenix, OR 97535-0359
Fax (541) 535-8889
800-553-2312
http://www.childcaremanager.com

Source: Reprinted by permission of Personalized Software, Inc.

AccuTrak

AccuTrak is an automated claims management system for sponsors of the Child and Adult Care Food Program. Family child care providers who wish to receive reimbursements for meals served complete special optical mark recognitions (OMR, or "bubble" forms) for children in attendance and menu items served. These forms are then scanned into the computer using an OMR scanner.

This data is analyzed for compliance with USDA regulations, and meals are totaled by tier for various claim reports. The system can either print reimbursement checks, create direct deposit files, or create files to interface with the sponsor's accounting system.

An Internet claims entry option is also available to providers. This option allows providers to go to a Web site and enter their current claim information, or review previous claims. Recent enhancements to the system analyze provider claims for possible fraud situations looking specifically for "block claiming." AccuTrak has been in production since 1998 and uses a Microsoft Access database allowing sponsors to create their own queries and reports. Available from

Millennium Computer Resources LLC
5376 Temple Court
Madison, WI 53705
608-233-7841
http://www.AccuTrak2000.com

Source: Reprinted by permission of AccuTrak 2000 Software.

ChildPlus Software

ChildPlus software is comprehensive management software for publicly funded child development programs such as Head Start, prekindergarten, and sponsored child care centers. ChildPlus software provides program managers with simple day-to-day procedures, executive monitoring reports, priority enrollment lists, and special critical indicator analyses to assess how well the program is doing. The following modules are included in the software: child outcome measure, child health and disabilities, educational development, attendance, family services, parent education and training, parent involvement, parent and state billing, and administrative procedures. The software generates over 500 standard programmatic reports including application procedures, health and dental, immunization, treatment, disability, transportation, child-adult care food program, enrollment, family services, home visit, and demographic reports. ChildPlus is designed for program staff with little or no computer knowledge. Available from

ChildPlus Software
750 Hammond Drive
Building 10, Suite 300
Atlanta, GA 30328
800-888-6674
fax 404-252-7337
http://www.childplus.com

Source: Reprinted by permission of ChildPlus Software.

Controltec™

Controltec™ is a custom systems software development and Internet business company with specific expertise in providing solutions to agencies serving children and families.

Controltec's suite of products for the child care market consists of KinderTrack™, a full subsidy management system; KinderWait™, an Internet-based waiting list for agencies servicing subsidized families; and KinderAttend™, an integrated system for paperless attendance tracking and accurate subsidy payment processing.

Our newest products are SchoolAttend™, HEAPTrack, and CenterTrack. Schools and child care agencies using SchoolAttend log in to a secured Web site to access their attendance data. Information tracked includes in and out times as well as meals and snacks. HEAPTrack is an Internet-based Home Energy Assistance Program that enables agencies to automatically authorize emergency energy subsidies to needy families living in cold weather areas. CenterTrack, currently being developed, is an Internet-based application that manages all facets of center-based operations.

Besides offering software solutions, Controltec has extensive experience as a software systems and integration consulting firm. In this capacity, Controltec has worked with social services staff at the agency, county, and state level.

Controltec is committed to becoming the premier supplier of software solutions to the child care subsidy market and related industries at the national level. Controltec can be contacted at

Controltec
330 South Main Street
Fallbrook, CA 92028
800-991-6120
http://www.controltec.com

Source: Reprinted by permission of Controltec, Inc.

EZ-CARE

Windows™

EZ-CARE is one of the most widely used solutions for center management. It offers tremendous flexibility to accommodate the unique needs of each organization. Data formats can be customized for each organization as well as in the product's easy-to-use report creator. Combining the point and click features of Windows with a simple file cabinet design, EZ-CARE is easy to use and easy to learn. Customizable screens and reports, versatile scheduling options, and complete control of sorting and selecting make EZ-CARE unique in its ability to be tailored to each center's needs. The software is sold in modules. The Data Management module includes customized family information, class lists, schedules, and a report generator. Accounts Receivable allows you to record a complete charge history, year-end statements, invoices, and revenue analysis. In addition, there are Computerized Time-Clock, Accounts Payable, Payroll, General Ledger, and Child Care Food Program modules. Some of the newest innovations incorporated into the software include door-release access control and automatic fee collection via electronic funds transfer or credit card.

The company offers a Full Support program that includes unlimited phone support, regular product enhancements, quarterly newsletter, users' meetings, and discounted training classes. Available from

SofterWare, Inc.
   540 Pennsylvania Avenue, Suite 200
   Fort Washington, PA 19034
   800-221-4111
   e-mail: info@softerware.com
   http://www.softerware.com/ezcare

Source: Reprinted by permission of SofterWare, Inc.

KidsCare for Windows™

KidsCare is a powerful, easy to use program that provides child care professionals with all the tools necessary for successful, efficient management in one integrated system. It allows you to control the daily affairs of a center, minimizing the amount of time spent on paperwork, as well as providing you with the ability to increase the center's efficiency and profitability.

KidsCare is appropriate for any size child care operation and provides the flexibility to track all of your center's critical information. The software includes everything needed to manage enrollment, control receivables, analyze center profitability, project future enrollment, increase revenue, and minimize staffing costs. Its unique e-mail capabilities allow you to send messages and/or statements to all or selected families. And, over 100 reports give you quick, easy access to all of the information you need for yourself, your teachers, your accountant, or your board of directors. As part of our professional support program, you will receive unlimited assistance, as well as free product enhancements. New features are being added all the time, such as Staff Development, which allows you to keep track of continuing education credits, certification, and much more. Available from

> KidsCare
> 540 Pennsylvania Avenue
> Fort Washington, PA 19034
> 800-836-3575
> e-mail: kidscare@softerware.com
> http://www.softerware.com/kidscare

Source: Reprinted by permission of SofterWare, Inc.

Maggey Deluxe for Windows™/Maggey for DOS

Separate Windows™ and DOS Versions Available

Maggey Deluxe for Windows™ contains all of the important data about your parents and children including address and telephone numbers, emergency names and numbers, immunization records, birthdays, and allergies. The menus and toolbar make data entry and retrieval fast and easy. This powerful program automatically calculates and posts tuition charges, maintains client ledgers, tracks accounts receivable, and bills subsidy/third party sponsors. Detailed weekly financial reports quickly provide you with an analysis of the center's performance. The automatic billing will save hours each week by calculating tuition and posting it to a ledger for each client. Maggey Deluxe for Windows will enable you to closely monitor your center's revenues with accurate billing receipts, deposit summaries, and income reports that can detail billing revenue by classes.

WinTime Deluxe is a unique time clock, which features a small keypad linked to your computer. Together with a monitor in the entrance to your center, WinTime Deluxe allows your parents to receive messages from the staff, see their current balance, and clock their children in and out quickly and accurately. Employees can also clock in and out providing accurate time information for your payroll.

Menus Deluxe allows you to create and maintain food menus in cycles up to six weeks long. From an inventory list, you can quickly create and change meal names and food items. Create meal calendars and USDA compliant worksheets with ease. Paired with WinTime, Menus Deluxe can even print weekly and monthly meal attendance reports that show how many children attended the meal, how many were disallowed according to current USDA reimbursement restrictions, and how many can be claimed.

Soon, Maggey Deluxe for Windows will include programs that will print paychecks, payroll detail reports, profit and loss statements, and balance sheets; allow inputting of checking and other cash expenses; and transfer all summary information to other locations or central offices via the Internet. These modules are currently available in Maggey for DOS. For more information and DEMO programs contact

CMSE., Ltd.
4641 N. 1st Avenue, Suite 1
Tucson, AZ 85718
800-462-4439
fax 520-292-2779
http://www.maggey.com

Source: Reprinted by permission of CMSE, Ltd., publishers of Maggey Software.

Office Center

DOS or Windows™

Office Center is both an accounting system and information manager. The Base program is simple in design, yet powerful, and is extremely flexible. Along with a wide variety of built-in accounting and database reports, the user can design reports to accommodate individual needs. Attendance-based charges can be calculated using Office Center's time-clock accounting system. The program generates customer statements, account balance reports, year-end customer summaries, and current deposit reports. It is also possible to record, define, track, sort, and print sign-in and roll-call sheets, class and bus schedules, allergy and immunization reports, date-activated future schedules, and family notes. Users may add their own data fields as well as create dozens of their own user-defined reports. The built-in word processing includes data merge, 26 letter templates, and some built-in letters. There are built-in network capabilities, designed for sharing information between computers. A program security system restricts access to information to those designated by the director.

Other modules that are available are Payroll and Advances, Accounts Payable, General Ledger, Timeclock Accounting, and USDA Food Program. Available from

Emerging Technologies
P.O. Box 1539
Mt. Shasta, CA 96067
800-729-4445

Source: Reprinted by permission of Emerging Technologies.

Pre-School Partner

Windows™ or DOS

The Pre-School Partner Combo module has been specifically designed for the daily administration of child care and pre school centers. It aids the provider in the functions of family and child registration, staff management, billing of services provided, collections of receivables, and conforming with HRS/government regulations. This one base package allows the user to accomplish most of the essential functions of operating a center.

Single modules can be purchased that will address specific functions. Registration tracks family, child, and staff information and generates lists, work schedules, funding sources, and secular denomination. There are also user-defined fields available for the specific needs of each situation. This module allows the user to store frequently used letters, memos, and facsimiles. There is also a mail-merge capability. Billing permits the user to prepare and print family invoices for child care and preschool services rendered. Quick Bill is used to print invoices for families that are on fixed recurring charges. Billable services and goods may be preset in order to speed the invoicing process, although predefined descriptions and charges can be changed at invoicing time. Accounts Receivable tracks each family's outstanding balance, and reports can be generated showing monthly activity and year-end analysis. Other modules available include Labels, Rolodex™, Envelopes; USDA Meal Program; Accounts Payable and Check Writer; Bank Reconciliation; and Report Writer. Available from

ON-Q Software, Inc.
13764 S.W. 11th Street
Miami, FL 33184
305-553-2400
fax 305-220-2666
http://www.on-qsoftware.com

Source: Reprinted by permission of ON-Q Software, Inc.

Private Advantage

Windows™ and Macintosh

Private Advantage is specifically designed to meet the demands and needs of large and small preschools, children's centers, and schools with widely varying needs. The software is available in two different versions, each having base features and add-ons. The Professional Series is the most powerful and flexible version. Private Advantage Light offers the basics but is designed for smaller facilities or for home-based programs.

The Professional Series features a Client Management module that allows the user to track family and child information, scheduling, waiting list, medical information, activity management, transportation management, and much more. The module has many reports including sign in/out sheets, birthday reports, attendance sheets, enrollment projections, weekly schedules, Full Time Equivalent (FTE) reports, emergency reports, immunization overdue reports/letters, birthday reports, some California Department of Education (CDE) reporting support, and much more. The Accounts Receivable module features family ledgers, co-family ledgers, agency ledgers, statements and receipts, reoccurring list and activity billing, pay sources tracking, tuition projections, vacation tracking, deposit tape, many useful reports, and more. The program accurately forecasts revenue that will be available for any given date in the future even if children leave the school, switch classes, or change tuitions. The Staff Management module features basic staff information, scheduling, emergency information, document tracking, staff/child ratios, vacation/sick tracking, contact log, training tracking, and more. The Meal Management module includes monthly meal calendars, eligibility status, flexible menu setup, shopping lists, meal count sheets, production report, meal attendance reports, meal total reports, and more. The Flexible Scheduling module allows children/staff to have a different schedule for every day of the year, hourly/daily billing, enrollment projections, staff/child ratios, integrated vacation/sick ledger tracks up to five user definable items, auto flex billing, and more. The Time Key module acts as a time clock for the capturing of child/staff times, allows messages to be received by the parents/staff, current child/staff ratios, many billing options, "who's here" report, child time lists and staff time cards, and more. There is a Word Processing feature that includes letter templates, mail merge, and the inserting of database fields in the letters. The Custom editors allow the creation of custom reports, graphs, labels, and the exporting of information to ASCII files (text files).

Available from

Private Advantage
   Mount Taylor Programs
   2777 Yulupa Avenue #302
   Santa Rosa, CA 95405
   800-238-7015
   fax 707-542-1521
   http://www.privateadv.com

Source: Reprinted by permission of Mount Taylor Programs.

Project KickStart

Windows™

Project KickStart is the fastest, easiest way to plan any project. Its eight-step planning process provides the framework for brainstorming, planning, and scheduling projects. You'll identify goals, anticipate potential problems, and assign tasks to resources. And it's incredibly flexible, accommodating hundreds of tasks and resources per project.

Some of the most powerful features of Project KickStart are the libraries of Phases, Goals, People, and Obstacles. You can drag and drop sample project terms from the libraries into your plan, finding issues you may have overlooked. Or save your own terms into the libraries. These libraries are a permanent pool of knowledge for future projects, making each successive project that much easier to plan.

An outline of your project is ready in 30 minutes or less. You can add Start and End dates to each task, print a wide variety of reports, and create a simple schedule with Project KickStart's Gantt chart. Or, click on the Hot-Link icon and transfer your project plan directly into Excel, Word, Power Point, Outlook, and Microsoft Project.

Use Project KickStart to plan an event, develop marketing campaigns, write proposals and business plans, create process templates, and much more. Project KickStart is the perfect combination of ease-of-use and affordability. Available from

Experience In Software
  2000 Hearst Avenue
  Berkeley, CA 94709
  800-678-7008
  fax 510-644-3823
  http://www.projectkickstart.com

Source: Reprinted by permission of Experience In Software.

RIVERS

Windows 95, 98, NT, ME, 2000, XP™

RIVERS is a computer software database system designed for child care programs, human service agencies, and educational institutions. RIVERS enables these agencies to track complete information for all of the children and adults they serve, and also for others, such as staff, volunteers, and outside service providers. All of RIVERS' features are included in a single modest price, with no extra modules to buy.

RIVERS contains an advanced "template" capability that enables agencies to customize RIVERS to exactly match their information needs. A template is a set of *data entry windows* together with a matching set of *printed reports*, all created using RIVERS' built-in menu commands. Agencies can modify existing templates or create new templates, without limit, at no extra cost.

RIVERS tracks complete families as well as all individual family members, making RIVERS ideal for case management strategies. RIVERS can track many different service programs concurrently, and any child or adult can be enrolled and tracked in several service programs at the same time. Summaries can be printed for each child (across programs), and for each program (across children).

RIVERS uses a simple and efficient windows design that allows new users to be trained in just 20 minutes to productively enter data. Users can send data from one RIVERS database to another, such as from centers to the central office, permitting total agency summaries across all centers. RIVERS has industrial strength capacity to track over a million children and adults at the same time, and follow them for many years. It has been used by agencies across the country since 1992. For a free demo and more information about the RIVERS computer software database system, contact

MOBIUS Corporation
  405 N. Henry Street
  Alexandria, VA 22314
  800-426-2710 or 703-684-2911
  fax 703-684-5649 or 703-684-2919
  e-mail: ddeloria@compuserve.com

Source: Reprinted by permission of MOBIUS Corporation.

School Minder

Windows™

School Minder® is the core product in a suite of school management software products from Hunter Systems. School Minder keeps detailed student, parent, and faculty records while handling payroll, medical information, discipline, attendance, grades, and much more. Add the billing module to manage tuition. Hunter Systems is partnered with Grade Quick®, the popular gradebook from Jackson Software, to provide data integration between the classroom and front office. School Minder integrates with other Hunter products to create a completely integrated and automated administrative environment where shared school data eliminates double entry, saves time, and creates other administrative advantages. Other available software includes Master Scheduling System®, Librarian's Edge®, Lunch Minder® (cafeteria Point of Sale [POS] and management), Accountrak® (for Federal Accounting Standards Board [FASB] compliant accounting), and Giftrak® (donor development). All software products are backed by a knowledgeable training and technical support staff. Available from

Hunter Systems
3500 Blue Lake Drive, Suite 400
Birmingham, AL 35243
800-326-0527
fax 205-968-6556
http://www.huntersystems.com

Source: Reprinted by permission of Hunter Systems.

SOFTWARE PROGRAMS WITH SPECIALIZED USES
Electronic Fee Collection

EZ-EFT

This software allows tuition information to be electronically transmitted for processing via bank draft or credit cards. Such a procedure can completely eliminate paper checks and ensure that payments are always received on the day they are due. Parents or guardians must sign an agreement to process fees by this method. The product integrates with SofterWare's EZ-CARE and KidsCare management software so that no reentry of data is required.

SofterWare Inc.
540 Pennsylvania Avenue
Fort Washington, PA 19034
800-220-4111

Internet Child Care Center Viewing

The following programs allow parents to view their children in their child care setting at any time during the day.

Kinderview

Kinderview
  8304 Clairemont Mesa Boulevard, Suite 202
  San Diego, CA 92111
  800-543-7075
  http://www.kinderview.com

I See You

Simplex Knowledge Company
  P.O. Box 1260
  White Plains, NY 10602
  914-328-9400
  http://www.skc.com

Watch Me!

Watch Me!
  4851 Keller Springs Road (#221)
  Dallas, TX 75248
  888-5WATCHME
  http://www.watch-me.com

APPENDIX B

Professional Organizations and Sources of Information

Action for Children's Television
  46 Austin Street
  Newtonville, MA 02160

Administration for Children, Youth
and Families (ACYF)
  Division of Child Care
  370 L'Enfant Promenade, SW
  Washington, DC 20447
  202-401-9326
  http://www.acf.dhhs.gov/programs/acyf/

Administration for Children, Youth
and Families (ACYF)
  Head Start Division
  P.O. Box 1182
  Washington, DC 20013
  http://www.acf.dhhs.gov/programs/acyf/

American Academy of Pediatrics
  141 Northwest Point Road
  P.O. Box 747
  Elk Grove Village, IL 60009-0747
  800-433-9016
  http://www.aap.org

American Association for Deaf Children
  814 Thayer Avenue
  Silver Spring, MD 20910
  301-585-5400

American Association for Gifted Children
1121 W. Main Street, Suite 100
Durham, NC 27701
919-683-1400
http://www.aagc.org

American Association of School Administrators
1801 N. Moore Street
Arlington, VA 22209
703-528-0700
http://www.aasa.org

American Council on Education (ACE)
1785 Massachusetts Avenue, NW
Washington, DC 20036
http://www.acenet.edu

American Educational Research Association (AERA)
1230 17th Street, NW
Washington, DC 20036-3078
202-223-9485
http://www.aera.net

American Federation of Teachers (AFT)
555 New Jersey Avenue, NW
Washington, DC 20001
202-879-4400
http://www.aft.org

American Foundation for the Blind
11 Penn Plaza, Suite 300
New York, NY 10001
212-502-7600
http://www.afb.org

American Medical Association
515 N. State Street
Chicago, IL 60610
312-464-5000
http://www.ama-assn.org

American Montessori Society (AMS)
281 Park Avenue South, 6th Floor
New York, NY 10010-6102
212-358-1250
http://www.amshq.org

American Speech-Language-Hearing Association
10801 Rockville Pike
Rockville, MD 20852

800-638-8255
http://www.asha.org

Association for Childhood Education
International
    11501 Georgia Avenue, Suite 315
    Wheaton, MD 20902
    800-423-3563
    http://www.udel.edu/bateman/acei

Bank Street College of Education
    610 W. 112th Street
    New York, NY 10025
    http://www.bnkst.edu

Centers for Disease Control & Prevention
    1600 Clifton Road, NE
    Atlanta, GA 30333
    404-639-3534
    http://www.cdc.gov

Center for Parenting Studies
    Wheelock College
    200 Riverway
    Boston, MA 02215-4176
    617-734-5200
    http://www.wheelock.edu/int/intendeavors.htm

Child Care Information Exchange
    P.O. Box 2890
    Redmond, WA 98073
    http://www.ccie.com/index.cfm

Child Care Law Center
    221 Pine Street, 3rd Floor
    San Francisco, CA 94104
    415-394-7144
    http://www.childcarelaw.org

Child Welfare League of America
    440 First Street, NW, 3rd Floor
    Washington DC, 20001-2085
    202-638-2952
    http://www.cwla.org

The Children's Book Council
    12 W. 37th Street, 2nd Floor
    New York, NY 10018-7480
    212-966-1090
    http://www.cbcbooks.org

Children's Defense Fund
25 E Street, NW
Washington, DC 20001
202-628-8787
http://www.childrensdefense.org

Council for Professional Recognition
2460 16th Street, NW
Washington, DC 20009-3575
800-424-4310
http://www.cdacouncil.org

Council for Exceptional Children
1110 North Glebe Road, Suite 300
Arlington, VA 22201
703-620-3660
http://www.cec.sped.org

Director's Network, Child Care Information
Exchange Press, Inc.
P.O. Box 3249
Redmond, WA 98073-3249
800-221-2864
http://www.ccie.com

Ecumenical Child Care Network
P.O. Box 803586
Chicago IL 60680
800-694-5443
http://www.eccn.org

ERIC Clearinghouse on Elementary and Early Childhood Education
University of Illinois at Urbana-Champaign
Childrens Research Center
51 Gerty Drive
Champaign, IL 61820-7469
800-583-4135
http://www.ericeece.org

ERIC Clearinghouse on Disabilities and Gifted Children
1110 North Glebe Road
Arlington, VA 22201-5704
800-328-0072
http://www.ericec.org

ERIC Clearinghouse on Teaching and
Teacher Education
1307 New York Avenue NW, Suite 300
Washington, DC 20005-4701
800-822-9229
http://www.ericsp.org

High/Scope Educational Research Foundation
  600 N. River Street
  Ypsilanti, MI 48198-2898
  734-485-2000
  http://www.highscope.org

Jean Piaget Society
  113 Willard Hall Building
  College of Education
  University of Delaware
  Newark, DE 19711
  http://www.piaget.org

Learning Disabilities Association of America
  4156 Library Road
  Pittsburgh, PA 15229
  412-341-1515
  http://www.ldanatl.org

National Academy of Early Childhood Programs (NAEYC)
  1509 16th Street, NW
  Washington, DC 20036
  800-424-2460
  http://www.naeyc.org

National Association of Child Care Professionals
  P.O. Box 90723
  Austin, TX 78709-0723
  512-301-5557
  http://www.naccp.org

National Association for the Education of
Young Children (NAEYC)
  1509 16th Street, NW
  Washington, DC 20036
  800-424-2460
  http://www.naeyc.org

National Association for Family Child Care
  5202 Pinemont Drive
  Salt Lake City, UT 84123
  801-269-9338
  http://www.nafcc.org

National Black Child Development Institute
  1023 15th Street, NW
  Washington, DC 20005
  http://www.nbcdi.org

National Center for Clinical Infant Programs
733 15th Street, NW, Suite 912
Washington, DC 20005

National Child Care Association
1016 Rosser Street
Conyers, GA 30012
800-543-7161
http://www.nccanet.org

National Coalition for Campus Children's Centers
119 Schindler Education Center
University of Northern Iowa
Cedar Falls, IA 50614
800-813-8207
http://www.campuschildren.org

National Council of Jewish Women
Center for the Child
53 W. 23rd Street (6th Floor)
New York, NY 10010
212-645-4048
http://www.ncjw.org

National Down Syndrome Society
666 Broadway
New York, NY 10012
800-221-4602
http://www.ndss.org

National Education Association
1201 16th Street, NW
Washington, DC 20036
202-833-4000
http://www.nea.org

National Head Start Association
1651 Prince Street
Alexandria, VA 22314
703-739-0875
fax 703-739-0878
http://www.nhsa.org

National Institute of Child Health and
Human Development
Bldg. 31, Room 2A32, MSC, 242
31 Center Drive
Bethesda, MD 20892-2485
http://www.nichd.nih.gov

Office of Human Development Services
U.S. Department of Health and Human Services
309F Hubert H. Humphrey Building
200 Independence Avenue, SW
Washington, DC 20201
http://www.hhs.gov

Parents Anonymous, Inc,
675 W. Foothill Blvd., Suite 220
Claremont, CA 91711
909-621-6184
http://www.parentsanonymous.org

School-Age Child Care Project
Center for Research on Women
Wellesley College
Wellesley, MA 02181-8201
617-283-1000

School-Age NOTES
P.O. Box 40205
Nashville, TN 37204
615-279-0700
fax 615-279-0800
http://www.schoolagenotes.com

Society for Research in Child Development
University of Michigan
3131 South State Street, Suite 302
Ann Arbor, MI 48108-1623
734-998-6578
http://www.srcd.org

United States National Committee of OMEP
World Organization for Early Childhood Education
1314 G Street, NW
Washington, DC 20005-3105
800-424-4310

Work and Family Life Studies, Research Division
Bank Street College
610 W. 112th Street
New York, NY 10025
212-875-4400
http://www.bankstreet.edu

APPENDIX C

Sources for Early Childhood Materials, Equipment, Supplies, and Books

ABC School Supply
   3312 N. Berkeley Lake Road
   P.O. Box 100019
   Duluth, GA 30136-9419
   http://www.abcschoolsupply.com

Angeles Nursery Toys
   9 Capper Drive
   Dailey Industrial Park
   Pacific, MO 63069-3604
   636-257-0533

Barron's Educational Series, Inc.
   250 Wireless Blvd.
   Hauppauge, NY 11788
   800-645-3476
   http://www.barronseduc.com

Caedmon Publishers
   Division of Harper & Row Publishers
   100 Keystone Industrial Park
   Scranton, PA 18512
   800-331-3761

Childcraft Education Corp.
   P.O. Box 3239
   Lancaster, PA 17604
   888-532-4453
   http://www.childcraft.com

Childswork/Childsplay
135 Dupont Street
P.O. Box 760
Plainview, NY 11803-0760
516-349-5520
http://www.childswork.com

Clarion Books
Division of Houghton-Mifflin
215 Park Avenue S
New York, NY 10003
212-420-5800
http://www.houghtonmifflinbooks.com

Community Playthings
359 Gibson Hill Road
Chester, NY 10918-2321
800-777-4244
http://www.communityplaythings.com

Constructive Playthings
13201 Arrington Road
Grandview, MO 64030-1117
800-448-7830
http://www.constplay.com

Corwin Press Inc., A Sage Publications Company
2455 Teller Road
Thousand Oaks, CA 91320
805-499-9734
http://www.corwinpress.com

Delmar Learning
Executive Woods, #5 Maxwell Drive
Clifton Park, NY 12065-2919
800-998-7498
http://www.earlychilded.delmar.com

Developmental Learning Materials
One DLM Park
Allen, TX 75002

Edumate-Educational Materials
2231 Moreno Blvd.
San Diego, CA 92110
619-275-7117
http://www.edumate.com

Environments, Inc.
P.O. Box 1348

Beaufort Industrial Park
Beaufort, SC 29901
843-846-8155

Facts on File
132 W. 31st Street, 17th Floor
New York, NY 10001
800-322-8755
http://www.factsonfile.com

Greenwillow Books
HarperCollins Publishers
10 East 53rd Street
New York, NY 10022
212-207-7000
http://www.harpercollins.com

Gryphon House, Inc.
Early Childhood Books
P.O. Box 207
Mt. Ranier, MD 20704
301-595-9500
http://www.ghbooks.com

Harcourt, Inc.
6227 Sea Harbor Drive
Orlando, FL 32887
407-345-2000
http://www.harcourt.com

Holcomb's Education Resources
3205 Harvard Avenue
P.O. Box 94636
Cleveland, OH 44101-4636
800-362-9907 ext. 2152
http://www.holcombs.com

Houghton-Mifflin Publishers
222 Berkeley Street
Boston, MA 02116
617-351-5000
http://www.hmco.com

Kaplan Early Learning Company
1310 Lewisville-Clemmons Road
Lewisville, NC 27023
800-334-2014
http://www.kaplanco.com

Lakeshore Learning Materials
  2695 E. Dominguez Street
  P.O. Box 6261
  Carson, CA 90810
  800-421-5354
  http://www.lakeshorelearning.com

Little Brown & Co.
  1271 Avenue of the Americas
  New York, NY 10020
  212-522-8700
  http://www.twbookmark.com

Nasco School Age
  4825 Stoddard Road
  Modesto, CA 95356-9318
  800-558-9595
  http://www.nascofa.com

New Horizons For Learning
  P.O. Box 15329
  Seattle, WA 98115
  206-547-7936
  http://www.newhorizons.org

Playtime Equipment and School Supply, Inc.
  5310 W. 99th Street
  Omaha, NE 68134
  402-571-1717

Redleaf Press
  450 N. Syndicate Suite
  St. Paul, MN 55104
  800-423-8309
  http://www.redleafpress.org

Scholastic
  557 Broadway
  New York, NY 10012
  212-343-6100
  http://www.scholastic.com

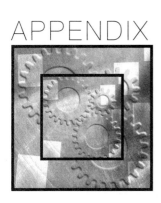

APPENDIX **D**

State Child Care
Licensing Agencies

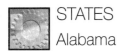 STATES

Alabama

Department of Human Resources
Child Day Care Partnership
50 North Ripley Street
Montgomery, AL 36130
334-242-1425
fax 334-353-1491
http://www.dhr.state.al.us/fsd/licresdv.asp

Alaska

AK Division of Family and Youth Services
P.O. Box 110630
Juneau, AK 99811-0630
907-465-3207
fax 907-465-3656 or 907-465-3190
http://www.eed.state.ak.us/EarlyDev/licensing.html

Arizona

Department of Health Services
Office of Child Care Licensure
1647 East Morten, Suite 230
Phoenix, AZ 85020
602-674-4220
fax 602-861-0674

Arkansas

Child Care Licensing
Division of Child Care and Early Childhood Education
P.O. Box 1437, Slot F150
Little Rock, AR 72203-1437
501-682-8590
fax 501-682-2317
http://www.state.ar.us/childcare/provinfo.html

California

Central Operations Branch
Department of Social Services
Community Care Licensing Division
744 P Street, Mail Stop 19-50
Sacramento, CA 95814
916-324-4031
fax 916-323-8352
http://ccl.dss.cahwnet.gov/docs/childcare/Provider/ccc.htm

Colorado

Department of Human Services
Division of Child Care
1575 Sherman Street, 1st Floor
Denver, CO 80203-1714
303-866-5958 or 800-799-5876
fax 303-866-4453
http://www.cdhs.state.co.us/childcare/licensing.htm

Connecticut

CT Department of Public Health
Child Day Care Licensing
410 Capitol Avenue
Mail Station 12
DAC, P.O. Box 340308
Hartford, CT 06134-0308
860-509-8045
fax 860-509-7541
http://www.dph.state.ct.us/BRS/Day_Care/day_care.htm

Delaware

Department of Services for Children, Youth and Families
Office of Child Care Licensing
1825 Faulkland Road
Wilmington, DE 19805
302-892-5800
fax 302-633-5112
http://www.state.de.us/kids/occlhome.htm

District of Columbia

Licensing Regulation Administration
Human Services Facility Division
614 H Street, NW, Suite 1003
Washington, DC 20001
202-727-7226
fax 202-727-7780

Florida

Child Care Program Office
Department of Children & Families
Child Care Services
1317 Winewood Blvd., Building 6, Room 389A
Tallahassee, FL 32399-0700
850-488-4900
fax 850-488-9584
http://www5.myflorida.com/cf_web/myflorida2/healthhuman/
childcare/licensingpermitting/index.html

Georgia

Department of Human Resources
Office of Regulatory Services, Child Care Licensing Section
2 Peachtree Street, NW
32nd Floor, Room 458
Atlanta, GA 30303-3142
404-657-5562
fax 404-657-8936
http://www2.state.ga.us/Departments/DHR/ORS/orsccl.htm

Hawaii

Department of Human Services
Benefit, Employment & Support Services Division
820 Mililani Street, Suite 606, Haseko Center
Honolulu, HI 96813
808-586-7050
fax 808-586-5229

Idaho

Department of Health & Welfare
Bureau of Family & Children's Services
450 W. State Street
P.O. Box 83720
Boise, ID 83720-0036
208-334-5691
fax 208-334-6664
http://www2.state.id.us/dhw/ecic/CC/Child_Ca.htm

Illinois

Department of Children & Family Services
Bureau of Licensure & Certification
406 East Monroe Street
Station 60
Springfield, IL 62701-1498
217-785-2688
fax 217-524-3347
http://www.state.il.us/agency/dhs/childcnp.html

Indiana

IN Family & Social Services Administration
Division of Family and Children
Bureau of Child Development—Licensing Section
402 W. Washington Street, Room W-386
Indianapolis, IN 46204
for *center-based child care* call: 317-232-4469
for *family child care and ministries* call: 317-232-4521
fax 317-232-4436
http://www.carefinderindiana.org/

Iowa

For center-based child care:

Department of Human Services
Division of Behavioral Development & Protective Services
Child Day Care Unit
Hoover State Office Building, 5th Floor
Des Moines, IA 50319
515-281-8746
fax 515-281-4597

For family child care:

Department of Human Services
Division of Behavioral Development & Protective Services
Child Day Care Unit
Hoover State Office Building, 5th Floor
Des Moines, IA 50319
515-281-8746
fax 515-281-4597

Kansas

Department of Health and Environment
Child Care Licensing & Registration
Curtis State Office Building
1000 SW Jackson, Suite 200
Topeka, KS 66612-1274
785-296-1270
fax 785-296-0803

Kentucky

For centers and family child care homes serving seven or more children:

Cabinet for Health Services
Division of Licensing & Regulation
C.H.R. Building
275 East Main Street, 5E-A
Frankfort, KY 40621
502-564-2800
fax 502-564-6546

For certification of family child care homes serving three to six children. No certification needed for less than three children.

Community Based Services
Division of Child Care
C.H.R. Building
275 East Main Street, 3C-F
Frankfort, KY 40621
502-564-2524
fax 502-564-3464

Louisiana

Department of Social Services
Bureau of Licensing
2751 Wooddele Blvd.
P.O. Box 3078
Baton Rouge, LA 70821
225-922-0015
fax 225-922-0014
http://www.dss.state.la.us/offos/html/licensing.html

Maine

Bureau of Child & Family Services
221 State Street
State House, Station 11
Augusta, ME 04333
207-287-5060
fax 207-287-5031

Maryland

Department of Human Resources
Child Care Administration
311 W. Saratoga Street, 1st Floor
Baltimore, MD 21201
410-767-7805
fax 410-333-8699

Massachusetts

Office of Child Care Services
One Ashburton Place, Room 1105
Boston, MA 02108

617-626-2000
fax 617-626-2028
http://www.qualitychildcare.org/licensing.shtml

Michigan

Department of Consumer & Industry Services
Division of Child Day Care Licensing
7109 W. Saginaw, 2nd Floor
P.O. Box 30650
Lansing, MI 48909-8150
517-373-8300
fax 517-335-6121
http://www.cis.state.mi.us/brs/cdc/home.htm

Minnesota

Refers family child care calls to counties.

Department of Human Services
Division of Licensing
444 Lafayette Road North
St. Paul, MN 55155-3842
561-296-3971
fax 561-297-1490
http://www.dhs.state.mn.us/Licensing

Mississippi

Department of Health
Division of Child Care
P.O. Box 1700
Jackson, MS 39215-1700
601-576-7613
fax 601-576-7813

Missouri

Department of Health
Bureau of Child Care, Safety and Licensure
1715 Southridge
Jefferson City, MO 65109
573-751-2450
fax 573-526-5345
http://www.health.state.mo.us/LicensingAndCertification/welcome.html

Montana

Department of Public Health and Human Services (DPHHS)
  Quality Assurance Division (QAD)
  Licensing Bureau
  Child Care Licensing Program
  P.O. Box 202953
  Helena, MT 59620-2953
  http://www.dphhs.state.mt.us/about_us/divisions/quality_assurance/
  quality_assurance.htm

Nebraska

NE Department of Health and Human Services
  Child Care
  P.O. Box 95044
  Lincoln, NE 68509-5044
  402-471-7763
  fax 402-471-9455
  http://www.hhs.state.ne.us/crl/childcare.htm

Nevada

Department of Human Resources
  Division of Child and Family Services
  Bureau of Child Care Licensing
  3920 E. Idaho Street
  Elko, NV 89801
  775-753-1237
  fax 775-738-0165

New Hampshire

NH Department of Health and Human Services
  Office of Program Support
  Bureau of Child Care Licensing
  129 Pleasant Street
  Concord, NH 03301
  603-271-4624
  fax 603-271-4782

New Jersey

Refers family child care calls to counties.

Division of Youth and Family Services
    Bureau of Licensing
    P.O. Box 717
    Trenton, NJ 08625-0717
    609-292-1018
    fax 609-292-6976
    http://www.state.nj.us/humanservices/dyfs/licensing.html

New Mexico

Child Services Unit/Licensing
    PERA Building, Room 111
    P.O. Drawer 5160
    Santa Fe, NM 87502-5160
    505-827-4185
    fax 505-827-7361

New York

NY State Department of Family Assistance
    Office of Children and Family Services
    Bureau of Early Childhood Services
    52 Washington Street
    Riverview Center 6th Floor
    Rensselaer, NY 12144
    518-474-9454
    fax 518-474-9617

For callers from the five boroughs of New York City: Manhattan, Queens, Brooklyn, Bronx, and Staten Island:

New York City Department of Health
    Bureau of Day Care
    2 Lafayette Street, 22nd Floor
    New York, NY 10007
    212-676-2444 (212-280-9251 for family child care registration only)
    fax 212-676-2424
    http://www.nyc.gov/html/doh/html/dc/dc.html

North Carolina

Division of Child Development
Regulatory Services Section
2201 Mail Service Center
Raleigh, NC 27699-2201
919-662-4499 or 919-662-4527 or 800-859-0829 (in-state calls only)
fax 919-661-4845
http://www.dhhs.state.nc.us/dcd/provider.htm

North Dakota

Department of Human Services
Early Childhood Services
600 East Boulevard
State Capitol Building
Bismarck, ND 58505-0250
701-328-4809
fax 701-328-3538

Ohio

Ohio Department of Job & Family Services
Bureau of Child Care and Development
255 East Main Street, 3rd Floor
Columbus, OH 43215-5222
614-466-1043
fax 614-466-0164 or 614-728-6803
http://www.state.oh.us/odjfs/cdc/

Oklahoma

Department of Human Services
Office of Child Care
P.O. Box 25352
Oklahoma City, OK 73125
405-521-3561
fax 405-522-2564
http://okdhs.org/childcare/ProviderInfo/provinfo_licensing.htm

Oregon

Employment Department
Child Care Division
875 Union Street, NE
Salem, OR 97311

503-947-1400
fax 503-947-1428
http://findit.emp.state.or.us/childcare/rules.cfm

Pennsylvania

Department of Public Welfare, Bureau of Child Day Care
Office of Children, Youth & Families
Bertolino Building, 4th Floor
P.O. Box 2675
Harrisburg, PA 17105-2675
717-787-8691
fax 717-787-1529
http://www.dpw.state.pa.us/ocyf/childcarewks/ccwreqccp.asp

Rhode Island

Rhode Island Department of Children, Youth, and Families
Day Care Licensing Unit
101 Friendship Street
Providence, RI 02903
401-528-3624
fax 401-528-3650
http://www.dcyf.state.ri.us/licensing.htm

South Carolina

Department of Social Services
Division of Child Day Care Licensing
P.O. Box 1520
Room 520
Columbia, SC 29202-1520
803-898-7345
fax 803-898-7179
http://www.hhs.state.sc.us/FAQ/providers_faq.htm

South Dakota

Department of Social Services
Child Care Services
Kneip Building
700 Governors Drive
Pierre, SD 57501-2291
605-773-4766
fax 605-773-7294
http://www.state.sd.us/social/CCS/Licensing/infolic.htm

Tennessee

Department of Human Services
    Child Care Services Unit
    Citizens Plaza—14th Floor
    400 Deaderick Street
    Nashville, TN 37248-9800
    615-313-4778
    fax 615-532-9956

Texas

Department of Protective and Regulatory Services
    Child Care Licensing
    P.O. Box 149030
    M.C. E-550
    Austin, TX 78714-9030
    day care hotline 800-862-5252 or 512-438-3267
    fax 512-438-3848
    http://www.tdprs.state.tx.us/Child_Care/

Utah

Department of Health
    Bureau of Licensing
    Child Care Unit
    P.O. Box 142003
    Salt Lake City, UT 84114-2003
    801-538-9299
    fax 801-538-9259
    http://www.health.state.ut.us/hsi/hfl/index.html

Vermont

Department of Social Rehabilitation Services
    Child Care Services Division
    Child Care Licensing Unit
    103 S. Main Street
    Waterbury, VT 05671-2901
    802-241-2158 or 3110
    fax 802-241-1220
    http://www.state.vt.us/srs/childcare/licensing/license.htm

Virginia

Department of Social Services
Division of Licensing Programs
730 E. Broad Street, 7th Floor
Richmond, VA 23219-1849
800-543-7545
fax 804-692-2370
http://www.dss.state.va.us/division/license/

Washington

Division of Child Care and Early Learning
Economic Services Administration
Department of Social and Health Services
P.O. Box 45480
Olympia, WA 98504-5480
360-413-3209
fax 360-413-3482
http://www.wa.gov/dshs/occp/license.html

West Virginia

Department of Health and Human Resources
Day Care Licensing
P.O. Box 2590
Fairmont, WV 26555-2590
304-363-3261
fax 304-367-2729
http://www.wvdhhr.org/oss/childcare/licensing.htm

Wisconsin

Division of Children & Family Services
Bureau of Regulation and Licensing
1 West Wilson Street
P.O. Box 8916
Madison, WI 53708-8916
608-266-9314
fax 608-267-7252
http://www.dhfs.state.wi.us/rl_dcfs/index.htm

Wyoming

Department of Family Services
Division of Juvenile Services
Hathaway Building, Room 343
2300 Capitol Avenue
Cheyenne, WY 82002-0490
307-777-6285
fax 307-777-3659

 TERRITORIES

Puerto Rico

Department of Family
Licensing Office
P.O. Box 11398
Santurce, PR 00910
787-724-0772
fax 787-724-0767

Virgin Islands

Department of Human Services
Child Care Licensing
3011 Golden Rock
Christiansted, St. Croix
U.S. Virgin Islands 00820-4355
340-773-2323
fax 340-773-6121

GLOSSARY

accreditation	National program for validating the quality of early childhood programs.
adventure play areas	Outdoor areas where children can use a variety of materials to build their own structures.
aesthetic appeal	Pleasant appearance derived from a well-designed environment.
AIDS	Acquired immune deficiency syndrome.
allergens	Environmental substances that cause a reaction such as asthma, hives, or hay fever.
anti-bias curriculum	Broader approach that includes not only cultural aspects, but also gender and physical ability differences.
attachment	The affectional tie that binds one person to another and that endures with time.
authoritarian manager	An administrator who makes decisions and determines policies for others.
authoritative director	An administrator who establishes rules, but is willing to discuss compromises with staff members.
budget	A statement of goals for one year stated in financial terms.
budget calendar	A schedule for compiling budget data.
business plan	A written document that describes a proposed venture in detail.
caregiver	One who provides a caring, nurturing environment for children who spend long hours away from home.
child abuse	Serious harm to children in the form of physical, emotional, or sexual mistreatment.
child care resource and referral network	Information service for parents seeking child care.
Child Development Associate (CDA)	A credential that certifies the holder has achieved a level of competency.
church-sponsored program	A child care center or preschool organized as an extension of the educational program of the church.

clique
A group formed by school-age children as a means for strengthening bonds with peers and to be free from adult supervision.

collegiality
An academic environment in which members work together as equals, cooperating rather than competing with one another.

concrete materials
Objects that children can touch, taste, smell, hear, and see.

contract
Written agreement between a child development facility and the employee that promotes job security.

cooperative school
Nonprofit enterprise, owned by all the parents who currently have children enrolled in the school.

corporate child care centers
Business corporation operating multiple schools at different sites.

creativity
Unique ways of reacting to a situation, not just imitating what others have done.

critical job elements
Things which, if not done, would seriously impede the total teaching process.

democratic manager
An administrator who involves others in decisions and policy-making processes.

developmentally appropriate infant-toddler program
Based on knowledge of the physical, emotional, social, and cognitive abilities of the children served.

developmentally appropriate practice
Based on a knowledge of universal sequences of growth and change and of each child's individual pattern and timing.

disaster plans
Detailed plans for evacuating children and managing a disaster.

egocentric
Children's inability to see things from more than one point of view.

employer-sponsored programs
On-site or off-site child care facilities supported by a company or business.

ethics
The study of right and wrong, duty, and obligation.

evaluation
Process to determine whether the goals of an early childhood center are being met.

expendable supplies
Items that are used up and have to be replaced.

family child care home
Child care service provided in a private residence.

family group
Children whose ages vary, sometimes by several years.

fixed expenses
Expenses that do not vary or change very little, over periods of time.

flexible
Ability to change as needed.

Food Guide Pyramid
Recommended daily servings of food developed by the U.S. Department of Agriculture in 1992.

for-profit proprietary school
School owned by one or more individuals, established to provide a community service but also to make a profit for the owners.

fringe benefits
Mandated or voluntary benefits that are added to personnel expenses.

goal
Expected long-term changes in a child's behavior.

industry versus inferiority	Erikson's middle childhood stage during which children acquire skills needed for adulthood.
knowledge	A familiarity with a particular subject or branch of learning.
laboratory school	Early childhood center that is part of the instructional program of a college or university.
maintenance	Major expenditures on the physical plant: painting, alterations, repair.
management skill	Ability to coordinate all the parts of an organization to meet common goals.
master teacher	Experienced, model teacher who can provide a positive learning environment for student teachers.
mentor	Someone who can serve as a role model to help an inexperienced teacher gain new skills and knowledge.
morality	Our view of what is good or right, how people should behave, and the kinds of obligations we have to one another.
multiculturalism	A program that provides opportunities for children to develop a positive self-concept, including an acceptance of their own differences and differences of others.
multipurpose equipment	Equipment that can be used in more than one way.
nonexpendable items	Equipment and toys that last a long time.
nonverbal messages	Facial expression, movements, and posture.
objective	Expected short-term changes in a child's behavior.
ongoing cost	Expected costs of operating a school.
operations	Recurring, day-to-day activities involved in the upkeep of a school.
parent conference	One-on-one meeting between teacher and parents to discuss a child's progress or resolve problems.
parent education	Activities designed to help parents become better informed about child-rearing and family life.
parent involvement	Sharing in the education of their children through participation in school activities.
peer	A person the same age as oneself.
peer group	Children who are close to the same age.
permissive manager	An administrator who remains passive, often leaving decisions to others.
philosophy	A distillation of ideas, beliefs, and values held by an individual, a group, or organization.
preschool period	Designates the years before a child enters elementary school.
probationary period	The time before the full contract goes into effect, usually from one to three months.
psychosocial area	Space that is planned to encourage interactions between adults and children, and among the children themselves.

scooter board	A 12-inch plastic or wooden square, with swivel casters (commercially produced boards are equipped with handles on the side).
self-concept	Children's understanding of their own characteristics.
sensorimotor period	Stage from birth to age two when children use all their senses to absorb the world around them.
sensory diversity	Objects and experiences that stimulate the senses.
skill	An ability that comes from knowledge, practice, or aptitude (sometimes called competency).
start-up costs	Expenses incurred before a new school can open.
statement of personnel policies	Written document covering employer-employee relations.
student teacher	College or university student who is enrolled in a practice teaching or field study course requiring placement in a school or child care center.
supervision	Overseeing staff members during the performance of their jobs.
synchrony	The back-and-forth interaction between infants and their parents or caregivers.
trust versus mistrust	Piagetian stage in which children learn to trust themselves and others.
values	The qualities that we believe are intrinsically desirable and that we strive to achieve in ourselves.
variable expenses	Expenses that vary and over which the director has some control.
volunteer	Unpaid person who offers his or her services freely.

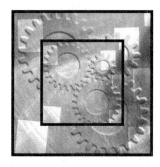

Index

CRUISIN' THE FOSSIL FREEWAY

AN EPOCH TALE

OF A SCIENTIST AND AN ARTIST

ON THE ULTIMATE 5,000-MILE

PALEO ROAD TRIP

WITH PALEONTOLOGIST **KIRK JOHNSON**

AND ARTIST **RAY TROLL**

FULCRUM

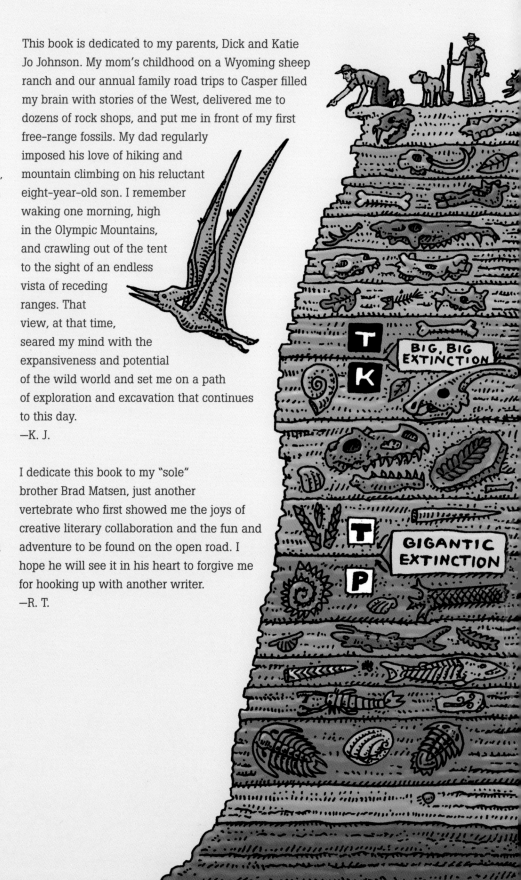

Library of Congress Cataloging-in-Publication Data

Johnson, Kirk R.
  Cruisin' the fossil freeway : an epoch tale of a scientist and an artist on the
ultimate 5,000-mile paleo road trip / by Kirk R. Johnson and Ray Troll.
    p. cm.
  Includes index.
  ISBN-13: 978-1-55591-451-6 (pbk. : alk. paper) 1. Paleontology--West (U.S.)
2. Dinosaurs--West (U.S.) 3. Fossils--West (U.S.) 4. West (U.S.)--Description and
travel. 5. United States--Discovery and exploration. I. Troll, Ray, 1954- II. Title.
  QE711.3.J64 2007
  560.978--dc22
                                        2007019480
Printed in China by P. Chan and Edward, Inc.
0 9 8 7 6 5 4 3

Editorial: Faith Marcovecchio, Haley Berry
Design: Ann W. Douden

Fulcrum Publishing
4690 Table Mountain Drive, Suite 100
Golden, CO 80403
800-992-2908 • 303-277-1623
www.fulcrumbooks.com

This book is dedicated to my parents, Dick and Katie Jo Johnson. My mom's childhood on a Wyoming sheep ranch and our annual family road trips to Casper filled my brain with stories of the West, delivered me to dozens of rock shops, and put me in front of my first free-range fossils. My dad regularly imposed his love of hiking and mountain climbing on his reluctant eight-year-old son. I remember waking one morning, high in the Olympic Mountains, and crawling out of the tent to the sight of an endless vista of receding ranges. That view, at that time, seared my mind with the expansiveness and potential of the wild world and set me on a path of exploration and excavation that continues to this day.
—K. J.

I dedicate this book to my "sole" brother Brad Matsen, just another vertebrate who first showed me the joys of creative literary collaboration and the fun and adventure to be found on the open road. I hope he will see it in his heart to forgive me for hooking up with another writer.
—R. T.

BIG, BIG EXTINCTION

GIGANTIC EXTINCTION

Era	Period/Epoch	Millions of Years Ago
CENOZOIC	HOLOCENE	10,000 YEARS
	PLEISTOCENE	1.8
	PLIOCENE	5.3
	MIOCENE	2.3
	OLIGOCENE	33.9
	EOCENE	55.8
	PALEOCENE	65.5
MESOZOIC	CRETACEOUS	145.5
	JURASSIC	199.6
	TRIASSIC	251
PALEOZOIC	PERMIAN	299
	PENNSYLVANIAN	318.1
	MISSISSIPPIAN	359.2
	DEVONIAN	416
	SILURIAN	443.7
	ORDOVICIAN	488.3
	CAMBRIAN	542
	PROTEROZOIC	2.5 BILLION
	ARCHEAN	

MILLIONS OF YEARS AGO

EARTH FORMS 4.6 BILLION YEARS AGO

TABLE OF CONTENTS

SABER-TOOTHED EVERYTHING

I woke with a jolt, soaked in sweat, in a stinky little cabin on a riverboat on the upper Amazon in Peru. Snarling animals with slashing saber teeth snapped at my heels, the remnants of a horrible dream. Stocked with images of all of prehistory, my paleontologist's brain had concocted appalling saber-toothed cats and tigers, saber-toothed marsupials, saber-toothed uintatheres, saber-toothed deer, and a staggering melee of other extinct creatures with saber teeth but no common names. I was 36 years old and suffering from another Lariam nightmare.

Lariam is a drug used to prevent malaria, but it is also renowned for its side effect of appallingly vivid slasher nightmares. Many users report murderous dreams where family members set on each other with knives or friends chop each other apart with machetes. Suffering a similar fate that morning, I heard the shrill "wree, wree, wree" from the shower scene in Hitchcock's *Psycho*, only my Janet Leigh had much bigger teeth.

As I shook off my terror and pondered this night-mare, two realizations suddenly hit me: walrus are saber-toothed seals, and only Ray Troll could paint my dream.

I first met Ray at the Burke Museum in Seattle in 1993, but the meeting had been destined for a long time. Ray is a fish-obsessed artist whose work is densely packed and jarringly unique. Early in his career, he found that it was easier to sell art if it was on a T-shirt, and his images can now be seen on more than a million chests up and down the West Coast. Growing up in Seattle, I spent my early 20s wearing those T-shirts. Ray remembers looking up from a lobe-fin fish–filled museum case that day to see

a hulking 6′ 3″ frame bearing down on him. I was really excited to meet the man whose "Spawn 'til you Die" and "Humpies from Hell" shirts filled my closet. Ray felt like he was about to get mugged.

Despite our shared interests, it wasn't until my 1996 Lariam dream that I realized I simply had to work with Ray. But how could I lure this artist into working with me? I knew that for the last 20 years he had lived in Ketchikan, a small fishing, logging, and tourist town on Revillagigedo Island off the southern tip of Alaska, and I figured it would be best if I went to him. So I tacked a few extra days onto a fishing trip and found myself in a phone booth in rainy Ketchikan, cold-calling the Troll.

I didn't really have a plan for my pitch, but I was aided by the fact that Ray has a curious habit shared by artists who dabble in the realm of natural history: he collects scientists. Between that and the fact that people in Ketchikan don't get many drop-in visitors, it wasn't much of a sales job after all. Ray answered the phone and invited me to the Soho Coho, his smart little art gallery on a boardwalk over a salmon stream. Our conversation went well, and we ended up in his

The Soho Coho gallery on a boardwalk over a salmon stream.

studio talking about fossils and fish. I told him about the Lariam dream and the fishy wonders of the Amazon, which I visit each year for an immersion in tropical biodiversity. By the end of the conversation, Ray had signed up for my next Amazon trip and we started plotting projects together.

But let me back up and start at the beginning, at least my beginning, of this whole paleo obsession. When I was five, there was a pretty redhead next door who owned a rock polisher, one of those metal cans on rubber rollers hooked up to a small engine. You fill the can with rocks, grit, and water, turn it on, and let it slowly rotate for a week. Then you change out the coarser grit for finer and repeat the process. Three times you change the grit, with the whole process taking a month. A month is an insanely inscrutable amount of time for a five-year-old. Kelsey, a mature nine-year-old, had the patience of a saint, and I remember clearly that sunny morning when she called me over to her porch. The month was finally up, and she let me watch as she lifted the can off the tumbler, opened it, and poured out a muddy slurry. I was stunned as she washed away the slimy polishing compound to reveal a trove of gorgeous glistening agates. It was one of those perfect Seattle summer mornings, and I remember the sun backlighting Kelsey's red hair and bouncing off the polished red agates. I fell in love with rocks, and girls, at that moment.

It took me many more years to even begin to get a grip on the girl thing, but the rocks got traction immediately. I pored over the gravel in driveways and on beaches. I planned and pouted so my parents would interrupt family road trips to stop at rock shops. My dad caved pretty quickly to my incessant pleading for a rock tumbler, and before long I had my own tumbling drums of grit and gravel. I discovered the 500 section of the local public library and was soon hauling home stacks of books about rocks, gems, and fossils.

Memorable stones began to present themselves to me. A fossil leaf on a trail at summer camp near Mount Rainier. A brachiopod from the top of Casper Mountain that I thought was a fossilized rattlesnake tail. A chunk of black limestone from the Canadian Rockies that was patterned with stark white bryozoans. Then, a little later, beautifully pyritized ammonites from the beach gravels of Lyme Regis on the Dorset Coast of England. By the time I was 12, I was a goner, hooked for life on this strange pastime of seeking and hoarding stones. Fossils owned me, and I owned a lot of them. It was around this time that someone showed me one of the fossil crabs from the Olympic Peninsula. These are still some of the most amazing and precious fossils I have ever seen. Crabs, complete with all of their legs and claws, preserved, sometimes with the original shell color intact, in tight round concretions. Little round tombs containing perfect crustaceans. I had to have one. I had to find one. Unlike most kids on the planet, I didn't give much thought to dinosaurs. Instead, I was passionately hooked on fossils that I thought I might have a chance of finding.

In time, probably not much time, friends of friends steered me to a man who knew how and where to find fossils: highway department maintenance man Bill Buchanan. His house was only a five-hour drive from ours. My dad and I drove to his smoky cottage at the edge of the town of Clallam Bay on the north coast of the Olympic Peninsula. He was a generous man who gave me fossils as well as information about how to find them.

Under his guidance, I learned how to walk down a rain-soaked, rocky beach with an eight-pound sledge-hammer, smacking likely boulders for the treasures they held. On our first venture together, Bill cracked open a soccer ball–sized concretion that contained a perfect crab. He didn't even hesitate to give me the precious rock. That's a kindness I remember with great clarity. In time, I too had a personal armory of sledgehammers and a keen eye for just the right kind of rock.

It was about this time that I met Wes Wehr, an impossibly quiet artist with an abiding passion for petri-fied wood. He had already worked his way into the Burke Museum as an unpaid curator of fossil plants and was busy collecting correspondence from distant paleobotanists. Bill Buchanan had found some fossil conifer cones in crab nodules, and, through me, Wes connected Bill with Chuck Miller, a professor at the University of Montana who spe-cialized in fossil cones. Wes and I began to gather cones, and eventually Chuck named a fossil cone after Bill.

Wes was a city artist who didn't know how to drive a car. The summer after I got my driver's license, he and I headed off in my parents' orange Audi for a weeklong drive across eastern Washington and Oregon to locate fossil sites that we had read about in library books. Early in the trip, we struck pay dirt in the little gold-mining town of Republic in northeastern Washington. A forgot-ten Eocene lake bed was exposed in the hills around town, and we blundered around asking the locals if they knew where to find fossils. They didn't, and we weren't having any luck ourselves, so we decided to leave. Our car was parked on the south end of the main street. As I walked around the back to get in, I kicked a little piece of

roadside shale. To my amazement, the rock fell open, revealing a stunning little sprig of dawn redwood foliage. We quickly dug into the drainage ditch, and the buff layers imme-diately began to yield beautiful fossil leaves, cones, insects, and flowers. On subsequent trips to this spot, we found so many perfect fossil flowers that I started giving them to girls I liked, and their sweet response made me realize that plants are the best kind of fossils.

On the way back to Seattle, we stopped at the Oregon Museum of Science and Industry in Portland, where we met a 21-year-old paleobotanical wunderkind named Steve Manchester. He was in a back room supervis-ing a team of six high-school kids who were using Elmer's glue to reassemble shattered fossil tropical rain forest leaves from eastern Oregon. Some of the leaves were in 20 pieces, and I was amazed at how diligently these kids struggled over their rocky jigsaw puzzles. I was more surprised, and a little bit dismayed, to realize that I wasn't the only kid in the world who thought about fossil leaves. I didn't realize it at the time, but this road trip sealed my fate and destined me to become a paleobotanist.

A few years later, as an interested but aimless junior studying art, geology, and rugby at Amherst College in central Massachusetts, I accepted a summer research assistantship that landed me in the tiny town of Marmarth in the southwestern corner of North Dakota. My job was to measure coal seams and trace them along hillsides to see how they thickened and thinned. The 65-million-year-old coal is soft and brown, and it lies buried in layers of sand and clay that just never got buried deeply enough to turn into rock. I spent the summer, much of it alone, wander-ing through a maze of buttes and gullies with a shovel, digging trenches through the shallow prairie soil to expose the coal seams. Sometimes the holes yielded fragments of fossil leaves. The utter remoteness of place and my daily grind of digging into the earth gave me an appreciation for the vastness of space and time. It also made me realize that it was pointless to like fossils without understanding geology.

Those months on the High Plains reawakened childhood memories of driving from Seattle to Wyoming to visit the ranch where my mother spent her childhood. I was rediscovering the things that I loved about the plains: the huge sky, where a cast of clouds plays out the continuous, overwrought drama of real weather; the smell of ozone that mixes with intense sage when a thunderstorm is imminent; the eternal search for arrowheads and rattlesnakes. That summer, I saw a tornado, I found arrowheads, and I grabbed a rattlesnake, but mostly, I realized that I could travel through time with a shovel. I began to understand Faulkner's lines "The past is not dead. In fact, it is not even past." By the end of August, I had converted to geology and to North Dakota with the fervor of the born-again.

Ray took another path. He grew up in the dinosaur frenzy of the late 1950s and, like every other kid on the planet, he was dinosaur-obsessed. But unlike the other kids, was really good at drawing the dinosaurs. As a nascent artist, his very first crayon drawings were of snarling *T. rex* and cowering, bloodied *Triceratops*. The first word he wanted and managed to spell was *dinosaur*; by the age of six, he knew the Latin names for dozens of them. Making sound effects that worried his mother, he spent countless hours drawing prehistoric animals. He bought every dinosaur toy available in the 1960s and collected cereal-box treasures and postcards of prehistoric creatures. He was one of those kids who found oddly shaped rocks in the playground and adamantly declared that he had

discovered rare dinosaur bones. As a museum curator, I see those kids every week, and it's my job to let them down easily as I explain that their dinosaur egg is a rounded chunk of granite. But aside from a lucky brachiopod found in his grandparents' driveway, Ray didn't collect his first real fossil until he was 40 years old.

Instead, he grew up as a fossil-obsessed but fossil-deprived military brat, bouncing from air force base to air force base. He had an innate talent for seeing and drawing, and his early paintings were elaborate battle scenes with casts of thousands. By the time Ray was in high school, his family had settled in Kansas, and he soon became aware of the phenomenal fossils of the Sternberg Museum in Hays. Fruits of the labors of a whole fossil-finding family, the collection at the Sternberg is beyond compare. Here, in an unremarkable town on the plains of western Kansas, are the remains of the fish, reptiles, and birds that swam in and flew over a huge salty sea that covered this area 85 million years ago. Whole sharks, mosasaurs, plesiosaurs, pteranodons, and giant fishes lived where today you only see farm animals. When he was in high school, Ray and his buddies road-tripped to the chalk beds of western Kansas to find their own fossils, but he didn't know how to look for them, so he didn't find any. Not long after, Ray hooked up with a retired schoolteacher who was making educational filmstrips, and soon he was being paid for his drawings of prehistoric creatures.

Ray was born in 1954, so technically he was part of the '60s. But the truth is, the '60s didn't get to rural Kansas until the early '70s, so Ray came of age just about the time the funk rolled into town. He went to a local college and studied art, photography, and rock 'n' roll. Avant-garde images and electric-guitar riffs were added to the battle scenes and dinosaurs in his head and, surprisingly, it all stayed in there. Graduate school and a stint in Seattle buffed off his midwestern edges and morphed him into an urban hipster who played in rock 'n' roll bands and camouflaged his love of fossils.

Ray's move to Ketchikan in the early '80s dumped him into the epicenter of the salmon fishery and the Haida and Tlingit Indian art revival. By the time I met him, Ray was 39, married with two kids, balding, and cranking out some amazing art. Best of all, he had recently reconnected with his childhood love of fossils.

A HARSH LESSON: No matter how hard young Raymond imagined it to be, the rock was simply NOT a fossil bone.

Xiphactinus, a 15-foot Cretaceous fish, being played on a dry fly by the artist.

Art and Fossils

Throughout the brief few hundred years of the discipline of paleontology, paleontologists have often worked with artists or were artists themselves. In a world of stony fragments, old bones, and flattened leaves, there's a real need for people with artistic talent, imagination, and the ability to bring lost worlds back as images. Museums and books are full of paintings of dinosaurs and their worlds.

As a curator, I have advised many artists as to what they could, and could not, legitimately include in prehistoric scenes. In these collaborations, our goal is always to create accurate, plausible, and realistic landscapes from deep time. For me, a wannabe artist, it's great fun to direct the conception of an image, to tweak its contents, and yet still be surprised by how the final image so often feels like a real place.

Ray is a different kind of paleoartist than I was used to. He's no photo-realist, he's a scientific surrealist. His art, while often paleontological, is infused with the rest of his life. In his images, extinct animals visit the modern world in daydreams, as if underground cartoonist R. Crumb time-traveled to the Cretaceous.

The Troll family explores the chalk.

Monument Rocks (also known as the Kansas Pyramids) of Gove County, Kansas, are made of layers of Cretaceous chalk. These stacks of fossil plankton are full of marine fossils that lived when Kansas was at the bottom of a sea.

In 1997, Ray, his wife, Michelle, and their two kids, Patrick and Corinna, flew to Denver for a few days of digging. We drove east to western Kansas and hooked up with Ray's friend Chuck Bonner. Chuck's dad, Marion Bonner, had worked with the famous Sternberg family and had himself collected a number of the giant fossil fish now on display at the Denver Museum of Nature & Science, where I am chief curator. Chuck walked in his father's footsteps. One of the first fossils I acquired for the museum was a coffee-table-size Cretaceous clam that came from Chuck. I had driven out to pick up the massive mollusk and asked Chuck if he would show me where he had collected it. "No problem," he replied, "it's just over the hill." Ten minutes later, I was standing at the edge of a little valley where the prairie had eroded away to expose a half-acre of flat-lying Cretaceous chalk. From where I stood, I could count a dozen of the meter-wide clams just lying there, waiting to be collected. I began to understand the charms of fossiling in Kansas.

The Troll family and I had a great time visiting the Bonners, who live in a small house far out on the prairie, next to an old stone church full of Chuck's fossil finds. Our expedition to the Cretaceous chalk beds was a blast, but

Ray seemed unable to unearth a single fossil. His daughter found a great pectoral girdle of a big mosasaur, and the rest of us were finding pieces and chunks of ancient fish and handfuls of sharks' teeth, but Ray kept getting skunked. Finally, he sat down in exasperation near the truck and gave up. I wandered over to harass him. The key to finding a fossil is knowing what a fossil looks like, I told him. It's about shape, color, and texture, and recognizing the anomalous fragment of biological form. Often, simply remaining motion- less and concentrating on a single piece of ground is all it takes. With that piece of advice, I bent over and picked up a beautifully sharp and shiny *Squalicorax* shark tooth that was about six inches from Ray's butt. It was clear that I had my work cut out for me with this fossil- lovin' but fossil-blind artist.

By 1999, Ray and I had installed a museum exhibit called *Cruisin' the Fossil Freeway* at the Denver Museum. It's a traveling show of Ray's art with a lot of cool local fossils from the museum's collections. As part of this exhibit, we bought an old Volvo station wagon and completely worked it over with fossils and evolutionary paraphernalia, and put Charles Darwin in the driver's seat. Ray called the tricked-out car an Evolvo, and that stylin' little fossil car started us thinking about taking a real fossil road trip around the American West.

Ray Troll and a team of volunteers painting a giant ammonite mural in Denver in 1999.

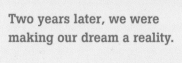

Two years later, we were making our dream a reality.

Our idea for a big fossil road map actually preceded our idea for a big road trip, but they quickly grew together. Ray jump-started the map by gluing a gigantic sheet of paper to the wall of his studio in Ketchikan and tracing some state lines on it. The shape of the paper was pretty arbitrary, and it dictated which states made it onto the final map. Our original idea was to do Colorado and Wyoming and all the states that touched them, but, because of the shape of the paper, we ended up shorting Arizona and New Mexico and adding a lot of real estate in Washington, Oregon, Nevada, and California. Each image on the map is based on an actual fossil from that spot. Ray, ever the fan of roadside eats, hid a drawing of a cheeseburger in every state.

The drawing took a solid nine months of Ray's time, with me working feverishly to supply accurate data to fill all the spaces. Hundreds of phone calls, faxes, and e-mails flew between our respective work spaces in Denver and Ketchikan. When the map was half done, I flew to Ketchikan to visit Ray. My first viewing lasted more than an hour. Despite the incredible density of prehistoric images, I was struck by the fact that fossils are so abundant, diverse, and widespread that we could have drawn dozens of different versions of this map, each populated by a completely different cast of characters. When the drawing was finally completed, Ray carefully cut the original in two to have it scanned at a local print shop. Terry Pyles, one of Ray's Ketchikan art pals, added digital color over the next few months. After a year's time, we had our map.

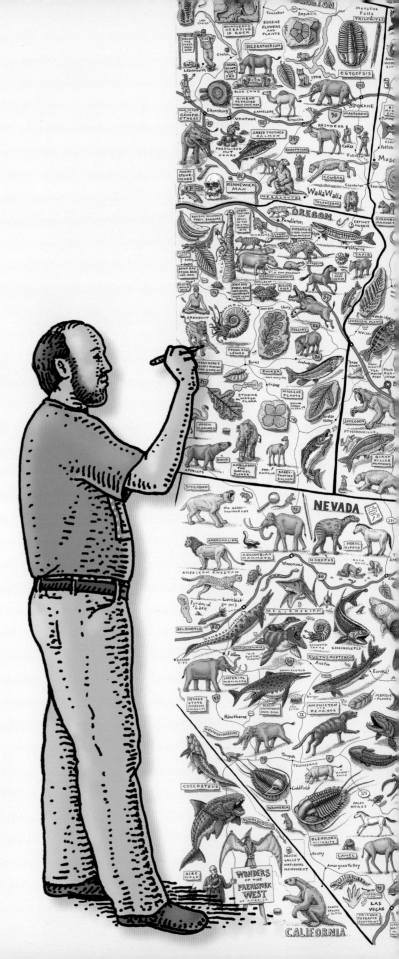

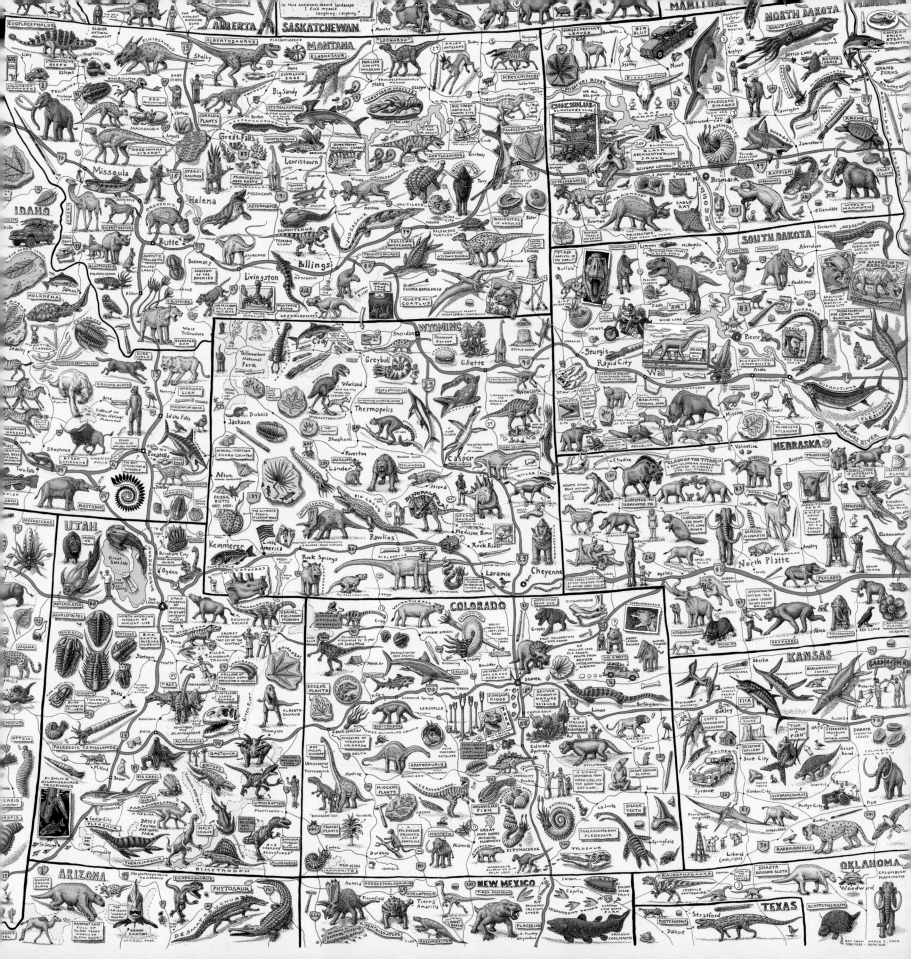

1
SUBURBAN REX

I found Ray at the baggage claim at Denver International Airport. He was sporting a jean jacket with a Haida Indian design, black jeans, shiny black shoes, and carrying a briefcase decorated with trilobites and dinosaurs. Not my idea of field clothes, but urban artiness is apparently tough to shed. Eventually Ray's huge duffel spewed onto the carousel. I remembered that I had asked him to bring the Troll family camping tent to keep our costs down, since we were going to be traveling on the cheap. We each grabbed an end of the bag, which felt like it held a corpse, and hauled it out to the parking garage to the museum's pickup.

A dark blue Ford F-250 with a partial crew cab, aluminum toolboxes, and a Tommy lift, Big Blue was purchased new into the Denver Museum's vehicle fleet back in 1983. Big Blue has an engine too small for its big body, a very finicky clutch and stiff gearshift, and a really big steel tailgate that makes it nearly impossible to see out the rearview mirror. For these reasons, most of the other museum employees hated driving it, and those who did could often be seen struggling with the bucking clutch or backing the truck into unseen obstacles. Mainly by default, it became my truck, and between 1991 and the moment I picked up Ray, Big Blue and I had visited more than 500 fossil sites in a dozen western states. Like the big kid I am, I delighted in the comic possibilities of the hydraulic tailgate, often lowering it to just the right level so that I could tie my bootlaces or roll a shopping cart full of groceries onto it to load into a cooler in the bed of the truck. Big Blue is a fossil-killing monster, and it seems only right that this beast would be our time-traveling machine.

As we rolled out of the parking garage and onto the flat plains of eastern Colorado, I began to explain the wonders of the land we were driving across on our way toward town. Today, Coloradoans are pretty comfortable with the concept that they live in a place that's a mix of mountains and plains, forests and prairies, cities, small towns, strip malls, and ranch land. But it doesn't take too much memory or too many generations to get back to the time before Lewis and Clark. We imagine endless herds of bison carpeting the plains and wish we could see how it used to be. But this is a slippery slope, because "used to be" isn't a destination, it's a journey. The world of paleontology allows us to slide that slippery slope all the way back to the beginning of life on Earth. Fossils are the remains of those days, and the fossils allow us to rebuild and understand those ancient and extinct ecosystems.

The Rocky Mountain West is the world's finest fossil field, home to *Tyrannosaurus rex*, *Apatosaurus*, *Allosaurus*, *Stegosaurus*, and countless other well-known dinosaurs. But that's just the beginning. The rocks and road cuts of the Rocky Mountain states contain fossils that hark back more than 500 million years. The West has not only dinosaurs but trilobites, giant beavers, American cheetahs, spiny clams, spiky plankton, killer pigs, shovel-tusked elephants, palm fronds, mammoth camels, rain forest primates, six-foot-wide ammonites, tens of billions of fossil leaves, and myriad plants and animals that haven't even been named yet. The region is bursting at the seams with cool fossils.

Some great finds have been made in and around the sprawling strip-mall city of Denver, where fossils have been known to show up in suburban backyards, on city street corners, and even at the airport. Denver was founded on the banks of the Platte River on November 22,

1858, a year and two days before Charles Darwin published *The Origin of Species*, but four years after Ferdinand Hayden found America's first dinosaur fossil on the banks of the Missouri River. On March 26, 1877, a man named Arthur Lakes was searching for fossil leaves near Golden, Colorado, when he came across a fossil bone the size of a log. He had found the first sauropod, or long-necked dinosaur, an animal that would come to be known as *Apatosaurus ajax*. Sauropods, the largest land animals this planet has ever seen, are awesome, enigmatic reptiles, deep-time denizens utterly different from anything alive today. Lakes's beast still tips the scales as one of the largest sauropods ever found. His discovery was followed that same year by even better dinosaur finds in Cañon City, Colorado, and Como Bluff, Wyoming. The western bone rush was on.

Ten years later, William Cannon, wandering up a gully about a mile west of downtown Denver, found a pair of long fossil horns. He shipped them to Othniel C. Marsh at Yale, who named them *Bison alticornis*, a new species of fossil bison. It only took two years and a more complete skull from Wyoming before Marsh realized that Cannon's bison horns were actually the business end of a *Triceratops*, and downtown Denver was credited with the first-known horned dinosaur.

It's been like that in Denver ever since. Someone walking around town or an alert backhoe driver digging a ditch finds a bone, and sooner or later somebody else realizes that it's a chunk of some huge extinct beast. The vaults at the Denver Museum of Nature & Science are full of these urban treasures. There's a fossil camel from the corner of 6th and Clermont, a group of Ice Age peccaries from the excavation for the Colorado capitol building, chunks of mammoths from the stream valleys, a dinosaur rib from home plate at Coors Field, and fossil palm trunks from all over town.

As I drove west, I reminisced out loud about my connection to a typical Denver fossil find.

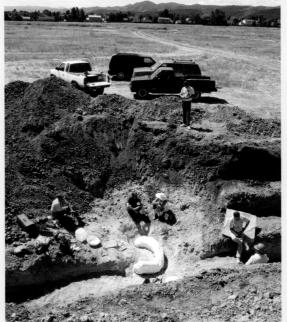

When I moved to Denver in 1990 to begin working at the Denver Museum, the city was building DIA, its completed white outline now fading in Big Blue's rearview mirror. One day in early spring, workers called the museum to report that they were finding giant fossil fish, or at least the tails of giant fish. When I rushed out to the site, I found that the fish tails were actually giant fossil palm fronds: the new airport was being built on a very old swamp! I watched helplessly as one grader buried a single frond that was 11 feet long and 7 feet wide. It was my second month on the job, and I didn't have the equipment or the chutzpah to collect the 20-ton fossil.

Two years later, the museum again received a call: a guy named Charles Fickle was walking his dog through a half-built neighborhood in the suburb of Littleton when the two of them crossed a lot that had recently been scraped clean to make way for a new home. Halfway across the lot, they found a huge bone sticking out of the ground. Fickle maintains that he saw the bone first, but I'm convinced that his dog beat him to it. Fickle ran home and got his truck, which he parked over the bone to protect it until museum staff arrived. Fickle's bone was associated with many more bones, and when the dust had settled, the museum team had excavated the entire right leg, 10 teeth, a shoulder blade, and a tail vertebra of a *Tyrannosaurus rex*. At the time, this was the 15th *T. rex* skeleton known in the world, but it was the first with its own street address.

What becomes apparent when you start to look at all these fossils is that the Rocky Mountain region has a long history, and a lot of that history is just lying around waiting to be bumped into. With that in mind, and our stomachs grumbling, Ray and I decided to stop for a bite of breakfast at the Walnut Café and contemplate the many possibilities of our trip.

A plaster-covered mammoth tusk at a construction site 10 miles south of Denver.

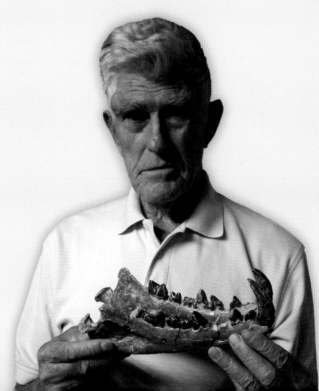

(left)
Museum volunteer John Shinton with a fossil palm from Denver International Airport.

(right)
Les Robinette, a retired wildlife biologist whose Denver basement is full of fantastic fossil jaws and skulls.

Ray was up to speed on geologic time, evolution, and extinct critters, but he had a lot to learn about other fossils, such as my beloved and much ignored plants. And when it came to rocks and geology, he was a babe in the woods. The waitress dropped off the menus as I explained to Ray, "If you want to find fossils, you've got to go where they are, you've got to understand geology. If you can understand the geometry of geology, then you're well on your way to being a successful fossil finder."

Without even cracking the menu, I decided to use pancakes to explain the idea of a geological formation. Food makes excellent geology. I once used a plate of mashed potatoes and gravy to explain plate tectonics to a table full of millionaires on a ship in Antarctica. I cut a Gondwana-shaped blob of potato into smaller pieces and pushed them away from each other with spoons. Oceans of gravy filled in between my potatoey southern continents, and soon I had created a credible polar view of Antarctica, Australia, Africa, India, and South America. Then I ate the caloric continents. The six-pack of CEOs seemed amused, and I realized that teaching geology is easy because everybody has to eat.

This is especially true for Ray. He loves his three squares. I like my meals too, but I'll often overindulge in the first round and sit out the second. But with Ray, before we even packed the truck for our trip, I knew I would be eating a regular breakfast, lunch, and dinner every day, and always in the most authentic local eatery we could find.

Giant tilted slabs of Pennsylvanian Fountain Formation at Red Rocks Amphitheatre, the best place in the world to see a concert.

By the time my stack of walnut pancakes and cup of coffee had arrived, the lesson had begun. As I told my fossil-finding partner, the key to understanding fossil-bearing rocks is to think about familiar layers. Think about stacks of pancakes, trays of lasagna, Dagwood sandwiches, and platters of baklava. Think about your undershirt, chamois shirt, sweater, and raincoat. Think about painting your bedroom with three coats of paint. Think about an Oriental rug store where the finely woven carpets are stacked in tall piles, and the one you want is always at the bottom. In all of these cases, the first coat, the first layer, the first carpet, the first pancake is the lowest one. Fossil-bearing rock comes in layers, big layers, which geologists group into formations. I like to think of a geological formation as a big stone pancake.

Formations, like pancakes, have a certain thickness and a certain lateral dimension. The walnut pancakes were about half an inch thick and nine inches in diameter. I was going to have a tough time eating this demonstration. But there is no typical formation; they range from 10 to 10,000 feet thick and are from 3 to 3,000 miles in diameter. They are rarely as round as a pancake, and they sometimes grade into each other at their edges. Like pancakes, they come in stacks, with the oldest ones at the bottom of the stack. I sliced my stack of pancakes in half with a knife and showed Ray the stack of formations. A similar thing happened when canyons were cut into the Rocky Mountains, exposing stacks of layers of rocks.

But unlike pancakes, which are uniform inside, the formations themselves are made of thinner layers. So

maybe a piece of baklava is a better analogy for a formation than a pancake. Like baklava, formations are named for the place where they were first described. Take the Chugwater Formation, first described near Chugwater Creek, Wyoming. The Chugwater Formation is about 1,000 feet thick and stretches over most of Wyoming. It's bright red and easy to distinguish from the layers above and below it. It's composed of sandstone and mudstone—rocks, by their name, that you can tell used to be sand and mud. This sediment was deposited by streams and rivers about 230 million years ago, when all of the continents were connected, forming the mother of all continents: a landmass known to geologists as Pangaea. Since it takes a flat place to make flat layers (remember, it's a flat griddle that makes a pancake flat), we surmise that the Chugwater was deposited on a flat surface. The very fact that most of the formations of the Rocky Mountains are composed of flat layers is enough to tell you that this region was primarily a flat place for much of its history. Of course, it's not flat now, so it's hard to imagine it that way.

The stack of rocky pancakes is called a geological column. That's the whole pile of layered rocks. In some places, because of uplifting mountains and the resultant tilt of the layers, it's possible to see the whole column at the surface. At other places, the surface of the Earth is the top of the stack and the rest of the pile is deeply buried. The Rocky Mountain region contains many examples of both. You can use the surface exposures to understand and predict the buried ones. The oil and gas industry has been doing just that for the last 100 years.

Now we were getting to the good part. Because different fossils are generally found in different formations, the rocks are the most important clue to understanding how to find fossils. Sitting there enjoying our third cup of coffee, Ray and I found ourselves in the middle of the Denver Basin, directly on top of nearly 12,000 feet of layered rock that geologists had grouped into 11 formations. A hole drilled straight down from the Walnut Café would penetrate all of these formations. The layer just below the building is about 50 feet thick and 12,000 years old. It's called the Cherry Creek Gravels, and it contains Ice Age fossils such as mammoths and peccaries. Just below that lies the 67-million-year-old Denver Formation, which produced the first *Triceratops* ever found. Continue drilling, and you pass through the Arapahoe, Laramie, Fox Hills, Pierre, Fort Hays, Benton, Dakota, Morrison, Lykins, and Lyons formations before reaching the bottom of the hole, where the 300-million-year-old Fountain Formation sits on top of granite. "In this café, you are literally sitting on a big piece of Earth history," I told Ray as he passed me the cream.

Ray's next question was how far down he would have to dig to find a *Stegosaurus*. It was a reasonable question, with a reasonable food analogy readily available. So I ordered a red onion from the kitchen. When it came, I sliced it in half and set one half on the table with the flat side facing up. Formations can be big, but the Earth is a lot bigger, I told Ray, so when the Earth moves, formations can be folded, flipped, or broken. The red onion was my model for the Denver Basin, a geological structure formed by a stack of formations that folded when the Earth moved and the Rocky Mountains were thrust out of the ground. Each concentric segment of the onion represented a formation. In the onion, the segments were horizontal in the center and tilted to nearly vertical at the edge.

The tilted slabs of stone along the front of the Rocky Mountains, such as Red Rocks near Denver or the Flatirons near Boulder, are like the edge of the onion. The horizontal stack of formations beneath the café is in the center of the onion. I put the tip of my fork on the middle of the flat top of the onion. "Here's the Walnut Café," I explained. "In the Rocky Mountains, if you can't see rocks, you're probably on top of them, sitting in a basin."

So the answer to the *Stegosaurus* question was simple. Ray could either dig straight down through the café floor to a depth of about 9,000 feet, or we could hop in Big Blue and drive 10 miles to the west, to the edge of the onion, where that layer poked out at the surface at a place called Dinosaur Ridge. We decided that after loading the truck, this would be our first stop.

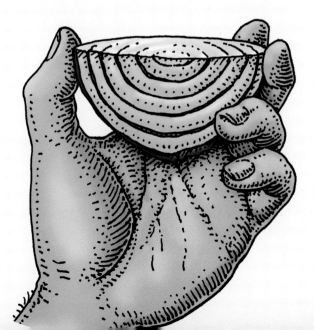

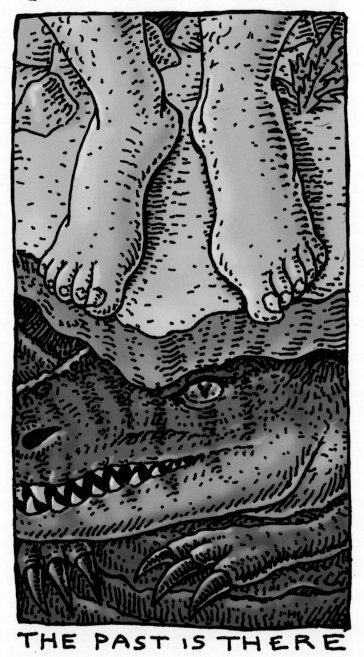

LOOK UNDER YOUR FEET

THE PAST IS THERE

2
ON THE ROAD

No matter how eager you are to leave, it's always a chore to make sure the right stuff gets into the truck. I needed hammers of all sizes, chisels and little picks, my personal pickaxe, sledgehammers, hoes, shovels, brooms, crowbars. Smaller boxes contained superglue, hand lenses, and Ziplocs. To make sure I knew where we were and where we were going, I loaded boxes of geological books, articles, and maps, GPS devices, and my Brunton compass. We packed the toolboxes of Big Blue with cardboard Coke flats, newspaper, tape, Sharpies, and dozens of rolls of restaurant-grade toilet paper (no perforations) to wrap and pack delicate fossils. Then there were lawn chairs, camping gear, propane tanks, coolers, sleeping bags, and the Troll family tent. I filled a couple of five-gallon carboys with water and then went back to my office to think about what I was forgetting. Ray wandered around the museum, looking at skeletons and getting wound up with thoughts of what it was going to be like to find one of his own. I remembered sunscreen, bandannas,

a spare hat, and the phone numbers of a bunch of people we hoped to visit. We were as ready as we'd ever be.

Fifteen minutes later we were standing next to Alameda Parkway and Ray had his hands on a *Stegosaurus* bone that was sticking out of a block of sandstone. We were only a mile from where Arthur Lakes had made his big discovery in 1877, and it was only 124 years later. The stone that encased the bone was hard as iron, a condition that by happenstance prevented vandals from chipping the bones out and hauling them away. A diligent group of interested citizens had built a little visitor's center and placed signs along the roadside on the long linear hill aptly named Dinosaur Ridge. This ridge is where the layers of the onion poke out at the surface. The western slope of the ridge exposes the 145-million-year-old Morrison Formation, and the eastern side of the ridge exposes the 105-million-year-old Dakota Group (geologically, a group is a package of associated formations). Since the layers

The famous I-70 roadcut west of Denver exposes the drab Dakota Group and the colorful Morrison Formation.

were tilted to the east and the slope of the eastern side of the hill was tilting at the same angle, the eastern side actually exposes rock that was the surface of the Earth when the Dakota Group was deposited. As we strolled down the road, we could see ripple marks and dinosaur tracks on the tilted surface. By walking only a few hundred yards, we had moved up the stack of pancakes into a younger formation, from *Stegosaurus* bones to *Iguanodon* footprints.

Layered rocks are also known as sedimentary rocks, because they began their history as unconsolidated sediment on a landscape. If the sediment is buried by more sediment (the next pancake), and if the weight of the overlying sediment is great enough, the lower layers can be compressed and cemented into stone. Later movements of the Earth can fold this stone and bring it toward the surface of the Earth, where erosion exposes it to the sky.

As we walked along, I pointed out other features in the cemented sand. We could see places where little sea creatures had burrowed into the ripples, leaving collapsed tunnels. In other spots, dents made by driftwood marred the sandy surface. Near the bottom of the hill and the top of the formation, we found layers of black shale that contained easily distinguishable fish bones and scales. It was becoming obvious to Ray that the features of the rock and the embedded fossils were clues about the nature of

this fossilized landscape. He realized, with some gentle prompting, that we were walking on a fossilized beach.

As Ray and I stood looking at our fossilized beach, I explained that depositional areas tend to be low-lying places, as Dinosaur Ridge once was, where water is standing or flowing slowly: rivers, lakes, ponds, swamps, and shallow seas. Sediment settles differently in different environments, and you can see this in the resulting sedimentary rock. The landscape is the canvas on which is painted an ever-changing panorama of ecosystems composed of an ever-changing parade of fantastic plants and animals. Subsequent landscapes bury earlier ones, and some of these beasts and broccoli become fossils.

The Dakota Group sandstone before us was once a beach at the side of a salty sea. But then the setting changed, and so did the formation: the region sank and the sea flooded the old beach, covering it with a layer of gray mud nearly 5,000 feet thick. This layer, known as the Pierre Shale, is itself covered by stark white sandstone known as the Fox Hills Formation, which deposited itself as the sea withdrew and beaches migrated across the top of the mile-thick pile of mud. The whole process only took about 20 million years, and each of those formations are chockablock full of the corpses of animals that died during that time and were buried in the mud and sand.

BEASTS AND BROCCOLI

TWO CONDITIONS ON OUR PLANET

EROSION | DEPOSITION

E WORLD | **D** WORLD

STUFF DISAPPEARS | STUFF PILES UP

It's a Very Simple Planet

I like to think that the world is composed of only two kinds of places: places where the land is eroding away and places where sediment is piling up. The first is Erosion-World (or E-World) and the second is Deposition-World (or D-World). Fossils form when corpses are buried in D-World; fossils are found when erosion exhumes them in E-World. The perfect place to find fossils is a place that was D-World for much of Earth history and then recently changed to E-World. That is the Rocky Mountain region. For most of the last 500 million years, this region was a flat, subsiding landscape that collected layer after layer of sediments and bodies. Then, about 70 million years ago, the Rocky Mountains themselves were shoved out of the ground, creating local zones of E-World on the mountaintops. The areas between the mountains received the debris that was shed from the rising mountains, and these little pockets, or basins, of D-World accumulated more sediment and more bodies. Finally, about 10 million

years ago, the whole region lifted up, and even the basins became E-World. This last burst of erosion has carved canyons and badlands, exposing 500 million years' worth of fossil-filled rocks. It would be hard to imagine a better setup for finding fossils than the history that shaped this region.

There's a close relationship between erosion and deposition, since the first creates the fodder for the second. Mountaintops suffer erosion, and rivers flowing off mountains carry sand and mud downhill and deposit them in places like New Orleans. The Big Easy should really be called D-Town. I've told my wife that I want to be buried at the mouth of the Mississippi River near New Orleans, because that's the place where I'll have the best chance of getting deeply and quickly buried by sand and mud eroded off the Rockies. It's the best place to actually become a fossil. Conversely, if you get buried in the mountains, you can kiss away your chances of ever being a decent fossil.

Ray, knowing from the interpretive signs that the sea had been a very shallow one, asked how it could accumulate a mile of mud. A good question with an interesting answer. The simple weight of sediment can cause the Earth to flex down. This flexing makes room for more sediment. That's how a 600-foot-deep sea can accumulate 5,000 feet of mud. It's like those spring-loaded plate-dispensing devices you see at cafeterias. You take a plate, and another rises into its place. When you load those things, you stick in plates one at a time, and the top of the stack stays in the same place because the increased weight of the stack of plates is pushing the whole thing down. In the same way, sediment layers can thicken, one formation can bury another, and the accumulating weight of sediments can cause the Earth to flex down. Ultimately, this is how the rock column came to be.

Ray's head was about to explode. He had come for fossils, and he was getting rocks and a long discourse on geology. But I had to make one more point. Because specific formations contain specific fossils, and because formations come in a predictable sequence, all you have to do to find the fossils you want is to pay attention to the formations. That way you know where you are in the geological column and, thus, where you are in geologic time.

Whenever I drive anywhere, I'm aware of the formation that I'm driving on, even when I can't see it. I do this by knowing where I started and paying attention to small road cuts and the direction the formations are tilting. That way, I know if I'm driving up the section into younger formations or down the section into older formations. Every once in a while, I may be lucky enough to see a great outcrop of an obvious formation, such as the bright red Chugwater Formation. This lets me check my bearings. I promised Ray that he could, at any point in the trip, ask me what kind of rock we were driving past and what type of fossil we would find if we stopped the truck. It's not that brash of a claim if you understand geology and know your formations.

Mountains Are Insignificant, Continents Wander, and Seas Come and Go

The world is really old, about 4.567 billion years. That's 4,567 million years, or 45.67 million centuries. This is a really big chunk of time. When you have a lot of time to work with, big permanent things don't seem so big or so permanent. Take mountains, for instance. Mountain ranges seem pretty big to us because they're so much bigger than we are, but we should really compare mountain ranges to the size of the globe. Then they don't seem so big. Mount Everest, the tallest mountain today, is 29,058 feet tall, or about six miles. Seems big until you realize that it's located on a continent that is almost 3,000 by 5,000 miles. In fact, if the Earth were the size of a billiard ball, it would be smoother than a billiard ball. So maybe mountains aren't that big. But how permanent are they?

We know that wind, water, and freezing and thawing cause rock to be slowly worn down over time. There are about 25 millimeters in an inch. If we assume that it takes a year to weather down one-quarter of a millimeter (one-hundredth of an inch) of rock, then it only takes 4 million years to wear down a kilometer of rock, or 6.4 million years to get rid of a mile of rock. At this rate, we could rasp Mount Everest off the face the Earth in less than 40 million years. Remember that the Earth is 4,567 million years old, more than enough time to get rid of Mount Everest a hundred times, and you begin to realize that mountain ranges can come and go. As Donovan sang,

"First there is a mountain,
then there is no mountain,
then there is."

That's important to realize, because mountains have come and gone in what we now call the Rocky Mountain region. In fact, this area has only been mountainous a couple of times in the last 400 million years. At other times, it has been as flat as a pancake. How mountains grow is a ques-

FIRST

THERE IS A MOUNTAIN

THEN

THERE IS NO MOUNTAIN

THEN

THERE IS.

tion that is still being worked on. For the moment, let's just say that mountains are pushed up by forces below. Some of these forces are related to plate tectonics, and others seem to be associated with the movement of heat within the Earth. Since mountaintops are E-World, it's often a race between how fast a mountain range is being pushed up and how fast it's being worn down.

The deepest point in all the world's oceans is about a mile and a half deeper than Mount Everest is tall, about 37,000 feet. Most of the world's oceans are much shallower than that, say 10,000 to 12,000 feet. But seas are shallow, on the order of 200 to 600 feet. Seas form when continents flex below sea level and seawater floods the continent. This situation occurs today in the North Sea, the Bering Sea, along the southeast coast of South America, and in many other spots along the edges of the world's continents. It has happened many times in the history of North America. The continent flexes down, and the sea comes ashore. Another way to drown a continent with a sea is for the volume

of the world's oceans to decrease due to volcanic eruptions on the ocean floor. Just like chucking a cinderblock into your bathtub, the water has to go somewhere, so it floods onto the continents. If the volume of the ocean basin increases, then reverse the process and the seas drain off the continent. The final obvious way that sea level changes is by the waxing and waning of the polar ice caps.

So just like that, seas and mountains come and go. I like to say that mountains are nothing and that seas are pretty undependable as well. For that matter, you can't count on continents to stay in one place for long either. For big things, continents actually move pretty fast. As I write these words, North America is headed west at nearly an inch a year. That may not sound like much, but at that rate, a million years would get North America nearly 16 miles down the road. With 4,567 million years to work with, North America could have lapped the globe three times. That is, if North America had been around that long, which it hasn't. It helps to have a pretty broad view of time to understand this stuff.

3
BONES GALORE

One of the worst things about digging fossils in Denver is driving a big field vehicle in heavy traffic. It was a stinkin' hot Friday afternoon when Ray and I pulled out of the parking lot at Dinosaur Ridge. But the slow stop-and-go start served to remind us that we were headed where people weren't. Fortunately, most roads that head east from Denver don't hold traffic for long, and soon we were sailing toward the northeast corner of Colorado on Highway 76. Our destination was a dig site seductively dubbed Bones Galore.

Bones Galore is located on the short-grass prairie, only 100 miles but a world away from bustling Denver. Though the U.S. Forest Service usually manages forests, somehow it also landed the responsibility for managing some huge swaths of the plains known as the national grasslands. It was on one of these patches that forest service staff noticed a scattering of white fossil bone emerging from the ground in an otherwise nondescript field near New Raymer, Colorado. They contacted the Denver Museum and used the lure of government grant dollars to entice Ice Age specialist Russ Graham to undertake a study of bones of animals that died more than 32 million years before the Ice Age began.

The Denver Museum has a long history of pulling bones from Colorado's upper right-hand corner. During the Depression, the museum used a team of WPA workers to excavate a quarry and retrieve the skeletons of 34-million-year-old rhinoceroses. Maybe it was the abundant free labor, maybe it was not knowing when to stop, or maybe it was good science, but between 1931 and 1933, the museum quarried the skeletons of nearly 70 rhinos. In the end, it was a good thing, since surplus skeletons

make for good trading stock. The Denver Museum was able to parlay its plethora of Colorado rhinos into a Montana duck-billed dinosaur, a Utah *Diplodocus*, and a giant fish skull from Ohio. Yet, while the excavation in the 1930s pulled a lot of skeletons from the ground, little thought was given to how they got there in the first place. That's where Russ Graham came in, albeit more than 65 years later.

Russ Graham has made a career of studying how animals die, get buried, and become fossils. For him, the Bones Galore site was close enough to the museum's old digs to suggest that he might be able to get some new information to perk up the old skeletons. As a forensic paleontologist, Russ was going to treat this fossil site like a crime scene.

After Ray and I had been driving for a few hours, we were passed by a grinning Russ, who was driving another museum truck. Rush hour had given way to the open road, and the person we were looking for had found us. We followed him to a gas station and then the next few miles toward his camp.

As we headed for the dig site, I began describing the landscape to give Ray a context for what we were seeing. The plains of northeastern Colorado are rolling grassy hills occasionally incised by deep, narrow gullies that expose the shallowly buried bedrock. The rock layer beneath this subdued landscape is the White River Group. White River rocks are indeed white, or at least a very light gray, a direct clue to their origin as airborne volcanic ash. Being from Seattle, I know what happens when volcanoes erupt. When Mount Saint Helens blew on May 18, 1980, snotty magma in the volcano's neck exploded into the sky and flash-froze into silt-sized particles of glass. This

big elephants had tusks on both their lower and upper jaws. And some, such as *Amebelodon*, had lower tusks that were flattened like shovel blades. What these shovel-tuskers did for a living is hard to say. In 1962, two workers laying an electrical line near Crawford, Nebraska, found a big bone sticking out of a bank. They took a chunk to nearby Fort Robinson, where a University of Nebraska paleontology crew was staying. The crew starting digging the site, and they identified the animal as a Colombian mammoth. They were initially confused when the skull appeared to have four tusks. Then they realized that they had found one of the most amazing fossils of all time. Instead of one mammoth, they had two bull mammoths that had died with their tusks locked together in a true fight to the finish.

Nebraska has 93 counties, and 90 of them have yielded elephant skeletons or bones. In fact, western Nebraska has so many fossil mammals that the state university has held contracts with the state highway department to salvage prehistoric skeletons that lie in the way of roads. The state museum in Lincoln has one of the finer displays of fossil mammals in the country. It features 11 different fossil elephants and an amazing 11-foot-tall camel known as *Gigantocamelus*. This humped giant weighed more than twice as much as any living camel, and it came from a 1936 discovery at a place called Lisco in Garden County. That same site produced bones from more than 70 individual skeletons: a giant herd of giant camels.

Another site in Antelope County preserves a herd of Pliocene rhinos (*Aphelops*), buried under an ashfall. The animals are so well preserved that one of the pregnant females actually has a full-term rhino fetus preserved in her rib cage. All this from a state whose population chooses to call themselves cornhuskers.

Ray had dreams of seeing the rhinos of the Ashfall site and the hall of elephants in Lincoln, but our destiny lay to the west, where we had a party to attend, so we rolled onto Interstate 80 and headed into Wyoming.

4
THIS CABIN WALKED

For me, when traveling in Wyoming, a stop at Little America is mandatory. What is for most people an elaborate truck stop–hotel–golf course combo is for me a family moment. My mom, who grew up in Wyoming, used to tell me about a sheepherder who was trapped by a blizzard west of Rock Springs in the 1890s. He prayed that if he survived, he would build an oasis for travelers on that very spot. He survived, and the original oasis opened in 1934. Now there is a chain of half a dozen overbuilt compounds where survival is no longer an issue. These are truck stops for the common man, with phones at the tables and sweet waitresses who call you "sugar" and serve up tuna sandwiches and ice cream. Whenever I'm at Little America, I honor my Wyoming survivalist heritage and call my mom to let her know that I'm okay. Ray is always good for a cup of coffee, so we grabbed a table and I had a nice chat with Mom. Then we headed up a long hill known as the Gangplank.

West of Cheyenne is the only place where erosion has not severed the connection between the Great Plains and the Rocky Mountains. The Rocky Mountains were built in several steps. First the core of each range was pushed up, folding the overlying layers and sending sheets of sediment out into the adjacent basins, partially filling them. Some of the basins filled to the brim and actually buried the ranges in their own debris. Then the whole region lifted, and erosive rivers cut deep canyons into the ranges and basins, carrying the debris out of the region and off to the drainage of the distant Mississippi River. This process scoured out the basins more rapidly than the more resistant mountains, and the mountains began to grow, this time more by the lowering of the basin floor than by the raising of the mountains. In many places in the Rockies, you can see smooth, sloping surfaces that ramp up toward the mountains. These ramps are the remains of the surfaces that existed when the basins were filled. The subsequent erosion has dissected the sloped surfaces, making tilted buttes. The result is a series of ramps that slope toward the mountains but never get there. The Gangplank is the best exception to this process. It's a place where the basin-filling slope is still intact.

Driving west on Interstate 80, which follows the Union Pacific railroad tracks, which follow the Oregon Trail, we were taking the simplest route to cross the Rockies. When we reached the top of the Laramie Range, we stopped at the Vedauwoo Campground and I unrolled the geologic map of Wyoming to continue Ray's rolling Geology 101 class. It was really important to me that my artist friend comprehend the geometry of geology.

Geologic maps look like you would need an artist to interpret them. Swirls and splotches of color overlay the familiar landscape. The patterns are the result of history, the culmination of D-World and E-World repeated again and again, with a bunch of other stuff mixed in.

The critical piece to understanding a geologic map is that each color is keyed to a distinct group of rocks exposed at the surface. Sometimes these rocks are the result of deposition and are layered. Other times the rocks are cooled lava that splatted out of a volcano, and they lie on the landscape like seagull poop on a pier. Faults break and move rocks; forces fold and deform rocks; new sediments bury old rocks; and recent erosion slices away overlying rocks to expose older ones. All of these processes live on the colored surface of a two-dimensional geologic map. Wyoming's was compiled by David Love, the geologist who is the central figure in John McPhee's book *Rising from the Plains*. The title of the book is a double entendre. The Rockies appear to rise from the plains and they literally rose from the plains. Since the individual ranges of the Rockies are oriented in a variety of directions and because they pushed up through thick overlaying piles of sedimentary rocks, Dave Love likened the formation of the Rockies to so many pigs waking up under a blanket.

Dave compiled the Wyoming map in 1950 and revised it in 1980. It's a phenomenal piece of work, and, with it, any trip to Wyoming is so much better because every hill, road cut, or distant vista starts to make sense. The details of the mountains, the basins, and the geologic formations are on the same sheet as the roads, towns, and rivers. The map really is a paleontological treasure map.

1. PIG SNOOZING UNDER A PALEOZOIC AND MESOZOIC BLANKET.

2. PIG WAKES UP AND STANDS... BREAKING THE BLANKET

3. BLANKET ERODES AWAY AND FILLS ADJACENT BASINS WITH REMAINS OF BLANKET.

But after a while, I could see that Ray's interest was waning, so I put the map away and we rolled down the vast slope of the Laramie Range and into Laramie, a town locked in time.

The University of Wyoming is a venerable institution, founded in 1886. My Uncle Leroy was a vaunted running back for the Wyoming Cowboys back in 1950, and the place doesn't look like much has happened since then. But that certainly doesn't mean it's not worth visiting. A one-room geology museum on campus has some of the greatest fossils from Wyoming. Laramie is not far from some of the best dinosaur country in the world, and the room is dominated by the skeleton of a monstrously huge *Apatosaurus*, one of the bulkiest of the long-necked dinosaurs to ever flatten a landscape. The museum is a one-man show, run by the extremely blonde Brent Breithaupt, who curates, tours, talks, and performs all of the museum functions. If you can get it, a tour of Brent's office provides a great example of how sediment accumulates. His desk was long ago buried in papers and books, and now all you see is a haystack of printed debris in the middle of the office. Sure enough, in keeping with the principles of basic geology, the youngest layers are on top.

The Denver Museum had borrowed a six-foot fossil garfish from Laramie for the *Cruisin' the Fossil Freeway* exhibit, and Ray had done a splendid job of painting the wooden museum case that held the giant fish. Ray was keen to see how Brent displayed the gar on its home field, and we also wanted to check in on the Laramie *Apatosaurus*, the biggest dinosaur in the smallest museum around. It was not to be. Brent had organized a *T. rex* run the day we arrived, so the museum was shuttered. We paused briefly to stock up on beer and beans and then headed north out of town toward Medicine Bow. We were determined to attend a party in the middle of nowhere, known as Dinopalooza.

About 40 miles out of Laramie, Highway 30 arcs around to the west and a rounded high hill fills the skyline. This is Como Bluff, the first true American dinosaur Shangri-la.

Dinosaur discoveries near Morrison, Colorado, in March 1877 had shown the Morrison Formation to be rich in bones, but the rock was hard as steel and the digging was extremely difficult and slow going. Later that year, a bored Union Pacific railroad employee realized that the mysterious loglike rocks on Como Bluff were actually ancient bones, and he contacted Yale paleontologist O. C. Marsh, who hired the man and immediately sent some others. At Como, the rock was soft and there was little overburden. Bones began to pour out. The spectacular *Apatosaurus* in the great hall of dinosaurs at the Yale Peabody Museum came from this hill, as did dozens of others. The rush for big dinosaurs was on, and it didn't abate until the 1930s.

In 1898, a group from the American Museum of Natural History led by Henry Fairfield Osborn, an imperious American aristocrat, and the impeccably dressed Barnum Brown, was prospecting for bones near Como Bluff. They stopped to ask directions from a lonely sheepherder who lived in a stone house on the desolate windblasted land to the north of Medicine Bow. The sheepherder didn't have any information, but then the bone diggers realized that the stone house was actually a bone house. So numerous were the bones that the sheepherder had inadvertently built his home out of chunks of fossilized dinosaur. The resulting Bone Cabin Quarry was excavated for the next decade and yielded tons of dinosaur bones, including the mighty *Apatosaurus* that was mounted by Osborn's men at the American Museum in 1905. This was the first sauropod dinosaur to be publicly exhibited, and the world took notice.

In November 1898, news of the American Museum discoveries at Bone Cabin Quarry caught the eye of steel magnate Andrew Carnegie. Reading the morning newspaper in his Manhattan mansion, he noticed a headline that proclaimed "Most colossal animal ever on Earth just found out West." He couldn't imagine not owning the biggest dinosaur in the world, so he penned a note to W. J. Holland, the director of the fledgling Carnegie Museum, with the famous line "Buy this for Pittsburgh." The $10,000 check that accompanied the note launched the Carnegie Museum dinosaur program. Holland's field men soon found a skeleton at Sheep Creek, Wyoming, that they named *Diplodocus carnegii*. Andrew was a proud man, and when the king of England requested a cast of the animal for the British Museum, Carnegie was more than happy to send an example of an American dinosaur bigger and better than anything found in old Europe. He got so much acclaim for this act that soon museums in Paris, Rome, Madrid, and La Plata sported their own plaster casts of Carnegie's *Diplodocus*.

The *Apatosaurus* at Laramie was collected in 1901 by the Carnegie Museum, repatriated to Wyoming in 1956, and installed in the University of Wyoming museum between 1959 and 1961. Repatriation is a sentiment that still has traction in Wyoming, where "Keep 'em in Wyoming" bumper stickers can be seen decorating the trucks of local bone diggers.

By the time Osborn retired from the American Museum in 1930, the blush was off the rose of American paleontology. The Great Depression depleted field budgets, and other types of science were on the rise. The first big bone rush was over.

Today, Como Bluff is the lair of America's best-known and most notorious paleontologist, Dr. Bob Bakker.

Bob was an undergraduate at Yale in 1968 when John Ostrom discovered a startling little dinosaur named *Deinonychus* near Bridger, Montana. The anatomy of the wolflike *Deinonychus* and a careful examination of the few specimens of the half-bird, half-dinosaur from Bavaria known as *Archaeopteryx* led Ostrom to reopen the discussion about the nature of dinosaur metabolism and the relationship between birds and dinosaurs. Ostrom was a meticulous and insightful anatomist. Bakker, clever and charismatic, was a quick study and a splendid artist who penned insightful and convincing drawings of dinosaur anatomy. With Bakker's art and vivid imagination and Ostrom's rock-solid anatomy, the two leveraged the rebirth of dinosaurs. What the Depression, World War II, the Manhattan Project, and the GI Bill had taken away by thoroughly distracting most everyone from paleontology, Bakker and Ostrom gave back. By the 1980s, the Dinosaur Renaissance was underway, and more than just children were paying attention to dinosaurs once again. Bakker's big book, *The Dinosaur Heresies*, published in 1986, is a beautiful, blustery tome that makes paleontology really fun and interesting. Ideas from this book found their way into Michael Crichton's *Jurassic Park*, which was a major best seller in 1990. Bakker started to challenge Stephen J. Gould as the world's best-known paleontologist.

Bob's ideas hit Hollywood in 1993 with the debut of the movie *Jurassic Park*, but Bob wasn't there with them. Steven Spielberg had tapped Montana dinosaur digger Jack Horner, not Bakker, to be the main adviser for the film. In the *Jurassic Park* sequel, *The Lost World* (1997), fatal injury was added to insult when a bearded Bakker-like character was eaten by a *T. rex*.

The real (and uneaten) Bakker always wears his signature outfit: an absolutely battered straw hat, a tan field vest, and a long-sleeved field shirt. The hat is the

BAKKER'S CLOSET

Flashdance sweatshirt of headgear, held together by tiny filaments in danger of disintegration at the slightest breeze. There can't be just one. He must have a room full of them, carefully crushed and tortured to achieve that casually mangled look. The more Ray and I thought about this, the more we started to wonder what Bakker's closet looks like.

Ray was eager to meet the great man, but there was a place we had to visit first. Walter Boylan, a roadside entrepreneur with an eye to making a quick buck, built a facsimile of the Bone Cabin in 1933 on the road south of Como Bluff. And it sits there today: a small building made almost exclusively of dinosaur bones. The place has definitely seen better days. The dream of easy money now an afterthought, some windows are broken and not a lot of attention has been paid to the place's retail potential. A water-stained card stuck in one of the windows reads "Two hundred million years ago, this cabin walked." We stopped, and for the first time in my memory, there was someone there.

Apparently the owners are looking to sell, but in the meantime, they let a laconic rock-picking cowboy named Mike Lewis run the place. Mike looked every inch the quintessential Wyoming cowboy, except for his pair of sandals. It's a challenge to run a place that used to walk, but Mike had some modest plans. Scattered around the bone cabin and adjacent house was a panoply of premium dinosaur artifacts: rusty metal *Brontosaurus* signs, *Stegosaurus* humerus doorstops, and cannonball concretions from nearby marine layers. Ray kept urging me to make an offer to Mike for the metal *Brontosaurus* sign. It felt like offering to buy the fireplace at Old Faithful Inn, and I just couldn't bring myself to do it. Mike told us of his plans to give the sign a fresh coat of paint, and that didn't sound so good either. We left, trusting the fate of the roadside attraction to natural processes, and drove into Medicine Bow.

There are places where time has stood still, and there are places where it's definitely losing ground. Medicine Bow, Wyoming, is clearly of the latter group. In 1885, Owen Wister, an East Coast dandy, rode west on the Union Pacific, saw the narrative potential of the place, and penned the first Western novel here. *The Virginian*, first published in 1902, spawned a genre that washed over into television and film and made John Wayne and Louis L'Amour some of the biggest names of my childhood. That wave has passed, but the Virginian Hotel, built in 1911, still stands in Medicine Bow, and it feels like Owen Wister just checked out. It is in this venerable establishment that Bakker often holds court.

Evening was approaching and the sky was beginning to darken ominously. Realizing that Dinopalooza wasn't going to be a Woodstock-size event, Ray began prodding, "How about a hotel, comfortable beds, and a big chicken-fried steak?" But I knew what he didn't, or at least thought I did, and we rolled north into the waning day and worsening sky. We had good instructions, and after a few miles of gravel we rolled into Dinopalooza. And there was Bakker, half-crammed into his beaten Toyota, fully garbed in his battered hat, and completely surrounded by the paleopaparazzi. The arrival of Big Blue caused a stir in the crowd of 30 or so. Ray hopped out and joined the crowd around the Toyota to stand in line to shake hands with the Dinosaur Renaissance man.

(left)
Mike Lewis, caretaker of the Bone Cabin, flanked by dinosaur bones at an adjacent building.

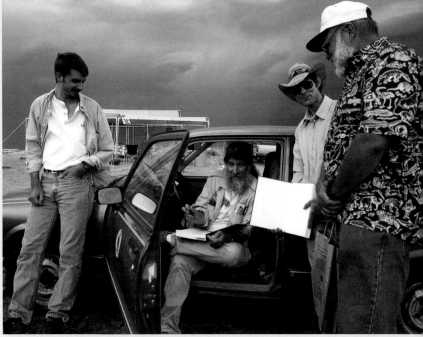

Dinopalooza is the brainchild of two guys who are living out their childhood dream of hunting dinosaurs. Chris Weege and Dave Schumde are Denver oilmen, each in their early 40s. Both are lanky, lean men, comfortable and smooth at the Petroleum Club, and, at first glance, not a bit nerdy. Using their ample geologic acumen and the curious American fact that if you own the land, you own the dinosaurs, Chris and Dave have leased their very

Bob Bakker surrounded by paleopaparazzi at Dinopalooza.

own dinosaur quarry. That's right, two boys and their very own dinosaur excavation. Chris literally has an *Allosaurus* in his garage. When I, as a museum guy, ask him what he's going to do with it, he just smiles and says he's still thinking about it.

One thing was sure: Chris and Dave know how to throw a good party in the middle of nowhere. Rock-n-Roll Ray, the childhood dinosaur nerd, was in heaven. Your own private dinosaurs *and* live music. Despite the gathering black clouds and what appeared to be a brewing tornado, the band, including at least one mandolin-toting paleontologist, was setting up. Chris showed us his quarry, from which he has extracted parts of a *Stegosaurus* and an *Allosaurus*. He described the plate-backed *Stegosaurus* as stubbier than usual and the *Allosaurus* as one of the oldest known. We scavenged some hotdogs from a thinly populated grill as the wind started to howl. The band started, the rain started, the wind and rain got really serious, the band stopped. Then the rain stopped and the band came back. But it stayed cold and wet. Given the state of the roads after the only serious rain of the year, there really was no place to go,

Dave Schmude and Chris Weege at Dinopalooza.

so the party went on. Dave's little brother, Doug, played some mean slide guitar, and a weird paleobluegrass riff got going. These guys were singing about fossils. "May the belemnite be unbroken, May the ammonite be exalted." Ray happily swilled some red wine he'd picked up in Denver, swaying gently in the gusts. Then a drunken group of partyers led by Chris and Dave lit a *Brontosaurus*-shaped panel of fireworks and the party continued. Late in the night, Chris and Dave told us about another claim they had staked in northern Wyoming, a site rich in fossil fish where they had found and reburied the body of a Jurassic ichthyosaur. This sounded like many of the lost-treasure stories that fueled my childhood lust for discoveries, but in this case, the guys were able to give us precise GPS coordinates so we could find the site for ourselves. Thinking about warm Jurassic seas, we unfurled the Troll family tent and crashed, hungry, cold, and wet, but strangely happy amongst this remote band of fossil fanciers.

We awoke with medium-size hangovers and huge hungers. We had stocked no real food in Laramie, so we were destined for breakfast back in town at the Virginian. Ray had elicited a sketchy promise from Bakker that he would join us for an omelet, so we rolled up the soggy tent and slid the muddy roads back to Medicine Bow. We spotted Bakker just pulling out as we pulled in, and Ray's breakfast with Bob turned into the diminishing north end of a southbound Toyota.

Fortunately, we had a plan B and had arranged to meet our friend Gary Staab and his pal Kent Hups in Medicine Bow and go hunting for ammonites by smashing them from giant concretions. Gary, one of the best paleoartists around, is an old friend of ours, but we had never met Kent. He turned out to be one of those highly focused and utterly driven finders of fossils. Gary and Kent had driven up from Denver joking about hunting squid, since ammonites are extinct

(right)
A trio of Morrison Formation killers (left to right): *Allosaurus*, *Ceratosaurus*, and the giant claws of a *Torvosaurus*.

42

shelled relatives of today's tasty calamari. We got our breakfast and headed out for the tiny town of Rock River, where, among other things, there's a fine mural of a not-too-luscious cowgirl riding a giant pink *Apatosaurus*.

Bashing concretions is about my favorite thing in the world. You get to wander around with as big a sledge-hammer as you can carry and smash open round balls of case-hardened mudstone that, every once in a while, will have a splendid fossil on board. This gets addicting fast, but it's also exhausting and dangerous. When I was a kid whacking concretions on West Coast beaches, I quickly learned that if you hit a concretion with a glancing blow, you have a pretty good chance of creating a deadly projectile. My shins still bear the scars. And if the concretion breaks, the flying shards can take on shrapnel-like properties that make even the most casual digger really think hard about the idea of safety goggles.

Kent and Gary had found a superb spot where giant nodules were eroding out of a ridgetop. These were basketball-size numbers, and most sledgehammers aren't up to that gauge of rock. I had a 12-pounder that just kept bouncing off the case-hardened concretions. But one of the things you learn is that rock gets tired. Hit it enough, and it'll break. Kent and Gary were whackos, literally. They just kept whacking on the rocks, and in not too

Gary Staab and Kent Hups, the squid hunters, and a *Placenticeras*.

long, we had accumulated some splendid ammonites and inoceramid clams, the shiny, ribbed oysters often found with ammonites. As a museum guy, I know that the most common kind of mistaken identifications are meteorites and dinosaur eggs. It must be once a week that somebody comes to the museum fully convinced that they have found one or the other. Round rocks are mistaken for eggs, and heavy or rusty rocks get called meteorites. Concretions, because of their amazing roundness, sometimes get picked for either. Both the roundness and hardness are artifacts of their formation. Most common in the drab gray shale that formed as mud at the bottom of Cretaceous seas, concretions appear to have formed rapidly, probably the result of a chemical reaction between a dead critter and the surrounding mud. A concretion didn't form around every dead body, nor do all concretions contain fossils, but there seems to be a connection nonetheless. It's possible to find fossils in shale that are crushed flat as cardboard, while those in concretions are perfectly three-dimensional and uncrushed. This observation argues that the rock balls hardened before much weight from overlying mud bore down on them. Recently, some marine geologists at Yale have found concretions forming around recently deceased crabs and clams in Long Island Sound. It's a useful natural process, and it's responsible for a lot of cool fossils.

Ammonites are nothing more than extinct shelled marine animals related to squid, octopi, and nautili, but they have a certain something that makes them very desirable. It's hard to explain our lust for ammonites. Like trilobites, ammonites are icons of extinction. So many kinds lived on Earth, and now none do. Ammonites are exquisite objects, coiled shells imbued with the sublime symmetrical essence of the Golden Mean. Ammonites are the shells that she sold by the seashore, she being Mary Anning of Lyme Regis, an English coastal town near sea cliffs made up of Jurassic marine shale loaded with gorgeous ammonites. Many of the ammonites from concretions still wear their iridescent and pearly shell. If the shell has broken away, the walls of its chambers trace an incredibly delicate dendritic pattern that, once seen, can never be forgotten.

Not all ammonites are smoothly coiled. Deviant species, known as heteromorphs, come in shapes ranging from the *G*-shaped *Scaphites* to the cyclindrical *Baculites* to the twisted saxophone–shaped *Didymoceras.* As we smashed the concretions, we were finding pieces of all of these types.

Hauling smashed concretions is a real chore, and it makes you very selective about the fossils you carry home. Kent had found a nearly perfect *Placenticeras,* a smooth, discus-shaped ammonite, and was happy as a clam. Ray and I had found half a dozen partial heteromorph ammonites and were likewise happy. Kent and Gary had to get back to Denver and Ray and I had to head north, so we parted ways. Like hard-core fishermen who always have to make just one more cast, or blue hairs who can't pull themselves away from the slot machines, none of us wanted to stop collecting ammonites.

Ray was tight on cash, and another night in the soggy Troll family tent wasn't an inviting thought, so I called my cousin Lisa in Casper and made arrangements to use her basement floor. After passing back through Medicine Bow and heading north, we drove by the Freeze-out Hills to the northwest and rolled into the broad and barren Shirley Basin. This is big, flat country, where cars come along very rarely and pronghorns are everywhere. The long spine of the Laramie Range makes the east wall of the basin, and the Early Eocene Wind River Formation makes its floor. Here and there are petrified logs, remains of the subtropical forests that used to grow here. For much of the '50s and '60s, this area saw strip-mining for uranium, and the not-so-subtle scars of reclamation are still visible. Lying above the Wind River Formation are the bright white beds of the White River Group, that familiar Late Eocene fossil paradise we saw in northeast Colorado. Forty miles north of Medicine Bow, the flats of the Shirley Basin end at an escarpment, the lip of a huge mud-floored hole named after a guy called Bates.

Bates Hole is central to my family's history. Herbert

Pearce, my mother's father, was born on the Salisbury Plain in the south of England in 1879. At the age of 12, he took a job to transport some horses to Rawlins, Wyoming. When he got back to England, he encountered the man who had hired him and greeted him like a friend. Bound by age-old class boundaries, my grandfather's employer refused to acknowledge him. Bert Pearce had seen the freedom of the open range, and this event made him realize that he couldn't stay in England. He returned to Wyoming the next year. By the time he was 28, he was working for the Freeland Livestock Company, which owned a big piece of Bates Hole. As the old family story is told, the owners let Bert in as a partner on credit, certain that he would never prove up. But since it's my family, the story ended well, and a Casper doctor came through with a loan that allowed Bert to buy his own ranch in 1908.

Cracking giant Milk Duds in search of ammonites.

(right)
Dreams of
Didymoceras.

The place was rough, stretching from the muddy gullies in the floor of the hole to the slot-canyon granite of the Laramie Range. My mother grew up on a ranch they called Headquarters and lived a childhood full of stories of odd old Basque sheepherders drinking vanilla extract for a cheap high and corralling wild mustangs. Her three brothers were wild ones, lowering themselves by rope into ice caves and racing each other backward in jalopies down dirt roads. Bert sold the ranch in 1948, the year my mom left for California, college, and a new life. When I was a kid, my old spinster aunt lived in the giant family house in Casper, and we would drive east from Seattle so we could "go out West." The house on Beech Street was an amazing warren full of treasures from a half-century of ranch life in Wyoming. I used to pore over cigar boxes full of arrowheads, polished pieces of Wyoming jade, and fragments of fossil teeth. Uncle Sid, an insurance salesman and my mother's brother, was great for stories about the old days on the ranch and the stuff they used to find, but he had become a townie, and I could never convince him to take me fossil hunting on the old place. I dreamt of finding my own treasures.

Casper, nonetheless, was a place of discoveries waiting to be made. My aunt introduced me to neighbors who collected rocks and to old codgers who were kind and generous with their collections. On a weekend drive to the top of Casper Mountain when I was five, I wandered away from the picnic and starting poking around a big white boulder. I found a sugar-cube-size chunk of rock with the impression of what I now know to be a brachiopod. At the age of five, I was convinced that I had discovered a fossil rattlesnake tail. It was my first big find.

Uncle Sid really annoyed me by telling me about a fist-size dinosaur tooth that he'd found near Headquarters in the '40s. If he still had it, he'd have given it to me. The part that nicked me was that he had given the tooth to a young geologist, and, worse still, he had forgotten his name. No matter how hard I pressed, Sid simply couldn't remember who got what I came to call "my tooth." It wasn't until 1991, a few years after John McPhee had published *Rising from the Plains*, his sublime book about Wyoming geology and Wyoming's premier geologist, David Love, that the mystery was solved. When I told my mom about this new book, she exclaimed, "That's him, that's the guy who has your tooth!"

I had just moved to Denver at the time and immediately got into my car and drove the hundred miles to Laramie, where I stormed into Dave Love's office, demanding my tooth back. The man had a mind like a steel trap. He remembered my uncle, told me some ribald stories about my aunt, and started hunting around in the collections for the tooth. Curation at the University of Wyoming wasn't as efficient as Dave's memory, so we never found it, but the encounter started a great friendship. As Dave pointed out, the geology of Bates Hole is such that the tooth likely didn't belong to a dinosaur. Bates Hole consists of Late Cretaceous marine rocks overlain by Early Eocene rocks overlain by late Eocene rocks, none of which would contain dinosaurs.

While we visited, Dave regaled me with stories of some old German homesteaders in Bates Hole who claimed to have found lots of "tushes" near their cabin. Dave surmised that they meant "tusks" and dispatched a University of Wyoming paleontologist to check out the site. The "tushes" turned out to be the six-inch-long teeth of the Early Eocene hippolike beast known as *Coryphodon*. From Sid's description and Dave's memory, it was more likely that my tooth fell out of the jaw of a Late Eocene titanothere, one of those great knob-nosed contemporaries of the killer pigs. In a later visit to the present owners of the ranch, I laid the family mystery to rest when I saw a toothy titanothere skull sticking out of the side of a hill.

Ray and I talked about my family as the sun set and Big Blue rolled through Bates Hole. Bates Creek, which drains the giant valley, is a tiny ephemeral creek that hardly seems up to the task of such a prodigious excavation, but Wyoming is full of stark and confusing topography. It's a state with some serious history. We stopped for a cup of coffee and to discuss politics with the present owners of Headquarters, then rolled into Casper long after dark.

THE GREAT TURTLE

6
DINOSAUR TRACKS AT 65 MPH

The day that dawned was a huge improvement over the previous night. It was one of those High Plains sparklers with a dark blue sky, not a cloud above, and no hint of too much heat. The road from Edgemont climbs up a long pine-topped ridge and into the Black Hills of South Dakota. The Hills are magical, thick stands of lodgepole pine giving way here and there to open parklands of tall grass. Formed in the classic Rocky Mountain style when a giant area of buried granite was pushed up through a two-mile-thick slab of Paleozoic and Mesozoic–layered rocks, the uplift makes one of the more spectacular geologic bull's-eyes in the Rocky Mountain region. With giant concentric rings of geologic formations, each ring of rock younger than the one inside it, the Black Hills Uplift is what geologists call a breached dome. It was just another place where one of Dave Love's pigs had woken up under a blanket of formations.

The granite core of the Black Hills has been irresistible to the makers of massive monuments, with Mount Rushmore as the first huge effort and the endlessly ongoing Crazy Horse as a second helping. Both of these monuments were the obsessions of individual white men who ended up donating their lives to the projects. Every time I see these giant granite carvings, I can't help but think of the Sioux people who successfully bartered with the U.S. government in 1868 so they could keep the Black Hills while allowing settlers to pass around them peacefully. George Custer's arrogant Black Hills expedition of 1874 was the first step toward the demolition of this agreement, and the fact that his prospectors found gold sealed the deal. I don't know what it feels like to be Sioux, but I can only imagine that these giant rock carvings cause a lot of Lakota stomach acid.

We'd left Edgemont without so much as even a cup of coffee, the memory of the bad meal driving us quickly out of town. Highway 18 heads north up the ramping flank of the Black Hills toward Minnekahta Junction. This is the site of one of paleobotany's greatest failures. In 1892, a guy named F. H. Cole from the town of Hot Springs discovered an amazing deposit of fossil cycadeoids just south of Minnekahta. Cycadeoids, better known as bennettites, are often incorrectly called cycads, because they have similar trunks and fronds, and are some of the most charismatic of all fossil plants. Big petrified trunks the size of fireplugs, they're often used in paintings of dinosaurian landscapes. In fact, it's rare to find a dinosaur painting that doesn't have one these overgrown pineapple–shaped plants somewhere. Their surface is patterned with diamond-shaped pits that are the remains of leaf bases, and embedded in the leaf bases are the remains of reproductive structures that are pretty close to being true flowers.

The Minnekahta cycadeoids were petrified and agatized, which allowed them to be sliced open to expose perfect anatomy. One of Marsh's field men, George Wieland, got so excited by this anatomy that he devoted his life to studying it and eventually published the giant two-volume *American Fossil Cycads,* the first volume in 1906, the second in 1916 (at that time, cycadeoids were still called cycads). The Minnekahta site was so rich that Wieland made plans for a fossil plant visitor center and, using his Yale connections, was able to influence the National Park Service to protect the site. In 1922, President Warren G. Harding dedicated a 320-acre patch of land just south of Minnekahta as Cycad National Monument.

Driving into town, Ray and I didn't see any signs for the national monument, the reason being that it's the only national monument to have ever been decommissioned. It's not clear whether it was rampant collecting (and Wieland did move hundreds of the fossil trunks back to New Haven) or simply a lack of anything to see, but in 1957, four years after Wieland's death, Cycad lost its national monument status. So much for the glory of paleobotany.

Digesting this sad tale did little for our growing hunger, so our first stop in Hot Springs was a local café that sported some very serious biscuits and gravy. We more than made up for the lost steaks of Lusk, slurped several cups of coffee, and talked about the Hot Springs mammoth site.

Located at the edge of town and looking for all the world like a giant gymnasium, the mammoth site is really worth a long drive to see. In 1974, an alert construction worker was moving earth when his backhoe hit a chunk of what turned out to be mammoth bone. There are two types of heavy-equipment operators in this world: those who care about what they are digging through and those who don't. Fortunately for the Hot Springs tourist industry, this guy was of the former persuasion. Now Hot Springs is more famous for its mammoths than it is for its hot springs.

The discovery site was on the top of a hill at the edge of town. The rock beneath Hot Springs is the soft red Triassic Spearfish Shale, but that rock is underlain by a layer of limestone that dissolves away to make

underground caves. Around 26,000 years ago, an underground depression collapsed, forming a 60-foot-deep hole in the slimy Spearfish Shale. The hole filled with water to become a lake, but it was a dangerous lake due to its slick and vertical shoreline. Then the fun began. One after another, dozens of mammoths let their curiosity override their caution and found themselves treading water. I don't know how long a mammoth can tread water, but I can tell you that it wasn't long enough, and one by one they drowned. Eventually, the lake silted up and filled the depression. And some 25,000 years later, a town was founded on the spot.

After the backhoe driver found the bones, word of the discovery made it to mammothologist Larry Agenbroad, who went to work with the town fathers to preserve and study the site. Now it's a bustling building full of tourists and eager interpreters. More than 100,000 people visit the site each year. After more than three decades, Agenbroad still shows up for work, now with teams of Earthwatch volunteers, to excavate more of the unfortunate mammoths. When Ray and I visited, more than 2,000 bones had been retrieved and the body count was up to 49 Colombian mammoths and three woolly mammoths, not to mention a smattering of wolves, coyotes, camels, and 22 other species of mammals that couldn't tread water forever.

We were amused to learn that most of the mammoth skeletons were young males.

commercial fossil operation in the country. Collectively, and with a tip of the hat to the Old West, Pete, Neal, and Bob are called the "Black Hills boys" or often simply "the boys." I've known Pete since 1982 and have shared a love of the Hell Creek Formation and the last days of the dinosaurs with him. Pete was born on the Rosebud Reservation and grew up collecting Fox Hills ammonites and the bones of sheeplike oreodonts from the White River badlands. When he was eight, he opened a fossil museum in a shed in his backyard. In eighth grade, he won the state science fair with a fossil exhibit. He went to college at SDSM and then started a fossil and mineral business with his buddy Jim Honert. Pete's big dream is to build a huge fossil museum in the Black Hills.

The Black Hills Institute grew on the backs of ammonites, but things got interesting when Pete got serious about dinosaurs. Pete found out about a bone bed near Faith, South Dakota, and soon leased the rights to dig the site, naming the quarry after the old ranch woman that owned the property. The Ruth Mason Quarry is a two-foot-thick layer of mudstone that's chocka-block full of hadrosaur, or duckbilled dinosaur, bones. Pete mined them, collecting thousands. From his inventory, he began to assemble skeletons and sold them to museums around the world. Initially, the price for a delivered and assembled *Edmontosaurus* was around 300 grand. Not bad, when you consider all the work that went into excavating and assembling it and the fact that you

were getting a real dinosaur.

On August 12, 1990, Pete and his crew were digging duckbills at the Ruth Mason Quarry. Pete's girlfriend at the time, Sue Hendrickson, decided to take a break from the tedious work of digging duckbilled dinosaurs with an X-Acto knife and took a stroll across the prairie to a distant clump of badlands. When she got to the muddy bluffs, she was confronted with the comfortable sight of a string of dinosaur vertebrae sticking out of the hill. There was something unusual about these bones, and she ran back to get Pete.

The dinosaur was a *Tyrannosaurus rex*, and it was a really nice one. Pete wrote a check for $5,000 to Maurice Williams, the landowner, and the boys dug like hell to remove the nearly complete skeleton from the ground in less than three weeks.

Once they got the skeleton back to Hill City and started chipping rock off of bone, they realized that they had a world-class find. Their lifelong plan to build their own natural history museum suddenly began to have some real potential.

But events didn't unfold as Pete had planned. A disgruntled acquaintance of Pete's contacted Williams and suggested that he had been ripped off. Williams was part Sioux and his ranch was within the bounds of the reservation, so the tribe began to take notice. Meanwhile, Vince Santucci, a paleontologist with a law enforcement degree who was

Peter Larson in the jaws of *Acrocanthosaurus*.

working for Badlands National Park, also got interested in the reservation rex. Vince was worried about the illegal collection of fossils from national park and Indian land and was suspicious about the activities of the Black Hills boys. It didn't help that a giant turtle from the reservation had ended up in Austria. With the landowner, the tribe, and the feds stirred up, a lot of different agendas started to crowd in on the simple concept of a natural history museum in Hill City, and a swarm of lawyers started getting paid to think about the legalities of dinosaur ownership.

On May 8, 1992, I visited the Black Hills Institute with my friend Wes Wehr to see what they were up to. They had just finished preparing the right side of the skull of the *T. rex* that they had named Sue and were preparing to ship it to Georgia for a CAT-scan. I photographed Wes next to the awesome five-foot-long head, and we headed back to Denver. Five days later, operating with a warrant from the state attorney of South Dakota, the FBI arrived in Hill City and seized Sue. They also seized other fossils and the business records of the Black Hills Institute. The city rallied in protest, but to no avail. The skeleton was plastered, crated, and hauled down the hill to a storage room on SDSM campus.

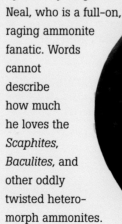

Wes Wehr and the skull of *T. rex* Sue.

More lawyers got involved. Eventually, the government ruled that the original sale had not been valid and that the dinosaur should be auctioned to the highest bidder, with the proceeds going to Maurice Williams. Based on the records seized at the institute, a 39-count indictment was placed on Pete, Neal, and Bob. Most were dropped, but the jury convicted Pete of failing to declare travelers' checks in excess of $10,000 when returning from Japan and sentenced him to two years in the minimum-security prison in Florence, Colorado.

(right)
Neal Larson being attacked by a *Placenticeras.*

Pete served 18 months and was released to a halfway house in Rapid City to serve the remaining six. I visited him in Florence when he was in month 12, and we spent a melancholy afternoon talking about *Triceratops*. It was a really sad situation. Even more so when the excavation of Sue wasn't even part of the conviction: her excavation itself had not been illegal. The feds had ruled that Williams, as an Indian with some of his land held in federal trust to avoid property tax, was not allowed to sell any of his property, land, or dinosaurs without prior approval. Williams claimed that the $5,000 check from Pete labeled "for theropod Sue" was not a sale anyway, just a fee to prospect.

Meanwhile, Sue was scheduled for auction in New York. I visited Sotheby's a few weeks before the big day and wandered through a warehouse full of antique furniture to inspect the plastered skeleton. On October 4, 1997, Sue went on auction, and 90 seconds later she was sold to the Field Museum in Chicago for $7.34 million ($8.36 million with the commission). The Field had arranged financial backing from Disney, McDonald's, and a number of other supporters. The dinosaur went to Chicago and was unveiled in Stanley Hall at the Field Museum on May 17, 2000, before mesmerized crowds. Pete, living in a halfway house in Rapid City, missed the opening.

The next morning, after a hearty breakfast, Ray and I wandered over to the institute for a tour. We were greeted by Pete's younger brother, Neal, who is a full-on, raging ammonite fanatic. Words cannot describe how much he loves the *Scaphites*, *Baculites*, and other oddly twisted heteromorph ammonites.

AMMONITES, TRILOBITES, AND ARROWHEADS

If you start talking to Neal about anything, you'll soon be talking with Neal about ammonites. Ray and I like ammonites; I'd even say we love ammonites. They're part of the holy trinity—ammonites, trilobites, and arrowheads—that shaped my adolescent fantasies of discovery. But if you want an overdose of ammonites, go to Neal.

In the last couple of years, Neal has sat at the feet of Bill Cobban and begun to learn the real science of ammonites. Cobban, a 90-year-old USGS paleontologist in Denver, is the reigning Zen master of ammonites. A thin slip of a man, Cobban has a flawlessly photographic memory. He can remember, with precision, sites that he collected at 60 years ago. Since the Pierre Shale is widely exposed over the Great Plains from New Mexico to Canada, Bill has collected hundreds of thousands of ammonites from nearly 14,000 localities. Neal would like to collect millions of ammonites, and he's well on his way. Neal regaled us with tales of *Solenoceras*, *Placenticeras*, *Spiroxybeloceras*, and *Sphenodiscus*; he

attacked Ray with a giant plastic *Placenticeras*; he told us about ammonite jaws and how holes made by limpets in ammonite shells can sometimes be mistaken for mosasaur bite marks. After a couple of dizzying hours, he passed us off to Bob Farrar, who took us into the storage room and showed us parts of dozens of dinosaurs. By this time, Ray was in a rhapsodic and blissful state.

Later, interviewing Pete, I tried to learn how many dinosaur skeletons he had collected. Not counting the inventory of enough bones to make 50 or so *Edmontosaurus* skeletons from the Ruth Mason Quarry, he ran off a list of at least a couple of dozen other skeletons and skulls, including a number of *Triceratops*, an *Ornithomimus*, and a huge *Acrocanthosaurus*. And in the years since Sue came and went from his life, he's collected half a dozen more *T. rex*. Regardless of how history treats him, Pete Larson will go down in the books as one of the most prolific dinosaur hunters of all time. And he's still dreaming of his museum in Hill City.

own research on fossil plants and the K-T boundary since I first visited late in the summer of 1981, when as a student, I learned how to be a geologist. Marmarth, named for sisters Margaret and Martha, has a very special something that has drawn me back summer after summer for more than 25 years.

The buttes of the Little Missouri River expose the flat-lying layers of the last Cretaceous landscapes, and these hills are loaded with the bones of the last dinosaurs. Dean Pearson and his team have found more that 10,000 fossils representing more than 60 species of dinosaurs, mammals, birds, crocodiles, turtles, fish, amphibians, lizards, and pterosaurs. These finds include a partial *Tyrannosaurus rex* that Dean, in his opposition to the commercialization of paleontology, refuses to name (although a dinosaur named Dean has a certain ring to it) and parts and pieces of several *Triceratops* and *Edmontosaurus*.

Over the last 20 years, I've brought teams of urban volunteers to Marmarth to work with Dean's homegrown crew. Together we've dug more than 150 quarries in the Hell Creek and Fort Union formations and have collected more than 25,000 fossil leaves. Both Dean and I have obsessive-compulsive disorder when it comes to collecting large numbers of fossils, but the result is a pretty clear view of an ancient world.

When Ray and I rolled into town, summer was ending and Marmarth was as deserted

as ever. The local historical society maintains the old Milwaukee Railroad bunkhouse, and 12 bucks buys you a clean, Spartan room with a guaranteed 4 A.M. train rumbling through. Evelyn Lecoe, the live-in host, welcomed us to town, and we dropped our gear and headed across the dirt-road main street to the Pastime Bar.

When I first came to Marmarth, the bar was owned by a guy named Shirley and run by a wanderer named Mike Luten. We called the place Rootin' Tootin' Luten's and knew that with the law 50 miles away, the bar could stay open all night.

Luten and the bar regulars called us bone pickers, but we called ourselves leaf diggers. Luten, a bit of a bone picker himself, showed us a *Triceratops* femur that he'd found sticking out of a gumbo butte. We showed him how to use plaster of paris and burlap strips to make a plaster jacket for the bone so he could carry it back to the bar.

Later that night, actually much later, the bartender from the lone bar in Rhame rolled in for a nightcap. He didn't need one, and the one he got put him out on the floor by the jukebox. Luten looked at me; I looked at my assistant, Rob; he looked at Luten's wife, Teresa; and she looked at the passed-out bartender. Then we all looked at the leftover plaster and burlap and, simultaneously, had a very bad idea. Twenty minutes later, a drunken bartender learned, for the first time, what it meant to be truly plastered.

Now the Pastime has a surprisingly great restaurant out back. It's a good thing, because my favorite spot, Mert's Café, had closed a few years before because of a leaky roof and a failed inspection. (In the early 1980s, Mert's had so many varieties of fried food products that my visiting Ph.D. adviser called it the "Loire Valley of the fried potato.") Troll and I murdered a couple of big T-bone steaks at the Pastime and headed to the buttes.

It seems that the settlers of the American West were sometimes challenged to devise original place names. Try counting the number of Cedar Mountains or Cottonwood Creeks. The place we went to is known quite uncreatively as Mud Buttes. I first saw Mud Buttes in 1988 with Dean. It's a wonderland of eroding Cretaceous and Tertiary mud and sand, a thickness of about 50 feet of Cretaceous rocks overlain by 150 feet of Tertiary rocks. It's a great place to look for the last fossils of the Cretaceous and the first fossils of the Tertiary.

I wanted to give Ray the joy of finding dinosaurs, and Mud Buttes is loaded with chunks of ancient carcasses. The good news is that bones were everywhere, the great majority of which were scattered bits and pieces. Paleontologists have a name for tumbled chunks of unidentifiable dinosaur bones: *Chunkosaurus*. The fragmentary nature of the fossil record was a surprise for Ray, who was expecting perfect bones, not tumbled chunks. The bad news for Ray was that the land is overseen by the Bureau of Land Management, and it's only legal to collect bones with a permit. We didn't have one, so Ray's first dinosaur bone, a *Triceratops* vertebra, is still lying where he found it. For a guy who grew up dreaming of dinosaurs, this was a bitter pill to swallow. He sulked for a while and pleaded with me to bend the rules, but I was having none of it.

Mud Buttes is also one of the very best places on Earth to try to answer the question "What killed the dinosaurs?" I've spent a lot of time beating on this question, and my approach has been a simple one: find lots of fossils below the K-T boundary and lots above, then compare them and see how different they are. This approach is predicated on the idea that I can recognize the K-T boundary when I see it, which turns out to be easier said than done.

THE WORLD IS FULL OF CHUNKOSAURUSES

(top)
Bartender Rootin' Tootin' Luten and his *Triceratops* femur.

(middle)
The plastered bartender.

(bottom)
Fossil leaves from the Hell Creek Formation.

The End of the World as We Know It

In 1980, Walter Alvarez, his dad, Luis, and colleagues Helen Michel and Frank Asaro discovered that a rare platinum-group metal known as iridium was anomalously abundant in a finger-thick layer of clay at three K-T boundary sites in Italy, Denmark, and New Zealand. Using this tiny bit of evidence and a lot of chutzpah, they suggested that the iridium came from an asteroid that hit the Earth and killed the dinosaurs. The scientific world chortled and suggested that abduction by little green men was a similarly valid suggestion, but the Alvarezes were on to something. Within a year, dozens of new K-T sites were discovered, some in rocks that had been deposited under seawater and some that had been deposited in swamps and lakes. In all of these places, chemists talked to paleontologists who showed them the precise stratigraphic level where diverse Cretaceous microfossils (plankton fossils for marine rocks; plant pollen and spores for freshwater rocks) gave way to nondiverse Tertiary microfossils.

In 1988, my longtime science buddy, USGS fossil pollen specialist Doug Nichols, had sampled the rocks at Mud Buttes, and his results showed that Cretaceous pollen was found only in the Hell Creek Formation and not in the overlying Fort Union Formation. This jibed with Dean's bones. He found abundant dinosaur fossils in the Hell Creek Formation but only turtles and crocodiles in the Fort Union Formation. Together, the plant and animal fossils point an accusing finger at an asteroid as the cause of the big extinction.

Ray and I dug a foot-deep trench that crossed the contact of the Hell Creek and Fort Union formations. Our intent was to find the precise layer that marked the debris from the dinosaur-killing asteroid. Usually this layer is subtle to the point of invisibility, and you can't even tell you have it without doing costly laboratory analyses. But Ray's luck was good, and the trench we dug had a strange tan layer. As we got down on our hands and knees to inspect it, my eyes focused and I realized the layer was composed of tiny round balls of clay about a half a millimeter in diameter. In a few rare K-T boundary sections in the Caribbean, the layer is composed of tiny glass beads known as microtektites that formed when molten droplets of target rock from the impact crater cooled as they flew through the air. On that day at Mud Buttes, Ray and I found microtektites that had been blasted all the way from the Chicxulub crater on the Yucatán Peninsula in Mexico to the southwestern corner of North Dakota. Sixty-five million years of weathering had reduced the glass to clay, but the characteristic teardrop and dumbbell shapes that are diagnostic of microtektites were clearly there.

After more than 20 years of work in North Dakota, this was one of my most exciting and most unexpected moments. We set the camera on selftimer and proudly posed by the tan layer of death. Later, lab work documented the presence of anomalous amounts of iridium in this layer and confirmed its origin as asteroid debris.

There are still some scientists who doubt that the dinosaurs met their demise at the fiery fist of an asteroid impact, but I don't think many of the doubters have had the profound experience we did of walking in a valley full of dinosaur bone and then finding the distinctive K-T boundary layer and realizing that the layers above didn't contain a single fragment of *Chunkosaurus*.

Back in Marmarth later that night, we stopped by to visit a local high-school wunderkind, Tyler Lyson. Tyler's uncles own a lot of gumbo, and Tyler, a lean, laconic 17-year-old, had spent a few summers learning how to dig bones with a commercial digger. Quickly figuring out that finding dinosaurs isn't rocket science and that nobody needs a middleman, he started hunting bones on his own.

His dad turned over the family workshop, and Tyler began to find amazing fossils. First it was a turtle jam: 35 turtle skeletons in an ancient streambed. Then he found a mummified hadrosaur, complete with scaly skin impressions. Then, not one but two *Thescelosaurus* dinosaur skeletons. Pretty soon he was hotdogging it: one night he showed us a hollow *Triceratops* horn full of baby *Tyrannosaurus* teeth. When I mentioned that I had always wanted to find a good *Triceratops* skull, he said that he'd seen dozens and took me for a hike where I found my own. By the time he was a senior BMOC at tiny Baker High School, Tyler had a regular stream of paleontologists making pilgrimages to his shop. The last time I checked, Tyler had parlayed his small-town smarts into scholarships at Swarthmore and Yale.

Most pictures that portray the landscapes of *Tyrannosaurus* and his buddies do a pretty poor job of it, focusing on the animals but not the plants with which they lived. Often, the only plants in the scene are distant conifers behind a field of brown, pounded-down dirt. I call this misleading iconography "Monkey Puzzles and Parking Lots" because in these paintings, it commonly looks like dinosaurs are wandering around a parking lot fringed by Chilean conifers known as monkey puzzles. When I quizzed artists as to why they were painting bare earth,

they told me that paleobotanists had forbidden them from using grass because it didn't evolve until the dinosaurs had gone extinct. Remove the grass and you're left with bare earth. This begs the question "What was the ground cover in the Cretaceous?"

I took Ray to another spot near Marmarth where I'd been digging since 1986. Here we dug into tilting mudstone layers that used to be a mud bar on a big lazy Cretaceous river, and we found the remains of a meadow. This new site was full of information about the ground cover, and what we found was surprising. Instead of ferns, cycads, or horsetails, we found herbaceous flowering plants. Many we didn't recognize, but others we could, including buttercups, nettles, hops, and even something that looked suspiciously like marijuana. On closer inspection, the marijuana-like leaf had features that suggested it might also be related to hops.

Hops (genus *Humulus*) and marijuana (genus *Cannabis*) are the only genera in the botanical family Cannabaceae. This is an obscure fact often missed by connoisseurs of the products of either of these two widely imbibed plants. The fact that the last dinosaurs might have been browsing on an extinct missing link between hops and marijuana led to some fertile conversations about

Monkey puzzles
and parking lots.

Deceptive fossil nettles from a Cretaceous meadow.

the real cause of their extinction. And it led to many more conversations about what to name these fossils.

One of the fun things about being a paleontologist is getting to name a new fossil species. If you can demonstrate that nobody has previously named a specific fossil, then you can do it yourself by publishing a careful description and illustrations in a scientific journal, provided you pass the scrupulous review process. Troll was really keen that this fossil get an appropriate name, one that reflected the widespread use and abuse of its descendants. But there was a problem. Since 1990, I've been enjoying the malted beverages of a Denver establishment known as the Wynkoop Brewing Company. One night several years ago over a free pitcher of Wynkoop's finest, I'd signed a contract with one of the bar's owners, on a napkin, of course, promising to name this Cretaceous hops ancestor after the brewpub.

Ray was adamant that the fossil have a different name, one that reflected the plant's apparent affinities with marijuana. He was so adamant, in fact, that when he and I later attended a Ziggy Marley concert in Philadelphia, he set up a meeting with the Rastafarian to make his case with a true ganja expert backing him up. Ray bribed the

stagehand, and we found ourselves standing in a small room backstage with Ziggy himself. Troll explained that I was a paleontologist and that we had great respect for Ziggy's dad, Bob Marley. Then he told Ziggy about the Cretaceous marijuana missing-link plant from North Dakota. Ziggy seemed puzzled by the concept of paleontologists backstage, but he was a surprisingly fossil-savvy guy. In retrospect, it was apparent that he knew that *Australopithecus afarensis*, the 3.5-million-year-old hominid fossil known as Lucy, was, like Haile Selassie, leader of the Rastafarians, from Ethiopia. He asked me, "Where de first mon from?" I was starstruck, didn't clearly understand his accent, and thought he had asked me where my fossil came from. I answered with two words: "North Dakota." The room was suddenly stone-cold silent. I looked at Ray, he looked at me, and I realized that I had just dissed Haile Selassie. Fortunately, Ray used his backstage ways to smooth out the misunderstanding, and we left a room full of slightly confused Rastafarians with the concept that maybe, just maybe, we might name a fossil plant after Ziggy's dad. In the end, the marijuana-like fossil turned out to be a lobe-leafed nettle, a disappointment to both the bar owner and the Rastafarian.

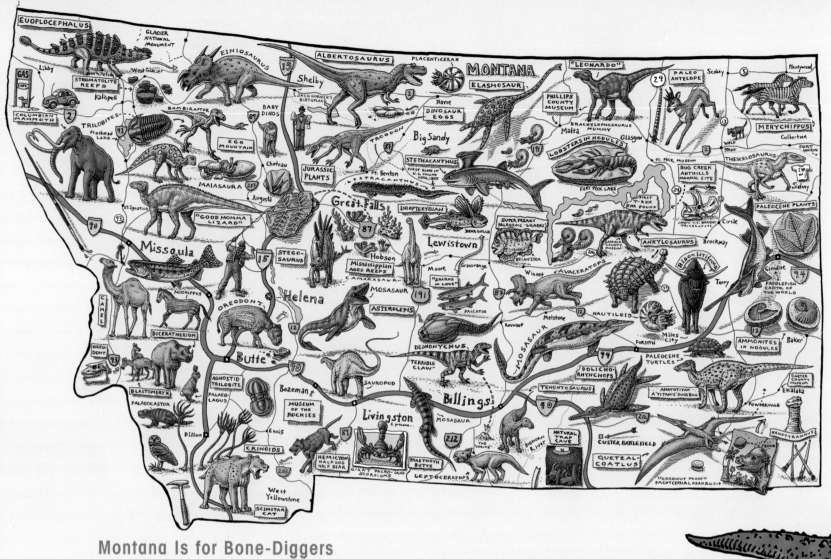

Montana Is for Bone-Diggers

Eastern Montana does not live up to the state's name. Instead, it's a huge expanse of grasslands and badlands and a high-speed drive-by for those headed for Seattle on Interstate 90. What it lacks in elevation, it more than makes up for in fossils. The Yellowstone and Missouri rivers drain the distant Rockies and lazily slice their way across the eastern half of the state. In the process, they've exposed Late Cretaceous and Paleocene rocks in some of the world's most extensive and fossiliferous badlands. The town of Glendive on the Yellowstone River near the North Dakota border is best known for its riverbed agates and for hundred-pound paddlefish, but it also hosts Makoshika State Park, a hoodoo heaven dripping with *Triceratops*. Jack Horner made himself, and the town of Choteau, famous when he found baby dinosaur bones in a coffee can in a rock shop and traced them back to their source, which turned out to be a dino-

saur nesting ground full of nests, eggs, and babies. Eventually he also discovered bone beds composed of thousands of duckbilled dinosaurs, which he named *Maiasaura*, "the good mother lizard." In time, the state of Montana was forced to acknowledge its riches and built the Museum of the Rockies in Bozeman. Although it tips its hat to settlers and Indians, this museum is really a tribute to the star power and dinosaur-finding ability of Jack Horner.

In the forgotten center of eastern Montana, the area around Jordan has been haunted by paleontologists ever since Barnum Brown found the first *Tyrannosaurus rex* skeleton there in 1902. Legendary amateur collector Harley Garbani scored a pair of *T. rex* for Los Angeles here in the 1960s, and in the 1970s the place was overrun by hunters of tiny Cretaceous and Paleocene mammals. In the 1980s it became ground zero for the K-T boundary debate, providing most of what we know about how dinosaurs and smaller animals responded to the Chicxulub impact. In the late 1990s, Horner began prospecting the southern shores of Fort Peck Reservoir (a dammed portion of the Missouri River). In the process, he discovered so many *T. rex* skeletons that he rendered the king of dinosaurs blasé in the process. In 2000, Phillips County coughed up a nearly perfect mummified *Brachylophosaurus* duckbill that was named Leonardo because of some 1917 graffiti on the rock near where it lay. Leonardo is cited by the *Guinness Book of World Records* as the world's best-preserved dinosaur because more than 90 percent of its skin is intact. Its promoter, Nate Murphy, godson of American Museum dinosaur guru Ned Colbert, has built a research program and museum around this world-class fossil in the tiny town of Malta.

In Ray's mind, the fossil epicenter of Montana is located near Livingston at a place called Bear Gulch in the Big Snowy Mountains. Discovered in 1967, this obscure 318-million-year-old pocket of platy limestone preserves an unbelievably cool equatorial seafloor. Known mainly for its insanely fine preservation, Bear Gulch has produced dozens of species of fish with intact skin, color patterns, gut contents, and even sexual organs. The pièce de résistance of this amazing site is a small slab with a pair of six-inch-long *Falcatus* sharks fossilized in the act of copulation. It is one of the rarest of fossils, an amorous couple engaged *in flagrante delicto.*

Drs. Dick Lund and Eileen Grogan have spent decades excavating the site along with the help of an army of mostly local volunteers. They've unearthed an astounding array of Paleozoic fishes, nearly all of them new to science. The Bear Gulch fauna was dominated by a wild menagerie of sharks that have long captivated Ray's artistic eye. In 1998, the Discovery Channel flew Ray out to meet Dick and Eileen live and on-camera at Bear Gulch. Since then, Ray has worked with the two to create lifelike reconstructions of their discoveries.

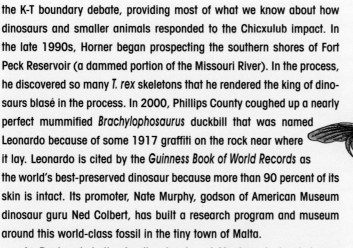

As we entered Montana, we rolled through the oil field town of Baker. From Baker, the road south is the world's longest 34-mile road. It consists of two 17-mile ruler-straight stretches. No matter how fast you drive, this road takes forever. To the west of the road is Medicine Rocks State Park, a maze of sandstone towers, spires, and pillars that are the remains of Paleocene stream channels. At the end of the road is the quirky town of Ekalaka, named for an obscure Indian princess.

Ekalaka is the home of Marshall Lambert, a high-school teacher turned dinosaur digger. Marshall and the Carter County Historical Society built a museum out of jagged chunks of petrified wood and filled it with odd skeletons from the Hell Creek. This museum has the only *Anatotitan* (a giant duckbill) skeleton outside of New York City and one of the finest *Triceratops* skulls ever found.

The badlands around Ekalaka have hosted bone hunters for years. The Cleveland Museum of Natural History has a splendid little tyrannosaur skull from this area that was renamed *Nanotyrannus*, "the microscopic ruler," by Bakker. Rumor has it that the beautiful little skull was perched on a hoodoo when it was found by Cleveland curator David Dunkle in 1942. Hoodoos are pillars of sedimentary rock capped with something more resistant to erosion than the rock of the pillar. Typically, the cap is just a zone of hardened rock, but in fossil-rich areas, fossils can cap the hoodoos. Collecting the skull required nothing more than strolling up to the hoodoo and snapping the skull free. Paleopurists dream of being the first to prospect an area, because the fossils will

(left)
The badlands of
the Little Missouri
River.

litter the ground and cap the hoodoos.

Ekalaka also produced one of the first skulls of the bone-headed *Pachycephalosaurus*. There's a great old newspaper clipping in the Carter County Museum that shows a cartoon of *Pachycephalosaurus* with a coconut bouncing off his bony head. It's still a mystery why these animals had skulls that were capped with bowling ball–thick wads of bone, and I've always liked the absurd idea that the skulls were for protection from falling coconuts.

You don't want to stay too long in Ekalaka, so we set off across the gumbo and into a dusty afternoon. The land to the south and west is a huge, empty corner of Montana, and our drive continued for hours as rolling thunderheads dumped periodic showers.

Around sunset, we realized that we were on the same path that Custer had taken to his demise at the Little Bighorn. About 8:45 P.M., with only minutes before closing, we drove into the Custer Battlefield monument. The massacre site was completely deserted except for one nervous security guard. Big Blue glided up to the top of the hill where a big concrete memorial marks the place where Custer fell. The moon was full, and we looked down the hill at the white headstones dotting the slope, each marking the spot where some poor trooper got his comeuppance in the form of a bullet, arrow, or tomahawk. Just then, a smooth, strong wind came up, and we both looked at each other and got truly spooked. We hurriedly hopped in Big Blue and headed to the little town of Ranchester, Wyoming.

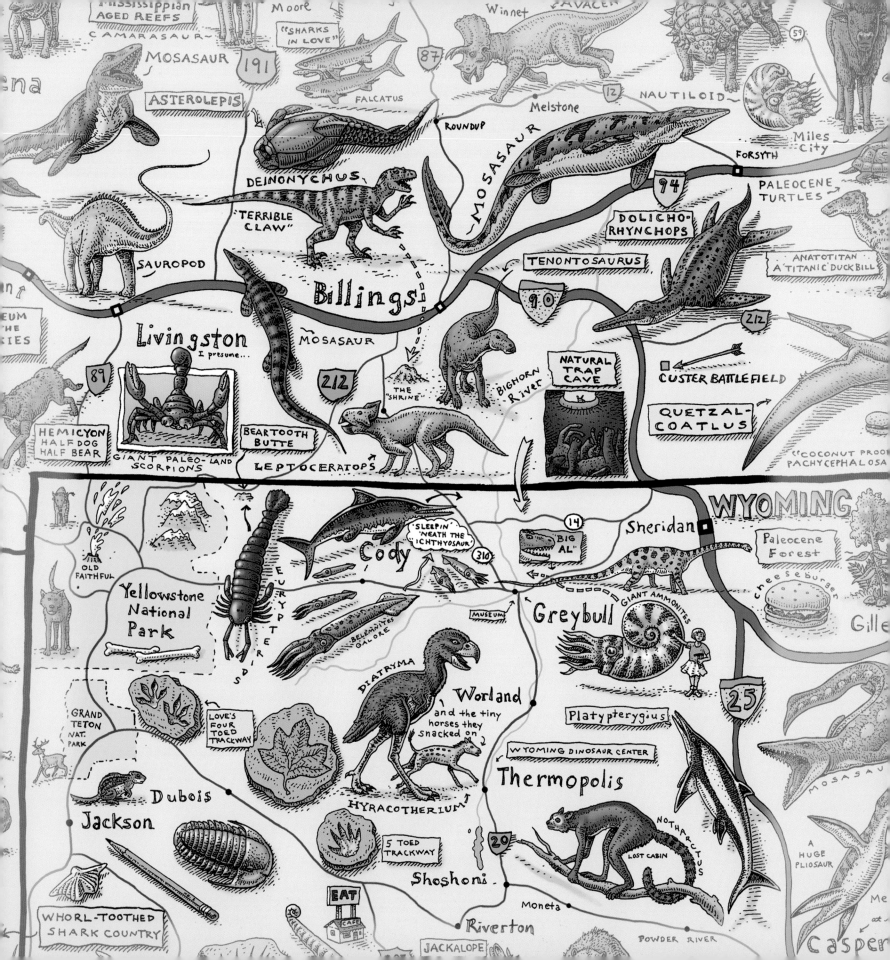

8
40,000 MAMMALS CAN BE WRONG

The top of the Bighorn Mountain range is bucolic, or at least a moosey version of bucolic, with meandering streams and green patches of mountain spruce. It was here, at the western edge of this rolling surface, that Indians arranged chunks of Bighorn Dolomite to make the famous Medicine Wheel. This stony pinwheel looks like a giant wagon wheel with 28 spokes. Its original purpose is obscure, but dozens of these stone circles also exist on the prairies of Montana and Alberta. The chunks of rock in this wheel contain fossils of animals that lived at the bottom of a sea 400 million years ago.

At the western edge of the planed mountaintop, the road begins its downward slide and suddenly, there is 7,000 feet of air below you. This giant hole in the ground is the Bighorn Basin. The structure is so big that you can easily see it on any map of North America that shows some topography. It's the northwest-southeast oval that dangles off the northern border of Wyoming. For paleontologists, it's also the promised land. Taken as a whole, the Bighorn Basin probably has more exposed rocks and more fossils from more formations than any other place in the world. I've often thought that if I could have only one place on Earth to tell the story of life on Earth, the Bighorn Basin would be it. The story isn't quite complete, missing most of the Precambrian, the Silurian, the Miocene, and the Pliocene. Nonetheless, the parts that are there are huge and magnificent and could make a book all by themselves.

The Bighorn Basin is dry and difficult to find. Surrounded by five mountain ranges and hostile Indians, this huge, dry depression was hard to get to and offered little incentive for those attempting to reach it. The Bozeman Trail missed it by going north, and the Oregon Trail missed it by going south. Jacob Wortman, the first paleontologist to reach this promised land, accessed the basin from the south in 1880. His spectacular finds of Eocene mammals inspired additional attempts. Paleontologists still come to the Bighorn Basin each summer, realizing that they've barely begun to scratch the surface of this amazing place.

After stopping at the U.S. Forest Service visitor's center at Burgess Junction and admiring large, chunky Paleozoic clams and corals, Ray and I hopped into Big Blue and headed down into the basin. The geology of the western flank of the Bighorns is textbook spectacular. As the mountains rose, the overlying drape of layered rocks was lifted high into the sky on top of the block but tilted, folded, broken, and overturned along the margins of the range. Driving down the steep road that passes for Alternate U.S. Route 14, we could see ancient seafloors now standing with perfect verticality. In places, the beds have literally been overturned. We stopped to look at this upside-down world and found 400-million-year-old marine creatures. Ray stood on his head to orient his body like an Ordovician clam.

Farther down, the road crosses the giant thrust fault that separated basin from mountain some

These vertical fins of Mississippian Madison Limestone along the flanks of the Beartooth Mountains near Red Lodge, Montana, are a great example of an ancient seafloor turned on its side.

60 million years ago. Here, upside-down Paleozoic sand dunes lie atop right-side-up Triassic red beds. The rocks in the fault zone are shot through with weak spots, and the road slides on a regular basis. The fault zone is easily recognized by fresh applications of asphalt. Once across the fault and into the basin, the layered rocks slope gently downhill. These endless exposures invited inspection, and we were soon off-road looking at the multihued layers of the Morrison Formation.

In the Bighorn Basin, the stack of formations is more than 10,000 feet thick, but there are several that are so distinctive that they orient you to where you are in the stack. The Morrison is one such formation, as it has brilliant red, white, and blue banding. Above the Morrison is a superthick sequence of Cretaceous marine mudstones. The mudstone weathers into gray rolling hills unencumbered with plant life.

Whenever I see Cretaceous marine shale, I think of ammonites. And when I think of them, I want to find one.

We drove down a long road into an area of bentonite mines. Bentonite is an altered form of volcanic ash. All throughout the Late Cretaceous, erupting volcanoes in Montana dusted the surface of the sea with a fine sifting of airborne ash. If the eruption was large enough, the ash would settle through the water column and form a soupy layer on the seafloor. Some bentonite layers are paper-thin, and others are as thick as a house.

Bentonite has a number of industrial uses: drilling mud is the most common, chocolate filler the most despicable. When bentonite at the surface is moistened by rain, it gets unbelievable slippery. Many people have learned this at their peril when driving across these old ash layers. Bentonite is moderately big business in the Bighorn Basin, and mining it's simply a matter of finding a layer and digging it out. These mines are good places to see freshly excavated blocks of old seafloor and to hunt for the remains of critters that got buried in the soup.

The day was plenty hot, so there was little danger of slipping anywhere. We drove into an old bentonite mine where desk-sized blocks of old seafloor were piled into huge jumbles. Ray and I searched for fossils by crawling from one block to the next and reading the surfaces. I found a knobby ammonite the size of a dinner plate, but it had been crushed flat when the shale compressed. We found a few fish scales, then decided to leave.

A mile or so down the dirt road, Ray demanded that I stop the truck. He had a feeling about the rolling hill of Cretaceous mud next to the road, and he needed to respect the feeling. I couldn't see any obvious concretions, and the site looked barren to me, but you can't find fossils if you don't look, so I stopped the truck and Ray grabbed a hammer and strolled off into the heat. By the time I'd begun to lace my boots, Ray was yelling that he'd found a plesiosaur. I ran up the popcorn slope, filling my open boots with Cretaceous crumbs. Ray was holding a beautiful three-inch fossil bone, a vertebra for sure, most likely from a plesiosaur, and he was grinning from ear to ear. We crawled around looking for more, but that was all she wrote. It was Ray's first "find based on a feeling," and he was pretty proud of himself. Being a vertebrate fossil on federal land, the specimen was not destined for Ray's pocket. But this time we did have a collecting permit, so I logged the vertebra into the museum's record book.

Continuing down the hill, we drove to the banks of the Bighorn River. This is a river that respects no mountain ranges, cutting through the Owl Creek and Bighorn Mountains en route to its confluence with the Yellowstone River. Like many rivers in the Rockies, the Bighorn is literally older than the surrounding mountains. Not just older than the hills, but older than the mountains. Evidence for this bold claim is plain to see. The headwaters of the Bighorn River start at

Togwotee Pass, the divide between the Wind River Basin and Jackson Hole (this is also the Continental Divide). Here it's called the Wind River. It flows southeast to Shoshoni, Wyoming, where it bends sharply north and flows directly into the Owl Creek Mountains through Wind River Canyon. At the north end of the canyon, the river abruptly changes its name to the Bighorn at a place oddly named the Wedding of the Waters and flows into the Bighorn Basin. Usually two rivers come together at places called Wedding of the Waters, but here a single river just changes its name. The Bighorn River performs a similar trick at the north end of the basin, slicing through the Bighorn Mountains and forming Bighorn Canyon. The only sensible explanation for this weird pattern is that the river is older than the mountains, the canyons, and the basins.

We crossed the river and headed into Lovell to visit the forest service visitor's center, which has a great relief map of the northern margin of the basin. By this time, the pleasant morning had morphed into one of those smoking hot Wyoming afternoons that melts the ice in your cooler and makes you want to retreat to the nearest dark bar. Instead, we headed back east, recrossed the Bighorn River, and drove north on a dirt road to find a legendary deep and deadly hole in the ground.

The road to Natural Trap is one of those roads that you drive not really knowing if it's drivable. After consulting a freshly purchased topographic map, we started up a steep valley. The road is made of solid rock that got narrower, steeper, and more rutted as Big Blue crept along. Eventually, I was hanging on to the door to keep from sliding across the bench seat, and Ray was imploring me to turn around, a maneuver that seemed utterly impossible and worse than carrying on and hoping for the best. In compound low, Big Blue was up to the task, and we emerged from

Troll at the grated mouth of Natural Trap Cave.

FORTY THOUSAND MAMMALS CAN BE WRONG

the rocky canyon onto a sage-covered plateau that stretched to the north. After a few miles, we pulled up to the gaping mouth of a cave that has killed more than 40,000 animals in the last 100,000 years.

Natural Trap Cave is shaped like a short-necked beer bottle. The opening, roughly 20 feet wide, appears as an ominous hole in the floor of a gentle valley on the top of a lime-stone plateau. The BLM has built a metal frame over the cave's gaping mouth, so we were able to walk out onto it and peer down into the inky blackness. Even though the spacing of the metal bars is so close that it would have been impossible to slip through, the fact that this cave was the site of so much fatality gave us pause as we considered its victims.

Natural Trap is the greatest pit trap of all time. Lying at the bottom of an 85-foot drop are the skeletons of woolly mammoths, horses, pronghorns, bighorn sheep, camels, musk oxen, bison, fox, wolverines, dire wolves, coyotes, gray wolves, red fox, lynx, weasels, American lions, short-faced bears, and American chee-tahs. Each one of these animals made a bad decision and fell into the hole. The drop was enough to kill them. Regardless, there was no way out. There was no way in for big-bodied scavengers either, so the bodies lay where they fell, essentially undisturbed. In time the floor of the cave was covered by a pyramid-like pile of fallen skeletons.

In order to study the site, Larry Martin and his crew from the University of Kansas built a staircase on scaffolding and climbed down into the hole. Each year from 1974 until 1985, they dug away at the pyramid pile of carcasses on the cave floor. Results of their digging show the census of bad luck. The University of Kansas Museum in Lawrence, Kansas, displays nearly perfect skeletons of a giant musk oxen (*Bootherium bombifrons*), an extinct big-horn sheep (*Ovis catclawensis*), and an American cheetah (*Miracinonyx trumani*) from the cave. Peering down into the dark hole, we looked at each other and smiled. Here was one of the best fossil sites in the world.

On the way back to town, we stopped at the mouth of Cottonwood Canyon. The Bighorns are a splendid example of Dave Love's metaphorical pigs waking up under a stony blanket. Thick Paleozoic limestone and dolomite layers are draped across the mountain margin. Deep canyons slice these layers and create a series of flatirons shaped like piranha teeth. Cottonwood Canyon is one of these canyons, a place that would be a national park if found in a less-endowed state. In Wyoming, it's just another spectacular canyon with a crappy gravel road that goes nowhere. Its walls are nearly 2,100 feet high. The canyon floor is made of Cambrian shale, layer after layer of mud and lime stacked to make a pile of marine rocks that's thicker than the canyon is deep.

The Beartooth Butte Formation, found all along the walls of Cottonwood Canyon, is a rare one, occurring only in a few places in Wyoming. The formation formed when a Silurian or Devonian river cut canyons into the top of the Ordovician dolomite. This happened during a brief interlude when the sea drained off the continent and old seafloors were high and dry. In the Early Devonian, the sea level came back up and the canyons were drowned with

water and filled with mud. The remains of this mud formed lenses of red rock incised into the dolomites. These layers have fossils of some of the first fish and land plants.

The potential of the Beartooth Butte Formation was discovered in 1931 by Princeton professor Erling Dorf, who led a team of students into the high Beartooth Mountains near Cooke City, Montana. His team had been alerted to the presence of "fossil butterflies" by local hunters, and they set out to inspect the report. The butterflies turned out to be the tails of trilobites in the Cambrian Park Shale. After correctly identifying them, Erling saw the red lens on the face of Beartooth Butte and climbed up to inspect it. He found a trove of twiglike land plants and the bony head plates of early fishes. At the time, these land plants were some of the earliest known, and Erling acquired some fame for finding them. Meanwhile, the game warden in Red Lodge heard rumors of Princeton students fishing without licenses in Beartooth Lake and set out to bag himself a bunch of eastern scofflaws. When he rode into Erling's camp and learned that the fish were not fresh trout but 395-million-year-old Devonian fossils, he gamely gave up and went home.

The exposure of the Beartooth Butte Formation in Cottonwood Canyon was discovered later. I had a hunch that this would be a great place to reconstruct a Devonian landscape and led a team to this site

The mouth of Cottonwood Canyon, home of giant scorpions and eurypterids.

He lay especially still, hoping the eurypterid wouldn't notice him.

in 1993. We camped at an old homesteader cabin at the mouth of the canyon and hiked into the site every morning. We were only a quarter mile from the quarry, but we were 1,000 feet lower, and each morning started with a grueling hour-and-a-half climb.

Our team of seven included the Patagonian field man Pablo Puerta, renowned on five continents for his ability to find amazing fossils. Pablo held the record for fastest trip from camp to quarry with a smoking 42-minute time, while none of the rest of us could even crack the one-hour mark. It was all the worse because he had enough energy and breath to sing as he climbed.

The quarry site had a magnificent view down the canyon and out into the Bighorn Basin. Digging was pretty straightforward, since the rock wasn't covered by much dirt and wasn't too hard. We just pried out blocks and split them with hammers and chisels. This site had abundant remains of early land plants and even some unmistakable fossil roots, some of the earliest in the world. A Field Museum excavation in the 1960s had yielded a complete skeleton of a bony-headed fish, and there were rumors of large fossil eurypterids, feared marine predators related to spiders and scorpions. We had luck finding chunks of bony-headed fish, but little else. On day three of the dig, I drove into town for supplies, and when I returned, the quarry was abuzz. Two of the team had found a giant claw. Unfortunately, the portion of the claw that connected to the body was oriented away from the cliff, meaning that the body had long ago weathered away. When I got a close look at the big chomper, I realized that I was looking at a piece of a eurypterid that must have been at least five feet long. I later learned that this site has also produced a rare land-roaming scorpion known as *Phaearcturus*, which was almost three feet long.

Three hundred and ninety-five million years ago, Wyoming lay south of the equator and was covered by a tropical sea. As those waters receded, streams flowing from the land carved shallow valleys onto exposed wave-cut platforms. The land would have looked barren at a distance, but closer inspection would have shown patches of plants, some as tall as a few feet. Wandering around in this miniature canopy were truly massive and murderous arthropods. The scorpions were bigger than badgers, and the eurypterids may have been amphibious. This was our world before our world even began to look vaguely familiar.

I explained all of this to Ray as we stood at the mouth of the canyon watching a glorious sunset light up the layers. Thoughts of enormous scorpions crawling into his bed sent Ray scurrying for his notebook. He wanted to climb into the land of the eurypterid, but I was keenly aware of the effort involved and tried to sate him with stories instead of firsthand experience. After horsing around and taking some pictures, with Ray quickly sketching giant murderous sea scorpions and armored fish swimming above the canyon walls, we set out from the sunset toward the beautifully named Sundance Formation.

Perhaps the most fossiliferous formation in Wyoming is the Sundance Shale. This gray mudstone was once the mud at the bottom of a Middle Jurassic sea full of oysters, shelled squid, and sleek, dolphin-shaped ichthyosaurs. Today, the shale weathers to form slopes and valley floors. Lying below the dinosaur-rich Morrison and above the distinctive bright-red Chugwater Formation, the Sundance is the easiest place to find a fossil, or your money back. Bullet-shaped belemnites and ram's horn *Gryphaea* oysters are the most common, but star-shaped crinoid stems and bits of marine lizard are also easy to find, with a modicum of patience. On the northern end of the Bighorn Basin, the Sundance Formation includes a layer of paper shale, the remains of some dried-up coastal lagoon. The fossil fish our Dinopalooza friends Chris and Dave were mining on their nearby ranch had come from this layer.

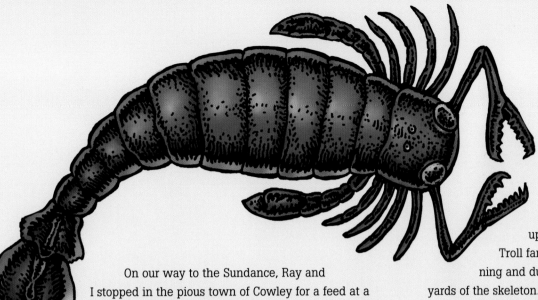

On our way to the Sundance, Ray and I stopped in the pious town of Cowley for a feed at a Mormon family restaurant and sampled a very credible chicken-fried steak. By the time we finished, the sun had set over our bottomless iced teas. Chris and Dave had given us good instructions to their site, but there's an art to finding a place out in the sage at night. We pushed on into the dark, and I followed the instructions as best I could, meandering for miles down dirt roads. After an hour of tentative creeping, we arrived at a spot that I figured was close enough, and we stopped the truck to pitch the Troll family tent next to the road. It was only our second camp on this outing, and we soon discovered that the tent stakes had been lost in the post-Dinopalooza hangover haze or, if on board, were too well hidden to be found. Not a problem, as the capacious toolboxes of Big Blue yielded a profusion of pickaxe heads and crowbars that soon pegged the tent to the soft soil. We tucked into our bags and began chatting about Jurassic seas. Ray was completely jazzed and couldn't stop talking about big-eyed, sleek marine lizards, wondering out loud if they breached like dolphins.

When morning came, I set about building a pot of coffee on the back of the truck. A bleary-eyed Troll poked his head out of the tent and complained that the ground was too rocky for a good night's sleep. We had pitched our tent on the Sundance Shale, and the bullet-shaped bumps under our bedrolls were fossils. Troll started collecting them while still in his sleeping bag, and soon he had a handful of belemnites. We sipped our coffee and read Chris's notes about the buried ichthyosaur. The instructions were good, and we had followed them well.

The modern world of paleontology is armed with GPS devices, so there's no excuse for bad directions. With Chris's coordinates, we soon unburied his marine lizard for a breakfast viewing high up on a slope directly above the Troll family tent. By a combination of cunning and dumb luck, we had camped within 50 yards of the skeleton. We reburied the find and ambled over to the conspicuous outcrops of the Hulett Paper Shale to find some fish.

Paper shale sometimes lives up to its name, and the Hulett is amazing in that way. It's possible to pull out book-sized and -shaped chunks and then split off the pages one at a time. The sheets are stable and sturdy, even when they're only a few millimeters thick. Using sharp knives, we sliced open pages of time and looked at what had been buried in a Jurassic lagoon when Wyoming was under the sea. In no time, we were finding fish and insects.

The concept of Middle Jurassic paper shale from a marine lagoon is particularly tantalizing when you stop to consider that one of the most famous fossils ever found came from Late Jurassic lagoonal deposits in Bavaria. *Archaeopteryx*, the first feathered dinosaur/earliest bird, was discovered in 1860, the year after Darwin published the *Origin of Species,* and provided one of the sweetest and best examples of a fossil animal with characteristics of two major animal groups: birds and dinosaurs. More than a century later, Bavaria's Solnhofen Limestone has coughed up only a half dozen more *Archaeopteryx* skeletons. Meanwhile, slightly younger paper shale from Liaoning Province in northeastern China has produced a whole flock of fossil birds and many feathered dinosaurs. What we don't yet have is a really credible feathered dinosaur/bird earlier than the Late Jurassic.

The same Larry Martin who revealed the joys of Natural Trap Cave has spent months splitting the paper

(right top)
Dialing in an
ichthyosaur
with a GPS. The
Troll family tent
and Big Blue
are located at
the left end of
the road.

(middle)
Pointing at
Sundance
belemnites.

shale of the Sundance Formation in the hope of finding such a creature. That's the way predictive paleontology works. Get a question, in this case, "What is the oldest bird?" then choose a strategy that might allow you to find it. Nice idea, but Larry is still splitting shale and has yet to find his bird. Still, the Sundance is a great place to look.

Another part of the *Archaeopteryx* story played out not far to the west of where we sat. The Cloverly Formation is an Early Cretaceous pile of sandstone and mudstone that's exposed several hundred feet up the section from the Sundance. The American Museum's ubiquitous Barnum Brown prospected the Cloverly late in his career and found a number of provocative dinosaur fragments that he never got around to describing. In the early 1960s, Yale's John Ostrom used Brown's field notes and worked his way around the southern end of the Pryor Mountains near Bridger, Montana, in search of new and interesting dinosaurs. On the last day of the field season in 1964, Ostrom found a skeleton of an animal that he later named *Deinonychus.* The deadly grace and implied pack behavior of this wolf-sized meat eater was yet another argument for the warm blood of dinosaurs and the dinosaur-bird link. *Deinonychus,* under the pseudonym of its cousin *Velociraptor,* would go on to be the star of *Jurassic Park.*

Though fish and insect fossils lay in sheets at our feet, we got bored with not finding any Jurassic birds, so we stopped splitting shale and drove to Greybull. This sleepy eastern basin town has a great local museum that displays some of the amazing fossil richness of the Bighorn Basin. My favorite fossil there is a giant ammonite collected from the nearby Cretaceous marine shale. The three-foot giant is displayed next to a picture of an even larger ammonite that must be stored out on someone's ranch. These are some of the largest ammonites ever collected in North America. The world record goes to the German *Parapuzozia,* which stretches the tape measure to an awesome six feet.

(left)
Sleeping
with the
ichthyosaurs.

Deinonychus.

The road east of Greybull heads back toward the mighty Bighorn massif, but we turned off to the north and wound our way back down through the gray Cretaceous shale and into the multihued Morrison. It was in this valley that one of the greatest dinosaur hunters of all time, Barnum Brown, made one of his biggest finds. Brown was told of the site by a rancher in 1932 and led a massive excavation there in 1934. The early photographs of Howe Quarry show an unbelievable jumble of bones. Paleontologists make detailed maps of quarries that show the position of every bone. The Sinclair Oil Company underwrote this expedition, and the famous green Sinclair dinosaur was a result of this collaboration. It's because of this history that many people today hold tenaciously to the misconception that oil is made from dinosaurs.

One of the common happenstances of the modern West is that commercial dinosaur diggers have realized that many of the classic quarries of the last century, such as Howe Quarry, were not dug to exhaustion. If the quarry sites can be relocated and if they're on private ranch land, then it's legal and often possible to make an arrangement with the rancher for the site to be reopened. In 1991, Kirby Siber, a Swiss dinosaur enthusiast, located the forgotten Howe Quarry and obtained a lease from the landowner to reopen it.

Oil Is Not Made of Dinosaurs

Big Blue was a gas hog, getting only 12 miles per gallon. Our 5,000-mile road trip used about 420 gallons of gas, releasing nearly four tons of carbon dioxide gas into the atmosphere. Eighty million years ago, during the Cretaceous, marine plankton extracted carbon dioxide from the warm sea that covered Colorado. Then the plankton died and sank to the seafloor, where it was buried and fossilized, eventually maturing into buried petroleum. Our trip was fueled by fossils from a greenhouse world, and Big Blue's emissions, which will hang in the atmosphere for the next hundred years, are doing their part to return our modern world to greenhouse conditions.

What was good for Barnum was also good for Kirby. The quarry was far from kicked, and bones once again began to roll out of the hill. Kirby's operation hit a snag when a BLM pilot spotted a new road near the old Howe Quarry and reported it to the BLM office in Worland. On the ground, Kirby and his team had located a splendid and unusually large *Allosaurus* skeleton with a nearly perfect skull. His mounting excitement morphed to utter dismay when BLM officials showed up and surveyed the

The multihued Morrison Formation near the Howe Quarry.

site. Kirby was digging on the correct side of the fence, but the rancher had mistakenly set his fence on BLM property. Kirby walked away from the *Allosaurus* and back onto private land. The BLM looked around for a paleontologist who would finish the excavation and curate the specimen at a federal repository. Eventually, Jack Horner and his

Everything else is pretty small. Mammals started small, and many of the lineages stayed small as they diversified. The Willwood Formation has a mixture of mammals from living groups such as rodents, primates, bats, insectivores, artiodactyls, perissodactyls, and carnivores, and from a smattering of extinct groups such as mesonychids, condylarths, creodonts, taeniodonts, and others with even odder names. Phil Gingerich from the University of Michigan has been returning to Wyoming since the early 1960s, and his crews have collected tens of thousands of these tiny jaws and bones from hundreds of fossil localities. The result is the most densely sampled records of mammal evolution on Earth. Through Phil's data, it's possible to see a clear example of the gradual process of evolution. Creationist apologists often claim that the fossil record is too episodic to show evolution. Phil has shown that the episodic appearance is an artifact of small sample size, not any reality of the fossil record.

While most of these fossils are fragmentary, diligent efforts by paleontologists have slowly assembled more-complete skeletons. In paleospeak, anything behind the skull is postcranial, and for most Paleocene and Early Eocene mammals, we know very little about their postcranial skeletons. For the last 30 years, a team from Johns Hopkins led by Ken Rose has been carefully collecting and assembling postcranial skeletons of fragmentary Eocene animals.

More recently, two students from the University of Michigan have found some truly spectacular fossil skeletons by dissolving blocks of limestone in weak acids. The limestone apparently formed in shallow ponds or depressions in Eocene forests. Somehow, the complete skeletons of exquisite tiny bats, primates, and insectivores have been completely preserved in these tiny, limy tombs.

You won't learn any of this while driving around the Bighorn Basin or stopping at the few museums in the basin. Practically the whole spectacular story of mammal evolution is played out on these hills, but, sadly, it's not part of the local lore, which trends more toward cowboys and Indians, Buffalo Bill, and Yellowstone. The town of Cody has been a tourist trap ever since Buffalo Bill opened the Irma Hotel, "just the sweetest hotel that ever was," on Main Street in 1902, just 22 years after Wortman discovered the adjacent fossil fields. Every summer, millions of tourists roll through town, sample the daily rodeo, and roll on to Yellowstone, ignorant of the fact that some of the world's best fossil sites are right there. Here we were, on this great trip through space and geologic time, seeing dozens of fossil sites every day, and everybody else on the road couldn't care less. We ducked into the palatial Buffalo Bill Museum, which had just added an entire wing, the Draper Museum of Natural History, dedicated to local nature. The focus of the museum was all ecology and no evolution. Didn't the designers of this new museum know that they were located in the best fossil basin in the world? Didn't they care that the living ecosystems of Wyoming are the result of billions of years of evolutionary change? We realized that ours was a simple quest. We just want people to know that the Earth has a long and exciting history and that life has persevered despite asteroids, glaciers, and volcanoes. The evidence for this vast drama is all around us: fossils are everywhere. We left Cody's strip-mall fast-food tourist hell and drove off into the lingering twilight feeling like the last of the paleosamurai.

Just to the north of Cody is one of the most unlikely mountains in the world. It's a mountain loved by creationists and much discussed by geologists. Geologically, it's a true conundrum. The jagged mountaintop consists of 350-million-year-old marine Madison Limestone, while the lower slopes are composed of the 55-million-year-old Early Eocene *Eohippus*-bearing Willwood Formation. Heart Mountain appears to defy the defining principle of stratigraphy, the one that says the oldest layers are found on the bottom. In its case, the oldest layers are clearly on

(left) Badlands of the Paleocene-Eocene boundary at the nose of Polecat Bench near Powell, Wyoming.

FORWARD INTO THE PAST . . .

top. For the "short-chronology" creationists who believe that the world is about 6,000 years old, this is a place where an exception to the rule tosses out the whole conceptual structure. To geologists, this site is damned interesting and not a little puzzling.

Detailed fieldwork now suggests that the mountain is the result of a giant horizontal fault and that the old rock of the mountaintop slid or was shoved into place sometime after 50 million years ago. The source of the mountain has been located near the northeast corner of Yellowstone, 50 miles away. What geologists can't agree on is how long it took to get there. One group argues that the mountain was pushed into place as the Absaroka Mountains were forming, but another argues that it slid into place in one massive, catastrophic landslide. Both ideas have compelling arguments and passionate proponents. I kind of like the idea of a mountain sliding 50 miles into place in a few moments. Talk about a change of scenery.

North of Heart Mountain and south of the Montana line is one of the most rewarding places in North America to look at geology. Clark's Fork Canyon is a gaping slice into the eastern margin of the Beartooth Mountains. Here, tipped on edge for perfect viewing, are nearly 10,000 feet of layered rock: a record of Earth from the Precambrian to the Paleocene, a time span of more than 500 million years. The road up the canyon is massively overbuilt, a highway

to nowhere. The original plan was to carve an access road to Yellowstone, but the realities of the canyon won out, and now the pavement stops a few miles inside it. Like many places in Wyoming, this world-class geological hot spot isn't labeled on maps or marked by signs. It's just there if you know what to look for. This is the subtle magic of the Cowboy State.

Ray and I continued our trip down the basin, aiming for the hot springs at Thermopolis. As Big Blue roared along through this open, endless, fossil-filled landscape, my only thought was, "How could I ever explore all of this country?" My sister, a documentary filmmaker who travels the world from Brooklyn, is baffled by the ease with which I travel through space and time without becoming overwhelmed by the immensity of it all. For me, it's the immensity that makes it interesting, because I know that we'll never find the last fossil. And the immensity is not overwhelming, because of the soothing spatial framework of geologic maps and the temporal comfort of geologic time. Yes, the Earth is 4.567 billion years old, but nonmicroscopic life-forms have only been around for 600 million years or so. I'm comfortable because I can map the infinity of fossils and fit it comfortably into my planet's timetable.

As we drove through the dark past Worland, I told Ray about all the cool digs we were passing. The basin is so rich that nearly every ridge has a story. For example, back in 1990, Scott Wing, a Smithsonian paleobotanist and my academic brother (we shared the same Ph.D. adviser, Leo Hickey), was working on Big Cedar Ridge in the southeast corner of the basin on a godforsaken piece of real estate known as the Honeycombs, a huge roadless area of brilliantly colored badlands composed of Paleocene and Eocene rocks. The sheer vastness of the Honeycombs had crushed the spirit of many an ambitious graduate student, but Scott had spent his entire career tracking the fossil plants of the Willwood Formation. He's not easily deterred by insane temperatures, long roads, and no water. He's keenly interested in what happened to plants at the Paleocene-Eocene transition, so he found himself wandering around the Honeycombs with shovel in hand, trying to find layers of fossil leaves.

It's simple geology that walking downhill in an area of flat-lying strata means you're going back in time, and that climbing the same hill means the rocks under your feet are getting younger. For me, this takes the sting out of climbing a hill, because I know that I can climb rocks a lot faster than it took to get them there in the first place. Assuming a reasonable sediment accumulation rate of 100 meters in a million years, that means you make or lose about 3,000 years for every foot of elevation that you gain or lose. A key point here is that sediment didn't always accumulate at a steady rate. Sometimes you can cross a horizon where time is missing, and sometimes that amount of time can be significant.

Geologists and paleontologists like to know how old the rocks are beneath their feet. I know that I'm always aware of this obscure information. Once I trained Ray, he knew that he could ask me at any point along the road and I would have a ready estimate of the age of the rock below the truck.

Back in the Honeycombs in 1990, Scott thought he knew where he was, but he didn't. He'd been working in 60-million-year-old rocks and had walked down a hill thinking that he was walking into 61-million-year-old rocks. In reality, he stepped over a time gap and ended up in 72-million-year-old rocks. No big deal; it could happen to anyone. But then he stuck his shovel into a weathered gumbo slope and flipped out an amazing fossil. Still not fully aware that he'd slipped out of the Paleocene and into the Cretaceous, he began to dig ferociously and realized

Paleobotanists Leo Hickey (left) and Scott Wing (right) at the edge of the Honeycombs near Worland, Wyoming.

that the whole ridgeline was made of fossil plants. He knew that he was digging into a rock that formed from volcanic ash, and he soon realized that the fossils were at the bottom of the ash layer. The more he dug, the more he realized that he was finding whole fossil plants: complete palmettos, whole ferns, darling little cycads. He had found a buried landscape, a plant Pompeii. Later, when he got the samples back to Washington, D.C., he realized that they were plants unknown in the Paleocene, and when he sent a sample of the ash to be dated, he learned that the site was 72 million years old and his fossils were from the Late Cretaceous Meeteetse Formation. Armed with this new information, he returned the next year with a

big team and opened up more than a hundred quarries, literally mapping a vegetational transect, or strip, through a Late Cretaceous landscape. It was the first time anybody had found such a site and followed the discovery with the absurd amount of work necessary to really reconstitute an ancient meadow. This kind of paleontology is a kind of time travel.

Today, the BLM office in Worland allows, even encourages, people to visit this site and to collect their own fossils. Unfortunately for Ray, it was another frustrating flyby, a cool fossil spot that we couldn't visit because we had other places to go.

It takes a paleobotanist to understand what the biggest herbivores of all time ate.

Instead, we rolled into Thermopolis, and the next morning we enjoyed Star Plunge, a very campy spigot for the world's largest hot springs. The geology of the nearby Owl Creek Mountains is such that rain falling on the mountains sinks into the ground and percolates to great depths, where the Earth's heat warms it up to over 100 degrees. Then a great fold in the rock layers beneath Thermopolis brings it right back to the surface, where it spews out at the rate of more than a million gallons a day. Smelling like rotten eggs, it's just the thing for the aching joints of a pair of road trippers. Taking the waters at Thermopolis is mandatory for all travelers, and the town has been a destination since mountain men soaked their stinky bones back in the 1830s.

In 1992, a wandering German fossil enthusiast-veterinarian named Burkhart Pohl was poking around for fossils in the Morrison Formation south of the Owl Creek Mountains. A rancher told him about similar outcrops in the hills behind Thermopolis. Burkhart could read a geological map better than the average Joe and learned that the same fold in the rock that brought the hot water to the surface also brought the thick and fossiliferous Morrison Formation to the surface. The rancher's relative was a realtor and, before he knew it, Burkhart found a ranch for sale for the right price and bought it for its dinosaur potential. Sure enough, the Morrison Formation produced, and Burkhart had a dinosaur quarry going by 1993.

People who like fossils often collect them. They also like museums and often have dreams of building them. Burkhart had a huge collection of European fossils and his own dinosaur quarry, so he decided to build his own museum. The Thermopolis city fathers were happy to entertain the idea of another tourist draw, and soon enough Burkhart built a giant square building. In 1995, he opened the Wyoming Dinosaur Center, another chapter in the great American dream (isolated paleonerd version). It seems it takes a German to keep Wyoming dinosaurs in Wyoming.

It's a big museum, full of wonderful European fossils and Jurassic dinosaurs from the ranch. There are daily tours to the dinosaur mines, where volunteers and employees are excavating the back side of a hill and finding tons of bones. Some of the bones go into the museum, but others have been sent overseas. The big *Apatosaurus* at the National Science Museum in Tokyo came from Burkhart's ranch. The quarry itself is a scary affair, since the layers of the Morrison Formation tilt into the hill and the huge sandstone blocks of the Cloverly Formation loom overhead. It seemed to me that the more Burkhart digs, the better his chances are of oversteepening the slope and bringing huge cubes of sandstone tumbling down on his dinosaur diggers. Not a place for a rainy day. We headed for the next basin.

reptile foot." Dave, while flattered, was also annoyed that he had missed the tracks when he was in the area in 1941. So it was that in his early 80s, he too climbed the ball-bearing hill to see the site of the four-toed tracks.

Just as I finished telling this tale to Ray, Dave and Jane rolled up their driveway in a green Subaru. They were delighted to see us, and Jane soon replaced our warm pops with ice-cold beers and crackers. Right off the bat, they told us that one of Dave's neighbors had found a fine fossil footprint in the red Triassic rock at the mouth of Dinwoody Canyon. This was interesting news, as these rocks were notoriously unfossiliferous. I remember reading a scientific paper from the 1930s about them that was more of a lament than a thesis. The authors talked about how they had searched the Chugwater and Popo Agie (pronounced "poh-pah-jah") formations around Riverton for months, expecting to find crocodile-like phytosaurs, small-headed herbivorous armored aetosaurs, and giant-salamander-like metoposaurs, the kind of fossils that are not uncommon in the Chinle Formation, the equivalent strata in northern New Mexico and Arizona. Instead, they found next to nothing. They talked about walking endless ridges for weeks, systematically dividing the outcrop and searching with great care. They knew that they wouldn't find anything if they didn't look, but they looked real hard and still didn't find anything.

So Dave's neighbor was especially lucky. Dave showed us a picture of the amazing five-toed track. It was about the size of my hand. Like the tracks that Hicks and I had found, this track was another example of a creature that left only footprints. A forensic mystery like so many fossils tracks, this was just one more example of how little we know about the past and how many more fossils there are to find and understand.

The perfect case in point regarded a site Dave had shared with me one memorable afternoon on a visit to Laramie. He had shown me tantalizing slides of a dinosaur bone bed from the high country south of Yellowstone. The images were yellowed, but the jumble of large bones was unmistakable. I asked him if a paleontologist had ever visited the site,

Saurexallopus lovei, a four-toed Cretaceous dinosaur known only from its tracks.

Macginitiea gracilis, an Eocene rain forest leaf named after Berkeley paleobotanist Harry MacGinitie.

and he was sure that none had. I started obsessing about Dr. Love's Lost Bone Bed and noted the coordinates.

Ray, knowing the story, quizzed Dave about the lost bone bed that afternoon. But Dave, in an impish way, derailed the topic and started talking about the evolution of the jackalope. He had a particularly fine mounted specimen of this uniquely western beast on his wall. It was clear that the conversation was going to be light that night. And so it was. We stayed too long and left too late to make it to Jackson, but we didn't want the Loves to think we were angling for a bed for the night. It was the last time I ever saw Dave, who died the next year.

I was quarrying fossils in Utah the week Dave died, and I drove alone across the length of Wyoming to attend his memorial service in Laramie. It was amazing to me how many outcrops I passed on that drive that he and I had discussed. I often think of Dave: his encyclopedic knowledge of Wyoming, his irreverent whimsy, and all the stories he didn't tell me. The big empty state of Wyoming will be a whole lot emptier without him. I've lost Dave, but one day I'm going to find Love's Lost Bone Bed.

West of Dinwoody, the valley of the Wind River narrows and becomes wooded. The evening sun lit up the brilliant red cliffs of the Wind River Formation on the north side of the road, and we rolled into Dubois just as the evening light was going flat. We stopped for gas, and I looked across the street at the old wooden sidewalk and storefronts that are typical of quasi-authentic western towns. Even though it was after nine, I noticed that there was a light on in the Two Oceans Bookstore.

What seems an odd name for a bookstore in the mountains of Wyoming is not so wrong when you realize that Togwotee Pass between Dubois and Jackson follows the Continental Divide. The water in the Wind River eventually makes it to New Orleans, while the water in the Snake River, which flows through Jackson Hole, will eventually reach the Pacific at Astoria, Oregon. I remembered that the owner of the bookstore had reprinted one of Dave Love's classic monographs on the geology of the Absaroka Mountains, so I wandered across the street and knocked on the locked glass door.

After a few moments, Anna Moschiki answered and invited us in. The store was closed, but she was picking something up and was curious about us. Ray was flattered to find that the store carried copies of his books, and Anna put him to work signing them. One thing led to another, and pretty soon we were headed to Anna's house up the valley for a beer and the chance to meet her husband, Mike Kinney. Mike is straight from central casting, a quintessential cowpoke with a big ol' mustache, and their cabin on the banks of the Wind River is packed with western literature. Soon the beer turned into a fine meal of bangers and mash, and they wouldn't hear of us pushing on. We spent the night talking about fossils, Mormons, and the fact that wolves from Yellowstone had been killing local dogs and horses. Anna and Mike, friends of the Loves, had been to visit the four-toed track site in the Bridger-Teton Wilderness and had found several more fine prints themselves. We talked on into the night about the possibility of someday mounting a packhorse expedition to find Dr. Love's Lost Bone Bed. The next morning, we had some strong mountain-cowboy coffee, said farewell to our new friends, and hit the road.

The valley of the upper Wind River is densely forested and densely fossiliferous. A number of Middle Eocene formations crop out amongst the trees. These outcrops contain fossil leaves and mammals from a time when tropical rain forests covered the slopes of the Wind River Mountains. This area has attracted generations of paleobotanists. One of my favorites is Roland Brown from the U.S. Geological Survey. Brown was a notorious penny pincher who wore the same pair of pants for many years, gradually adding panels of cloth as he added pounds of flesh. Like many a paleobotanist, he was a deft hand with a trimming hammer. When you collect hundreds of fossil leaves, you want to minimize the rock-to-fossil ratio to lighten your load. On an expedition in the Wind River Valley, he found a fossil site that produced a splendid fossil bird feather. Much to the horror of the geologists he was with, he proceeded to neatly trim the rock with a large hammer, not pausing to wonder "what if" he were to shatter the feather. He didn't. This is a skill that I've tried to learn over the years. It's come at the expense of many a fine fossil, but that's why they invented glue.

We crested Togwotee Pass and coasted down into Jackson Hole. The outcrops on the west side of the pass are from the Harebell Formation and have yielded the teeth of the enigmatic dinosaur known as *Leptoceratops,* a modest little cousin of *Triceratops* that seems to be more common in deposits formed near ancient mountain ranges. Maybe this little guy was the Rocky Mountain sheep of his day. At Moran Junction, we faced the option of heading north to Yellowstone or south to Jackson.

Yellowstone is hard to pass up. Difficult to get to and the source of many a mountain man tale, the high plateau region of northwest Wyoming is a volcanic wonderland that started erupting more than 50 million years ago and has been catastrophically active as recently as 700,000

years ago. An army expedition into Yellowstone in 1871 confirmed rumors of hot springs and geysers, which led to the place being called "Colter's Hell" after one particularly loquacious mountain man. In 1871, 42-year-old Ferdinand Vandiveer Hayden led a group that included scientists, surveyors, the painter Thomas Moran, and the photographer William Henry Jackson into Yellowstone. Hayden had been exploring the West since he graduated from college, and he already had a string of discoveries under his belt. On the banks of the Missouri River on one of his first trips west in 1854, he collected pieces of the first dinosaur ever found in North America. He loved natural history, and even though his primary goal was to survey land and resources, he sensed that the general public really wanted to hear about and see images of the amazing American West. On this trip, Hayden had some great artists with him and he made the most of their images. Armed with paintings and

Bluffs of the Eocene Wind River Formation near Dubois, Wyoming.

forests in church bulletins. I remember pained discussions in Sabbath school about the implications of these stacked forests and their conflict with Bishop James Ussher's 1658 proclamation that the first day of Creation was Sunday, October 23, 4004 B.C.

Interest in the Yellowstone fossils led the Seventh Day Adventist researchers to Mount Saint Helens after the great eruption of 1980. Here they made an interesting discovery. The blast from the eruption had blown down thousands of giant trees, and many of these trees ended up floating on the surface of nearby Spirit Lake. Eventually, the trees got waterlogged and started to sink. Since the base of the trunks were wider and heavier, they sank first, and many of the trees ended up floating vertically in the water column. Some of the trees sank and embedded themselves in the muddy lake bottom, creating a submerged standing forest that was buried where it didn't grow. In creationists' desire to compress time and confirm a biblical catastrophe, they discovered an interesting volcanic process. Despite this discovery, the presence of fossil soils and the fact that many of Yellowstone's petrified trees were actually rooted in the fossil soils showed that the Yellowstone forests really were stacked sequential forests, not transported ones. On a 4.567-billion-year-old planet, 6,000 years is simply not enough time to get serious work done.

It was ironic that my fundamentalist upbringing

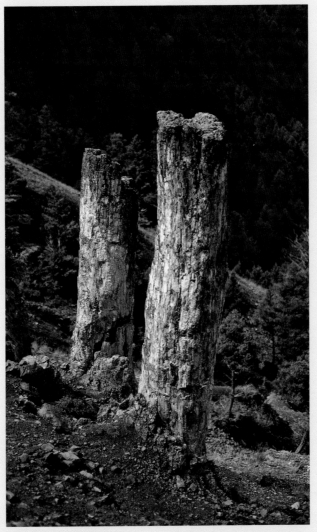

brought me into contact with the study of strata long before most kids even know that rock layers were once landscapes. In a church where Noah's flood was the default answer for any geologic problem, I started to think for myself. I remember standing by a road in British Columbia collecting fossil fish from a hill of paper shale. It occurred to me that each thin layer, or varve, might have been a year's deposit. I counted the varves in a foot of rock and guessed the thickness of the road cut. By my own teenage calculation, I was looking at 30,000 years. All teenagers rebel against something, and that day I sank Noah's ark. To their credit, my naturalist parents supported my observations and didn't let the dogma of their upbringing affect the progress of mine.

We resisted Yellowstone and turned south, driving into the valley of the Snake River, one of the prettiest places on the continent. My parents used to bring me to Jackson Hole in the summer, and it was here, in a parking lot near Jenny Lake, that I learned the pure joy of successful searching. I must have been about 10 years old at the time, and I got it in my mind that I could find an arrowhead. My mom was patient, but she had limits, so she told me I had five minutes to find an arrowhead and then we had to leave. I sprinted out of the car and began scanning the ground. Somehow I knew that I would have better luck in the bushes than on the open ground.

I crawled under a dense willow thicket and there, to my amazement, lay a beautiful obsidian arrowhead. I rushed back, well within the five-minute limit. My mom could not have been more surprised. Ever since that time, I have set out to find things with the faith that I will find them. For a paleontologist, this is a useful mind-set.

I can also remember riding the gondola at Teton Village to the top of the range and finding fossil marine brachiopods more than 10,000 feet above sea level. This was startling to me at the time, but now I know that mountains and seas come and go and marine fossils on mountaintops are the norm rather than an exception.

Jackson, like Cody, has been a western tourist town for a long time. Unlike Cody, however, the area around Jackson has been taken over by the insanely rich. In 2000, the median house price in Teton County was more than $565,000, a tenfold increase from 1980. The result is yet another western town where the townspeople can't afford to live. Jackson is full of overpriced trinket shops and wildlife art galleries. We could easily see why Dave and Jane Love had moved east. Nonetheless, I am full of childhood nostalgia for Jackson because it's a town that always had a rock shop, and who can argue with the four archways of elk antlers that bracket the central square or the staged gunfight that breaks out every summer afternoon. Still, the eternal traffic jam of motor homes and the relentless commercial strip south of town made us want to flee.

We broke out of Jackson around five and headed over Teton Pass to Victor, Idaho. We had arranged to meet my friends Susan and Mayo at their house in the country. Susan greeted us with a freshly baked apple pie that was topped with a toothy dough dinosaur. Mayo's murdering ways supplied us with a dinner of dinosaur descendants in the form of a brace of tasty grouse. After a splendid meal, I hit the pillow hard. But Ray was restless, because the next day we were headed to a place that he had longed to visit for years.

There is a bizarre fossil known as *Helicoprion* that had possessed Ray's artistic soul and piqued his thirst for the insanely weird since he first encountered it nearly 20 years ago. It's a whorled thing, ranging from a few inches to a few feet in diameter. From even a short distance, *Helicoprion* looks like a beautifully coiled ammonite. But let your eyes focus, and you'll see that the whorl is made of teeth. This wicked spiral is the business end of a Permian shark, and some of the best specimens in the world come from the eastern edge of Idaho. Ray first learned of *Helicoprion* when he saw one being used as a doorstop at the Natural History Museum of Los Angeles County in the late 1980s. Ray can be obsessive, and *Helicoprion* became his obsession. He'd visited whorl-tooth specialists and worked with them to make credible reconstructions of the animals, but he'd never found one in the wild.

Susan and Mayo joined us the next day, and we drove south along the long valleys, slipping back and forth between Idaho and Wyoming. The Idaho-Wyoming border country is composed of long linear ridges that run north and south and are the result of a messy geologic bust-up where nearly flat faults sliced and shifted rock layers like a deck of cards. This is the overthrust belt, a place where the layers of sedimentary rock are faulted but the basement rock doesn't come to the surface. Geologists call this kind of deformation thin-skinned, as opposed to the thick-skinned Rocky Mountains where the basement rock is shoved to the surface. Some of the same layers are here, but instead of being laid out in an orderly fashion, they're sliced like deli meat, and it can be real tough to know where you are in the geologic column. This, of course, made me edgy and unhappy. Ray didn't really care about the sordid details of the rock formations; he was fixated on his freak show of a shark.

Ray had a *Helicoprion* pen pal that he'd written to on a number of occasions, a fellow by the name of Jay Muir who worked in a phosphate mine near Afton. So we pulled into the home of the world's largest elk antler arch around noon, planning to meet up with him. The Phosphoria Formation, not surprisingly, has a lot of phosphate, the legacy of its origin as mud on the bottom of a Permian sea. Jay had worked the mines for 38 years, and he'd seen his share of *Helicoprion*. Ray was nervous and excited as we closed in on his "whorl-tooth blind date." We followed the instructions that Jay had given over the phone and soon pulled up in front of a two-story house at the edge of a foggy cow pasture. Susan, Mayo, and I hung back as Ray met Jay. Jay, a lean and lanky 60-year-old with a trimmed gray beard, caught his first glimpse of Ray and said, "I knew that you would have a gray beard just like mine." He invited us in, introduced us to his wife, and showed us some of his rock collection. Out in his yard, he had a giant concretion from the mine. Apparently, the whorls are found in the middle of concretions, just like the ammonites Ray and I had collected at Rock River. But Jay's was a gigantic concretion, the size of a beanbag chair. And it was very, very hard. I started calculating the size of the sledgehammer that would be needed to crack it open and soon realized that I wouldn't be able to lift such a hammer.

Jay took us to a local café for a hearty lunch. Ray ordered a chicken-fried steak and burrowed deeply into conversation with Jay. The date was going very well indeed, and Ray was bonding with his whorl-tooth brother. We discovered that in his 38 years in the mine, Jay had seen only six *Helicoprion* whorls, but we were feeling lucky, so we decided to visit the mine after lunch.

A whorl of shark teeth.

There was excitement in the air as we drove back into Idaho and up the road to the Smoky Canyon Mine. As we approached, we saw huge piles of concretions lining the road. These giant indestructible Milk Duds were a pain to the miners, but they made good riprap, so the mine used them to stabilize slopes. We stopped and looked at a few, but soon realized that there was no way we would ever get them open. Ray looked like he might burst into tears as it dawned on him that there must be shark spirals inside some of the hundreds of impregnable beanbag boulders that littered the hill, but he was never going to see them.

We parked at the entrance to the mine and signed in at the office where a big bear of a man gave us a safety test and issued us bright pink hard hats and shockingly yellow steel toes for our shoes. He was the local wrestling coach, and he told us to watch out for his boy, Rulon, in the upcoming Olympics. You might remember that Rulon Gardner went on to win the gold medal in 2000 by unexpectedly upending a giant Russian wrestler. At the time, we didn't think anything about it.

Garbed in our absurd pink hats, we toured the garage where the giant mining trucks were repaired. Ray was wondering if the ridiculously colored safety gear wasn't a way to humiliate city slicker visitors. We thought we saw more than one dust-covered miner chuckling to himself.

The immense mine produced phosphate ore, which was ground into a slurry and pumped to Pocatello, where it's used as fertilizer. It's sort of odd to think that your French fries are made from potatoes that are fertilized by ground-up Permian whorl-toothed sharks. Piles of concretions were all over the place. Some of them were eight feet in diameter. We scrambled over the mine spoils, convinced that we would find a whorl-tooth in a naturally cracked concretion. We hunted until it was starting to get dark and found a few fragments of fossil shell, but the sharks were elusive and our hammers were simply not up to the task. Reluctantly and with damp spirits, we left the mine and headed back to Afton without having seen even a fragment of a whorl-tooth. It was then that Jay mentioned that, years before, he had given one to a local elementary school.

The next morning, Jay, Ray, and I drove to the Osmond Elementary School, named after Donny and Marie's grandfather. School was in session, but we soon found the principal, Kelly Tolman, and asked him where he kept his shark. He really didn't know what we were talking about but said that there was a big rock out by the Dumpster. With mounting excitement, we rounded the building, and there, lying forlornly on the asphalt next to the Dumpster, was half of a big Phosphoria concretion. On its surface was a glorious 18-inch whorl. Ray fell to his knees. Kids had been jumping on the rock for years and there was some blue paint splattered on it, but nothing could hide the fact that this was still a fine fossil. It even held the impression of the shark's skin. Ray explained the significance of the fossil to Principal Tolman, who soon had us in a classroom in front of all of the teachers. Then the kids were released from class for an impromptu whorl-tooth presentation, and Ray got a stick of chalk and starting drawing a full-scale whorl-tooth on the concrete playground. Excitement was building as we explained to them just how rare these fossils were. By this time, Ray and Jay had fully bonded and were sharing secret whorl-tooth handshakes that looked like a cross between gang signs and rotating dishwashing maneuvers.

The team name for Osmond Elementary is the Star Valley Braves. Apparently it used to be Star Valley Cheesemakers, but that was just asking for a beating. Ray started berating the poor elementary school principal, telling him that if they had changed the name once, they could change it again, this time to the Osmond Elementary Fighting Whorl-Tooths. He promised to design a hip logo that could grace school jerseys. Principal Tolman was diplomatic, and we left town thinking we might actually have a chance at changing the mascot.

Ray and his whorl-tooth buddy, Jay Muir.

The children of Osmond Elementary doing the sign of the whorl.

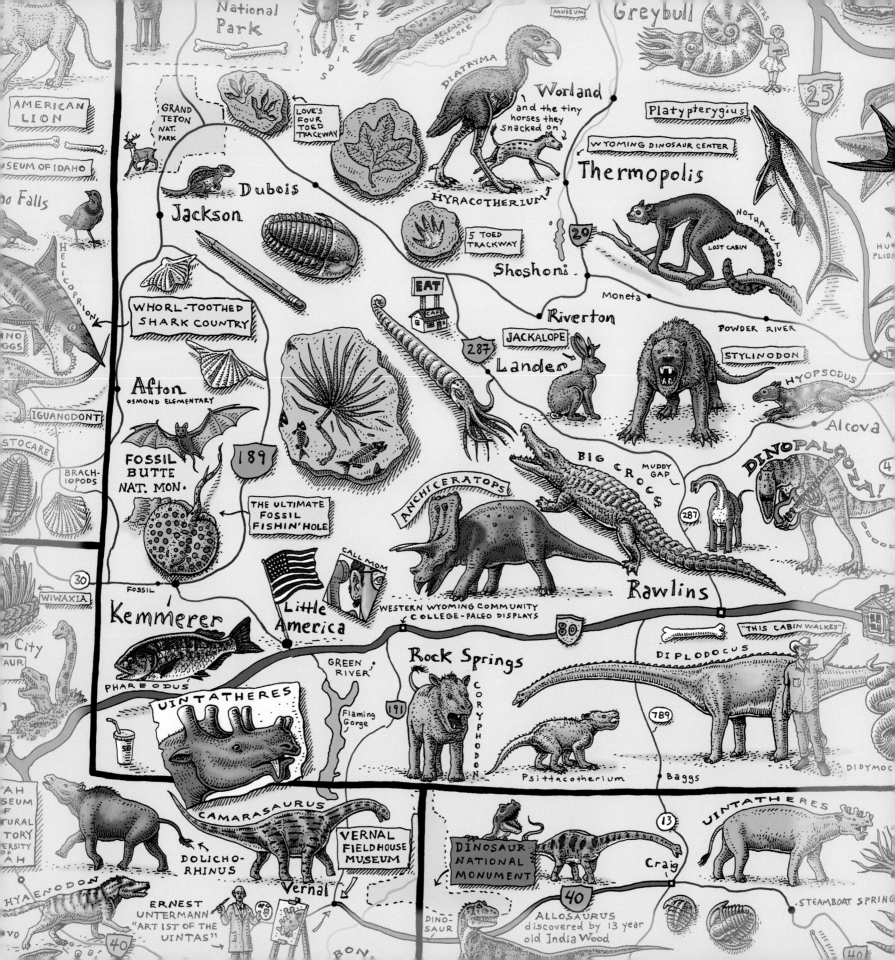

10
SURF AND TURF

There are few fossil sites more famous than the Green River fish beds near Kemmerer, Wyoming. The Green River Formation is a huge sequence of lake bed sediments that started to form as the Rocky Mountains were uplifted during the Paleocene. The mountains at the corner of Wyoming, Utah, and Colorado formed in such a way as to surround a huge area of low-lying land between them. It was a time when the climate was warm and wet and the runoff from the mountains had nowhere to go but into the land between the mountains. The great rivers that would eventually carve the Continental Divide didn't yet affect this area, and a series of huge lakes formed as the space between the mountains filled with water.

The southwest corner of Wyoming is also where the modern Rockies are their most gentle and aren't a formidable barrier to travelers. As a result, this area saw some of the first westbound explorers and, by the 1840s, became the path for the Oregon Trail. For this reason, Green River fossils were discovered very early in the game. The first paleontologists in southwestern Wyoming came by rail, and they couldn't miss the spectacular cliffs that paralleled the rail line (now Interstate 80). When they found fish in many of the layers, they realized that they were looking at the bottom of a huge lake.

Kemmerer, a hamlet that advertises itself as a "small town with a population of 103 pronghorn antelope, 113,000 fossil fish, and 3,000 people," is close to the Idaho line and a 50-million-year-old lake that formed between two ridges of the overthrust belt. Somehow, the lake's chemistry and sediment input were just right for fish to live, die, and be buried, three necessary ingredients for any fossil. A zone in the middle of the formation known as the 18-inch layer is the main pay zone. The fish from this layer are spectacular fossils, chocolaty brown bone on a creamy matrix that pulls up in sturdy table-sized sheets. The prepared fossils look like works of art, and they're often sold in frames.

There's skill and persistence in the excavation and preparation of these spectacular fossils, because the shale doesn't split cleanly away from the bone. Usually a few millimeters of the matrix coat the bone in such a way that you see a ghostly raised apparition of a fish skeleton in the rock. It takes a sure hand with a pocketknife, needle, or stiff brush and countless hours of patience to flake away the matrix and expose the fish.

Digging into the 18-inch layer is tricky. The rock is nearly white, so digging during the day can cause you to miss the subtle fossils due to the blinding reflection of the Wyoming sun. Some of the old-timers will get around this by working at night, using the low-angle light of a lantern to highlight the obscure lime-draped skeletons. One of my most surreal nights was spent digging the 18-inch layer from 10 P.M. until 4 A.M. with 82-year-old Lloyd Gunther and his 80-year-old wife, Freida. I was 31 at the time and happy to be there, but also dead tired and bone cold. It was all I could do to keep up with the tenacious octogenarians as they popped fish after fish out of the old lake bed and gave me a good look at marital bliss.

FISHES OF THE GREEN RIVER FORMATION

There's another zone, more suited for lazy men, called the "split fish" layer. Here the bone is apparent when the rock splits, but the fossils are not as pristine or beautiful as those from the 18-inch layer.

The fossil quarries in the valley are of two different types: those on private land and those on Wyoming state land. No regulations apply to the former, but the latter are administered by the Wyoming state geologist. Fossils deemed rare are supposed to be turned over to the state collections in Laramie. The federal government also manages BLM land in the valley, and, in 1972 Fossil Butte National Monument was commissioned from 8,720 acres of federal land. The stories about the fish diggers and their disputes are enough to fill a book, and Ray and I talked about all of this as we drove into the basin from Idaho. We'd both been here before, but we knew different diggers.

Our first stop was Carl Ulrich's house and shop at the head of the road that leads to the monument. Carl has been prying up shale and selling fish since 1947, and he's the senior fish digger in the valley. He has a prime quarry lease on state land and a skilled hand for preparing the fossils. He prepares the fish with an eye for artistic composition and then frames them like fine paintings. You can always tell an Ulrich fossil because Carl signs the lower right-hand corner, just like an artist signs a piece of art. Carl also had the bright idea of selling unprepared fish to would-be junior paleontologists. I spent much of my youth needling away on Carl's U-prep-it fish. I can tell you firsthand that Carl is one very patient person.

I met Carl's son, Wally, in Jackson when I was 12. He treated me like an adult, taking me to lunch and talking fossils at a local deli. Thirty-two years later, I walked into his Jackson fossil gallery with my new wife. He glanced at me for hardly a second before saying, "You've grown since I saw you last." Apparently, he kept track of the kids he took to lunch. Wally is also in the fish business, but he has branched into selling fossil fish from the tougher brown layers of shale, where the fish are hard to extract. He treats the stone like wood, sawing and planing it into slabs, exposing the fish by sanding and polishing the

Stingrays of Wyoming.

stone. The resulting pieces are hung as art or built into heavy but appealing furniture. The top of the bar at the Phantom Canyon Brewing Company in Colorado Springs is made of this stone, but few of the patrons realize that they are raising their pints from a surface that used to be the bottom of an ancient lake in Wyoming.

Many other families of diggers have also worked the valley, and more move in all the time, pulled by the lure of fossil fishing and the hope of finding something fantastically rare. Guys such as Jimmy Tynsky, Tom Lindgren, and Rick Hebden compete with the Ulrichs. They all dig for a living, but they also dig because they love finding the really rare stuff.

The meat and potatoes of the Green River fish business are five common species: *Knightia*, *Diplomystus*, *Priscacara*, *Phareodus*, and *Notogoneous*. They can be sold from the state leases without accounting. Species such as the big scaly garfish *Lepisosteus*, stingrays, paddlefish, and catfish are considerably rarer and are managed by the state of Wyoming. Of course, if you own or lease a quarry on private land, there are no restrictions on the rare fossils.

Besides the ubiquitous fish, there are some stunningly rare and fantastic plant and animal fossils from the 18-inch layer. These include whole alligators and crocodiles, turtles, complete palm fronds, birds, mammals, lizards, crawfish, insects, leaves, flowers, and even snakes. In 2004, Jimmy Tynsky, a longtime Green River digger, flipped over a four-foot slab and found a nearly perfect and wholly complete fossil horse skeleton. The little five-toed steed was laid out on the slab as though it were sleeping, and the rest of the slab was sprinkled with fossil fish in a sweet little surf-and-turf composition. The last time I checked, this fine fossil was residing in a bank vault in downtown Kemmerer.

The market has always lusted for these rare beauties, and many of the very best fossils have been spirited out of the basin and into private collections. Sometimes they're photographed or cast, but other times they simply vanish from the public eye. Today, a rare Green River fossil can easily fetch a six-figure sale price, and some are even in the seven-figure range.

One of the best ever found was a fossil bat collected in 1935 by Clarence Cushman and given to Princeton in 1941. It's an exquisite gem of a fossil, only about three by six inches but utterly complete. Princeton paleontologist Glenn Jepsen took his time and prepared the bat from both sides, eventually describing details as fine as the hammer, anvil, and stirrup bones of the tiny mammal's inner ear in a paper in *Science* in 1966. Wally told me that Jepsen used to carry these tiny bones around in a vial. When Princeton University decided to toss in the towel on paleontology in 1984, they gave their fossil mammal collection to the Peabody Museum at Yale. Today, the bat resides in a secure safe in New Haven. A few years ago, I made an appointment with dinosaur paleontologist and Yale curator John Ostrom to view the fossil. After much fussing, he pulled the tiny slab from the safe and handed it to me. I was surprised how small and perfect it was. To my delight, there, by its foot, was a fossil flower.

The fate of other Green River treasures is more obscure. A beautiful fossil boa constrictor was cast and replicated, but the whereabouts of the original are unknown. In the last decade alone, I've laid eyes on several bats, birds, and a couple of complete four-legged mammals. All of these specimens were destined for market and are now largely out of reach of science.

When Ray and I stopped to see Carl, we were amazed to discover that he had a small *Helicoprion* on display. Carl wasn't around, and the clerk had no idea where the fossil came from. Ray insinuated to the woman that he was prepared to pay any price for the whorl, but the hired help was well trained and politely rejected his entreaties. We admired a giant garfish that has graced Carl's shop for years and then headed for the national monument.

Fossil Butte National Monument has done an excellent job of working with both local commercial diggers and the scientists who do the primary research in the basin. Lance Grande, a bowfin fish specialist from the Field Museum in Chicago, is the reigning expert on the fossil fish of the Green River Formation, and his handbook to the fossils of the basin is like a bible to those who dig this pale rock. Lance has taken the time to get to know the diggers. As a result, the Field Museum has the best publicly owned Green River fossil collection.

We checked out the visitor's center, which does a good job of showing what the monument looked like when it was at the bottom of a lake, then we asked to see the collections. Sadly, we were told that the curator had gone and taken the keys with him. As we were about to leave, I recognized a face I knew in one of the offices down the hall: Vince Santucci, who had been on the other side of the fence from Pete Larson in the Sue incident. Vince is an odd duck: part hard-nosed cop and part practicing paleontologist. I first met him when he worked at Petrified Forest National Monument in Arizona. There he set up stings to catch people who stole souvenir pieces of petrified wood. He oversaw experiments in which they would spray a section of ground with paint that was invisible to the naked eye but showed up well under special lights. Then they would rephotograph the section of ground over time and calculate how much wood had been removed by stealthy tourists. The results were staggering: tons of fossils were being hauled away each year. Vince had also been stationed at Big Badlands National Monument in South Dakota, where he began enforcing the unenforced laws against collecting fossils.

Ray and I spent a couple of hours listening to Vince talk about protection of fossils on federal land. One of the main fronts of the controversy over who should and should not access the fossils occurs in southwestern Wyoming, which is spectacularly barren, chock-full of vertebrate fossils, and largely managed by the BLM. Vince told us about a zealous flying sheriff who ran a sting operation called Operation Rockfish in which he flew over the southwest corner of Wyoming in a Cessna looking for people out illegally collecting fossil fish. The Green River Basin is a gigantic area where rock hounds have long gone to collect the superabundant fossil herring known as *Knightia*. In one area near the tiny town of Farson, a fossil fish site looks like a heavily cratered World War I battlefield. But over the last 35 years, what was once common hobbyist practice has become illegal, and oblivious rock hounds have inadvertently become criminals. Crime and paleontology just seem like such odd bedfellows.

Ray and I talked about Rodney King and his infamous plea "Can't we all just get along?" It seemed silly to us that with so many fossils and so few people who love fossils, we can't find a better way to manage the resource. We both agreed that the best hope is clearly explaining the rules and regulations to as many people as possible.

We had lunch in Kemmerer and drove south along Fossil Ridge, a 50-mile-long ridge of the 92-million-year-old Frontier Sandstone. Fossil Ridge got its name because in places it is literally made of fossil oysters that lived along the shore of the Western Interior Sea. Many long ridges of Cretaceous sandstone in Wyoming are the remains of old beaches that have been tipped on end. At a place called Cumberland Gap, we cut through Fossil Ridge and into the Green River Basin. The Frontier Formation at Cumberland Gap is famous because the Frémont expedition of 1843 passed through this very spot. Here, Frémont himself found a layer full of spectacular fossil ferns.

We hoped to make it to Rock Springs by evening, so we sailed along, but we were passing over hallowed

Fossils and the Man

As it presently stands, there are no laws that concern collecting fossils on private land. For this reason, there's a legitimate commercial industry of fossil collectors who work on land they own or lease. Different states have different laws and regulations for state-owned land, and each one is slightly different. In addition, there are several kinds of federal land—Bureau of Land Management, Forest Service, National Park, Bureau of Reclamation—and each of them has slightly different rules and regulations as well. Indian reservations also have their own rules.

Perhaps the most controversial type of federal land is managed by the Bureau of Land Management (BLM), whose mandate is multiple use. Presently, private individuals can collect reasonable amounts of plant and invertebrate fossils for personal use on BLM land, and scientists may collect significant invertebrate, plant, and vertebrate fossils, as long as they obtain a permit and give all of the fossils to a federal repository. No form of commercial paleontology is permitted.

The BLM was formed to manage the land that was left over after the more arable acreage was homesteaded and the forested land was placed under the jurisdiction of the U.S. Forest Service. BLM land comprises much of the fossiliferous badlands of the American West. Commercial diggers would like access to this land and argue for multiple use.

Amateur paleontologists are allowed to collect on BLM land but must beware that they don't accidentally collect vertebrate fossils. Museum and university paleontologists can collect on BLM land but must make sure their permits are in order.

ground. The southern part of the Green River Basin is known as the Bridger Basin. The Bridger Basin was the site of one of the first mountain man rendezvous in 1825, and these crusty old beaver-trapping boys apparently knew a fine fossil when they saw one. Rumors of the region's fossils traveled back East. The completion of the Union Pacific Railroad in 1869 made it possible for an eastern academic to hop a train in Philadelphia and be in the Bridger Basin less than a week later. For this reason, the Bridger became a proving ground for the budding young field of American paleontology; nearly all of the important early workers cut their teeth on the badlands of the Bridger.

Joseph Leidy, naturalist extraordinaire from the Academy of Natural Sciences in Philadelphia, was one of the first, arriving in Bridger Basin in 1872. The blue-gray badlands of the Bridger are full of 50-million-year-old fossils, and here Leidy found the bizarre skulls of the knob-headed, saber-toothed herbivore known as the uintathere. Within a few years, both Edward Cope from Philadelphia and O. C. Marsh from Yale arrived in Fort Bridger and started collecting, describing, and naming uintatheres. In their haste to outpublish each other, they described fragments rather than complete skeletons and made a mess out of the scientific literature. Leidy grew disgusted with the antics of his junior colleagues and retired from the field, leaving Cope and Marsh to battle it out. Cope's work resulted in the publication of a massive 1,009-page, 16-pound, 5-ounce volume, *The Vertebrata of the Tertiary Formations of the West*, published in 1883. This monster of a book has come to be known as Cope's Bible. Marsh, in order to outfox Cope, led a group of Yale students over the Uinta Mountains into the Uinta Basin in 1870, and he published the results of that trip in a two-volume set in 1886 that named even more uintathere species.

In 1876, three Princeton undergraduates, avoiding exams by lounging in the shade along a canal in New Jersey, decided that rumors of fossils out West were just too good to be ignored and organized their own expedition. Two of these guys, Henry Fairfield Osborn

A shattered fossil turtle shell in the Bridger Basin. Turtles and turtle fragments are some of the most common vertebrate fossi

and William Berryman Scott, were to become towering figures in the study of fossil mammals. Osborn went on to establish the American Museum as the premier vertebrate paleontology museum in the world, and Scott returned to Princeton to build their program and launch a series of successful expeditions to the fossil fields of Patagonia. Each wrote a major book about fossil mammals: Osborn's *The Age of Mammals* was published in 1910 and Scott's *A History of Land Mammals in the Western Hemisphere* was published in 1937.

Ray and I were surprised to learn that Scott traveled with a paleontologically inclined artist named R. Bruce Horsfall. Now largely forgotten, Horsfall's images of the extinct mammals of North America are some of the finest ever drawn. The scientist-artist duo is one that we had originally thought was pretty

Hauling a cast of the strange skull of a uintathere.

novel, but the more we read, the more we realized that we were just reliving an old tradition of natural history.

Succumbing to the same passion for extinct mammals, Ray was nuts about uintatheres. If you're an artist, you naturally gravitate to the unusual or spectacular, and the knobby-headed uintathere has long been a favorite for the visually inclined. Uintatheres first originated in Asia and migrated to North America via the Bering Land Bridge. They flourished here through the middle years of the Eocene before becoming extinct. Uintatheres were big beasts, the size of rhinos but with incredibly wide pelvic bones; in other words, they were shaped like pears. These were the easy fossils to find because the weathered skeletons could be seen for miles. But the Bridger Basin is also rich in smaller mammals. And whereas one could easily find a uintathere from horseback, it took careful crawling to find the other critters. Leidy found and described the skeleton of a monkeylike primate that he called *Notharctus*. Fossil turtles and crocodiles were common. And the most common mammal was the *Hyopsodus*, or tube sheep, which are so abundant in the Bighorn Basin.

Like the Bighorn Basin, the Bridger Basin has remained a mecca for fossil mammalogists for the last century. In the early 1990s, Richard Stucky of the Denver Museum began working in the Bridger Basin. By then, most of the easy-to-find fossils had been collected, so he concentrated on the small stuff. I joined the crew for two different seasons and was amazed by the number of crushed fossil turtles that littered the landscape. In one place we found a layer of crushed turtles nearly a meter thick. This interbedded mud and turtle lasagna really made me think about why turtles make such extraordinarily common fossils.

It's likely that when you're searching for fossil bone in the American West, the first fragment you find will be from a poor deceased turtle. The more I thought about it, the more I realized that turtles are the perfect animal for fossilization. First, they live in ponds, lakes, and streams: places that are always accumulating mud and sand. Second, the turtle's shell is like

a heavy box that sinks to the bottom of the pond when the animal dies. It dawned on me that turtles wear their own coffins and live in their own graveyard. Looking at these piles of crushed turtles, I couldn't help but think of Dr. Seuss and Yertle the Turtle, the king of the turtles who stacked all of his subjects in a huge pile so he could climb to the top and see all that he owned. And here we were, 50 million years later, looking at the fossilized remains of Yertle's folly.

Ray and I continued east on Interstate 80 across the north side of Bridger Basin and stopped at the original Little America truck stop for soft ice cream and to call my mom. A few miles later, we rolled down the hill into Green River and saw the majestic cliffs of the Green River Formation. These same cliffs had inspired 34-year-old Thomas Moran when he stepped off the train from Cheyenne in 1871. He fell in love with this view and sketched and painted it many times. His classic image, *The Cliffs of Green River,* was painted in 1874, and he was still painting versions 44 years later. Also here was the spot where on May 24, 1869, John Wesley Powell and his brave crew launched wooden boats that they would eventually run through the unknown Grand Canyon.

We had an appointment to meet Dave Love's son Charlie in Rock Springs. Any son of Love's is bound to be interesting, and Charlie delivered in spades. Part geologist, part archaeologist, Charlie has made a career at Rock Springs Community College, where, oddly, he researched the giant stone statues of Easter Island in the South Pacific. He was trying to solve the age-old problem of how the Easter Islanders moved their monuments. His approach was pure small-town common sense with a dose of big think. He began by building full-scale concrete models of the statues. Then, with rolling logs,

A stack of Eocene turtles. (below) This full-size concrete replica of an Easter Island stone head can be found on the grounds of Western Wyoming Community College.

ropes, and Rock Springs students, Charlie showed how easy it was to move the massive stones. He had parked one of the giant concrete heads out behind the college, and I parked Big Blue next to it. Ray was impressed by the absurdity of it all.

Charlie knows the power of fossils, and he's turned an otherwise obscure community college into a flashy destination museum by working with a local welder to mount stylish and acrobatic casts of dinosaurs around the campus.

The student lounge features a dynamically posed *Tyrannosaurus rex*, and the hallways are lined with a giant Green River turtle, a huge Cretaceous Kansas fish, a graceful Colorado plesiosaur, and a variety of dinosaurs. The lawns around the school support huge boulders from the Wind River Mountains, Charlie's attempt to bring the older rocks from the mountains' flanks to Rock Springs, where lazy geology students bump into them on their way to class.

Rock Springs is situated at the western edge of a geological structure called the Rock Springs Uplift. Like a smaller version of South Dakota's Black Hills, the uplift is an oval structure with the oldest rock layers in the center. Unlike the Black Hills, which expose Precambrian basement rock at their core, the center of the Rock Springs Uplift exposes Late Cretaceous marine shale. The flanks of the uplift are formed by interbedded marine shale and coastal sandstone deposits, and the town of Rock Springs sits on the sandstone and coal of the Rock Springs Formation, an 80-million-year-old complex of beaches and swamps. As a result, Rock Springs has a long history as a coal miners' town; an old but surprisingly stylish neon sign down by the tracks still advertises the virtues of Rock Springs coal. The old downtown is a trip back to a time when Rock Springs was a coal-mining town on the Union Pacific line. Now the trains roll through every hour or so, but they no longer stop, and the classic old downtown buildings are occupied by tanning salons and junk shops.

A few blocks away are the archaeological ruins of a rock shop from my childhood. Den's Petrified Critters is a building that looks like it was made from log mill scrap. Ray and I peered through the broken glass and saw the remains of a once-thriving business of fossil fish. Doors hung lazily open on a couple of sheds in the backyard, and shards of fossils mixed with weeds along the battered wooden sidewalk. I remembered Den as a crusty fossil dealer known for using paint to enhance the charms of the fossil fish he sold. From all accounts, it looked like Den had left town. A few blocks away, at the slightly less dilapidated and still inhabited Tynsky Rock Shop, we learned that Den had headed to Arizona one autumn and never returned.

Tynsky is a big name in the fossil fish fields of southwestern Wyoming, but Tynsky namesakes were absent from this operation. The shop had traded owners a few times, and none of them had bothered to change the sign. The yard around the shop was piled deeply with chunks of petrified wood and *Turritella* agate. The owners, with an eye on the bottom line, had also branched out into aromatherapy, giving me yet another reason to mourn the decline and fall of the great American rock shop.

There was a time when almost every small town in the American West had a rock shop or two, evidence of the dual opportunities of the prospector and the treasure hunter. All you had to do was load up the camper, go out into the desert, and collect rocks. Somebody would eventually stop by to buy them. As a kid, I used to pore over the pages of *Lapidary Journal* and *Rock and Gem*. These magazines always included bad maps to remote spots where you could find your own rocks and minerals. In every city in the West, there was a network of rock and mineral clubs that would meet monthly to compare their finds and handiwork.

Many of these groups still exist, and they host annual gem and mineral shows. The largest by far is the February monster of a show in Tucson. All across the Rocky Mountain West, when a rock enthusiast says he's "going to Tucson," you know exactly what he means. It seems that every guy in the world with a cool rock or two loads up a van and heads to southern Arizona in the spring. Including everything from sprawling lobbies full of amethyst geodes to a couple of guys sitting quietly in a hotel room with a fossilized elephant skeleton, the Tucson show is one overwhelmingly weird nosedive into the world of the rock and fossil obsessed. Ray and I had "done Tucson" a couple of times, so we shared memories of the big event. In a lot of ways it's like the old mountain man rendezvous. Crusty old diggers come pouring out of the hills to sell the goods they've accumulated over a hard year and whoop it up with the similarly inclined. I suppose the addition of crystal healers, museum curators, schoolkids, and wealthy collectors makes the Tucson show an imperfect analogy. But driving east, we yukked it up talking about the fossil man rendezvous and decided that once again, we'd be there.

11
THE RAGING UINTATHERES OF VERNAL

There aren't many paved roads south of Rock Springs. This region contains the Sand Wash and Washakie basins, areas revered by paleontologists for their fossil mammals. In the middle of this 5,000-square-mile forgotten quarter is a haunting maze of fossil-filled badlands known as Adobe Town. About 60 miles south of Rock Springs, as the road started to head downhill, we rounded a corner and saw a deep basin of brick-red badlands.

We had entered Utah. Almost immediately, the geology began to play ball. As we approached the Uinta Mountains, the layered strata older than the Wasatch Formation had been tilted up so that it dipped north and exposed as a series of east-west ridges, each older than the previous one as we headed south. By the time we reached Dutch John, we'd driven all the way from the Eocene back into the Precambrian. We paused at the dam to glance at Flaming Gorge Reservoir, which was buzzing with ski boats, Jet Skis, and small cruisers. We spotted a geologic road sign that claimed to explain the local geology, and eagerly pulled over to inspect it. The sign was pretty, but the geology was so miserably explained it virtually guaranteed that curious travelers would walk away confused and uninterested. We harrumphed loudly and jumped back into Big Blue for the steep climb up the Uinta Mountains.

The Uintas are the odd mountains out when it comes to the Rockies. To start with, they're oriented east-west. Then, unlike all the rest of the Rockies, which are cored by Precambrian crystalline rocks, the Uintas are cored by Precambrian sedimentary rocks. The Precambrian Uinta Mountain Group is a nearly three-mile-thick pile of layered fossil-free sandstone that formed at the bottom of a shallow sea back when the largest living thing on the planet was smaller than the period at the end of this sentence. Apparently, this chunk of east-west terrain along the Wyoming-Utah border was a huge tear in the Earth's crust that allowed sand to accumulate while the rest of the region was suffering the ravages of E-World.

Downstream from the dam, the Green River winds lazily through Brown's Park, a rolling, drab landscape floored with Miocene sediments. Then the river does that amazing thing the Rocky Mountain rivers do: it flows directly into a mountain range, once again demonstrating that the river is older than the mountains. At the Gates of Ladore, the Green flows into a 2,000-foot-deep canyon whose walls are composed of layer after layer after layer of 1.6-billion-year-old Uinta Mountain Group sandstone. If you were to launch a raft at Ladore and float the Green, you would literally float across the mountain range. After crossing the center point of the range, the bedrock begins to dip to the south, so the river climbs up through the layered rocks.

After a long grind up through a thick pine and cedar forest, we crested onto a high plateau covered with patches of lodgepole pines and aspen. Once the road started downhill, we began to notice highway signs that pointed out the geological formations. The first few signs were odd, because they'd been placed in the woods, where it was impossible to see any rocks. We had pity for the hapless geological tourists who tried to make heads or tails of these wretched signs.

Then, as the road steepened, the rocks came into view, and we rolled down the south face of the range and climbed into younger and younger rock layers, because the tilt of the layers was steeper than the grade of the road. The main descent occurred over half a dozen switchbacks that snaked along the margin of an active phosphate mine. We realized as we drove that this was the Permian Park City Formation, a lateral equivalent to Ray's beloved Phosphoria Formation. This meant that the miners, unbeknownst to themselves, might be having casual encounters with whorl-toothed sharks. To my knowledge, no one has ever found one of these sharks in this mine, but they must be there, just like they're in the mines near Afton, Wyoming.

At the bottom of the hill, just past the mine entrance, the highway flattened out and rock layer after layer came splendidly into view. As I drove past the formations, I chanted the strange and evocative rock-reciting poetry of a driving geologist to my bemused artist friend. Ray cranked James Brown on the CD player, and I belted out the names of the formations as we passed them: "Dinwoody, Moenkopi, Shinarump, Chinle, Navajo, Carmel, Entrada, Curtis, Morrison, Cedar Mountain, Dakota, Mowry, Frontier, Mancos." In the 20 miles between the mine and the edge of the town of Vernal, we drove through 13 different Mesozoic formations, from the brick-red 225-million-year-old Dinwoody to the 80-million-year-old monotonous dark gray Mancos Shale. We stopped several times to look at the layers, finding bits of fossil fish in the black flaky shale of a fresh Mancos road cut and feeling like the funk from the CD had called the fossils from the hill.

We gave up when the sun went down. Hungry and happy, we rolled into the dinosaur-obsessed town of Vernal and got a room at the Best Western Dinosaur Inn, where we found small plastic dinosaurs next to the complimentary toiletries. After a

few gin and tonics poolside and a bona fide ranch-sized meal at the 7-11 Ranch Café, we made our way back to the hotel and slumped into the hot tub.

Apparently, a bunch of local high-school kids knew the code to the hot tub room, and we were soon joined by a trio of teenage Vernalites. After our attempt to change the school mascot in Afton, Wyoming, to a whorl-toothed shark, we thought that we'd have a go at changing the Uintah High School mascot to the Raging Uintatheres. It's tough to convince someone to give up their team mascot, but we figured that the present name, the Uintah Utes, wasn't really politically correct anyway, so Ray broached the idea with the kids. They looked at us like we were completely out of our gourds and slid off to the other side of the pool in embarrassed silence.

Like many of Utah's lost corners, Vernal is a remote and unremarkable town made exquisite by its geologic setting. Located just south of the Uinta Mountains on the northern margin of the Uinta Basin, it lies at the center of a paleontological paradise. This treasure was initially discovered by O. C. Marsh, who focused on the flat-lying Eocene rocks in the middle of the basin and was handsomely rewarded with a hoard of Eocene mammals and a jackpot of uintatheres. But it was Andrew Carnegie's man Earl Douglass who really made the place famous. In 1909, he found a string of giant vertebrae on a tilted ridge of Morrison Formation sandstone high above the north bank of the Green River where it spews out of the Uintas at Split Mountain. Douglass excavated his way into the tough sandstone, and soon the ridge was a veritable dinosaur mine, producing splendid skeletons of *Apatosaurus, Camarasaurus, Diplodocus, Stegosaurus,* and *Camptosaurus.*

His efforts stocked the Carnegie Museum with dinosaurs, and there were enough left over for the Smithsonian and the University of Utah. After all the smoke had cleared, nearly 40 skeletons had been chipped and blasted out of the ridge, and parts of dozens remained embedded in the mountain wall.

In 1915, the place was named Dinosaur National Monument. Douglass built a cabin on the banks of the Green River and spent the rest of his life collecting Jurassic dinosaurs and Eocene mammals. In 1958, a building was constructed over the remnants of the Douglass Quarry. Regardless of the huge number of skeletons that

have been removed, this still remains the best place in the world to see dinosaur bones in place, a virtual gateway to the Jurassic. In a response to the dinomania that swept the region, the state of Utah decided to open a small museum of its own in Vernal. The Utah Field House of Natural History State Park opened its doors in 1945. At the time of our visit, the state of Utah was planning a major renovation to the old building. I'd been retained by a Seattle design firm to act as the paleontologist for the renovation, so I'd recently made several trips to Vernal and was familiar with the collections and the museum. The old building was still intact and open for business, and I was anxious to show Ray the highlights of this classic old joint.

We woke to a nearly perfect day that happened to be the Fourth of July and ate a substantial breakfast. We finished up just in time for the parade down Main Street. Vernal is an all-American town, but it's also a dinosaur town, so the parade combined the usual rodeo queens and veterans in convertibles with a whole host of giant papier-mâché dinosaurs. We thought they were missing a beat by not exploiting the uintathere theme.

It was starting to boil and I was raring to show Ray the treasures of the Field House, so we walked half a block from the Dinosaur Inn to the squat, square brick building. The entry foyer was nondescript, but it contained five notable objects: two petrified trees, two paintings, and a stone transom inscribed with the words "A knowledge of the past makes understandable the present and serves as a guide to future." It was a nice invitation indeed.

The paintings were fantastic. One showed a Triassic phytosaur lounging in a compelling and realistic yet strangely Dr. Suessian forest. In my mind, most prehistoric landscape paintings are ruined by the irresistible pull of the present. Who can blame the artist who paints familiar landscapes populated by extinct animals? Artists, after all, are animals of the modern landscape themselves, and there are very few good references to work from when reconstituting extinct ecosystems. Nonetheless, I almost always feel that these paintings look too modern, too "today." But not these strange pastel-colored canvases hanging freely at the Field House entry. We had entered the world of Untermann.

Ernest Untermann was a friend of Jack London and translated London's work into German. He was an ardent Communist who also translated Marx into English. Born in Germany in 1864, Untermann went to sea on American sailing ships at the age of 17 and had the misfortune but romantic good luck to be twice shipwrecked in the South Seas. After the second wreck, he drifted alone in an open boat for 21 days before washing ashore on an island. He lived there with the locals for more than a year before being rescued. By the time he was 29, Untermann had come ashore, studied geology and paleontology, and was working in the Rockies, briefly visiting Vernal in 1919. This was followed by stints in the 1920s and 1930s collecting zoological specimens for scientific supply houses in Brazil and East Africa. His interests in paleontology and animals led him to pursue art. He studied at the Chicago Art Insti-

tute and later under a painter named William Heine, who was famous for painting grand battle panoramas. Tireless and versatile, Untermann embroiled himself in politics on one hand and animals and art on the other, ending up as the director of the Milwaukee Zoo. In 1940, after a controversial tenure no doubt soured by his politics, he retired from his position and, in his 75th year, moved to Vernal to live near his son George, also known as Getty, who was a ranger at Dinosaur National Monument. In 1945, when the Field House opened its doors, Getty was appointed its first director, Getty's wife, Billie, was named staff scientist, and old Ernest was appointed an unsalaried staff artist.

Untermann was a man who saw the past clearly. His paintings of the area around Vernal are crisp and colorful. They depict the local landscapes, Native Americans, and the lost worlds that are preserved as fossils. He was a man obsessed with *Allosaurus* and uintatheres. His canvases were covered with herds of titanotheres, *Triceratops* goring *T. rex*, frolicking plesiosaurs, and playful creodonts. In some of the images, he painted subtle figures of naked women into the clouds or the desert outcrops. The paint-

ings are equal parts Grandma Moses, Henri Rousseau, and ribald paleontologist. In the nearly 20 years between his move to Vernal and the day he died at the age of 92 in 1956, Untermann painted hundreds of canvases. These paintings had spread around town, showing up in restaurants and private collections, some changing hands at yard sales, but most of the vast body of work staying where he worked, stashed in the fossil museum.

While Ernest painted, Getty and Billie built the museum into a local treasure. They fanned the local dinosaur frenzy and oversaw the construction of a dinosaur garden populated by huge fiberglass dinosaurs of dubious proportions. They even acquired a cast of *Diplodocus carnegii*, the animal from Sheep Creek, Wyoming, that Carnegie had sent around the world. For years, the big concrete *Diplodocus* graced the front yard of the Field House, and Vernal had the opportunity to say, "London, Paris, Rome, Buenos Aires, Vernal." Of course, it didn't think to say that, but it could have.

While dozens of the paintings were hanging on the walls of the museum, there were scores more gathering dust in the museum's antiquated attic, an odd space that was no more than five feet tall. The museum's curator, Sue Ann Bilbey, led us to them. We made our way up a rickety wooden ladder into a room full of paintings. Sue Ann had a wheelchair that allowed her to wheel around the stunted room, and, one at a time, we wheeled ourselves past a huge and partially crushed uintathere skeleton on our way to Untermann's art. Sue Ann told us that the big uintathere skeleton was loaded with uranium ore and was "hot." A second uintathere skeleton was mounted high on the wall. Apparently this one, a papier-mâché model, had been purchased from Ward's Scientific Company sometime in the distant past. The paper was actually shredded money from the mint. Then came the paintings. Ray was in heaven, trying to channel Untermann through his images of Eocene mammals. We found an amazing self-portrait of the old commie with a tiny uintathere posed regally above one shoulder and a snarling Allosaurus gnashing its teeth over the other. "Oh my God, it's like a Van Gogh with two dueling muses," Ray murmured. He had clearly

met his own muse, and we spent the afternoon pulling one masterpiece after another from the rickety rope contraption that held the frames. Funky old paintings, radioactive uintatheres, and uintatheres made of cash: this place was too good to be true.

We returned to the main part of the Field House to admire the fossils on display. In one case there was the skull and jaws of an animal

Kirk and a taeniodont, the bizarre Eocene mammal that seems to be all about teeth.

that would come to captivate us both. It was a stylinodontine taeniodont, a beast whose lineage appeared around 65 million years ago and lasted until 42 million years ago when it checked out for good. Taeniodonts are leopard-shaped mammals with massive claws on front and back feet. Their jaws are crammed full of pluglike teeth. The result is a buck-toothed wombat with a catlike tail. Ray goes for the creatures that no one has ever reconstructed, or at least reconstructed well, and the taeniodonts would become an obsession.

Later, in the cool of the evening, we wandered down Main Street to the middle of town. All around us the locals were lining up lawn chairs in vacant lots, anticipating the fireworks. There was a half-block-long white building on the south side of the street that I wanted to check out. I'd been there once before back in the early '90s when the building had housed a truly amazing fossil shop. I bought a beautiful fossil crab from the Cretaceous of Tennessee and a stunning finned ammonite from the chalk beds near Fort Worth; both of these fossils are prizes of the *Prehistoric Journey* exhibit at the Denver Museum of Nature & Science. The proprietor was a tough-talking woman named Lace Honert. Based on the fantastic fossils I saw in her shop that day, it was clear that Lace was a bona fide digger. I was curious if she was still around.

(right) Taeniodont skull.

The storefront windows were covered with white paper, and the shop was clearly no longer in business, yet the wonderful sign on the side of the building still displayed the name of the store, "Remains To Be Seen," high above the street. I knocked on the door. Nothing. I pounded. This time Lace materialized and invited us in. She had friends over, and they were sitting on the big, flat tar roof drinking beers and waiting for the fireworks to start. We climbed over her toilet and wriggled out the bathroom window to join them. Ray and I told Lace that we were driving around the West looking for the best fossil stories. She lifted an eyebrow and squinted at us. Sizing us up, she handed out beers and said, "Well, I've got a few stories for you."

In the off-season (the non-digging season, that is), Lace lives in Texas. She's married to a guy named Jim who was once Pete Larson's partner. Lace told us that she decided to marry Jim because of his "localities." Ray said, "Localities?" "Localities," Lace replied, clearly annoyed that Ray didn't understand she had chosen her mate because of his knowledge of where to find fossils.

Somehow Lace had learned about Untermann and had driven out to Vernal with the hope of acquiring one of his paintings. Instead, she ended up buying the building on Main Street and a piece of fossil-rich land near the town of Dinosaur, Colorado, where she runs her very own dinosaur quarry. She often works alone, wrestling giant dinosaur leg bones out of the ground when the need arises. She remains the only woman I know who owns her own backhoe. Tellingly, her female fashion sense is intact but a bit warped. The Imelda Marcos of the fossil-hunting set, Lace owns more than 30 pairs of field boots.

After a few more beers, Lace could see that what Ray and I were really after was an adventure of some sort. She started talking about a truly fantastic fossil site that she had stumbled across while hiking near Dinosaur National Monument. As the fireworks started up, she promised to take us there the next day.

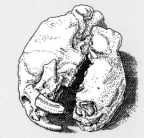

The next morning dawned a sizzler. Lace pulled up in a very large truck, and we rolled down the road from Vernal to Jensen, a long commercial stretch festooned with vintage commercial dinosaur sculptures. After entering the monument, we crossed the Green River and drove until the road changed to red dirt. Lace parked at the base of a large slope, and we climbed a couple of hundred feet up to the base of a huge sandstone cliff. Because I'm a big guy

and I like climbing hills, I moved faster than Lace and Ray and was standing at the base of the cliff when they huffed into view. Just then, I realized that the rock face was covered with subtle petroglyphs.

Lace pointed to my right where a huge chunk of the cliff had broken away, creating a giant fissure. The opening was less than a yard wide, but the crack was easily a hundred feet high. I stepped into the opening and stopped, realizing that spooky life-sized guardian figures were engraved on both facing walls.

I know that a lot of people get the willies around big petroglyphs. Ray is one of them. He could feel the power of the art, and he started to freak a little. Lace smiled and said, "See, cool place," then sauntered up the crack. Ray noticed that there were giant spirals etched on either side of the fissure. "The Indians must've dug whorl-toothed sharks too," he said as he stepped into the big hallway of rock.

The floor of the crack sloped steadily up, and within about 100 yards we were at the top of the cliff standing at the edge of a stunted juniper forest. Lace took off and we followed her for at least a mile, dodging trees and sandstone slabs until we came to a small canyon. We lowered ourselves down the rock walls and followed them up valley for a couple of hundred yards to a 10-foot overhang. Lace hung back and said, "Check it out."

I crawled under the overhang and looked up. There, above my head, projecting down from the flat sandstone surface, were the polygonal projections of fossil mud cracks. Scattered across the surface were a medley of small tracks, some three-toed, others four. The mud between the tracks was a lovely bright green, and the rock itself was red. I looked down and

saw the sandstone slab that had fallen to create the overhang. Its surface was the mirror image of the surface from which it had fallen. The rock was just so beautiful, the colors, the polygons, the tracks. Lace really had known what we were after.

The three of us sat there, imagining the little Jurassic dinosaurs skittering across a drying lake bed, a moment from 180 million years ago frozen in time. I tried to picture the rest of their world. The cliff was part of the Navajo Sandstone, a Jurassic formation known because it's largely composed of lithified sand dunes. It's thought to represent a Sahara-like sand sea that covered much of the Four Corners region around 180 million years ago. Few complete skeletons are known from the Navajo, and fossil plants are even more rare, although the occasional fossil tree trunk does show up. These tracks, perfect as they were, represented an incomplete message from a lost time. Truly impressed, we climbed back out of the canyon and headed back into the 21st century.

Although we'd all been there before, we decided we shouldn't pass up the opportunity to see the giant quarry wall at Dinosaur National Monument. The fact is, Earl Douglass really did discover one of the greatest fossil sites in the entire world. We drove up the winding road from the valley of the Green River, back through the tilted

(right)
The enigmatic taeniodont.

Fossil leaves are like potato chips: you can't have just one. These *Macginitiea* leaves were recovered from a 47-million-year-old lake bed.

layers of time, and joined the throngs of tourists already streaming into the large building that enclosed a dinosaur-studded rock wall. For years, park service employees wearing campy white jumpsuits and hard hats crawled around on the bone-infested surface and chipped away at the hard rock, exposing more bones and posing for funky postcard photographs. The result is a Jurassic sandbar frozen in time and laid out for our viewing pleasure. Parts of dozens of incomplete dinosaurs jumble the surface: a leg here, a section of tail there, and near the top of the wall a length of neck terminated by a nearly perfect *Camarasaurus* skull. The Morrison Formation is known for its diversity of long-necked sauropods, and it's crazy to see how these 50- to 80-foot-long beasts fell apart. They fossilized in segments of tail vertebra, neck bones, and timberlike piles of legs.

Despite the richness of fossils on the wall, the setting that caused the fossils to be there is not immediately clear. The park service signage suggests that it was the lithified and tilted sandbar of a giant river. Not implausible, but why are there so many skeletons? It still baffles me. Sadly, the discovery of cracks in the building's foundation in 2006 has caused the National Park Service to close this magnificent attraction indefinitely.

After the visit, we dropped Lace in Vernal and headed due south to the nearly abandoned town of Bonanza. Along the way, the road from Vernal cuts across the middle of the Uinta Basin and rolls through the drab gray badlands of the Uinta Formation. Both the Uinta and the overlying red beds of the Duchesne Formation are known for their larder of Eocene mammals. This was country that's been heavily visited by museums for more than a century. As we continued south, the rolling badlands gave way to sagebrush flats with occasional sandstone hills. We crested a final hill and rolled into Bonanza.

Bonanza is really more of a mine than a town. The mineral of choice is a bizarre hydrocarbon known as gilsonite, used for paints and plastics. The really strange thing about this shiny black asphalt-like substance is that it occurs in long vertical veins that track across the landscape in a northwest-southeast orientation. The Bonanza seam was a whopper, nearly 20 feet thick, and it stretched for miles. During the heyday of gilsonite mining, workers dug straight down into the seams, building a wooden lattice to keep the resulting trench open. Eventually, some of these narrow trenches ran for miles. The roads around Bonanza cross these immense slits, and for the casual weekend driver, the scars beg nothing but questions.

South of Bonanza, we plunged down a valley into the canyon of the White River, then up a long sandstone ridge and back down into the valley of Evacuation Creek.

Once we dropped to creek level, we descended from the Uinta Formation to the top of the Green River Formation and back into the remains of the old Eocene lakes.

Back in 1991, a Vernalite named Bruce Handley invited me out to dig fossil leaves near Evacuation Creek. He'd perfected the art of popping up big slabs of ancient lake bed and revealing fantastic leaf fossils. This is no easy trick. The hard shale of the Parachute Creek Member of the Green River Formation is finicky stuff. It splits readily into thin sheets after it has weathered for a while, but the freshly exposed rock is hard as Hades and breaks into rounded, conchoidal chips rather than perfectly flat surfaces. Bruce figured out how to judge the slope of the hill just right so that he could pop up plywood-sized sheets that had weathered to just the right degree of split.

The fossils that he found were exquisite leaves, flowers, and insects, preserved as a sweet carbon black on a creamy matrix. Using my old adage that "you can't find a big leaf on a small rock," Bruce mastered the art of pulling table-sized slabs from the earth and finding whole fossil branches.

During the planning for the new Vernal museum, I got the idea that it would be stunning to make an entire museum wall out of slabs of this stone. I wanted to scout an appropriate site to quarry the fossils. Bonanza has been discovered by fossil hounds, and the sage-covered slopes are pocked by quarries made by their efforts. Ray and I walked around one of my old quarries and split a few slabs. Fossils were pretty easy to find, and it's not too hard to imagine that this was once the bottom of a Lake

Hell Hole Canyon near Bonanza is a superb exposure of the Green River Formation.

Erie–sized lake. Later that year, I would return with a team of 30 volunteers and a couple of prisoners from the Vernal jail to dig for a full week and retrieve 300 square feet of fossiliferous lake bed, which now hang on the museum wall in Vernal.

On the day Ray and I were there, it was still plenty hot and I wasn't up for a major quarry effort. Instead, we drove up a two–track to the top of a nearby ridge and peered off the other side. One of the great things about the American West is how you can find your own vistas and think, because of the remoteness and the emptiness, that you're the first person to ever see them. The view into Hell Hole Canyon, which lay before us, is like this: smooth and nondescript on the west side, but on the east one of the great natural outcrops in the world. Nearly a thousand feet deep, the canyon walls are composed entirely of thinly bedded Green River Shale.

India Wood's *Allosaurus* skeleton.

If there's one place on Earth where the metaphor "pages of time" is a reality, this is it. When ancient Lake Uinta stood at this spot, mud settling to the lake bottom accumulated steadily enough to help overburden the Earth's crust. The result was that the bottom of the lake sank even as it was accumulating layers of mud. This went on for millennia, and the result was a 1,000-foot pile of mud at the bottom of a 100-foot-deep lake. Hell's Hole slices through this huge fossil phone book. It's a hard spot to find but well worth the effort.

After finding our way back to Bonanza, we headed out of the Uinta Basin toward Rangely, Colorado, passing through the distinctly odd town of Dinosaur. This is a place that has tried to make dinosaurs pay, but there just isn't enough real traffic through this dusty corner of Colorado for anyone to break even, much less get rich. I must admit that I'm touched by the genuine Dinosaur Cemetery, which is full of deceased human residents, but Brontosaurus Street doesn't quite do it for me. The city park does have a splendid pair of incredibly ugly dinosaur sculptures: an

overhorned *Triceratops* and an extra-bony bone-headed *Pachycephalosaurus.* Ray thinks highly of such roadside works of art and posed me for a snapshot by these battered monuments. "It's pretty cool that some old guy out in the middle of nowhere would be so moved by dreams of prehistory that he was driven to resurrect these beasts. Think of all the bags of cement," Ray mused.

East of Dinosaur, Highway 40 is a long empty road that eventually leads to Craig and Steamboat Springs, but the first 60 miles contain absolutely nothing save a few grassed-over sand dunes. In this barren corner of Colorado, one of the more colorful dinosaur finds was made. In 1979, a single mother dropped her only daughter off at a friend's ranch for a summer. The girl, 13-year-old India Wood, was an independent and brainy youngster who liked to ride horses and had a lot of time on her hands. At some point during that summer, India found some black dinosaur bones weathering out of an exposure of the Morrison Formation and started to dig into the hill. With the help of the ranchers, who knew a fossil when they saw one, and a few library books, India educated herself in the ways of paleontology and set about excavating a skeleton that she correctly identified as an *Allosaurus*. Over the course of the next three years, India pulled more than half of the skeleton out of its muddy matrix and carefully hauled the bones back to her home in Colorado Springs. By the time India was 16, her mom was beginning to worry about the volume of rock in her bedroom and suggested that she find a new home for her dinosaur. That's when India called Don Lindsey at the Denver Museum and said, "I've got an *Allosaurus* in my bedroom, do you want to see it?" Much to Lindsey's credit, he headed down to Colorado Springs with the museum's videographer to check out India's claim. The video footage, still in the museum's archive, shows a young girl's room full of plastic horses and a pink bedspread. Then young India starts to pull box after box of beautifully collected dinosaur bones from beneath her bed.

The museum hired her on the spot, and for the next few summers, India guided a museum crew back to the site to collect the rest of the skeleton. At the end of the day, Lindsey wasn't a very good mentor, telling India that there was no future for her in paleontology. She took him at his word and went off to get an MBA. Thirteen years later, the *Allosaurus* was pulled from a dusty storeroom and installed next to the Colorado state fossil *Stegosaurus* as the centerpiece of my museum's *Prehistoric Journey* exhibit.

Acting on some old information, I tracked India down in Cambridge, Massachusetts, where she was living with her husband and two kids, and flew her to Denver for the opening of the exhibit. India and I became friends, and eventually, she and her family moved back to Boulder. A few years ago, I finally had the chance to visit the site of her childhood discovery with her and stand in the hole where she came of age digging her own *Allosaurus*.

On that memorable visit, I drove out from Denver in my Saab and followed some tortured directions that took me down several long dirt roads to a ranch house. The place was a museum in its own right, as the ranchers had collected all manner of hides, heads, fossils, rocks, artifacts, and bones, filling their living room. India cooked me a fantastic steak, then we drove out along a long valley and camped in a juniper forest. The next morning, we woke up and hiked over to the spot where India found her animal. More bones were exposed nearby, and India showed me where she'd found a *Camarasaurus* vertebra the day before. Nearby, a truly bizarre excavation was underway. A group of Texas creationists were busy excavating a *Stegosaurus*. It wasn't clear whether they knew they were proving themselves wrong or if they thought they were testing a theory about the packing of large animals onto Noah's ark. I could tell that she was a bit unnerved to be back at the site of her childhood discovery. My presence there seemed like an unmerited intimacy, and the creationist dig seemed sacrilegious in an anti-intellectual way. I quietly cursed Lindsey for dissuading this talented woman from entering the field of paleontology.

A year later, Ray and I passed the turnoff on the dusty ranch road to India's *Allosaurus*, and I told him about the creationist dig. He thought for a moment and said, "What blows my mind is that evolution is the biggest puzzle mankind has ever solved, and it took generations to do it. Everything, and I mean everything, falls into place when you perceive the world through evolutionary eyes. How can these guys not see the logic of what they're denying?" I agreed.

It was nearing dusk when we hit Rangely for a family-style Italian meal of spaghetti and meatballs at Mangilino's Diner. It was one of those nights when we hadn't really decided where to sleep, and it was still light after our big meal, so we headed down Highway 139 with the thought that we might camp on Douglas Pass. The road south from Rangely runs straight south through increasingly high cliffs of Mesaverde Sandstone. Several times in the waning evening light, I spotted what looked to be dinosaur footprints in sandstone outcrops along the side of

the road. We inspected a few by the headlights, but never really convinced ourselves that we'd found a good one.

Douglas Pass is at an elevation of over 8,000 feet. A spruce and aspen forest closed around us as we gained elevation and lost the last of the daylight. At the top of the pass, we turned off the pavement to the east. I shifted Blue into low gear and slowly climbed a steep but oddly wide gravel road that gained several hundred feet before leveling off on a forested ridgeline. We drove down the ridge for about a mile, then I pulled Big Blue off the road into a little meadow. It was delightfully cool as we laid our sleeping bags out on the ground, and soon we were dreaming about finding the perfect Eocene leaf.

At dawn the next morning, we were awakened by the sounds of pots and pans banging nearby. Then, voices started discussing fossils. Inadvertently, we had camped within 40 yards of some other fossil freaks. I walked over to their car and recognized some of my own volunteers from the Denver Museum of Nature & Science. I'd completely forgotten that there was a big field trip to Douglas Pass over the July Fourth weekend. For years these guys had been asking me to join them, but other July Fourth events had always intervened. Now, with absolutely no intention whatsoever, I had accidentally shown up for the dig. I cleared my throat and brazenly lied that I'd been planning to be here all along. A quick nod to Troll and a subtle blurry-eyed wink back assured me that he was in on the ruse. "Got any coffee?" were his first doleful words of the day.

Like the site near Evacuation Creek, Douglas Pass is an exposure of the Parachute Creek Member of the Green River Formation. This is one of the richest horizons of oil shale in world. Oil shale is a tight, hard rock that is black and smells of oil when it's fresh but is nearly white and splits into perfectly flat, thin sheets when weathered. There was a lot of interest in oil shale in the 1970s during the Middle East oil crisis, and a lot of money was spent gearing up to make the area around Rifle and Parachute, Colorado, into a major petroleum-producing region. Kuwait, Qatar, and Parachute—it had a nice ring to it. There certainly was enough of the stuff to get people whipped into a get-rich-quick frenzy. The oil shale formed as algae and other organics sank to the bottom of the Green River lakes way back in the Eocene. The lakes were huge, and in the Uinta Basin of Utah and the Piceance Basin of Colorado, the conditions were just right to bury a huge amount of shale.

The problem was that the shale didn't want to give up its oil. You could drill a well right into the middle of the oiliest, blackest, richest layer, lovingly called the Mahogany Zone, and nothing would happen. No gushers, no Jed Clampett bubblin' crude, no Texas tea, nothin'. The rock was simply too tight; the oil was there, but they just couldn't get it out.

Pretty frustrating to be sitting on the next Prudhoe Bay and have no way to make it pay. All manner of schemes were cooked up to make the shale yield its treasure. One thought was to mine the shale, crush it, and cook it so the oil would ooze out. Another was to drill a

hole, then set off an explosion at the bottom of it, thereby fracturing the rock and releasing oil. In principal, these approaches worked, but they always cost lots more than the oil was worth. The culmination of effort and absurdity happened when in 1969, a consortium drilled a well in the Piceance Basin and lowered a thermonuclear device to a depth of 7,000 feet. They set the device off, Colorado's only nuclear explosion, and sat back and waited for the bubblin' crude. But it never came. The idea had been to create a huge underground cavity into which the oil would flow. The problem was that the bomb, known as the Rulison blast, fused the bedrock into a huge mass of glass. Probably a good thing, as it's not clear to me what you would do with radioactive petroleum. To this date, the state restricts drilling in this area to prevent inadvertent release of radioactivity.

Finally, in 1979, Shell Oil, the major player in the big boondoggle, pulled the plug and walked away from the oil shale boomtowns of Parachute and Rifle, leaving the economy to scramble for new foundation. Here and there you could still see small experimental operations where oil shale is baked to make road-grade asphalt, but, by and large, the exploitation of the oil shale had to wait until we were really desperate for gasoline, as has occurred with the current situation in the Middle East.

In the meantime, oil shale fanatics had become the fossil diggers of Douglas Pass, paleonerds like Ray and me, as well as whole families from Salt Lake and Denver. The most famous fossil site is known as Radar Dome, because the FAA has one of its distinctive giant–golf ball microwave facilities located at the top of the large round hill. The hill is made of oil shale, and the Mahogany Zone is about 150 feet below the dome. The west side of the hill drops away precipitously. The rocks above the Mahogany Zone are full of gorgeous fossils, and the land is owned and managed by the BLM, so it's legal to collect reasonable amounts of plant and invertebrate fossils for noncommercial purposes.

It used to be that you could drive right to the dome and start digging, but then some clever person realized that having fossil-finding families milling around directly in front of the giant microwave transmitter wasn't the best thing for everybody's well-being, so they gated the road. The fossil diggers just moved their digs along the access road and around the back side of the hill.

At the Denver Museum of Nature & Science, we name our fossil sites as well as number them. Numbers are great for the computer database, but it's just easier for my brain to remember names. The museum name for the fossil quarry along the west side of this hill is "Da purdiest fossil site in the world," and the collection drawers at the museum bear this happy moniker. We named it on a perfect summer day back in 1993 when we were popping up sled-sized sheets of half-inch-thick shale that were covered with extra-fine fossil leaves. It was a sunny day but not too hot, not too much overburden, no biting insects, no wind, a cliffside view that looked out west past the Utah border, a happy crew of good-lookin' young diggers—who could ask for more than that? We had a photographer from *U.S. News and World Report* with us that day. They published a photo and a small blurb about fossils, but I doubt that any of the millions of readers of that little piece had any idea of what a fine time they were missing.

Mike Graham (right) at Douglas Pass.

The light rock and dark imprints in oil shale make for really pretty fossils, and the chance of finding something rare gives the site what we call "that Green River feeling." This feeling is the fairly legitimate hope that you might actually find something spectacular. It's like buying a lottery ticket, but with great odds. Yet unlike buying a lottery ticket, the process itself is lots of fun.

The bread-and-butter fossils of Douglas Pass are leaves and insects, common enough that people who've never dug before can expect to go home with boxes of them. The rare stuff comes in several forms. It can simply be a fossil that is extremely well preserved: a leaf that shows tiny veinlets in great detail; an insect with a stinger still intact; or a fossil flower with perfectly preserved and obvious pistils, stamens, and anthers. Or, it can be a whole fossil branch complete with attached leaves and sometimes even flowers. Every once in a great while, someone will find a small fish, but they tend to be guppy-like things. If you really want fossil fish, go back to the private quarries in Wyoming.

The jackpot fossils at Douglas Pass are things such as whole moths and butterflies with the patterning of their wings preserved. Once, at the fossil show in Tucson, I was shown a hand-sized slab from Douglas Pass with a complete but flattened baby bird, its tiny pin feathers, bony feet, and pointy beak all clearly visible. But there's a rub. The BLM regulations say that it's legal to collect plant and invertebrate fossils for noncommercial uses. So you can't collect vertebrate fossils, and you can't sell or trade the plants and invertebrates you find. It's sort of like saying, "Play the lottery, but only keep the payouts that are worth less than a hundred bucks." The collector of the baby bird defied those rules, and another rare fossil was lost to science.

The group from Denver that Ray and I ran into were members of a group known as WIPS, short for the Western Interior Paleontological Society. WIPS is one of a number of fossil clubs around the country that gathers monthly to talk about the many joys of loving fossils. The trip leader was a determined man named Mike Graham who had made Douglas Pass the focus of his hobby life. Mike is a computer database whiz who has collected every scrap of science that has ever been written about the plants and insects of the Green River Formation. Mike and the BLM put their heads together and worked out a plan to allow people to collect responsibly. At the end of each trip, Mike brings all of the unusual fossils to Denver, where we evaluate which pieces are so rare or scientifically signifi-

13
THE DINOSAUR DIAMOND

Grand Junction, a peach-growing town located in the Grand Valley at the confluence of the Gunnison and Colorado rivers, is a place where fossil-obsessed citizens have had a century of field days. Mount Garfield, named for the assassinated president, towers high above the northeast side of the town. Capped by thick sandstone layers, its flanks are smooth gray slopes nearly devoid of vegetation. This is the Mancos Shale, mud from the bottom of the Cretaceous Sea. This formation is full of marine fossils, and is the westward equivalent of the super-fossily Niobrara chalk beds of Kansas, both part of an 80-million-year-old sea that stretched from western Utah to at least Saint Louis.

Our museum collected a 13-foot-long *Xiphactinus* fish from the Mancos at an elevation of over 7,000 feet near Snowmass Village in 1967. "Dino Jim" Jensen pulled out a 50-foot-long mosasaur, *Prognathodon stagmani*, near Cedaredge, and giant clams and ammonites can be found with diligent digging. The Mancos also hosts the exquisite Cretaceous crinoid called *Uintacrinus.* There's debate about whether these gorgeous creatures lived on the seafloor or dangled from floating logs. Fossils like these transform gray shale hills into libraries of lost worlds. Approaching Grand Junction, we saw that the Mancos, which towers above the town and is what underlies it, is now regularly victimized by dirt bikers whose ubiquitous tracks had scarred even the steepest slopes.

The road south from Junction leads to the Black Canyon of the Gunnison and the giant dinosaur site known as Dry Mesa. A local couple, Eddie and Vivian Jones, found the site in 1971 and showed it to Dino Jim. He toiled for more than a decade there, collecting enough bones to fill the basement of the football stadium at Brigham Young University. In addition to the standard Morrison fauna, he found the huge theropod *Torvosaurus* and the giant sauropods *Brachiosaurus* and *Supersaurus.* Jim made himself famous with a picture of his stocky frame dwarfed by a huge shoulder blade.

Grand Junction itself is home to 45,000 enterprising souls who make a living in agriculture and the service industry. In 1900, Chicago-based paleontologist Elmer Riggs wrote letters to people in Grand Junction asking if they'd seen any old bones. A dentist wrote back with affirmation, and on July 4, 1900, Elmer found a giant dinosaur just a few miles outside of town. Then and there, Grand Junction became part of the expanding world of dinosaurs.

The beast from Riggs's Hill, *Brachiosaurus altithorax*, was the same species of long neck that sneezed on the little girl in the first *Jurassic Park* movie. Although Riggs's skeleton was only about 20 percent complete, it was enough to qualify as North America's largest dinosaur skeleton, and, for many years, a cast of this absurdly large beast was mounted in Stanley Hall at the Field Museum.

When the Field acquired *T. rex* Sue, the giant plastic brachiosaur was shipped to United Airlines Concourse B at O'Hare Airport. I was always so impressed at the skeleton when it was at the Field, especially at how much larger it is than the *Diplodocus* we have on display in Denver. Yet somehow, the setting at O'Hare diminished the old boy. His tail pokes out over the security area, his head looks longingly at a Starbucks. I'm not sure that dinosaurs and air travel mix. Then again, since we now know that birds are dinosaurs, maybe they do.

Grand Junction is the largest town on the Colorado Plateau and, as such, is also a center for the mineral exploration that has rocked the region since the

Manhattan Project ramped up demand for uranium. Al Look's 1956 book, *U-Boom*, chronicles the craziness that came down as every Tom, Dick, and Harry grabbed a Geiger counter and became a prospector. All that prospecting led to a lot of incidental fossil finds, and a lot of old prospectors eventually turned into rock and fossil hounds.

The uranium deposits of the plateau were formed as uranium-rich groundwater seeped through bedrock and found places to precipitate. A lot of those places turned out to contain buried dinosaur bones and fossil logs. People were mining dinosaur bones for their uranium content or simply finding radioactive bones as they searched for ore. But uranium was not the only mineral to precipitate in the bones and wood: often fossils were agatized with a beautiful red silica. Pretty soon, prospectors were cutting cabochons out of agatized dinosaur bone or fossil logs.

Today, Grand Junction is full of rock hounds, dinophiles, and fossil nuts. My friend Dick Dayvault, a reclamation specialist contracted by the Department of Energy, collects petrified logs, seeds, cycads, bennettites, and cones on this western edge of Colorado and the adjacent Colorado Plateau in Utah. His friend Frank Daniels, a former district attorney, has become one of the finest collectors and photographers of polished petrified wood. In 2006, Frank and Dick published *Ancient Forests: A Closer Look at Fossil Wood*, a full-color, 456-page exposé of two men's obsession with gorgeous fossils.

In Denver, I get e-mails from Grand Junction physicians and math professors who hunt fossil

leaves in the nearby Book Cliffs. Either there really is nothing to do in Grand Junction, or the fossils are really that good. Could be a little of both.

Ray and I stopped at the Museum of Western Colorado in Fruita. It used to be in downtown Grand Junction, but when a competing museum run by a company called Dinomation failed, the Museum of Western Colorado took over the Fruita space 10 miles west of Grand Junction. The new operation, christened Dinosaur Journey, has a highway exit and is next door to a McDonald's. It is poised for tourist success.

Dinomation is a California-based company that makes robotic dinosaurs—big rubberized beasts that move a little and roar a lot. During the heyday of *Jurassic Park*, when Hollywood finally realized that 99.9 percent of all children love dinosaurs, Dinomation provided quasi-accurate beasts that traveled the country appearing in museums. These popular exhibits seemed really thin on science but drew big crowds. When Dinomation closed up shop in Fruita, they left the big rubber models, and the Museum of Western Colorado, itself a legitimate museum with actual research collections, inherited an odd legacy of oversized toys.

Among the first monsters that greeted us as we walked into the museum was a roaring *Utahraptor* in the process of ripping the head off a hapless baby sauropod. It was hard to escape the tawdry thrills of the cheap horror-flick sensation. We chatted with the curator, John Foster, who was working hard to nurture a group of retired volunteers.

Hunger gripped the Troll and me, so we stepped out of the cool museum into an asphalt-melting 106-degree midday scorcher and headed across the interstate into the Fruita town center, a quaint touristy place replete with dinosaur sculptures, dinosaur murals, dinosaur paintings, and dinosaur street names. Thankfully, we found an air-conditioned Mexican restaurant on Main Street, because the heat was slowing us down. Western Colorado in early July was a little more than Ketchikan-based Troll had bargained for. The restaurant was really good and we took advantage of it, eating bowl after bowl of tortilla chips. The second we sauntered back out onto Main Street, we realized we were toast. Acknowledging that really full bellies and summer heat are why the siesta was invented, we started rearranging plans.

My friend Rob Gaston lives near Fruita, and I had never lived up to my many threats to visit him. I rummaged around in the toolbox of Big Blue and found my trusty paleontologist's little black book. We called, he was home, and we headed over, perfectly ready for a slow, lengthy, indoor, preferably air-conditioned conversation. Rob and his wife, Jennifer, greeted us like they'd been planning our visit for months. Rob is a lanky Tennessee boy with the trace of an accent and a casual style. He runs a business selling exquisitely detailed plastic casts of prehistoric animal parts.

Rob is one of those paleo-obsessed natural history buffs who has found a novel way to make his obsession pay the bills. Wandering around his studio was very much like walking around a candy store, or a chocolate store, to be precise. Rob uses a nice hard plastic, makes beautiful molds, and generates replicas that look indistinguishable from the real thing. But because he makes multiples, the little rows of brown raptor claws, *Allosaurus* teeth, and oviraptor skulls really looked like tasty little chocolates from the Rocky Mountain Chocolate Factory.

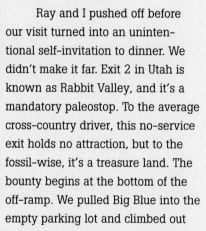

Rob had his start working for Lin Ottinger, a rock shop owner in Moab, and while working for Lin, Rob discovered a dinosaur bone bed in the Cedar Mountain Formation. Some of the bones belonged to an odd armored ankylosaur that was new to science. In time, Utah paleontologist Jim Kirkland named the new genus *Gastonia* after Rob. The site, known as the Yellow Cat Quarry, was extensively dug by teams from the College of Eastern Utah in Price and eventually yielded the first good specimens of the giant raptor known as *Utahraptor*. We talked about this as we drank our iced tea. It wasn't a siesta, but Rob's southern style was just the slowdown we needed.

Ray and I pushed off before our visit turned into an unintentional self-invitation to dinner. We didn't make it far. Exit 2 in Utah is known as Rabbit Valley, and it's a mandatory paleostop. To the average cross-country driver, this no-service exit holds no attraction, but to the fossil-wise, it's a treasure land. The bounty begins at the bottom of the off-ramp. We pulled Big Blue into the empty parking lot and climbed out into the still, hot afternoon to take a walk. I love this spot because it's possible to literally stand on a 20-foot-long sauropod neck without knowing it.

Sauropods are not called long necks for nothing. Because their necks are so long, it's easy to ignore the incredible intricacies of each vertebra.

Rob Gaston and the skull of *Gastonia*.

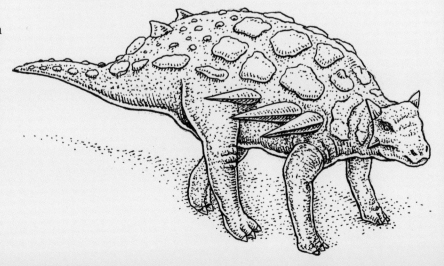

(right)
The Book Cliffs
of Utah with
badlands of the
Mancos Shale in
the foreground.

In fact, for long necks to function, each of the component bones had to be an engineering wonder. A single neck vertebra on a garden variety *Camarasaurus* might be the size of a keg of beer, but it's an intensely elaborate bone composed of a central disk and a whole series of projections of thin bone. Fossils of elaborate things are tricky to interpret because the sediment that buries the bone eventually hardens to rock that breaks in a manner that's irregular with respect to the convoluted bone. Sauropod necks are really bad this way.

I strolled ahead of Troll and sauntered onto the neck. He ambled up after me, mumbling something about the heat before he grumbled, "So, professor, where in the heck is this cool fossil site?" I mentioned that he ought to be more careful when standing on a dinosaur's neck. We spent the next half hour crawling around the enigmatic fossil as the interstate traffic roared below us.

After leaving Rabbit Valley, we drove up-section through the Cedar Mountain Formation and the Dakota Sandstone before ramping onto the broad plain of the Mancos Shale. This really is the land of buried treasure. Over the long years of the uranium boom, prospectors scoured this landscape, and barroom tales of whole dinosaurs and perfect fossil logs abounded.

As we continued west, the north side of the road revealed an endless rampart of stepped cliffs. Known as the Book Cliffs, these sandstone ramparts stretch all the way from Grand Junction to Price, almost a hundred miles. I explained to Troll how the filling and emptying of the great Cretaceous Seaway had paved layers of beach sands on top of the seafloor mud. The sea slowly filled and emptied, the region slowly sank, and each time the sea refilled, mud would be deposited on top of sand. When the sea emptied again, sand would be deposited on top of mud. In this way, hundreds of feet of alternating sand and mud accumulated. The mud was full of marine fossils, the sand full of beach and swamp fossils. Then, when the sediment turned to stone, the sand hardened more than the mud, so that when erosion carved the Book Cliffs, the sandstone made vertical cliffs while the mud made slopes. The layers of the Book Cliffs each have their own name,

but collectively they're known as the Mesaverde Group, a reference to the giant sandstone cliffs near Durango that are famous for their cliff dwellings.

Over the years, I'd explored a number of the canyons that sliced through the cliffs in my search for Cretaceous fossil leaves. Up Thompson Canyon, the remains of old coal mines were telltale signs of ancient vegetation, and there we found fossil leaves from the forests that grew on the shore of the sea. Broadleaf trees, palms, ferns, and conifers related to bald cypress composed the flora. Even though it was 75 million years old, the vegetation would have looked pretty similar, at first glance, to what you'd see today if you boated around the swamps near New Orleans.

The Book Cliffs layers formed at the same time as the rocks at Dinosaur Provincial Park in Alberta, which is the richest dinosaur site in the world, yielding more than 40 different kinds of dinosaurs. This would make you think that the Book Cliffs should be a real dinosaur mecca. It hasn't been, probably because the acid groundwater associated with swamps is a strong chemical deterrent to the fossilization of bone. Dinos were here but were not so commonly fossilized. To be sure, there were some exceptions; geologists have found a few foot bones of a tyrannosaurid, possibly *Albertosaurus*, and a Utah student found the back end of a mummified hadrosaur. The reality is that the dinosaur fossil action to be had was to the south of the interstate, not the north, in what is called the Cedar Mountain Formation.

Long a fairly obscure formation sandwiched between the Morrison and the Dakota, the Cedar Mountain Formation is exposed from the Colorado state line all the way to Price, Utah, and from there to the south along the eastern side of the San Rafael Swell. It's been a tricky formation to understand because its thickness is variable and the fossils found in it suggest that the Cedar Mountain was deposited at several distinct times during the Cretaceous. So where the Hell Creek Formation was deposited in a 1.5-million-year time span at the end of the Cretaceous, the Cedar Mountain may have been laid down in as many as five pulses, each perhaps a million years in duration, but spread over as much as 30 million years.

Flower Power

The beginning of the Cedar Mountain Formation was in the earliest Cretaceous, between 125 and 95 million years ago. This was a critical time in Earth history, because it was when the first flowering plants appeared. Flowering plants are confusing because their technical name, angiosperms, is poorly known, and their common name places so much emphasis on the flower. A lot of flowering plants have very subtle flowers, so you couldn't be faulted for missing them. For example, all of the broadleaf trees are flowering plants, as are all of the grasses, rushes, palms, and most aquatic plants. Of the eight major groups of living land plants, flowering plants account for more than 80 percent of the nearly 300,000 species. Number two are ferns, with about 20,000 species, and third place goes to the conifers, with a few hundred species. Cycads, gnetales, and lycopods have just over 100 species each; horsetails a few; and ginkgo just one. So flowering plants are by far the most species-rich and, in general, the most common plants on the Earth today. In a general rule of thumb for botanists, if it's not a fern or conifer, it's likely a flowering plant. The fact that flowering plants date back only to the Early Cretaceous means that the Jurassic landscape probably looked a whole lot different from any landscape you can find on Earth today.

KEN'S
THUNDERING
HERD OF
THIGH-HIGH
ANKYLOSAURS

Since the first gasp of the Cedar Mountain Formation was being deposited during the first years of flowering plant evolution, you would think that it would be a great place to tell the story of the origin of flowering plants. Unfortunately, the chemistry of the formation is poor for plant fossilization: only trunks were preserved with any regularity. One of the sad ironies of paleontology is that the rock layer that you'd guess would answer a specific question often doesn't. Some formations were acidic when they were deposited, and the bones were dissolved but the plants weren't. Other formations were just the opposite: leaves and flowers are destroyed, but bones are well preserved. The Cedar Mountain is a formation that's good for bones and logs but bad for leaves and flowers.

The Cedar Mountain Formation appears to have as many as five different dinosaur faunas, each composed of a different group of animals. Not bad for a layer of rock that was largely ignored during the first, second, and third rounds of dinosaur exploration in the American West. In fact, the heyday of Cedar Mountain dinosaur exploration appears to be underway as we speak. Sparked by Gaston's find at Yellow Cat Quarry in 1990, teams from BYU, the College of Eastern Utah in Price, the Museum of Western Colorado (now Dinosaur Journey), and the Denver Museum of Nature & Science have been searching for new sites in this formation and quarrying with great energy. I had visited my museum colleague Ken Carpenter and his volunteer crews at their quarries in the Cedar Mountain Formation and quickly learned that I have neither the skill nor the patience to be a bone digger. At one of his sites, Ken has been excavating a fossilized herd of thigh-high *Gastonia*. The skeletons were scattered during burial, and their remains form a continuous layer 75 yards wide.

Ever aware of our paltry budget, Ray and I checked into a markedly substandard hotel in Green River and lowered our body temperature by sliding into a pool that hadn't been cleaned since the Cretaceous. As the sun finally set and the temperature became reasonable, we emerged back onto land and wandered over to a burger joint appropriately named Ray's. Having followed Ray into greasy spoons in a dozen states in search of the perfect hamburger, I wondered if he would be tempted to rank this one higher because of its name.

The next morning, we backtracked a bit to visit Moab. The road from Interstate 70 runs downhill and into lower rocks. We passed rapidly down through the Dakota and Cedar Mountain formations. These exposures of the Cedar Mountain are known to produce beautiful petrified plants. It was near here in the early 1980s that Moab poet and rock hound Frank Lemmon and his wife, Leona, had discovered a petrified cycadeoid trunk that wasn't squat and round like other cycadeoids. It was cylindrical, almost two feet in diameter, and eight feet long. The trunk was brutally heavy, but it had already broken into portable sections. The Lemmons hauled the telephone pole of a rock back to Moab, where it caught the attention of BYU paleobotanist Don Tidwell. The quality of petrifaction was good, so he was able to see the anatomy of the plant on the broken surfaces. What he saw baffled him.

Cycadeoids, similar to many living cycads and palms, armed their squat trunks with persistent remains of old leaf bases, and this trunk was no different. Unlike cycads, which produce cones, and palms, which produce flowers, cycadeoids produced flowerlike structures that were nestled in between the persistent leaf bases. There was a lot of debate about whether these structures ever opened and looked like flowers or if they stayed closed and looked more like pods embedded in the surface of the trunk. Some detailed anatomy on the specimens collected in the Black Hills seems to suggest the latter, a finding that ruined a lot of beautiful prehistoric paintings by artists who had chosen to reconstruct the trunks to look like pineapples covered with daisies. The thing that

stunned Don about this fossil was that every single leaf base had an associated flowerlike structure. Did the plant grow to full stature before forming its flowers? Were there leaves all over the thing or just at the top? Why weren't the flowers at the bottom of the pole more mature than the ones at the top? Here he had the most perfectly preserved and unusual Early Cretaceous plant ever found, and it was too complicated to figure out.

We continued toward Moab, passing the entrance to Arches National Park, where Edward Abbey penned his revolutionary tome *Desert Solitaire*. The line of RVs queuing at the ticket booth seemed to mock the book. Abbey was always so mad at people for not taking the time to appreciate the landscape. I always wondered how much he appreciated the vanished landscapes that had come before, the ones that had shaped his world.

Moab is now exactly what Abbey feared: a giant outdoor theme park. I'm sure that most of the slickrock mountain bikers, ATV jockeys, and jeepers have no clue about the prehistoric underpinnings of their red-rock playground. There's at least one major exception to this rule. We'd driven to Moab to meet Lin Ottinger, proprietor of Ottinger's Rock Shop, a squat building surrounded by piles of rocks on the north side of town. Rob Gaston had told us enough about the man that we just had to meet him.

By the time the second the bell on the front door had stopped ringing, we knew we had walked into a real rock shop. Most rock shops these days buy their stock wholesale at the big show in Tucson. For that reason, you can be at a rock shop in Steamboat Springs or Jackson and see nothing but the same fossils from China, Morocco, and Brazil. Like the rest of the American economy, the rock shop business is globalizing. The problem with that is you learn nothing about the local area. Refreshingly, Ottinger's place was a sampling of the local landscape. There were shelves of gorgeous acid-etched horn corals from the Permian Rico Formation, which is exposed just to the north of town, and big agatized dinosaur bones from the Morrison.

We overheard a kid whining, "I really want a prehistoric thing," and we approved. "One of our peeps," smiled Ray. After slowly working our way around the room, Ray took advantage of a lull at the cash register and engaged Lin in conversation. A lanky no-nonsense man, Lin had been selling rocks for 68 years. He was born in Casper, Wyoming, in 1927. His family moved around a bit, and Lin was selling rocks and arrowheads in Tennessee during the Depression, when he was seven. A few years later, his family visited Peterson's Rock Garden, an early rock shop near Prineville, Oregon, and Lin started making career plans. In 1939, at the age of 12, he first visited the Denver Museum. Philip Reinheimer had just completed the Hall of Dinosaurs, displaying a *Diplodocus* from Dinosaur National Monument, a *Stegosaurus* from Cañon City, and an *Edmontosaurus* from Montana. The dinosaurs had a big effect on young Lin.

By the 1950s, he was prospecting for uranium on the Colorado Plateau. He rode the boom and rode out the bust, realizing that this was the place for him. He opened his own rock shop and started taking visitors on backcountry jeep trips and rock and fossil safaris. He appeared in a 1962 issue of *National Geographic*. In 1973, he found a dinosaur in the Cedar Mountain Formation that was new to science, and in 1979, Dino Jim Jensen named it *Iguanodon ottingeri*. Lin combines the crusty seen-it-all crankiness of an old-timer with a true curiosity about rock and fossils. His time is passing. Globalized fossils and regulations that prevent the sale of fossils from federal lands have changed the rules for rock shops on the Colorado Plateau. Nonetheless, Ottinger's story is integral to how we have come to see fossils in the American West.

After taking advantage of the presence of a good latte in jetsettin' Moab, we headed back to the interstate and west to Price. Past Green River we veered north, avoiding the topography and geology of the San Rafael Swell, and rolled into the sleepy town of Price in the late afternoon.

As the fourth corner of the "dinosaur diamond" that includes Vernal, Grand Junction, and Moab, Price seems aware of its past. "Dino" is the high-school mascot, so we felt no need to start our usual mascot campaign, and signs to the College of Eastern Utah Museum are everywhere. The museum is a modern building full of not only fossils, but also some really interesting archaeological exhibits. We'd come to see paleobiologist Don Burge, but he was away, so the registrar, a pleasant fellow named Dwayne Taylor, took the task of showing us around. He told us that in 1988, the museum acquired a spectacular and nearly complete mammoth from Huntington Canyon north of Price. The mammoth was discovered at an elevation of 9,500 feet by an alert backhoe driver. Ray started riffing about enlightened backhoe drivers who have the good sense to stop. "How many times do you hear this story in the ever-expanding western suburban sprawl: 'Backhoe operator finds prehistoric wonder.' Think of how many times they don't stop! I think museums should launch an outreach program geared to construction workers!" Ray was building up steam. Just as he was about to step on the next soapbox, Dwayne interrupted with, "Want to see something really interesting?"

Then Dwayne took us to the museum's off-site storage facility in an old hospital. It seemed appropriate to be storing old broken bodies in an old hospital. You could tell that Burge and his team had been busy in the Cedar Mountain by the room after room of prepared dinosaur bones Dwayne showed us. The museum had worked three main quarries in the Cedar Mountain Formation: the Yellow Cat, which we already knew about based on our conversations with Rob Gaston, the Mussentuchit, and the Price River #2. The Mussentuchit had produced a different fauna that included a group of juvenile orthnithopods known as *Eolambia* as well as an armored dinosaur known as *Cedarpelta*. There was a whole room full of the shiny black bones of baby *Eolambia*.

The Price River #2 is located in the Ruby Ranch Member of the Cedar Mountain, about 20 miles from Price. This quarry had a lower level that gave up parts of five brachiosaurs. Its upper level produced a huge nodosaur, an armored dinosaur nearly 35 feet long.

Besides Gaston's *Gastonia* and Ottinger's *Iguanodon*, the Yellow Cat Quarry had also yielded *Nedcolbertia*, a cute little carnivore named after Ned Colbert, the discoverer of the big *Coelophysis* bed at Ghost Ranch, New Mexico. The big Yellow Cat find for Burge came in 1992 when his team found parts of a huge raptor that would later come to be known as *Utahraptor*. The timing of the discovery could not have been better. That was the summer of *Jurassic Park*, and Steve Spielberg had a problem. Michael Crichton had loved the name *Velociraptor*, a dinosaur first found at the Flaming Cliffs of the Gobi Desert by Roy Chapman Andrews in 1924, and had shaped the book around a pack of those dinosaurs gone bad. No mind that *Velociraptor*, though probably vicious, was smaller than a turkey. Crichton had amplified his ideas from John Ostrom's work on *Deinonychus*, the nasty wolf-sized dinosaur from Montana, so it wasn't too egregious to borrow the wicked-sounding name *Velociraptor* for the larger but less aggressively named *Deinonychus*. The problem started during preparation for filming, when Spielberg decided that even

Utahraptor, the giant raptor from the Cedar Mountain Formation that made Steven Spielberg an honest man.

Deinonychus wasn't big enough for the sense of threat he wanted to impart. Remember, this was the guy who made *Jaws*. So Spielberg did what any self-respecting filmmaker would do, he invented a larger dinosaur, a double-sized *Deinonychus* that he called *Velociraptor*, or "raptor" for short. Enter Don Burge, the Yellow Cat Quarry, and *Utahraptor*. By the time the movie had opened, giant raptors were a reality rather than a Hollywood exaggeration. *Utahraptor*-mania blazed in the hearts of paleonerds across Utah. Soon T-shirts and books were plastered with its snarling visage.

We asked Dwayne about *Utahraptor*, and he invited us into one of the museum's inner collection rooms where an old bank vault stood. We stood back as he rolled the tumblers, and within a minute Ray was holding the giant six-inch slashing claw of the original *Utahraptor* in his shaking hands. It really was better than holding one of Rob Gaston's near-perfect reproductions. This was the real thing, the business end of what was very clearly an animal that neither Ray nor I would like to meet in any other form than stone-cold dead. We thanked Dwayne profusely for the opportunity to shake hands with the killer and wandered back into the museum exhibit area.

Before we headed out, we admired a display of dinosaurs from the nearby Cleveland-Lloyd Quarry, a famous Morrison site that we planned to visit later in the trip. Parts of an *Allosaurus*, a *Camarasaurus*, a *Stegosaurus*, and a *Camptosaurus* lay strewn on the exhibit floor, testimony perhaps to the lack of a person with the skills to mount them upright. It was not the last time that we would see this type of lay-'em-flat exhibitry.

Price is coal mining country. The Cretaceous rocks of the Book Cliffs are coal rich, and, to the north and west of Price, underground coal mining has been active since the 1920s. These coal mines are world famous because of their dinosaur tracks. When the coal was a swampy forest, it was apparently quite a busy place, with a variety of dinosaurs—mainly hadrosaurs—marching around in the muddy water, leaving tracks all over the peaty floor of the swamp. Eventually floods brought in mud and sand, which filled in the tracks and buried the peat. Seventy-five million years later, when the peat had changed to coal and the sand and mud was the roof of the coal mine, Price-based coal miners noticed that when they removed the coal, giant three-toed rocks would fall off the ceiling of the mine. This was a bit of a worry, because a miner's hard hat is pretty useless if a 100-pound rock is dropped on top of it. The dinosaur tracks became a safety hazard, and there are unconfirmed rumors of miners who were actually killed by the tumbling tracks, perhaps the only humans ever killed by dinosaurs.

We loaded back into Big Blue and headed up Price Canyon en route to Ogden, Utah. As we passed over Soldier Summit, we encountered deposits of the westernmost edge of the giant Eocene Green River lakes. Sheets of lakeside shale from this area are covered with fossil bird footprints. Big Blue made its own tracks as the Rolling Stones, blasting from the stereo, carried us out of the Colorado Plateau.

Breathing Some Life into Those Old Bones

"Mounting" a dinosaur skeleton is not an easy feat. Heavy, because they're petrified, and often distorted, crushed, or cracked by the process, dinosaur bones are a real challenge to the would-be museum designer. There are museums that dodge this problem by mounting plastic or plaster casts. Some scientists argue against mounting real bone, because it makes it less accessible for scientific study. But people's valid desire to see the real thing continues to encourage museums to mount actual skeletons. It's done with supporting steel bars and cables, and a good mount does a thorough job of minimizing the obvious-ness of the supporting steel while maximizing the vitality of the dinosaur's pose.

Ken Carpenter at the Denver Museum of Nature & Science is the Zen master of dinosaur mounting. For 25 years I've watched him breath life into tortured fossil bones, creating skeletal mounts whose vitality belies their fossilized reality.

14
THE MORMON TRILOBITE CHOIR

We burst out of the Rockies and into the Basin and Range at Ogden. The huge Salt Lake was hidden from sight, and the swell of the rapidly growing urban sprawl of the Wasatch Front quenched any sense that we were on a drive in the Old West.

Stop number one was the Eccles Dinosaur Park in Ogden. Utah has the dinosaur sickness bad, and this place is one of the symptoms. Like the dinosaur garden in Vernal, Eccles Park has gone to great pains to rebuild the old boys in fiberglass. The number of different dinosaurs that you see when you walk around the park is quite amazing. Director Brooks Britt is a serious dinosaur paleontologist, and he's added a smallish museum to the front of the operation where a few skeletons are lying around on the floor. It was a nice afternoon, so we wandered around the grounds trying to figure out why people pay to walk among plastic dinosaurs. But there were moments of discovery as we rounded a bend and saw a few vaguely lifelike models. Ray posed and roared beside the *Parasaurolophus*, and we experienced an intimidating sense of scale by standing beneath a life-sized *Brachiosaurus*.

We'd come to this part of Utah to see the Gunthers, a fossil-finding family that lives in nearby Brigham City at the foot of the Wellsville Mountains. Three active generations of Gunthers are fossil fanatics, and the fourth generation is now playing in the quarries and is well on its way to joining the family hobby. The patriarch of the tribe is Lloyd Gunther, who, though he's nearly 90, has the handshake of a grizzly bear, the result of years spent with hammer, crowbar, and shovel in the search of trilobites.

When I first met Lloyd in 1991, he was married to his second wife, Freida, and the two of them, with their combined families, had a sum of 120 children and grandchildren. I asked Freida how she remembered their birthdays, and she said that it didn't really matter because there was one every few days. Lloyd's son Val and Val's son Glade round out the central triad of the bug-digging clan. The Gunthers' forte is trilobite hunting, and no one does it better. For years they headed south to the Cambrian beds west of Delta and prospected thousands of feet of Cambrian shale in search of better bugs. Unlike the masses that returned time and time again to the known trilobite holes in the Wheeler Quadrangle, the Gunthers explored new areas, making fantastic discoveries and passing on their finds on to museums around the country. In 1981, BYU published the Gunthers' *Some Middle Cambrian Fossils of Utah*, a definitive text on the more than 40 species of trilobites found in central Utah.

I met the Gunthers shortly after they made a major discovery a few miles from their house. The Wellsville Mountains are the northern extension of the Wasatch Front, and they rise abruptly and steeply off the flat surface of old Lake Bonneville, the Ice Age lake that made the Great Salt Lake look like a puddle. Knowing that the Spence Shale was Middle Cambrian in age, Lloyd and Val surmised that they might be able to find trilobites there. It was really

Lloyd Gunther, patriarch of the Gunther trilobite tribe.

Trilobite Subculture.

tough work, because the rocks of the Wellsville Mountains are steeply tilted and the layers are angled into the hill. This is the worst possible configuration for digging. To make matters even worse, the Spence Shale is very hard rock. But the Gunthers are nothing if not persistent, and they managed to find a thin vein of shale that was rich in trilobites. Then, to their amazement, they started finding more than trilobites. They found worms, hyolithids, bizarre arthropods, and scalelike sclerites and realized that they were finding Burgess Shale creatures.

The Burgess Shale is a world-famous Cambrian site from the Cambrian shale of the southern Canadian Rockies. Originally discovered by Charles Doolittle Wolcott in 1911, a single quarry at an elevation of nearly 12,000 feet preserved a whole host of bizarre animals that had their popular debut in Stephen J. Gould's book *Wonderful Life*. The Burgess fauna was thought to be unique, but then a similar assemblage known as the Chenjiang was found in China. Shortly after that, the Gunthers found yet another assemblage a stone's throw from their own backyard. I visited them in 1991 and Val, Lloyd, and Glade took me and a couple of my elderly volunteers to see their site. It was a brutally steep and slippery climb up a talus slope of hard shale, and I was impressed that Lloyd's old limbs seemed immune to fatigue.

I was further amazed when Glade whipped a heavy rock drill out of his pack, fired it up, and started boring a hole into the mountainside. A little while later, Val ran a wire down the hole and poured liquid in behind it. Then he backed away, crouched behind a rock, whispered, "Fire in the hole," and set off a detonation that blew rock and dust high into the sky. This came as a huge and unwanted surprise to my crew, who were looking for trilobites in the talus slope just below the cliff. But for just a moment, it was raining trilobites.

Later on that same trip, I learned how fast an 80-year-old could move. Apparently, in the congenial but competitive world of rock hounds, there's an unspoken fossil-hunting rule that whoever puts his hand on a fossil first is the one who gets to keep it. Lloyd and his son Val had taken me and some museum volunteers to a few of their favorite trilobite holes so that we could collect material for the *Prehistoric Journey* exhibit. In addition to trilobites, I was particularly keen to get a few of the rarer Cambrian fossils, things such as the shrimplike phyllocarids or arms of the predatory *Anomalocaris*. I was talking to Lloyd about this as we stood next to our vehicles, which were parked at the edge of a trilobite hole in the middle of a huge sagebrush flat. As we spoke, we both gazed over at a pile of shaley slabs. At the same instant, we both saw the big phyllocarid on top of the pile. I started to point it out, but I was interrupted by a quiet "whoosh" as the large grandfather lunged past me. Lloyd covered 10 yards in an instant, and the next thing I knew, he was holding the fine fossil in his hand. Never mind that he'd brought the museum to this spot to find this very kind of fossil. This one was his. Lloyd and Val eventually loaded my truck with fossils for our exhibit, so I didn't begrudge him his phyllocarid, but it did teach me a lesson about the stealth and speed of spry octogenarians.

The Gunthers are shale diggers of the first order, and they'll dig anything that's preserved in flat fissile rock. Lloyd had found a Cretaceous fossil leaf site near Henefer, Utah, less than an hour's drive from his house. Whenever he got the fossil-digging bug, which was fairly often, he would head out to Henefer with his hammer and crowbar and bust up the road cut. As a result, he'd acquired a huge collection of these leaves. Knowing that I studied Cretaceous fossils, he offered me the collection. I drove to Brigham City to pick it up and haul it back to Denver.

Now, a few years later, Lloyd had filled his workshop again, generously offering me this new collection, so I was back for another load. Ray and I spent an hour or so with the hand truck loading the back of Blue with almost 60 Coke flats full of fossil leaves.

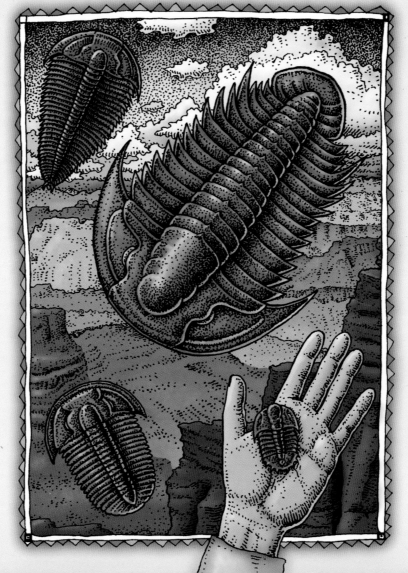

Coke flats, usually seen next to Coke machines, are the box of choice for fossil hounds. Cheap and easy to find, the flats also hold a reasonable weight of fossils.

After we were finished loading, Val came over and we spent some time looking at the display cases that crowd Lloyd's living room. Although he'd recently given the majority of his collection to a new museum in Cedar City, Utah, Lloyd had held back a substantial selection of premium bugs. His third wife, DeEsta, joined us and brought out some paintings that she'd been working on. Here was a real Grandma Moses, only her paintings were of family fossil digs rather than family picnics. Glade joined us and chanted an old Pavant Ute Indian saying about trilobites: "Timpe-Konitza-Pachuee." Roughly translated, it means "Little water bug living in a house of stone."

It took a while to disengage from the Gunthers, and when we got back on the road, the truck was substantially heavier with all the fossils we were hauling. We headed south, wishing that there were more family fossil dynasties in our great nation.

We arrived in Salt Lake and headed up the hill to the Utah Museum of Natural History at the University of Utah. This is a classic university museum, with little thought given to how the public might actually visit it. Testimony to this

(left)
Parasaurolophus
plays the blues.

are the five parking spaces available to the public. Luckily, we scored one. Our goal was to visit the chief curator, Scott Sampson, to hear about his work in the North Horn and Kaiparowits formations. Scott is a tall, handsome guy who looks far too normal to be a dinosaur paleontologist. We sat down in his office and discussed dinosaurs. Ray was particularly impressed because Scott was part of the team that named a new species of dinosaur from Madagascar after Mark Knopfler, the guitarist for Dire Straits. Scott said that the same Dire Straits tape was playing over and over again in the quarry when they found the skeleton, and there really wasn't much choice in the matter.

Scott's team had recently recovered a partial *Tyrannosaurus rex* skeleton from the North Horn Formation at North Horn Mountain in central Utah. This was really exciting news, because the original excavations at North Horn by Smithsonian paleontologist Charles Gilmore in the 1930s had yielded the ceratopsian dinosaur *Torosaurus*, the titanosaurid sauropod *Alamosaurus*, as well as a bunch of three-foot-long lizards and a big tortoise. The discovery of a *T. rex* here meant that the legendary carnosaur and sauropods had coexisted. This was music to Ray's ears. "Wow, so artists can now draw *T. rex* and long necks in the same image without fearing ridicule. Cool!"

The possible existence of the K-T boundary layer in central Utah was of interest to me, because it would represent the westernmost exposure of the boundary in North America. If there were any geographic variation to the way plants and animals responded to the killer asteroid, this would be a good place to look for it. We got instructions to the site before heading off with Scott and his grad student Mark Loewen, a rounded bear of a guy, to a nice dark cave of a student bar where we drank a few tall beers and inhaled some pizza.

After the first round of beers, Scott's student opened up a bit and told us about his efforts to find dinosaurs in the huge expanse of Grand Staircase National Monument near Escalante, Utah. I had driven through the area in the 1980s, and I remembered how a bend in the road had revealed an awesome vista of blue badlands steeper and more ominous than anything South Dakota has to offer.

The Blues are composed of the Late Cretaceous Kaiparowits Formation. A Berkeley turtle paleontologist named Howard Hutchison told me he was prospecting the Blues and came across a chunk of dinosaur bone that had fallen out of the outcrop. When he picked it up, he realized that he was holding a nearly complete and almost perfect *Parasaurolophus* skull in his hand. *Parasaurolophus* is a duckbilled dinosaur with an exceptionally long skull projection, or crest, that is an extension of its nasal chamber. Duckbill specialist David Weishampel has speculated that *Parasaurolophus* was the Pavarotti of the dinosaurian world and was able to use the crest as a kind of trombone or saxophone. By adjusting its breath, the animal could probably have had quite the melodic range.

This area used to be one of Utah's big backcountry secrets, but when the Clinton administration declared it a national monument at the end of 1996, a spotlight was thrown on this beautiful and remote place. The administrative switch to national monument status led to the imposition of a whole new set of regulations and a mandate to catalog the fossil resources of the region. This was

Tom Williamson of the New Mexico Museum of Natural History and Science in Albuquerque sports a skull of *Parasaurolophus* that he collected in the badlands of the San Juan Basin.

both good and bad news for Scott. His team was funded to search for and excavate dinosaurs, but they weren't allowed to use vehicles to do it. They had spectacular luck finding a host of new dinosaurs, including an unusual ceratopsian, an albertosaur, and a *Parasaurolophus*, but they had to hand-carry all of their heavy field gear deep into the wilderness.

Scott's dinosaurs were beginning to suggest that the Grand Staircase was the southern equivalent of Dinosaur Provincial Park in Alberta. By collecting plants and animals up and down the spine of the Rocky Mountains, he stood a chance to resurrect an ancient geography and see how it varied. After days of hot roads and plastic dinosaurs, it was nice to be in a museum where science was driving the questions. It was also nice to be in a cool basement drinking cold beer.

Ray had been corresponding with Jim Madsen (*Allosaurus jimmadseni*, a little dinosaur found at Dinosaur National Monument, was named after him), who operates a dinosaur casting business out of a warehouse in the Salt Lake industrial area. Lots of museums need fake dinosaur skeletons, and Jim is one busy man. Even when you find a pretty good skeleton, you usually need some spare parts to round out the mount. When we were mounting India Wood's *Allosaurus* for the *Prehistoric Journey* exhibit, for example, we had to "order out" for all sorts of extra ribs, arm bones, and feet to make the poor thing whole. Ray wanted to scope out Jim's operation, and I had never been there, so we called ahead and told them we'd be coming around. Jim wasn't in, but his son was in charge of a crew of half a dozen guys diligently working away on a variety of molds. The shop was strangely still, because everyone was listening to a book-on-tape about World War II. We could tell that we'd arrived at some point during an invasion, because Jim's son was reluctant to leave the main room and seemed really distracted. He eventually warmed up, put the tape on pause, and showed us around the warehouse, where parts of all manner of prehistoric creatures lay stocked in multiples on large shelves. Their product list boasts 50 different mammals and 60 different dinosaurs. Ray started angling for a freebie,

and, amazingly, a few months after he returned home to Ketchikan, he received a box containing a lovely plastic Eocene killer pig skull of his own.

We continued south along the Wasatch Front and stopped near American Fork to visit a new museum, The North American Museum of Ancient Life. It's an absolutely gigantic box of a building located next to Interstate 15 in the middle of a big, themed, mall-like commercial development. Coincidentally, we had arrived for the museum's first anniversary, and one of its founders, Cliff Miles, was happy to tour us around.

Cliff is another art-paleo guy. He started his career with an art undergrad degree and found himself working as a fossil preparator at BYU. Later, he and two of his buddies split off from BYU and opened their own fossil quarrying and preparation business. They had reopened the famous Bone Cabin Quarry near Como Bluff, Wyoming, and were making a decent living selling dinosaurs to Japanese museums. I'd seen some of their fossils when I visited the Gunma Museum of Natural History in Japan and had met Cliff when he and his partners generously donated a new Jurassic ankylosaur to the Denver Museum. The animal was new to science, and Ken Carpenter named it *Gargoylesaurus parkpinorum* after Jeff Park and Tyler Pinegar, the two guys who found the skeleton.

I was eager to see Cliff's new museum for a number of reasons. The place was huge and reputed to be full of cool fossils, including the country's first *Supersaurus* mount. They'd built the museum with amazing speed, from bare ground to open doors in less than two years. And the thing that really fascinated me was that it was a for-profit museum without an explicit collections or research mandate. In a way, it was the logical extension of the commercial fossil trade.

Cliff was a lively and proud tour guide. We could see that he'd really thrown his heart into the effort and had made a credible showing. The side-by-side mounts of *Brachiosaurus* and *Supersaurus* were truly awesome because of their insane size. We were also particularly taken by a sweet uintathere skeleton from the BYU collections. The skeleton took on larger stature when we learned that the guy who had found it later fell to his death off a cliff. Fortunately, you don't hear that too often in paleontology.

The museum also had moments of tragicomedy, like the reconstructed massive head of the shark *Charcarodon megalodon* that was blasted through a wall as if in an attempt to eat the visitors, or the skeleton of a mammoth being attacked by a bunch of human skeletons. Cliff told us that one was inspired by the film *Jason and the Argonauts*, a favorite of his from childhood, which featured a gigantic battle of skeletons.

We made a fleeting stop in Provo to see the BYU fossil collection and decided it was time to get back to the real outcrops. Our immediate goal was North Horn Mountain, and I insisted on taking the scenic route through Fairview, which put us on the very dusty and slow Skyline Road that creeps along a gorgeous ridgeline. We got nowhere fast and ended up pitching camp in an alpine meadow. The next morning, we squeezed Big Blue down a jeep trail and eventually found ourselves on the north shore of Joes Valley Reservoir. All we had to do to get to North Horn was drive to the south end of the lake and a few miles up the valley. As we approached, smoke began to cloud the sky, and by the time we reached the south end, we found our path blocked by a forest service truck. He pointed to the southeast where flames could be clearly seen licking up the slopes of North Horn Mountain. A helicopter was dipping water out of the lake and working the fire, and the road was truly closed. There wouldn't be a North Horn *Tyrannosaurus* for us that day.

It ended up being a blessing in disguise. We were feeling more like a big breakfast than a big hike, and there were other theropods in our immediate future anyway. A steep drive down the canyon from Joes Valley Reservoir abruptly spilled us from the mountain forests onto the desert of central Utah. Soon we were happily raiding our cooler for a midmorning picnic at the Cleveland town park.

Sated, we headed for the Cleveland-Lloyd Quarry, one of the most enigmatic of all the Morrison deposits. The road to the quarry is a long gravel drive from Cleveland across fairly featureless sage flats that eventually give way to a small escarpment. At the foot of the escarpment is a trio of small and markedly unimpressive buildings. We parked and went in to the one-room visitor's center. A laconic ranger chewing on a soggy unlit cigar and two tiny, extremely cute Hispanic women greeted us. Mike Leschin, the ranger, was in his fifth season at this lonely post, and Celina and Marina Suarez are twins from San Antonio, Texas, who'd somehow managed to catch the dinosaur bug. In addition to greatly increasing the ratio of women and twins in Utah paleontology, they were studying stegosaurs with Scott Sampson. The trio had been forewarned by Scott that we were coming, so they were clearly waiting to entertain us. Away we went on a private tour of a very odd quarry.

Celina and Marina Suarez, stegosaur-studying sisters from San Antonio.

Cleveland-Lloyd doesn't look like much until you lay eyes on the quarry map, a spectacular diagram that shows all 12,000 bones that have been dug out of the quarry. Most of the bones have been removed, and all that remain are a few bones and a big conundrum.

Carnivorous dinosaurs are far more common at this site than herbivorous dinosaurs. The quarry has produced parts of 44 *Allosaurus*, 2 *Marshosaurus*, 2 *Stokesosaurus*, and 1 *Ceratosaurus*. That's a lot of meat-eaters when you consider that the herbivores in the quarry are represented by only 5 camptosaurs, 4 stegosaurs, 3 camarasaurs, 1 *Barosaurus*, and 1 ankylosaur. That's 49 carnivores to 14 herbivores, hardly a fair fight. Mike didn't stand a chance in our eyes either, as the tour belonged entirely to Celina and Marina, who told us the tale of carnivore death at high speed, each talking over the other in a steady stream of dinosaureze. I'll admit that the story was a lot more interesting in stereo, but at the end of the day, the murder mystery had a pretty unsatisfactory resolution.

The superabundance of carnivores suggests that there was some sort of trap that lured them to their death. The classic example of this is La Brea Tar Pits, where Ice Age carnivores got caught in sticky tar. Other carnivores couldn't resist the opportunity to dine on their mired colleagues, and they too got trapped. The result is a deadly chain letter

of treacherous dinner invitations. The tar at La Brea has yielded far more saber-toothed cats and dire wolves than bison, horses, or sloths, and it really looks like the place was a classic predator trap.

The problem with Cleveland-Lloyd is that there's no obvious trap: no tar, no natural trap cave, just a bunch of bodies buried in a three-foot-thick layer of mudstone. This was not a mystery that Ray and I were about to solve that day and, if you can believe it, even Ray was reaching the dinosaur saturation point. We bid adieu to Mike and the charming Suarez sisters and turned once again to the road. It was time for trilobites.

For the last 40 years, there's been one go-to place for trilobites in North America: Delta. I'd blown through Delta once back in the early '80s and had remembered seeing trilobite safari signs. We arrived in town with the thermometer hovering around 105 and immediately sought refuge in a café, making the problem worse by eating a big greasy lunch. The Gunthers had told us that a local banker owned a necklace made of trilobites that had been found in a local archaeological site in Delta, but it was a Saturday and the banks were closed. We looked through the yellow pages and found a few places that advertised trilobite trips, but nobody was home. I was starting to feel like I should have been more prepared when I remembered Robert Harris. His number was in the white pages, and when he answered the phone, I said, "Are you the King of Trilobites?" He responded that indeed, he was, and that he was going to be down at his shop on Main Street in an hour or so if we felt like dropping by. We killed the hour lying in the shade at the city park and then slowly strolled over to his store.

The King of Trilobites holds court in what must have once been a pharmacy. Behind the plate glass window are a pair of giant plywood cutouts of trilobites wearing crowns. The cutouts clearly refer to *Elrathia kingii*, the little black trilobite that's the coin of the realm of commercial paleontology. Described by one of the earliest American paleontologists, Fielding Meek, *Elrathia kingii* was noted for its unusual mode of preservation. Most trilobites preserved in shale are preserved as impressions. These *Elrathia* were different, having suffered a mineral enhancement that perfectly captured and preserved their upper surface while thickening the body itself. The result is a perfect little shiny black button of a fossil. They weather out of the shale and lie on the surface like so many shiny black scarablike bugs. Collecting them is like picking up coins. These little guys are everywhere, gracing many a bolo tie. There was a Civilian Conservation Corps camp out in the Wheeler Quadrangle in the 1930s, and with lots of workers wandering around the desolate landscape picking up bugs and taking them home, the

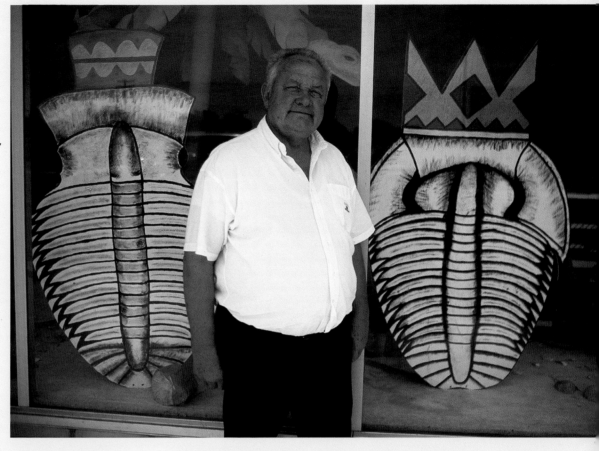

trilobites began to get a reputation outside of western Utah. They were a rock shop standard from Fresno to Fargo when I was a kid.

Harris got into the business of mining and selling bugs the same year I was born. He'd been working for Fawcett Ant Farms, the company that supplied ants for ant farms. They used straws to collect ants by the thousands, and they also collected fossils. Robert learned the trade from Fawcett and then went big-time. By the 1970s the state of Utah was leasing land in the Wheeler Quadrangle so that people could mine trilobites. Harris estimates that something like half a million trilobites are mined in this tiny patch of Utah each year.

Visiting Harris seemed like going to the heart of commercial paleontology. The man was a brick. Late middle aged, solid around the middle, wearing a white polyester shirt and gray trousers, he could have passed for a small-

Robert Harris, the King of the Trilobites.

town banker. He was in the back of his large shop pricing stones and wasn't very welcoming as Ray and I picked our way around the shop looking at baskets of rocks. Ray, whose Soho Coho Gallery in Ketchikan sells the occasional polished stone and fossil, started going into shopkeeper mode when he found out Harris was willing to sell wholesale. Soon Ray was picking out polished stone hearts made from septarian nodules and Harris started to warm up.

Here was a man who'd been there and done that. Having mined and marketed bugs for almost 40 years, he was probably responsible for getting more than 20 million trilobites into private hands. I asked him if he liked trilobites. "Not really," he replied. "Just a way to make a buck. I'm not even really into rocks. Ten-year-old girls are into rocks." Then he showed us a framed picture of a really nice trilobite with a stylish tapering pygidium (the technical term for the back half of a trilobite). The name, *Alokistocare harrisii* (by the vagaries of scientific naming, the bug is now known as *Altiocculus harrisii*), suggested that some scholar had once admired Harris enough to name a new species after him. The scientist was Dick Robeson, a local boy from Fillmore, Utah, who parlayed an interest in trilobites into a career as a paleontologist at the University of Kansas. I asked Harris what he thought of paleontologists. "Academics are all a bunch of damn liars," he replied. I tried to remember how I had introduced myself. Meanwhile, Ray was taping up flat after flat of polished hearts and handing over his credit card.

Harris, an active commercial paleontologist, was voicing a sentiment commonly heard at the Tucson and Denver shows, where sellers of fossils meet each year to make their big wholesale deals. Academics see fossils as data integral to the understanding of life's history, while dealers see fossils as part of making payroll. Pure academics and pure commercialists don't see eye to eye over a pile of fossils. As a fossil-loving and fossil-buying kid-turned-museum-curator, I see value in both sides and am always trying to broker a middle ground. It wasn't clear whether Harris didn't really understand that I was an academic or whether he sensed that my interest in him was genuine, but he began to warm up to me as well.

We asked Harris if he had any recommendations about seeing the famous trilobite digs. He said we should just drive out to his claim in the Wheeler Quadrangle, and it was just fine with him if we dug a few bugs. "I've got a little man named Jimmy out there, tell him I sent ya." Ray shot Harris's portrait in front of the *Elrathia kingii* plywood plaque and we bid him farewell. The King of Trilobites was a man who didn't seem to enjoy the life of a fossil digger. Ray, laden down with 400 bucks' worth of stone hearts, sighed, "Bugs are nothing but business to that guy."

In the truck, Ray fiddled with his pencil as he pored over the Gunthers' trilobite book. "For some people, like me, trilobites are inherently beautiful objects of mystery, grace, and beauty, elegant symbols of deep time," he sighed. "After all, these are critters from half a *billion* years ago. They're so damn pretty!" I had to agree. Trilobites are the pocketable poster children of prehistory. Thousands of species of these little guys attest to a healthy residence on Earth from 545 million years ago until 252 million years ago, a run of 293 million years. The human family, at 7 million years and counting, should be so lucky.

It hadn't cooled a bit, and I stopped at the store for a big bag of cherries and some ice. As we headed out of town, we noticed that the local high-school mascot was the jackrabbit. Ah, the mighty rabbits of Delta. It seemed like the Delta Trilobite Kings might win a few more games, and we added yet another school to our list that needed to go paleo with its mascot. Ray asked if I thought Harris

followed high-school football.

The road out to the trilobite hole was long, straight, and dusty, and it took us about an hour to get there. Not a soul nor a vehicle was around as we pulled up the draw to a building-sized heap of shale next to a hole that was about 50 feet deep. We parked the truck and walked down the ramp into the trilobite quarry. There was a beach umbrella at the bottom of the hole, and hunkered beneath the umbrella, chipping away with a hammer, was a small, shirtless, bronzed man. He glanced up as we approached and returned to his work without saying a word. There was no radio playing, no sound at all, just this guy, his umbrella, and a cooler.

Ray approached and said that Harris had sent us. Jimmy didn't say anything. We awkwardly started poking around the shale. Every minute or so, Jimmy would find a trilobite and toss it into a five-gallon plastic bucket. We started splitting shale, but with no luck. Then Jimmy said, "Here's a big one," prying up a dinner plate–sized slab with a three-inch trilobite. Ray flipped. Jimmy said, "You just have to let your eyes adjust and you'll start to find 'em." We started finding 'em.

Jimmy was a wiry piece of lean jerky who probably didn't weigh more than 125. He'd been a blaster for road crews, the guy they hang off the side of cliffs to set the charges. Now he liked working for Harris, getting paid for what he found, about a buck a bug, sometimes more, depending on the size. Harris was a good man

who cut a fair deal and left Jimmy alone. On a good day, he could put a hundred bugs in his bucket.

Buck-a-bug Jimmy eventually started talking to us, and the insanely hot day started to cool. It was nice popping bugs and eating cherries. Pretty soon we each had about a dozen bugs and Ray made a deal with Jimmy for the three-incher. We waited until the sun started to set before we left, and Jimmy was still digging when we drove away.

In our push back to Denver, we wound our way through the San Juan Mountains and took time only to dig fossil leaves in Creede. This little 19th-century silver-mining town sits right in the bottom of a huge volcanic caldera, a great collapsed ring that formed a lake 25 million years ago. The lake did as lakes do, and the caldera-filling sediments also trapped fossils. Creede is an unusual fossil site because the caldera lake formed when the San Juan Mountains were already at significant elevation. Here was the rarer sort of depositional setting, a little spot of D-World high in the Miocene E-World mountains. The Creede fossils reflect their elevation, and we found needles and cones of pines and spruces. They looked just like the plants that were growing at the fossil site. Ray and I liked splitting the beautifully thin paper shale, but good fossils were few and far between. Denver beckoned and we headed back to town to clean the truck and prepare for the last leg of the trip.

Buck-a-bug Jimmy Corbett.

15
THREE HANDSHAKES FROM DARWIN

Thirty minutes south of Denver we hurtled past the town of Castle Rock and a fossil site that was definitely not a bust. In 1994, Steve Wallace, a paleontologist employed by the Colorado Department of Transportation, found an amazing site on the side of the interstate in Castle Rock. He brought me a box of fossil leaves, and every single one represented a new species. We went to the site, a road cut on the busiest road in Colorado, and dug into the side of the hill. Leaves began to pour out of the hill, and in a matter of days we had collected dozens of species. The leaves were fantastic and huge, some of them more than 24 inches long and 18 inches wide. More than half of them had long skinny tips known as drip tips. This sort of leaf tip is found in tropical rain forests where the annual rainfall is more than 100 inches.

By the end of the third day, we realized that we were digging in an intact layer of fossilized leaf litter, and we started to recognize the remains of upright tree trunks. Near the end of the fifth day, we started finding cycad leaves. As the abundance of cycad leaves increased, I realized that we'd uncovered the edge of a whole cycad plant. Ever the media hound, I called the museum, which alerted Denver's television channels.

It must have been a slow news day, because all three channels sent cameras to the site. We cracked open the final slab "live at five." The split was no disappointment: as we lifted the manhole cover–sized slab of rock, it revealed a spray of 25 three-foot-long cycad fronds. From my live-feed earphones, I could hear the baffled anchors trying to decide why a fossil cycad was newsworthy, and I have to admit that I understood their confusion. Cycads, after all, are tropical and subtropical plants known mainly to specialists and usually seen only in the rare-plant col-

lections at botanic gardens. But this one was special. We eventually excavated the fronds, the trunk, the whole root system, and even a sweet little cycad seedling. When the dust had cleared, we'd collected the most complete fossil cycad plant ever found.

The Castle Rock rain forest is now recognized as the oldest and best-preserved fossil rain forest in the world. Its occurrence in Colorado raises really interesting questions about the origin and antiquity of tropical rain forests and drives home the point that the fossil record is nowhere close to giving up all of its secrets.

In order to figure out the age of the Castle Rock rain forest site, I collaborated with Bob Raynolds, a lanky, side-burned, goat- and yak-owning petroleum geologist who is curious about more than just finding oil. Denver is full of people who have and are making their living by understanding Rocky Mountain geology. The layers of rock in the Denver Basin and other Rocky Mountain basins are full of oil and gas that accumulated as the result of the burial and decay of ancient organic matter. Being able to see the third dimension of the Earth allows people like Bob to find oil and natural gas. He was curious about what the fossil rain forest said about ancient climates and how it related to the formation of the Front Range. It seemed to us that the layered rocks in the Denver Basin probably held some secrets about the history of the region. So we cooked up the idea of drilling a well at the tiny plains town of Kiowa, in the center of the Denver Basin, to retrieve a continuous core sample to test our ideas.

With funding from the National Science Foundation and the state of Colorado, we drilled the hole in the spring of 1999. For a simple idea, execution was a real pain. We drilled round the clock for seven weeks, pulling up a 2.5-

Fossil leaf from the Castle Rock rain forest.

inch-diameter tube filled with precious cylinders of rock. Five feet at a time we worked our way back in time. The first 65 feet were sand and gravel from the last few thousand years. Then the core penetrated bedrock that was something like 54 million years old. At a depth of 340 feet, the rock was 64 million years old. At 990 feet, we crossed the K-T boundary layer and found evidence of the asteroid that killed the dinosaurs. At a depth of 1,680 feet, we found the lowest occurrence of ground-up granite. Below this level we were drilling into rock that had been deposited at the surface before the uplift of the Rocky Mountains. At 1,800 feet, we were pulling up coal from ancient coastal swamps. At 2,000 feet, we were drilling through a buried beach. Around 2,200 feet, we were pulling up cylinders of gray mudstone that had formed at the bottom of a salty sea. Some of these cores cracked open to show fossil ammonites, extinct marine animals that were 69 million years old. We stopped drilling at 2,256 feet, confident that we had extracted an adequate sample to record the retreat of the Cretaceous Seaway, the uplift of the Rocky Mountains, the extinction of the dinosaurs, the formation of tropical rain forests along the flanks of the mountains, and a second pulse of mountain building.

The drill rig that took us 2,256 feet from the grass of the Colorado prairie to the seafloor mud of a 69-million-year-old sea.

We're still doing science on the core and using it as a method to date the fossils in the Denver Basin. The core confirms that the Castle Rock rain forest is 64 million years old.

Sixty miles south of Denver, Colorado Springs has one of the most impressive geologic settings of any prairie town in the world. Built at the extreme western edge of the Great Plains, the city looks straight up at towering Pikes Peak, which is only 20 miles away but more than 8,000 feet higher than downtown. Most of the citizens of the Springs look west and see rocks but forget that the city is built on them as well.

For more than a decade, I've been excavating fossils from Colorado Springs's city parks. It all started when a guy was digging a barbecue pit in his backyard in 1993 and bumped into a big Pierre Shale concretion. He was describing what he found over the phone when it occurred to me what it was. I hopped in the car and drove down to see him that day. He'd unburied a complete yard-long, pearly shelled, giant baculite, one of the straight ammonites. *Baculites* are common, but complete ones are vanishingly rare. He donated the fossil, which went right onto permanent display in *Prehistoric Journey*.

The south half of the Springs is built on the Pierre Shale. Ammonites and sharks' teeth are common there—"urban fossils," as I like to call them. The north half of town is built on rocks that were shed as sediments when the Rockies were starting to uplift at the end of the Cretaceous. Dinosaur bones show up in construction sites and in the parks on the north end. The K-T boundary itself traces a northwest–southeast line through the middle of town. The parks out to the east contain a menagerie of animals that survived the great extinction. In 1998 we collected a nearly complete alligator skull from a sweeping series of hills known as the Corral Bluffs, an area now slated for more subdivisions.

Despite all of this, the real story is on the west side of town, where the famous Garden of the Gods park displays some of the most breathtaking geology in the world. The park exposes the entire sequence of rocks from the Fountain Formation through the Pierre Shale, each formation tipped on end. I was eager to keep moving, so Ray was forced to glimpse the giant vertical planks of red sandstone through the truck window rather than wander amongst them. On the west side of Manitou Springs, we briefly stopped to admire an outcrop of the Sawatch Sandstone that lies directly on the 1-billion-year-old Pikes Peak Granite. I made Ray get out of the truck and put his finger on the contact so he could span 500 million years with just a few millimeters of skin.

Troll with urban ammonites on his mind.

The remains of an eight-foot tree stump preserved as a ring of carbon in one of the Castle Rock fossil rain forest quarries.

The Florissant Fossil Beds National Monument is located on the west side of Pikes Peak at an elevation of about 8,400 feet and about an hour's drive from the Springs. This is sacred ground for American paleontology. The site was discovered in the 1860s, and scientists working for Ferdinand Vandiveer Hayden's survey made it there in 1873. What Hayden's men found at Florissant was a fossil forest beyond compare. Giant fossil logs, some more than 10 feet in diameter, blocked the Florissant Valley to such a degree that it was hard to negotiate a wagon through them. The site also revealed an amazing fossil lake full of insects, fish, leaves, and birds. The paper shale was so fine that even butterflies, moths, and caterpillars were preserved. Some of the moths and butterflies still retained the pattern of the markings of their wings.

Many scientists and museums have benefited from this rich site. Samuel Scudder, a prolific paleoentomologist from Cambridge, Massachusetts, described hundreds of different species of fossil insects from Florissant. In 1877, Henry Fairfield Osborn, William Berryman Scott, and Frank Speir passed through Florissant on their famous Princeton College paleontological expedition, collecting fossils that can be seen to this day in the Peabody Museum in New Haven, Connecticut. In 1915 the Colorado Museum of Natural History actually bought a piece of property near Florissant, and the first fossils added to the Denver Museum collections were from that site.

By the 1940s, most of the obvious wood had been carted away, and the petrified forest was turned into a tourist trap that was divided into two warring concessions, the Pike Petrified Forest and the Colorado Petrified Forest. It was an ugly competition as each owner vied for tourist dollars. Eventually the rivalry grew violent, and one of the owners caught a bullet in the gut. Only the Pike Petrified Forest survived.

In the 1950s, a big black sedan pulled into the parking lot of the petrified forest, and the driver got out and introduced himself as Walt Disney. He wandered around for a while before leaving, but Mrs. Disney didn't even get out of the car. A few months later, Mrs. Disney wrote to say that Walt was obsessed with the place and would it be possible to buy a stump. A deal was struck and to this day, you can see a chunk of Florissant at Frontierland in Disneyland.

By the 1960s, Pike Petrified Forest had failed and the land was scheduled to be subdivided. Three formidable women, Estella Leopold, daughter of the environmentalist Aldo Leopold; Vim Wright; and Betty Willard worked with a Long Island lawyer to craft a campaign to save the land as a federal park. In 1969 the federal government purchased the property and established the national monument.

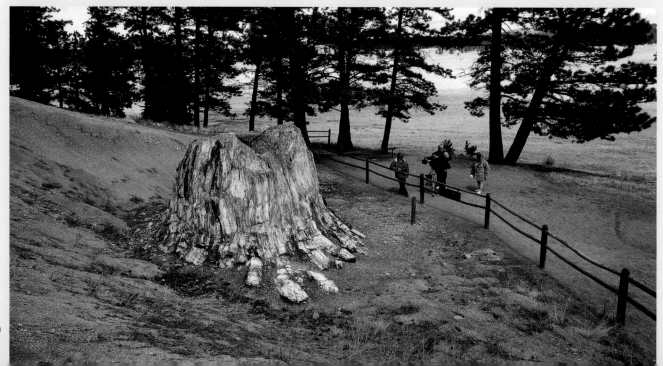

"The Big Stump," the most impressive fossil *Sequoia* trunk at Florissant, was nearly sawed up and hauled off to the 1893 World's Fair in Chicago.

Farm, a place where they take advantage of natural hot springs to grow alligators. By the time we hit Antonito, Jack Dempsey's hometown, the sky had darkened. It began to rain in Chama, and by Tierra Amarilla the rain had given way to a Seattle overcast. By Cebolla, pink cliffs had risen on both sides of the road. Eventually we pulled up to the understated entrance of Ghost Ranch, a place named for a hanging that occurred there once upon a time.

Ghost Ranch is a place where paleontology and art have brushed shoulders. An adventurous correspondent of Edward Cope explored this valley in 1881 and sent back a smattering of fossil bones, including the bones of a small theropod that Cope named *Coelophysis*. Cope himself passed briefly through the area in 1874 on his way to collect fossil mammals near a town called Cuba in the middle of the San Juan Basin. In 1927, Charles Camp from Berkeley led field trips to Ghost Ranch, where they collected skulls of the big crocodile-like phytosaurs from the late Triassic red beds of the Chinle Formation. But the big find came in 1947, when American Museum paleontologist Ned Colbert dropped by Ghost Ranch for a few days on his way out to do fieldwork at Petrified Forest National Monument. It had taken him some effort to obtain the permits

to work in the monument, so he meant not to tarry long at Ghost Ranch. That changed on his third day, when Colbert stumbled upon the find of his life, a bone bed consisting of many skeletons of the coyote-sized *Coelophysis*. This was a breathtaking find, because the little meat-eaters were whole, were many, and were Late Triassic.

Colbert realized that his life had changed, cancelled his plans for the monument, and spent the next several seasons at Ghost Ranch excavating his find. It was an embarrassment of scientific riches, so much so that it wasn't until 1989 that, at the age of 84, he finally published his definitive description of the little dinosaur. *Coelophysis* is now a well-known little beast that populates scenes of the Triassic. In 1995, Colbert published a sweet swan song of a book entitled *The Little Dinosaurs of Ghost Ranch* in which he tells the story of how *Coelophysis* changed his life. In 1998, *Coelophysis* became the second dinosaur in space when a skull was taken to the MIR Space Station (a Montana *Maiasaura* made it in the 1980s).

There is also an artistic connection to Ghost Ranch, as Ray was well aware. Georgia O'Keeffe was already a famous artist when she first visited New Mexico in 1929. She saw Ghost Ranch in 1934 and was taken by the stark and brilliant landscape and old bones that she found in the arroyos. In 1940 she purchased a small house from the ranch's owners. Her distinctive paintings and famous guests, including D. H. Lawrence, Ansel Adams, Charles and Anne Lindbergh, and Joni Mitchell, brought notoriety to the obscure ranch.

Desmatosuchus, an armored herbivorous aetosaur.

We'd driven to Ghost Ranch neither for *Coelophysis* nor O'Keeffe. We came to see a little animal whose name could not be said. Scientists name new species by the time-honored practice of designating a type specimen and publishing a detailed and illustrated description in a scientific journal. A name is not considered valid until the journal is published. This system has worked well for more than 300 years, and it's the basis for the science of taxonomy. But problems can arise when species names are given to poorly preserved or partial fossils. In some of those cases, there may not be enough biological information to merit a distinct species, and later scientists have the option to come along and "sink" the name.

This became an issue for Ray and me when Bryan Small from the Denver Museum showed us a photograph of a gorgeous and enigmatic little skeleton that had been collected from the Ghost Ranch Quarry in the early 1990s. The animal looked like a cross between an armadillo and an alligator. Bryan, who was working on the description of the animal with the Ghost Ranch paleontologist, Alex Downs, was cagey about the affinities of the animal, but he already had a name for it, a name that wouldn't be valid until the description was published. So Bryan told us the name and then told us we couldn't repeat it. This only increased our desire to see the actual fossil located at Ghost Ranch.

We turned into Ghost Ranch and drove up the muddy road. As we crested a hill, a sweeping vista of New Mexico cliffs came into view: red muddy hills of the Chinle Formation overlain by massive sandstone cliffs of the Entrada capped by the gray gravelstone of the Todolito. Trees covered the higher slopes of the Morrison Formation, and even farther away, a cliff of Dakota Sandstone shaped the horizon.

We'd called ahead to make sure that Alex Downs knew we were coming, and he greeted us at the door. Before us stood a sprawling bear of a man, his broad sloping frame wrapped in a pair of dueling striped long-sleeved dress shirts, one over the other. His head was hidden under a baseball cap, he wore big, round glasses, and he sported a tangle of alternately light and dark gray scraggily hair that merged into an unkempt beard and mustache. His swollen eyes were watering, and he was wheezing and sneezing. Alex said it was fortunate that we'd called ahead, because he felt like he was going to die, and, were it not for our arrival, he would have gone to the local health clinic. He had clearly made a bad decision on our behalf. We simultaneously warmed to him and gingerly backed away.

He'd been briefed about our obsession with the unnamed animal and ushered us directly to a display case that contained a photograph of the skeleton, a plasticine model of what the animal looked like, and a label that listed the unmentionable name. He said, "Please don't use this name, since it's not published yet." Ray, rightfully, was confused that we couldn't use it when it was posted in a public place. Alex told him that a poorly preserved skeleton was found in the 1960s in Petrified National Forest and had been named *Vancleavea*, but the specimen was too poorly preserved to be a name holder. Their new specimen was probably the same thing as *Vancleavea*, but it was hard to tell. Once they described the creature in a published article, we were free to use the name. Until then, he requested that we call it an "undescribed archosaur." Still confused, we agreed.

The little paleontology museum at Ghost Ranch is a single room chock-full of the lore of Ghost Ranch and its fossils. There were photos of the early Berkeley expeditions, pieces of skeletons, an ugly diorama of what the place looked like 225 million years ago, and, in the center of the room, a dining room table–sized block of red mudstone completely and utterly covered with bones and skeletons. Apparently, the block had preceded the building, since it was far bigger than any of the doors. The block had been

(top)
"An undescribed archosaur."

Alex Downs and the skull of the "undescribed archosaur."

186

brought down from the *Coelophysis* quarry and was the centerpiece of the room. In the summer, Alex can be found chipping away at it. It was on this block, inside the museum, that he had uncovered the "undescribed archosaur." Ray, ever the fish lover, was delighted to learn the *Coelophysis* quarry was also full of the bones of coelacanths and gars.

Ray became fascinated with another plasticine reconstruction of a long-legged terrestrial crocodile called *Hesperosuchus*. Only a few feet long, the thing reminded us both of the horrible little Gollum in the *Lord of the Rings*. Alex confirmed that Phil Burcheff, the sculptor, leaned toward the Dungeons and Dragons end of things. I asked Alex about Ned Colbert, who had died in 2001 at the ripe Triassic age of 96. He told us that Ned had been around long enough to have worked with Henry Fairfield Osborn, who had met Charles Darwin. By knowing Colbert, Alex was only three handshakes away from Darwin himself. We were about to shake Alex's hand to join this queue of famous paleontologists when Alex exploded into a frenzy of sneezes and hacking coughs. Braving a host of viruses, we both shook hands with Alex.

Finally, Alex ushered us into another building to see the "undescribed archosaur." We entered a cluttered corner room filled with boxes. In the center of the room was a rolling table, and on the table was a tire-sized block of rock nestled in a plaster and burlap jacket. Alex opened a wooden drawer, pulled out a small box, and unwrapped a piece that he then fitted onto the big slab. It was the nearly perfect skull of a most unusual animal. The flattened toothy skull fit neatly into Alex's paw, and he snugged it up against the scaly skeleton. The body was doubled back on itself but was maybe three feet long if extended. There was enough there to imagine the whole animal, and it looked like nothing I had ever seen in my life: the body was covered with diamond-shaped scales and the legs were quite short relative to the body. It looked like a swimmer, which made some sense in the context of all the fish in the quarry. Suddenly, fossil skull

in hand, Alex let loose with another sneezing attack, and I didn't move quickly enough to avoid being sprayed. It was time to leave.

The sun was breaking through the clouds, and the wet outcrops of bright-red Chinle Formation screamed with saturated color as we headed toward Abiquiu. The moon was rising, and a brilliant sun from the west lit up a bank of white clouds above a group of small adobe buildings. I remarked to Troll that the scene reminded me of that famous Ansel Adams photograph, *Moon over …* something. I couldn't remember the name, and neither could Troll. We spent most of the rest of the drive trying to scare up the name from our rusty art history memories. A few days later, Ray suddenly said, "Hernanadez, it's *Moon over Hernandez*." I looked at a map and realized, to my amazement, that we'd been in Hernandez when we saw the reminiscent scene.

Near Taos, we finally turned Big Blue back toward Denver. The sun set and it grew dark as coal. Bruce Springsteen was singing, "I am the nothing man." It was reassuring when, a few hours later, we finally saw the lights of Raton, a town named with the Spanish word for "rat." I'd last been in Raton with my friend Chuck Pillmore, the USGS geologist who capped his career by locating the K-T boundary in the Raton Basin. When Walter Alvarez found the iridium layer in marine limestone near the Italian mountain town of Gubbio in 1980 and proposed the hypothesis that an asteroid had wiped out the dinosaurs, it was Chuck who knew where to look for the same layer in sediments deposited on land. His work with Carl Orth and Bob Tschudy, published in 1981, was the first resounding support for the asteroid hypothesis. After he retired from the survey in Denver, Chuck bought a home high on Raton Pass, not far from the K-T boundary. He was an endless source of guidance for people who wanted to see the thin but deadly layer.

In 1992, I took Denver-based dinosaur-track specialist Martin Lockley down to Raton Pass to search for dinosaur tracks below and above the K-T boundary. His premise, and it was a good one, was that there should be more dinosaur tracks than dinosaur skeletons. Watching

A mess of Triassic metoposaurs. These six-foot-long amphibians have been found in large groups.

some of my dieting friends rack up 10,000 strides a day on their pedometers, I had to agree. In addition, dinosaur tracks were sure traces of a living dinosaur, while dinosaur bones could have come from a long-dead dinosaur. This all became important as the dispute over the time of the dinosaur extinction grew and some scientists argued that dinosaurs had survived the K-T extinction.

There's a small but vocal band of scientists who claimed that dinosaurs became extinct just before the asteroid hit. Another bunch argue that they survived for a while after the impact. I was of the opinion that they disappeared as a direct result of the deadly impact. Martin and I went to sites where Chuck had located the thin boundary layer and found abundant dinosaur tracks below the K-T boundary but only alligator, salamander, and bird tracks above the boundary. The track record seems to show the same pattern that we were seeing with the fossil leaves and bones in North Dakota and Montana.

On one of these trips, Martin located a particularly nice *Triceratops* track hanging off the bottom side of a giant rock that projected from a road cut above the highway. He crawled under the projecting rock and started to scrape away the underlying sediment to better expose the track. I was standing above him watching the top of the rock. As he dug, I noticed a thin but widening crack had appeared in the dirt above the rock. I realized that

Martin was undermining the rock that he was lying beneath. I screamed at him to move and, thankfully, he did, because a moment after he rolled out of the hole, the 600-pound rock smashed down on the spot where he'd been lying only seconds before. The rock tumbled down the hill, breaking into smaller chunks as it went. A 100-pound piece complete with the intact *Triceratops* track skidded to a stop within three feet of Big Blue's tailgate, where we easily loaded it up. I'd saved Martin from being killed, and he was appropriately grateful at the averted irony of a dinosaur tracker being crushed by a dinosaur track.

The next morning, Ray and I woke early and sat in the coffee shop at the Oasis. It was a classic old roadside joint with a steady flow of Raton cops and New Mexico state troopers tanking up on their morning coffee. It was the last morning of our road trip, and neither of us were that eager to hit the highway. We had two more famous fossil sites and a long drive between us and Denver, and there was a dinner party waiting for us at the other end. We finished our coffee and headed east to the site of the Denver Museum's greatest find.

Founded in 1900, the Denver Museum of Nature & Science has long been a large regional museum with a bit of a chip on its shoulder. Jesse Dade Figgins, an artist, paleontologist, zoologist, and archaeologist, left New York to become the museum's director in 1910. We were headed

to the town of Folsom to see the site of Jesse's biggest success. In the 1920s, the dogma of the archaeological elite stated that humans had not arrived in North America until 3,000 years ago. There was a dearth of archaeological sites to challenge the dogma. Figgins found spear points associated with Ice Age bison bones in Texas but made the mistake of not collecting them in context. As a result, his find had been dismissed as the uneducated screwup of a hick amateur. Figgins had a sense that he was right, and he knew that what he needed was a site where bona fide artifacts were in direct association with the bones of Ice Age animals. It took nearly 20 years, a curious cowboy, and a Raton banker to deliver Jesse's dream.

Driving east from Raton, we passed Capulin Peak, a near perfect 60,000-year-old volcanic cone sitting on the plains of northern New Mexico, and wound down a road that seemed too narrow for two-way traffic. A few minutes later, we pulled into Folsom and back into the 19th century. A summer of driving through little western towns had not prepared us for the perfect little ghost town that we encountered. It was still early and there was no sign of life. When I told Ray we were going to Folsom, he

naturally thought of Johnny Cash. This wasn't California, nor was it 1968, but it was clear that time had been draggin' here as well. We got out of the truck and wandered around, wondering when there'd last been signs of life in the town. We quickly found the Folsom Museum, located in a classic old western storefront. A card in the window gave a number to call and said the museum would be opened on request. It was a nice idea, but there didn't seem to be any phones around.

Then I noticed a little post office. I walked in and met a man about my age named Alfred Newkirk. Alfred, wearing a plaid shirt, rodeo buckle, and baseball cap, looked like he should be driving a tractor rather than sorting letters. He told me that in a town of 57, working for the postal service was the best job in town. His parents had owned the general store across the street, which closed in 1987. The nearest doctor was in Des Moines, New Mexico, 45 miles to the east. Of course he knew about the Denver Museum and their big find in 1927, clearly the biggest thing that ever happened in Folsom. He told me that the museum in town was run by two sisters, and he was sure one of them would be happy to meet us.

The white layer in this outcrop on the margin of Interstate 25 north of Raton, New Mexico, is the Cretaceous-Tertiary boundary.

He made a phone call, and about 20 minutes later, Kay Thompson met us in front of the museum. Kay, a short woman in her 70s, wore a huge patterned fleece coat and the face of a pioneer's daughter.

Kay opened the door and let us into a perfect time capsule. The museum had opened in 1967 in the old mercantile. It contained kitchen gear, bison skulls, saddles, old rifles, barbed wire, arrowheads, rattlesnake rattles, old photographs, magazines, and newspapers. It was as though anything that ever happened in this little town had been saved for posterity. Ray found an old *Newsweek* with "The Sick World of Son of Sam" blazoned across the front. I found a photograph of Francis Folsom, a wasp-waisted beauty for whom the town was named. She was born during the Civil War and died in 1947. There was a shocking photograph of the hanging of Black Jack Ketchum, a luckless crook who tried to hold up a train near Folsom in 1899. On the east wall hung a sign that remembered "Those hardy pioneers who traveled the Santa Fe Trail."

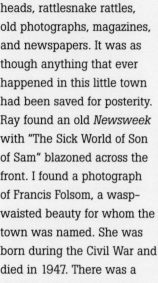

Kay Thompson holding a cast of a Folsom point and standing next to a statue of George McJunkin.

The museum was great and Kay couldn't have been more helpful, but we'd come to trace the story of a cowboy named George McJunkin, and we were in luck. George was born in Texas in 1856, the son of a slave who saved enough money from blacksmithing to buy his own freedom. George wandered west and learned how to handle horses and cattle. By the turn of the century, he'd settled near Folsom, was managing the Crowfoot cattle ranch, and had a reputation for being well read and curious. It also seems that he was a rock hound. One day in 1908, he found a freshly cut arroyo with bones sticking out of the side of the hill. He mentioned this find to Carl Schwachheim, a blacksmith, and Fred Howarth, a banker, in Raton and got them thinking about it as well. Howarth had recently found a mammoth tusk and was interested in ancient stuff.

George died in 1922, and it wasn't until later that year that Schwachheim and Howarth actually got around to confirming the story of an arroyo full of bones. It took them another couple of years to mention the find to someone who cared: Figgins, who enthusiastically embraced their discovery in 1926. Figgins and Harold Cook visited the site in March and decided that it was worth returning in the summer to excavate. They started digging in May 1926 with the intent of collecting a skeleton they could mount for display. In July, the workers found a spear point, but it wasn't in place. Now Figgins knew he was on to something, and he urged the workers to proceed with extreme caution. On August 27, 1927, they found an unusually fine fluted spear point lying in place in a spray of Ice Age bison ribs. Figgins ordered Schwachheim to guard the point and let no one touch it. Schwachheim duly sat down and awaited the arrival of "Scientists, Anthropologists, Zoologists, or other bugs."

Figgins wired New York, and, as luck would have it, Barnum Brown, the great dinosaur finder and the American Museum's number-one field man, was in Grand Junction. Brown joined Figgins at Folsom on September 4, 1927, and confirmed that Figgins was right. Humans had been in North America at the end of the Ice Age and they had been hunting the big animals. The advent of carbon dating showed the site to be 10,500 years old. A few years

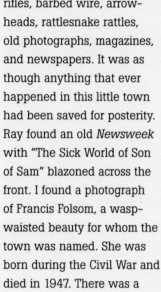

later, Figgins followed this discovery with a mammoth kill site at a place near Denver called Dent.

The fact that George was a black cowboy has tainted the telling of the story. He was clearly much loved in Folsom. A three-by-five card in the museum included this little tribute: "George must have been a very knowledgeable cowboy with other very special cowboy qualities to have been a Negro foreman, a noted achievement for his day and time. George was the Ben Franklin scientist of his time and the Folsom area." A plaster statue of George is actually a stock rendering of a white cowboy dipped in black paint with the clothing painted gold. Both Kay and Alfred had grown up in the lore of the Folsom discovery, and Alfred's curiosity had once built to the level that he actually visited the arroyo a few miles from town. Like a lot of western towns, time keeps draggin' on in Folsom, and things that happened a long time ago are a lot closer to the surface than they are in cities.

Kay showed us the Folsom point replicas that they had on display, and we stuffed some cash in the donation box and left town feeling we'd just had one of the more authentic experiences of our whole trip.

We crossed back into Colorado through a tight, winding valley called Tollgate Canyon. The walls of the canyon are sandstone and occasional dark gray mudstone layers. Ray now recognized the 100-million-year-old Dakota Sandstone when he saw it. He was able to predict that the land would flatten when we popped out of the canyon and up into the marine shale, and moments later, we were speeding along on the tabletop plains of southern Colorado near Branson. The sky was classic Colorado blue and the paired snowcapped Spanish Peaks in the distance pulled us west, but we turned east to make our rendezvous with Bruce Schumacher.

After 90 minutes of straight, dry road and blasting U2, we pulled up next to Bruce's green forest-service pickup at the turnoff for Vogel Canyon. Ray had hosted Bruce in Ketchikan the previous year and had seen him eyeing his son Patrick's drum set. On this day, Bruce was sporting a ponytail, scraggily goatee, blue jeans, and a black T-shirt without a single dinosaur reference. "Finally,

a hip federal employee," said Ray. As we hopped out of the truck, Bruce loped over and welcomed Ray with the phrase, "You're standing on plesiosaurs, *Xiphactinus*, and mosasaurs." A federal employee who knew what he was standing on. We got into Bruce's truck and headed off across the plains toward Purgatoire Canyon.

Called "Picketwire" by the locals who have no truck with French, Purgatoire Canyon was explored by Spanish conquistadors in the 16th century. A number of the Spanish soldiers had the misfortune to die without the benefit of attending clergy, and their souls were thus condemned to purgatory. The canyon was thus given the name El Rio de las Animas Perdidas en Purgatorio ("the river of lost souls in purgatory"). French trappers changed it to Purgatoire. The canyon is there because the Purgatoire River cut down through the thousands of feet of soft marine shale and chalk and then sawed into the much tougher and more resistant Dakota Sandstone and the underlying Morrison Formation. On most of the rest of the plains of southeastern Colorado, the Dakota lies deeply buried beneath the soft marine sediments. So soft are they that they weather flat, forming the monotony of the landscape that keeps most Coloradoans oriented toward the mountains. From a fossil lover's perspective, the eastern plains are one huge sushi platter, literally covered with the remains of marine life that lived here during the late Cretaceous.

Bruce did a doctorate on the Cretaceous marine rocks of South Dakota, and Ray is certifiable when it comes to Cretaceous marine creatures, so the conversation went submarine fast. The unit directly above the Dakota is the Graneros Shale, and it has produced skeletons of *Brachauchenius*, a horrifically big pliosaur with a head the size of a sperm whale. We weren't too far west from Pritchett, where Harvey Markman collected a nearly complete long-necked plesiosaur in 1939. A WPA worker named Fred Roth had found the 45-foot-long skeleton weathering out of a stream bank. Locals came from all around to see the beast, and many of them collected souvenirs. By the time the local high-school principal finally wrote the museum to report the find, pieces were scattered around two counties. The first step in Markman's excavation was to visit all the souvenir collectors and retrieve the scattered bones.

The specimen was described and named by Sam Welles, who named it after the president of the Denver Museum board, Charles Hanington. *Thalassomedon haningtoni* is an animal I see every day, because we have two casts of this graceful swimmer hanging from the ceiling of the entry atrium of the Denver Museum of Nature & Science. Visitors often peer up at the skeleton and remark that its shape is odd for a flying animal. Long-necked plesiosaurs are the real beasts that loaned their form to the imaginations of those who would claim to see the Loch Ness and other lacustrine monsters around the world.

Picketwire Canyon is a very well-kept secret. For many years, the army used it for training exercises, and they still use some of the surrounding area, so tank tracks and 50 mm cartridges from airborne warthogs litter the landscape. Because people have been excluded for so long, most people don't even know that southeastern Colorado has its own amazing canyonlands. The army transferred a big part of the canyon to the forest service in 1992, and the service began the long process of evaluating their new resource.

With cholla cactus, coyotes, and roadrunners, the canyon seems like the set of a Warner Brothers cartoon. But a closer inspection shows that the canyon was occupied by early Native Americans, conquistadors, and Spanish settlers, and the rock walls are lathered with petroglyphs. Federal archaeologists are a special breed, and the assessment of the archaeological resource has been a labored process. The riches have convinced the forest service to keep public access to a minimum. When Bruce took the job, he was essentially walking into a lost valley of paleontology.

He and his team of volunteers have been surveying the fossils and beginning to excavate the best ones. They recently recovered a roadside *Allosaurus* with a belly full of 86 gastroliths, or stomach stones, a real anomaly for a carnivorous dinosaur. With hundreds of square miles of unprospected Morrison Formation, the future is bright for more finds. We drove for about five miles, stopping here and there to look at archaeological sites before we arrived at the most spectacular dinosaur footprint site in the country.

The Picketwire track site is a flat-lying sheet of limy sandstone in the Morrison Formation that forms the bed of the Purgatoire River for a couple of hundred yards. The river is continually sweeping the bedrock clean, then covering it, then ripping it up. The site is dynamic. Famous dinosaur tracker Roland Bird apparently found the site back in the 1930s before he got distracted by the Glen Rose track site in Texas. He lost interest, and the closure of the valley by the army pulled the curtains of obscurity over the site. It wasn't until the forest service started to survey the valley in the early 1990s that the site came back to light. Martin Lockley studied it, and his fame was magnified when Louie Psihoyos photographed him at Picketwire for *National Geographic*.

The Purgatoire River was running fast but not deep, so we waded the channel in our bare feet. Because the channel bottom was smooth sandstone, there was no problem with big cobbles. "But," Bruce said, "watch out for the dinosaur tracks. If you step in one you could go in up to your waist." With that, he slowly waded across the 30-yard channel. Ray followed him, and so did I. Once on the other side, the size and magnificence of the site became apparent.

A sauropod dinosaur foot is shaped like the bottom of a telephone pole, basically a big round cylinder, like the foot of an elephant. The exposed sheet of sandstone

on the far side of the river was as wide as a two-lane road and perhaps a hundred yards long. The surface was marked by many very clear sauropod trackways. Most of the animals had been walking in the same direction, and I had the sudden and powerful feeling that I was standing on a Jurassic Serengeti. Ray and Bruce paced alongside the trails while I shot photographs. Two things were immediately clear: the absence of tail-drag marks meant that sauropods kept their tails in the air, and the narrow gauge of the tracks meant they walked with their feet directly beneath their bodies. These were two insights of the Dinosaur Renaissance and here they were, literally cast in stone. The third piece that struck me hard was that all of the trails were going the same direction. It was at least possible that we were seeing evidence of a herd of animals moving together.

Wading the Purgatoire River.

Ray marveled at the huge surface. By taking our time and moving slowly and gingerly in our bare feet, we began to notice the smaller three-toed tracks of a medium-sized theropod. These sauropods had not been alone. *Allosaurus* or some other large three-toed predator had walked on the same lakeshore, perhaps with not the best of intentions.

Wading back across the river, I stepped into a submerged dinosaur track and stumbled into thigh-deep water. I'd been warned, so I couldn't complain about my jeans being soaked. Bruce took us to one last site, a place where he and his volunteers had, on the last day of a survey, found the edge of a nice big *Apatosaurus* skeleton. "How many hundreds of sauropod skeletons are there in this valley?" mused Ray.

(right)
The Purgatoire sauropod trackway, about as clear as a fossil site could possibly be.

As we drove out of the canyon, Bruce put Jimmy Cliff in the CD player and we rolled back up to army training grounds with Jimmy singing, "Sittin' Here in Limbo." I'd made dinner plans with my wife and a couple friends who wanted to meet Ray, so we knew that this trip would end on schedule. It's at least 200 miles from Lamar to my condominium in Denver's Capitol Hill. We broke free from Bruce's Lost Valley of Paleontology around 3:00 P.M. Dinner was scheduled for 7:30, so we had to hoof it. Fortunately, the roads of eastern Colorado are straight, flat, and empty. I set my bearings for the quaintly named town of Punkin Center and let 'er rip. Ray played with the video feature of his digital camera and we conspired to prevent this endless road trip from ending. The sun was out and it felt fantastic. The sky was beginning to light up with a classic Denver Bronco sunset: blue sky and orange clouds. I remarked, for perhaps the hundredth time, that we were driving over the top of the Pierre Shale and that ammonites surely were to be found beneath us. Ray pulled out a five-dollar bill and said, "Prove it." I rolled the truck to a stop next to a small road cut and walked across the road with my hammer in my hand. The cut wasn't much taller than the truck, and it was almost completely grassed over. I picked my way through the roadside trash and climbed to the crest of the cut. A blazing red sun was lying right on the horizon and shining directly into my eyes, so I backed down the slope to get back into the shade. I spotted a piece of harder rock standing out against the weathered gray shale, picked it up, and split it with the hammer. One rock, one hammer blow, and one perfect pink, pearly ammonite. I uttered, "Got one" to Ray and walked over to where he was rummaging in the dirt.

"Dr. J," he swore as he handed over the fiver, "fossils really are everywhere."

Every Road Cut Asks a Question

Every road cut asks a question
Every fossil tells a story
All the rocks that lay around us
They speak of prehistoric glory

Of mighty mammoths on endless
   plains
And dancing herds of dinosaurs
Sauropods with necks entwining
Ammonites schooling by the shore

Pterosaurs circling high above
Thunderheads on open seas
Killer pigs and brontotheres
Mountains building by degrees

Once a swampland, dark and dreary
Then burning deserts so severe
Winding rivers carving valleys
Waters rolling blue and clear

Take me back to
Where I've never been,
Oh take me back!

Once an incline now a fault
Distant landscapes melt like rain
Eroding mysteries they channel deeply
Ice caps shrinking once again

Trilobites squirming in the mire
Lizards leaping through the waves
Giants striding across the beaches
Sending echoes from their graves

Where once walked titans now is
   concrete
We all are driving down this road
Sing it loudly, sing it proudly
The wildest story ever told

Every outcrop is a puzzle
Crying out to you and me
If you listen it will tell you
About our planet's long history

Take me back to
Where I've never been,
Oh take me back!

—R. T.

ACKNOWLEDGMENTS

This road trip could not have happened without the support and cooperation of a host of enablers, friends, fossil fanatics, and family members. Ray thanks his wife, Michelle, and their kids, Patrick and Corinna. Kirk thanks his wife, Chase DeForest. Russ Graham authorized the use of Big Blue and some of Kirk's museum time for the trip. Jim Curtis kept Big Blue running. Both Ray and Kirk mourn the loss of people whom they encountered along the way who did not live to see the book published: Freida Gunther, Dave Love, Donna Engard, Bob Akerley, Wes Wehr, and Bill Bateman. Big Blue herself died in the spring of 2006. Other losses include Denver's Walnut Café, which closed before its pancakes could become famous, and the famous Douglass Quarry at Dinosaur National Monument, which closed indefinitely due to a faulty foundation.

This book was originally acquired for Fulcrum by Marlene Blessing and shepherded into print by Faith Marcovecchio, Sam Scinta, and Ann Douden. The text was improved by comments from Bruce Schumacher, Peter Larson, Dina Venezky, Doug Nichols, Peter Heller, Ken Carpenter, Greg Wilson, Kirsten and Dick Johnson, and Chase DeForest.

There would have been no story if it weren't for the thick mesh of fossil finders, watchers, and keepers that covers the western landscape like a prehistoric national guard. In rough order of their occurrence in the text, we thank Chuck Bonner, Barbara Sheldon, Les Robinette, John Shinton, Russ Graham, Emmett Evanoff, Brent Breithaupt, Mike Lewis, Dave Schmude, Chris Weege, Kelli Trujillo, Bob Bakker, Kent Hups, Gary Staab, Lisa and Stan Icenogle, Dave Brown, Bill Wahl, Russell Hawley, Lee Campbell, Julia Sankey, Peter and Neal Larson, Bob Farrar, Mike Triebold, Bill Stein, Dean Pearson, Tyler Lyson, Patty Perry, Marshall Lambert, Nate Murphy, Darren Tanke, Phil Gingerich, Kirby Siber, Burkhart Pohl, Dave and Jane Love, Anna Moschiki,

Mike Kinney, Tom Rush, Renée Askins, Susan and Mayo Lykes, Jay Muir, Wally Ulrich, Tom Lindgren, Rick Hebden, Vince Santucci, Charlie Love, Steve Sroka, Sue Ann Bilbey, Lace and Jim Honert, Randy Fullbright, Carol McCoy Brown, Ann Elder, India Wood, Mike Graham, Bill Bateman, Frank Rupp, Bob Akerley, Dick Dayvault, Rob Gaston, Jennifer Schellenbach, Lin Ottinger, Dwayne Taylor, Scott Sampson, Mark Loewen, Celina and Marina Suarez, Mike Leschin, the Gunthers (Lloyd, Val, Freida, DeEsta, Glade), Don Tidwell, Cliff Miles, Robert Harris, Buck-a-Bug Jimmy Corbett, Toni and Nancy Clare, Herb Meyer, Donna Engard and Pat Monaco, Alex Downs, Josh Smith, Tom Williamson, Matt Celesky, Alfred Newkirk, Kay Thompson, and Bruce Schumacher.

Kirk also thanks those geologists and paleontologists who have trained him and welcomed him to their western field camps, fossil sites, and quarries: Sid Ash, Ed Belt, Bill Bonini, Tom Bown, Robyn Burnham, Ken Carpenter, Bill Clemens, Bill Cobban, Phil Currie, Erling Dorf, Dave Fastovsky, Bob Giegengack, Phil Gingerich, Russ Graham, Leo Hickey, Jack Horner, Steve Manchester, Hans Nelson, Doug Nichols, Gomaa Omar, Pete Palmer, Reuben Ross, Richard Stucky, Don Tidwell, Wes Wehr, Peter Wilf, and Scott Wing. He also thanks Kelsey Martin for causing the rock problem in the first place.

Ray and Kirk toiled over the big map for nine months and are grateful for help from John Alroy, Howard and Darlene Emry, Larry Martin, John Hoganson, Matt Celesky, Chuck Bonner, Clark Markell, David Elliott, Russell Hawley, Bob McChord, Ken Carpenter, Jerry Smith, George Stanley, Neal Larson, Ron Eng, and Jim Baichtal. Fellow Alaskan artist Terry Pyles added the glorious digital color.

Ray would like to thank Marjorie Leggitt for the original leaf composition on *Leaves of the Apocalypse* on page 73.

INDEX

183; South Dakota School of Mines, 64; Tate Museum, 49–51; University of Kansas Museum, 86; University of Utah Museum, 130; University of Wyoming, 38–39; Utah Field House, 130–131, 137–138; Utah Museum of Natural History, 167; Wyoming Dinosaur Center, 51, 101. *See also* Denver Museum of Nature & Science; *Prehistoric Journey* exhibit

Museum of the Rockies, 78

Museum of Western Colorado (now Dinosaur Journey), 154–155, 158

Mussentuchit Quarry, 161

N

Nanotyrannus, 81

Natural Trap Cave, 85–86, 89

Nebraska: and abundant mammal fossils, 35; Agate Fossil Beds National Monument, 31, 33

Nedcolbertia, 161

nettles, 76

Nevada, volcanoes and calderas in, 29

Newkirk, Alfred, 189, 191

New Orleans, and D-World, 23

New Raymer, Colorado, 27, 29

Nichols, Doug, 75

North American Museum of Ancient Life, 170–171

North Carolina Museum of Natural Sciences, 71

Notharctus, 122

Notogoneous, 119

Nyctosaurus, 193

O

ocean, 25

Ogden, Utah, Eccles Dinosaur Park, 165

oil shale, 143, 149; formation of, 141; and thermonuclear explosion, 141

O'Keefe, Georgia, 185

Okefenokee Swamp, Georgia, and Sentinel Butte Member, 72

Old Woman Anticline, 53

onion as a metaphor for strata, 19

Ornithomimus, 67

Orth, Carl, 187

Osborn, Henry Fairfield, 39, 121–122, 180, 187

Osmond Elementary School, *Helicoprion* at, 115

Ostrom, John, 40, 91, 119, 161

Ottinger, Lin, 155, 160–161

Ottinger's Rock Shop, 160

outcrop analysis, 31

overthrust belt, 112, 117

oviraptor dinosaurs, 70

Ovis catclawensis, 87

P

Pachycephalosaurus, 81; roadside sculpture, 138

paddlefish, 78, 119

"pages of time" metaphor, 138

paleoartists, 42, 44–45, 49–50, 104, 122, 130, 170

paleobotany, 99; advantages of, 54; greatest failure of, 59; Late Cretaceous vegetation, 52

Paleocene-Eocene (P-E) boundary, 95, 99; and warm climate, 94

paleonerds, 49–50, 64, 101, 143, 162

Paleozoic fish fossils with intact skin, 79

Pangaea, 17

Parapuzozia, 91

Parasaurolophus, 165, 168–170

Park, Jeff, 170

Patterson, Bryan, 149

Pawnee Buttes, Colorado, 31

Peabody Museum, 39, 52, 119, 180; and *Archelon*, 64

Pearce, Herbert, 45

Pearce, Sid, 46

Pearson, Dean, 71, 73–75

peccary, 14, 18

petrified trees, 14, 45, 154, 159; at Field House Museum, 130; at Florissant Fossil Beds, 180–181; in Yellowstone, 110–111

Phaearcturus, 88

Pharodeus, 119

Phenacodus, 64

Phillips County Museum, 79

phyllocarid, 166–167

phytosaurs, 185

"Picketwire" Canyon. *See* Purgatoire Canyon

Picketwire track site, 192

Pierre Shale, 18, 67, 69–70, 72, 179; ammonite in, 194; *Baculites*-bearing concretion from, 178; Bill Cobban's ammonite zonation, 53, 55

piglike animal (*Archaeotherium*), 29–30

pigs, killer, 170; and Oligocene gazelle camels, 51; at Tate Museum, 50

pigs, scavenging behavior of, 30

pig-under-blanket metaphor, 38, 59, 87

Pillmore, Chuck, 187–188

Pinegar, Tyler, 170

Pine Ridge Indian Reservation, South Dakota, and *Archelon* discovery, 64

Pioneer Trails Regional Museum, 71

Placenticeras, 44, 45, 66, 67, 145–146

plastered bartender, 73–74

plate tectonics and mountain uplift, 25

plesiosaur, 4, 131, 182, 191–192; at South Dakota School of Mines, 64

pliosaur, 51, 191

Pohl, Burkhart, 101

pollen at K-T boundary, 75

Powell, John Wesley, 123

Prehistoric Journey exhibit, 132, 166, 170, 178; *Stegosaurus* in, 139

Price, College of Eastern Utah Museum, 161

Price, Flora Ellen, 145

Price River #2 Quarry, 161

primates: rain forest, 104; in Wyoming Eocene rocks, 104

Priscacara, 119

Prognathodon stagmani, 153

prongbuck, 32–33, 51

protection of fossils, 85, 92, 119–121, 142

Protosphyraea, 193

Psihoyos, Louie, 192

pteranodon, 4, 55

pterosaurs, 73

Puerta, Pablo, 88, 105

Purgatoire Canyon, 191–192

Pyles, Terry, 8

R

Rabbit Valley, Utah, 155–156

Radar Dome fossil site, 141–143

radioactive bones, 131, 154

Ramoceros, 33

Rapid City, South Dakota, 64

Raton, New Mexico, and K-T boundary, 187

Raymer, Colorado, 27, 29

Raynolds, Bob, 177

Redbird, Wyoming, and the Cretaceous Interior Seaway, 53

Red Rocks near Denver, 16, 19

Reinheimer, Philip, 160

Reptile Gardens, South Dakota, and *Archelon*, 64

rhinoceroses: and Agate Springs Ranch, 31; from northeast Colorado, 27; Pliocene, 35

Riggs, Elmer, 153

road maps, fossil, 8–9; Colorado, 20, 26, 116, 126, 144, 152, 176; Idaho, 102; Kansas, 26, 176; Montana, 68, 78, 82; Nebraska, 26; New Mexico, 176; North Dakota, 68; Oklahoma, 176; South Dakota, 58, 68, 176; Texas, 176; Utah, 102, 116, 126, 152, 164; Wyoming, 26, 36, 48, 68, 82, 102, 116, 144

Robeson, Dick, 174

Robinette, Les, 15

rock art, 133–134, 192

Rock River, Wyoming: *Didymoceras* from, 51; mural at, 44

Rock Springs, Wyoming, 37; formation of rocks and uplift, 124; museum, 124

Rocky Mountain Dinosaur Resource Center, 182–183

Rocky Mountain region: Earth history, 24, 178; geologic development of, 17, 19, 37, 55, 59, 117

Roosevelt, Teddy, 72

Roper, Clyde, 146

Rose, Ken, 97

Roth, Fred, 191

Rousseau, Henri, 131

Rulison blast for oil shale, 141

Rupp, Frank, 146

Russell, Dale, 71

Ruth Mason Quarry and *Edmontosaurus*, 65, 67

S

saber-toothed cats, Pennsylvanian, 147

Sacrison, Stan and Steve, 70

Salt Lake City, Utah Museum of Natural History, 167

Sampson, Scott, 169–171

Sankey, Julia, 64

Santucci, Vince, 65–66, 120

Saurexallopus lovei, 106, 107

sauropod, 14, 32, 155, 169; from Bone Cabin Quarry, 39; gigantic vertebra of, 183; trackways in Arkansas River, 192, 194

Scaphites, 45, 66

Scaptohyus, 64

Schellenbach, Jennifer, 155

Schumacher, Bruce, 191–192, 194

Schumde, Dave, 41–42, 88–89

Schumde, Doug, 42

Schwachheim, Carl, 190

Science Museum of Minnesota, Saint Paul, 72

scientific names, 32

scorpion, 149

Scott, William Berryman, 53, 122, 180

Scudder, Samuel, 180

seas, definition of, 25

sedimentary rocks, definition of, 22

Seismosaurus from Morrison Formation, 50

sequoias, 181

Seventh Day Adventists, 110–111

sexually dimorphic ammonites, 146

shark, whorl-toothed. *See Helicoprion*

Shinton, John, 15

shovel-tusked elephants, 13, 35

Siber, Kirby, 64, 92–93

Sioux people and Black Hills, South Dakota, 59

Skinner, Morris, 33

Skyline Drive, 184

Slim Buttes, South Dakota, battle at, 69–70

Small, Bryan, 183, 186

Smithsonian Institution, 130, 146, 183

Soho Coho Gallery, 1, 174

Solenoceras, 67

South Dakota School of Mines, 64

Sparactolambda, 149

spawning ammonites, 147

spear point in Ice Age bison ribs, 190

species: explanation of, 32; number of different plant, 157

Speir, Frank, 180

Sphenodiscus, 67

Spielberg, Steven, 40, 161–162

Spirit Lake submerged forest, 111

Spiroxybeloceras, 67

Squalicorax, 7; at South Dakota School of Mines, 64

Staab, Gary, 42, 44–45

stacked fossil forests in Yellowstone, 110–111

Stegosaurus, 13, 19, 22, 42, 93, 162; at Denver Museum, 160; at Dinosaur Ridge, 21; from Morrison Formation, 128; in *Prehistoric Journey* exhibit, 139

Stein, Bill, 182

Stenomylus, 33

Sternberg family, 6, 53

Sternberg Museum, Hays, Kansas, 4

Stokesosaurus, 172

stromatolites, 143

Stucky, Richard, 95, 104, 122

Suarez, Celina and Marina, 171–172

Subhyracodon, 29

subtropical forests, 45

Sundell, Kent, 50–51

Supersaurus, 153, 170; from Morrison Formation, 50

T

taeniodont, 132

Tate Museum, Casper, Wyoming, 49–51

Taylor, Dwayne, 161–162

Teton Village gondola and mountaintop brachiopods, 112

Thalassomedon haningtoni, 192, 193

Theodore Roosevelt National Park, 72

"There is a mountain" (Donovan), 24–25

thermonuclear blast for oil shale, 141

Thermopolis: hot springs, 98, 101; Wyoming Dinosaur Center, 51, 101

Thescelosaurus, 76; with a heart, 71

Thompson, Kay, 190–191

three-step method, 31

Tidwell, Don, 159–160

time, geologic, 24

Titanoides, 149

titanothere, 28, 46, 131

Torosaurus, 43, 169

Torvosaurus, 153

tracker of dinosaurs almost killed by dinosaur track, 188

tracks, 106–108; dinosaur, 62–63, 134, 163, 184, 187, 192, 194; *Iguanodon*, 22; and K-T boundary survivors, 188

Triceratops, 14, 18, 67, 76, 78, 109; depicted goring *T. rex*, 131; from Hell Creek Formation, 69; from Little Missouri River buttes, 73; at Mud Buttes, North Dakota, 74; near Lusk, Wyoming, 51–52; roadside sculpture, 138; track of, 188

Triebold, Mike, 70, 182

Trigonias (rhinoceros): absent at Bones Galore, 29; and Denver Museum, 27

trilobites, 165–166; ancient necklace of, 172; at Delta, Utah, 172; icons of extinction, 44; Pavant Ute saying about, 167; in Wheeler Quadrangle, 173–175

Tschudy, Bob, 187

Tully Monster, 64

turtles: discovery of *Archelon*, 64; jam, 76; from Little Missouri River buttes, 73; mud and turtle lasagna, 122–123; from Wannagan Creek Quarry, 72

Twain, Mark, 149

Tynsky, Jimmy, 119

Tynsky Rock Shop, 125

type specimen: definition of, 32; "undescribed archosaur," 186–187

Tyrannosaurus rex, 13, 15, 171; baby teeth of, 76; Buffalo, South Dakota, named individuals, 70; depicted being gored by *Triceratops*, 131; from Hell Creek Formation, 69; from Little Missouri River buttes, 73; named Sue, 65–67, 120, 153; from Utah, 169

U

U-Haul trucks and *Archelon*, 64

Uintacrinus, 153

Uintascorpio meyershawesi, 149

uintatheres, 121–122, 170; skeleton loaded with uranium ore, 131

Ulrich, Carl and Wally, 118, 120

University of Kansas Museum, 86

University of Utah Museum, 130

Untermann, Billie, 131

Untermann, Ernest, 130–132

Untermann, George (Getty), 131

U-prep-it fish fossils, 118

uranium deposits: formation of, 154; and radioactive bones, 154

Ussher, Bishop James, 111

Utah, volcanoes and calderas in, 29

Utah Field House of Natural History State Park, 130–132, 137–138

Utah Museum of Natural History, 167

Utahraptor, 154–155, 161–162

V

Vancleavea, 186

Van Gogh, 131

varves, 105

Velociraptor, 91, 161–162

velociraptors, 70

Vernal, Utah, Field House, 130–132, 137–138

Virginian Hotel and Bob Bakker, 41–42

volcanic ash: altered to bentonite, 84; and fossil plants, 100; and Mount Saint Helens,

29; now gumbo, 70; and Pawnee Buttes, 31; rhinos buried in, 35; and White River Group, 29

volcanic ash deposits: in Colorado, 29; in North Dakota, 69; in Wyoming, 84–85

volcanoes: in Colorado, 181; in Montana, 70; in Utah and Nevada, 29

W

Wahl, Bill, 49–50

Wallace, Steve, 177

Wannagan Creek Quarry, reptiles of, 72

water holes and starvation, 30

Watson, Frank, 64

Weege, Chris, 41–42, 88–89

Wehr, Wes, 3, 66

Weishampel, David, 169

Welles, Sam, 192

Western Interior Paleontological Society (WIPS), 142–143

Western Interior Sea. *See* Cretaceous Interior Seaway

Wheeler Quadrangle and trilobites, 165, 173–174

White River Group, 27, 31, 50; oreodonts from, 65; volcanic ash, 29

Wieland, George, 59–60; and *Archelon*, 64

Willard, Betty, 180

Williams, Maurice, 65–66

Williamson, Tom, 169

Wing, Scott, 99

Wister, Owen, 41

Wolcott, Charles Doolittle, 166

wolves and missing ribs of prey, 30

Wood, India: and *Allosaurus*, 139–140, 170; and *Camarasaurus*, 139

Woodland Park, Colorado, Rocky Mountain Dinosaur Resource Center, 182

Wortman, Jacob, 83, 94, 97

Wright, Vim, 180

Wyoming Dinosaur Center, 51, 101

X

Xiphactinus, 5, 64, 153, 191

Y

Yellow Cat Quarry, 155, 158, 161–162

Yellowstone National Park, 109; stacked fossil forests in, 110–111

READY TO CRUISE
THE FOSSIL FREEWAY YOURSELF?

Let Ray's road map be your guide.

This 4' X 5' masterpiece is filled with hundreds

of prehistoric images based on actual fossils

found across the West

and just waiting to be discovered.